"Deckers' text provides a broad overview of several theories and empirical findings in the field of motivation. Deckers' style is approachable and conversational, making this text an excellent introduction to the philosophical and scientific study of motivation."

Sean Laraway, *Professor of Research and Psychology,*
San Jose State University

"There have been numerous developments in the field of motivation and emotion since the publication of the fourth edition in 2014. The updated fifth edition of Deckers' *Motivation: Biological, Psychological, and Environmental* highlights and integrates these new developments and the latest empirical work across each of the considered topic areas. Additionally, the fifth edition also presents some of the most important classic and historical theories. The addition of weblinks to the topics related to motivation in the media and online will be of interest to both instructors to stimulate discussion in the classroom and to students to enhance their experience with the text. Thus, the fifth edition is an excellent resource for an undergraduate course focused on examining human motivation."

Erica D. Musser, *Department of Psychology,*
Florida International University

"This text is a classic! Dr. Lambert Deckers uses an engaging narrative along with excellent empirical and real-life examples to articulate complex motivation theories and models. A wonderful recipe for learning—which also complements my teaching."

Steven J. Kohn, *Department of Psychology, Counseling,*
and Family Therapy, Valdosta State University

Motivation

This textbook provides a complete overview of motivation and emotion, using an overarching organizational scheme of how biological, psychological, and environmental sources become motivation—the inducement of behavior, feelings, and cognition. It combines classic studies with current research and uses numerous real-world examples to engage the student and make often-difficult theoretical concepts come to life. By understanding and applying the principles of motivation described in the text, students will not only discover insights into what motivates their own behavior but also how to instigate self-change.

Thoroughly revised and updated throughout, this fifth edition provides a major review of recent research, with over 225 new references, including expansion in the areas of goal motivation and emotion psychology. Other updated topics include new findings and interpretations on how evolution affects our preferences, how personality traits determine motivation, and how self-control depends on a cost/benefit analysis. The addition of individual chapter glossaries and an increased number of links to additional resources supplement student learning. This textbook is suitable as a primary text for courses on motivation.

For additional resources, please consult the companion website at www.routledge.com/cw/deckers.

Lambert Deckers is a professor emeritus of psychological science at Ball State University in Muncie, Indiana. He taught psychology courses for 45 years, with 40 years devoted to teaching a course in motivation and emotion. He also taught courses in the psychology of learning, and history and systems of psychology. Professor Deckers is a charter member of the Association for Psychological Science and a member of the Society for the Study of Motivation.

Motivation

Biological, Psychological, and Environmental

Fifth Edition

LAMBERT DECKERS

Routledge
Taylor & Francis Group

NEW YORK AND LONDON

Fifth edition published 2018
by Routledge
711 Third Avenue, New York, NY 10017

and by Routledge
2 Park Square, Milton Park, Abingdon, Oxon, OX14 4RN

Routledge is an imprint of the Taylor & Francis Group, an informa business

First edition published by Pearson Education, Inc. 2005
Fourth edition published by Routledge 2014

Library of Congress Cataloging-in-Publication Data
A catalog record for this book has been requested

ISBN: 978-1-138-03632-1 (hbk)
ISBN: 978-1-138-03633-8 (pbk)
ISBN: 978-1-315-17861-5 (ebk)

Typeset in Bembo and Frutiger
by Florence Production Ltd, Stoodleigh, Devon, UK

Visit the companion website: www.routledge.com/cw/deckers

To Lisa, Erik, and Cindy

Contents

Preface

TO INSTRUCTORS

In this text, motivation means "to be moved into action," or, for a more cognitive orientation, to be moved into cognition, feeling, and action. If motivation refers to inducement of action, feelings, and thought, then what is the source of this inducement? As conveyed by the title, this book provides answers by describing biological, psychological, and environmental sources of motivation. Biological refers to the material aspects of the body, nervous system, and brain. Psychological refers to drives, psychological needs, and personality traits. Environmental sources are composed of incentives and goals. The anticipation of their occurrence motivates behavior. These domains of motivation guided the selection of the eclectic topics that are covered in this text. There are a vast number of topics that could be included in the study of motivation. After all, the task of psychology is to describe behavior and cognition and the circumstances in which they occur. The study of motivation in its many guises attempts to describe and explain how this happens.

FIFTH EDITION

The fifth edition continues with the same eclectic approach as the four prior editions but with many changes and updates. There are over 225 new references that describe many new topics, findings, and theories about motivation and emotion. Older topics that are no longer current have been deleted to provide space for this newer material. In addition, each chapter contains its own glossary. This new edition also contains many web addresses, which have been checked for accuracy and accessibility, where students can find additional information about a topic.

TO STUDENTS

Motivation refers to the "why" of behavior, not the "how." Why do we engage in certain behaviors and have certain feelings and thoughts but not others? Do some events motivate us while other events do not? I hope that reading this book will provide answers and contribute to your self-discovery. It may help you understand what motivates some of your behaviors and not others and what motivates some individuals but not others. By applying the principles of motivation, a person can institute self-change. Are there ways you wish to behave, or do you act in ways that you wish you didn't? In the process of change, do people change the environment or alter something about themselves in order to make these changes happen? Perhaps you will find insights and answers in the following pages.

Acknowledgments

I would like to acknowledge that trying to understand the "why" of behavior is probably one of the most fascinating endeavors that a person can pursue. Thanks to Ball State University, it has been possible for me to do this. I would like to thank all former students in my motivation and emotion course who read the book and provided feedback. An appreciation also goes to my former colleagues, Thomas Holtgraves, David Perkins, Stephanie Simon-Dack, Anjolii Diaz, and Guy Mittleman, who were sounding boards for my ideas. An expression of gratitude goes to my wife, Cindy Ruman, for her expertise and help.

CHAPTER 1

Introduction to Motivation and Emotion

"There's no free will," says the philosopher; "to hang is most unjust." "There is no free will," assents the officer; "we hang because we must."

Ambrose Bierce, 1911

Whether you think you can, or think you can't, you're right.

Henry Ford, 1863–1947

To prepare the groundwork for motivation and emotion, consider these questions:

1. What is the definition of motivation?
2. What is the difference between motives, incentives, and goals?
3. Does motivation consist of anticipating future events, future behaviors, and future feelings?
4. How is motivation reflected in thinking and behaving?
5. What is emotion? How does it motivate behavior?
6. How is research conducted in motivation and emotion?

MEANING OF MOTIVATION

When their train engine broke down in the story *The Little Engine That Could*, the toy dolls asked various passing engines if they would pull their train the remaining distance over the mountain to the next town. This was their goal. Shiny New Engine came, and the dolls asked it to pull their train. Shiny New Engine replied, "I pull the likes of you? Indeed not!" Later, Big Strong Engine came by, and the dolls asked it to pull their train. Big Strong Engine very importantly said, "I won't pull the likes of you!" Subsequently, Rusty Old Engine chugged by, and the dolls asked it for help. Rusty Old Engine complained of being tired and answered, "I cannot." Soon Little Blue Engine passed along. Although not very strong, it was moved by the tearful pleading of the dolls and importance of the goal of getting the train to the town. While working hard going up the mountain, Little Blue Engine repeated the famous line, "I think I can" over and over, and on achieving the goal, finished by saying, "I thought I could" over and over (Piper, 1954/1961). The difference among the engines illustrates the differences between could (can) and would (will). Shiny New Engine and Big Strong Engine undoubtedly could but would not; they were not motivated to do the job. They were not moved by the pleading of the toy dolls or by the goal of getting the goods over the mountain. Rusty Old Engine perhaps would but could not. It may have been motivated to do the job but lacked the capability to do so. Only Little Blue Engine both could and, more importantly, would. It was both capable and motivated to do so.

Are people like the trains in the story? Must they be both motivated and capable for goal-directed behavior to occur? Is motivation linked to internal events such as wants, desires, and emotions as well as to external events such as incentives and goals? Are the characteristics of could and can linked to ability and knowledge?

To Be Moved into Action

Consider the implication for motivation of the following statements:

> Hunger drives a person to raid the refrigerator for food.
> Music provides the impulse to dance.
> The residence hall students enjoyed playing volleyball Sunday afternoon.
> If you pay your credit card bill on time, then you will avoid an interest charge.
> Students attend classes at the university in order to earn a bachelor's degree.

The individuals in these examples, who ate, danced, played volleyball, paid their bills when due, and attended classes, were motivated to do so. Individuals who did not were not motivated to do so or were motivated to do something else. According to the philosopher Arthur Schopenhauer (1841/1960), to be **motivated** is to be moved into action, or into a change in action. It comes from being pushed by the past and pulled by the future. The past resides in our internal motives and the future exists in anticipated external goals and incentives. The past and future define three categories of motivation: motive, goal, and incentive. A **motive** is a person's relatively stable internal disposition to be concerned with and approach positive incentives and avoid negative incentives (Atkinson, 1958/1983; McClelland, 1987). For example, people have a stable disposition or motive to eat over their lifetime. Sometimes the motive to eat can be strong, which occurs when a person is hungry. A **goal** is represented as the internal image of a future outcome that a person plans to achieve: an end-state. A goal guides the behavior necessary for achievement. For instance, students have an image of their goal of graduating from a university. This image guides the academic behavior necessary to achieve that goal. People's goals can stem from their motives. The goal of a motive is the satisfaction of that motive (Atkinson, 1958/1983; McClelland, 1987). For instance, hunger motivates eating because that achieves the goal of satisfying hunger. Similarly, gaining friends is the goal of the need to affiliate because friends satisfy that need. An **incentive** is an anticipated reward or aversive event available in the environment. It is also contingent on behavior, which means that a person must perform the prescribed behavior to attain or avoid it. Goals and incentives are connected. While goals are the focus of motivation, incentives can contribute to that motivation. Incentives contribute by making a goal seem more attractive or valuable. For instance, grades, parental approval, and feelings of self-esteem are positive incentives that help motivate (incentivize) a student to work toward the goal of graduation. A late charge is a negative incentive that helps motivate the goal of prompt bill paying. Sometimes, however, the distinction between motives and incentives or goals is not clear. For example, in a murder mystery, detectives may ask, "What was the perpetrator's motive?" when they meant to say, "What was the goal of the crime?" In life, the motivation of behavior is a function of all three: motives, goals, and incentives.

Push and pull. Is motivation the result of being pushed, pulled, and their combination? The Little Blue Engine's motive (desire) pushed it to the next town, while the importance of that destination pulled it there. Likewise, motives (desire, want, longing) push individuals toward some end-state while external objects, referred to as incentives and goals, pull individuals there. Figure 1.1 illustrates this push/pull view of motivation toward different end-states. A person's internal disposition specifies the nature of this end-state or goal. Internal dispositions may consist of biological motives such as hunger, psychological motives such as the need to belong, or a value system that confers worth on an incentive or goal. Figure 1.1 illustrates that hunger pushes a person toward a goal of eating food and a psychological need to belong pushes a person toward a goal of being with good friends or family members. In addition, a person's values determine

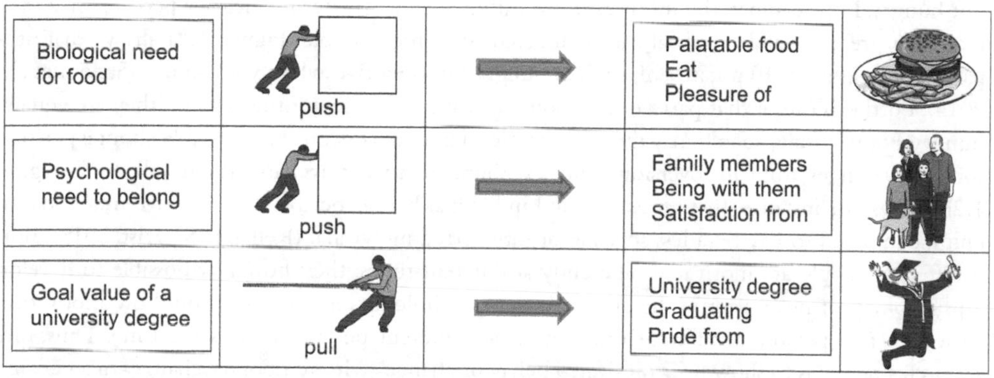

FIGURE 1.1 Push/Pull Motivation. Motives such as biological needs and psychological needs act like a push motivation, while external incentives and goals act like a pull motivation. The actions of push/pull bring individuals to the desired end-states.

the pulling power of a particular incentive or goal, such as the value placed on a university degree. From the combination of push and pull, individuals are motivated toward the appropriate end, where motives and goals become linked together. There, for example, eating satisfies hunger, relating to others fulfills the need to belong, and completing university requirements achieves the valued goal of graduation.

Emotions as motives. Emotions are a special case of push motivation. For example, fear, anger, disgust, and sadness push individuals toward end-states defined by the aim of the emotion. However, those end-states also act like goals and pull the individual. An **emotion** is a universal integrated reaction that involves channels of behavior, thoughts, feelings, and physiological responses. These channels function in unison to effectively cope with a challenging environmental event and thus enhance an individual's chances of survival (Keltner & Shiota, 2003). First, notice that several channels or response variables are motivated to occur in an integrated manner to achieve the aim (or goal) of the emotion. An emotion involves physiological changes that make behavior possible, while it also guides thought processes and provides the subjective feel of the emotion. Second, the integrated set of responses is designed to aid survival as individuals deal with environmental demands, such as danger, a blocked goal, or a significant loss. Finally, emotions are universal, which implies that all people experience them similarly.

Purpose of a Motivation Psychology

Can there be grand theories of motivation that would apply equally to everyone, such as the law of gravity? For example, imagine a tall, heavy person and a short, light person jumping, simultaneously, off the high platform into the swimming pool. Regardless of their difference in height and weight, both will hit the water simultaneously. A simple explanation is based on the law of gravity; it applies equally to all objects regardless of their size or weight. Unfortunately for psychology, things are not so simple. What motivates a person at one time may not do so at another time. And, what motivates one person may not motivate another.

For example, food motivates people to eat when they are hungry but less so when they are not hungry. Furthermore, the motivation for eating may be greater for heavier people, since they require a greater number of calories compared to lighter people. Figure 1.2a shows that at a party, you might eat 10 potato chips when hungry but only five when you are not (Sadoul et al., 2014). Furthermore, at that party one person may eat more than another, even if they are equally hungry. For example, people may differ in their level of extraversion. This variable about a person's sociability ranges from introversion (quiet, withdrawn) to extraversion (bold, talkative). Figure 1.2b shows, for instance, that an extraverted individual being sociable and talkative might eat 10 chips, compared to five by a less sociable or introverted individual (Keller & Siegrist, 2015). But, if different people are motivated differently at different times, then how is it possible to develop a psychology of motivation? The answer is that psychologists attempt to show how motivation varies *within* a person at different times or *among* different people at the same time. Thus, one research strategy is to show how motivated behavior changes with temporary changes in a person's internal motives, such as hungry versus not hungry (see Figure 1.2a). A second research strategy is to show how motivated behavior varies among different individuals, such as introverts versus extraverts (Figure 1.2b).

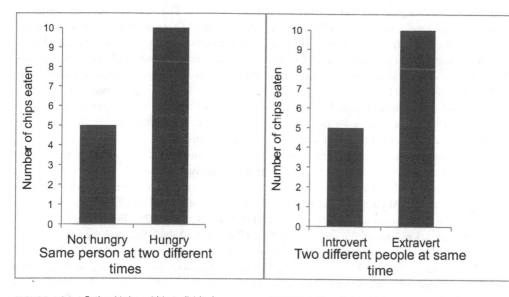

FIGURE 1.2A Eating Varies within Individuals. An individual eats more when hungry compared to when not hungry.

FIGURE 1.2B Eating Varies among Individuals. One individual eats more than another; an extravert eats more at a party than an introvert does.

Motivation as Anticipation of the Future

Think of motivation as a journey that takes you to an end-state or destination of your choosing. This journey idea implies that individuals are capable of looking ahead and visualizing their future. In fact, philosophers and early psychologists have long been aware that humans are motivated by the anticipated outcomes of their actions. In the first general psychology book, from 1797 (Hatfield, 1998), *Anthropology from a Pragmatic Point of View*, Immanuel Kant (1797/ 1978) describes the faculty of foreseeing. "Among all the prospects which man can have, the most comforting is, on the basis of his present moral condition, to look forward to something permanent and to further progress toward a still better prospect" (p. 78). A person may never have experienced the event before, but may have thought about various aspects of it.

Figure 1.1 illustrates motivation as being pushed or pulled toward end-states that highlight things, behaviors, or feelings. For example, the end-state can be a thing such as food, a behavior such as eating food, or a feeling such as the pleasure that food provides. However, an intermediate step has been left out. An individual is motivated not by the actual end-state but by the expectation and anticipation of it. People go to a restaurant expecting that food is there, visit family and friends expecting their need to belong will be satisfied, and attend universities expecting to earn a degree. If the end-states in Figure 1.1 are not expected, then the behaviors will not occur. Motivation can depend on things or entities. Thus, why enter a restaurant, visit friends, or enroll in a university if things or entities such as food, friends, and a degree are not expected? Motivation can also depend on visualizing the end-state as **consummatory** (to consummate = to finish)

behavior, which signals the end of the motivational sequence. The consummatory behaviors in Figure 1.1 are eating, associating or being with others, or graduating. Finally, the end-state could consist of the subjective feelings that are part of consummatory behavior, such as the pleasure of eating, the happiness from relating to others, and the pride felt on graduation. Sometimes, however, the expectation or anticipation of the end-state receives little attention or occurs below the level of awareness. Habits are examples of behaviors that occur with little conscious awareness of their end-states. Psychologists have used various types of analyses to account for motivation in terms of expecting an end-state or goal. Cognitive analyses, behavioral anticipation, and affective devices are broad views of how to understand motivation.

Cognitive motivation. The pizza restaurant in Figure 1.3 illustrates the function of anticipation in pull motivation. One pull mechanism is **cognitive motivation**, which works by visualizing an end-state as a goal and executing a plan or following a script to achieve that goal (Miller et al., 1960; Schank & Abelson, 1977). This visualization is easiest to perform for concrete aspects of the goal and accompanying consummatory behavior (Shepard, 1978). For example, it is easy to form a mental picture of the concrete goal in Figure 1.3: a restaurant, a pizza, and eating. To reach the goal, however, requires a plan of action or series of behaviors to achieve it. These can also be visualized. The plan involves a hierarchy of steps or a sequence of specific behaviors that when performed bring individuals closer and closer to their goal (Miller et al., 1960; Schank & Abelson, 1977). For example, if a student's goal is to reach the restaurant, then the first stage is to locate it on her cognitive map. The next stage is to select a route and then to walk or drive to the restaurant until she arrives, orders, and eats.

Anticipatory behavior and simulation. Behavioral anticipation is a second mechanism by which pull motivation occurs. Over half a century ago, neo-behaviorists formulated an **anticipatory response mechanism** to account for goal motivation (Lachman, 1960; Spence, 1956). According to this mechanism, the goal evokes excitement in the form of minuscule consummatory behaviors that would occur to the actual goal. For example, the goal in Figure 1.3 consists of eating pizza, which is referred to as consummatory behavior because it consummated (finished) the motivation

What motivates a person to go to a pizza restaurant and eat pizza?

Cognitive motivation: Visualize pizza restaurant and follow plan to arrive there.

Anticipatory response mechanism: Stimuli that predict arrival at the restaurant elicit responses that motivate and guide an individual to go there.

Simulation: Visual, sensory, and behavioral imaginary for reenactment of pizza eating. This experience motivates and guides individuals to go to the restaurant.

Affective forecasting: Presumed pleasure from eating pizza is pleasant and this anticipated feeling motivates approaching the restaurant.

FIGURE 1.3 Motivation as Anticipation. Motivation for pizza involves anticipating the following: (1) Visualizing a pizza, which is the goal object; (2) visualizing eating pizza, which is the consummatory behavior; and (3) visualizing the pleasure of eating the pizza, which is the subjective feeling.

sequence that began with hunger, the thought of food, and choosing the restaurant. The anticipatory response mechanism consists of imaginary responses that resemble actually eating pizza: handling pizza, chewing, and salivating. These responses occur involuntarily to events that predict or are associated with eating pizza, such as dinner time, rumbling of stomach, someone saying "pizza," pizza advertisement, and the location of the restaurant. An individual is aware of this anticipation, which serves as a stimulus that pulls the individual toward the restaurant. Furthermore, anticipation becomes more intense the closer a person gets to actually eating the pizza. In this sense, the anticipatory response mechanism becomes a case of pull motivation, since the stimuli associated with the goal pull individuals along to the pizza restaurant.

Motivation toward a specific end-state also occurs by way of simulation; an elaboration of the anticipatory response mechanism. **Simulation** refers to an array of anticipated psychological experiences that occur as if the individual were actually experiencing the end-state. These experiences could consist of visualizing the end-state, mentally interacting with it, or imagining what it would feel like (Barsalou, 2008, 2009). In addition, different aspects of simulation are linked to different brain regions. Thus, in anticipating the various features of the end-state, their corresponding brain areas become active. For example, in the case of food, one set of interconnected areas respond to the sensory and hedonic qualities of food, while other brain areas are involved in the expected perception and interaction with food (Barrós-Loscertales et al., 2012; Decety & Grèzes, 2006; Lewis, 2006; Simmons et al., 2005). In the case of simulating the goal of eating pizza, several motivational features are present (see Figure 1.3). First, there is the imagined perception of what the pizza looks like upon arrival at the table. Second, there is the simulated sensory experience of smelling and eating pizza. In addition, part of the simulated environment includes the location and social setting. All of these psychological experiences emerge from brain regions that give rise to these visions, sensations, pleasures, and behaviors. Thus, simulation is the psychological reenactment of an actual eating pizza experience that motivates the individual toward the restaurant.

Affective forecasting. Anticipating how we will feel, our affect, is the fourth motivational mechanism. **Affective forecasting** resembles a weather report but concerns the individual's expected subjective feelings of pain and pleasure in the future. These feelings arise from achieving a goal and from the accompanying consummatory behavior, such as the pleasure of eating pizza when hungry. Thus, affective forecasting is an important determiner of motivation, since people's choices and future behaviors are based on their anticipated feelings. Troland (1928/1967), for instance, claimed that the present anticipation of future pleasure is pleasant and the present anticipation of future pain is unpleasant. Thus, anticipating a positive goal is associated with pleasant feelings, while expecting a negative outcome is associated with unpleasant feelings. People are usually accurate in forecasting whether their feelings will be unpleasant or pleasant. However, they are more likely to err in predicting the intensity and duration of those feelings (Wilson & Gilbert, 2005).

What are the implications for errors in affective forecasting? For instance, try to forecast your level of positive affect during a 15-minute walk on campus. This walk could either be indoors by way of buildings and tunnels or outdoors on a path between a road and a river at the edge of campus. Before starting out, forecast your positive affect by rating, for example, how active, excited, and interested you would be on the indoor walk or on the outdoor walk. Then, after completing the walk, rate your positive affect again. Figure 1.4 shows the forecasting errors that

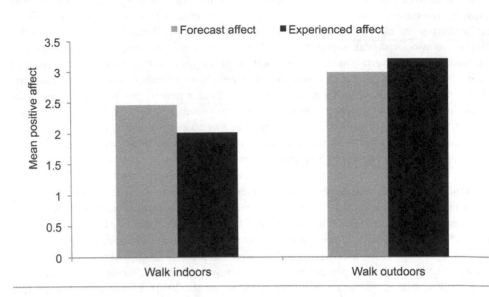

FIGURE 1.4 Predicted and Experienced Affect for a Walk. Participants made forecasting errors in how they would feel during a walk. A walk indoors in buildings and through tunnels created less positive affect than forecast. A walk outdoors created more positive affect than forecast.

Source: Adapted from "Underestimating Nearby Nature: Affective Forecasting Errors Obscure the Happy Path to Sustainability" by E. K. Nisbet and J. M. Zelenski, 2011, *Psychological Science, 22*, Table 2, p. 1104.

were made: Participants overestimated their positive affect for the indoor walk and underestimated their positive affect for the outdoor walk (Nisbet & Zelenski, 2011). One implication is reduced happiness that results when an individual chooses an indoor path rather than an outdoor one. In another example, imagine being an introverted, reserved, quiet individual who is asked to act like an extravert by being bold, talkative, and assertive. Forecast what your positive affect (excited, interested) and your negative affect (worried, nervous) would be prior to acting in this manner. Then rate yourself afterwards. Results of such research indicate that introverted individuals, when required to act extraverted, underestimated their positive affect and overestimated their negative affect (Zelenski et al., 2013). As a result of these affect prediction errors, introverted individuals may tend to avoid social settings where extraverted behavior is expected. But in doing so they miss opportunities for a good time.

Aspects of Motivation as a Journey

If motivation is like a journey from a current position to a selected end-state, then how is the end-state chosen and how does an individual arrive there? The answer lies in Table 1.1. Choice, the first consideration, refers to selecting the motive or outcome from those vying for satisfaction. The choice becomes the goal. A senior in high school has several choices to make, including whether to enter the armed forces, seek employment, or attend a vocational college or a university.

TABLE 1.1 Major Indicators of Motivated Behavior

Behavior	Definition and Example
Choice	What an individual actually chooses or selects from among possible alternatives. Example: a student chooses to major in psychology rather than some other discipline.
Activation	An individual is spurred or induced into action from a previously inactive state or a change in action or behavior. Example: a seated individual gets up and walks to class but then runs in order not to be tardy.
Frequency	This refers to how often (rate) a specific behavior occurs during a fixed time interval. Example: some individuals might check their email accounts five times per hour.
Intensity	This refers to the effort, exertion, force, or vigor with which motivated behavior or thought is performed. Example: when the door did not open when pulled, he thought hard, then pushed on it with great force.
Persistence	Also known as perseverance, it is revealed by the duration of motivated behavior. Example: after 10 job interviews in six months without success, the applicant was finally hired after the eleventh interview during the seventh month.

Which option is chosen depends on the intensity of the motive, the attractiveness of the incentive and goal, the likelihood of success, and the amount of effort required. However, choice is only the first step. Next, an individual must be motivated to do what is required to realize her chosen goal. **Instrumental behaviors** are those motivated activities in which a person engages to satisfy a motive, attain an incentive, or achieve a goal. Working for money, studying to pass a test, and acting kindly toward people are all examples of instrumental or motivated behavior. Working, studying, and acting kindly are instrumental in earning money, passing exams, and being liked. Often, an individual can also choose from among several different ways of satisfying a motive. For instance, in the process of finding a job a person may choose from among reading want ads, visiting an employment agency, accessing online job sites, attending job fairs, or consulting the university placement office.

Instrumental behaviors that reflect motivation include activation, frequency, intensity, and persistence (see Table 1.1). Activation may be the most basic aspect of motivation, since it indicates being spurred into some kind of action or a change in action. For example, a person proceeds from doing nothing to doing something, such as from sitting to walking and then to running. Frequency refers to the rate of a particular behavior, such as class attendance, going to the gym, or sending text messages. For example, what percentage of your classes do you attend? How many days per week do you exercise? And how many text messages do you send per day? Intensity or effort of behavior varies directly with motivation. For example, a person's depth of concentration may make him impervious to incoming text messages. Intensity may also imply yelling rather than talking and running rather than walking across the street. Persistence or duration refers to the amount of time a person persists in order to satisfy a motive or achieve a goal. For example, how many years is a person willing to spend preparing for a chosen career or how many hours for typing a course paper?

Auxiliary Assumptions about Motivation

Knowledge and competence are two hidden assumptions regarding motivation. Even if all sources of motivation are in place, behavior may not occur if these assumptions are not met. A motive will not be satisfied or a goal will not be achieved if a person lacks the knowledge and competence to do so.

A student may be motivated to obtain summer employment to pay tuition, to earn a university degree, and to eventually become a practicing psychologist, but being motivated is not the sole factor for these events to be realized. The student must also know how to accomplish these goals and be competent or capable of doing so. Knowledge is important because it enables the individual to evaluate potential goals, understand how to achieve them, and assess the chances of success. *Competence* means being capable of performing the behavior necessary to achieve a desired end. Thus, individuals may fail to accomplish a task because they did not know how or were not able. For instance, what determines whether a person makes her or his bed in the morning? Knowledge implies that a person knows how. A person must know how to make a bed, such as straightening the covers and tucking in the sheets. Competence implies being able to execute the behavior. An individual may not be capable of making the top bed of a triple bunk even if he possesses the knowledge. Even with knowledge and competence, motivation is still the impetus or reason for doing the behavior; it initiates the action. So, did you make your bed this morning? If not, the reason most likely is a lack of motivation and not a lack of knowledge or competence. In the study of motivation, we assume that a person has the knowledge and competence to perform the behavior. Whether the behavior occurs, however, depends on motivation.

Section Recap

To be *motivated* means to be induced or moved into action or thought toward some end-state by either the push of a motive or the pull of an incentive or goal. A *motive* is an internal disposition that pushes an individual toward a desired end-state where the motive is satisfied. A *goal* is the cognitive representation of a desired outcome that an individual attempts to achieve. The goal guides the behavior that results in achieving it. An *incentive* is an anticipated feature of the environment that pulls an individual toward or away from it. Incentives enhance motivation for goal achievement. *Emotions* act like motives. They motivate an individual in a coordinated fashion along multiple channels (affect, physiology, behavior) to adapt to significant environmental changes. The purpose of the psychology of motivation is to explain what motivates the same person at different times and different people at the same time.

Motivation is based on anticipation of the future. It is represented by a journey, which means that an individual tries to reach or achieve various features of an end-state, like a material goal, consummatory behavior, or subjective feelings (affect). *Consummatory behavior* refers to the completion of a motivational sequence as in eating consummates the progression of planning and preparing a meal. End-states are anticipated by either being visualized cognitively as objects, experienced as anticipatory behaviors, or felt as affect. *Cognitive motivation* involves visualizing an end-state or goal as concrete objects, such as food or people. The *anticipatory response mechanism* is an imaginary consummatory response that serves as a sign of an individual's expectations about the interaction with the goal object. *Simulation* refers to anticipating the end-state as if an individual were actually experiencing, visualizing, or imagining it. *Affective forecasting* refers to predicting positive or negative future feelings that occur in expectation of goal achievement. These predicted feelings promote behavior toward or away from the goal. Motivation can also be represented as a behavioral journey that begins with the *choice* of a motive to be satisfied or goal to be achieved. Once a choice is made, a person is motivated to engage in *instrumental behavior* that will eventually satisfy the motive or achieve the goal. Behaviors that indicate motivation are the choices people make plus the activation, frequency, intensity, and persistence of behavior. Although motives and incentives are the causes of behavior, knowledge and competence are also necessary if behavior is to occur.

SOURCES OF MOTIVATION

Motivation refers to the sequence of events that starts with motives or anticipated incentives and goals and finishes at end-states. Here motives are satisfied, incentives are attained, and goals are achieved. In order to understand how motivation works, scientists sometimes concentrate on a person's internal dispositions (motives) and sometimes on external events. In Figure 1.1, internal dispositions are hunger, the need to belong, and the value system about a university degree. The external events are palatable food, friends and family, and a university degree. Internal dispositions that push are classified either as biological variables or as psychological variables, while external sources that pull the person are labeled environmental variables—that is, as incentives and goals. These variables compose the title of this book.

What are the biological and psychological sources of motivation? In other words, what gives rise to motives? What are the sources of incentives and goals? That is, why do we value certain incentives and goals over others?

Internal Sources

Internal dispositions divide into biological states (variables) and psychological states (variables) that determine what will be motivating.

Biological variables. Biological variables refer to material characteristics of the body and brain that serve to motivate behavior. In Figure 1.1, hunger, when considered as a biological variable, correlates with a particular state of the human body, such as little food in the stomach, a rapid decline in blood glucose, and the circulation of various hormones. The hormone ghrelin is an example of a specific biological variable. Ghrelin is released in the stomach and promotes hunger and eating. This hormone travels in the bloodstream, is high before meals, and decreases after eating (Cummings et al., 2004). In one experiment, Wren and coresearchers (2001) injected ghrelin into the bloodstream of one group of participants and saline (placebo) into another group. To determine the effects of ghrelin, participants rated their hunger and then were provided a buffet lunch, during which they could eat as much as they wanted. The results indicated that participants given ghrelin reported greater hunger and ate more than participants infused with saline. In addition, prior to their lunch ghrelin participants also indicated that they would eat more.

Psychological variables. Psychological variables refer to properties of the mind, such as its motives. These are studied indirectly through measurable indicators. For example, perspiration and smiles are used to indicate anxiety and happiness, respectively. Psychological questionnaires can also indicate the amount of a psychological variable, much like stepping on a bathroom scale indicates a person's weight. Higher scores indicate a greater amount of a psychological variable, such as a psychological need or motive. As a general rule, as a psychological motive increases there are accompanying increases in the motivation for need-relevant incentives, consummatory behaviors, and associated feelings.

For example, individuals who have an unsatisfied need to belong should prefer to work with people who show a willingness to work with others. This willingness is exhibited by a genuine smile compared to a polite but fake smile. Thus, individuals with an unsatisfied need to belong should prefer individuals who show genuine smiles because those individuals would satisfy one's need to belong. To test this hypothesis, Bernstein and coresearchers (2010) created a strong need to belong in their participants by having them write about an instance when they had felt excluded and rejected. The researchers created a low need to belong by having participants write about an instance of being included and accepted, while a neutral control group of participants wrote about yesterday morning. Next, participants were shown a series of brief videos of individuals exhibiting a polite but fake smile or a genuine smile. Participants indicated the degree they wanted to work with those individuals: *not at all* = 1 to *very much* = 7. Participants with the unsatisfied need to belong preferred to work much more with people showing genuine smiles compared to those showing fake smiles. This preference was much less pronounced for participants with a satisfied need to belong and for participants in the neutral group. Thus, individuals whose need to belong had been aroused through writing about social exclusions were more motivated to work with individuals who signaled social inclusion with a genuine smile.

How to spot genuine from fake smiles is demonstrated in the YouTube video titled "Can you spot a fake smile?" here: www.youtube.com/watch?v=7SqlilB1w3g.

External Sources

The environment is an obvious source of motivation. Environmental variables refer to those characteristics of incentives and goals that have the ability to attract or repel. Positive characteristics attract or pull us toward the incentive, while unattractive ones repel us. As a general rule, incentives and goals with higher values of attraction or repulsion are more motivating than those with smaller values. Thus, if the value of an incentive can be determined then its motivational power is known.

One example of the relationship between incentive value and motivation occurs between the value of the academic experience and student behavior, such as attending classes and studying. With a questionnaire approach, students could be asked the extent they found their coursework interesting, valuable, and important, and if they had reasons for doing it. Using such an approach, Legault and coresearchers (2006) found that declines in the value of schoolwork were associated with lower GPAs, less time spent studying, and greater intentions to drop out. An instance of the perceived value of university courses refers to their perceived *instrumentality*—that is, their function in rendering future rewards (Miller & Brickman, 2004). The instrumental value of a course is measured by requiring students to rate such statements as "Good grades lead to other things that I want (e.g., money, graduation, good job, certification)" (Greene et al., 1999, p. 431). Higher endorsements of such statements reflect a greater valuation of academic courses. Researchers have found that students earned higher grades in more valued courses (Greene et al., 1999) and indicated a greater willingness to do the required academic work (Miller et al., 1999).

Linking Biological, Psychological, and Environmental Variables

How do these biological, psychological, and environmental variables motivate behavior and thought? Scientists examine the mind and brain and their interaction with the environment to find answers to this question. Consider a classic topic in the study of motivation: the relationship between hunger and eating. Will the mind, brain, or the environment provide an understanding of the motivation for this common behavior? An environmental factor that contributes to hunger is food deprivation. People's personal experiences plus research show that longer periods of food deprivation increase the psychological value of food, the amount eaten, and efforts to obtain food (Polivy, 1996; Raynor & Epstein, 2001). Food deprivation also produces a number of psychological sensations related to hunger. These sensations are measured with scales that ask: How hungry are you? How much can you eat? How full do you feel? How strong is your desire to eat? These sensations of hunger increase with the time that has elapsed since a person's last meal (Friedman et al., 1999). Furthermore, stronger hunger sensations are associated with eating more food or more food energy (Sadoul et al., 2014). Do these psychological sensations of hunger have parallel events that occur in the body and brain?

The brain and mind are intertwined. According to the concept of **reductionism**, the mind's psychological processes can be reduced to the activity of billions of neurons in the brain. Neurons are cells that specialize in conducting electrical impulses. The brain's neurons receive information about the environment and information about the body. They process this information and communicate it via these electrical impulses among different parts of the brain. This communication is possible because neurons are interconnected to one another via complex networks. For example, neurons process and communicate information about the body's energy stores, about hunger sensations, and about the availability of food. However, neurons also require energy to perform their task of communication. Just as a car uses fuel when its engine is idling, a brain at rest uses fuel also. Furthermore, as a car uses more fuel when driven, the brain also uses more fuel in locations where its neurons are most active. Scientists use this feature of energy expenditure to determine what brain areas are currently processing information. For example, what areas of the brain show increased energy use that corresponds with hunger, the anticipation of food, and the pleasure of eating? Two procedures, known as brain imaging techniques, are able to measure increased energy use in active areas of the brain. One procedure is *positron emission tomography* (PET scan). It produces a three-dimensional picture indicating areas of the brain that are most active. The picture is obtained by measuring positrons. These are particles emitted by radioactive substances that have been injected into a person's bloodstream and carried to the brain. The particles concentrate in those brain areas that have the highest blood flow for transporting oxygen or the highest utilization of glucose. Another procedure for detecting brain activity makes use of *functional magnetic resonance imaging* (fMRI). This technique obtains high-resolution images of the brain from energy waves that are emitted from hydrogen atoms, which are released when the brain is surrounded by a strong magnetic field. The energy waves are influenced by the amount of oxygen in the blood of brain tissue. Increased blood flow and oxygen as detected by the fMRI indicate an active brain area.

Brain scanning techniques are demonstrated in the YouTube video titled "Discovering the Human Brain: New Pathways to Neuroscience (Davidson Films, Inc.)" here: www.youtube.com/watch?v=RREoQJUHSYE.

Reductionism is the process of linking psychological events to brain events. Scales and behaviors reflect psychological events, while PET scans and fMRIs measure brain events. Reductionism links the two events together. However, the brain is a basic biological entity and psychological events are reduced to it. For instance, the measurements of various hunger sensations are reducible to parallel events that happen in the brain. The brain monitors various substances in a person's blood, stomach, and small intestine in order to determine the level of the body's energy supply. Changes in the brain's registration regarding the amount of these substances parallel the ratings of various hunger sensations (Lemmens et al., 2011; Page et al., 2011). Furthermore, activity in certain brain areas predicts the amount of food consumption. For example, Nolan-Poupart and coresearchers (2013) had participants rate the pleasantness of a milkshake while simultaneously scanning their brains with an fMRI. Following the scanning procedure, participants were offered a milkshake to drink. The amount of milkshake consumption was predicted by activity in the center of the brain and in the orbitofrontal area, which is located behind the forehead. These results demonstrate the explanation of behavior via reductionism. The amount of milkshake consumed was reduced to or explained by the increased activity of neurons located in those brain areas. Applying reductionism to psychology means that the motivation of behavior may be reduced down to the activity of neurons in the brain. However, way more than this is required for understanding motivation. We also need to consider the role of cognitive activities and of characteristics of the environment.

But what if the workings of the brain do not reach consciousness—that is, we do not experience hunger sensation? Are we still motivated to eat? According to the concept of **emergence**, the brain's neuronal activity issues forth mental processes—that is, the mind is an emergent property of the brain. Based on emergence, the status of the body's energy supply emerges as hunger in a person's consciousness. Some parts of the brain have a more crucial role in the emergence of hunger, such as the orbitofrontal cortex (Malik et al., 2008). The mind-versus-brain distinction is important because scientists sometimes use the mind and sometimes the brain to explain the motivation of behavior. For example, hunger is a feeling in the mind that determines how motivated a person is to eat. Yet, the amount of food in the stomach or other bodily indicators of energy are registered by the brain. These bodily events also determine the motivation to eat. In the first example, the mind is used; in the second, the brain is used to explain the motivation of hunger and eating.

The Past as a Source of Motivation

Recall that internal dispositions refer to biological and psychological motives that push individuals into action. But how did biological and psychological motives develop and what are their function? Recall, also, that environmental variables describe the value of incentives and their ability to attract or repel. How do values concerning incentives develop?

Evolutionary and personal history. Push motivation depends on characteristics of the body, brain, and mind—that is, on biological variables and on psychological variables. These two variables are the result of our evolutionary history and personal history. **Evolutionary history**, or the remote past, refers to the effects of millions of years of natural selection in shaping motives and emotions that aided survival of the individual and the species. As a consequence of natural selection, relevant motives or emotions increase in frequency in the population. For example, motives that promote eating and drinking aid the survival of the individual, while motives that promote sexual behavior help perpetuate the human species. The emotion of fear motivates individuals to avoid danger or dangerous animals such as black widow spiders, pythons, and Komodo dragons.

The field of **evolutionary psychology** attempts to understand current human behavior by relating it to our evolutionary past (Buss, 2015; Cosmides & Tooby, 2006). Applying evolutionary psychology to motivation is an attempt to describe and understand the origin of psychological motives through natural selection. How do biological and psychological motives aid the survival of the individual or humans in general? Fear of snakes, gender differences in what provokes jealousy, the universal appeal of music, and our preferences for sweets are all examples of behaviors that evolutionary psychologists have tried to explain in terms of natural selection. In other words, these motives presumably evolved because they aided human survival.

Personal history, in contrast, refers to an individual's experience from conception to the present. These experiences help shape an individual's motives and value system that involves determining the utility of goals and incentives. *Utility* refers to how useful something is to increase satisfaction and happiness, and decrease dissatisfaction. The greater an item's utility, the greater its value. Utility becomes an important explanatory concept when the incentive or goal is not linked to any obvious psychological or biological motive as in the case of money and course grades. Value or amount of utility is the pulling quality of an incentive or goal. Individuals learn that $100 is more valuable or useful than $10 and that an A grade is more valuable or useful than a B. The greater value determines that individuals are motivated to labor longer for $100 than for $10 and to study harder for an A than for a B.

Individual differences. Psychological differences among people provide a challenge in determining what motivates them. People with different psychological needs and different personality traits are motivated differently. Figure 1.2b illustrated this idea by showing that introverts reacted differently, by eating fewer chips than extraverts ate. In addition, individual differences in motivation become apparent from the fact that humans create the environments in which they live. According to Bandura's (2006) **agentic theory**, rather than merely reacting, humans also intentionally create the circumstances of their lives. People are not slaves to their environments and instead seek out or create environments to satisfy their different psychological motives (John & Robins, 1993; Winter et al., 1998). For example, one could speculate that most individuals who possess a stable need to belong will seek careers that will allow them to affiliate with others (Winter et al., 1998). In the case of people who differ in the level of extraversion, extraverts are more likely to prefer large parties than introverts are likely to prefer (Argyle & Lu, 1990).

Combined Internal and External Sources Motivate Behavior

The push/pull metaphor of motivation also suggests that internal and external sources combine to motivate behavior in both animals and humans. This joint effect is illustrated by the combined effects of a thirst drive (motive) and a water reward. Kintsch (1962), for example, produced various levels of a thirst drive by limiting rats' access to water. He then conditioned rats to run to the end of an alley, where different amounts of a water reward were available. The rats' response speed depended on the combined effects of the thirst drive and water reward. Notice in Figure 1.5 that rats responded fastest with a high thirst drive and a high water reward. Responding was slowest for the combination of a low thirst drive and small water reward. As a

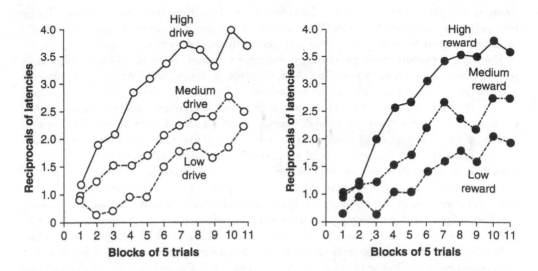

FIGURE 1.5 Drive and Reward Motivate Behavior. On the left, starting speed increases as the magnitude of the thirst drive increases. On the right, starting speed increases as the magnitude of the water reward increases. Response speed was fastest when high thirst drive combined with high water reward, and was slowest when low drive combined with low reward.

Source: From "Runway Performance as a Function of Drive Strength and Magnitude of Reinforcement" by W. Kintsch, 1962, *Journal of Comparative and Physiological Psychology*, 55, Figures 1 and 2, p. 883. Copyright 1962 by American Psychological Association.

general rule, as the size of the internal motive (thirst drive) and external reward (water) increases, motivated behavior increases.

The interacting effects of motives and incentives are much more complicated for humans. For instance, the same substance can serve as both. This dual effect occurs for money and food. Money deprivation can produce a motive that affects the value of food and food deprivation can produce a motive that affects the value of money. Money, obviously, can be used to buy food in order to satisfy hunger. So, as a person's hunger increases she is willing to spend more money for food. Yet, the reverse also seems to be true; hunger determines the incentive value of money. To illustrate, Briers and coresearchers (2006, exp. I) compared hungry and sated men for their willingness to donate money to charity. The results showed that hungry men were less likely to donate to charity than nonhungry men were likely to do. In experiment 2, the researchers induced hunger in female participants with the scent of freshly baked brownies. The results showed that hungry participants were less likely to donate money as part of a computer game than nonhungry participants were willing to donate. Thus, in both experiments hunger increased the incentive value of money. Because money was now considered more valuable, participants were less willing to part with it. In experiment 3, a desire for money was manipulated by asking both male and female participants to "list all of the things they would dream of buying if they won" a lottery. The dream of winning a large lottery (25,000 euros, about $26,500) presumably created a strong motive, while the dream of winning a small lottery (25 euros, about $26.50) presumably created a weak motive for money.

Then as part of a taste test, participants were allowed to eat as many M&M candies as they wanted. Participants with a strong motive for money ate more M&Ms than did participants with a weak motive. In this case, an increase in the motive for money was associated with an increase in the value of food (M&Ms) and consequently participants ate more.

The results in Figures 1.5 and 1.2a and those of the preceding paragraph about hunger and money illustrate why motivated behavior comes and goes. Behavior depends on internal states, which determine what incentives motivate behavior. Internal states refer to an individual's inner feelings (states), such as sleepiness, hunger, thirst, warm/cold, pain, sexual arousal, boredom, excitement, drug withdrawal, or an emotional feeling. It is as if the pulling power of an incentive depends on those states. For example, a person is pulled to food when hungry, to a sweater when cold, to a bed when sleepy, and to safety when afraid. The draw of those incentives will be negligible in the absence of hunger, cold, sleepiness, and fear. In this manner, what is motivating is constantly changing because people's internal states are constantly changing. Figure 1.2a illustrated this idea. Other incentives, on the other hand, motivate behavior independent of internal states and instead rely on a more stable value system. Thus, how motivated an individual is to obtain shoes, a smartphone, a tablet, or a college education depends on what those are worth—that is, how much value is placed on the utility of those items. So the study of motivation is to determine how internal states and value systems link up with external events. These links motivate behavior.

Emotions

Sensations such as cold, hot, thirst, hunger, and pain can invade a person's consciousness. These sensations serve to motivate specific actions in order to alleviate their unpleasantness. In addition to these sensations, however, there are other distinct feelings that serve as a source of motivation. These are known as emotional feelings or affect, such as happy, love, sad, anger, fear, shame, and disgust. Like the word motivation, which means to be moved into action, the term *emotion,* from the Latin word *emovere,* means to move out. When people experience an emotion, they are ready to move in a certain way (Leeper, 1948), as if emotional feelings ready a person for actions that are crucial for the experienced emotion (Frijda, 1986, 2007). The action is motivated to achieve the goal of the emotion. Thus, when experiencing anger in an unpleasant situation, for example, a person may be moved to verbally or physically aggress toward an intended target (Berkowitz & Harmon-Jones, 2004). But when experiencing an opposite emotion, say fear, a person is moved to behave differently, such as to withdraw in order not to incur harm. The behaviors differ because the goals of anger and fear differ.

Section Recap

The sources of motivation are either internal in the case of push motivation or external in the case of pull motivation. For push motivation, biological variables describe a person's brain and nervous system while psychological variables describe properties of a person's mind, such as psychological needs. Biological and psychological variables are conceptually linked through reductionism and emergence. *Reductionism* is the principle that concepts from psychology can be explained by reducing them to principles based on the body's physiology or brain. *Emergence* is the reverse of reductionism and represents the view that the brain's neuronal processes generate psychological feelings, which can motivate people to act. Environmental variables describe external sources of motivation, such as the value or utility of an incentive or goal. As value or utility increases, motivation increases. Motivation has different origins. One is the *evolutionary history* of humans, which embraces our remote past. The purpose of *evolutionary psychology* is to describe and explain motivated behavior in terms of human evolution. *Personal history* refers to a person's lifelong experiences that shape a person's motives and determine the utility of goals and incentives. Utility is the ability of a goal to increase satisfaction and happiness and decrease dissatisfaction and unhappiness. Motivation also depends on stable individual differences, such as psychological needs and personality traits. In addition, people do not merely react but also act by anticipating, selecting, creating, or altering their environments according to *agentic theory*. Internal sources like drives and needs interact with external sources like incentives and goals to motivate behavior. Furthermore, the same substance can serve as a drive source in one situation and an incentive in another. Motivation by an incentive depends on the internal state of the individual as when food motivates behavior provided a person is hungry. The Latin word emovere (to move out) is the origin of the word emotion. Emotions also serve as motives. When a person experiences an emotional feeling she is ready to act in a manner that motivates her to accomplish the aim of the emotion.

STUDY OF MOTIVATION AND EMOTION

For individuals to determine what motivates their behavior, they need only observe the link between it and prior events. The philosopher René Descartes made this recommendation in 1649 regarding the study of emotions. Everyone feels emotions, and so there is no need to make use of observations about emotions from elsewhere. Similarly, the philosopher Jeremy Bentham (1789) made observations regarding aspects of incentive motivation 90 years before the beginning of a science of psychology in 1879 (Boring, 1965). According to Bentham, characteristics of stimuli such as intensity, duration, certainty, and closeness enhance pleasure and thus increase their power of motivation. However, there are several problems with relying on personal insights or those of philosophers to uncover principles of motivation and emotion. For example, is what is true of one individual also true of another? Are people aware of all of the events that motivate their behavior? How certain can individuals be about what motivates their behavior? Psychology as the science of cognitive processes and behavior can help answer these questions. The content of this book is based on information that was obtained by psychology's use of the scientific method.

Imagine the goal of earning a coupon from a fast-food restaurant versus earning a bachelor's degree. Both goals motivate behavior, but they cannot be investigated in the same manner. A psychologist can study the extent a food coupon motivates performance on some laboratory task. For instance, how many anagrams or arithmetic problems will a participant solve in 10 minutes in order to earn a coupon? However, studying how a bachelor's degree motivates behavior over several years cannot be done in the laboratory. In this case, it is necessary to use questionnaires and survey a group of students over a number of semesters. Perhaps it will be discovered that the likelihood of earning a bachelor's degree depends on how intrinsically motivated students are to study the material in their classes. Thus, all questions about motivation cannot be studied with the same method.

Conduct the following thought experiment: Re-create in your mind as vividly as possible a situation in which you were greatly embarrassed. Now concentrate on these memories long and hard. Do you feel embarrassed all over again? Is your face getting warm and red? Would this be an effective way to study emotions by re-creating them from memory? Maybe you are not feeling this emotion at the same intensity but only as a weak reminder of what you originally experienced. If psychologists wanted to study intense emotions, it would not be ethical to embarrass, frighten, or anger someone in a laboratory to study these emotions. It might be possible to study mildly felt emotions in the laboratory, but extremely intense emotions likely would have to be investigated as they occur naturally in people's lives.

Research in Motivation

Psychologists use two different methods to research motivation and emotion. *Experimental research* is usually conducted in a laboratory. It involves manipulating a motivational variable to determine the effects on any behaviors, such as those described in Table 1.1. *Correlational research*, in contrast, is different, since it does not manipulate a variable. Instead, it involves measuring an existing motivational variable to determine how the measured values are associated with behavioral indicators of motivation from Table 1.1. Whether experimental or correlational research is employed depends on the phenomenon being investigated but also on the feasibility and ethics of doing so.

Experimental versus correlational research. An **experimental variable** is one whose values are created. For instance, an experimenter can establish different values of incentives and goals, such as a $1 versus a $10 incentive or an easy versus difficult goal. A **correlational variable** is one whose values already exist. Researchers only measure preexisting values of a correlational variable, such as measuring people to classify them as introverts or extraverts. For example, both experimental and correlational variables were employed during an investigation of how introverts and extraverts react to leisurely activities (Matz et al., 2016). The experimental variable defined the activities: one involved spending a $10 voucher on buying a book and reading it. The other activity involved spending a $10 voucher at a bar while remaining there. The correlational variable considered differences among people in terms of their level of extraversion. A personality test measured a participant's level of extraversion before the start of the investigation. Based on this measurement, introverts were defined as individuals who performed in the bottom third of the test and extraverts in the top third. Do individuals react differently to the bookstore versus bar experience? And does this difference depend on whether the individuals are introverted or extraverted?

People's reaction to the bookstore or bar experience is the dependent variable. A **dependent variable** refers to behavior that depends on the experimental variable but is only assumed to be associated with the correlational variable. In the bookstore versus bar experiment, the dependent variable consisted of the participants' subjective reaction to receiving the voucher, using it, and then staying at the bookstore or bar. Participants rated their positive affect on several adjectives both before and after each experience. For example, how happy are you now on a 1 to 5 scale? Introverts and extraverts reacted differently to the bookstore versus bar. Figure 1.6 shows that introverts had a strong increase in positive affect to the bookstore experience and a slight decrease to the bar experience. Extraverts, on the other hand, had a mild increase in positive affect to both experiences. The correlational variable of extraversion shows one way that people

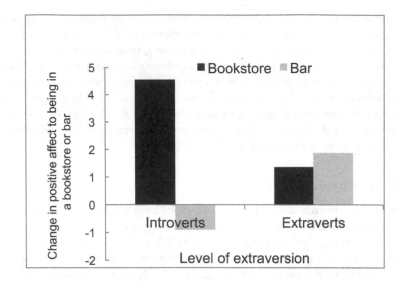

FIGURE 1.6 Introverts and Extraverts React Differently. Introverts exhibited a strong increase in positive affect to the bookstore experience and a slight decrease in positive affect to the bar experience. Extraverts showed a slight increase in positive affect to both experiences.

Source: Adapted from "Money Buys Happiness When Spending Fits Our Personality" by S.C. Matz et al., 2016, *Psychological Science, 27*, Table S3.

differ in what motivates them. In this case, introverts strongly prefer to go to bookstores rather than bars, while extraverts are content in both places.

Feasibility and ethics. It is neither feasible nor ethical to study some motivational phenomena in the psychology laboratory. In experimental research, different intensities of a motive can be created to determine how this will affect behavior. However, there is a limit to how intense the motive can be. With correlational research, a greater range of motive intensities is possible. Many motives occur naturally, and their intensity is measured along with changes in behavior. One question that arises is whether the results from laboratory experiments are the same as those from correlational studies done in natural settings. Anderson and associates (1999) have concluded that research from laboratory studies and from natural settings provides similar results.

The questions about feasibility and ethics arise, for example, in research on the effects of hunger on behavior. Different degrees of hunger can be created experimentally or can be measured from the amount that people experience voluntarily. For example, does food deprivation produce an image of food that guides the search for food (Warden, 1931)? Would the strength of the image and the motivation for food change with the degree of hunger? But how long could human participants practically and ethically be deprived of food to study this? Because of practicality and ethics, these two questions may be answerable partly in the psychology laboratory and partly from events that happen in the world. Some motivation experiments are appropriate in the psychology laboratory because the conditions studied are not too severe for the human participants. Biner and associates (1995, 1998) manipulated hunger by asking one group of students not to eat breakfast or lunch and asking another group to eat both meals prior to reporting for a 1:00 p.m. experiment. Students complied voluntarily with the requests. Would it have been ethical to ask human participants to go for even longer periods without food?

Research in a natural setting. Yet there are people who deprive themselves of food for long periods of time of their own volition. For example, people with anorexia and hunger strikers go voluntarily without food for much longer periods of time than do participants in the typical psychology experiment. Brozek and associates (1951) studied the effects of a semistarvation diet on a group of male conscientious objectors during World War II. The men were put on a very restricted diet for 24 weeks, during which time they lost an average of 37 pounds. Over the 24 weeks, their motivation for food increased, while that for sex and activity decreased. In addition, their thoughts and actions were preoccupied with food the entire time. Food assumed the dominant theme in conversation, was the focus of their attention at movies, was involved in daydreaming, and was the subject in reading matter, such as cookbooks and recipes. By the end of the experiment, almost 59 percent of the participants reported being hungry most of the time. However, in O'Malley's (1990) description of hunger strikers, feelings of hunger eventually go away. Does this mean that the preoccupation with food and its images disappears also? This question is not answerable by an experiment, since it would not be practical or ethical to subject individuals for such long periods of time without food but instead may be answerable by investigating this phenomena when it occurs naturally. For example, people with anorexia and hunger strikers could be interviewed to determine the extent of their hunger symptoms and preoccupation with food.

Research in Emotion

An emotion consists of an interconnected pattern among subjective feelings, facial expressions, physiological changes, and emotion-linked behavior. Each of these components of emotion unfold in reaction to external changes or mental events. For instance, an insult induces anger, seeing old friends creates happiness, walking on a dark deserted street elicits anxiety, or the memory of an old friend triggers sadness. Emotions when studied in the psychology laboratory are evoked by the techniques described in Table 1.2. These have been shown to effectively elicit the various components of emotion (Lench et al., 2011). But how realistic are the emotional experiences

TABLE 1.2 Laboratory Methods Used to Induce Emotions

Method	Description
Autobiographic	Recall or write a personal memory of an intense emotional experience
Behavioral	Act in a way that is synonymous with a specific emotion
Films	Watch a brief video clip that was selected to elicit a discrete emotion
Imagination	Imagine being in the emotional situation that you read or hear about
Life Manipulation	Participate in an actual situation that would elicit emotion in real life
Music	Listen to musical excerpts that were selected to induce discrete emotions
Pictures	View a single picture that was designed to elicit a discrete emotion
Priming	React to emotion words, pictures or puzzles presented below awareness
Reading Text	Read a printed passage that is aimed to induce an emotional response
Velten	Read statements about self that refer to discrete emotional experiences

Source: Based on "Discrete Emotions Predict Changes in Cognition, Judgment, Experience, Behavior, and Physiology: A Meta-analysis of Experimental Emotion Elicitations" by H. C. Lench et al., 2011, *Psychological Bulletin, 137*, pp. 836, 837.

that are evoked in the artificial setting of a psychology laboratory? Can experimentally induced emotions match the intensity of emotions felt in life, such as parents grieving the death of their child, the joy felt in response to a wedding proposal, or the anger felt when a thief steals your identity? As in the case of motivation, feasibility and ethical concerns prevent the study of intense emotions in the laboratory, and thus such emotions can only be investigated as they occur naturally.

Sources and Scope of Motivation

If motivation is the inducement of an individual's actions, thoughts, and feelings, then what is the source of this inducement? As the book's title implies, psychologists can look to the biological —that is, the nature of the body and specifically the structure and workings of the brain. Part of the biological view is the consideration of how the brain evolved. What function did it play in our evolutionary past and how does that function affect human motivation today? The psychological refers to properties of the human mind, in contrast to the body and brain. The psychological is represented by motives, such as psychological needs, wants, and desires, but also by other characteristics, such as personality traits. And, finally, the environmental can be divided into two categories. The first concerns the objective environment—that is, material things, such as money, grades, or prizes. The second concerns the cognitive representation of some external event, which is a case of cognitive motivation. For example, graduation is not a thing but the mental representation of some event that a student can visualize in her mind's eye. The mental representation is the goal that attracts or draws a student toward it. However, if a mental representation is viewed negatively, then it would actually repel the individual and provide motivation for behavior so that it would not happen.

Furthermore, the sources of motivation cut across various disciplines within psychology. Biological sources are a main consideration in disciplines that examine motivation and emotion in terms of an organism's autonomic and central nervous systems. These areas are covered in biological psychology, in cognitive and affective neuroscience, and in neuroscience outside of psychology. The relationship between arousal and performance is considered in sports psychology, and the relationship between stress and well-being is covered in health psychology. Internal sources, such as psychological needs, personality traits, and self-esteem, are included in the areas of social psychology, personality, and personal growth. Psychological needs are also examined in consumer psychology and advertising. In addition, social psychology often covers emotions, since other individuals are a major source of emotional experiences. Environmental sources of motivation, such as incentives, are found in courses on learning, conditioning, and behavior analysis. Behavior modification, for instance, relies heavily on external incentives to change behavior. Incentives and goals also receive treatment as a part of industrial psychology and work motivation. Finally, clinical psychology and the study of psychopathology also include the topic of motivation. For instance, amotivation (the complete absence of any motivation) and the overpowering motivation for drugs (as in addiction) are two opposite ends of the motivation continuum studied in these fields.

Section Recap

Feasibility and research ethics determine whether a phenomenon is studied using an experimental or correlational method. Experiments involve a researcher manipulating an *experimental variable* to create different values. Participants are subjected to the conditions or treatments that represent the different values of the manipulated experimental variable. Characteristics of people, such as their personality traits and psychological needs, define *correlational variables*. Psychologists measure the amount of an individual's trait or need with a psychological scale; they do not create the amount. The *dependent variable* refers to behavior that depends on the experimental variable or is associated with the correlational variable. Moderately intense motives and emotions are studied in the laboratory. To this end, a wide variety of procedures are used to create emotional experiences in the laboratory. Very intense motives and emotions, however, are less feasible and also unethical to create in the laboratory. Instead, they are studied in actual situations using correlational research methods. The study of motivation involves the study of biological variables—that is, what do the body and brain contribute? The study of psychological variables involves examining how mental processes contribute to motivation. Environmental variables are examined to determine how material incentives, goals, and their mental representations motivate individuals. Finally, the study of motivation is applicable to many different disciplines.

GLOSSARY

Term	Definition
Affective Forecasting	When a person predicts his or her subjective feelings (affect), much like the weather reporter forecasts the weather
Agentic Theory	Bandura's theory that humans willfully create or alter their circumstances, which in turn affect behavior
Anticipatory Behavior	Minuscule responses that resemble actual consummatory responses that occur when the goal is achieved
Anticipatory Response Mechanism	Minuscule consummatory responses elicited by stimuli associated with the goal; the mechanism describes prediction or looking forward to the goal
Biological	Characteristics of the material body or brain and how that relates to motivation
Biological Variables	Biological are internal body dimensions or brain properties that affect motivation, e.g., ghrelin
Cognitive Knowledge	Knowledge or know-how in the form of a cognitive map, a plan, or script that is necessary in order to achieve a goal or satisfy a motive
Cognitive Motivation	Visualizing the end-state or goal of the motivation sequence and mentally perceiving a plan or script to achieve that goal
Competence	Capability or skill necessary to perform the instrumental behavior that is necessary to achieve a goal or satisfy a motive
Consummatory Behavior	From the verb to finish, as in finishing the motivation sequence when the person interacts with the goal, e.g., eating or affiliating
Correlational Research	Research designed to describe the relationship between behavior and measures of an existing person or environmental variable
Correlational Variable	A variable the researcher measures in order to determine the different values on this variable
Dependent Variable	Behavior that depends on the different values of the experimental variable or is associated with different values of the correlational variable

continued ...

GLOSSARY Continued

Term	Definition
Duration or Persistence	An index of motivation that refers to the amount of time a person works to achieve a goal or to satisfy a motive
Emergence	Brain processes appear or materialize into consciousness as mental awareness
Emotion	An evolved coordinated effort among physiological, psychological, and behavioral dimensions in order to cope with an environmental demand or problem
Environmental Variables	Dimensions that characterize external incentives, such as quantity and quality and their effects on motivation
Evolutionary History	Accumulations of the effects of millions of years of natural selection that reside in a person's genes
Evolutionary Psychology	Trying to understand cognition, motivation, and behavior by examining our evolutionary past
Experimental Research	Research designed to describe the relationship between behavior and created or manipulated values of a person or environmental variable
Experimental Variable	A variable the experimenter manipulates in order to create different values on this variable
Forecasting	The prediction of an end-state as in affective forecasting resembles a weather report of a person's future subjective feelings
Frequency	An index of motivation that refers to the rate of performing an instrumental behavior that leads to goal achievement or motive satisfaction
Functional Magnetic Resonance Imaging (fMRI)	A brain imaging procedure that detects active brain areas from the increased blood flow and oxygen use detected from hydrogen atoms
Ghrelin	A hormone residing in the stomach that promotes hunger and eating; example of a biological variable
Goal	The cognitive representation of a selected end-state that a person commits to and is pulled toward achieving
Incentive	A valued feature of the environment that pulls an individual toward it if positive and repels an individual if negative
Instrumental Behaviors	A person's actions that are designed to achieve the goal or satisfy a motive; behavior that results in goal attainment
Instrumentality	The ability of an activity to provide future rewards
Knowledge	Understanding or comprehension that is necessary to achieve a goal or satisfy a motive; see "cognitive knowledge"
Motivated	To be moved into action or change in action by the push of a motive or the pull of an incentive
Motivation	A journey typified as motivated behavior from a beginning to a selected end-state comprised of a concrete goal, consummatory behavior, and subjective feelings
Motive	An internal disposition (hunger, desire, want) that pushes an individual toward a desired end-state or goal

continued . . .

GLOSSARY Continued

Term	Definition
Personal History	Accumulation of a person's experiences from his or her conception until the present
Physical Energy	Material energy, such as glucose that is used to power the brain and muscles
Positron Emission Tomography (PET)	A brain imaging procedure that detects active brain areas based on the highest blood flow and use of glucose, which is detected from measuring atomic particles
Psychological Variables	Dimensions of the mind or mental process that affect motivation, e.g., psychological needs
Push/Pull Motivation	Idea that motives push and incentives or goals pull people into action
Reductionism	Using the brain as a more basic entity to explain the workings of the mind, which is considered a less basic entity
Simulation	Anticipated psychological experiences that occur as if the individual were actually visualizing, interacting, or imagining an end-state
Utility	How useful something is to increasing satisfaction and happiness, and decreasing dissatisfaction

REFERENCES

Anderson, C. A., Lindsay, J. J., & Bushman, B. J. (1999). Research in the psychological laboratory: Truth or triviality. *Current Directions in Psychological Science, 8,* 3–9.

Argyle, M., & Lu, L. (1990). The happiness of extraverts. *Personality and Individual Differences, 11,* 1011–1017.

Atkinson, J. W. (1958/1983). Towards experimental analysis of human motivation in terms of motives, expectancies, and incentives. In J. W. Atkinson (Ed.), *Personality, motivation, and action: Selected papers* (pp. 81–97). New York, NY: Praeger.

Bandura, A. (2006). Toward a psychology of human agency. *Perspectives on Psychological Science, 1,* 164–180.

Barrós-Loscertales, A., González, J., Pulvermüller, F., Ventura-Campos, N., Bustamante, J. C., Costumero, V., & Ávila, C. (2012). Reading salt activates gustatory brain regions: fMRI evidence for semantic grounding in a novel sensory modality. *Cerebral Cortex, 22,* 2554–2563.

Barsalou, L. W. (2008). Grounded cognition. *Review of Psychology, 59,* 617–645.

Barsalou, L. W. (2009). Simulation, situated conceptualization, and prediction. *Philosophical Transactions of the Royal Society B: Biological Sciences, 364,* 1281–1289.

Bentham, J. (1789/1970). *An introduction to the principles of morals and legislation* (J. H. Burns & H. L. A. Hart, Eds.). London: Athlone.

Berkowitz, L., & Harmon-Jones, E. (2004). Toward an understanding of the determinants of anger. *Emotion, 4,* 107–130.

Bernstein, M. J., Sacco, D. F., Brown, C. M., Young, S. G., & Claypool, H. M. (2010). A preference for genuine smiles following social exclusion. *Journal of Experimental Social Psychology, 46,* 196–199.

Biner, P. M., & Hua, D. M. (1995). Determinants of the magnitude of goal valence: The interactive effects of need, instrumentality, and the difficulty of goal attainment. *Basic and Applied Social Psychology, 16,* 53–74.

Biner, P. M., Huffman, M. L., Curran, M. A., & Long, K. L. (1998). Illusory control as a function of motivation for a specific outcome in a chance-based situation. *Motivation and Emotion, 22,* 277–291.

Boring, E. G. (1965). On the subjectivity of important historical dates: Leipzig 1879. *Journal of the History of the Behavioral Sciences, 1,* 1–9.

Briers, B., Pandelaere, M., Dewitte, S., & Warlop, L. (2006). Hungry for money: The desire for caloric resources increases the desire for financial resources and vice versa. *Psychological Science, 17*, 939–943.

Brozek, J., Guetzkow, H., & Baldwin, M. V. (1951). A quantitative study of perception and association in experimental semistarvation. *Journal of Personality, 19*, 245–264.

Buss, D. M. (2015). *Evolutionary psychology: The new science of the mind* (5th ed.). New York, NY: Routledge.

Cosmides, L., & Tooby, J. (2006). Evolutionary psychology: Evolutionary theory, paleoanthropology, adaptationism. Retrieved August 26, 2015, from University of California, Santa Barbara, Center for Evolutionary Psychology: http://cogweb.ucla.edu/ep/

Cummings, D. E., Frayo, R. S., Marmonier, C., Aubert, R., & Chapelot, D. (2004). Plasma ghrelin levels and hunger scores in humans initiating meals voluntarily without time- and food-related cues. *American Journal of Physiology: Endocrinology and Metabolism, 287*, E297–E304.

Decety, J., & Grèzes, J. (2006). The power of simulation: Imagining one's own and other's behavior. *Brain Research, 1079*, 4–14.

Friedman, M. I., Ulrich, P., & Mattes, R. D. (1999). A figurative measure of subjective hunger sensations. *Appetite, 32*, 395–404.

Frijda, N. H. (1986). *The emotions*. Cambridge: Cambridge University Press.

Frijda, N. H. (2007). *The laws of emotion*. Mahwah, NJ: Lawrence Erlbaum.

Greene, B. A., DeBacker, T. K., Ravindran, B., & Krows, A. J. (1999). Goals, values, and beliefs as predictors of achievement and effort in high school mathematics classes. *Sex Roles, 40*, 421–458.

Hatfield, G. (1998). Kant and empirical psychology in the 18th century. *Psychological Science, 9*, 423–428.

John, O. P., & Robins, R. W. (1993). Gordon Allport: Father and critic of the five-factor model. In K. H. Craik, R. Hogan, & R. N. Wolfe (Eds.), *Fifty years of personality psychology* (pp. 215–236). New York, NY: Plenum.

Kant, I. (1797). *Anthropology from a pragmatic point of view* (V. L. Dowdell, trans.). Carbondale, IL: Southern Illinois University.

Keller, C., & Siegrist, M. (2015). Does personality influence eating styles and food choices? Direct and indirect effects. *Appetite, 84*, 128–138.

Keltner, D., & Shiota, M. N. (2003). New displays and emotions: A commentary on Rozin and Cohen (2003). *Emotion, 3*, 86–109.

Kintsch, W. (1962). Runway performance as a function of drive strength and magnitude of reinforcement. *Journal of Comparative and Physiological Psychology, 55*, 882–887.

Lachman, R. (1960). The r_g–s_g mechanism. *Psychological Review, 67*, 113–129.

Leeper, R. W. (1948). A motivational theory of emotion to replace "emotion as disorganized response." *Psychological Review, 55*, 5–21.

Legault, L., Green-Demers, I., & Pelletier, L. (2006). Why do high school students lack motivation in the classroom? Toward an understanding of academic motivation and the role of social support. *Journal of Educational Psychology, 98*, 567–582.

Lemmens, S. G., Martens, E. A., Kester, A. D., & Westerterp-Plantenga, M. S. (2011). Changes in gut hormone and glucose concentrations in relation to hunger and fullness. *American Journal of Clinical Nutrition, 94*, 717–725.

Lench, H. C., Flores, S. A., & Bench, S. W. (2011). Discrete emotions predict changes in cognition, judgment, experience, behavior, and physiology: A meta-analysis of experimental emotion elicitations. *Psychological Bulletin, 137*, 834–855.

Lewis, J. W. (2006). Cortical networks related to human use of tools. *The Neuroscientist, 12*, 211–231.

Malik S., McGlone, F., Bedrossian, D., & Dagher A. (2008). Ghrelin modulates brain activity in areas that control appetitive behavior. *Cell Metabolism, 7*, 400–409.

Matz, S. C., Gladstone, J. J., & Stillwell, D. (2016). Money buys happiness when spending fits our personality. *Psychological Science, 27*, 715–725.

McClelland, D. C. (1987). *Human motivation*. Cambridge: Cambridge University Press.

Miller, G. A., Galanter, E., & Pribram, K. H. (1960). *Plans and the structure of behavior*. New York, NY: Henry Holt.

Miller, R. B., & Brickman, S. J. (2004). A model of future-oriented motivation and self-regulation. *Educational Psychology Review, 16*, 9–33.

Miller, R. B., DeBacker, T. K., & Greene, B. A. (1999). Perceived instrumentality and academics: The link to task valuing. *Journal of Instructional Psychology, 26*, 250–260.

Nisbet, E. K., & Zelenski, J. M. (2011). Underestimating nearby nature: Affective forecasting errors obscure the happy path to sustainability, *Psychological Science, 22*, 1101–1106.

Nolan-Poupart, S., Veldhuizen, M. G., Geha, P., & Small, D. M. (2013). Midbrain response to milkshake correlates with ad libitum milkshake intake in the absence of hunger. *Appetite, 60*, 168–174.

O'Malley, P. (1990). *Biting at the grave: The Irish hunger strikes and the politics of despair*. Boston, MA: Beacon Press.

Page, K. A., Seo, D., Belfort-DeAguiar, R., Lacadie, C., Dzuira, J., Naik, S., . . . Sinha, R. (2011). Circulating glucose levels modulate neural control of desire for high-calorie foods in humans. *The Journal of Clinical Investigation, 121*, 4161–4169.

Piper, W. (1954/1961). *The little engine that could*. New York, NY: Platt & Munk.

Polivy, J. (1996). Psychological consequences of food restriction. *Journal of the American Dietetic Association, 96*, 589–592.

Raynor, H. A., & Epstein, L. H. (2001). Dietary variety, energy regulation, and obesity. *Psychological Bulletin, 127*, 325–341.

Sadoul, B. C., Schuring, E. A. H., Mela, D. J., & Peters, H. P. F. (2014). The relationship between appetite scores and subsequent energy intake: An analysis based on 23 randomized controlled studies. *Appetite, 83*, 153–159.

Schank, R. C., & Abelson, R. P. (1977). *Scripts, plans, goals and understanding*. Hillsdale, NJ: Lawrence Erlbaum.

Schopenhauer, A. (1841/1960). *Essay on the freedom of the will* (K. Kolenda, trans.). Indianapolis, IN: Bobbs-Merrill.

Shepard, R. N. (1978). The mental image. *American Psychologist, 33*, 125–137.

Simmons, W. K., Martin, A., & Barsalou, L. W. (2005). Pictures of appetizing foods activate gustatory cortices for taste and reward. *Cerebral Cortex, 15*, 1602–1608.

Spence, K. W. (1956). *Behavior theory and conditioning*. New Haven, CT: Yale University Press.

Troland, L. T. (1928/1967). *The fundamentals of human motivation*. New York, NY: Hafner.

Warden, C. J. (1931). The Columbia Obstruction Method. In C. J. Warden (Ed.), *Animal motivation: Experimental studies on the albino rat* (pp. 3–16). New York, NY: Columbia University Press.

Wilson, T. D., & Gilbert, D. T. (2005). Affective forecasting: Knowing what to want. *Current Directions in Psychological Science, 14*, 131–134.

Winter, D. G., John, O. P., Stewart, A. J., Klohnen, E. C., & Duncan, L. E. (1998). Traits and motives: Toward an integration of two traditions in personality research. *Psychological Review, 105*, 230–250.

Wren, A. M., Seal, L. J., Cohen, M. A., Brynes, A. E., Frost, G. S., Murphy, K. G., . . . Bloom, S. R. (2001). Ghrelin enhances appetite and increases food intake in humans. *The Journal of Clinical Endocrinology and Metabolism, 86*, 5992–5995.

Zelenski, J. M., Whelan, D. C., Nealis, L. J., Besner, C. M., Santoro, M. S., & Wynn, J. E. (2013). Personality and affective forecasting: Trait introverts underpredict the hedonic benefits of acting extraverted. *Journal of Personality and Social Psychology, 104*, 1092–1108.

CHAPTER 2

The History of Motivation and Emotion

He that would know what shall be, must consider what hath been.

H. G. Bohn, 1855

We hold these truths to be self-evident, that all men are created equal, that they are endowed by their Creator with certain unalienable Rights, that among these are Life, Liberty and the Pursuit of Happiness.

Declaration of Independence, July 4, 1776

How does psychology's past pave the way for the study of motivation and emotion? Consider these questions:

1. What is hedonism and how is it a source of motivation?
2. How did Darwin's concept of evolution contribute to understanding motivation?
3. What was Sigmund Freud's contribution to understanding motivation?
4. How did philosophers and early psychologists describe internal and external sources of motivation?
5. How did philosophers and early psychologists describe emotion?

BRIEF HISTORY OF MOTIVATION

Eve saw that the tree in the Garden of Eden bore delightfully edible fruit, which would provide wisdom when eaten. These qualities motivated her to eat the fruit. This scene from Genesis provides a very early demonstration of motivation, specifically external motivation by a meaningful incentive. Historically, people were already thinking about what motivates behavior certainly long before the beginning of psychology.

Philosophers and early psychologists speculated on a variety of ideas that are still pertinent to the study of motivation today. Their ideas include: sources of motivation, hedonism, instincts, unconscious motivation, drives, psychological needs, and incentives.

Aristotle's Theory

If to motivate is to induce or to cause a change in behavior, then the ancient philosopher Aristotle (384–322 BC) was probably one of the first to advocate a theory of motivation. Writing between 347 and 335 BC, he described four different types of causes: efficient, final, formal, and material (Peck, 1942). These four causes are still relevant for psychology (Killeen, 2001) and provide insight into sources of motivation. Aristotle's efficient causes refer to triggers of behavior. These are a person's current motives and incentives. For example, the sight of your favorite dessert triggers eating it. His final causes refer to the aim or purpose of motivated behavior. It is the goal of behavior. The aim of eating, for example, is to provide nourishment to the body. Formal causes refer to integrating the concept of motivation into models, hypotheses, or theories of behavior. Continuing the eating example, Darwin's theory of evolution maintains that humans evolved a preference for sweets during a time of scarcity. People were motivated to eat sweets since that provided a rich source of energy that was beneficial for survival. Finally, Aristotle's concept of material causes refers to the material of which a thing is made. The brain can be considered the material cause of motivated behavior. For instance, the material cause for eating dessert refers to the events occurring in the brain. In this case, the sight of dessert activates the brain's hypothalamus and contributes to the desire and the anticipated pleasure for sweets.

Hedonism

Two bumper stickers from times past read, "If it feels good, do it" and "If it's no fun, why do it?" Are these edicts accurate descriptions of human conduct? If so, are we merely pursuers of pleasure and avoiders of pain? Some early philosophers and pioneer psychologists agree that we are. We can see from Table 2.1 that this view has a long history.

Ancient sources. Nearly 2,400 years ago Greek philosophers were already discussing motivation under a principle known as **hedonism**—the pursuit of pleasure and the avoidance of pain. Although today the term hedonism often refers to sensory pleasures derived from food, drink, and sex, for philosophers the term meant striving for the greater good. The phrase "the Pursuit of Happiness" from the Declaration of Independence means striving for the greater good. It is doubtful that the signers of the Declaration meant for people to stop working and party all the time. While it is true that sensory pleasure might be attained from spending your tuition money to pay for nightly partying, a hedonically greater benefit would result if that money were used

TABLE 2.1   Quotes Illustrating the History of Hedonism as Motivation

Socrates (470–399 BC): "The right choice remains that in which the pleasures exceed the pains; this is the preferred course. The wrong choice remains that in which the pains outweigh the pleasures; this course is to be rejected" (Weiss, 1989, p. 518)

Democritus (460–370 BC): "The good is the same for all men in the sense that it is good for them to pursue pleasure and avoid displeasure or pain" (Hyland, 1973, p. 291)

Epicurus (341–271 BC): "We do not choose every pleasure either, but we sometimes pass over many pleasures in cases when their outcome for us is a greater quantity of discomfort" (Long & Sedley, 1987, p. 114)

Thomas Hobbes (1640): "This motion, in which consisteth pleasure or *pain,* is a *solicitation* or provocation either to draw *near* the thing that pleaseth, or to *retire* from the thing that displeaseth" (Hobbes, 1640/1962, p. 31)

John Locke (1690): *"Good,* the *greater good,* though apprehended and acknowledged to be so, does not determine the *will,* until our desire, raised proportionately to it, makes us uneasie in the want of it" (Locke, 1690, p. 35)

Jeremy Bentham (1789): "Nature has placed mankind under the governance of two sovereign masters, *pain* and *pleasure.* . . . The general tendency of an act is more or less pernicious according to the sum total of its consequences" (Bentham, 1789/1970, pp. 11, 74)

Herbert Spencer (1899): "Those races of beings only can have survived in which . . . agreeable . . . feelings went along with activities conducive to the maintenance of life, while disagreeable . . . feelings went along with activities destructive of life" (Spencer, 1899, p. 280)

Edward Lee Thorndike (1911): "The Law of Effect is that: *Of several responses made to the same situation, those of which are accompanied . . . by satisfaction to the animal . . . will be more likely to recur; those which are accompanied . . . by discomfort to the animal will be less likely to occur*" (italic in original; Thorndike, 1911, p. 245)

Sigmund Freud (1920): "[The pleasure principle] does not abandon the intention of ultimately obtaining pleasure, but it nevertheless demands and carries into effect the postponement of satisfaction, the abandonment of a number of possibilities of gaining satisfaction and the temporary toleration of unpleasure as a step on the long indirect road to pleasure" (Freud, 1920, p. 10)

Roger Brown and Richard Herrnstein (1975): "Barring the rare inborn movements, human behavior obeys the law of effect, *and nothing else*" (Brown & Herrnstein, 1975, p. 169)

to pay for your tuition and subsequent education. One of the first promoters of hedonism was the famous Greek philosopher Socrates (470–399 BC), who claimed that a person should follow a course of action for which pleasure exceeds pain (see Table 2.1). Further, Socrates claimed that the only reason a person would not do so is because he lacks complete knowledge of the pleasure or pain that can result. For Democritus (460–370 BC), it was both natural and good for people to follow this course (see Table 2.1), although he could not identify what was pleasurable or painful independent of a person's behavior. Something was pleasurable if an individual strived for it, and something was painful if an individual avoided it. So what is pleasurable or painful could differ for each individual. No matter what these things were, pleasure was to be pursued and pain was to be avoided (Hyland, 1973).

One might get the impression that Socrates and Democritus meant that we should "eat, drink and be merry as if there is no tomorrow." On the contrary, they felt that our pursuits should be followed in moderation, since this leads to greater pleasure in the long run. The idea of moderation was developed further over a century later by Epicurus (341–271 BC), who maintained that pleasure and pain average out. Thus, we might forgo certain intense pleasures if subsequent pain of greater magnitude is a result (see Table 2.1). For instance, an individual might drink alcohol in moderation, thereby avoiding the painful aftereffects of overindulgence. Similarly, moderation may require experiencing pain prior to pleasure. An individual may endure immediate pain because more enduring pleasure may be a consequence (Long & Sedley, 1987). To illustrate, a university student might forgo the immediate benefit of earning money at an unskilled job in hopes that spending her time earning a university degree will provide more meaningful and fruitful employment later. Or a student may forgo a party Thursday night in order to study for Friday's exam on the assumption that good exam performance will produce greater pleasure than a good party. The party, although providing immediate pleasure, may result in a hangover and poor exam performance the next day, thus compromising long-term gain.

Later philosophers. Things in the environment can produce pain or pleasure. For example, extra credit for doing additional coursework is a positive incentive that provides pleasure, while a fine for exceeding the speed limit is a negative incentive that produces pain. These examples of **incentive motivation** have their roots in the writing of Thomas Hobbes in 1640 (see Table 2.1). Incentives are anticipated events that are approached if pleasurable and avoided if painful. Our ability to anticipate that an incentive will be pleasant or unpleasant depends on our remembrance of a similar incentive that produced that feeling in the past. Thus, Hobbes (1640/1962) reasoned that a feeling of pleasure leads us to approach the situation responsible for that feeling, while an unpleasant feeling leads us to avoid the situation that produces it.

Incentives are in the future, and their power to provoke approach or avoidance behavior depends on how delayed they are. For example, does a person want an unchallenging minimum wage job immediately after high school graduation or is she willing to wait for better-paying and more challenging work after college? The often-cited conflict between a small immediate reward versus a large delayed reward is evident in the writings of John Locke in 1690 (see Table 2.1). He stated that a person may acknowledge that there may be a greater good or goal than those immediately available. These immediate rewards, however, appear to evoke a desire so strong that a person is unable to resist. Thus, for the delayed greater good to motivate behavior, it must evoke a desire stronger than the desire for immediate pleasure. Locke gives the example of an alcoholic who acknowledges that his health and estate are of greater value than drink. This same alcoholic, however, is unable to resist the lure of immediate drink and drinking companions (Locke, 1690).

The eighteenth-century philosopher Jeremy Bentham (1789/1970) put it bluntly: we are the servants of pain and pleasure (see Table 2.1). Like Hobbes before him, Bentham described motivation in terms of the positive and negative consequences of our actions. In this vein, he anticipated the notions of cognitive motivation and affective forecasting, described in Chapter 1. For him, *cognitive motivation* involved the perception of an external event that could happen. For example, a person could perceive holding a winning lottery ticket or perceive his house being on fire. *Affective forecasting* was intertwined with cognitive motivation. Thus, feelings of pleasure accompany one's imagination of holding the winning lottery ticket, while anxiety is associated with the thought "my house is on fire." Motivation results from the prospects or the anticipated consequences of a person's action (Bentham, 1789/1970). Either unpleasant or pleasant anticipated consequences determine the likelihood of our behavior. And if there is more than one possible outcome, the individual has the choice of which one to bring about.

Here we see the beginning of *decision theory*: of possible end-states, which should we choose to make our goal? To illustrate, in making a decision about what university to attend, one weighs both the pleasant and unpleasant aspect of each. The outcome of weighing both the visualized events and anticipated affect determines a person's decision (Bentham, 1789/1970). Bentham also uses the phrase **principle of utility** to describe the idea that our actions are determined by whether they decrease or increase our happiness. An incentive has utility if it is useful, benefits us, or induces pleasure or happiness, but it also has utility if it prevents pain or reduces unhappiness. Money, cell phones, and computers, for example, have utility because these objects provide the means to increase our happiness.

Sigmund Freud. Listed in *Time* (March 29, 1999) as one of the 20 most influential minds of the twentieth century (Gay, 1999), Sigmund Freud wrote on hedonism, instincts, and unconscious motivation. Although his theories have been criticized for their lack of scientific rigor, his ideas are still influential today in psychology, literature, and the arts. The theme put forth by Democritus and Epicurus—that of postponing immediate pleasure or enduring immediate discomfort for subsequent greater pleasure later—is repeated by Freud (1920). He postulated two principles relevant for increasing pleasure and decreasing pain (see Table 2.1). For Freud, pleasure was in contrast to unpleasure. In his **pleasure principle**, he referred to a person's pursuit of pleasure, which is attained from a decrease in psychological tension, especially when it follows from a sudden increase in tension. While pleasure results from reducing or keeping psychological tension as low as possible, unpleasure results when tension increases. Pleasure is also obtained from gratifying unconscious instinctual impulses or desires. According to Freud's **reality principle**, circumstances may force the individual to postpone immediate pleasure or endure discomfort if the result is greater pleasure later.

Edward Lee Thorndike. Pain and pleasure motivate behavior when those feelings reach our consciousness. Herbert Spencer (1881/1977) claimed that humans strive to bring feelings of pleasure into consciousness while also trying to drive out feelings of pain. In addition, he contended that pleasure supports behaviors that benefit life, while pain prevents behaviors that harm life. Furthermore, assume that the ability of cognitive forecasting is absent—that is, an animal or person lacks the ability to foresee future events. Then, Spencer claimed, the anticipation of pain or pleasure is the only guide for that individual's behavior. For such a creature, acts that give rise to pleasure will persist while acts that give rise to pain will cease. Is it possible to empirically demonstrate that pain and pleasure motivate behavior? In an early empirical demonstration, Thorndike (1898, 1911) rewarded a cat with food for escaping from a box. Thorndike observed that over a series of attempts the cat's escapes occurred faster and faster. In applying Spencer's formulations, escape brought forth a feeling of pleasure into the cat's consciousness and the behavior that brought it about was beneficial to the cat. Based on his research, Thorndike (1898, 1911) formulated an idea, similar to Spencer's, which was the **law of effect**: the cat escaped because of the satisfaction that resulted from escaping, whereas remaining in the box was associated with less satisfaction or with dissatisfaction (see Table 2.1). In general, a satisfying effect strengthened behavior, and a dissatisfying effect weakened behavior. Thorndike, of course, was faced with the problem that the cat could not tell him whether escape and food provided pleasure. Thorndike assumed that an animal behaves to attain a satisfying state and to remove a dissatisfying state. Can this assumption alone explain the cat's behavior? Another way of explaining behavior began when John Watson (1913) introduced *behaviorism*. This school of psychology emphasized observable behavior and its consequences rather than the subjective experiences of pain and pleasure. Thus, whereas Thorndike emphasized the pleasure or satisfaction derived from the cat's escape, Watson would have emphasized the actual freedom as the source of motivation for the cat.

A reenactment of Thorndike's famous puzzle box experiment is presented in the YouTube video titled "thorndike-puzzle box" here: www.youtube.com/watch?v=BDujDOLre-8.

Law of effect today. Thorndike's law of effect is widely accepted today but with an emphasis on the observable consequences of behavior, which are referred to as reinforcers and punishers. The current law avoids the subjective and unobservable nature of hedonism. Instead, reinforcers are defined as observable consequences that increase and maintain behavior. For example, a food pellet that results from a lever press is a reinforcer, provided the pellet increases or maintains the rat's lever pressing. A punisher is a consequence of behavior that reduces the frequency of the behavior. A loss of privileges for a child as a consequence of misbehavior is a punisher, provided that the misbehavior decreases. Today, many psychologists accept the view that human behavior is determined by the law of effect (Brown & Herrnstein, 1975; see Table 2.1). This law may sound similar to hedonism as proposed by the Greek philosophers some 2,400 years ago. However, hedonism emphasizes the subjective nature of motivation: pursue pleasure and avoid pain. The law of effect, however, emphasizes the objective nature of motivation: some stimuli increase behavior and other stimuli decrease it. There is no claim in the law of effect that the stimuli we approach provide some degree of pleasure or that those we avoid produce varying degrees of discomfort or pain if we fail to do so. The two principles emphasize different sources of motivation: internal and external.

Current trends. Current research has expanded the study of hedonism to include the function of self-control. In 1690, Locke had already noted that the distinction between pleasure and pain is easy to make when they are compared, side by side, in the present. The distinction becomes obscure, however, when trying to compare present feelings with future feelings. For example, compare the pleasure of spending this evening with friends versus the pleasure from earning a high exam score next week. If these sources of pleasure occurred simultaneously, Locke would argue that a student would have no trouble deciding which pleasure was greater. However, the decision becomes more difficult, according to Locke, because the pleasure from a high exam score is obscure owing to its distance in the future. Over 300 years later psychologists are researching what characteristics determine a person's choice between rewards that bring immediate smaller pleasure at the expense of larger delayed pleasures, such as the pleasure of friends tonight versus the pleasure of exam success next week.

Current research uses the term *impulsiveness* to describe individuals who display the tendency to choose smaller rewards, while self-control (self-discipline) describes those who choose larger but delayed rewards (Logue, 1988, 1998). Research shows that greater self-control provides benefits, such as better academic achievement. For example, Duckworth and Seligman (2005) employed several measures of self-discipline including the *Brief Self-Control Scale*. This scale permits individuals to rate themselves on such abilities as being able to resist temptation, think through the alternatives of their actions, and work toward long-term goals. A higher score on the scale means a person has a greater ability to exercise self-control. Duckworth and Seligman found that eighth graders with greater self-control earned higher GPAs regardless of their level of intelligence. Tangney and coresearchers (2004) also found that higher scores on the *Brief Self-*

Control Scale were associated with higher grades for university students, a better degree of adjustment, less alcohol abuse, and better interpersonal relationships and skills.

A copy of the *Brief Self-Control Scale* titled *"brief self-control scale"* is provided here: www.good medicine.org.uk/files/assessment,%20self-control,%20brief.pdf.

Current research also examines a version of Freud's reality principle by examining the utility of emotion regulation for goal achievement (Tamir, 2009). Freud (1920) realized that people are willing to experience discomfort, such as negative emotions, if greater benefits are derived later, such as positive feelings that accompany goal achievement. For instance, Tamir and Ford (2009) demonstrated that participants were willing to endure negative emotions of fear and anger to help achieve a goal. In their research, participants were led to believe that they would play a computer game that involved an avoidance goal of preventing being killed by flying monsters or aliens from outer space. Other participants played a computer game with a confrontational goal of avenging a murder or inflicting pain on an opponent. Participants were then provided with a choice of what music and memories they wanted to experience in order to experience fear, anger, or general excitement. The researchers discovered that for the avoidance goal computer game participants preferred the fear-inducing stimuli, while for the confrontational goal computer game they preferred the anger-inducing stimuli. A conclusion from this research is that participants were willing to endure the unpleasant emotion induced by these stimuli if they believed it would help them achieve their goals.

Positive psychology is another new front in the study of hedonism. Recall that there are two aspects to hedonism: decrease unhappiness or pain and increase happiness or pleasure. Locke would argue that unhappiness has a greater motivational impact because, when experienced, an individual is motivated to reduce that feeling. Happiness, however, is a future promise based on a person's current actions. As a result of the immediacy of unhappiness, psychologists have been mostly concerned with its reduction by treating, for example, depression, grief, anxiety, and distress. There had been little concern in going beyond the alleviation of unhappiness. However, 1999 marked the formal beginning of the discipline of positive psychology with the publication of a series of articles that addressed positive experiences, positive personality, and the social context for positive feelings (Seligman & Csíkszentmihályi, 2000). **Positive psychology** is the scientific investigation of possible factors that promote people, groups, and institutions to function at their best (Gable & Haidt, 2005). These factors may provide people with a prescription for what is good for them. For example, how should students spend their discretionary income, which is what remains after paying for tuition, books, and lodging? One piece of advice is that greater happiness ensues when money is spent on experiences, such as concerts, sporting events, and movies, rather than on material possessions, such as televisions and clothes (Van Boven, 2005).

Evolution and Motivation

Recall from Chapter 1 that evolutionary psychology attempts to understand current human behavior by relating it to our evolutionary past (Buss, 2015; Cosmides & Tooby, 2006). Evolutionary psychology assumes that humans are born with existing motives or are disposed to develop motives that prompt behaviors beneficial for survival. But how did these motives and dispositions originate? The answer to these questions comes from one of the most influential theories ever devised to help us understand motivation.

Charles Darwin. Do hedonism and a disposition toward utility occur in all animals and humans? Is this universal? Would the bases for these psychological traits have evolved over millions of years? Charles Darwin, as one of the originators of a **theory of evolution**, introduced in his book *On the Origin of Species by Means of Natural Selection* (1859/1936) two concepts that may answer these questions. *Variation* means that different values of a particular trait vary in frequency in the population. *Selection* means that certain trait values are selected by the environment and aid survival (Endler, 1986). The evolution of the running speed of cheetahs is an example (see Figure 2.1). Cheetahs vary in running speed: slow, medium, and fast. The ability of a cheetah to obtain food depends, in part, on how fast it runs. When all their prey are slow, all cheetahs are able to eat. Even the slowest cheetah is fast enough to run after the slowest prey. However, if all the slow prey are eaten, then only faster-running cheetahs will survive, since only they are going to be able to catch the remaining faster-running prey. Thus, the faster-running prey selects for faster-running cheetahs and selects against slower-running cheetahs. Consequently, faster-running cheetahs have a greater chance of survival than slower-running cheetahs, since the faster ones are more likely to capture the prey they need for food. Darwin (1859/1936) also reasoned that

Original population		Evolved population

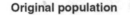

 The percentage of slow-running cheetahs in the population has been reduced to near zero because they were not fast enough to catch their prey.

Slow running speed

 The percentage of medium-fast cheetahs has remained constant in the population because they were just fast enough to catch the slowest prey.

Medium running speed

 The percentage of fast cheetahs has increased in the population because they were fast enough to catch more of the prey they pursued.

Fast running speed

FIGURE 2.1 Variation and Selection in Evolution. The percentage of slow-, medium-, and fast-running cheetahs changes over succeeding generations. Slow-running cheetahs decrease in the population because they are not fast enough to catch even the slowest prey. Medium-fast cheetahs hold their own, since they can catch the slowest prey. Fast-running cheetahs increase in the population because they can catch a greater amount of the prey they pursue.

physical traits are inherited. Thus, the physical equipment for fast running, such as powerful muscles, strong heart, and lung capacity, is transmitted to succeeding generations.

Darwin also introduced the concept of **population thinking**, which refers to the idea that every individual in a population is different (Mayr, 2001). Thus, rather than emphasizing that individuals are similar, population thinking emphasizes that individuals are unique. An implication of population thinking is that various aspects of motivation do not apply equally to all individuals, much like the average-size shoe does not fit everyone. Population thinking justifies phrases such as one person's pain is another person's pleasure. In psychology, population thinking translates into the area of individual differences, such as psychological needs (Chapter 8) and personality traits (Chapter 9). For example, people vary in their need to affiliate and thus each person expends different amounts of effort in order to associate with others. People also vary in personality traits. For instance, more extraverted individuals might expend additional effort to attend parties than less extraverted individuals would.

The complete works of Charles Darwin is available on the web page titled "DARWIN ONLINE" here: http://darwin-online.org.uk.

Herbert Spencer. As described earlier, Spencer stated that pleasurable behavior benefitted life, while painful behavior did not. Spencer believed that this function of pain and pleasure resulted from evolution (see Table 2.1). Suppose there was variation in the amount of pleasure or discomfort produced by a particular behavior and that this behavior is important for survival. Pain and pleasure become selecting agents for those behaviors, much like fast-running prey selects for fast-running cheetahs. Pleasure selected behaviors that promoted survival, while pain selected behaviors that protected the organism from harm. Fear and the pleasure of sweets support Spencer's idea. Fear may have evolved by natural selection as a motive to avoid dangerous animals. Assume variation in children's level of fear that is evoked as a dangerous-looking animal approaches. Children who become easily afraid are more likely to avoid dangerous creatures and survive. Children who react with little fear may draw closer to these creatures and be harmed. For another illustration, consider the fact that spoiled food produces a bitter taste, while nutritious food has a more pleasing taste. Now imagine that children differed in their preferences for sweet versus bitter foods. Young infants prefer a sweet taste over a bitter taste and are therefore more likely to eat nutritious food and reject spoiled food (Steiner, 1977). If this ability and preference had not evolved, then a lack of preference would cause infants to accept food indiscriminately, including that which produces potentially life-threatening diarrhea and dehydration. In contrast, infants who preferred sweet over bitter would have a greater chance of survival, since they would reject bitter food.

Instincts. Hedonism can motivate a variety of behaviors. Other motivational sources, however, provide the impetus for only a limited class of behaviors. **Instinct**, for instance, is an internal stimulus that induces a specific pattern of behavior in a species. It is considered to be an inherited disposition that shows itself as behavior in the presence of a limited range of stimuli. Instincts are characteristic of an entire species, are influenced little (if at all) by learning, and have survival value for the organism (Fletcher, 1966). Although instincts are evoked by external stimuli, early psychologists considered them responsible for energizing or powering the muscles into a fixed pattern of behavior. One early proponent of human instincts was William James (1890/1950), who emphasized that the impulse to action was an important component of instinct. William McDougall (1908), another popularizer of instincts, also felt they were the principal instigators of human behavior and that without instinct humans would be incapable of any type of action. James (1890/1950) postulated 38 instincts, which ranged from sucking, crying, and smiling to play, jealousy, and love. An important characteristic of instincts for James was that "instincts are implanted for the sake of giving rise to habits" (p. 402). In order for a particular behavior pattern to become habitual, it is helpful if the behavior already occurs naturally. To illustrate, walking is the most efficient way for humans to get around, and it is probably much easier for a child to learn to walk if it is instinctive to do so. Even before a child is able to walk on its own, a young infant will make reflexive walking movements (not under voluntary control) when it is held upright with its feet touching the floor (Eibl-Eibesfeldt, 1989).

Current trends. A shift in thinking regarding instincts has led to the concept of **species-typical behavior**. Stimuli in the environment known as sign stimuli are capable of eliciting such behavior. Since all members of a species exhibit the behavior, it is considered to be universal—that is, to occur all over the world. Furthermore, such behavior is assumed to have resulted from natural selection. In other words, instincts or species-typical behaviors evolved to solve recurring problems of survival. Love is an example of such behavior that has begun to interest psychologists. They propose that love is an instinct or species-typical behavior that evolved to solve a set of specific survival problems, in this case the difficulty of trying to survive on your own. The idea that love evolved is not that new and was already in the mind of William James over 120 years ago.

More specifically, however, what recurring problem of survival does love solve? The answer is the **commitment problem** (Buss, 2006; Frank, 1988). This problem refers to the necessity of one individual to be loyal and faithful to another for the survival benefits of each. For example, a mother's commitment to her infant promotes the infant's survival and carries on the mother's genes to the next generation. What survival advantages arise from commitment? First, imagine a person who moves next door to a couple. The new neighbor is better looking, wittier, more thoughtful, and richer. Or imagine that one member of the couple becomes sick, loses employment, or becomes depressed. Frank (1988) and Buss (2006) maintain that in such instances the likelihood increases that one member of the pair will leave for the more attractive neighbor. This switch would occur if people were strictly rational and without emotion. However, that is not the case. Love will tend to keep the two individuals together—that is, to remain committed, even when there are more attractive alternatives elsewhere. Second, parents' love for their children helps ensure the children's survival especially when children are young and vulnerable. For example, young infants can be very demanding: they cry, scream, fuss, need attention, demand hugging, cuddling, and need diaper changes. Love commits parents to do all of those things for their children.

Another current trend is integrating the law of effect into natural selection. Recall that in natural selection the environment chooses those traits that aid the animals' survival and reproduction. These traits increase in frequency. For example, leaves high up in the tree select for long-neck giraffes, since only they can reach them. Eventually, the trait of long necks increases in frequency compared to short necks, which become extinct. The law of effect chooses behavior in a similar fashion. Certain consequences of behavior known as reinforcers increase the likelihood of that behavior as if it were selected. For example, Thorndike's cat tried various ways of escape but only one way worked—that is, was reinforced. The successful escape route occurred more frequently, while unsuccessful attempts extinguished—that is, the cat no longer tried them. In other words, behaviors are selected by the consequences they provide. This view has become known as **selection by consequences** (Catania, 2013; Skinner, 1981; Wasserman, 2012). Thus, if a particular goal is the desired consequence, then it selects behaviors that will achieve that goal. The success provided by these achievement behaviors makes them part of an individual's repertoire of goal behaviors. Other behaviors that do not result in goal achievement extinguish—that is, they are no longer maintained in the person's repertoire.

To illustrate with a practical example, imagine the goal of successfully completing the requirements for a college course. Students behave in various ways but only preparing for class leads to success while socializing, sleeping-in, or playing computer games does not. Preparing for class, say, a minimum of two hours per week provides minimal success. Increasing the time spent preparing for class definitely increases the chances of success. Thus, success in a course selects such behaviors as studying, reading, writing, analyzing data, rehearsing, and doing lab or homework. Furthermore, doing more of these academic behaviors leads to greater success, such as higher grades, scholarships, and graduate school acceptance. As a result of selection by consequences, time spent on class preparation increases to an average of nearly 15 hours a week for seniors (NSSE, 2015). Thus, longer class preparation becomes ingrained in a student's academic behavior repertoire. Other behaviors such as socializing, sleeping-in, or computer games extinguish and fade from the student's repertoire of course achievement behaviors. Thus, selection by consequence means that the desired end-state selects for those behaviors that allow the end-state to be reached.

Unconscious Motivation

Are we always aware what motivates our behavior? A person may explain a raid on the refrigerator by saying "I was hungry" or explain her choice of a particular movie by stating "My favorite actor was in it." In these examples, the person is aware of the motives for her behavior. Yet there are instances when the motives and incentives for some actions are inferred or are incorrectly stated (Nisbett & Wilson, 1977). Inaccessibility to one's motives characterizes unconscious motivation.

Freud's conscious–unconscious distinction. Sigmund Freud (1920/1943) described a very influential theory of unconscious motivation in his book *A General Introduction to Psychoanalysis.* According to Freud, awareness results when motives have entered consciousness from either the preconscious or the unconscious. Using two rooms as a metaphor (see Figure 2.2), the **preconscious** part of a person's mental apparatus is represented by the small room, which contains thoughts, feelings, sensations, and memories. A person's "consciousness as a spectator" (p. 261) resides in this small room and serves as the focus of awareness. The large room represents the **unconscious**, "in which the various mental excitations are crowding upon one another, like individual beings" (p. 260). This part of the mental apparatus is unavailable to a person. It contains instinctual impulses, repressed thoughts, and other mental stimuli. For material to proceed from the large room (unconscious) to the small adjoining room (preconscious), it must pass through the doorway separating the two rooms. Here stands a doorkeeper or censor who determines what mental excitations are allowed entry into the room of the preconscious. If some mental events have gained entry, then they may yet be driven out if found to be unacceptable or anxiety provoking. Freud uses the term **repression** to refer to those mental excitations that have made it to the doorway and have been turned back by the doorkeeper. This makes them incapable of becoming

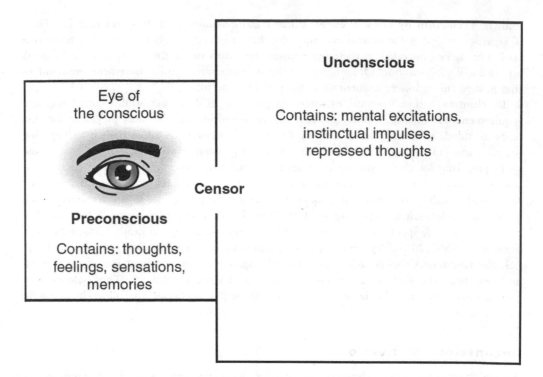

FIGURE 2.2 Freud's Concept of Motivation. Freud used two adjoining rooms separated by a doorway as a metaphor for his unconscious and preconscious motivation. Unconscious thoughts and impulses reside in the large room and try to enter the preconscious by slipping by the censor, who is standing guard between the two rooms. Thoughts and impulses in the smaller room of the preconscious compete for the attention of the conscious.

conscious. Freud (1915b) conceived repression as a means of protecting us from unpleasures that would result if we became aware of some of the impulses residing in our unconscious. The idea of unpleasure means that the instinct might produce anxiety, embarrassment, or punishment from others. In certain circumstances, however, these instinctual needs can reach awareness in jokes, dreams, slips of the tongue, and neuroses (Freud, 1920, 1920/1943). However, if mental events cross the threshold into the small room (preconscious), it does not mean that an individual is automatically aware of them. A person becomes aware of these mental excitations or thoughts only if they attract "the eye of consciousness" (Freud, 1920/1943, p. 260).

Motivational instincts and the unconscious. Motivation for Freud was based on the satisfaction of unconscious instinctual impulses (Freud, 1915a). Originating in the body, instincts reach consciousness, where they exert pressure, which is really their demand for satisfaction. The aim or goal of every instinctual need is for the reduction of this pressure. The object of the instinct is the incentive that allows the instinct to meet its aim. The object can be external or can be a body part that provides for the reduction of the instinctual need. The source of the instinct is the body part or perhaps a chemical change in the brain from which the instinct originates.

However, we are only aware of the aim or goal of the instinct in our mind (Freud, 1915a). According to Freud (1924), there are three groups of instincts. Sexual or life instincts are those that operate to maintain and transfer life to successive generations. Death instincts, in contrast, manifest themselves as aggressive and destructive impulses. Sexual and death instincts mix and fuse together in living creatures but also compete for supremacy so that at times one instinct is dominant and then the other. A third type includes the ego or self-preservation instincts. Freud saw motivation as an increase and decrease of instinctual excitation invading our minds. An increase in excitation produces unpleasure (pain), and a decrease produces pleasure. The ultimate pleasure is to keep excitation as low as possible or at least keep it constant. Low excitation is the aim of the death instinct. Yet Freud (1920, 1924) recognized that people also experience pleasure from an increase in excitation, such as that occurring with heightened sexual tension and its sudden release. He also theorized that there were instances when tension could be pleasurable and that the lowering of tension in some cases could be painful (Freud, 1924).

Satisfying unconscious impulses. Much of Freud's writing is concerned with the satisfaction of instinctual needs that may be considered socially unacceptable or even personally unacceptable. An example of an unacceptable impulse is a "desire to see the organs peculiar to each sex exposed" (Freud, 1905, p. 98). Many of our sexual and aggressive instincts, for example, are repressed because awareness of them would produce anxiety or social punishment. Thus, Freud's theorizing concerned how these unacceptable instinctual needs are reduced and satisfied. In *Jokes and Their Relation to the Unconscious* (1905), Freud describes humor as one way of satisfying instinctual impulses. Consider his riddles: "What is a cannibal who has eaten his father and his mother?— An orphan—And if he has eaten all his other relations as well?—The sole heir.—And where will a monster of that kind find sympathy?—In the dictionary under 'S'" (p. 153). Laughing at these riddles results in a partial satisfaction of the death instinct, which is preferable to actually committing a murder. The sex instinct can also be satisfied by laughing at jokes containing sexual themes. A second source of pleasure in jokes lies in saving the energy that is expended in repression. Since the repressed impulse is manifested momentarily in the joke, there is a corresponding saving in psychic energy. The energy used for repression is now no longer needed and can thus be expended in other ways, such as laughing at the joke (Freud, 1905).

Dreams are another way instinctual impulses are satisfied. During sleep there is a relaxation of censorship, and so it is easier for unconscious impulses to enter into consciousness. Even during sleep, however, the unconscious impulse undergoes some censorship whereby the impulse is disguised. The reason for the censorship is that it protects our sleep from being disturbed. If the dream were too real, we would awaken. The actual dream, as reported, is known as the *manifest content*, while the unconscious impulses the dream represents are known as the *latent content*. Sticks, umbrellas, knives, and guns are manifestations of the penis, according to Freud. Ships, caves, jars, and boxes are manifestations of the vagina:

> The act of mounting ladders, steep places, or stairs is indubitably symbolic of sexual intercourse. On closer reflection we shall notice that the rhythmic character of this climbing is the point in common between the two, and perhaps also the accompanying increase in excitation the shortening of breath as the climber ascends.
>
> (Freud, 1920/1943, p. 141)

41

Thus, dreams about sex, even when disguised, allow for the satisfaction of our sexual urges (Freud, 1915b, 1920/1943).

Current trends. Unconscious motivation in Freud's theory favors a push orientation. The aim of an instinct is to reduce the pressure that is felt, much like the aim of hunger is to push a person to reduce feelings of hunger. However, because instincts reside in the unconscious, individuals are not aware of the source of these pushing effects. They are only aware of being pushed. Current research trends on unconscious motivation, however, have emphasized a pull rather than push orientation. Goals are in the unconscious or below the level of awareness. When goals are activated into consciousness they are then acted on. For example, suppose during class your professor says, "Check to see that your cell phone is off." You did not hear your professor because you were talking to your neighbor. Several minutes later, for no reason that you could discern, you check your cell phone. In this example, check cell phone reached consciousness in the form of a goal on which you acted. However, you were not aware of how it reached consciousness.

Today unconscious refers to "the influences or effects of stimulus processing of which one is not aware" (Bargh & Morsella, 2008, p. 74). In other words, certain deliberations carried out by the brain are not accessible to consciousness yet those deliberations affect behavior. There are several ways of examining how unconscious processes can influence behavior. One way is to measure the relation between a person's conscious intention to respond and the brain's preparation for that response. The brain prepares for a response prior to a person's conscious intention for doing so as if a person is not conscious of this preparation (Haggard, 2008). In the first of such research, Libet and coresearchers (1983) attached electrodes on a participant's skull over the brain's motor cortex. In this area of the brain, neurons produce the impulses that control movement, such as pressing a button. While motor neuron activity is being measured, a participant notes on a clock when she feels the urge (intent) to push a button. The fascinating result of this procedure is that the motor cortex showed a preparation for button-pushing prior to the participant's conscious intention to push. Individuals were not aware that their motor cortex was already activated for button-pushing prior to their conscious intention to make that response.

An illustration of this experiment about awareness to move and intention to move is presented in the YouTube video titled "Neuroscience and Free Will—Libet's Experiment" here: www.youtube.com/watch?v=IQ4nwTTmcgs.

Another demonstration of unconscious motivation involves presenting stimuli below the level of awareness. Stimuli presented in this manner, for example, can increase the reward value of a goal and thereby increase an individual's motivation. In addition, there are automatic processes that refer to behaviors occurring with little conscious control or awareness. For example, a person drives the same route to school or work with little conscious awareness, control, and effort—in effect, being on automatic pilot. Also, seeing another person or situation can trigger an intention. This intention, in turn, is linked to actual behavior. This whole chain occurs automatically, without the person being consciously aware of what triggered her intention and subsequent behavior (Bargh & Williams, 2006; Custers & Aarts, 2010).

Early Views on Drives, Needs, and Incentives

What potentials within people compel them into action? Psychologists have long wondered whether there are drives and psychological needs that motivate behavior from within. In addition, are there inducements in the environment that somehow initiate behavior? Philosophers and psychologists have long been aware that the environment provides incentives and goals to both guide and motivate behavior.

Drive. How does one become a world-renowned actor, a popular musician, a Nobel Prize-winning scientist, or a gold medal athlete? To reach this level of achievement, it is probably necessary to be a genius, such as an acting, musical, scientific, or athletic genius. With this provision in place, one source of motivation for these achievements is the value placed on financial rewards, fame, winning, or the adoration received from others. The philosopher Schopenhauer (1851/1970), however, suggests that these incentives are not enough. The money may not be worth it and fame is too uncertain. In addition, the possibility that these incentives will be the result of one's actions is vague, uncertain, and far in the future. Schopenhauer instead suggests that there are processes inside these individuals that will explain their motivation. He reasons that some inner force or drive compels them toward their achievements. Schopenhauer likens this inner drive to an innate instinctual process that compels these individuals into action toward their goals as if they had no choice in the matter. This inner force is today labeled drive because it refers to that internal push, urge, or desire that moves a person into action.

Moreover, drive has also been used to describe the push toward a goal. Hunger and thirst drives that result from food and water deprivation persist until the goals of eating and drinking have been achieved. Drive is the initial inducement of behavior and remains in effect—that is, it remains in some part of our nervous system until behavior eventually results. Experimental research focused on drive as the deprivation of some incentive. For example, Figure 1.5 (in Chapter 1) shows the effects of thirst drive on the speed at which rats begin to run toward a water reward.

Psychological needs. **Psychological need** was an early motivational concept similar to drive. Whereas drive was often viewed as the result of deprivation of some incentive, a psychological need was considered to be an inherent characteristic of humans. While different levels of drive could be experimentally manipulated within an animal, need was assumed to already exist in different amounts in individuals. Need intensity was thus measured via some scale, questionnaire, or projective test (see Chapter 8). Georges Le Roy (1764/1974) claimed the existence of the need for food, clothing, shelter, love, external stimulation, and rest. The psychologist Henry Murray (1938) formalized the study of needs and concluded that needs are a major source of human motivation. According to Murray, *primary needs* are physiological in nature and are characterized by bodily satisfaction. These would include the need for air, water, food, sex, lactation, urination, rest and sleep, defecation, and physical stimulation and the need to avoid harm, noxious stimuli, heat, and cold. *Secondary needs* are concerned with mental or emotional satisfaction and depend on or are derived from primary needs. Murray considered that all needs are hypothetical processes referring "to an organic potentiality or readiness to respond in a certain way under given conditions" (p. 61). Once initiated, a need will persist as an electrical chemical process in the brain, which corresponds to a feeling of desire. Behaviors prompted by need cease when the goal of satisfying the specific need has been achieved. Needs can be evoked by an internal physiological process but also by environmental demands. To illustrate, a person's need for affiliation is brought on by the presence of other people and causes her to seek out individuals to connect with. Murray (1938) postulated the existence of some 22 secondary needs. Table 2.2 defines six of his needs that are still of interest today along with sample statements from different scales he used to measure the level of each need.

TABLE 2.2 Six of Murray's Needs and Sample Statements from Murray's *Psychological Insight Test*

Instructions	Read each statement carefully and make up your mind whether it is more or less for you than it is for the average. Use the following rating scale: Below average = –3, –2, –1 Above average = +1, +2, +3
Achievement	To accomplish difficult tasks, surpass self and others Sample statement: "I am driven to ever greater efforts by an unslaked ambition"
Affiliation	To approach others, win their affection; to remain loyal to friends Sample statement: "I am in my element when I am with a group of people who enjoy life"
Autonomy	To be independent and free, to resist coercion Sample statement: "I am unable to do my best work when I am in a subservient position"
Dominance	To control your environment, to influence and direct others Sample statement: "I enjoy organizing or directing the activities of a group—team, club, or committee"
Order	To put things in order, to organize, to be neat and clean Sample statement: "I know what I want to say without having to fumble about for the right word"
Understanding	To ask questions, to seek answers, to analyze events, to enjoy using theory, logic, or reason. Sample statement: "I enjoy reflection and speculation as much as anything"

Source: Adapted from *Explorations in Personality* by H. A. Murray, 1938. New York, NY: Oxford University Press.

Current trends. A very basic psychological need is one that should be shared by all people. An example is **existential concerns,** which are about life's most basic challenges (Koole et al., 2006). Existential concerns become paramount as a consequence of some tragic event, such as a death, illness, accident, natural disaster, or act of terrorism. They cause people to ask questions about why this happened and what it means, and make them change the course of their lives in profound ways. There are five major existential concerns that can motivate people in different ways. A concern about one's own death promotes a desire to maintain life. A concern with isolation emphasizes that we have a need to associate with others rather than be isolated and be unable to share meaningful experiences. Identity concerns deal with self-insight, a person's role in the world, and the boundaries between the self and others. A concern with freedom questions the extent to which individuals have free will and are responsible for their actions versus being controlled by external factors. A final concern involves the question of whether life has meaning or if it is merely a series of randomly occurring meaningless events (Koole et al., 2006). It may be possible that many psychological needs are derivable from these five existential concerns. For example, a need for safety comes from a concern about death. Affiliation and belonging needs are derived from a concern about isolation. Concerns about freedom promote a need for autonomy.

In addition, psychologists are discovering news ways that people satisfy their psychological needs. For instance, Chen (2011) postulated a *need to connect*, which she derived from Murray's need for affiliation (see Table 2.2). An individual's need to connect is satisfied by the use of Twitter, an Internet social network site that allows users to send and read messages (tweets) of 140 characters or less. With a five-item scale, she measured the degree that the use of Twitter satisfied people's need to connect. Her results showed that increases in time spent using Twitter were associated with increases in satisfying the need to connect.

Incentives. Even though a person may know how to do something, this does not mean that she will. A person might say, "I know how to make my bed but why do it?" A reason for doing something is provided by incentives, which are external stimuli that attract or repel an individual, such as anticipated rewards or punishers. Tolman and Honzik (1930) provided one of the first empirical demonstrations that the presence or absence of an incentive affects behavior. First, they had rats run through a maze for 10 trials with or without a food incentive in the goal box. Then, on the eleventh trial, the incentive conditions remained the same for some rats, but for others the incentive conditions were switched. Their results in Figure 2.3 show that the number of errors the rats made in traversing the maze depended on experience gained over trials and on the presence or absence of the food incentive or reward. The fewest number of errors per trial occurred for the continuous reward group (i.e., "food"), which benefitted from the food incentive on every trial. The most errors were made by the continuous nonreward group (i.e., "no food"), which never benefitted from the food incentive on any trial. The motivational benefits of the incentive were most apparent for the other two groups when a reward was suddenly introduced or removed. In Figure 2.3, when food became available on trial 11 for the nonreward-reward group (i.e., "food available"), there was a rapid drop in the number of errors. When food

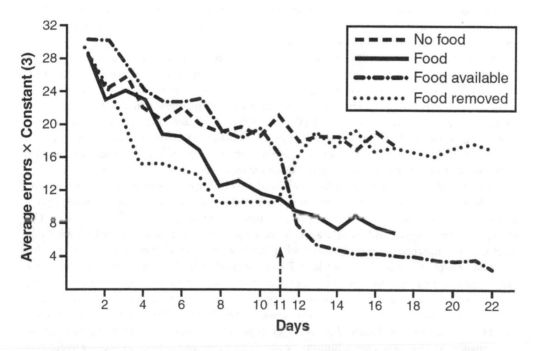

FIGURE 2.3 Incentive Change and Performance. When a food incentive becomes available on trial 11, there is a sudden decrease in the number of errors rats made in traversing a maze. However, when a food incentive is removed on trial 11, there is a sudden increase in the number of errors in traversing a maze.

Source: From "Introduction and Removal of Reward, and Maze Performance in Rats" by E. C. Tolman and C. H. Honzik, 1930, *University of California Publications in Psychology, 4*, Figure 4. Copyright 1930 The Regents of the University of California.

suddenly disappeared on trial 11 for the reward–nonreward group (i.e., "food removed"), there was a rapid increase in the number of errors. Changes in behavior reflected changes in the absence or presence of the incentive. Maze errors increased when the incentive was absent but decreased when the incentive was present.

Early Views that Drives and Incentives Interact to Motivate Behavior

Figure 1.1 (Chapter 1) illustrated push motivation as the need for food and as the need to belong. It illustrated pull motivation with palatable food and friends and family. Unspecified, however, is how a specific need becomes associated with a relevant incentive. For example, how does food become relevant for hunger but not thirst? How do people become relevant for the need to belong but not for the need for autonomy? Early psychologists were aware that both internal motivation such as drive and external motivation such as incentive combined to motivate behavior. Neither drive nor incentive alone sufficed. How has this association between internal and external motivation played out in the history of psychology?

Warden's drive–incentive link. Warden (1931) delineated the difference between internal and external sources of motivation based on his work with rats. For Warden, motivation involved both internal or drive factors and external or incentive factors. Drive was an aroused action tendency that resulted from deprivation and led the animal to seek out the appropriate incentive. An incentive was an external object that also operates to arouse some internal physiological state or tendency on the part of the organism to approach or avoid it. Warden's **drive–incentive link** holds that drives and incentives match up, like hunger matches with food, thirst with water, and curiosity with novel stimuli. These drive–incentive match-ups mean that drive is "a reaction tendency directed toward an incentive" (Warden, 1931, p. 15) and that both are necessary for motivating behavior. Again referring to Figure 1.5 (Chapter 1), notice the match-up between thirst drive and water reward. Furthermore, as thirst drive increases behavior increases, but also as the amount of water incentive increases behavior increases.

Lewin's field theory. Lewin (1936, 1938) postulated **psychological force** as a way of accounting for push and pull motivation. According to Lewin's (1936) field theory, human action takes place within a person's life space, which is the person's current internal and external environment. The *life space* contains objects and possible activities of which a person is aware and which attract or repel him. For instance, you may be aware when reading this book that you are hungry and that you have a date at a pizza restaurant later. Forces or motivational factors within the life space cause a person to move from one object or activity to another. Objects or activities that have *positive valence* attract the individual; they are approached or wanted. Objects that have *negative valence* repel the individual; they are avoided or not wanted. Lewin (1938, p. 160) cites the Tolman and Honzik results (see Figure 2.3) as an example of the effects of incentive valence on performance. According to Lewin, humans are also forced from one activity to another depending on the valences of those activities. A scheduled exam forces you to keep reading, but as time for your pizza date draws near you will instead be heading for the restaurant. In addition to incentive valence, psychological force depends on the psychological distance to the incentive. *Psychological distance* can refer to both physical space and time. The nearness of a toy to an infant illustrates psychological distance in terms of physical space. An infant may prefer a closer toy over one that is farther away, which to Lewin meant that the preferred toy had a shorter psychological distance (Lewin, 1933). Thus, the more interesting your date and the tastier the pizza, the stronger the forces that attract you to this outing. The farther away in time your date is, however, the weaker the force that attracts you to it.

Tension is the term Lewin (1936) used to label a deficit in the person's internal environment. Tension can result from an unfulfilled intention, a physiological need, or a psychological need. For example, being deprived of food or not knowing the course material well enough to pass an exam puts a student in a state of tension. The result of tension is to instill valence on relevant environmental objects. Tension from hunger increases the positive valence of pizza, and tension from being unprepared increases the negative valence of poor exam performance. When the desired object or incentive is attained, then tension dissipates and the valence of the incentive approaches zero. Combining the internal and environmental factors of motivation in Lewin's (1938) system results in the formula:

$$\text{Psychological force} = \frac{\text{Valence of goal properties and tension in person}}{\text{Psychological distance between person and goal}}$$

(Lewin does not claim that this formula is always correct, but it is a good approximation to help in remembering the relationship among force, valence, tension, and psychological distance.) Although it is not clear whether valence and tension should be added or multiplied together, what is important is that force or inducement to action depends on both incentive valence or goal value and tension. Force, however, changes with psychological distance. Usually, the closer in time an individual is to attaining the incentive, the shorter the psychological distance. To illustrate the formula: how hard a student is forced to study for an exam depends on how important it is for the student to do well (valence), how unprepared she is at the moment (tension), and how many days away the exam is scheduled (psychological distance). In Lewin's system, tension equals push motivation and incentive or goal valence equals pull motivation. Lewin claims that tension increases the valence of a relevant goal object. This dependence of valence on tension is the basis of motivation. For with increases in tension, motivation for the appropriate goal object increases (Lewin, 1938).

Tolman's purposive behavior theory. Tolman also acknowledged the necessary connection between drives and their corresponding goal objects. Tolman (1932) uses the term *demand* for why goal objects motivate behaviors that relieve physiological drives. For him, demand hinges on two properties: characteristics of the physiological drives and characteristics of the incentives or goal objects. First, physiological drives depend on their intensity to motivate behavior, such as the degree of hunger drive. Hungry rats will run in a maze faster and learn it faster compared to nonhungry rats. Second, incentives motivate behavior, while their absences demotivate behavior as demonstrated by Tolman's research shown in Figure 2.3. In addition, Tolman (1932) also reports that some goal stimuli are more motivating than others. For example, rats run faster and learn a maze faster for a reward of bran mash compared to a reward of sunflower seeds. But is it the connection between the drive push and the incentive pull that motivates behavior? Tolman indicates such a connection. Motivation stems from seeking relief from physiological drives and keeping away from threatening physiological experiences such as pain. But this can only be accomplished with the appropriate goal objects. Thus, only when animals experience physiological drives or physiological disturbances (such as fear) do they seek to consummate (interact with) the goal objects that will relieve the drive or rid them of the disturbance. The animal is vaguely aware what goal object provides this relief, how to consummate (interact with) the goal object, and how to explore the environment in order to obtain the critical goal object. Through experience animals associate drive relief with the necessary goal object. Similarly, the animal would learn to stay away from negative goal objects that produce a negative physiological experience (Tolman, 1932).

Hull's behavior theory. Clark Hull also provided an early theory on the integration of drive and incentive for the motivation of behavior. For him, psychological drive emerges from physiological need (Hull, 1943, 1951, 1952). Like Warden's theorizing, for Hull drive (D) was the motivational construct that results when an animal is deprived of a needed substance, such as when a hunger drive results from food deprivation. In addition to drive, an incentive (K) was necessary for the drive to be satisfied. Furthermore, the mere presence of D and K were not enough; the organism must also know what to do. Hull used the construct of habit strength (H) to represent learning the behavior necessary for attaining the incentive. Thus, for Hull,

$$Behavior = D \times K \times H$$

Drive has several properties or characteristics (Hull, 1943, 1951, 1952). First, it energizes behavior by intensifying all responses in a particular situation. The more intense the drive, the more intense the behavior (Hull, 1943, 1952). This point is illustrated in an experiment by Hillman and associates (1953), who deprived two groups of rats of water for either two or 22 hours and then measured how long it took them to run a 10-unit T maze for a water reward. After 10 trials, one half of each group remained at the original deprivation level, while the other half switched to the other deprivation level. For example, group 2–2 and group 22–22 remained at two and 22 hours of water deprivation, respectively, throughout the experiment. Group 2–22 switched from two to 22 hours of water deprivation after the first 10 trials, while group 22–2 switched from 22 to two hours of water deprivation. According to Hull's theory, 22 hours of water deprivation corresponds to high thirst drive, while two hours of water deprivation corresponds to low drive. High drive should multiply or intensify instrumental behavior much more than low drive. As shown in Figure 2.4, the rats took less time to run the maze under high drive than under low drive. The interpretation based on drive theory is that high drive exhibits more intense push motivation than low drive does.

A second characteristic is that each drive has its own unique internal sensations that serve as stimuli for guiding behavior. For example, hunger and thirst feel different and provide the basis for knowing when to eat and when to drink. Leeper (1935) used thirst and hunger drives as cues for rats to choose the correct goal box when water- or food-deprived. In his experimental apparatus, rats had to make a choice between an alley leading to food and another alley leading to water. The rats learned to choose the alley leading to food on food-deprived days and to choose the alley leading to water on water-deprived days. Thus, hunger drive stimuli became associated with the location of food, and thirst drive stimuli became associated with the location of water. A third characteristic is that behavior is motivated to reduce the intensity of a drive. Hull considered drive to be unpleasant. In fact, he felt that "Bentham's concept of pain is equated

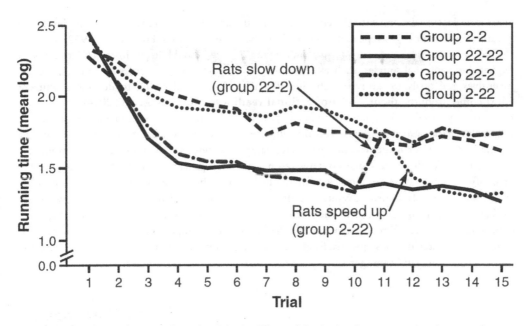

FIGURE 2.4 Intensity of Drive and Running Behavior. Effects of deprivation time on mean log time to run a 10-unit T maze for a water reward by water-deprived rats. Note the increase in running time immediately after the 22–2 hour shift and the decrease in running time after the 2–22 hour shift.

Source: From "The Effect of Drive Level on the Maze Performance of the White Rat" by B. Hillman et al., 1953, *Journal of Comparative and Physiological Psychology, 46,* Figure 1. Copyright 1953 by American Psychological Association.

substantially to our own [Hull's] concept of need" (Hull, 1952, p. 341). Recall that Bentham (1789/1970) is the utilitarian philosopher who claimed that people are under the governance of two masters: pain and pleasure. Humans are motivated to reduce drive—that is, to get rid of any painful or unpleasant feeling. Since drive is characterized as being painful, the behavior that reduces it will be more likely to occur. Eating reduces an unpleasant hunger drive and drinking reduces an unpleasant thirst drive. The importance of Hull's drive concept is that drive motivates voluntary behavior. Drive motivates an individual to reduce feelings of hunger or thirst, thus maximizing the conditions necessary for well-being and life.

Incentives were the other motivational component of Hull's theory. The incentive or potential reward depends on its objective features, such as amount and quality, but also on its prior associations with drive. Incentives are those substances or commodities offered by the environment that will reduce the organism's drive. However, not until the incentive has reduced a drive does that incentive come to motivate future behavior (Hull, 1943, 1952). In addition, compared to other early psychologists, Hull was more descriptive of how drives become associated with their relevant incentives. First, there are innate drive–incentive connections. In other words, there was an existing evolutionary connection between certain drives and their relevant incentives, such as hunger with food, thirst with water, and relief with the reduction of intense stimulation. Second, organisms acquire the connection between drives and their associated incentives. In other words, organisms learn what incentives reduce a currently active drive. This association developed because drive intensity is repeatedly reduced by the same incentive (Hull, 1943, 1952).

Current trends. The theories of Warden, Lewin, Tolman, and Hull are historical attempts to explain how internal sources, such as tension or drive, combine with external sources, such as incentives and goals, to motivate behavior. Psychologists are still trying to do this. A current effort comes from the **theory of motivational readiness** (Kruglanski et al., 2014). The theory refers to a person's willingness to attain a specific end-state similar to the idea expressed in Figure 1.1. Motivational readiness depends on a person's want and expectancy the want will be satisfied. *Wants* refer to desires, motives, drives, needs, or wishes. An individual's environment, such as Lewin's (1936) life space, contains resources called *affordances* that are potentially capable of satisfying wants. An expectancy is an individual's belief about the likelihood that an available affordance can satisfy a current want. The effectiveness of an affordance depends on how closely its features match or complement the features of a want. This match determines the degree of expectancy that the affordance will satisfy the want. For example, food is a better match for hunger than water is. Consequently, food produces a greater expectancy than water does for the ability of food to satisfy hunger.

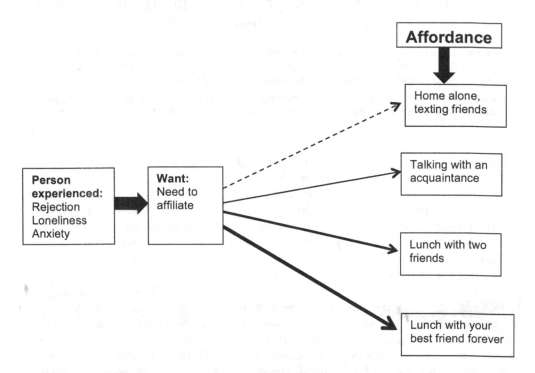

FIGURE 2.5 Degree of Match between Want and Affordances. The want varies to the extent it matches onto the four environmental affordances. The degree of match between the want and the affordances increases from top (dashed arrow) to bottom (wide arrow). As the match increases, the expected likelihood of satisfying the want increases. Furthermore, with increasing degrees of match, the affordance approaches an incentive or becomes the most effective incentive (Kruglanski et al., 2014).

Figure 2.5 uses the need to affiliate to illustrate motivational readiness. Imagine the end of your romantic relationship, being new on campus, plus awaiting notice of your acceptance into a fraternity/sorority. These three events may create feelings of rejection, loneliness, and anxiety, which in turn give rise to the need to affiliate (see Table 2.2). This need is classified as a want in motivational readiness theory. An individual's life space may contain any of the affordances on the right side of Figure 2.5. These affordances, however, vary in their capacity to satisfy the want. Lunch with your best friend forever has the capacity to satisfy all features of the need to affiliate, whereas the other affordances can satisfy only some of them. For example, your best friend can console you better about the romantic breakup and reduce your loneliness more, and a delicious lunch can momentarily relieve your anxiety. The other affordances in Figure 2.5 can only satisfy some of the features of the want. Based on motivational readiness, increases in the match between the want and the affordance increases the individual's expectancy that the need to affiliate will be satisfied. In such a case, the best affordance becomes the most effective incentive.

Section Recap

Ideas about motivation long proposed by philosophers and early psychologists are still under consideration today. First, Aristotle's four causes are analogous to four sources of motivation: efficient, final, formal, and material. Other ancient philosophers thought hedonism might be an explanation. *Hedonism* refers to the pursuit of pleasure and the avoidance of pain as averaged over the long run. According to Hobbes (1640/1962) and the concept of *incentive motivation*, positive incentives are approached because they produce pleasant feelings, while negative incentives are avoided because they produce unpleasant feelings. Bentham's (1789/1970) *principle of utility* describes behavior as being governed solely by the pursuit of pleasure and avoidance of pain. The utility of an object refers to its capacity to increase happiness or decrease unhappiness or pain. Freud proposed his *pleasure principle*, which refers to a person's pursuit of pleasure. This pursuit was guided by his *reality principle*, which asserts that pleasure may have to be postponed until a later, more opportune, time. Thorndike (1898) used a cat's escape from a box to provide an empirical demonstration of hedonism. From his work he formulated his *law of effect*: behavior followed by satisfaction is stamped in while behavior followed by dissatisfaction is stamped out. Currently, the law of effect emphasizes the role of observable reinforcers to increase behavior and observable punishers to decrease behavior. The new field of *positive psychology* is concerned with what factors promote the beneficial effects of pleasure for individuals and the groups and institutions to which they belong.

Darwin (1859/1936) was one of the originators of the *theory of evolution*, which accounted for the change in frequency of some physical trait. From variation among traits, the environment selected or favored some traits because they specifically aided in the organism's survival. *Population thinking* stems from the concept of variation and emphasizes that each individual is unique, which translates into individual differences in psychological needs and personality traits. According to Spencer (1899), preferring pleasure to pain may be an attribute of living creatures that has aided their survival. Pleasure is linked with behavior beneficial to life and pain is linked with behavior detrimental to life. *Instinct* is an inherited predisposition that has survival value for the animal. It resembles an internal stimulus that induces a specific pattern of behavior in a species. Species-typical behavior is a current version of instincts. Sign stimuli elicit species-typical behavior as an innate reaction exhibited by all members of a species. Love is an instance of an instinct that evolved to solve the *commitment problem*, which refers to the necessity of a pair of individuals to remain loyal for their mutual survival benefits. *Selection by consequences* derives from combining evolution and the law of effect. It means that a desired end-state or goal selects the behavior that makes achievement of the goal possible. Freud relied on instinctual impulses residing in the unconscious to account for motivation. According to Freud, the *conscious* refers to awareness of thoughts and impulses that are residing in the *preconscious*, which contains thoughts, feelings, and memories. The *unconscious* is the part of one's mental apparatus that is unavailable to the individual and contains instinctual impulses, repressed thoughts, and other mental excitations. Anxiety- and shame-provoking impulses and thoughts are prevented from reaching the pre-conscious or awareness through a process known as *repression*. Currently, unconscious motivation refers to not being aware of processing information and not being aware of how that affects behavior.

Other internal sources of motivation involve drives and primary and secondary needs. *Drive* is the internal stimulus that motivates action and remains in effect even after the instigating stimulus has been removed. Primary needs have a physiological basis and include the needs for air, food, water, and sex. Secondary needs are derived from primary needs and relate to psychological satisfaction of physiological desires but also to psychological motives, such as achievement and affiliation. Currently, psychologists are investigating a basic psychological need referred to as *existential concern* that centers on questioning the meaning and implications of one's life. The need to connect illustrates how Twitter can be used to satisfy this derivative of the need to affiliate.

In regards to external motivation, incentives are external stimuli that attract or repel, such as anticipated rewards and dreaded punishers. The action of incentives depend on a *drive–incentive link*, which joins external and internal sources of motivation. According to this concept, incentives and drives coordinate so that the appropriate incentive satisfies the corresponding drive, like putting on a sweater alleviates feeling cold. Lewin's concept of *psychological force* also ties external and internal sources of motivation together. Force motivates behavior. It becomes stronger based on incentive valence and on tension within the person but weakens as the psychological distance of the incentive increases. Tolman's theory employed the term demand to describe why goals motivate behavior. Demand was determined by the intensity of physiological drive and the characteristics of the goal. For Hull, motivation was linked to drive, which was the psychological counterpart of a physiological need. *Drive* was felt as unpleasant and motivated behavior to seek incentives that would reduce that need. *Motivational readiness* is a current elaboration of the drive–incentive link. Readiness refers to the expectancy that a person's want will be satisfied by affordances (potential incentives) that are available to a person.

BRIEF HISTORY OF EMOTION

The word emotion has undergone a change in meaning regarding its reference to movement. Initially, it meant movement of a physical phenomenon. For instance, in 1690 Locke wrote of how exercise stirs the emotion of a person's blood or pulse (see the Oxford English Dictionary). By the 1800s, emotion was used in reference to movement of events that were not visible but were inferred (Gillis, 1988). Philosophers and psychologists have long commented on the meaning of emotions in people's lives. What were their views on the subjective feel, categories, physiological arousal, and facial expressions of emotion? Their views, however, were based on thoughtful opinions rather than on scientific observations.

Emotion as Subjective Feeling

As a state of mind, the subjective "feel" of emotion has been separated from feelings produced by other bodily processes. According to the Greek philosopher Aristotle (384–322 BC), mixtures of pain and pleasure could arise solely from the body, such as itches and tickles, or from the body and soul, such as hunger and thirst. Emotions, however, were mixtures arising only in the soul (Fortenbaugh, 1975). For the seventeenth-century philosopher Descartes (1649/1968), emotions were feelings but not like those resulting from environmental stimuli like smell, sound, or vision or from internal stimuli like hunger or thirst. He also excluded feelings regarding thoughts or intentions. One of the first American psychologists to write eloquently about emotion was William James (1892), who referred to emotions' subjective part as "mind stuff" (p. 378). In fact for James, the mind stuff of emotions was our awareness of accompanying bodily symptoms. If those were somehow removed from awareness, then the only content remaining would be a cold, neutral state of intellectual perception. For example, what would grief feel like if tears, sobs, and pangs in the heart were removed? For James there would be no feeling but only a cold cognition about some terrible circumstance. As part of subjective feeling, Woodworth (1921) added the conscious awareness of the behavioral impulse that accompanies emotion. In his book *The Laws of Feeling*, F. Paulhan (1887/1930) claimed that an emotion floods consciousness, thereby directing a person's attention specifically to the experience.

Basic Emotions

The idea that there is a basic set of emotions from which all other emotions can be derived was discussed as early as 300 BC. Greek philosophers such as Aristotle (384–322 BC) and Epicurus (341–271 BC) mentioned the basic emotions of joy, fear, envy, love, anger, and hatred, with additional emotions being combinations of these more central ones (Fortenbaugh, 1975; Long & Sedley, 1987). Much later, the seventeenth-century philosopher René Descartes (1649/1968) devised a similar list of six basic or primitive emotions: wonder, love, hatred, desire, joy, and sadness. In addition, he maintained that the emotion of hope stems from the desire that certain events will happen. Fear, by contrast, is the desire that certain events will not happen. Descartes also provided a possible answer as to why there are more negative than positive emotions. He stated that it is more important to escape and avoid things that may destroy us than to acquire things that are beneficial but not necessary for existence. Indeed, negative emotions are signals of things that are harmful. For example, when afraid it may be wise to run away and thus increase the likelihood of surviving. Negative emotions can prompt beneficial action. For instance, anger may force people to stand up for their rights rather than being taken advantage of. Happiness and joy may be beneficial as well, but they are often not as important for our immediate survival. James (1892), however, disputed the value of trying to categorize emotions. He felt that it was more important to explain why events could produce physiological arousal in the individual rather than fixate on determining the different categories of emotions.

Philosophers were also aware that certain events and their interpretation triggered emotional experiences. Aristotle reasoned that the thought of imminent danger caused fear, that being unjustly insulted resulted in anger, and that the thought of disgrace brought about shame (Fortenbaugh, 1975). An example of a cognitive interpretation is Aristotle's *superiority theory of humor*, which was also endorsed by Hobbes (1640/1962). According to this theory, laughter and amusement arise when a person perceives a prominence in himself or herself in comparison to the inferiority of other individuals (Fortenbaugh, 1975). An example is the sight gag of an individual slipping and falling on a banana peel.

Emotion as Motive for Action and Thought

The impression that emotions serve as motives that push individuals into action is also apparent in the writings of early Greek philosophers. Zeno (350–258 BC) and Chrysippus (280–206 BC) described emotion as providing irrational and excessive impulses (Long & Sedley, 1987). These impulses provide a push for people to act irrationally and without reason or judgment, such as when a person acts in anger and regrets it later. This idea that emotions push us was continued by Descartes (1649/1968), who wrote that "the principal effect of all the passions [emotions] is that they incite and dispose the mind to will the things to which they prepare the body." As Descartes illustrated, fear wills a person to flee and courage wills a person to fight. This observation by Descartes serves to tie emotions to motivation—that is, emotions are an internal source of motivation that push humans into action toward a specific aim. In one of the first psychology textbooks, Stout (1903) remarks that "the typical varieties of emotion are each connected with certain characteristic directions of collation trends of activity" (p. 190). Later, Woodworth (1921) repeated this theme, stating that emotion is an impulse toward a specific action or certain result and not just a preparation for action in general. Disgust is the impulse to escape and avoid a noxious substance or idea, while anger is the impulse to strike an offending person. Currently, the term **action readiness** refers to the tendency of an emotion to serve as motive for an action specific to the emotion being experienced (Arnold, 1960; Frijda, 1986, 2007). However, Margaret Washburn (1928), the first woman to receive a PhD in psychology (Scarborough, 1990), challenged this view with her concept of motor explosion. This refers to nonadaptive muscular responses that occur during intense emotion. For example, "jumping for joy" is a motor explosion that seems to have no purpose. Furthermore, although emotion can aid thinking, it can also cause mental panic, such as having "the effect of making our brain whirl" (Washburn, 1928).

TABLE 2.3 Stout's View of the Class of Ideas Revived by Emotions

Emotion	Ideas Revived by Emotion
Joy	"success and gratification"
Grief	"loss and defeat"
Fear	"danger"
Anger	"insult and injuries"
Jealousy	"encroachment of others on . . .our own peculiar possessions"

Source: Adapted from *The Groundwork of Psychology* by G. F. Stout, 1903. New York, NY: Hinds & Noble.

Early psychologists were also aware that emotion directs thought. In *The Groundwork of Psychology*, Stout (1903) posed the consideration that emotion directs our thinking, an idea currently receiving attention from psychologists (Frijda, 1994, 2007; Niedenthal & Kitayama, 1994). According to Stout, each emotion revives a certain class of ideas that are congruent with that emotion (see Table 2.3). Thus, depression directs an individual's mind to the dark side of things, while a cheerful disposition brings forth thoughts of success and progress. When angry, one's mental meanderings encourage ideas of injury, neglect, or persecution, while fear activates thoughts of danger and insecurity.

Accompaniments of Emotion

The early view of emotion was that of a movement of events along physiological channels and facial expressions. Emotions were thought to move a person physiologically and facially, according to philosophers and early psychologists.

Physiological arousal. "A broken heart" is a frequently used metaphor for disappointment and sadness in popular songs. The heart as the seat of emotion has had a long history. According to Aristotle (384–322 BC), blood boiling around the heart causes a person to turn red with anger. "The quaking of the heart causes the whole body to quake, following the heart's motion and from this comes stammering and hesitation in speech," wrote Luis Vives in *Of the Soul and Life* (1538/1974). Descartes (1649/1968) also considered bodily manifestations of emotion to involve changes in the heart and blood flow. The nature of the link between subjective emotions and patterns of physiological arousal began in the writings of Francis Bacon (1627/1974). For him, certain emotions produced their manifestations by arousing the body. Table 2.4 provides views from the seventeenth century on the relationship between physiological arousal and associated subjective feelings. Current research in the twenty-first century has verified the importance of these physiological reactions for emotions (Levenson, 2014). In addition, Descartes reasoned that subjective experience provided the body with useful information on how to act, with physiological arousal being the basis for that action. The physiologist Walter Cannon (1929/1953) later elaborated the view that arousal energizes emotional behavior. For example, fear energizes running and anger energizes fighting. For William James (1890/1950), bodily arousal was the source of information for the subjective feel of an emotion. He maintained that an exciting event produced reflexive bodily changes. An individual's perception of these changes in consciousness

TABLE 2.4 Ideas on the Physiological Accompaniments of Emotion of Bacon and Descartes

Emotion	Physiological Accompaniments
Fear	Paleness, trembling, hair erection, startle, screeching
Grief	Sighing, sobbing, groans, tears, distorted face, grinding of teeth
Joy	Vigor of eyes, singing, leaping, dancing, at times tears
Anger	Paleness, blushing, trembling, foaming at mouth
Lust	Flagrancy in eyes, priapism
Love	Pulse is fuller and stronger; heat in breast
Hate	Pulse is feebler and quicker; cold alternates with heat in breast
Sadness	Pulse is feeble and slow; feel constriction around heart

is the emotion. Also writing about emotion in the same vein as James was Francis Sumner, who was the first African-American in the United States to earn a PhD in psychology (Guthrie, 1998). Sumner (1924) surmised that consciousness registered an aggregate of bodily changes in order to generate an emotion. However, a person is unable to state the specific origin of these bodily changes even though they provide for a distinction among different emotions, such as love, fear, and anger. However, sometimes bodily changes are the same, such as tears of joy or of sorrow. Hence, other bodily information must be available for a person to feel these separate emotions.

Facial expression. It is difficult to conceive of emotional experiences without accompanying facial expressions. Both Bacon (1627/1974) and Descartes (1649/1968) viewed changes in facial expressions as outward signs of emotion. The social importance of these expressions was elaborated at about the same time by Marin Cureau de La Chambre (1663/1974). He felt that facial expressions of emotions were more likely to occur in the presence of others because of their effects. He reasoned that women and children are quicker to cry in order to make known their need for help when in the presence of others than when alone. Similarly, laughter is more likely to occur in a social setting and is a social instrument that acts to make our feelings known. In *The Expression of the Emotions in Man and Animals* (1873), Darwin wrote that the expression of emotion was mostly innate, although some expressions require practice before they are fully developed. Darwin felt that expression serves to communicate our emotions and "reveal the thoughts and intentions of others more truly than do words" (p. 364). A current debate regarding the relationship between emotion and facial expression is described in Chapter 14. One view is that facial expressions are like dials reflecting our internal subjective emotions (Buck, 1984). Another view is that facial expressions serve more as signals to others to satisfy social motives (Fridlund, 1991, 1992). For example, a sad face means "help me," while an angry face means "don't mess with me."

Current trends. According to William James (1884/1948), an emotion is synonymous with the subjective awareness of bodily actions. Also, each shade of emotion would have a unique bodily reverberation or its own profile of physiological responses. James's theory led to a long history of research trying to demonstrate the parallel between emotional feelings on the one hand and specific activity of the nervous system on the other. In an early experiment along these lines, Ax (1953) frightened and angered his participants while simultaneously recording their heart rate, respiration, face and hand temperature, and electrodermal (skin conductance) responses. The results were promising for James's theory. Ax discovered different physiological profiles for anger and fear. Nevertheless, in spite of this early promise, 60 some years and many experiments later, psychologists have concluded that discrete emotions "cannot be fully differentiated by visceral activity alone" (Cacioppo et al., 2000, p. 184; Larsen et al., 2008). Nevertheless, the issue has been revived and it still may be that each basic emotion is defined by a unique pattern of physiological responses (Levenson, 2014).

The search for the bodily basis of subjective feelings has shifted to the brain. A current research strategy uses fMRI to identify brain maps that correspond to emotions. But what do these maps consist of? One possibility is that each basic emotion would correspond to a distinct brain location where there is greater activity as shown by increased use of oxygen and glucose (Vytal & Hamann, 2010). Another possibility is that various brain regions interact to construct an emotion with different brain regions participating to represent any one basic emotion (Kassam et al., 2013;

Lindquist et al., 2012). Perhaps eventually neuroscientists will discover that each emotional experience will have a unique brain map, as James had imagined would be the case with physiological response profiles.

Section Recap

Initially, emotion meant observable movement but later it came to mean the unobserved movement of feelings. Currently, an emotion consists of the integration of affective feelings, physiological arousal, behavior, and facial expressions. Early philosophers and psychologists formulated a list of basic emotions, which, like today, involves more negative than positive emotions. Each emotion was thought to have an accompanying physiological profile but also a set of accompanying thoughts. The appraisal of certain situations was linked to specific emotions. Aristotle and Hobbes, for example, felt that appraising ourselves as superior to others produced amusement and laughter. There are two early interpretations of physiological arousal: providing information for the subjective feel of emotion (according to James) and serving as a readiness for action (according to Cannon). In fact, for philosophers emotion provided an impulse to action or a motive for action. The term *action readiness* means that emotions yield tendencies to act in a manner distinctive of a particular emotion in order to fulfill the aim of the emotion. Facial expressions have been interpreted as a way of making our feelings or social intentions known to others. In addition to each emotion having a specific physiological profile, researchers are looking for networks of activated neurons in the brain that would correspond to emotional feelings.

GLOSSARY

Term	Definition
Action Readiness	The tendency of an emotion to serve as a motive for behavior that is specific to satisfying the aim of the emotion
Affective Forecasting	When a person predicts his or her subjective feelings (affect), much like the weather reporter forecasts the weather
Affordance	In motivational readiness theory, it refers to resources in the environment that are potentially capable of satisfying wants. Affordances resemble incentives
Behaviorism	A school of psychology that emphasizes observable behavior and observable consequences of behavior; not subjective pain or pleasure
Brief Self-Control Scale	Psychological scale that measures a person's degree of self-control, i.e., to resist temptation, to consider alternative, and to work toward long-term goals
Commitment Problem	Necessity of one individual being loyal and faithful to another for the survival benefit of one or both of them, e.g., mother commits to her infant
Conscious	Freud's term for that part of the mind that contains thoughts, desires, and impulses of which the individual is aware or conscious
Decision Theory	Theory derived from Bentham for the process by which an individual chooses from among possible end-states. The choice becomes the person's goal

continued . . .

GLOSSARY Continued

Term	Definition
Demand	For Tolman, it refers to characteristics of goals to motivate behavior, which depended on the animal's physiological drive and characteristics of the goal
Drive	Motivation construct that results from being deprived of a needed substance. It acts like an internal stimulus that motivates action to reduce drive
Drive–Incentive Link	Warden's term that a physiological drive matches up with the appropriate incentive, such as hunger matches food and curiosity with novel stimuli
Evolution (Theory of)	According to Darwin, from differences among traits, the environment seemingly selected traits that aided in the organism's survival
Existential Concern	A psychological need that centers around questions regarding the meaning and implications of one's life
Forces	Lewin's term for the motivational factors in a person's life space that motivate the person from one object or activity to another
Habit Strength (H)	In Hull's theory, habit strength represents learning the behavior that is necessary for attaining the incentive
Hedonism	Motivation principle that emphasizes the pursuit of pleasure and the avoidance of pain
Impulsiveness	Trait of heightened sensitivity to immediate rewards rather than larger delayed rewards; tendency to act now and inability of foresight
Incentive Motivation	To be motivated to approach positive environmental events (incentives) and to avoid negative environmental events (incentives)
Incentives	A valued feature of the environment that pulls an individual toward it if positive and repels an individual if negative; designated K in Hull's theory
Instinct	An inherited disposition or impulse that shows itself as species-typical behavior in the presence of a limited range of stimuli
Latent Content	The meaning of the dream or significance of the dream that is represented by the dream's manifest content
Law of Effect	Thorndike's idea that behavior followed by satisfying consequences is strengthened and if followed by unsatisfying consequences is weakened
Life Space	Lewin's term for a person's current internal and external environment of which the person is aware
Manifest Content	The content of the dream of which a person is aware; the part of the dream that can be reported
Motivational Readiness (Theory of)	It is the expectancy that an individual's wants will be satisfied by possible available incentives known as affordances
Need to Connect	Derived from the need to affiliate, it refers to the motive to be in contact with other people via Twitter
Pleasure Principle	Freud's term that humans are motivated by the pursuit of pleasure, which was viewed as a sudden decrease in tension

continued . . .

GLOSSARY Continued

Term	Definition
Population Thinking	Based on Darwin's concept of variation; it emphasizes how each individual is unique, as in differences in psychological needs and traits
Positive Psychology	Area of scientific investigation that investigates factors that promote people and groups to function at their best in order to maximize their happiness
Preconscious	The accessible part of a person's mind that contains thoughts, feelings, and memories
Primary Needs	Murray's term for physiological needs like the need for food, water, sex, sleep
Principle of Utility	Motivation principle that our decisions and actions are motivated by the utility or usefulness of incentives to increase pleasure or decrease pain
Psychological Distance	Lewin's term for the physical distance or time interval to an available incentive; decreases in distance will increase motivation for the incentive
Psychological Force	Lewin's term for the ability of goals, incentives, and needs in a person's life space to be able to motivate the person's behavior
Psychological Need	Similar to drive, it referred to an existing psychological deficit. People are motivated to reduce the deficit—that is, satisfy the need
Punisher	An observable stimulus consequence of behavior that decreases the behavior
Reality Principle	Freud's term for the environment dictating when pleasure could be attained or that a person might experience pain in order to achieve pleasure later
Reinforcers	An observable stimulus consequence of behavior that maintains or increases the behavior
Repression	A Freudian term for keeping anxiety- and shame-provoking impulses and thoughts in the unconscious so as to keep them from awareness
Secondary Needs	Murray's term for needs derived from primary needs, such as achievement and affiliation
Selection	Certain values of a trait are favored or selected by the environment and aid survival
Selection by Consequences	The reinforcing consequence of behavior acts to select the behavior and make it more likely to occur, e.g., a goal selects goal achievement behavior
Self-Control	Trait of being able to control impulses, having foresight, and the tendency to choose larger delayed rewards over smaller immediate rewards
Species-Typical Behavior	The modal pattern or characteristic pattern of behavior elicited by a stimulus; considered innate behavior or instinctive
Superiority Theory of Humor	A theory proposed by Aristotle that laughter and amusement arise when individuals perceive themselves grander in comparison to the inferiority of other individuals
Tension	Lewin's term for unfulfilled physiological need or psychological need; a deficit in a person's internal environment
Unconscious	That part of the mind of which the person is unaware or is not open to introspection and contains repressed thought and instinctual impulses

continued . . .

GLOSSARY Continued

Term	Definition
Unconscious Motivation	Motivation that stems from unaware part of a person's mind that is unavailable for introspection and that contains instinctual impulses and repressed thoughts
Valence	Positive and negative features of an incentive. Positive valence attracts individuals to and negative valence repel individuals from the incentive
Variation	Different values of a particular trait that vary in frequency in the population
Wants	In motivational readiness theory, it refers to desires, motives, drives, needs or wishes

REFERENCES

Arnold, M. B. (1960). *Emotion and personality: Vol. I. Psychological aspects*. New York, NY: Columbia University Press.

Ax, A. F. (1953). The physiological differentiation between fear and anger in humans. *Psychosomatic Medicine, 15*, 433–442.

Bacon, F. (1627/1974). Sylva sylvarum. In S. Diamond (Ed.), *The roots of psychology* (pp. 523–525). New York, NY: Basic.

Bargh, J. A., & Morsella, E. (2008). The unconscious mind. *Perspectives on Psychological Science, 3*, 73–79.

Bargh, J. A., & Williams, E. L. (2006). The automaticity of social life. *Current Directions in Psychological Science, 15*, 1–4.

Bentham, J. (1789/1970). *An introduction to the principles of morals and legislation* (J. H. Burns & H. L. A. Hart, Eds.). London: Athlone.

Brown, R., & Herrnstein, R. J. (1975). *Psychology*. Boston, MA: Little, Brown.

Buck, R. (1984). *The communication of emotion*. New York, NY: Guilford.

Buss, D. M. (2006). The evolution of love. In R. J. Sternberg & K. Weis (Eds.), *The new psychology of love* (pp. 65–86). New Haven, CT, & London: Yale University Press.

Buss, D. M. (2015). *Evolutionary psychology: The new science of the mind* (5th ed.). New York, NY: Routledge.

Cacioppo, J. T., Berntson, G. G., Larsen, J. T., Poehlmann, K. M., & Ito, T. A. (2000). The psychophysiology of emotion. In M. Lewis & J. M. Haviland-Jones (Eds), *Handbook of emotions* (2nd ed., pp. 173–191). New York, NY: Guilford.

Cannon, W. B. (1929/1953). *Bodily changes in pain, hunger, fear and rage*. Boston, MA: Charles T. Branford.

Catania, A. C. (2013). A natural science of behavior. *Review of General Psychology, 17*, 133–139.

Chen, G. M. (2011). Tweet this: A uses and gratifications perspective on how active Twitter use gratifies a need to connect with others. *Computers in Human Behavior, 27*, 755–762.

Cosmides, L., & Tooby, J. (2006). Evolutionary psychology: Evolutionary theory, paleoanthropology, adaptationism. Retrieved August 26, 2015, from University of California, Santa Barbara, Center for Evolutionary Psychology: http://cogweb.ucla.edu/ep/

Custers, R., & Aarts, H. (2010). The unconscious will: How the pursuit of goals operates outside of conscious awareness. *Science, 329*, 4750.

Darwin, C. (1859/1936). *On the origin of species by means of natural selection*. New York, NY: Random House.

Darwin, C. (1873). *The expression of the emotions in man and animals*. London: John Murray.

de La Chambre, M. C. (1663/1974). Of weeping, fear, and despair. In S. Diamond (Ed.), *The roots of psychology* (pp. 526–528). New York, NY: Basic.

Descartes, R. (1649/1968). The passions of the soul. In E. S. Haldane & G. R. T. Ross (Eds.), *The philosophical works of Descartes*. Cambridge: Cambridge University Press.

Duckworth, A. L., & Seligman, M. E. P. (2005). Self-discipline outdoes IQ in predicting academic performance of adolescents. *Psychological Science, 16*, 939–944.

Eibl-Eibesfeldt, I. (1989). *Human ethology*. New York, NY: Aldine de Gruyter.

Endler, J. A. (1986). *Natural selection in the wild*. Princeton, NJ: Princeton University Press.

Fletcher, R. (1966). *Instincts in man*. New York, NY: Schocken.

Fortenbaugh, W. W. (1975). *Aristotle on emotion*. New York, NY: Harper & Row.

Frank, R. H. (1988). *Passions within reason*. New York, NY: W. W. Norton & Company.

Freud, S. (1905). Jokes and their relation to the unconscious. In J. Strachey (Ed.), *The standard edition of the complete psychological works of Sigmund Freud* (Vol. 8). London: Hogarth.

Freud, S. (1915a). Instincts and their vicissitudes. In J. Strachey (Ed.), *The standard edition of the complete psychological works of Sigmund Freud* (Vol. 14). London: Hogarth.

Freud, S. (1915b). The unconscious. In J. Strachey (Ed.), *The standard edition of the complete psychological works of Sigmund Freud* (Vol. 14). London: Hogarth.

Freud, S. (1920). Beyond the pleasure principle. In J. Strachey (Ed.), *The standard edition of the complete psychological works of Sigmund Freud* (Vol. 18). London: Hogarth.

Freud, S. (1920/1943). *A general introduction to psychoanalysis*. Garden City, NY: Garden City Publishing.

Freud, S. (1924). The economic problem in masochism. In E. Jones (Ed.), *Sigmund Freud: Collected papers* (Vol. 2). New York, NY: Basic.

Fridlund, A. J. (1991). Evolution and facial action in reflex, social motive, and paralanguage. *Biological Psychology, 32*, 3–100.

Fridlund, A. J. (1992). The behavioral ecology and sociality of human faces. In M. S. Clark (Ed.), *Review of personality and social psychology: Vol. 13. Emotion* (pp. 90–121). Newbury Park, CA: Sage.

Frijda, N. H. (1986). *The emotions*. Cambridge: Cambridge University Press.

Frijda, N. H. (1994). Emotions are functional, most of the time. In P. Ekman & R. J. Davidson (Eds.), *The nature of emotion* (pp. 112–122). New York, NY: Oxford University Press.

Frijda, N. H. (2007). *The laws of emotion*. Mahwah, NJ: Lawrence Erlbaum.

Gable, S. L., & Haidt, J. (2005). What (and why) is positive psychology? *Review of General Psychology, 9*, 103–110.

Gay, P. (1999, March 29). Sigmund Freud. *Time, 153*, 66–69.

Gillis, J. R. (1988). From ritual to romance: Toward an alternative history of love. In C. Z. Stearns & P. N. Stearns (Eds.), *Emotion and social change: Toward a new psychohistory* (pp. 87–121). New York, NY: Holmes & Meier.

Guthrie, R. V. (1998). *Even the rat was white* (2nd ed.). Boston, MA: Allyn and Bacon.

Haggard, P. (2008). Human volition: Towards a neuroscience of will. *Nature Reviews Neuroscience, 9*, 934–946.

Hillman, B., Hunter, W. S., & Kimble, G. A. (1953). The effect of drive level on the maze performance of the white rat. *Journal of Comparative and Physiological Psychology, 46*, 87–89.

Hobbes, T. (1640/1962). *Human nature*. Cleveland, OH: Bell & Howell.

Hull, C. L. (1943). *Principles of behavior*. New York, NY: Appleton-Century-Crofts.

Hull, C. L. (1951). *Essentials of behavior*. New Haven, CT: Yale University Press.

Hull, C. L. (1952). *A behavior system*. New Haven, CT: Yale University Press.

Hyland, D. A. (1973). *The origins of philosophy: Its rise in myth and the pre-Socratics*. New York, NY: G. P. Putman's.

James, W. (1884/1948). What is an emotion? *Mind, 9*, 188–204. Reprinted in W. Dennis (Ed.), *Readings in history of psychology* (pp. 290–303). New York, NY: Appleton-Century-Crofts.

James, W. (1890/1950). *The principles of psychology*. New York, NY: Dover.

James, W. (1892). *Psychology*. New York, NY: Henry Holt.

Kassam, K. S., Markey, A. R., Cherkassky, V. L., Loewenstein, G., & Just, M. A. (2013). Identifying emotions on the basis of neural activation. *PLOS ONE, 8*(6), e66032.

Killeen, P. R. (2001). The four causes of behavior. *Current Directions in Psychological Science, 10*, 136–140.

Koole, S. L., Greenberg, J., & Pyszczynski, T. (2006). Introducing the science to the psychology of the soul. *Current Directions in Psychological Science, 15*, 212–216.

Kruglanski, A. W., Chernikova, M., Rosenzweig, E., & Kopetz, C. (2014). On motivational readiness. *Psychological Review, 121*, 367–388.

61

Larsen, J. T., Berntson, G. G., Poehlmann, K. M., Ito, T. A., & Cacioppo, J. T. (2008). The psychophysiology of emotion. In M. Lewis, J. M. Haviland-Jones, & L. F. Barrett (Eds.), *Handbook of Emotions* (3rd ed., pp. 180–195). New York, NY: Guilford.

Le Roy, G. (1764/1974). Letter on man. In S. Diamond (Ed.), *The roots of psychology* (pp. 564–567). New York, NY: Basic.

Leeper, R. (1935). The role of motivation in learning: A study of the phenomenon of differential motivational control of the utilization of habits. *Journal of Genetic Psychology, 46*, 3–40.

Levenson, R. W. (2014). The autonomic nervous system and emotion. *Emotion Review, 6*, 100–112.

Lewin, K. (1933). Environmental forces in child behavior and development. In C. Murchison (Ed.), *Handbook of child psychology* (2nd ed., Chap. 14). Worcester, MA: Clark University Press.

Lewin, K. (1936). *Principles of topological psychology* (F. Heider & G. Heider, trans.). New York, NY: McGraw-Hill.

Lewin, K. (1938). *The conceptual representation and the measurement of psychological forces.* Durham, NC: Duke University Press.

Libet, B., Gleason, C. A., Wright, E. W., & Pearl, D. K. (1983). Time of conscious intention to act in relation to onset of cerebral activity (readiness-potential). *Brain, 106*, 623–642.

Lindquist, K. A., Wager, T. D., Kober, H., Bliss-Moreau, E., & Barrett, L. F. (2012). The brain basis of emotion: A meta-analytic review. *Behavioral and Brain Sciences, 35*, 121–143.

Locke, J. (1690). *An essay concerning human understanding.* Retrieved March 10, 2008, from http://humanum.arts.cuhk.edu.hk/Philosophy/Locke/echu

Logue, A. W. (1988). Research on self-control: An integrating framework. *Behavioral and Brain Sciences, 11*, 665–709.

Logue, A. W. (1998). Laboratory research on self-control: Applications to administration. *Review of General Psychology, 2*, 221–238.

Long, A. A., & Sedley, D. N. (1987). *The Hellenistic philosophers* (Vol. 1). Cambridge: Cambridge University Press.

Mayr, E. (2001). *What evolution is.* New York, NY: Basic.

McDougall, W. (1908). *An introduction to social psychology.* London: Methuen.

Murray, H. A. (1938). *Explorations in personality.* New York, NY: Oxford University Press.

National Survey of Student Engagement (2015). NSSE 2015 Summary Means and Standard Deviations by Class and Sex. Retrieved September 3, 2015, from http://nsse.indiana.edu/2015_institutional_report/pdf/Means/Mean%20-%20Sex.pdf

Niedenthal, P. M., & Kitayama, S. (1994). *The heart's eye: Emotional influences on perception and attention.* San Diego, CA: Academic Press.

Nisbett, R. E., & Wilson, T. D. (1977). Telling more than we can know: Verbal reports on mental processes. *Psychological Review, 84*, 231–259.

Paulhan, F. (1887/1930). *The laws of feeling* (C. K. Ogden, trans.). London: Kegan Paul, Trench, Trubner.

Peck, A. L. (1942). *Aristotle: Generation of animals.* Cambridge: Harvard University Press.

Scarborough, E. (1990). Margaret Floy Washburn (1871–1939). In A. N. O'Connell & N. F. Russo (Eds.), *Women in psychology: A bio-bibliographic sourcebook* (pp. 342–349). New York, NY: Greenwood.

Schopenhauer, A. (1851/1970). On philosophy and the intellect. In R. J. Hollingdale (Ed.), *Essays and aphorisms* (pp. 117–132). New York, NY: Penguin Classics.

Seligman, M. E. P., & Csíkszentmihályi, M. (2000). Positive psychology: An introduction. *American Psychologist, 55*, 5–14.

Skinner, B. F. (1981). Selection by consequences. *Science, 213*, 501–504.

Spencer, H. (1881/1977). *The principles of psychology.* Boston, MA: Longwood.

Spencer, H. (1899). *The principles of psychology* (Vol. 1). New York, NY: D. Appleton.

Steiner, J. E. (1977). Facial expressions of the neonate infant indicating the hedonics of food-related chemical stimuli. In J. M. Weiffenbach (Ed.), *Taste and development* (pp. 173–189). Bethesda, MD: U.S. Department of Health, Education, and Welfare.

Stout, G. F. (1903). *The groundwork of psychology.* New York, NY: Hinds & Noble.

Sumner, F. C. (1924, June). The nature of emotion. *Howard Review*, pp. 181–195.

Tamir, M. (2009). What do people want to feel and why? Pleasure and utility in emotion regulation. *Current Directions in Psychological Science, 18*, 101–105.

Tamir, M., & Ford, B. Q. (2009). Choosing to be afraid: Preferences for fear as a function of goal pursuit. *Emotion, 9*, 488–497.

Tangney, J. P., Baumeister, R. F., & Boone, A. L. (2004). High self-control predicts good adjustment, less pathology, better grades, and interpersonal success. *Journal of Personality, 72*, 271–324.

Thorndike, E. L. (1898). Animal intelligence: An experimental study of the associative process in animals. *Psychological Review Monographs Supplements, 2*(8).

Thorndike, E. L. (1911). *Animal intelligence*. New York, NY: Macmillan.

Tolman, E. C. (1932). *Purposive behavior in animals and men*. New York, NY: Appleton-Century.

Tolman, E. C., & Honzik, C. H. (1930). Introduction and removal of reward, and maze performance in rats. *University of California Publications in Psychology, 4*, 257–275.

Van Boven, L. (2005). Experientialism, materialism, and the pursuit of happiness. *Review of General Psychology, 9*, 132–142.

Vives, L. (1538/1974). Of the soul and life. In S. Diamond (Ed.), *The roots of psychology* (pp. 521–523). New York, NY: Basic.

Vytal, K., & Hamann, S. (2010). Neuroimaging support for discrete neural correlates of basic emotions: A voxel-based meta-analysis. *Journal of Cognitive Neuroscience, 22*, 2864–2885.

Warden, C. J. (1931). The Columbia Obstruction Method. In C. J. Warden (Ed.), *Animal motivation: Experimental studies on the albino rat* (pp. 3–16). New York, NY: Columbia University Press.

Washburn, M. F. (1928). Emotion and thought: A motor theory of their relations. In M. L. Reymert (Ed.), *Feelings and emotions: The Wittenberg symposium* (pp. 104–115). Worcester, MA: Clark University Press.

Wasserman, E. A. (2012). Species, tepees, scotties, and jockeys: Selected by consequences. *Journal of the Experimental Analysis of Behavior, 98*, 213–226.

Watson, J. B. (1913). Psychology as the behaviorist views it. *Psychological Review, 20*, 158–177.

Weiss, R. (1989). The hedonic calculus in the *Protagoras* and the *Phaedo*. *Journal of the History of Philosophy, 27*, 511–529.

Woodworth, R. S. (1921). *Psychology: A study of mental life*. New York, NY: Henry Holt.

CHAPTER 3

Evolutionary Antecedents of Motivation

Human nature is the same all over the world, but its operations are so varied by education and habit that one must see it in all its dresses in order to be entirely acquainted with it.

Lord Chesterfield, 1747

Human action can be modified to some extent, but human nature cannot be changed.

Abraham Lincoln, 1809–1865

Does human nature refer to characteristics of motivation that all people have in common? Is there a core of motives and goals that all people share? Also, consider the following:

1. What is human nature, and how does it relate to motivation and emotion?
2. Are there dispositions that serve as universal motives for all humans?
3. How did evolution and the social environment contribute to mate preferences, reproductive behavior, and jealousy?
4. What is the contribution of evolution to fear, food preferences, and the enjoyment of music?

EVOLUTIONARY PERSPECTIVE ON MOTIVATION

Where in people's past is the origin for the motivation of their current behavior? By way of analogy, what caused the fall of the last domino pictured in Figure 3.1? Some event must have

FIGURE 3.1 A Metaphor for Evolutionary History and Personal History. The toppling of the initial dominoes represents evolutionary history, which topple later dominoes that represent personal history. The tenth or last domino represents motivated behavior in the present.

toppled the first domino, which eventually led to the fall of the last one. Is the immediately preceding domino responsible for the fall of the last one or is it the one prior to that one and so on back to the initial event? In the case of a person's current behavior, is the motivation in the recent past like the fall of an immediately preceding domino or in the remote past like the very first domino?

Evolutionary History and Personal History

How do evolutionary history and personal history determine an individual's current motivation and emotion? Does our evolutionary past combine with individual environmental and cultural experiences to determine what is motivating?

What shaped human nature? From an evolutionary perspective, motivation pushes and pulls people toward the most basic of goals: the survival and transmission of their genes to the next generation. Achieving this goal involves surviving, finding and keeping a mate, producing children, and raising them successfully so that they can repeat the process for the next generation (Bernard et al., 2005). This process has been repeated over and over during human evolutionary history. The result has been a set of behaviors that all humans have in common in spite of vast geographical, social, and cultural differences. **Human nature** refers to the behavioral, motivational, and emotional similarities among people that have resulted from their common evolutionary history. They are disposed to behave in a particular fashion, depending on their situation. Human nature is most striking when similarities occur in spite of environmental and cultural differences. It is shaped by natural selection or sexual selection and is genetically transmitted from one generation to the next. Human nature is universal, which means it is the same in societies all over the world. Finally, the behavioral expression of human nature tends to be innate—that is, it is influenced little by experience.

Evolutionary and personal history interact. Evolutionary history created human nature, which in turn interacts with our personal history, much like the fall of later dominoes depend on the fall of earlier ones (Figure 3.1). The interaction between evolutionary history and personal history is another way of stating that the interaction between heredity (nature) and environment (nurture) motivates behavior. The nature of this interaction was recognized over 130 years ago by Sir Francis Galton (1883). He claimed that it was difficult to distinguish between the part of human character that results from education and circumstances and that which results from the human constitution. Today, we accept that both heredity and environment interact to determine behavior (Plomin et al., 2013).

The relative contribution of heredity and environment is different for various behaviors. Some behaviors are genetically disposed to occur and thus require little environmental experience. Other behaviors are genetically neutral and require much environmental experience to occur. For instance, learning to eat is almost automatic, whereas it takes a lot of practice to master long division. Figure 3.2 uses a series of rectangles to illustrate the interaction between heredity and environment for motivating behavior (Plomin et al., 2013). A rectangle's length and width both contribute to its area, since area = length × width, although the relative contribution of each may vary. Similarly, heredity and environment both contribute to behavior, but their relative contributions may also vary. Changes in the contribution of heredity and environment are illustrated by rectangles a through d in Figure 3.2: the contribution of length (heredity) decreases, and the contribution of width (environment) increases. Although the change from rectangle a

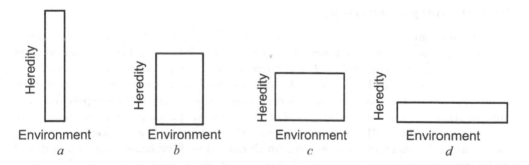

FIGURE 3.2 Relative Contributions of Heredity and Environment. Length and width both contribute to the area of a rectangle, since area = length × width. The relative contribution of length decreases, and width increases from a to d, yet both length and width still contribute to the total area of each rectangle. Similarly, heredity and environment both contribute to the motivation of behavior. The relative contribution of heredity decreases and that of environment increases from a to d, yet both heredity and environment still contribute to the motivation of behavior.

to rectangle d represents a decrease in heredity and an increase in environment, both heredity and environment contribute. Behaviors that are strongly influenced by heredity (rectangle a) are known as innate, which means not taught or not benefitting from experience.

It is important to remember, however, that heredity can influence behavior in more than one way. First, inherited physical features affect a person's behavior, such as the relationship between the thumb and fingers. How difficult would it be to write, tie a ribbon, or grasp a ball without the use of either a thumb or fingers? Or consider how size and strength differences between men and women contribute to a general division of labor. Men, on average, are bigger and physically stronger and so tend to do heavy work, such as farming, mining, and construction. Women, on average, are smaller and have less muscle mass and so tend to do lighter work, such as cooking and clerical tasks. Second, the hereditary nature, or innateness, of certain feelings or motives disposes humans to react in one way rather than another to various stimuli. The influence of these seemingly innate feelings becomes apparent in the prevalence of sexual behavior, certain fears, a baby's taste preferences, and the universal pleasure of music.

Experience and motives. As the rectangles in Figure 3.2 illustrate, even behaviors that appear to be totally innate may actually require at least some minimal environmental experience to occur (rectangle a). Other behaviors require the benefit of additional experiences (rectangles b through d). To illustrate, we might think of walking as being innate, but some prior experience in sitting upright and crawling appears necessary for walking to occur in a timely manner (Dennis, 1960). Other examples are an infant's crying to indicate hunger or distress. This behavior is fairly complete immediately following birth. As new parents quickly learn, their baby requires little if any practice at this activity. Facial reactions to taste stimuli also seem to be in place in the first few hours of an infant's life. Little practice, if any, is needed to indicate whether something is tasty or awful (Mennella & Beauchamp, 1998; Steiner, 1977). Finally, an individual's innate disposition and personal experience usually operate in tandem, which happens for example in the development of gender roles. Infants identified as girls and boys are nurtured along feminine and masculine roles, respectively.

Evolutionary Psychology

Human minds are not blank slates at birth upon which experience writes. Neither are minds passive recipients of experience. Instead, human minds have been shaped by evolution to adapt to their environment. Our evolutionary past interacts with people's experiences to determine current motivation. This interaction is the view of evolutionary psychology, which analyzes universal motives in the context of evolution. According to evolutionary psychology, **psychological mechanisms** have evolved through natural selection to solve specific problems of adaptation to the environment (Buss, 2015). *Universal motives* are a particular type of psychological mechanism that refers to the commonality of motives, which resulted from evolution. Fear, such as that of snakes, for instance, evolved to motivate behavior to escape or avoid such dangerous creatures. Food preferences for sugar and fat evolved to ensure a person liked food that provided adequate calories. Women evolved a preference for mates who had the economic resources to provide for them and their children. Male attraction to beauty and desire for sexual variety evolved to ensure the selection of fertile mates and to motivate the seeking of more sexual partners. The function of male sexual jealousy developed to increase a man's confidence regarding the paternity of his children. Each human motive can be considered an instance of a psychological mechanism that evolved because it aided humans in adapting to their environment.

Extensive information about evolutionary psychology is available at a website hosted by the University of California, Santa Barbara titled "Center for Evolutionary Psychology" here: www.cep.ucsb.edu.

Universal motives. For a motive to be considered universal, it must occur in all countries and cultures of the world even though it might be expressed differently. Different geographical regions, climates, societies, and cultures exist around the world. These differences produce differences in the foods people eat, in social customs, and in educational practices. In spite of these geographical, climatic, and social differences, universal motivation and behavior are presumably the same for food, custom, and learning. Brown (1991) uses the term **universals** to describe traits that are found in almost all cultures and societies. Some items in his list can be categorized together for their relevance to universal motives and universally valued incentives (see Table 3.1). Emotional behaviors seem to dominate the list as reflected by the presence of fears, emotions, and their accompanying facial expressions. The social nature of human motives is exhibited in categories of sexual interactions and the social milieu. Universals with external characteristics express themselves in terms of controlling the environment and setting goals for preventing and alleviating stress. Universals that seem more removed from human biology are beliefs about aesthetics and concepts about the self. The universal motive categories in Table 3.1 are taken for granted. We forget that entire institutions and customs have developed to satisfy these motives or attain these valued incentives in today's societies.

Inherited structures for behavior, motives, and emotions. How can universal motives, such as fear or food preferences, evolve and pass on to succeeding generations? They do so by way of natural selection (see Chapter 2), which operates at the level of the individual. In turn, an individual's genes transmit universal motives to the next generation (Mayr, 2001). **Genes** are those parts of a person's DNA content that provide the information necessary for the construction of proteins. In turn, proteins form the brain and nervous system. Humans receive one-half of their genes from each parent at conception. At this time the sperm containing the male's genetic information unites with the ovum (egg), which contains the female's genetic information. The resulting combination contains information from each parent, which in turn came from their parents, and so on. Our genes or our genetic past do not influence motivation or behavior directly. Genes

TABLE 3.1 Categories of Universal Motives

Universal Motive/Incentive	Characteristics
Aesthetics	art, hygiene, music, standards of beauty
Control Environment	fire, mood altering substances, shelter, tools
Emotions	anger, contempt, disgust, fear, happy, sad, surprise
Facial Expressions	for emotions, for communication, and are modifiable
Fears	loud noises, snakes, strangers in childhood
Goal Setting	predict and plan for the future
Self-Concept	self as subject, object, and different from other persons
Sexual Interactions	attraction, sexual jealousy, and regulation
Social Milieu	live in social units, rights, obligations of membership, and status

Source: Based on *Human Universals* by D. E. Brown, 1991, Chapter 6. Philadelphia, PA: Temple University Press.

provide the information for the building of proteins that are used to "create the skeletal system, muscles, the endocrine system, the immune system, the digestive system, and most important for behavior, the nervous system" (Plomin et al., 2013, p. 44). To say that genes or heredity influence behavior is really a shorthand way of stating that genes are the recipes for various proteins, which in turn produce neurophysiological systems that determine the particular reaction to environmental stimulation (Plomin et al., 2013). Thus, the genetic inheritance of motives or psychological mechanisms simply means that the brain or body appears sensitive to the stimuli that evoke or satisfy those motives. For example, different neurons in the tongue and brain react to sweet and bitter stimuli such that infants prefer sweet tastes. Genes carry the information for how the tongue's neurons and the brain's structure are constructed. At a more global level, however, variation and selection occur at the level of behavior. After all, behavioral and environmental events are visible, while genes are not; only their end results are visible.

Section Recap

The motivation for current behavior has its roots in our evolutionary and personal history. Evolutionary history refers to a person's genetic makeup or nature, and personal history is the person's experiences or nurture. Both nature and nurture contribute to what motivates behavior, just as length and width both contribute to the area of a rectangle. Usually tendencies that are part of human nature operate in tandem with personal experiences as in the development of gender roles. Evolutionary history created *human nature*, which encompasses all the behavioral, motivational, and emotional characteristics that all people have in common despite environmental and cultural differences. Evolutionary psychology supposes that part of human nature consists of *psychological mechanisms*, which have evolved to solve problems of adaptation to the environment. Universal motives are psychological mechanisms that refer to similarities in what motivates people, such as a set of basic needs, valued incentives, and social interactions. Societies formed to express and regulate *universals*, which are traits found the world over such as fears, emotions, facial expressions, environmental control, goal setting, and beliefs about aesthetics and the self. *Genes* are DNA segments that provide information from each parent on how to build the child's neurophysiological structures. These structures, in turn, are the physical basis for psychological mechanisms or universal motives. These mechanisms, according to evolutionary psychology, evolved so that humans could adapt efficiently to long-term environmental problems in their evolutionary past.

UNIVERSAL MOTIVES FOR RELATIONSHIPS AND SEX

How are universal motives satisfied in the current environment? Specifically, how did sexual motives evolve? And how do sexual motives cause individuals to form relationships in their social environments?

Motivation for Relationships

"They stroke, kiss, nip, nuzzle, pat, tap, lick, tug, or playfully chase this chosen one. Some sing. Some whinny. Some squeak, croak, or bark. Some dance. Some strut. Some preen. Some chase.

Most play" (Fisher, 2004, p. 27). In her book *Why We Love*, Fisher gives many behavioral examples of various animals engaging in behaviors that we anthropomorphize as romantic love. In addition to this love play, animals, like humans, exhibit choosiness. They do not mate indiscriminately with members of the other sex. A further similarity is that animals, like humans, appear possessive and guard their mates closely. How do the psychological mechanisms of sexual desire, romantic love, mate choice, and jealousy help start and maintain relationships?

Motives of sexual desire and romantic love. Two universal motives have evolved that are important for the continuation of the human species: sexual desire and romantic love. These are separate and independent motives that induce different behaviors (Berscheid, 2010; Diamond, 2004). If it were not for **sexual desire**, humans might consider sexual intercourse as requiring too much time or effort or as being too dangerous. This universal motive evolved, however, in order to motivate the sexual behavior that is necessary for conception and the eventual birth of a baby (Eastwick, 2009). Without sexual desire and subsequent sexual intercourse, there would be few, if any, offspring.

In addition to sexual desire, another incentive and reinforcer for sexual intercourse is orgasm (Gould, 1987). For males, the pleasure of orgasm is usually always associated with ejaculation, at which time semen and sperm are expelled from the penis. Even though men may achieve orgasm close to 100 percent of the time during sexual intercourse, women experience orgasm much less frequently. In a summary of 32 published reports, Lloyd (2005, p. 36) concludes that as a result of sexual intercourse 25 percent of women always have orgasm, 55 percent have it more than half the time, 23 percent sometimes do, 33 percent rarely or never do, and 5–10 percent never do. Thus, although men are reinforced consistently for sexual intercourse, the reward for women is inconsistent. This may be the reason why the value of orgasm for women has been pondered more extensively (Lloyd, 2005; Symons, 1979). Even though women might not attain orgasm, they still enjoy intercourse because it provides feelings of excitement, intimacy, and closeness with their partners (Lloyd, 2005).

Feelings of sexual desire and orgasm help contribute to an accompanying emotion of **romantic love**. This emotion refers to a strong attachment that individuals have for one another and promotes long-term commitment. These feelings motivate the search for a long-term mate, which provides immediate and evolutionary benefits. First, an immediate benefit is the very pleasant feelings that an individual's partner elicits. In contrast, a partner's absence produces feelings of anguish, distress, and longing: a feeling to reduce or avoid (Shaver et al., 1996). A number of psychologists also maintain that, in addition to sexual attraction, romantic love involves emotional bonds and commitment (Fletcher et al., 2015), factors that motivate a couple to remain together. Second, romantic love corresponds with the evolutionary perspective of motivation: survival and the passing on of one's genes. Romantic love occurs worldwide; it is universal. For example, Jankowiak and Fischer (1992) consulted ethnographic files for the presence of romantic love in 166 societies from around the world. In 88.5 percent of them, they were able to document its occurrence. Romantic love may have evolved from the strong bond that exists between mother and child, which increases the likelihood of the child's survival. This bond was then adapted to serve as the glue that binds a couple together and thus helps prevent one member of the couple from leaving for a more attractive alternative (Buss, 2006; Frank, 1988). Romantic love also reduces the motivation to search for another mate and to pay less attention to other potential partners. Another evolutionary benefit of romantic love is that it promotes the division of labor, which also aids the survival and health of the couple and their children (Eastwick, 2009; Fletcher et al., 2015).

Sexual selection. The trouble with sex, according to the humorists Thurber and White (1929), is the other person. In other words, the true fulfillment of sexual desire and romantic love requires another (cooperative) person. So why and on what basis do people seek that other person for a mate? The point of natural selection is to ensure survival and longevity. However, living a long time because of natural selection may benefit an individual but may not benefit the species. For a species to receive the benefits of natural selection, adaptive traits must be passed on to succeeding generations. This requires short- and long-term cooperation between men and women. Short-term cooperation is required for sexual intercourse that leads to conception, and long-term cooperation is necessary for the care of any infants. Consequently, a major area of interest in evolutionary psychology concerns the establishment and maintenance of human relationships. In terms of pull motivation, what characteristics do men and women look for or select in the other sex to establish a relationship and to maintain that relationship?

Darwin (1859/1936) used the term **sexual selection** to refer to the "struggle between males for possession of the females; the result is not death to the unsuccessful competitor, but few or no offspring" (p. 88). The male could be very aggressive and fight off all other males, thereby having a harem of females all to himself. However, if he could not be the most aggressive then maybe he could be the most charming and attract the most females in that manner. In such cases, the female acts as the selecting agent because it is what she likes about the male that determines whether she allows him to mate with her. For example, the number of copulations performed by a peacock correlates positively with the number of eyespots he has on his train of tail feathers. The greater the number of eyespots, the more likely a peahen is to consent to copulation (Petrie et al., 1991).

Peahens sexually selecting peacocks for their train of tail feathers is shown on a YouTube video titled "Natural Selection Tale of the Peacock" here: www.youtube.com/watch?v=gKybAp--n7M.

Good Genes and Bad Genes Hypotheses

From an evolutionary perspective, humans are motivated to seek individuals with whom to mate, with whom to produce children, and with whom to raise the children successfully (Bernard et al., 2005). What characteristics in a potential mate promote the achievement of this goal?

Mate value. A person's mate value refers to the possession of characteristics that are desired by the other sex. The higher your mate value, the greater is your appeal to others. Table 3.2 is an inventory of mate characteristics that determine a person's mate value (Kirsner et al., 2003). What is desired in a mate consists of physical features (attractiveness) and psychological characteristics (ambition, sense of humor, loyal) but also a value system. An attractive face and body are immediately noticeable in a person but fade with time and are ones to which the other person habituates. Psychological characteristics take time to discover and are less likely to fade. Finally, when interests and values are shared, it increases people's attraction to each other. The characteristics in Table 3.2 signal good genes, being a good mate, and being a good parent.

It is probably safe to state that both women and men prefer attractive partners, who have high mate value. But what is the reason for this preference? One answer is that attractiveness is a universally valued incentive that arose during our evolutionary past as a result of sexual selection.

TABLE 3.2   Mate Value Inventory

Describe yourself as accurately as possible on the traits listed below. Use the following scale:
Extremely low on this trait = –3 –2 –1 0 +1 +2 +3 = extremely high on this trait

Ambitious* ___	Faithful to partner ___	Kind and understanding ___
Attractive face* ___	Financially secure* ___	Loyal ___
Attractive body* ___	Good sense of humor ___	Responsible ___
Desire for children ___	Generous ___	Shares my values ___
Emotionally stable ___	Healthy ___	Shares my interests ___
Enthusiastic about sex ___	Independent ___	Sociable ___

Notes:
* Indicates that similar traits were used by Buss (1989) in 37 different cultures.
To compute your mate value, sum your scores on all of the items. The total score reflects the amount of a person's mate value.

Source: Adapted from "Self, Friends, and Lovers: Structural Relations among Beck Depression Inventory Scores And Perceived Mate Values" by B. R. Kirsner et al., 2003, *Journal of Affective Disorders, 75*, pp. 135, 147.

This choice is based on the assumption that these characteristics signal genes for health, fertility, and intelligence according to the **good genes hypothesis**.

Attractiveness for mates. Facial attractiveness increases a person's mate value but what makes a face attractive to the other sex? One feature is that attractive faces are more symmetrical, which means the right and left half of a face match up. Another feature is sexual dimorphism, which refers to differences in the form or structure between men and women. More attractive male faces show greater masculinity and more attractive female faces show greater femininity. A third feature is that an attractive face represents the average of many facial configurations that occur in the population. It is a face that has average lip, eye, and nose size, for example (Rhodes, 2006). However, the average does not tell the whole story. An attractive female face, compared to the average, has redder lips, darker eye lines, and less mass around the upper neck and cheeks. An attractive male face, compared to the average, has a darker brow, eye lines, and skin and also more beard and less mass around the upper neck and cheeks (Said & Todorov, 2011).

Research on beauty and attractiveness can be found at the website titled "Beauty Check" here: www.beautycheck.de/English.

Does an attractive face and body help you acquire a partner? If facial and physical attractiveness are determinants of mate value, then one obvious question is whether increases in attractiveness increase one's chances of attracting a mate. Rhodes and coresearchers (2005) investigated this question in an Australian sample of men and women. As a measure of success in attracting a mate, the researchers asked the individuals to report their number of sexual partners, age of first intercourse, and the length of each relationship. Photos of the participants were rated for attractiveness, sexual dimorphism, averageness, and symmetry by a separate group of people. Do these indicators of physical attractiveness correlate with sexual experience? The results showed that they did. Individuals with higher physical mate values had more relationship experiences. Men with attractive faces and attractive and masculine bodies had more sexual partners and also became sexually active at an earlier age. Women with attractive faces became sexually active at an earlier age and had more relationships that exceeded 12 months. The results provide some evidence that as one's mate value increases the likelihood of attracting others also increases.

Attractiveness for reproductive success. Does your attractiveness help determine your reproductive success—that is, how many children you will have? One way to proceed is to rate the attractiveness and sexiness of women's faces when they are young and of an age to enter long-term relationships. Then, when the women are older, determine how many children they have. Using this approach, Pflüger and coresearchers (2012) had male university students rate the photos of 20-year-old women for attractiveness and sexiness on a scale from 1 = *not* to 100 = *highly*. When the women were much older, the researchers counted their number of children. Women rated as being more attractive and sexier when young experienced more pregnancies and gave birth to more children. This relationship was true only of women who did not use contraception. Other researchers have also found evidence between attractiveness and the number of offspring. Jokela (2009) had people rate the facial attractiveness of 1,000 men and over 1,000 women from their yearbook photos. Based on these ratings, the faces were divided into four categories of attractiveness: not attractive, moderately attractive, attractive, and very attractive. The level of attractiveness at age 18 predicted how many children a person would have 35–38 years later. Women categorized as attractive had 16 percent more children than women categorized as not or moderately attractive, while women characterized as very attractive had 6 percent more children. Only for men in the not-attractive category was there an effect on the number of children. These men had 13 percent fewer children than the rest. The evolutionary interpretation is that beauty signals reproductive capacity—that is, the ability to bear healthy children.

An inverse of the good genes hypothesis is that individuals reject those people whose physical appearance suggests the possibility of bad genes—that is, genes that signal potential disease and low intelligence (Zebrowitz & Rhodes, 2004). According to this **bad genes hypothesis**, the emphasis is on rejecting people, not attracting them. Zebrowitz and Rhodes (2004) tested this hypothesis with longitudinal data from individuals for whom facial photos, intelligence test scores, and health indicators were available at 10, 11–15, 17, and 30–40 years of age. The photos were rated for facial quality, such as attractiveness, symmetry, averageness, and sexual dimorphism. To examine whether people with unattractive faces are rejected, the researchers divided the photos at the median based on attractiveness. Individuals categorized below the median (lower 50 percent) were judged as less attractive at all ages and had less facial symmetry, and male faces showed less masculinity. The researchers reasoned that if facial attractiveness correlates with health and intelligence then this correlation is evident only for faces below the median in attractiveness, since those above the median all had acceptable levels of attractiveness. In other words, to be selected as a mate one must possess a face with a minimal level of attractiveness, which indicates some minimal level of health and intelligence. The results showed a positive correlation between facial attractiveness, intelligence, and health, but only for individuals whose faces were below the median. For these faces, as rated attractiveness decreased, judgments of the individuals' health and intelligence decreased correspondingly. This relationship was also true when actual indicators of health and intelligence were used: faces with lower attractiveness were associated with poorer health and lower intelligence. Thus, according to the bad genes hypothesis, people avoid mating with individuals who have extremely poor physical appearance or low facial attractiveness. In regard to sexual selection, it is not that people are pulled toward a face with high mate value but instead are repelled by one with poor mate value—that is, one that signals poor health and low intelligence.

Universality of beauty and health. Facial attractiveness evolved through sexual selection. Consequently, the basis of attractiveness and its relationship to health is assumed to be universal and not culturally specific. This claim is based on research that has resulted in several convincing conclusions (Langlois et al., 2000). First, people agree on who is beautiful and who is not within their culture. Second, people agree on the standards of beauty for faces in cultures other than their own. Third, people agree on the degree of attractiveness among children. Presumably, then, the association between an evolved set of features and physical health or intelligence should be similar everywhere. For example, a runny nose and watery eyes that are linked to a cold would be assumed to be unattractive compared to the same face when a person does not have a cold. However, there may be instances of cultural standards of beauty that are not linked to health. For example, thinness in women is associated with beauty and health, although extreme thinness is associated with poor health (Weeden & Sabini, 2005).

Value of a sense of humor. The *Mate Value Inventory* in Table 3.2 also presents psychological characteristics that people value, such as good sense of humor, generous, kind, loyal, and being responsible. A unique indicator of mate value is sense of humor. What is its evolutionary significance for mate value? Sense of humor, along with being kind, loyal, and responsible, are cognitive traits signaling that an individual is genetically fit and intelligent (Klasios, 2013). In fact, intelligence is one of the mostly highly desired traits people seek in a mate (Lippa, 2007). In other words, by possessing these traits individuals signal their intelligence and their potential as good providers and parents. If a sense of humor adds to an individual's mate value, then that trait should correlate with people's sexual experiences or short-term mating success. To test this hypothesis, Greengross and Miller (2011) measured the sense of humor in male and female university students based on their ability to create cartoon captions. Funnier captions indicated a greater sense of humor. Participants also completed a questionnaire that measured their short-term mating success, such as frequency of intercourse and number of sex partners. The results showed that the ability to create humor correlated with short-term mating success. Individuals with a greater sense of humor had more sexual experiences. Thus, in addition to being attractive, it helps to be witty to attract a mate.

Long-Term Mate Selection

Once mates are selected and relationships are formed, then the birth of offspring and parenthood is frequently the next step. Thus, other aspects of mate value besides physical beauty are important because evolutionary success depends on leaving the most number of surviving offspring. Furthermore, the biological differences between men and women determine what mate values are important. What are these differences?

Men and women differ in the amount of time they invest in their offspring (Buss, 1989). After sexual intercourse, a woman invests an additional 38 weeks as her baby develops, so that at birth the woman already has invested much more time in the child than the man. In addition, since she can produce many fewer children than a man, it is more important that a woman help each child to survive; by doing so, she increases her reproductive success. Since a man is capable of having innumerable children, he may not invest as heavily in each individual child as a woman would. He increases his reproductive success by having intercourse with as many women as possible, thereby conceiving many children. Thus, the strategies a woman employs to ensure the survival of her children and hence the perpetuation of her genes is different than the strategies a man employs for the perpetuation of his genes. Consequently, we would expect a woman to value characteristics in a man that indicate greater commitment and help in raising children. Men should value characteristics related to reproductive success, such as a woman's physical health and youth. In mating with a fertile woman, a man can maximize his reproductive success by having many children with her (Buss, 1989).

This difference in what men and women value in long-term mates is assumed to have universal appeal and has led evolutionary psychologists to concentrate on three mate value characteristics: ambition and industriousness, good financial prospects, and good looks (Buss, 1989). These three characteristics are marked with an asterisk in the *Mate Value Inventory* in Table 3.2. If differences in sexual preferences between men and women are universal, then ratings that indicate these differences should be similar in societies all over the world. This is exactly what Buss (1989) attempted to show by surveying men and women in 37 cultures from 33 different countries.

The survey results showed that in nearly all cultures women rate both ambition and industriousness and good financial prospects as more important in a mate than men rate those characteristics. These characteristics are good ones for a woman to look for if she expects her mate to be mature enough to commit to the relationship and to be a good provider of material things necessary for family life. The survey also found that men overwhelmingly rate good looks to be more important than women consider them to be. If young age and good looks are considered signs of health and fertility, men consider these important because they imply that the woman is capable of producing many children. Recall the research cited earlier that more attractive women bore more children (Jokela, 2009; Pflüger et al., 2012).

Biosocial Theory

Does evolutionary psychology place too much emphasis on our evolutionary past to explain mate selection? Doesn't an individual's current social environment also play a role? Mate value preferences do not remain constant as an evolutionary emphasis suggests (Buss et al., 2001). Differences in mate value preferences among countries or changes in those preferences over time suggest the influence of culture. **Biosocial theory** emphasizes this shift from evolution to culture. This theory stresses the interaction between social experiences and the evolved sex differences of strength and reproductive capacity. This interaction helps explain gender differences in long-term mate preferences and jealousy. What is important in biosocial theory is that men are physically bigger and stronger and that women can bear and nurse children. What is not relevant in this theory are the evolved psychological mechanisms that are postulated by evolutionary psychology. According to Wood and Eagly (2002; Eagly & Wood, 1999), the biological sex differences in strength and in reproductive capacity interact with societal expectations that men should have greater power and status, while women should accommodate to a lesser role. One consequence is that in adjusting to these expectations, men become providers and heads of households, while women become homemakers, cooks, and primary child-raisers. Thus, the biological differences between men and women contribute to the increase in psychological differences, because each sex tries to adjust to their expected social roles. According to biosocial theory, this adjustment is based on the cost-benefit analysis that typical sex roles provide greater satisfaction with lesser effort than would non-typical sex roles. Thus, it is less costly and more beneficial for men to enter male-dominated occupations such as construction worker, farmer, and warrior and for women to enter female-dominated occupations such as office manager, nurse, and childcare worker. However, the bulk of professions in our society may be staffed equally well by both sexes. Furthermore, although male and female genetic dispositions remain constant, society's views are constantly changing. As a consequence, men and women can enter professions that have been dominated by the other sex.

The evolutionary psychology explanation of why women prefer industrious men has been challenged further on the basis of how society affects the earning power of men and women (Buss, 1989; Caporael, 1989; Tattersall, 1998; Wiederman & Allgeier, 1992). According to the **structural powerless hypothesis**, both men and women want the same financial resources. However, since women are relatively powerless to achieve these in the working world, they do so in one of the ways available—that is, by marrying men who have these resources. If this is the case, reasoned Wiederman and Allgeier (1992), then as women earn more money a man's financial prospects should become less important to them. However, based on a sample of working women, the researchers found no relationship between how much money women personally earned and the importance to them of good financial prospects in a prospective mate. In other words, all women regardless of their income wanted a long-term mate who had good financial prospects. Eagly and Wood (1999) have challenged these results by reexamining some of the data from Buss's (1989) original survey of 37 cultures. Do men's preferences for good housekeepers and cooks and women's preferences regarding earning potential depend on the degree of inequality in power and earnings between the sexes? Using various indicators, Eagly and Wood found that, as gender equality increases, differences in preference decrease. For example, in countries with greater equality, men's preference for mates with good housekeeping and cooking skills decreases and women's emphasis on a spouse's income potential decreases.

Further evidence for biosocial theory comes from a worldwide survey of what people value in a long-term mate. The British Broadcasting Corporation (BBC) conducted a survey regarding the following traits: "age, ambition, communication skills, dependability, domestic skills, face attractiveness, fitness, fondness for children, hands, health, honesty, humor, industriousness, intelligence, kindness, money, all around good looks, parenting abilities, prosperity, religion, social status, teeth, and values" (Lippa, 2007, p. 197). From this list, participants were to select the first, second, and third most important trait that they wanted their mates to possess. Participants responded from all over the world with 53 countries having sample sizes of 90 or higher. The top nine traits listed by 120,000 men and 98,000 women (in order of importance) were: intelligence, humor, honesty, kindness, good looks, face attractiveness, values, communication skills, and dependability (Lippa, 2007).

The results of this BBC survey provide further insights into the evolutionary and social aspects of mate choice. Figure 3.3 shows the degree of difference in rankings between men and women for 12 different traits (Lippa, 2007). First, like the Buss (1989) survey of 37 cultures, men rated good looks and facial attractiveness as more important than women did in all 53 countries. This worldwide difference in the importance of looks is attributable to our evolutionary past. Second, women rated ambition to be more important in a mate than men rated that trait, which also replicates the findings from the Buss survey. Third, women, compared to men, also show a strong preference for what Lippa terms *niceness*. This collective trait consists of communication skills, dependability, kindness, humor, and honesty (see Figure 3.3). However, unlike good looks, sex differences in the niceness traits were not universal because their rankings varied widely across countries. This variability implies that there are social factors at work. Interestingly, both women and men indicated a higher preference for niceness in a mate when they lived in more economically developed countries with greater gender equality. Lippa's interpretation for these findings is that niceness traits are a luxury that is available only after necessities have been obtained. In less developed countries, traits indicating responsibility, such as ambition and money, are necessities. However, the material goods that ambition and money provide are more easily obtainable by women in economically developed countries with greater gender equality. As a consequence, they can now afford the luxury of seeking a nicer mate.

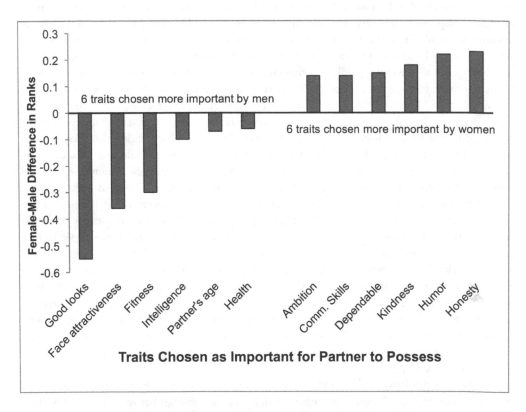

FIGURE 3.3 Female–Male Differences for Partner Traits. "What feature do you consider most important in a partner?" (Lippa, 2007, p. 197). Men chose the left six traits to be more important than women did. Women chose the right six traits to be more important than men did.

Source: Adapted from "The Preferred Traits of Mates in a Cross-National Study of Heterosexual and Homosexual Men and Women: An Examination of Biological and Cultural Influences" by R. A. Lippa, 2007, *Archives of Sexual Behavior, 36,* Table 2, p. 199.

Cultural environments also change over time and so does the relative value placed on mate characteristics. In a series of six surveys from 1939 to 1996, several traits have changed in importance (Buss et al., 2001). First, ambition and industriousness has decreased in importance for women, while it has remained stable for men. Second, good financial prospects have increased in importance for men while it remained relatively stable for women. Nevertheless, over the span from 1939 to 1996 both traits were still considered more important for women. Good looks increased in importance for both men and women, although still of greater importance to men. Mutual attraction and love went from fourth or fifth in importance in 1939 to first place in 1996 for both men and women. Dependability, which ranked in the top 10 of the BBC survey, was among the first three from 1939 to 1996 for both men and women. However, as Figure 3.3 shows, women value dependability more, such as faithful, loyal, and responsible in the mate value scale (Table 3.2). Dependability is an important trait because it means individuals can rely on their mates, which is important for child rearing. It is a biological fact that women become pregnant and bear children. Thus, if women engage in sexual behavior, they want to be able to depend on the man in case any children result from their union. The alternative is to become a single parent, of which women are a majority. In 2016, for example, in a survey of households with children under age 18, 24 percent were headed by single mothers and only 6 percent by single fathers (United States Census Bureau, 2016).

Guarding Relationships

Boy meets girl. They fall in love. They marry, have children, and live happily ever after. Maybe! Relationships can end. Why can this happen and what emotion has evolved to prevent it?

Mate poaching. Relationships can end through death but also from desertion, especially when someone has stolen your partner. **Mate poaching** refers to the attempt to attract someone who is already in a romantic relationship. The purpose is to form either a short-term or long-term relationship with the poached individual (Schmitt et al., 2004). Mate poaching occurs worldwide based on a survey of nearly 17,000 mostly college students from North and South America; Western, Eastern, and Southern Europe; the Middle East; Africa; Oceania; and South, Southeast, and East Asia. In the survey, nearly 60 percent of men and 40 percent of women have reported attempts at poaching. In addition, men are more likely than women to succumb to the temptations of short-term poaching. Thus, individuals who are currently in a romantic relationship need to be on guard for potential poachers. Buss (2007) reasons that people poach individuals who have high mate value. These individuals are not available for long and may already be in a relationship. Consequently, they are victims of mate poaching by virtue of their higher value. The necessity for a guard against poachers was the evolutionary reason for jealousy.

Jealousy. Known as the "green eyed monster" (Shakespeare's *Othello*), jealousy is a negative emotion triggered by an actual or suspected loss of a mate's sexual services or a mate's affection. These two losses produce different degrees of jealousy in men and women because of the biological fact that a woman is always certain of her maternity but a man is less certain of his paternity. According to evolutionary psychology, the reproductive strategies for men require knowing that they fathered the children they are helping to raise. Hence, a man is worried about any sexual infidelity on the part of his mate. If she was sexually unfaithful, then he is in doubt about his paternity of the children; they may not be carrying his genes. Since a woman obviously knows that her baby is carrying her genes, her major reproductive concern lies in successfully raising it. Hence, a woman is worried about any emotional infidelity on the part of her mate. To illustrate the differences in jealousy between men and women, imagine being asked some questions regarding the person with whom you are in love or with whom you are in a committed romantic relationship. One day you discover that your partner has become interested in another person. Which of the following statements from each pair would upset you more—that is, evoke the most jealousy?

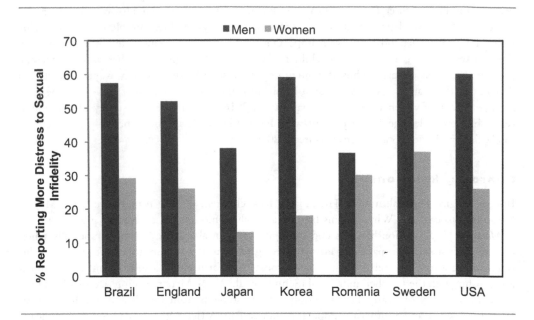

FIGURE 3.4 Sexual versus Emotional Infidelity. The percentage of students who reported more distress from imagining their partner enjoying passionate sexual intercourse with another person than by imagining their partner forming a deep emotional attachment to that person. Results are shown separately for men and women from Brazil, England, Japan, Korea, Romania, Sweden, and the USA.

Source: Adapted from:

"Emotional and Sexual Jealousy as a Function of Sex and Sexual Orientation in a Brazilian Sample" by A. A. L. de Souza et al., 2006, *Psychological Reports, 98,* p. 531.

"Sex Differences in Responses to Relationship Threats in England and Romania" by G. L. Brase et al., 2004, *Journal of Social and Personal Relationships, 21,* p. 770.

"Jealousy and the Nature of Beliefs About Infidelity: Tests of Competing Hypotheses About Sex Differences in the United States, Korea, and Japan" by D. M. Buss et al., 1999, *Personal Relationships, 6,* based on Figure 1, p. 131, pp. 139, 141.

USA estimates based on median of three samples from "Sex Differences in Jealousy: Evolution, Physiology, and Psychology" by D. M. Buss et al., 1992, *Psychological Science, 3,* p. 252.

Sex Differences in Jealousy: Comparing the Influence of Previous Infidelity Among College Students and Adults" by M. J. Tagler, 2010, *Social Psychological and Personality Science, 1,* p. 356.

"Evolution, Sex, and Jealousy: Investigation with a Sample from Sweden" by M. W. Wiederman & E. Kendall, 1999, *Evolution and Human Behavior, 20,* p. 127.

Emotional infidelity: "Imagining your partner forming a deep emotional attachment to that person."

Sexual infidelity: "Imagining your partner enjoying passionate sexual intercourse with that other person" (Buss et al., 1992, p. 252; Buunk et al., 1996, p. 360).

These statements contrast emotional infidelity with sexual infidelity. The prediction, based on evolutionary psychology, is that men should be more distressed regarding sexual infidelity. In these situations a man would be more uncertain of being the father and thus may be supporting children that are not carrying his genes. Women, however, should consider the emotional infidelity scenario to be more distressing. It represents the possibility of losing her mate's parental investment, protection, and commitment. When these questions were asked of male and female students, the results showed that men consider imagining sexual infidelity to be more distressing, whereas women consider imagining emotional infidelity to be more distressing. These findings have been replicated in many countries. Researchers have presented these choices to individuals in the United States, Germany, the Netherlands, Spain, and Chile (Buunk et al., 1996; Fernandez et al., 2006). In all five countries, men are more distressed when they suspect their partners of sexual infidelity rather than emotional infidelity. Women, in contrast, are more distressed by emotional infidelity. Similar results were found in additional countries: Brazil, England, Japan, Korea, Romania, Sweden, and again in the United States (Brase et al., 2004; Buss et al., 1999; de Souza et al., 2006; Tagler, 2010; Wiederman & Kendall, 1999). Figure 3.4 graphs results from seven different countries. This consistent difference in types of jealousy between men and women supports an evolutionary interpretation.

Section Recap

Sexual desire is a universal motive that motivates sexual behavior for the production of offspring, while *romantic love* is the universal motive that bonds individuals together for their mutual benefit and that of their offspring. However, before sexual behavior can begin a person must find a mate. According to Darwin's concept of *sexual selection*, relationships are formed by members of one sex choosing individuals of the other sex based on the latter's characteristics. *Mate value* refers to those characteristics of a person that are desired by the other sex, such as good looks, dependability, ambition and industriousness, and niceness. Good looks, according to the *good genes hypothesis*, is a universal trait that signals a woman has genes for intelligence, good health, and can produce many babies. Individuals select others either because their attractiveness signals good genes or reject individuals whose unattractiveness signals bad genes for these traits according to a *bad genes hypothesis*. As a woman's attractiveness increases, the likelihood of her bearing more children also increases. In the case of sexual selection for long-term relationships, women universally prefer ambitious and industrious men because they will provide the material means to support a family. Men usually prefer young and beautiful women because these features signal health and fertility. According to *biosocial theory*, gender differences result from biological differences between men and women in physical strength and reproductive capacity. These biological differences interact with societal expectations for men and women to take on sex-relevant social roles, which in turn increase their psychological gender differences. An alternative to gender differences in preferred mate value is the *structural powerless hypothesis*, which maintains that women are ineffectual in obtaining the same level of financial resources in the working world as men are. Therefore, women can gain access to resources by marrying men who can provide these. However, as income inequality between men and women declines, ambition and industriousness and good financial prospects become less important and instead the importance of niceness (dependability, kindness, honesty) traits increases for women. Established relationships can end as a result of *mate poaching*, which occurs when an outsider attempts to attract someone who is already in a romantic relationship. Poaching is a threat to the maintenance of a relationship and *jealousy* is the negative emotion that evolved to protect against it. Emotional infidelity elicits more jealousy in women, while sexual infidelity elicits more jealousy in men.

FEAR, FOOD PREFERENCES, AND MUSIC AS UNIVERSAL MOTIVES

Fear, food, and music serve as motives from our evolutionary past that affect current behavior. What is the survival value of fear and what stimuli do humans avoid as a consequence? Why is there an innate tendency to prefer certain basic foods and reject others? Finally, there is the puzzle of music. Why do people the world over enjoy music?

Fear as a Universal Motive

Are there certain stimuli that make you feel afraid or anxious? These feelings are beneficial because they motivate avoidance and escape behavior. Many stimuli that evoke fear come from evolution rather than from learning. "What do you fear most?" (Muris et al., 1997, p. 929). In response to the question, nine- to 13-year-old Dutch children responded with a number of fears, the top 10 of which are listed in Figure 3.5. These fears ranged from being burglarized to encountering spiders. When 11- to 14-year-old Australian children listed their three greatest fears they duplicated five of the ones from Figure 3.5: parents dying, being hit by a car or truck, snakes, the dark, and spiders (Lane & Gullone, 1999). When American adults were asked to pick their fears from a list presented to them, snakes and spiders were selected (Roper Report, 1984). Several fears included in these three surveys are attributable to our evolutionary past: spiders, the dark, snakes, height, death of a loved one, and thunder and lightning. One interesting feature from the survey with the Dutch children was that many of them did not know how their fears began (Muris et al., 1997). For example, 33 percent did not know how their fears originated when asked, "How did your fear of . . . begin?" (p. 931). In addition, 46 percent did not know how their fear of spiders began. Either the children did not remember what conditioning experiences produced these fears or the fears were innate and resulted from evolution. Other individuals have also reported being unable to recollect any particular conditioning incidents that would account for their fears of heights, spiders, and water (LoBue & Rakison, 2013).

Survival value. What stimulus features trigger escape and avoidance behavior? Learning what to avoid may be inefficient, since a single unsuccessful avoidance leads to death. Thus, we are programmed by evolution to innately avoid stimuli that produce fear and represent danger (Bolles, 1970). For example, Marks (1987), in his book *Fears, Phobias, and Rituals*, reports on his two-and-a-half-year-old son's reaction to seaweed on the beach. The seaweed skeins looked like tiny snakes. As soon as his son saw them:

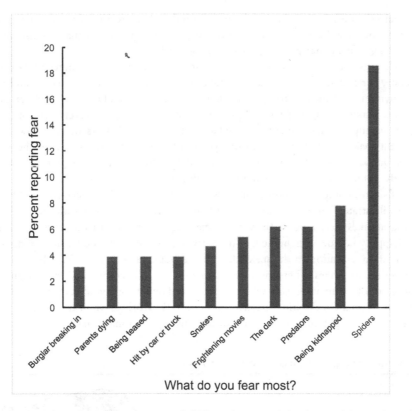

FIGURE 3.5 What Do You Fear? The percentage of children who responded with one of the 10 shown fears to the question "What do you fear most?" Notice that 23 percent of the children responded with a fear of either snakes or spiders.

Source: Adapted from "Common Childhood Fears and Their Origins" by P. Muris et al., 1997, *Behaviour Research and Therapy, 35*, Table 2, p. 932.

he screamed in terror and clutched me tightly, trying to stop me from sitting on the sand. When I touched the seaweed he shrieked and refused to do the same. His panic increased when gentle waves rolled the seaweed nearby or when I held him over the water to show him the moving fronds.

(p. 40)

Why is feeling fear or anxiety in our evolutionary history? The major reason is that fear evolved because it helped animals cope with danger in their environment (Öhman & Mineka, 2001; Plutchik, 1980). First, fear motivates the preparation for escape or avoidance responses. Depending on the species, escape may consist of freezing, scrambling, flying, running away, or tonic immobility. Second, animals have evolved to fear specific stimuli. The prevalence of a fear of reptiles, for example, may be an archaic remnant of when mammals tried to avoid being eaten by large reptiles (Öhman, 1986). Öhman (1993) speculates that feature detectors in the brain are naturally selected because of their sensitivity to stimulus characteristics of reptile predators. These feature detectors may be located in the amygdala, a part of the brain that is sensitive to stimuli that are ambiguous or that predict probable threat (Whalen, 1998).

The ability to detect threatening stimuli occurs early in life, which indicates its evolutionary significance. For instance, children are sensitive to fear-relevant stimuli (snakes) and are able to identify them more quickly than other stimuli. LoBue and DeLoache (2008) embedded the picture of a snake among eight other pictures of flowers, frogs, or caterpillars on a computer screen, for example a snake picture embedded among eight flowers or one flower embedded among eight snakes. Children three to five years old were instructed to touch the single target picture as quickly as possible. The results showed that the snake target pictures were touched significantly faster than any other stimuli. In addition, even infants are more likely to attend to pictures of snakes compared to other animals when those stimuli are accompanied by sounds of distress. To illustrate, DeLoache and LoBue (2009) showed seven- to 18-month old infants pairs of moving animals (see Table 3.3). At the same time, infants heard nonsense words spoken in either a happy voice or a frightened, distressed voice. Since frightened voices signal danger, do infants pay more attention to the snake than to the elephant (see Table 3.3)? Indeed, infants pay more attention to snakes when the pairs of pictures were accompanied by a frightened voice but looked at both animals equally when accompanied by a happy voice. An interesting discovery from this experiment is that this selective attention only worked when the snake was slithering. The effect of the frightening voice was not effective for stationary snakes.

TABLE 3.3   Pairing Happy and Frightened Voices with Animals

Demonstrating an infant's sensitivity to specific fear stimuli:

1. An infant sees pictures of a moving snake and a moving elephant
2. Simultaneous an infant hears nonsense words spoken with a happy or frightened voice
3. The experimenter measures the infant's looking time toward each animal

Results: Infants look longer at slithering snakes when hearing a frightened voice
Infants look equally long at both animals when hearing a happy voice

Source: Adapted from "The Narrow Fellow in the Grass: Human Infants Associate Snakes and Fear" by J. S. DeLoache & V. LoBue, 2009, *Developmental Science, 12,* 201–207.

But, in addition to slithering, are there other features to which humans are sensitive in detecting danger, especially in the case of evolutionary laden stimuli? One possibility is the curved features that characterize snakes and spiders. To test this possibility, LoBue (2014) presented on a computer screen a single wavy line embedded among eight straight lines or a single jagged line embedded among eight straight lines. College participants were instructed to touch the single wavy or jagged line as quickly as possible. The results indicated wavy lines were responded to more quickly than jagged lines. An interpretation is that humans have evolved a bias to detect wavy lines because they most resemble the curvilinear shapes of snakes and spiders. Furthermore, when participants were made fearful by a scary film clip, they responded even faster to the wavy lines than to the jagged lines (LoBue, 2014).

Preparedness. Learning, however, may still play a role in what we fear. After conditioning his daughter to fear a caterpillar after a single association with a loud whistle, Valentine (1930) concluded that fear is "*an instinct lurking ready to appear when the occasion arises*" (p. 404; italics in original). In this case, the instinct was a fear of woolly caterpillars that could be awakened when paired with a loud sound from a whistle. This awakening idea is similar to Seligman's (1971) concept of prepared learning, or **preparedness**, to describe the ease with which a behavior is learned. Behaviors for which humans are prepared are ones that occur easily as a result of experience, as if they are disposed toward learning them. *Contraprepared* behaviors are ones that occur with difficulty and only after much experience. Thus, to assume that certain fears are the result of evolution means that there are things of which humans are prepared to become afraid. If humans are prepared to become afraid of snakes, then it will take little experience to learn to fear them. Humans are contraprepared to become afraid of flowers. Seligman (1971) points out that humans are more likely to fear insects, heights, and the dark rather than their pajamas, grass, electrical outlets, and hammers.

In summary, fear is a universal motive that is shaped by evolution. It is a prepared tendency or psychological mechanism in humans that is ready to occur in response to certain stimuli, such as reptiles or the dark. Fear motivates the analysis of unusual stimuli and motivates escape and avoidance behaviors such as freezing, hiding, and fleeing. The evolutionary value of fear is that it increases a person's chance of survival.

More information about fears and phobias is available at the website titled "HELPGUIDE. ORG: Trusted guide to mental & emotional health" here: www.helpguide.org/articles/anxiety/phobias-and-fears.htm.

Preferences and Liking for Foods

Our food preferences are another example of a universal motive. The characteristics of this motive are uncovered from examining young children's innate dispositions toward and away from edible substances. The reason for studying children is that their preferences are not yet unduly [*excessively*] influenced by the food environment that parents provide. The effects of this environment are immediate, since in making the transition from milk, infants are disposed toward learning to accept the foods associated with their country and culture (Birch, 1992). Food acceptance is possible because humans are **omnivorous**, which means that they are able to eat a variety of foods. In fact, nutritionists recommend that people should do this to obtain all the nutrients that they need.

Being omnivorous allowed humans to make use of whatever food sources a geographical area has to offer, in spite of any innate taste preferences.

Food neophobia. As an introduction, there are several generalizations regarding innate food preferences. First, as many parents have discovered, in the transition from milk to solid foods, children often show **food neophobia**, which is the tendency to avoid novel foods and prefer familiar foods. Second, children innately prefer sweet and later salty foods. They avoid sour and bitter foods. Third, children are prepared to avoid food associated with negative digestive consequences and prefer those with positive consequences (Birch, 1999). Fourth, humans have a preference for fatty foods (Birch, 1992).

Would you like to eat some hummus, halvah, or funistrada? A "no" answer may be indicative of the universal motive of food neophobia. People vary in their degree of this neophobia and hence their willingness to try new foods. Pliner and Hobden (1992) constructed the *Food Neophobia Scale* to measure the extent individuals avoided or were reluctant to eat novel foods. Individuals who scored in the upper 15 percent of the *Food Neophobia Scale* were labeled neophobics, and those who scored in the lower 15 percent were labeled neophilics (individuals willing to try new foods). Raudenbush and Frank (1999) asked neophobics and neophilics about their potential reactions to familiar foods (yogurt, icing, applesauce, and peanut butter) and unfamiliar foods (hummus, a chickpea paste; halvah, crushed sesame seeds in honey; and funistrada, a fictitious food). Their reactions to these foods were measured on a 12-point scale on several dimensions: willingness to try, expected liking, actual liking, and willingness to try the foods again. Analyses of the ratings indicated that both neophobics and neophilics were less favorably disposed toward novel foods than toward familiar foods. The unfavorable ratings for novel foods were very apparent for neophobics. Compared to neophilics, neophobics were less willing to try novel foods, expected and actually liked novel foods less, and were less willing to try them again. Also, both groups ate less unfamiliar than familiar food, and neophobics ate significantly less than neophilics.

An explanation for neophobia is based on its survival value. Neophobia protects a person from eating a toxic substance that can cause illness and even death (Birch, 1999). By avoiding novel foods, an individual is less likely to be poisoned or to become very ill. However, neophobia also has some negative consequences. It can be a problem for individuals required to make dietary changes in support of good nutrition. Individuals may be reluctant to switch from familiar foods to new foods that provide diet and health benefits. The extent of food neophobia diminishes with the amount of experience a person has with other foods (Birch, 1999).

Innate preference and aversion for substances. Our innate preference for sweet and aversion for sour and bitter becomes apparent during the first few hours and days of life. Evidence for this comes from observing facial expressions made by newborn infants to various taste stimuli. For example, three-day-old infants show distinctive facial reactions to sweet-, sour-, and bitter-tasting stimuli but show indifference to salt (Mennella & Beauchamp, 1998). However, by four months of age a salt preference has developed (Birch, 1999). Additional evidence for innate taste preferences comes from research by Steiner (1977), who showed that infants were sensitive to the taste of sweet, sour, and bitter prior to their first feeding. He placed a drop of flavored liquid on the tongues of infants, who then clearly showed whether they liked it or not. Compared to a resting face or the reaction to distilled water, the sweet stimulus produced a retraction of mouth corners resembling a smile, a sucking response, and a licking of the upper lips. The reaction to the sour stimulus, however, produced a pursing of the lips, a wrinkling of the nose, a blinking of the eyes, and increased salivation. The reaction to the bitter stimulus produced protrusion of a flat tongue, salivation, spitting, and an expression resembling dislike and anger. The instinctive or innate nature of these expressions is also demonstrated by the finding that infants do not rely on higher cortical brain processes. Steiner (1977) tested four infants born without a cortex and with only a brain stem and midbrain. They reacted to taste stimuli in a fashion similar to that of normal infants: a preference for sweet and an aversion for sour and bitter.

A compilation of YouTube videos categorized as showing infants' first reactions to solid food, is available here: www.youtube.com/results?search_query=infants+first+reaction+to+food.

Evolutionary value of tastes and facial expressions. In addition to showing positive reactions to sweets, infants will also eat more of a sweet-tasting substance. Desor and associates (1973) offered one- to three-day-old infants plain water or sugar solutions of varying degrees of sweetness. Infants drank more of a sugar water solution than a plain water solution; the sweeter the solution, the more they drank. In fact, one way parents make adult food acceptable to infants is to add sugar (Jerome, 1977). However, infants will eat less of a substance the more bitter or sour it tastes. Desor and associates (1975) found that putting sufficient citric acid in a sugar solution to give it a sour taste led to a reduction in the amount infants drank. However, adding urea for a bitter taste or sodium chloride for a salty taste did not seem to suppress the amount of drinking. Perhaps bitterness is a more complex taste, although Steiner's (1977) research clearly shows that infants make an aversive response to bitter tastes.

Liking sugars and disliking sour or bitter foods are assumed to result from our genetic past for several reasons. First, the facial expressions reflecting infants' likes or dislikes are likely innate, or inborn, to use Steiner's (1977) term. It does not seem possible that these expressions are learned by infants during their first few hours of life or while in the womb. However, this possibility does exist. For instance, Mennella and Beauchamp (1998) summarized the results of research showing that infants can detect and prefer the odor of their own amniotic fluids during their first few days of life. Amniotic fluid surrounds the unborn fetus in the mother's womb. Second, even infants lacking a cortex for learning more complex material are able to make these facial expressions. Third, there is an evolutionary advantage to liking sweets. In our evolutionary past, sugar was only available in fruit, berries, or honey. It did not come neatly packaged in cakes, pies, ice cream, and soft drinks. A sweet taste is associated with ripe fruits, berries, some vegetables that are ripe, and mothers' milk (Mennella & Beauchamp, 1998). The sweet taste comes from complex carbohydrates, which are an essential nutrient for the body's growth, repair, and maintenance. Thus, by eating more sweet-tasting substances, early humans obtained essential nutrients, which aided in their survival. Sour and bitter tastes are associated with bark, dirt, and unripe fruits, berries, and vegetables that are not ready to eat. If eaten, these things are likely to make a person ill. In addition, a bitter-tasting substance is probably associated with toxins or poisons that can kill an individual. Thus, a bitter taste serves as a warning to avoid bad food.

In addition to innate taste preferences, the accompanying facial expressions also have survival value. A newborn infant is totally dependent on its mother for nutrients and can only communicate its likes and dislikes using facial expressions. These expressions are readable and clearly resemble the reactions made by adults if they were to taste identical stimuli. Steiner (1977) demonstrated this by having a panel of observers interpret what emotion the infant was showing when tasting various stimuli. The panel viewed either a videotape or still photograph of the infant's facial expression. The expression elicited by the sweet stimulus was interpreted as appreciation, enjoyment, or liking. The expression elicited by the bitter stimulus was interpreted as disgust, aversion, or dislike. Thus, an infant "knows" what is good based on the idea that what an infant likes is nutritious and what an infant does not like is not nutritious.

The various facial responses that accompany different tastes also serve other functions (Rosenstein & Oster, 1988). Sucking responses in reaction to sweet stimuli are a means of ingesting what is presumably a nutritive substance. The increased salivation to a sour stimulus may be an attempt to dilute its concentration, thereby making it less aversive. In an experiment with two-hour-old infants, Rosenstein and Oster (1988) observed infants' attempts to block swallowing a bitter liquid by allowing it to drain from their mouths. These responses presumably are an adaptive way to get rid of bitter substances. These investigators also tested infants using a salty substance and found no distinctive facial responses. The lack of distinctive responding may have occurred because infants cannot consume enough salt to be dangerous or because they have not yet developed a taste for salt.

Early experience interacts with innate preference. Innate taste preferences are presumably a function of our evolutionary past. However, taste may be affected by very early flavor experiences, which could affect food preferences later. Some flavors from foods that pregnant mothers eat may come to reside in the amniotic fluid that surrounds their babies. Consequently, when unborn babies swallow amniotic fluid they experience these flavors. What is the evidence that this early flavor experience affects an infant's later food preferences? In order to answer this question, Mennella

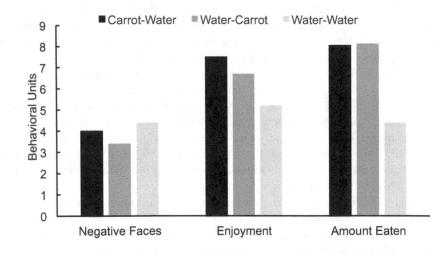

FIGURE 3.6 Effects of Early Taste Experience. When mothers drank carrot juice while pregnant (carrot–water) or during nursing (water–carrot), their infants preferred carrot-flavored cereal over plain cereal. When mothers drank water while pregnant or during nursing (water–water), their infants preferred carrot-flavored cereal less. Amount eaten is reported in decagrams.

Source: Adapted from "Prenatal and Postnatal Flavor Learning by Human Infants" [Electronic version] by J. A. Mennella et al., 2001, *Pediatrics, 107, e88,* Table 2, p. 3.

and coresearchers (2001) had pregnant women drink either water or carrot juice during their last three months of pregnancy or during the first month of breastfeeding their babies. Other mothers drank water both during their pregnancy and during breastfeeding. When ready to eat cereal, would infants prefer carrot-flavored over plain-flavored cereal? The infants' preference was measured in three ways. One made use of infants' negative facial expressions while eating, such as nose wrinkling or head turning. Presumably fewer negative expressions implied greater acceptance of a cereal. A second measure involved the mothers' ratings of their infants' enjoyment of the cereal on a scale from 1 (*not at all*) to 9 (*very much*). Third was the amount of cereal the infants ate. The results in Figure 3.6 indicate that the mothers' intake of carrot juice while pregnant or nursing increased their infants' acceptance of carrot-flavored cereal. Infants made fewer negative facial responses, showed more enjoyment, and ate more of the carrot-flavored cereal than the plain-flavored cereal. However, the amount eaten did not differ significantly among the three groups.

Early experience from the taste of amniotic fluid can remain for years, especially for garlic. For instance, Hepper and coresearchers (2013) compared the children of two groups of mothers. One group ate garlic during the last four weeks of pregnancy, while the other group did not. Eight to nine years later, their children were offered a meal of potatoes flavored with garlic. The children exposed to garlic in the womb ate significantly more garlic-flavored potatoes than the children not exposed to garlic. An important implication of these findings is that this initial exposure to a flavor, even prior to birth from the mother's amniotic fluid, disposes an infant to accept the solid foods of its culture. The result is a smoother transition from nursing to eating solid foods (Hepper et al., 2013; Mennella et al., 2001). In summary, innate preferences for sugar, salt, and fat plus very early flavor experiences determine adult food preferences.

Universal Appeal of Music

According to evolutionary psychology, psychological mechanisms evolved because they increased the survival chances of individuals and their offspring. However, there are also some evolutionary puzzles—mechanisms that evolved as by-products but do not seem beneficial for survival. Music may be in this category of mechanisms for which the evolutionary benefits are not obvious.

Evolution of music. Music refers to organized patterns of sound that are both regular and periodic. This organized pattern allows an individual to keep time, which is what distinguishes music from other patterns of sound such as speech (Cross, 2001). Being able to keep time is known as **entrainment**, which refers to body movements that synchronize with an external auditory beat. But why is listening to music enjoyable? The pleasure of eating, drinking, and sex are obvious. These pleasures motivate individuals to behave in ways that are conducive for their individual survival and that of the species. However, the function of pleasure derived from listening to music is unclear. Darwin (1871/1981) had no clear explanation. He wrote in *The Descent of Man* that

> neither the enjoyment nor the capacity of producing musical notes are faculties of the least use to man in reference to his daily habits of life, they must be ranked among the most mysterious with which he is endowed.

(p. 733)

Nevertheless, music seems to be part of human nature. Peretz (2006) describes several reasons why this is so. First, music is not a recent invention but has been part of human culture for at least 30,000 years. Second, music, although in different forms, is present in all cultures the world over. Third, the human response to music seems innate—that is, learning how to respond is not necessary. For example, infants respond to music and they can discriminate between music and other sounds, while most animals cannot. Fourth, music is a source of pleasure for most members of a culture, which is especially the case for popular music.

But why did the enjoyment of music evolve? One possibility is that music appreciation is a by-product that resulted from the evolution of something else. For example, male nipples might be considered the by-product of the evolution of female nipples, which are necessary for nursing children (Gould, 1987). Evidence for music appreciation as a by-product comes from the discovery that some parrots and cockatoos can entrain to music—that is, they are able to keep time (Schachner et al., 2009). These birds are able to engage in vocal mimicry, which is being able to imitate the sounds of other birds or humans, as in the case of a parrot who speaks. Thus, reproducing a sound one hears requires being able to create a link between that auditory stimulus and movement, such as foot tapping. Perhaps in this way the natural selection of vocal mimicry also resulted in entrainment to music as a by-product (Schachner et al., 2009). However, do parrots and cockatoos also enjoy listening to music? You can decide this by looking at the YouTube video of the dancing cockatoo.

A YouTube video of a dancing cockatoo is from an article in *Current Biology* (2009) by Patel et al.—the video is titled "Cockatoo Dances to the Beat"—here: www.youtube.com/watch?v=ERpIWTh18cY&feature=related.

There are other possibilities for why humans enjoy music. First, as Darwin (1871/1981) noted, music arouses emotions that are usually positive (like love) and not negative (like fear or rage). Because music has this effect, it can be used as a means of mood regulation: alleviate negative moods and boost positive moods (North et al., 2004; Thayer, 2001). A second possibility is that those feelings promote group or social bonding that can occur while listening to or creating music. Examples would include listening to patriotic music during Fourth of July celebrations or singing the happy birthday song. Another interpretation, however, is that music is the result of sexual selection rather than natural selection. In the words of Darwin (1871/1981), the purpose of music was to charm the other sex. Thus, individuals who could make music were more likely to be sexually selected based on their ability to charm or instill positive feelings in their listener (Klasios, 2013).

Source of music preference. One test of whether behavior is innate is to determine if it occurs prior to any experience. In the case of music, is our preference of consonant over dissonant music innate or the result of experience? For adults, dissonant music sounds unpleasant, disagreeable, and inconsistent. An early experiment with infants demonstrated that they prefer consonant (harmony) over dissonant (nonharmony) music (Zentner & Kagan, 1998).

A demonstration of consonant versus dissonant music is available on a YouTube video titled "Consonant and Dissonant Music" here: www.youtube.com/watch?v=b1Ph0sa0Gc0.

However, it is not possible to rule out infants' early experiences, including those in the womb. These experiences may have affected their musical preferences. For instance, Partanen and coresearchers (2013) had one group of mothers listen to the melody "Twinkle, Twinkle, Little

Star" an average of 171 times during the last three months of their pregnancy. A control group of mothers did not listen to the melody. When born, the experimenters measured how the infants' brains responded to the melody. The musical experience in the womb clearly affected the infants' responses. Infants previously exposed to the melody in the womb showed stronger brain responses than infants who had not been exposed. Thus, learning to recognize melodies can occur in the womb. But is recognizing a melody the same as enjoying that melody?

In addition to recognizing a melody, early experiences also influence preferences. Plantinga and Trehub (2014) familiarized six-month-old infants with three minutes of either consonant or dissonant music. This familiarization was followed by short segments of either dissonant music followed by consonant music or the reverse, with consonant music followed by dissonant music. If consonant music is preferred, then infants should focus more on its source, regardless of whether it was heard first or second. However, if familiarization is important, then the infants should focus more on the type of music they heard earlier. The experimenters measured the length of time infants fixated on the source of the music. The results showed that, when familiarized with consonant music, infants fixated more on the consonant music source than on the dissonant source. However, when familiarized with dissonant music, infants fixated more on the dissonant music source than on the consonant source. These results contradict the hypothesis that infants innately prefer consonant music. They preferred music similar to what they have been familiarized with.

Music preference is also shaped by culture rather than by evolution. In other words, humans like the music they grew up with, rather than as the result of any evolutionary disposition. To investigate this possibility, McDermott and coresearchers (2016) played consonant and dissonant music to people who had different degrees of exposure to Western music. The researchers examined people in the United States as well as people in a major city and town in Bolivia, but also the Tsimane'. These individuals lived in a remote section of the Amazon rain forest. The Tsimane' had no TV and little access to music by radio. In other words, they had little, if any, exposure to Western consonant music. When asked to rate the pleasantness of consonant versus dissonant music, Americans, city dwellers, and town dwellers in Bolivia all rated consonant music as more pleasant than they rated dissonant music. The Tsimane', however, showed no difference in preference. They could detect the difference in the two types of music, but preferred them equally. Thus, not all cultures prefer consonant music more than dissonant music. One conclusion is that music preferences may not be innate but instead result from early musical experiences in the culture.

The Massachusetts Institute of Technology YouTube channel has a video of this experiment titled "Are musical tastes cultural or hardwired in the brain" here: www.youtube.com/watch?v= IMjlZ-0Qm2Q.

But what motivates infants to prefer familiar music regardless of whether it is consonant or dissonant and for the Tsimane' to prefer each type of music equally? Plantinga and Trehub (2014) propose processing fluency as an explanation. **Processing fluency** refers to the ease with which information is recognized, evaluated, categorized, and stored in memory, as based on its symmetry, contrast, and typicality, or familiarity owing to past experience. In the case of music, processing fluency refers to the ease with which music is recognized and listened to. Stimuli that are easier to process are considered more aesthetically pleasing (Reber et al., 2004). Thus, infants derived more pleasure from consonant music because they were familiar with it owing to early exposure, such as from lullabies sung by their mothers. Infants are not exposed to dissonant music and hence are less familiar with it. The greater exposure to consonant music compared to dissonant music extends into adulthood. Consequently, appreciation of music depends on processing fluency that people acquire from music heard in their culture (Reber et al., 2004).

Section Recap

Fear and food preferences are categories of universal motives that resulted from natural selection. Music enjoyment may be a by-product of the evolution of other psychological mechanisms. Survey research indicates that some fears are more prevalent than others, especially ones that have survival value, such as the fear of snakes and spiders. Thus, individuals are more sensitive to dangerous stimuli that are remnants of our evolutionary past. Adults can identify snakes and spiders more rapidly in a background of harmless stimuli. Infants look longer at snakes than other animals when accompanied by frightened voices. Not all fears occur the first time in a dangerous situation but can arise quickly, with little previous experience, depending on the preparedness of the behavior. *Preparedness* refers to the ease with which behavior is conditioned. Some stimuli are easy to condition (prepared), such as fear stimuli, whereas other stimuli are difficult to condition (contraprepared).

Another set of universal motives revolves around our interaction with food. Humans exhibit food *neophobia*, which is the tendency to avoid novel foods and select familiar foods. Another related universal motive is the human preference for sugar and fat, which indicate high caloric value. Work with infants just a few hours old shows that they prefer sweet substances over sour and bitter substances. Early taste preferences for solid foods may also result from flavors that babies experienced from their mothers' amniotic fluid or breast milk. Fortunately, humans are *omnivorous*, which means they can eat a variety of foods to obtain the necessary ingredients for growth and maintenance.

The appreciation of music evolved as a by-product of *entrainment*, which is necessary for the ability to speak and allows for keeping time to a musical beat. The appreciation of music is not innate but depends on early experiences in the womb and from our culture. *Processing fluency* is the ease with which individuals recognize different stimuli based on their familiarity or typicality, as in the case of familiar music. Individuals not exposed to Western music prefer consonant and dissonant music equally.

GLOSSARY

Term	Definition
Bad Genes Hypothesis	Facial and physical appearance of people that indicate they carry genes for disease, low intelligence, and poor parenting skills. Such individuals tend to be rejected as long-term mates
Biosocial Theory	Sex differences in physical strength and reproductive capacity interact with society's expectations about social roles in order to produce gender differences

continued . . .

GLOSSARY Continued

Term	Definition
Consonant vs Dissonant Music	Consonant music is acceptable, pleasant, and harmonious in contrast to dissonant music, which is unacceptable and sounds unpleasant or harsh, and is inharmonious
Contraprepared	Behaviors that are learned with great difficulty and only after much experience
Emotional Infidelity	A person's mate is forming a deep emotional attachment to another person
Entrainment	Body movements that synchronize with an external auditory beat as in keeping time with the beat of the music
Evolutionary History	The cumulative effects of evolution that all humans have in common. It shows our human nature
Food Neophobia	A tendency (usually of a child) to avoid novel foods and prefer familiar foods
Genes	Parts of a person's DNA that provide information for the construction of proteins, which form the building blocks of the brain and bodily structures
Good Genes Hypothesis	Facial appearance of symmetry and sexual dimorphism that signal health, fertility, and intelligence. Such individuals are desired as long-term mates
Human Nature	Behavioral, motivational, and emotional similarities among people as a result of their common evolutionary history
Innate	Describes behavior that is strongly influenced by heredity; behavior that is not taught or not the result of experience
Jealousy	A negative emotion triggered by an actual or suspected loss of a mate's sexual services or a mate's affection
Mate Poaching	Attempts to attract someone as a romantic or sexual partner when that someone is already in a romantic relationship
Mate Value	Those characteristics of a person that are desired by the other sex, such as good looks, dependability, ambition, and industriousness
Neophilics/Neophobics	Neophilics are individuals willing to try new foods, while neophobics are individuals unwilling to do so
Niceness	A collection of mate value traits that consist of communication skills, dependability, kindness, humor, and honesty
Omnivorous	Human tendency to be able to eat a variety of foods, e.g., grains, vegetables, dairy, and meats
Personal History	Each person's unique experiences that have accumulated over his or her lifetime
Preparedness	The ease with which a behavior is learned. It ranges from being prepared (easy) to being contraprepared (difficult) to learn a behavior
Processing Fluency	The ease with which information is recognized, categorized, evaluated, and stored in memory. Easily processed music is enjoyed more
Psychological Mechanisms	A set of behavioral tendencies that evolved through natural selection in order to solve recurring problems of adaptation to the environment
Romantic Love	An emotion that involves a strong attachment between individuals and strong sexual desire, and promotes long-term commitment

continued . . .

GLOSSARY Continued

Term	Definition
Sexual Desire	A universal motive that motivates sexual behavior in a couple for the production of offspring
Sexual Infidelity	When a person's mate is engaging in and enjoying passionate sexual intercourse with another person
Sexual Selection	Darwin's term for the member of one sex choosing a mate from the other sex based on the characteristics of the latter
Structural Powerless Hypothesis	Women are not as effective in today's society at obtaining the same level of financial resources as men
Universal Motives	A psychological mechanism regarding the universality of evolved human motives, such as fear of snakes and the preference for sweets
Universals	Brown's term for psychological mechanisms that are found in almost all societies and cultures of the world, e.g., emotions, fears, goal setting, self-concept

REFERENCES

Bernard, L. C., Mills, M., Swenson, L., & Walsh, R. P. (2005). An evolutionary theory of human motivation. *Genetic, Social, and General Psychology Monographs, 131*, 129–184.

Berscheid, E. (2010). Love in the fourth dimension. *Annual Review of Psychology, 61*, 1–25.

Birch, L. L. (1992). Children's preferences for high-fat foods. *Nutrition Reviews, 50*, 249–255.

Birch, L. L. (1999). Development of food preferences. *Annual Review of Nutrition, 19*, 41–62.

Bolles, R. C. (1970). Species-specific defense reactions and avoidance learning. *Psychological Review, 77*, 32.

Brase, G. L., Caprar, D. V., & Voracek, M. (2004). Sex differences in responses to relationship threats in England and Romania. *Journal of Social and Personal Relationships, 21*, 763–778.

Brown, D. E. (1991). *Human universals*. Philadelphia, PA: Temple University Press.

Buss, D. M. (1989). Sex differences in human mate preferences: Evolutionary hypotheses tested in 37 cultures. *Behavioral and Brain Sciences, 12*, 1–49.

Buss, D. M. (2006). The evolution of love. In R. J. Sternberg & K. Weis (Eds.), *The new psychology of love* (pp. 65–86). New Haven, CT, & London: Yale University Press.

Buss, D. M. (2007). The evolution of human mating. *Acta Psychologica Sinica, 39*, 502–512.

Buss, D. M. (2015). *Evolutionary psychology: The new science of the mind* (5th ed.). New York, NY: Routledge.

Buss, D. M., Larsen, R. J., Westen, D., & Semmelroth, J. (1992). Sex differences in jealousy: Evolution, physiology, and psychology. *Psychological Science, 3*, 251–255.

Buss, D. M., Shackelford, T. K., Kirkpatrick, L. A., Choe, J. C., Lim, H. K., Hasegawa, M., . . . Bennett, K. (1999). Jealousy and the nature of beliefs about infidelity: Tests of competing hypotheses about sex differences in the United States, Korea, and Japan. *Personal Relationships, 6*, 125–150.

Buss, D. M., Shackelford, T. K., Kirkpatrick, L. A., & Larsen, R. J. (2001). A half century of mate preferences: The cultural evolution of values. *Journal of Marriage and Family, 63*, 491–503.

Buunk, B. P., Angleitner, A., Oubaid, V., & Buss, D. M. (1996). Sex differences in jealousy in evolutionary and cultural perspective: Tests from the Netherlands, Germany, and the United States. *Psychological Science, 7*, 359–363.

Caporael, L. R. (1989). Mechanisms matter: The difference between sociobiology and evolutionary psychology. *Behavioral and Brain Sciences, 12*, 17–18.

Cross, I. (2001). Music, cognition, culture, and evolution. In R. J. Zatorre & I. Peretz (Eds.), *Annals of the New York Academy of Sciences: Vol. 930. The biological foundations of music* (pp. 28–42). New York, NY: New York Academy of Sciences

Darwin, C. (1859/1936). *On the origin of species by means of natural selection*. New York, NY: Random House.

Darwin, C. (1871/1981). *The descent of man, and selection in relation to sex*. Princeton, NJ: Princeton University Press.

de Souza, A. A. L., Verderane, M. P., Taira, J. T., & Otta, E. (2006). Emotional and sexual jealousy as a function of sex and sexual orientation in a Brazilian sample. *Psychological Reports, 98*, 529–535.

DeLoache, J. S., & LoBue, V. (2009). The narrow fellow in the grass: Human infants associate snakes and fear. *Developmental Science, 12*, 201–207.

Dennis, W. (1960). Environmental influences upon motor development. *Journal of Genetic Psychology, 96*, 47–59.

Desor, J. A., Maller, O., & Andrews, K. (1975). Ingestive responses of human newborns to salty, sour, and bitter stimuli. *Journal of Comparative and Physiological Psychology, 89*, 966–970.

Desor, J. A., Maller, O., & Turner, R. E. (1973). Taste in acceptance of sugars by human infants. *Journal of Comparative and Physiological Psychology, 84*, 496–501.

Diamond, L. M. (2004). Emerging perspectives on distinctions between romantic love and sexual desire. *Current Directions in Psychological Science, 13*, 116–119.

Eagly, A. H., & Wood, W. (1999). The origins of sex differences in human behavior. *American Psychologist, 54*, 408–423.

Eastwick, P. W. (2009). Beyond the Pleistocene: Using phylogeny and constraint to inform the evolutionary psychology of human mating. *Psychological Bulletin, 135*, 794–821.

Fernandez, A. M., Sierra, J. C., Zubeidat, I., & Vera-Villarroel, P. (2006). Sex differences in response to sexual and emotional infidelity among Spanish and Chilean students. *Journal of Cross Cultural Psychology, 37*, 359–365.

Fisher, H. (2004). *Why we love: The nature and chemistry of romantic love*. New York, NY: Henry Holt.

Fletcher, G. J., Simpson, J. A., Campbell, L., & Overall, N. C. (2015). Pair-bonding, romantic love, and evolution: The curious case of homosapiens. *Perspectives on Psychological Science, 10*, 20–36.

Frank, R. H. (1988). *Passions within reason*. New York, NY: W. W. Norton.

Galton, F. (1883). *Inquiries into human faculty and its development*. London: Macmillan.

Gould, S. J. (1987). Freudian slip. *Natural History, 96*, 14–21.

Greengross, G., & Miller, G. (2011). Humor ability reveals intelligence, predicts mating success, and is higher in males. *Intelligence, 39*, 188–192.

Hepper, P. G., Wells, D. L., Dornan, J. C., & Lynch, C. (2013). Long-term flavor recognition in humans with prenatal garlic experience. *Developmental Psychobiology, 55*, 568–574.

Jankowiak, W. R., & Fischer, E. F. (1992). A cross-cultural perspective on romantic love. *Ethnology, 31*, 149–155.

Jerome, N. W. (1977). Taste experience and the development of a dietary preference for sweet in humans: Ethnic and cultural variations in early taste experience. In J. M. Weiffenbach (Ed.), *Taste and development* (pp. 235–248). Bethesda, MD: U.S. Department of Health, Education, and Welfare.

Jokela, M. (2009). Physical attractiveness and reproductive success in humans: Evidence from the late 20th century United States. *Evolution and Human Behavior, 30*, 342–350.

Kirsner, B. R., Figueredo, A. J., & Jacobs, W. J. (2003). Self, friends, and lovers: Structural relations among Beck Depression Inventory scores and perceived mate values. *Journal of Affective Disorders, 75*, 131–148.

Klasios, J. (2013). Cognitive traits as sexually selected fitness indicators. *Review of General Psychology, 17*, 428–442.

Lane, B., & Gullone, E. (1999). Common fears: A comparison of adolescents' self-generated and fear survey schedule generated fears. *Journal of Genetic Psychology, 160*, 194–204.

Langlois, J. H., Kalakanis, L., Rubenstein, A. J., Larson, A., Hallam, M., & Smoot, M. (2000). Maxims or myths of beauty? A meta-analytic and theoretical review. *Psychological Bulletin, 126*, 390–423.

Lippa, R. A. (2007). The preferred traits of mates in a cross-national study of heterosexual and homosexual men and women: An examination of biological and cultural influences. *Archives of Sexual Behavior, 36*, 193–208.

Lloyd, E. A. (2005). *The case of the female orgasm*. Cambridge, MA: Harvard University Press.

LoBue, V. (2014). Deconstructing the snake: The relative roles of perception, cognition, and emotion on threat detection. *Emotion, 14,* 701–711.

LoBue, V., & DeLoache, J. S. (2008). Detecting the snake in the grass. *Psychological Science, 19,* 284–289.

LoBue, V., & Rakison, D. H. (2013). What we fear most: A developmental advantage for threat-relevant stimuli. *Developmental Review, 33,* 285–303.

Marks, I. M. (1987). *Fears, phobias, and rituals.* New York, NY: Oxford University Press.

Mayr, E. (2001). *What evolution is.* New York, NY: Basic.

McDermott, J. H., Schultz, A. F., Undurraga, E. A., & Godoy, R. A. (2016). Indifference to dissonance in native Amazonians reveals cultural variation in music perception. *Nature, 535,* 547–550.

Mennella, J. A., & Beauchamp, G. K. (1998). Early flavor experiences: Research update. *Nutrition Reviews, 56,* 205–211.

Mennella, J. A., Jagnow, C. P., & Beauchamp, G. K. (2001). Prenatal and postnatal flavor learning by human infants. *Pediatrics, 107,* e88. Retrieved June 22, 2007, from www.pediatrics.org/cgi/content/full/107/6/e88.

Muris, P., Merckelbach, H., & Collaris, R. (1997). Common childhood fears and their origins. *Behaviour Research and Therapy, 35,* 929–937.

North, A. C., Hargreaves, D. J., & Hargreaves, J. J. (2004). Uses of music in everyday life. *Music Perception, 22,* 41–77.

Öhman, A. (1986). Face the beast and fear the face: Animal and social fears as prototypes of evolutionary analyses of emotion. *Psychophysiology, 23,* 123–145.

Öhman, A. (1993). Fear and anxiety as emotional phenomena: Clinical phenomenology, evolutionary perspectives, and information-processing mechanisms. In M. Lewis & J. M. Haviland (Eds.), *Handbook of emotions* (pp. 511–536). New York, NY: Guilford.

Öhman, A., & Mineka, S. (2001). Fears, phobias, and preparedness: Toward an evolved module of fear and learning. *Psychological Review, 108,* 483–522.

Partanen, E., Kujala, T., Tervaniemi, M., & Huotilainen, M. (2013). Prenatal music exposure induces long-term neural effects. *PLOS ONE, 8,* e78946.

Peretz, I. (2006). The nature of music from a biological perspective. *Cognition, 100,* 1–32.

Petrie, M., Halliday, T., & Sanders, C. (1991). Peahens prefer peacocks with elaborate trains. *Animal Behaviour, 41,* 323–331.

Pflüger, L. S., Oberzaucher, E., Katina, S., Holzleitner, I. J., & Grammer, K. (2012). Cues to fertility: Perceived attractiveness and facial shape predict reproductive success. *Evolution and Human Behavior, 33,* 708–714.

Plantinga, J., & Trehub, S. E. (2014). Revisiting the innate preference for consonance. *Journal of Experimental Psychology: Human Perception and Performance, 40,* 40–49.

Pliner, P., & Hobden, K. (1992). Development of a scale to measure the trait of food neophobia in humans. *Appetite, 19,* 105–120.

Plomin, R., DeFries, J. C., Knopik, V. S., & Neiderhiser, J. M. (2013). *Behavioral genetics* (6th ed.). New York, NY: Worth.

Plutchik, R. (1980). *Emotion: A psychoevolutionary synthesis.* New York, NY: Harper & Row.

Raudenbush, B., & Frank, R. A. (1999). Assessing food neophobia: The role of stimulus familiarity. *Appetite, 32,* 261–271.

Reber, R., Schwarz, N., & Winkielman, P. (2004). Processing fluency and aesthetic pleasure: Is beauty in the perceiver's processing experience? *Personality and Social Psychology Review, 8,* 364–382.

Rhodes, G. (2006). The evolutionary psychology of facial beauty. *Annual Review of Psychology,* 57, 199–226.

Rhodes, G., Simmons, L. W., & Peters, M. (2005). Attractiveness and sexual behavior: Does attractiveness enhance mating success? *Evolution and Human Behavior, 26,* 186–201.

Roper Report. (1984). *Public Opinion, 7,* 32.

Rosenstein, D., & Oster, H. (1988). Differential facial responses to four basic tastes in newborns. *Child Development, 59,* 1555–1568.

Said, C. P., & Todorov, A. (2011). A statistical model of facial attractiveness. *Psychological Science, 22,* 1183–1190.

Schachner, A., Brady, T. F., Pepperberg, I. M., & Hauser, M. D. (2009). Spontaneous motor entrainment to music in multiple mimicking species. *Current Biology, 19,* 831–836.

Schmitt, D. P., & 121 Members of the International Sexuality Description Project. (2004). Patterns and universals of mate poaching across 53 nations: The effects of sex, culture, and personality on romantically attracting another person's partner. *Journal of Personality and Social Psychology, 86*, 560–584.

Seligman, M. E. P. (1971). Phobias and preparedness. *Behavior Therapy, 2*, 307–320.

Shaver, P. R., Morgan, H. J., & Wu, S. (1996). Is love a "basic" emotion? *Personal Relationships, 3*, 81–96.

Steiner, J. E. (1977). Facial expressions of the neonate infant indicating the hedonics of food-related chemical stimuli. In J. M. Weiffenbach (Ed.), *Taste and development* (pp. 173–189). Bethesda, MD: U.S. Department of Health, Education, and Welfare.

Symons, D. (1979). *The evolution of human sexuality*. Oxford: Oxford University Press.

Tagler, M. J. (2010). Sex differences in jealousy: Comparing the influence of previous infidelity among college students and adults. *Social Psychological and Personality Science, 1*, 353–360.

Tattersall, I. (1998). *Becoming human*. New York, NY: Harcourt Brace.

Thayer, R. E. (2001). *Calm energy*. New York, NY: Oxford University Press.

Thurber, J., & White, E. B. (1929). *Is sex necessary?* New York, NY: Harper & Brothers.

United States Census Bureau (2016). *Current population survey, annual social and economic supplement, 2016*. Retrieved January 2, 2017.

Valentine, C. W. (1930). The innate bases of fear. *Journal of Genetic Psychology, 37*, 394–419.

Weeden, J., & Sabini, J. (2005). Physical attractiveness and health in western societies: A review. *Psychological Bulletin, 131*, 635–653.

Whalen, P. J. (1998). Fear, vigilance, and ambiguity: Initial neuroimaging studies of the human amygdala. *Current Directions in Psychological Science, 7*, 177–188.

Wiederman, M. W., & Allgeier, E. R. (1992). Gender differences in mate selection criteria: Sociobiological or socioeconomic explanation? *Ethology and Sociobiology, 13*, 115–124.

Wiederman, M. W., & Kendall, E. (1999). Evolution, sex, and jealousy: Investigation with a sample from Sweden. *Evolution and Human Behavior, 20*, 121–128.

Wood, W., & Eagly, A. H. (2002). A cross-cultural analysis of the behavior of women and men: Implications for the origins of sex differences. *Psychological Bulletin, 128*, 699–727.

Zebrowitz, L. A., & Rhodes, G. (2004). Sensitivity of "bad genes" and the anomalous face overgeneralization effect: Cue validity, cue utilization, and accuracy in judging intelligence and health. *Journal of Nonverbal Behavior, 28*, 167–185.

Zentner, M. R., & Kagan, J. (1998). Infants' perception of consonance and dissonance in music. *Infant Behavior and Development, 21*, 483–492.

CHAPTER 4

Addictions and Addictive Behaviors

Tobacco surely was designed
To poison and destroy mankind.

Philip Freneau, 1786

Thou hast the keys of Paradise, O just, subtle, and mighty opium!

Thomas De Quincey, 1821

Some feelings and the substances or activities that produce them are so motivating that little else seems to matter. What are these feelings and activities? Allow this question along with the following to guide your reading of this chapter:

1. What can drugs of abuse and addictive behaviors tell us about the brain as a source of motivation?
2. How do drugs differ from natural incentives in motivating behavior?
3. Why are there pleasure networks in the brain and how do they work?
4. What are the psychological theories for starting and maintaining drug use?
5. How can strenuous exercise, gambling, and Internet use become addictive behaviors?

DRUGS OF ABUSE AND ADDICTION

A young man has just left his mother's apartment and is strolling around his old neighborhood. He is delighted to be free after a year in prison. While walking, he reflects on the time he spent there undergoing heroin detoxification. This very unpleasant process left him free of any drug cravings. As he walks along familiar streets and sees familiar buildings, however, his intestines begin to rumble, his eyes begin to water, and he starts yawning. He also begins to sweat and becomes nauseated, as symptoms of his old withdrawal agony returns. These are symptoms that he has not experienced for over a year. "How is this possible?" he asks himself. "I haven't felt this way for so long." Although feeling panicky and anxious, he knows how to alleviate this old sickness. He turns the corner and begins walking toward a familiar apartment building, where relief awaits.

A young woman drives her car uptown to visit her girlfriend. Inside her friend's apartment she notices a mirror lying face-up on the coffee table. She can't take her eyes off the mirror. It elicits a mounting excitement that seems to take over her body. Does her friend have any cocaine, she wonders? Her whole body tingles in delightful waves of anticipation. She can almost taste the cocaine at the back of her throat. "If I am feeling a rush just from seeing this mirror, why do I bother using cocaine at all?" she thinks. The reason, she answers herself, is that there is no substitute for the drug. "Nothing in any way, shape, or form can make me feel this good."

Aspects of Addiction

These two scenarios depict addicted individuals, who engage in behaviors that run counter to their long-term well-being. Their addiction is the consequence of separating the experience of pleasure from its evolutionary function. Recall from Chapter 2 that *hedonism* refers to the pursuit of pleasure and the avoidance of pain. However, as Herbert Spencer (1881/1977) claimed, the function of pleasure was to support behaviors that benefit life. For example, pleasure maintains behaviors like eating, drinking, and sex. But now it is possible to experience pleasure for its own sake by using psychoactive drugs or engaging in addictive behaviors.

Addiction or substance use disorder? **Addictions** or addictive behaviors are compulsive and provide short-term pleasure at the expense of severe and long-term negative consequences. The everyday term addiction, however, is referred to as a **substance use disorder** (APA, 2013). Table 4.1 provides the criteria that define these disorders. Addicted individuals seem helpless in trying to curb their drug use. Their drug craving is so strong that it results in extensive effort toward drug procurement and use in spite of intentions to do otherwise (*impaired control*). Drug use is continued in spite of it interfering with a person's work, social, and academic life and resulting interpersonal problems. In addition, the individual withdraws from social interactions, work, and leisure activities (*social impairment*). Addicted individuals still use their drugs in spite of potential physical dangers and adverse physical or psychological consequences (*risky use*). Finally, drug use leads to tolerance and withdrawal (*pharmacological criteria*). Can the criteria of substance use disorder also apply to exercise, gambling, and Internet use?

Psychoactive drugs. These are any chemical substance that alters a person's mood and behavior as a result of the drug's effect on the function of the brain. The psychoactive drugs listed in Table 4.2 produce strong pleasurable effects that motivate compulsive use in spite of later negative

TABLE 4.1 Substance Use Disorders

Impaired Control	Uses larger amounts of the drug for longer than intended
	Multiple unsuccessful attempts to quit
	Extensive time, effort, and preoccupation to obtain and use the substance
	Craving often triggered by environmental stimuli
Social Impairment	Failure to meet obligations at work, school, and home
	Persistent use despite negative consequences socially and interpersonally
	Withdraw from important social, occupational, recreational activities, and family
Risky Use	Use substance in situations that are physically dangerous
	Unable to stop using despite negative physical or psychological consequences
Pharmacological Criteria	Tolerance: individual requires increasing amounts of substance for same effect as earlier
	Withdrawal: abstaining produces unpleasant feelings or unpleasant physical symptoms

Source: American Psychiatric Association (APA). (2013). *Diagnostic and Statistical Manual of Mental Disorders* (5th ed.). Arlington, VA: American Psychiatric Association.

TABLE 4.2 Psychoactive Drugs

Psychoactive Drug	*Source*	*Effects*
Caffeine	Coffee beans, tea leaves, coffee, tea, soft drinks	Alert, energetic, lively, clear-headed, experience well-being
Alcohol	Ethanol in beer, wine, distilled spirits	Euphoria, releases inhibitions, which may produce aggression and promiscuity
Nicotine	From tobacco leaves and smoked as cigarettes, cigars, pipe, and electronic cigarettes	Pleasurable, stimulating, but also relaxing when reducing withdrawal
Marijuana	Tetrahydrocannibol (THC) derived from hemp (cannabis) plant	Feel euphoric, relaxed, drowsy, and detached from reality
Psychotherapeutics	Obtained by prescription as pain relievers, tranquilizers, but also stimulants	Induce mild euphoria, reduce anxiety, calming effect, and as a stimulant increase alertness, attention, and wakefulness
Cocaine	Crystal or powder derived from leaves of coca plant native to South America	Injected or inhaled produces a short intense high, euphoria, feeling energetic and alert
Hallucinogens	Known as angel dust, ecstasy, LSD, mescaline, and peyote	Enhance perception and mental stimulation but also cause delusions, distort reality, and experience visions
Methamphetamines	Derived from amphetamine obtained from Khat plant	Taken orally, nasally, injected, or smoked to produce an initial rush, long high, euphoria followed by alertness and wakefulness
Opioids	Sap derived from seeds of opium poppy to make opium, morphine, codeine, and heroin	Intense rush, euphoria, relief of tension, relaxation, warm drowsiness

consequences. The drugs described in Table 4.2 are controlled substances, which means that their manufacture, possession, and distribution are regulated by the federal government of the United States. *Illicit drugs* are ones whose use is prohibited by state or federal law. Marijuana, for example, is an illicit drug in some states but legal in others, whereas heroin is illicit (illegal) in all states. Caffeine is not controlled by any state and may even be used by children in soft drinks.

Extent of drug use. Impaired control (see Table 4.1) refers to a drug becoming the entire focus of a person's life to the extent that it interferes with other behaviors. To determine the extent that this can become a national problem, an annual National Survey on Drug Use and Health (NSDUH) assesses the extent people are motivated to experiment, use, and eventually abuse psychoactive drugs. Figure 4.1, for example, shows the number of 18–22-year-old university students out of nine million who tried a psychoactive drug on a typical day. Alcohol was tried the most frequently and heroin the least. Other NSDUH surveys show that alcohol is the most frequently used drug, followed by cigarettes. The frequency of cigarette smoking is declining. On the other hand, marijuana use is increasing, probably because it is allowed for medicinal purposes in over half of the states and recreationally in many others. Tracking initial drug use is

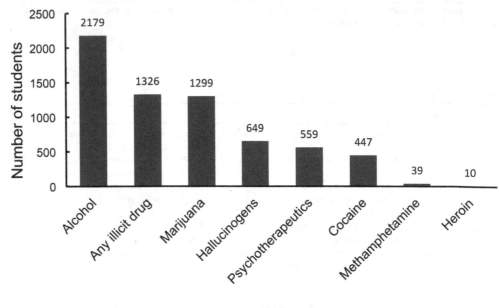

Psychoactive drug

FIGURE 4.1 Number of College Students Who Used a Drug for the First Time on an Average Day. National Survey on Drug Use and Health conducted between 2011 and 2014 estimates that annually there are nine million university students aged 18–22 years. Of this population of students, the graph shows the number who used a psychoactive drug for the first time on an average single day. When calculated by year, 9.9 percent of the students drank alcohol and 6.0 percent of the students used an illicit drug for the first time in the past year.

Source: SAMHSA, Center for Behavioral Health Statistics and Quality, National Surveys on Drug Use and Health (NSDUHs), 2011 and 2014. www.samhsa.gov/data/sites/default/files/report_2361/ShortReport-2361.html.

important, since it provides information regarding the percentage of the population that will become dependent users. From the initial use of drugs in Figure 4.1, who will come to use habitually? Is there any way of predicting who that will be?

The Substance Abuse and Mental Health Services Administration (SAMHSA) provides extensive national statistics of psychoactive drug use based on their National Survey on Drug Use and Health (NSDUH) here: www.samhsa.gov/data.

Specifics of Drug Addiction

What are some major characteristics of addiction—that is, of craving, tolerance, and withdrawal (see Table 4.1)?

Craving. People's lack of control over their substance use is apparent from their **craving**. It refers to the overpowering, uncontrollable urge for the drug a person is using. Koob and Le Moal (2008) define craving "as memory of the rewarding effects of a drug superimposed on a negative emotional state" (p. 38). Craving can arise from a previous drug experience or from stimuli that have been associated with drug use such as the familiar street and buildings or mirror in the opening vignettes. These stimuli intensify craving, especially when they overlay negative feelings, such as anxiety, dysphoria, or withdrawal (Koob & Le Moal, 2008). However, what are the separate effects of a drug's reward versus its ability to relieve negative feelings? This question is similar to "why does a person eat?" Is it the pleasure of eating food or to reduce hunger? To find an answer to this question, drug researchers asked alcohol, opiate, and cocaine patients what the feeling of craving meant to them. Their answer depended on the drug the patient used. For alcoholics and opiate patients, craving was associated more with getting rid of negative withdrawal symptoms and less with any positive feelings the drug may have provided. However, for cocaine patients, the pattern of findings was reversed. For them craving was associated more with getting the positive feelings derived from cocaine and less with removing negative feelings (Childress et al., 1992). Thus, on the whole, craving seems linked to reducing unpleasant feelings or negative drug effects as well as with a desire to experience a drug's specific euphoric effects.

Tolerance and withdrawal. Tolerance and withdrawal are two other striking characteristics of drug addiction (see Table 4.1). **Tolerance** means that the body habituates to the effects of a drug because of repeated experiences. Tolerance is a case of stimulus (drug) habituation and is shown by an increase in the amount of drug dosage needed to achieve the same desired effect. Figure 4.2 shows increased dosages needed to offset the tolerance developed by an individual with a history of drug abuse (Griffiths et al., 1980, p. 17). This person was allowed to request any drug as often and in any amount. He chose intravenous morphine injections for 112 consecutive days, after which he was instructed to detoxify himself.

A **withdrawal syndrome** is a second characteristic of drug dependence. It refers to a drug-opposite effect. A drug produces a rush or pleasant experience. However, when the drug wears off a person experiences feelings that are by contrast opposite: dysphoria, headache, fatigue, anxiety, irritability, and bodily distress. Withdrawal can range from mild to extreme and depend on the length of time since the last drug use. For example, caffeine withdrawal may result in a headache and lack of energy, while opiate withdrawal may involve dysphoria, depressed mood, nausea, and feelings of distress. In addition, there are increased cravings for the drug that was responsible for producing the withdrawal.

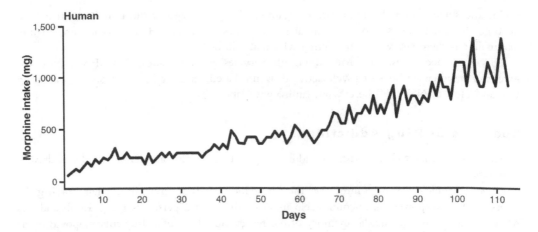

FIGURE 4.2 Drug Tolerance. Patterns of opiate intake in a human under conditions of continuous drug availability. The graph shows the amount of the drug taken over consecutive days.

Source: From "Similarities in Animal and Human Drug-Taking Behavior" by R. R. Griffiths et al. (Figure 3, p. 17), 1980, in N. K. Mello, Ed., *Advances in Substance Abuse*. Greenwich, CT: JAI Press. Copyright 1980 by JAI Press. Reprinted by permission.

From Experimentation to Addiction

How does the path toward drug addiction begin? It begins with experimentation (see Figure 4.1). Individuals may be attracted to the novelty of drug use and to its anticipated pleasure, and be influenced by the availability of drugs along with observing the actions of their peers. From this point forward, however, some individuals will stop, continue to use occasionally, or become compulsively addicted. How do *person characteristics*, such as genes and personality, shape the path from drug experimentation to dependence?

Genetic disposition. Will a person get sunburned while indoors on a hot, sunny day? Obviously not; there is no exposure to the sun. Will a person get sunburned while outside on a hot, sunny day? It depends. People with fair skin are susceptible to sunburn and so will burn when exposed to the sun. Other people, however, are not susceptible and so will not burn. In other words, the combination of exposure to the sun plus skin that is genetically disposed to burn results in a sunburn. A similar line of thought applies to addiction. An addiction depends on both exposure to an environment that promotes drug use and on a genetic disposition toward addiction.

"Everyone in my family smokes" and "alcoholism runs in my family" are observations that illustrate the combination of a genetic disposition and a drug-facilitating environment. **Behavioral genetics** of addiction attempts to untangle these effects. It is based on the assumption that drugs have their effects on structures in the brain. These structures are genetically transmitted from one generation to the next. Furthermore, greater genetic similarity between two individuals is associated with greater similarity in their brains and nervous systems, which in turn is associated with corresponding resemblances in their vulnerability to drugs of abuse (Goldman et al., 2005; Plomin et al., 2013). For example, identical twins are 100 percent genetically similar, while fraternal twins are like siblings and are only 50 percent genetically similar. A parent has a 50 percent genetic similarity with his or her biological children but 0 percent genetic similarity with his or her adopted children. Is drug use and abuse **heritable**—that is, as the genetic similarity between individuals increases, does their similarity in drug use behaviors increase also? Yes, the use of the psychoactive drugs in Table 4.2 are heritable (Agrawal & Lynskey, 2008; Kendler et al., 2003). Dependence on gambling is also heritable (Goldman et al., 2005; Lessov et al., 2004). Nevertheless, how genes interact with the environment is what determines drug use (Lessov et al., 2004).

The behavioral genetics of addiction uses different methods to separate the influence of genes and environment. One method involves comparing identical twins with fraternal twins. In the case of identical twins, if one member is alcoholic then the other identical twin will likely be also. In the case of fraternal twins, this shared alcoholism is less likely to occur (McGue, 1999). The same findings are true for smoking. Identical twins are more alike in their smoking habits than fraternal twins are (Broms et al., 2006). Even when twins are separated early in their lives and are adopted by different families, identical twins are more alike in their smoking habits than fraternal twins are (Kendler et al., 2000).

A second method uses adoption to study the effects of genetic dispositions on drug use. In the case of alcohol, for example, this method involves comparing the home environments of adopted children, who came from nonalcoholic or alcoholic parents. Alcoholic biological parents provide the genetic disposition, but what is the effect of the children's home environment? A genetic disposition toward alcoholism lies along a quantitative continuum termed **liability**. When the degree of liability exceeds some threshold amount, then individuals are most likely alcoholics (McGue, 1999). However, the environment also plays a critical role—that is, the environment puts individuals at risk for alcohol use and abuse. For instance, in one investigation conducted in Sweden, males adopted as young children were sorted into four categories: their biological parents were alcoholic and they were adopted in homes that placed them (1) at risk for alcohol use or (2) in the absence of such risk. Or their biological parents were not alcoholic and they were also adopted in homes that placed them (3) at risk for alcohol use or (4) in the absence of such risk. The likelihood of alcohol dependence later in life was greatest for men of alcoholic parents who had been adopted into homes placing them at risk for alcohol use. Only being a child of alcoholic parents or only being adopted into a home at risk for alcohol use had little effect on subsequent alcohol abuse (McGue, 1999; Sigvardsson et al., 1996). The combination of a genetic disposition and an at-risk environment also applies to smoking (Kendler et al., 2000). In fact, all illicit drug use seems to follow a similar pattern (Agrawal & Lynskey, 2008; Kendler et al., 2003).

There are, of course, different forms of environmental influences on psychoactive drug use and abuse (Maes et al., 2006; McGue, 1999). To illustrate, parents set examples for cigarette and alcohol use, which children may follow or rebel against. Furthermore, based on agentic theory (Bandura, 2006; see Chapter 1), individuals select the environments that determine the extent of their exposure to psychoactive drugs (Kendler et al., 2000, 2003). For example, children create their own environments at school and among their peers, which determine their risk of psychoactive drug use. Thus, environments interact with genetic dispositions to determine the likelihood of drug use as summarized in Figure 4.3. This figure illustrates that the interaction between a genetic disposition with an at-risk environment determines the likelihood of drug use, dependence, and abuse.

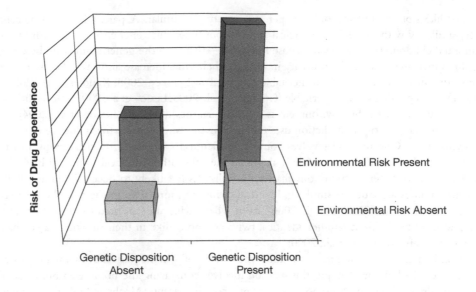

FIGURE 4.3 Gene X Environment Interaction. The risk of drug use and abuse depends on the joint presence of a genetic disposition and an environment placing a person at risk for drug use.

Personality disposition. In addition to examining genetic dispositions, psychologists have also examined the association between personality traits and drug use. There is no single addictive personality but there are several personality traits that are associated with addiction (Ball, 2005). Two such personality traits are sensation-seeking and impulsiveness. *Sensation-seeking* refers to a trait that is associated with seeking varied, intense, and novel sensations and the willingness to take various risks to experience those sensations (Zuckerman, 1994). In a review of the literature, Zuckerman (1994) concluded that sensation-seekers' curiosity and need for novelty motivated them to experience a variety of drugs. Disinhibition is another characteristic of sensation-seeking that is particularly associated with the use of alcohol and nicotine. Disinhibition is characterized by reduced social restraint, which is associated with partying, gambling, and engaging in sexual activities. Hittner and Swickert (2006), in a review of studies on sensation-seeking that involved over 37,000 participants, discovered that disinhibition is the strongest predictor of alcohol use. Nicotine use is also associated with disinhibition. Perkins and coresearchers (2000) administered a nasal spray of nicotine to nonsmokers who varied in sensation-seeking. The intensity of the individuals' positive and negative reactions to the spray depended on the level of sensation-seeking. Also, individuals high in disinhibition reacted to the spray with more pleasure, a greater head rush, tension, confusion, and arousal. These differences in the initial reaction to nicotine may help explain why high-sensation-seekers are more likely to end up as smokers compared to low-sensation-seekers (Zuckerman et al., 1990).

Impulsiveness is the other personality trait associated with psychoactive drug use. **Impulsiveness** consists of two components: heightened sensitivity to rewards and lack of foresight and planning (Dawe et al., 2004). Impulsive individuals are more sensitive to the rewarding pleasures that drugs provide. But they are also less aware of any negative consequences of their drug use. These two components are responsible for the relationship between impulsiveness and the use of drugs like alcohol, nicotine, and marijuana (Dawe et al., 2004). The *Barratt Impulsiveness Scale* (Patton et al., 1995) is one method that psychologists use to measure an individual's degree of impulsiveness. Five items sampled from this 30-item scale are presented in Table 4.3. Impulsiveness is the inverse of self-control as measured by the *Brief Self-Control Scale* (see Chapter 2; Tangney et al., 2004). Does the *Barratt Impulsiveness Scale* show a difference between individuals who abuse psychoactive drugs and those who do not? It does. Substance abuse patients, for example, scored significantly higher than did a large sample of university students. Other studies have also indicated that individuals who score higher on the *Barratt Impulsiveness Scale* are more prone to abuse drugs. For example, patients who became dependent or abused alcohol before and after age 25 were compared on their impulsiveness scores. Individuals who developed alcohol problems prior to age 25 had higher impulsiveness scores than those who developed problems after age 25 (Dom et al., 2006). Smoking is also affected by impulsiveness. Greater impulsiveness in beginning smokers was associated with greater expectations of the positive and negative reinforcing effects of smoking. More impulsive individuals expected smoking to be very pleasurable, would smoke more frequently, and would be less motivated to quit (Doran et al., 2007).

The complete *Barratt Impulsiveness Scale* is available on the website of the International Society for Research on Impulsivity here: www.impulsivity.org/measurement/bis11.

Two additional characteristics of impulsivity contribute to experimenting and using psychoactive drugs (de Wit, 2008). One is that impulsive individuals have greater difficulty inhibiting their drug cravings, especially in situations associated with drug use. They also have difficulty inhibiting their habitual responses to use drugs, such as using a drug out of habit. For example, an individual habitually smokes a cigarette in certain situations without thinking. Second is the tendency to have lapses in attention. When abstaining from drugs, individuals must constantly focus their attention on inhibiting any drug cravings or inhibiting habitual drug-using responses. Any lapse in attention away from inhibition increases the likelihood of renewed drug-taking.

Personality traits such as sensation-seeking and impulsiveness are not psychological abstractions but are heritable—that is, they have a genetic basis. Thus, although these personality traits are associated with drug use, they are also under the partial control of our genes (Hur & Bouchard, 1997; Zuckerman, 2002). Genes help contribute to a person's level of sensation-seeking and

TABLE 4.3 Items from the 30-Item *Barratt Impulsiveness Scale*

I "squirm" at plays or lectures
I act on impulse
I plan tasks carefully*
I like to think about complex problems*
I often have extraneous thoughts when thinking

Rate how true each item is of you:
1 = rarely/never, 2 = occasionally, 3 = often, 4 = almost always/always
* means reverse score: 1 = 4, 2 = 3, 3 = 2, 4 = 1. Sum your scores. A higher score means greater impulsiveness

Source: Adapted from "Factor Structure of the Barratt Impulsiveness Scale" by J. H. Patton et al., 1995, *Journal of Clinical Psychology, 51*, Table 1, p. 771.

impulsiveness, which then makes those individuals susceptible to drug experimentation and abuse (Goldman et al., 2005).

Affective forecasting errors for drug use. Chapter 1 described affective forecasting as anticipating how we will feel in the future. Does the accuracy of affective forecasting about drug use predict drug dependence? For example, would you steal from your roommate, your parents, or your romantic partner? Most likely, everyone will answer "no." However, individuals might do so in a state of drug withdrawal because they underestimate the intensity of their drug cravings. This underestimation is prevalent in beginning smokers. DiFranza and coresearchers (2007) administered the *Hooked on Nicotine Checklist* to 1,246 sixth graders. The *Checklist* measures the extent an individual feels a loss of autonomy over smoking. A higher score from 0 to 10 indicates a greater loss of autonomy—that is, reduced self-control of whether to smoke. The loss of autonomy can occur quite soon. For example, half of the sixth graders had lost some autonomy by the time they were smoking seven cigarettes per month and for some less than two days after inhaling. Doubeni and coresearchers (2010), analyzing the same data, showed that a strong desire for a cigarette is the first symptom to develop. The presence of a strong desire promotes smoking the next cigarette, which promotes further desire in an ever escalation of symptoms. Desire was followed by withdrawal symptoms during abstinence, feeling addicted, and finally difficulty controlling smoking.

The National Cancer Institute makes the *Hooked on Nicotine Checklist* available on its website, here: https://cancercontrol.cancer.gov/brp/tcrb/guide-measures/honc.html.

The *Hooked on Nicotine Checklist* is also available here: www.livingwellseontario.ca/livingwell/assets/File/Webinars/Hooked%20on%20Nicotine%20Checklist.pdf.

Heroin addicts also underestimate the force that craving has. Badger and coresearchers (2007) worked with patients who were being treated with Buprenorphine to help control their addiction to heroin. Buprenorphine is a drug that helps reduce heroin withdrawal symptoms and also produces a milder similar high. The researchers measured the patients' cravings for a second dose of Buprenorphine either before or after receiving the first dose. A single dose produces a "high" but a second dose will also increase that feeling. How strong is the craving for that second dose? The results showed that craving for a second dose of Buprenorphine was stronger prior to receiving the first dose but weaker afterwards. In other words, craving is weaker when addicts are drug-satiated, which occurs after the first dose. However, craving is stronger when drug deprived, which happens prior to the first dose. Badger and coresearchers reasoned that addicts underestimate the strength of their craving when satiated and do not realize how strong their cravings will be when they become drug deprived. Similarly, beginning drug users are more likely to become addicted because they underestimate the intensity of future cravings during a state of drug deprivation. They assume they will be able to abstain from drug use following experimentation. However, they do not realize how difficult this is because of underestimating the strength of their later cravings.

Section Recap

Addictions or addictive behaviors are compulsive actions in pursuit of short-term pleasure in spite of long-term negative consequences. Addiction is referred to as a *substance use disorder* of psychoactive drugs. The disorder is characterized by impaired self-control, social impairment, and risky use, and results in drug tolerance and withdrawal. Addictive behavior involves taking either legal or illegal (illicit) *psychoactive drugs*, which are chemical substances that can alter a person's mood. Caffeine has a stimulating effect and is the most widely used in the world. Nicotine is the psychoactive drug found in tobacco, and alcohol is found in beer, wine, and distilled spirits. Psychoactive drugs include opiates, such as morphine, codeine, and heroin, and cocaine, a powdery substance derived from coca plants. Smoking marijuana arouses feelings of euphoria and drowsiness. Psychotherapeutics are originally used for medical relief but now are hijacked for euphoric purposes. Hallucinogens are drugs such as ecstasy and LSD that produce altered senses of reality. Amphetamines and methamphetamines produce alertness, euphoria, and subjective well-being and are seemingly more powerful than cocaine. According to the National Survey on Drug Use and Health for individuals aged 18–22 years, the most frequently used drug (excluding caffeine) is alcohol and the least frequent is heroin.

Craving, drug tolerance, and a negative withdrawal syndrome are the most salient symptoms of addiction. *Craving* refers to an overpowering, almost uncontrollable urge for the drug a person uses in order to obtain the euphoric effects or to reduce withdrawal effects. *Tolerance* means that a person habituates to the effects of the drug, while the *withdrawal syndrome* refers to a drug-opposite effect resulting from drug use abstinence. Several factors contribute to people's experimentation and subsequent addiction. According to *behavioral genetics*, the likelihood of a person becoming addicted is *heritable*, which means that an increase in the genetic similarity between individuals is linked to an increase in their similarity of drug use. *Liability* refers to the likelihood of becoming alcoholic as a result of one's genetic propensity. However, a genetic disposition must combine with an at-risk environment in order to result in drug abuse and addiction. Personality traits such as sensation-seeking, which promotes experimentation and impulsiveness, are also associated with drug use. The trait of *impulsiveness* is linked to heightened drug pleasures and a lack of foresight regarding the consequences of drugs. Impulsiveness is also associated with lowered inability to inhibit cravings and to refrain from drug use. Finally, craving following drug experimentation is much stronger than individuals realize because of an error in affective forecasting.

THE ADDICTION PROCESS

What is the motivation behind drug use? In what way do changes in the environment, in conscious awareness, and in the brain motivate drug use? To an addicted individual, some environmental stimuli trigger drug positive cravings, while other stimuli trigger unpleasant feelings associated with withdrawal. In the case of withdrawal, ingesting drugs replaces unpleasant feelings with pleasant ones. These changes that occur in consciousness parallel ones that occur in the brain. Thus, conscious feelings of pleasure or withdrawal are reducible to the events in the brain from which these feelings emerge. This interplay between conscious feelings and brain processes give rise to two kinds of theories. One set of theories emphasizes what drugs do in the brain in order to explain what happens in consciousness. A second set of theories emphasizes what happens in the environment to explain conscious feelings about drugs without recourse to brain events.

Psychological Theories of Drug Addiction

How can the environment evoke drug craving and wanting? How do drugs make a person feel and how do those feelings change with repeated drug use? Several psychological theories answer these questions.

Positive and negative reinforcement. The nature of the pleasure that drugs provide changes from positive reinforcement to negative reinforcement (Koob & Le Moal, 2008). Initially, positive reinforcement motivates drug use through the pleasure or euphoria that results. However, when drug use ceases an individual begins to experience withdrawal symptoms, which are characterized by anxiety, dysphoria, and irritability. Now, negative reinforcement motivates drug use through the relief of withdrawal symptoms.

As positive reinforcers, what pleasurable feelings do drugs produce? In a test of the positive feeling produced by various drugs, Garrett and Griffiths (2001) gave different concentrations of caffeine, nicotine, or a placebo (nondrug) to their participants. Next, they asked them questions relevant to positive reinforcement, such as "How high are you?" and "Do you feel a rush?" The results showed that stronger doses of caffeine and nicotine were associated with reports of greater "highs" and "rushes."

Drug abstinence produces withdrawal symptoms felt as negative affect or dysphoria (APA, 2013; Baker et al., 2004). Negative reinforcement motivates drug-seeking behavior and use because it reduces withdrawal symptoms according to the **affective model of negative reinforcement** (Baker et al., 2004). Several considerations support the model. First, negative affect characterizes a general withdrawal process along with drug-specific withdrawal symptoms. Specifically, alcohol withdrawal may involve tremors and sweating and cocaine withdrawal may involve fatigue and increased appetite, while nicotine withdrawal involves anxiety and insomnia (Jaffe & Anthony, 2005). Accompanying these withdrawal symptoms is a craving for the very drug that produces the withdrawal. Thus, negative affect along with craving motivates seeking and using a variety of drugs. Second, withdrawal symptoms that are the basis for negative affect can occur early in drug use. A person need only use drugs for a short period of time to experience negative affect during withdrawal. For example, unpleasant withdrawal symptoms can occur after a first use of an opiate such as heroin or after only a few cigarettes (Doubeni et al., 2010; Harris & Gewirtz, 2005). Consequently, negative reinforcement as a motivator for drug use may accompany positive reinforcement early in the process of drug experimentation. Third, the intensity of negative affect increases with the duration of abstinence from drugs. As abstinence increases, there is greater relief from negative affect—that is, a greater amount of negative reinforcement.

Negative reinforcement implies escape, not avoidance behavior. The addict escapes or reduces negative affect that results from drug withdrawal. However, the anticipation of negative affect can motivate drug use as a case of avoidance behavior. An addict uses a drug to prevent negative affect. One possibility is that an addicted individual is motivated to reduce the frequency with which withdrawal occurs. Addicts may not be able to avoid withdrawal every time but they can reduce the frequency of it happening. Furthermore, the affective model of negative reinforcement states that the process of addiction involves many repetitions of the following cycle: drug levels drop in the body, negative affect follows, and drug use reduces negative affect. An addict becomes sensitive to the drop in drug levels and experiences it as bodily cues. These cues signify the initial emergence of negative withdrawal into conscious awareness. Consequently, these bodily cues set the occasion for drug use in order to avoid aversive withdrawal symptoms (Baker et al., 2004).

Opponent-process theory. This psychological theory integrates the interaction of two processes to account for drug-induced euphoria and withdrawal (Solomon & Corbit, 1974; Solomon, 1980). One process is the initial hedonic reaction produced by a drug, which is then opposed or counteracted by a second process. This second process is the drug-opposite effect, which has negative hedonic properties. The initial positive reaction is always the same and quickly subsides when the drug wears off while the opponent process is slow to take effect and continues after the drug wears off. The opponent process counteracts the disruptive effects of a drug reaction in an attempt to restore homeostasis (balanced internal environment; see Chapter 5). Subjectively, an individual experiences the algebraic sum of the initial hedonic reaction and the drug-opposite opponent reaction. For example, inhaling nicotine produces positive feelings, which are counteracted by opponent processes. When the nicotine wears off, the positive feelings cease and the negative opponent feelings become dominant, which is felt as a craving for nicotine (Solomon & Corbit, 1974). Repeated drug use strengthens the opponent process, while the strength of the initial positive process remains constant. The changes between these two processes explains drug tolerance, as shown in Figure 4.2, and explains the withdrawal syndrome. Tolerance develops because more drug is required to overcome the stronger drug-opposite effect. Negative withdrawal effects prevail because the drug-opposite reaction remains after any pleasurable effects have worn off.

Incentive sensitization theory. Drug cravings are ignited from the negative affect associated with drug withdrawal and also from environmental stimuli associated with drug use (Koob & Le Moal, 2008). Craving refers to wanting the drug for the pleasurable effect that the drug provides—that is, liking the drug. **Incentive sensitization theory** explains drug addiction by separating wanting a drug from liking it. Wanting or craving stems from incentive salience, which refers to the properties of drug-associated stimuli that evoke searching, approaching, and consuming drugs. Liking stems from a drug's hedonic value, which are those properties that determine the degree of pleasure a drug provides (Robinson & Berridge, 2003). Over the course of drug use, wanting drugs increases while liking or hedonic pleasure declines as shown in Figure 4.4 (Berridge et al., 2009; Robinson & Berridge, 1993, 2008). Liking decreases because addicts habituate to the pleasure that a drug provides. One line of evidence in support of incentive sensitization theory comes from comparing changes in the wanting and liking of beer. The amount of beer that individuals drink depends little on how much they like it and much more on how much they want it. Liking beer declines over the years an individual has been drinking beer (Ostafin et al., 2010).

Several reasons explain how a drug's incentive salience determines the strength of wanting or craving (Berridge et al., 2009; Robinson & Berridge, 2008). First, drug withdrawal states and drug-associated stimuli evoke craving responses that are extremely strong. Months and years of drug use have sensitized the addict's brain to drug-associated stimuli. Furthermore, the craving elicited by drug stimuli is not willfully chosen. Addicted individuals have no control over their craving even though they are consciously aware of it. Second, a drug's incentive salience contributes to the ability of drug-associated stimuli to act like motivational magnets. Individuals react to drug stimuli as if they were actual drugs (Berridge et al., 2009). Addicted individuals also show *attentional bias* for drug stimuli, which means they pay more attention and remember drug stimuli better. And when addicts show attentional bias they are more likely to drop out of drug treatment programs and are more likely to relapse (Stacy & Wiers, 2010).

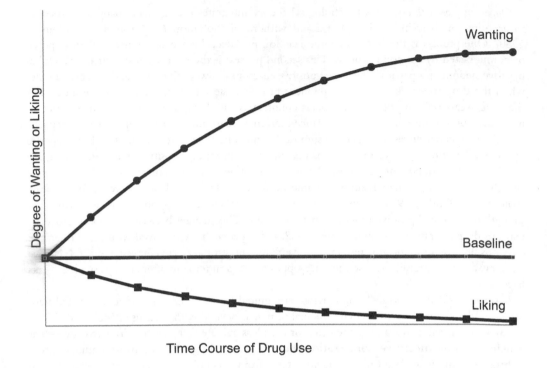

FIGURE 4.4 Changes in Wanting and Liking. Increased drug use over time leads to an increase in drug wanting or craving and a small decrease in the drug liking.

Source: Adapted from "Dissecting Components of Reward: 'Liking', 'Wanting', and Learning" by K. C. Berridge et al., 2009, *Current Opinions in Pharmacology, 9,* Figure 5, p. 69, and "The Neural Basis of Drug Craving: An Incentive-Sensitization Theory of Addiction" by T. E. Robinson & K. C. Berridge, 1993, *Brain Research Reviews, 18,* Figure 3, p. 265.

Brain Correlates of Addiction

Can drug craving, tolerance, and withdrawal be reduced to events in the addicted individual's brain? In other words, what events occur in the brain that parallel the psychological feelings of craving, euphoria, and withdrawal?

Drugs and natural incentive effects. First, artificially produced psychoactive drugs have the ability to provide pleasurable effects that are unmatched in nature. The ingestion of drugs provides no pleasurable sensory effects like those of natural incentives (Stewart et al., 1984). Only when drugs reach the brain do they have rewarding effects. Certain foods and drinks provide pleasure by their smell and taste, and the touch of the right person is pleasure to our skin. Drugs, however, do not provide pleasure to our taste buds and touch receptors. In fact, their routes of administration can be downright unpleasant. Cocaine powder is inhaled into the nose to penetrate the nasal membrane. Hypodermic needles allow addicts to inject drugs (morphine, heroin) directly into their veins for transport to the brain. Nicotine is absorbed into the bloodstream from the lungs when tobacco is smoked. In the 1800s, opium was smoked in specially made pipes, as is crack cocaine today. Alcohol is a drug taken by swallowing and is one that humans flavor heavily. Putting powder up the nose, pricking the skin, and filling the lungs with smoke are unpleasant experiences. Yet, individuals are willing to endure these procedures in order for drugs to reach the brain.

Neurons and neurotransmitters. How do drugs operate on the brain? Neuroscientists have discovered that psychoactive drugs activate certain brain sites. This results in the emergence of pleasurable feelings. This activation is possible because the brain and its various sites are composed of billions of neurons, which are interconnected to one another in a complex communication network. In this network, at the end of each neuron there is a small gap or synapse between it and the next neuron. Communication across the synapse is made possible with chemicals known a **neurotransmitters**. These substances diffuse across the synapse from one neuron to the next. When enough neurotransmitter is released into the synapse from a sending neuron, then the next or receiving neuron fires its own electrical impulse. Once the neurotransmitter has done its job, it is reabsorbed into the sending neuron through a process known as *reuptake*. *Dopamine* and *opioids* (resembling opium) are two neurotransmitters that interact with drugs at the synapses. Here psychoactive drugs activate or alter the firing of neurons in the brain's reward circuitry to produce pleasure.

Common brain pathway. Each psychoactive drug has its own specific effect. For example, cocaine, nicotine, and caffeine stimulate the central nervous system so that people feel excited, energetic, and more alert. Alcohol, in contrast, is a depressant, which means that it slows the function of the central nervous system. Alcohol makes a person feel less anxious, lowers stress, lowers social inhibitions, and increases relaxation. In addition, drugs differ in their method of ingestion and hence sensory stimulation—that is, by smoking, drinking, or injecting.

However, in spite of their different routes of administration, psychoactive drugs act on the synapses that lie in a common brain reward circuitry, a part of the larger communication network (Hyman et al., 2006; Koob & Le Moal, 2008; Nestler, 2005). This reward circuit is composed of neurons deep in the brain that connect different reward sites, such as the *nucleus accumbens* and the *ventral tegmental area*, but it also connects to the prefrontal cortex, which is located behind one's forehead. Neurons that fire in the nucleus accumbens and the ventral tegmental areas are responsible for much of the euphoric effects that come from using drugs (Hyman et al., 2006; Koob & Le Moal, 2008). In addition, the nucleus accumbens is thought to contain hedonic hotspots (Smith et al., 2010). When neurons in such a spot are stimulated by drugs, a feeling of pure pleasure emerges (Berridge, 2007; Hyman et al., 2006; Koob & Le Moal, 2008; Nestler, 2005).

Psychoactive drugs, however, vary in how they affect various neurotransmitters and neurons in the reward circuitry (Nestler, 2005, Pierce & Kumaresan, 2006). Cocaine and amphetamine work by blocking the reuptake of dopamine back into neurons located in the nucleus accumbens. Hence, dopamine remains constantly available to stimulate the neurons there that produce their euphoric effects. For instance, Cox and coresearchers (2009) had 10 nonaddicted individuals self-administer cocaine through their nose and then monitored the effects on the release of dopamine in the subjects' brains. Brain imaging showed an increase in the release of dopamine in areas that contained the nucleus accumbens. Along with this increase in dopamine, the subjects reported an increase in both the wanting and liking of cocaine. Similarly, Boileau and coresearchers (2007) used amphetamine to obtain similar results. Their subjects ingested amphetamine in capsule form on three separate days. Brain scans showed a resulting increase in the release of dopamine in regions containing and surrounding the nucleus accumbens. Simultaneously subjects reported increased feelings of being high, euphoric, energetic, and liking the drug. The researchers also demonstrated that dopamine can be released by stimuli associated with amphetamine. An example would be a placebo capsule, which is one that does not contain amphetamine. When subjects ingested the placebo capsule they also reported an increase in wanting dopamine along with liking.

Opiates (morphine and heroin) act differently from cocaine to produce pleasure. When an opiate is injected into the bloodstream, it reaches the brain and attaches to neurons that use a set of neurotransmitters known as opioids. The opioid neurons in turn release the neuronal brake that inhibits the release of dopamine in the ventral tegmental area. With the brake off, more dopamine is released, and pleasure is the result (Pierce & Kumaresan, 2006). Opiates can also directly stimulate opioid receptors located on the nucleus accumbens, which results in feelings of pleasure (Nestler, 2005). Moderate amounts of alcohol also take the brakes off of the release of dopamine in the ventral tegmental area and then the nucleus accumbens in order to provide its pleasurable effects (Pierce & Kumaresan, 2006). Nicotine is able to activate the release of dopamine in both the nucleus accumbens and the ventral tegmental area (Koob & Le Moal, 2008; Nestler, 2005; Pierce & Kumaresan, 2006). A major conclusion is that cocaine, opiates, alcohol, and nicotine evoke pleasurable feelings because of their ability to stimulate major centers in the brain's pleasure circuitry even though this is accomplished in different ways.

ALILA MEDICAL MEDIA provides a YouTube video titled "Mechanism of Drug Addiction in the Brain, Animation" here: www.youtube.com/watch?v=NxHNxmJv2bQ.

The National Institute on Drug Abuse provides a YouTube video titled "Brain Reward: Understanding How the Brain Responds to Natural Rewards and Drugs of Abuse" here: www.youtube.com/watch?v=7VUlKP4LDyQ.

Blocking drug effects. If psychoactive drugs are blocked from binding with their appropriate neurons, then their pleasurable effects are reduced. This blocking effect is made possible by drugs known as **antagonists**. Various antagonists have been used to curb people's appetites for a variety of psychoactive drugs. Naltrexone is one such antagonist that shows promise in helping humans curb their cravings to overcome various addictions (Johansson et al., 2006; O'Brien, 2005). In one experiment, O'Malley and coresearchers (2002) investigated the effects of naltrexone on 18 alcohol-dependent individuals, who consumed 20 to 40 drinks per week. During a six-day period prior to the experiment, half the participants took a daily dose of naltrexone while the other half took a daily placebo (nondrug). Six hours after the last dose, they were tested in a laboratory for their alcohol craving with the *Alcohol Urge Questionnaire* (Bohn et al., 1995). Next, in order to prime the desire for alcohol, participants were provided drinks of their favorite alcohol mixed with fruit juice. A test for any priming effects required the participants to make a choice eight times between receiving a drink now or receiving $3 tomorrow. Thus, the participant could consume a maximum of eight drinks or earn up to $24. If naltrexone effectively reduced the reinforcing value of alcohol, then the naltrexone participants should consume fewer drinks than the placebo participants should. This prediction was confirmed. The results in Figure 4.5 show that naltrexone reduced the urge for a drink and reduced the number of drinks that were consumed. In addition, naltrexone had the effect of making individuals drink more slowly. The researchers concluded that naltrexone reduced the reinforcing value of alcohol for alcohol-dependent individuals.

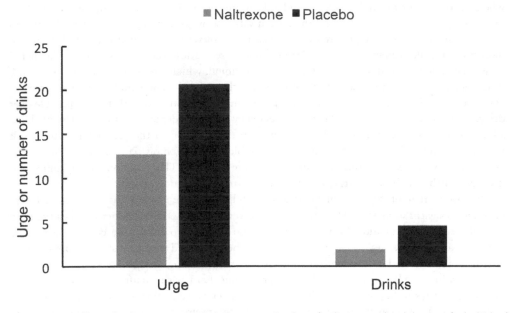

FIGURE 4.5 Effects of Naltrexone on Alcohol. Six consecutive days of naltrexone reduced the urge for a drink of alcohol and reduced the number of drinks consumed during a two-hour period.

Source: Adapted from "Naltrexone Decreases Craving and Alcohol Self-Administration in Alcohol-Dependent Subjects and Activates the Hypothalamo-Pituitary-Adrenocortical Axis" by S. S. O'Malley et al., 2002, *Psychopharmacology, 160,* Table 1, p. 22.

Naltrexone has also effectively curbed the craving for amphetamines and heroin (Comer et al., 2006; Jayaram-Lindström et al., 2008). For instance, patients who were seeking treatment for amphetamine dependence or heroin dependence showed several benefits from naltrexone compared to a placebo (no naltrexone). When receiving naltrexone, patients reduced their drug cravings. They also abstained from the drugs more during treatment, and were more likely to remain in the treatment program.

Loss of Self-Control

"Giving up smoking is the easiest thing in the world. I know because I've done it thousands of times," said Mark Twain. His struggle is that of many addicted individuals, who quit but then relapse. An explanation resides in the workings of the prefrontal cortex, which is part of the brain's reward circuitry. Located in back of the forehead, the prefrontal cortex engages in goal-setting, planning, decision-making, inhibiting impulses, and evaluating the consequences of behavior. The use of psychoactive drugs undermines this ability in several ways to the detriment of an individual trying to abstain from using drugs (Goldstein & Volkow, 2011). Foremost, addicted individuals lose self-control, as shown by the inability to manage their impulses. Consequently, they have impaired control over their drug use and often use compulsively (see Table 4.1). Also, when distressed, for example, addicted individuals are more likely to use drugs for relief. As a result, the prefrontal cortex evaluates the reward value of drugs as being greater than the reward value of alternatives. Consequently, there is increased motivation to obtain drugs and decreased motivation for alternative sources of pleasure, such as recreation, music, or friends. An addicted individual's attention is drawn toward drug-related stimuli, which strengthens the impulse to use drugs but also directs their attention away from other stimuli that could serve as sources of enjoyment. Finally, addicted individuals prefer the immediate gratification that drugs provide over delayed alternatives of pleasure. There is a tendency to be in denial and thus be less likely to admit the necessity of treatment. These changes in the function of the prefrontal cortex result from a reduction in the density of its neurons (Goldstein & Volkow, 2011). This reduction in neural density makes self-control of drug use more difficult. The function of dopamine also decreases in the prefrontal cortex, which results in increased drug cravings.

The involvement of the prefrontal cortex in the self-control of craving was demonstrated with *transcranial magnetic stimulation*. This procedure involves placing a coil near a person's head to send a small electric current into the region of the brain adjacent to where the coil is placed. The result is reduced activation of the brain's neurons in the stimulated area. Hayashi and coresearchers (2013) used this technique to determine if it would affect craving in cigarette smokers. First, the researchers increased craving in smokers by presenting them with pictures of smokers and the assurance that soon they would be allowed to smoke. However, prior to smoking, the smokers either received transcranial magnetic stimulation to the prefrontal cortex or a sham procedure as a control treatment. The magnetic stimulation reduced the smokers' cravings for cigarettes compared to the sham procedure. Furthermore, brain imaging showed that the reduced craving also occurred in other areas of the pleasure circuit (George & Koob, 2013; Hayashi et al., 2013).

Role of Environment in Addiction via Conditioning

Both psychological and neurological explanations describe what happens to the individual while craving and feeling euphoric from drug use. Both types of explanation, however, must still incorporate the role of the environment. In the case of craving, it never seems to disappear but lies dormant until the appropriate trigger emerges. Thus, it is important to know what promotes craving and how it develops. Conditioning theories go a long way in explaining how environmental stimuli can trigger craving and result in drug relapse. Although opponent-process theory implies that withdrawal and drug cravings eventually cease, it provides an incomplete picture (Solomon & Corbit, 1974). As noted by the young man in the example that opened the chapter, he was drug-free for over a year yet his withdrawal symptoms returned. In the other example, the young woman's craving for cocaine, dormant at the time, was suddenly activated on seeing the mirror. Thus, although an addict is not using drugs, craving in one form or another can be reinstated by the appropriate reminders.

Classical conditioning. Classical conditioning combined with opponent-process theory can explain the return of withdrawal symptoms and druglike euphoria. In his experiments on conditioned reflexes, Pavlov (1927) reports how a dog's reaction to morphine is conditionable. A dog's natural reaction to morphine (an unconditioned stimulus) consists of salivation, nausea, vomiting, and sleep (unconditioned responses). Preparation for the injection, such as seeing the removal of the syringe from its container, becomes the conditioned stimulus. After several days of repeated injections, the conditioned stimulus produces salivation and nausea (conditioned responses) before the actual injection. According to Solomon and Corbit (1974), during the process of repeated drug experiences, stimuli in the environment can become associated with a moderate degree of euphoria, as in the young woman's case, and also with withdrawal symptoms, as in the young man's case. Consequently, addicted individuals become motivated for their drug of choice.

To help understand classical conditioning, Stella Bastone in Toronto, Canada, created a YouTube video titled "Classical Conditioning: The Basics" here: www.youtube.com/watch?v=cP5l CleK-PM.

Conditioned compensatory versus conditioned druglike responses. How is it possible that conditioned responses can be similar to withdrawal symptoms at one time yet be similar to drug-unconditioned responses at another? The answer lies in the nature of the conditioned response. In classical conditioning, the conditioned response and the unconditioned response are usually the same. However, in the case of *paradoxical conditioning* the conditioned response is the opposite of the unconditioned response (Black, 1965). These conditioned responses are called *conditioned compensatory responses.* Thus, two types of drug-conditioned responses are possible. One conditioned response is the opposite of a drug reaction, while the other one mimics a drug reaction. According to a **conditioned compensatory response model**, a conditioned drug response is in the opposite direction of the unconditioned drug response. The compensatory response offsets the effects of a drug (such as morphine) and returns the body to its normal state to maintain homeostasis (Siegel, 2005). Siegel's (2016) compensatory model helps explain why nearly 13,000 people died from using heroin in 2015 according to the American Society of Addiction Medicine (2017). According to this model, the compensatory response occurs prior to the administration of a drug in order to prepare the body for the effects of the drug itself. One such effect is preparation for depressed breathing. However, in the absence of conditioned stimuli, compensatory responses will not occur. In this case, there is no preparation for depressed breathing. As a consequence, heroin injections can be fatal, as when the individual stops breathing completely. In contrast, the **conditioned druglike response model** proposes that conditioned drug stimuli are reminders that elicit conditioned responses similar to those evoked by the drug itself (Stewart et al., 1984). In either model, the desire for drugs returns.

Events that Lead to Drug Relapse

The motivation for drugs comes and goes. Even when an individual has quit using drugs for a time, she can *relapse*, which means going back to using drugs. Priming and the relief from stress are two major factors that contribute to drug relapse.

Drug priming with an unconditioned stimulus. "I'll bet you can't eat just one" is the slogan of a potato chip commercial. The slogan implies that the first bite increases your craving so strongly that further resistance is futile. **Priming** means that a strong craving for a drug can be reinstated with a single dose of alcohol, nicotine, cocaine, or heroin. Kirk and de Wit (2000) demonstrated priming with alcohol for social drinkers. During each experimental session, 22- to 25-year-old university undergraduates drank either a nonalcoholic beverage (a placebo) or one containing a 0.2-, 0.4-, or 0.8-gram dose of alcohol mixed with tonic water and lime juice. Participants were not informed what the beverage contained. After drinking, participants rated their reactions for "feel" the effect, "like" the effect, feel "high," and "want more" on a visual scale that ranged from 0 = *Not at all* or *Dislike a lot* to 100 = *A lot* or *Very much*. The results showed that all the ratings of the beverages increased above the placebo as the amount of alcohol increased. Participants felt the effects of the alcohol more, liked it more, experienced a greater high, and wanted more. All these effects indicate priming (Kirk & de Wit, 2000).

Human addicts who are trying to quit their drug habit also run into the problem of priming. A single cigarette, drink of alcohol, or drug injection can reestablish craving and reestablish the drug habit. For example, following their participation in a stop smoking program, participants smoked their first cigarette 58 days later. They smoked their second cigarette only nine days after that, with about half of the participants smoking their second cigarette within 24 hours after the first (Brandon et al., 1990). The first cigarette primed a craving for more cigarettes. Thus, it appears that, in trying to stop drinking, smoking, or using illicit drugs, one drink, smoke, or drug injection elicits the urge for another and another (Stewart et al., 1984). In other words, the motivation for the person's drug of choice returns.

Priming with a conditioned stimulus. Priming is also possible with conditioned stimuli that are intimately associated with the drug-taking procedure. In this chapter's opening vignette, the buildings and mirror on the coffee table are examples of conditioned stimuli associated with the use of cocaine. Drug-associated stimuli have been incorporated into virtual reality technology, which refers to a realistic environment created on a computer screen. Individuals interact with the environment visually but also through sound via headphones and by means of a mouse, keyboard, or joystick. Baumann and Sayette (2006) primed the desire for cigarettes by embedding them in a virtual reality neighborhood scene. They had smokers navigate a virtual environment that began from an apartment building to the street, past a news stand, and then into a restaurant/bar filled with patrons. During the first run through the virtual environment, cigarette stimuli were absent but those stimuli were present during the second run. On the second run, participants saw an open pack in the apartment, smokers on the street, and cigarettes for sale at the news stand, and entered the bar filled with patrons who smoked. The participants rated their urge to smoke at the start and end of each run and at specific locations where cigarettes were either absent or present. The smoking urge was measured with a 100-point scale that ranged from 0 = *absolutely no urge* to 100 = *the strongest urge I have ever experienced*. The smoking-associated stimuli indeed increased the urge to smoke. Figure 4.6 shows that, even when cigarette stimuli were absent, the urge to smoke increased from the beginning to the end of the virtual run. Many participants mentioned that, in spite of the absence of cigarettes, "there were many numerous unintentional and idiosyncratic cues that triggered their urges" (p. 486). Figure 4.6 also shows that the increase in the urge to smoke was greater when the virtual reality scenes were filled with the presence of cigarettes. The strongest smoking urges occurred in the presence of the bar scene that contained patrons who smoked.

Stress and drug cravings. Stressful events can vary in intensity and duration. The stress they induce comes from adverse life events, such as strained interpersonal relationships, the end of relationships by death or divorce, and also from neglect, abuse, violence or natural disasters. Stress is accompanied by the release of the stress hormones adrenaline (epinephrine) and cortisol, which arouse and energize the body. One of the consequences of stress is that individuals are more prone to begin drug use, to relapse, or to increase their frequency of use (Goeders, 2004; Sinha, 2008). Not only are real-life stressors responsible for increased drug use, but laboratory stressors can also contribute.

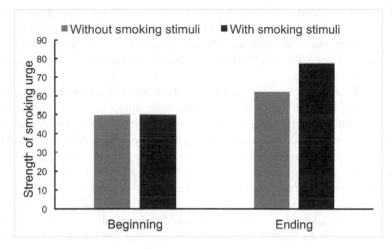

FIGURE 4.6 Priming Effects of Smoking Cues. Smokers traveled through a virtual neighborhood on a computer screen. When they encountered cues associated with smoking or cigarettes, their craving for a cigarette increased.

Source: Adapted from "Smoking Cues in a Virtual World Provoke Craving in Cigarette Smokers" by S. B. Baumann & M. A. Sayette, 2006, *Psychology of Addictive Behaviors, 20,* Table 2, p. 487.

To illustrate, Sinha and coresearchers (2006) induced stress in patients undergoing treatment for cocaine addiction by presenting an audio script of a very stressful situation, such as a romantic breakup, argument with family members, or being fired or laid off from work. On other days, patients listened to scripts of neutral situations, such as being at the beach, in the park, or a bubble bath. For each script, patients were to imagine the situation as it was being described. Afterwards, the patients' stress hormone levels were measured, as well as their anxiety level and cocaine cravings. The stressful situation increased the level of stress hormones, anxiety ratings, and the craving for cocaine. During a 90-day follow-up, greater laboratory stress was associated with quicker relapse and greater cocaine use. Using similar procedures, Sinha and coresearchers (2009) induced stress in individuals undergoing treatment for alcohol dependence. Their results showed that stress induction increased negative emotions (anger, fear, sadness), anxiety levels, and behavioral distress. These feelings were accompanied by an increased craving for alcohol. The use of alcohol from stress is negatively reinforced by the reduction of negative emotions. Moreover, stress also sensitizes an individual to the euphoric effects of a psychoactive drug, such as alcohol, thereby increasing its positive reinforcement value (Goeders, 2004).

Cognition and Addiction

The descriptions of drug addiction given thus far have been mostly mechanistic, with no mention of the role of cognitive processes. The addicted individual was described as reacting to stressful events and to drug-associated stimuli that evoke craving or withdrawal symptoms. The person was not seen as making an active attempt to approach or avoid these situations. Furthermore, mechanistic models minimize the possibility of a person willfully quitting. Therefore, trying to reduce or eliminate drug dependence would be difficult to accomplish. Bandura's (2006) agentic theory may be a way out of this difficulty. According to this theory, humans can intentionally create their circumstances. Thus, individuals have control over whether they want to continue exposing themselves to drugs.

A feature of the interplay between cognition and addiction is the **motivation for change** (DiClemente, 1999; DiClemente et al., 2004). This motivational factor represents change as a series of stages: willfully contemplating change, preparing for it, acting on it, and maintaining that change. For instance, a drug abuser begins by contemplating a change in his drug use by considering the pluses and minuses of such an action. Next, an individual might commit to change. As part of that commitment, for example, he might say, "I am planning to reduce my cigarette consumption by 10 percent, beginning next month." Then, when the time arrives, he initiates the plan and maintains his reduced cigarette intake, perhaps quitting eventually. His plan might be to start the day with a certain self-imposed cigarette allotment. If those are smoked prior to the end of the day, he will not seek more cigarettes. DiClemente (1999; DiClemente et al., 2004) points out that the success of motivation for change and eventually quitting depends on the incentives that are employed at each stage. Incentives imposed from outside are less effective than self-imposed ones. For example, court-ordered drug treatment is less effective than if a person decides for himself to seek treatment. Personal reasons for quitting are much more effective.

Section Recap

The main motivation for drug use is based on attaining pleasure (positive reinforcement) or reducing withdrawal symptoms (negative reinforcement). Various psychological theories have been proposed to explain these reinforcements. According to the *affective model of negative reinforcement*, repeated drug uses allow addicts to be sensitive to the symptoms that predict withdrawal. As a consequence, drug use occurs to prevent the anticipated negative affect. For *opponent-process theory*, the initial pleasurable reaction to a drug is held in check by an opponent process or drug-opposite effect characterized by dysphoria and withdrawal. The strengthening of the opponent process is responsible for drug tolerance and withdrawal. *Incentive sensitization theory* emphasizes that individuals are motivated by a drug's incentive value (anticipated pleasure) more than by its hedonic value (actual pleasure).

Psychological descriptions of drug abuse are reducible to parallel events in the brain, from where feelings of craving and euphoria emerge. Reinforcing events from psychoactive drugs emerge from the activation of neurons located in the brain's reward circuitry, which contains the nucleus accumbens and ventral tegmental area. Neurons in these areas communicate among themselves by way of chemicals known as *neurotransmitters*. These chemicals at the end of one neuron diffuse across a tiny gap to activate the next neuron. Psychoactive drugs affect neurotransmitters (such as dopamine) located in the nucleus accumbens, for example, where they activate neurons responsible for feelings of pleasure. Psychoactive drugs also produce their effects by either blocking the reuptake of dopamine or promoting its release. Drugs also interact with other neurotransmitters known as opioids to produce pleasure or alleviate withdrawal. *Antagonists* are substances capable of blocking the pleasurable effects of psychoactive drugs. As a consequence, antagonists can be used to reduce the motivation for cocaine, heroin, or alcohol. A consequence of long-term drug use is a reduction in the density of neurons of the prefrontal cortex. This results in poorer self-control over drug use. The involvement of the prefrontal cortex has been shown with transcranial magnetic stimulation. This procedure sends an electric current to the prefrontal cortex, which has been shown to lower the craving for cigarettes.

Much of craving is attributable to stimuli associated with drug use. For the *conditioned compensatory response model*, stimuli associated with drugs evoke conditioned responses that indicate withdrawal and are the opposite of drug-unconditioned responses—that is, they prepare the person for the effects of a drug. The *conditioned druglike response model*, on the other hand, states that the conditioned drug response is similar to the unconditioned drug response—that is, pleasure. Either model accounts for *priming*, which refers to the development of cravings whether by being exposed to the drug itself or to stimuli associated with the drug. Stress can also increase craving and increases the likelihood of drug use or relapse. Drugs now serve as negative reinforcers because their use alleviates painful stressful feelings. However, feelings of stress may also increase the positive reinforcing value of drugs. Based on agentic theory, a person can effect a *motivation for change*. This change represents states from willfully planning to reduce and eventually stopping drug use.

BEHAVIORAL ADDICTIONS

This is the case of a 20-year-old woman who had been running since age 10 and was now in leg casts because she severely sprained both ankles:

> I would sit all day and let my thoughts build up—I would go out at night to drink, I became so frustrated and confused I didn't realize what was important anymore. I ended up sick in bed for 2½ months because of my involvement in drinking and drugs because of my inability to run.
>
> (Morgan, 1979, p. 63)

This individual appears to demonstrate many of the symptoms of addiction described in Table 4.1. She craves running, suffers unpleasant withdrawal feelings because she is unable to run, and runs despite adverse consequences, and will probably relapse and start running again before she is fully recovered. This case raises the possibility that, in addition to drug addiction, there are behaviors that people can become addicted to. Do the characteristics of addiction listed in Table 4.1 also apply to exercise, gambling, and Internet use? Perhaps, although of these only gambling is considered an addictive disorder by the American Psychiatric Association (APA, 2013).

Exercise Addiction and Drug Addiction

Drugs are considered negative addictions because their use has long-term negative consequences. **Positive addiction** (Glasser, 1976), however, refers to compulsive behaviors that result in positive health consequences. This is a term applied mainly to runners and strenuous exercisers. Like drug use, running or strenuous exercise produces a runner's high or **exercise high**. This refers to a state of euphoria involving exhilaration, mood improvement, and eventually relaxation. People can become addicted to this feeling, and the effect of compulsive running or exercise can be equated with drug addiction.

Reinforcers. The rewards for running are the consequences that maintain this activity. Summers and associates (1983) asked marathoners who had been running about two years why they ran. Their reasons fell into three categories: physical health (being physically fit, losing weight), psychological health (feeling relaxed, enjoying life), and goal achievement (meeting a challenge, training for a marathon). Some reasons were classified as negative reinforcers, such as relieving depression and tension. The most rewarding consequence, however, was runner's high, which occurred in the latter part of or when finished with a run. Some runners reported experiencing "spin out," which is a detached, dreamy state of mind (Carmack & Martens, 1979; Summers et al., 1982). The length of a run seemed to correlate with the feelings characteristic of spin out. For example, runners who ran 40 minutes or more experienced spin out with a greater frequency than those who ran a shorter length of time. Other exercisers report "feeling high" or feeling like being "on speed" following periods of intense training (Griffiths, 1997).

The relationship between exercise intensity and "feeling high" has been verified in the laboratory. For instance, Blanchard and coresearchers (2002) had female university students exercise for 15 minutes on a stationary bicycle. Students felt significantly more positively engaged (happy, enthusiastic, upbeat) and revitalized as a result. These positive feelings seemed to increase with exercise intensity. Cox and coresearchers (2006) had women run on a treadmill for 33 minutes at either 60 percent (low intensity) or 80 percent (high intensity) of their maximum aerobic capacity, which refers to the body's ability to use oxygen. Post-exercise, the participants rated their positive well-being on a seven-point scale. The ratings showed that, as exercise intensity increased, positive well-being increased compared to a nonexercise control condition. In addition, positive well-being remained significantly high even 80 minutes post-exercise.

Exercise tolerance. While drug tolerance refers to the diminishing effects of a constant drug dose, running tolerance means a decline in the euphoric effects that result from running. One cause of this decline is that a person becomes physically conditioned so running becomes less stressful. To experience the same level of runner's high, a runner has to increase the mileage, frequency, or pace of running (Morgan, 1979). The upper limit of this increase, however, is the body's ability to tolerate such stress. When mileage increases, running injuries develop, such as hip pain, stress fractures, Achilles tendonitis, foot problems, and knee and back injuries. For example, a woman who appeared addicted to jujitsu exhibited exercise tolerance. She started training once a week, but after five years she now exercises every day of the week for longer and longer periods of time (i.e., six hours) (Griffiths, 1997).

The concept of tolerance points out one fundamental difference between exercise addiction and drug or alcohol addiction. Exercise addiction requires the individual to make considerable physical and mental effort, in contrast to what is required for drug or alcohol addiction (Cockerill & Riddington, 1996). In the case of exercise, an individual must become physically fit in order to experience euphoria, whereas drug or alcohol addiction requires less effort for the individual to experience any positive effects. Furthermore, when individuals are forced to withdraw from exercise owing to injuries, they are not likely to quickly resume their exercise addiction. It will be necessary for them to retrain to achieve a level of fitness necessary to again experience any euphoric effects (Cockerill & Riddington, 1996).

Withdrawal. For individuals who chronically exercise, deprivation results in symptoms akin to physiological and psychological withdrawal. These symptoms appear to reflect a dependence on exercise (Adams & Kirby, 2002). In an exercise-withdrawal experiment, Mondin and coresearchers (1996) paid regular exercisers $50 not to run, jog, or swim on Tuesday, Wednesday, and Thursday. Participants filled out various psychological scales each day in order to measure their moods before, during, and after their exercise deprivation. The results showed that state anxiety, tension, and depression increased from Monday to Wednesday and then decreased. These three indicators of the negative effects of exercise deprivation were greatest on the second day of deprivation, which indicates that withdrawal symptoms begin to occur after 48 hours. The decline in anxiety, tension, and depression on Thursday may indicate the participants' awareness that they could resume exercising the next day (Mondin et al., 1996).

In another exercise-withdrawal experiment, one group of regular male runners was paid not to run for two weeks. A control group of regular runners continued their usual running routine (Morris et al., 1990). Both groups filled out questionnaires measuring anxiety and depression before and during the enforced abstinence interval and after running resumed. The two groups did not differ in anxiety and depression before the abstinence interval and after running resumed. The effect of running deprivation became apparent during the second week, when the deprived runners reported greater anxiety and depression. In addition, the deprived runners complained of more social dysfunction and somatic (body) symptoms that developed during their first week of deprivation (Morris et al., 1990).

Addiction. Exercise dependence or addiction resembles the characteristics of substance use disorders summarized in Table 4.1. Ogden and associates (1997) found several similarities during the development of their *Exercise Dependence Questionnaire.* In the case of social impairment, exercise interfered with family, social, and work life. For instance, a person would report missing work in order to exercise. Individuals also experienced withdrawal, such as negative feelings from having missed exercising for some reason. A person would report being agitated or irritable when an exercise session was missed or hating being unable to exercise. In the case of risky use, people would exercise compulsively even though they were aware that their dependence on exercise was causing problems. For instance, a person would report feeling guilty about the amount of exercise, realize it was ruining her life, but feel unable to cut back. Ogden and associates (1997) found that these factors became more severe with either an increase in the number of years of exercise or an increase in the number of weekly hours of exercise, which reflects the tolerance component. Another scale, named the *Exercise Dependence Scale*, contains 21 questions that measure additional components of exercise addiction (Hausenblas & Downs, 2002). For instance, an individual's impaired control are probed by the extent he continues to exercise despite physical problems and the extent he feels unable to reduce the frequency of exercise, which is a case of compulsive exercise. A question relevant for exercise tolerance asks the extent a person feels a lack of benefit from his current level of exercise.

A copy of the *Exercise Dependence Scale-21* by Hausenblas & Downs (2002) is available here: www.personal.psu.edu/dsd11/EDS/index.html.

Opioids and Exercise-Induced Euphoria

Exercise such as running induces positive feelings. Are these feelings of an exercise high reducible to the actions of neurotransmitters associated with the brain's pleasure neurons? One hypothesis revolves around a set of opioid neurotransmitters, such as endorphins. The term endorphin refers to internal morphine (*endo* for endogenous or internal and *phin* for morphine). Endorphins are primarily located in the pain pathways and are responsible for reducing the negative effects of pain stimuli and stressors. Endorphins and opioids in general are released during strenuous exercise, which then act on pleasure neurons and neurons that are linked to them (Adams & Kirby, 2002; Nestler, 2005). Different experiments have demonstrated that exercise is linked to increases in subjective euphoria along with an increase of endorphins in a runner's blood. In one running experiment, higher levels of endorphins circulating in the runner's blood accompanied greater feelings of pleasure (Wildmann et al., 1986). In a later experiment, runners' positive mood increased and negative mood decreased following a 15-kilometer (9.3-mile) run. These mood changes were accompanied by increases in endorphins circulating in the runners' blood (Harte et al., 1995).

However, endorphins' and opioids' circulation in a runner's blood is not the same as their actions in the brain. It would be more convincing to show that increases in a runner's opioid level occur in those brain areas responsible for feelings of pleasure (runners' high). To investigate this possibility, Boecker and coresearchers (2008) scanned the brains of 10 runners during days without running and on other days following a two-hour run. Using positron emission tomography (PET) scans, the researchers measured opioid availability in the brain on both no-run and run days. In addition, the runners also reported their moods, especially euphoria on a visual scale that ranged from *no euphoria* (value = 0) to *strongest euphoria imaginable* (value = 100). Figure 4.7 shows that feelings of euphoria increased after the two-hour run compared to before

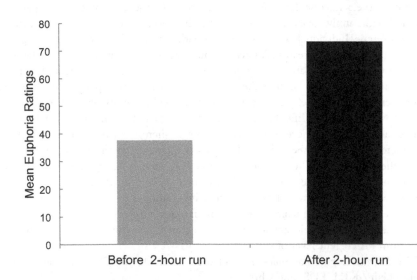

FIGURE 4.7 Effect of Running on Euphoria. Runners rated their level of euphoria on a 100-point scale before and after a two-hour run. Feelings of euphoria increased significantly following the two-hour run. In addition, PET scans showed a parallel increase in the release of opioids in three different brain regions.

Source: Adapted from "The Runner's High: Opioidergic Mechanisms in the Human Brain" by H. Boecker et al., 2008, *Cerebral Cortex, 18,* p. 2525.

the run. Ratings of happiness also increased. More important, however, is the association between the level of runners' high (euphoria) and the release of opioids in the brain. The degree of post-run euphoria correlated with the amount of opioids that had been released in three different brain regions—that is, greater euphoria was associated with more opioids.

Gambling Addiction

Gambling is an addictive disorder that shows the characteristics described in Table 4.1. It resembles substance use disorders, since it activates the brain's reward circuit similar to that of psychoactive drugs (APA, 2013). People may begin to gamble for fun and pleasure but then it becomes the most salient activity in their lives at the expense of other activities. For instance, individuals with a gambling disorder bet with increasing amounts of money, are unsuccessful in cutting back, and become preoccupied with gambling. They also crave gambling and become irritable when unable to do so. Furthermore, they risk social relationships, job security, or career opportunities as a result. According to Gamblers Anonymous, the first step in a 12-step recovery program for addicted gamblers is to admit that they are acting compulsively and are powerless over gambling.

The incidence of gambling addiction in society has grown as a result of increased gambling opportunities over the last few decades. Whereas previously illegal, now most states allow casinos, lotteries, and scratch-off cards. Gambling has also attained more social acceptance, especially when states use their gambling profits for the greater social good, such as education and counseling for gambling addicts. Shaffer and colleagues (1999) examined estimates of the prevalence of individuals with gambling problems. Prior to 1993, an estimated 0.84 percent of surveyed adults reported experiencing pathological gambling problems during the preceding year. This estimate rose significantly to 1.29 percent after 1993. Estimates of less severe gambling problems also rose significantly during this time. More recent surveys taken between 2005 and 2013 of over 13,000 university students estimated problem gambling at 10 percent (Nowak & Aloe, 2014).

Characteristics of addicted gamblers. One strategy for determining the powerful motivational effects of gambling is to uncover characteristics of addicted gamblers and the psychological costs incurred. With these goals in mind, Grant and Kim (2001) interviewed 131 individuals who had been diagnosed as pathological gamblers. These individuals played slot machines, cards, blackjack, and the lottery for an average of 16 hours per week and had lost an average of 45 percent of their annual income during the preceding 12 months. Interview results attest to the addictive nature of gambling. Nearly two-thirds of the individuals had maxed out their credit cards. After losing nearly all of their assets, nearly one-fourth of the addicted gamblers engaged in at least one form of illegal activity, such as writing bad checks, embezzling money at work, and committing tax fraud. Negative social consequences involved lying to friends and family members and experiencing marriage or work difficulties.

Gambling cravings. Like drug addiction, the urge or craving to gamble is a good predictor of whether or not an individual will gamble. If individuals can control their cravings, they can control their gambling. In an attempt to determine the influence of such urges on gambling, Young and Wohl (2009) constructed the *Gambling Craving Scale*. It consists of nine items measuring the strength of a person's need to gamble, how enjoyable it would be for them to gamble, and how much gambling would relieve any negative feelings. The researchers found that *Craving Scale* scores were greater for problem gamblers compared to non-problem gamblers.

In addition, individuals with higher scores were more likely to continue gambling in spite of experiencing losses. Another instrument for measuring a person's urge to gamble is provided in the Gamblers Anonymous home page. It consists of 20 questions that can help individuals decide if they are compulsive gamblers.

Gamblers Anonymous has a home page on the web here: www.gamblersanonymous.org.

Alcoholics Anonymous has a home page on the web here www.aa.org.

What sorts of stimuli can prime or trigger gambling urges? In a survey of 77 problem gamblers, Grant and coresearchers (2008) found that the most common triggers were having money (73 percent), followed by stress, loneliness, and advertisements for gambling (51 percent). The sights and sounds of casinos also prime gambling (Grant & Kim, 2001). These stimuli are capable of physiologically arousing compulsive gamblers. An example of an arousing stimulus occurs in slot machines, where wins are accompanied by the simulated sound of coins dropping into a metal tray. These sounds produce arousal when they accompany wins but also when they accompany losses disguised as wins (Dixon et al., 2010). For example, during one spin on a slot machine both wins and losses are possible. A person who bets $1 may win back only 70 cents, which is actually a loss of 30 cents. The slot machine still produces the noise accompanying the 70 cents. In such situations, if these sounds are pleasantly arousing (Sharpe, 2002), then they will reinforce gambling behavior even while the gambler is losing money (Dixon et al., 2010). Not all cues are equally effective in the priming of gambling, however. Most effective are cues associated with an individual's usual gambling activities. For instance, Wulfert and coresearchers (2009) showed experienced scratch-off lottery players and horse race bettors two videos. One video portrayed a person scratching off a lottery ticket and later another video portrayed a neck-to-neck finish in a thrilling horse race. Following each video, the individuals rated their urge to gamble on a 0–100 scale. Urges to gamble were much stronger when the gamblers had been exposed to cues associated with their preferred gambling activities. For example, horse race bettors had a greater urge to gamble when seeing a horse race compared to seeing the scratching of lottery tickets. The reverse was true for those who preferred to gamble with lottery tickets.

Dopamine and gambling. Like drugs and running, the pleasure derived from gambling may also depend on the extent that this activity activates dopamine and the pleasure circuits in the brain (Blum et al., 2000; Sharpe, 2002). However, not much is known about how gambling relates to dopamine. Gambling addiction does not occur in isolation but is often associated with other drug activities. For example, DeCaria and colleagues (1996) cite studies that compulsive gamblers are also likely to have problems with alcohol and illicit drugs. In their survey of 131 pathological gamblers, Grant and Kim (2001) found that 27 percent also suffered from alcohol dependence or abuse and 8.4 percent suffered from other forms of drug dependence or abuse. This association between pathological gambling and other forms of licit and illicit drug use warrants the search for common brain sites.

The drug naltrexone has been used effectively to help curb a person's appetite for heroin, cocaine, and alcohol (O'Brien, 2005). Naltrexone has also been employed to curb compulsive gambling. Kim and coresearchers (2001) tested the hypothesis that pathological gambling is triggered by its potential reward, which involves the actions of dopamine. Therefore, if naltrexone inhibits the release of dopamine, the impulse to gamble should decrease. The researchers gave one group of pathological gamblers a daily pill of naltrexone for 11 weeks, while another group of pathological gamblers received a placebo. Weekly evaluations showed that naltrexone reduced the symptoms of pathological gambling more than the placebo did. Naltrexone reduced the urge to gamble and reduced the subjective pleasure that gambling provided. In a follow-up investigation, Grant and coresearchers (2008) tested the effects of naltrexone for 18 weeks. They recruited 77 compulsive gamblers, who gambled an average of 13 hours and lost an average of $535 dollars per week. The researchers gave one group of pathological gamblers a daily pill of naltrexone for 18 weeks, while another group received a placebo. Beginning at week six and until the end of the program, naltrexone reduced urges and thoughts about gambling as well as reduced the amount of gambling. These results and the association of gambling with psychoactive drugs support the idea that the brain's reward circuitry involving dopamine is responsible for gambling addiction.

Internet Addiction

Internet addiction is new to the scene compared to drug and gambling addiction. But it is not officially recognized as an addictive behavior disorder (APA, 2013). However, some Internet users show many of the addiction characteristics described in Table 4.1 (Tao et al., 2010). This resemblance was noted by Block (2008), who emphasized four characteristics of Internet addiction. *Excessive use* of the Internet means that a person has less time to devote to other important activities, such as hygiene, social interactions, work, and school. Excessive use indicates impaired control (Table 4.1), since now the Internet dominates the person's time and behavior. *Withdrawal* results when a computer is inaccessible. It is accompanied by negative feelings, such as depression, tension, and anger. *Tolerance* of Internet use indicates that the individual needs more hours of computer use and better computer hardware and software. Finally, *negative repercussions* involve social impairment but also lying, fatigue, and low achievement.

Studies evaluating the extent of excessive Internet use began in the mid-1990s (Widyanto & Griffiths, 2006). Since then several questionnaires have been developed to measure the degree of an individual's Internet addiction. The *Internet Addiction Test* (developed by Kimberly Young) probes an individual's Internet use with 20 questions about salience, excessive use, neglect of work and of social life, and lack of control (Widyanto & McMurran, 2004). Another test, the *Compulsive Internet Use Scale*, employs 14 items to probe whether use interferes with sleep or social obligations, and whether it is mood altering (Meerkerk et al., 2009). It also measures how often a person finds it difficult to stop using the Internet, which implies a lack of control. People who scored high on the *Use Scale* spent more time on the Internet. Those individuals also reported that they felt their Internet use was a problem for them and that they felt addicted to the Internet (Meerkerk et al., 2009).

A copy of the Internet Addiction Test (IAT) created by Dr. Kimberly Young is available here: www.globaladdiction.org/dldocs/GLOBALADDICTION-Scales-InternetAddictionTest.pdf.

What is the prevalence of Internet addiction in the population? Aboujaoude and coresearchers (2006) conducted a random telephone survey of 2,513 individuals aged 18 or older. The survey asked questions that followed the indicators of behavioral addictions (Table 4.1) and questions from the *Internet Addiction Test* and the *Compulsive Internet Use Scale*. Figure 4.8 provides the percentage of respondents who felt various effects from excessive nonessential Internet use. The most frequently reported characteristics were the difficulty of staying away and being online too long. Preoccupation with the Internet while offline is the characteristic that resembles craving. It was the symptom most predictive of the other characteristics listed in Figure 4.8. The label

Internet addiction means that an individual acknowledges the following: nonessential use interferes with social relationships and preoccupies one's mind when offline, cutting down was unsuccessful, and often they stay online longer than intended. With these criteria as the bases, 0.7 percent of the sample was categorized as Internet addicts.

Related to Internet addiction is *compulsive texting*. This social phenomenon refers to an inordinate amount of time individuals devote to sending and receiving text messages. Lister-Landman and coresearchers (2015) investigated whether the frequency of texting could be considered compulsive, an indication of addiction. Under criteria listed in Table 4.1 on substance use disorders, compulsive texting results from impaired control—that is, the inability to reduce the frequency and time spent on the behavior. The researchers developed the *Compulsive Texting Scale* derived from the *Internet Addiction Test*. The *Scale* asks questions such as how often do you "Text longer than intended" or "Check your texts before doing something else that you need to do" or "Find yourself frustrated because you want to text but you have to wait" (p. 6). How often was measured on a five-point scale from 1 = *never* to 5 = *always*. The researchers asked 403 eighth- and eleventh-grade students how many text messages they sent per day. In addition, the researchers measured the students' adjustment to school, such as their grades, attitude, and perceived academic self-competence. They hypothesized that these measures were negatively associated with texting. The results showed that the students sent between 41 and 50 text messages

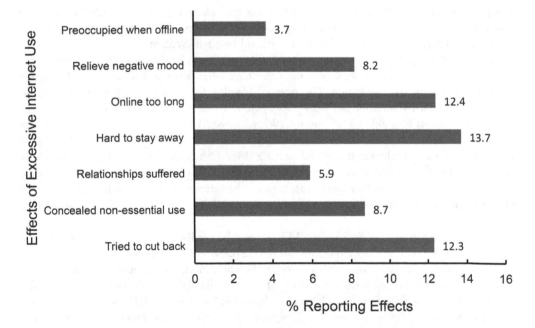

FIGURE 4.8 Stated Effects of Internet Use. Percentage of individuals reporting various detrimental effects of excessive Internet use.

Source: Adapted from "Potential Markers for Problematic Internet Use: A Telephone Survey of 2,513 Adults" by E. Aboujaoude et al., 2006, *CNS Spectrums, 11,* p. 751.

per day. Furthermore, there was evidence that the degree of compulsiveness, as measured by the *Compulsive Texting Scale*, and frequency of texting were associated with lower grades, poorer attitudes toward school, and lower academic self-confidence.

Section Recap

The use of psychoactive drugs is a negative addiction, while repeated strenuous exercise is a *positive addiction* because of the health benefits. However, extensive exercise also has characteristics of negative addiction. Exercise addiction is similar to drug addiction. Humans can develop a tolerance for exercise, show withdrawal symptoms when unable to exercise, and behave as if they are addicted. Exercise dependence scales measure the extent of a person's addiction. Strenuous exercise provides several positive reinforcers, the major one being the *exercise high*, which involves feelings of euphoria, exhilaration, positive mood, and relaxation. Based on brain imaging research, strenuous running releases opioids, which bind with neurons that are responsible for feelings of euphoria and exhilaration, known as runners' high.

Gambling is another addictive behavior that is pleasurable because it activates neurons in the brain's pleasure circuitry. This claim is based on the association between gambling behavior and drug or alcohol use. Naltrexone reduces the pleasure of alcohol, but can also reduce the urge to gamble and reduce the pleasure derived from gambling.

Finally, Internet addiction is a new entry into the scene of addictive behaviors, although it is not recognized as an addiction by the APA. Internet addiction is characterized by excessive use, which results in neglecting other aspects of life, and impaired control. Less than 1 percent of individuals are thought to be addicted to the Internet. Compulsive texting refers to a high frequency of texting and is associated with poor academic performance and attitude.

GLOSSARY

Term	Definition
Addiction	Also known as substance use disorder, it is characterized by the craving, compulsive use, loss of control, tolerance of psychoactive drugs and withdrawal symptoms due to drug abstinence
Addictive Behaviors	Compulsive activities often involving drugs that produce short-term pleasure at the expense of later negative consequences such as tolerance and withdrawal
Affective Model of Negative Reinforcement	Repeated drug use makes an addict sensitive to the unpleasant symptoms that predict drug withdrawal and thus takes drugs to avoid anticipated withdrawal
Alcohol	A psychoactive drug in the form of ethanol and served as beer, wine, or distilled spirits, such as vodka, rum, or gin
Antagonists	A drug that blocks the euphoric effects of psychoactive drugs and thus can curb people's cravings for drugs such as cocaine and alcohol
Attentional Bias	Addicted individuals pay more attention and remember drug stimuli better; more drawn to drug stimuli

continued . . .

GLOSSARY Continued

Term	Definition
Behavioral Genetics	A field of study that attempts to attribute behavior differences to genetic similarities/differences among people, as in the case of drug addiction
Cocaine	A psychoactive drug obtained from the coca plant. It produces a positive euphoric effect sometimes termed a full body orgasm
Conditioned Compensatory Response Model	A classically conditioned response that is opposite to the response produced by the unconditioned stimulus. The response prepares the individual for the actual drug experience
Conditioned Druglike Response Model	A classically conditioned response that mimics the actual response to the drug stimulus (drug-unconditioned stimulus)
Craving	An overpowering, uncontrollable urge for the drug that a person uses in order to experience the euphoric effect or to reduce withdrawal effects that result from abstinence
Disinhibition	Reduced social restraint especially in high-sensation-seekers that leads to alcohol and nicotine use, the tendency to party, gamble, and to engage in sex
Dopamine	A neurotransmitter that activates neurons in the brain's reward circuitry to produce feelings of pleasure and euphoria
Endorphin	Internal morphine located along pain pathways in the brain and responsible for producing exercise high
Exercise High	A positive euphoric feeling brought on by strenuous exercise, such as running producing runner's high
Hallucinogens	A psychoactive drug that enhances perception and mental stimulation and causes people to experience delusions, reality distortion, and hallucinations
Heritable	The idea that as the genetic similarity among people increases, their behavior similarity, such as the likelihood of drug experimentation and use, increases
Illicit Drugs	Their use is prohibited by the federal government. It is illegal (illicit) to use them
Impulsiveness	A characteristic of a person of heightened sensitivity to drug rewards and lack of foresight about the negative consequences that drugs produce
Incentive Sensitization Theory	The theory that repeated drug use becomes motivated more by a drug's incentive value (anticipated pleasure) than by its hedonic value (actual pleasure)
Internet Addiction	Internet use characterized by excessive use, withdrawal symptoms from not using, tolerance of use, and negative repercussion from too much use
Liability	The threshold along a genetic continuum at which people become susceptible to alcoholism when placed in an at-risk environment for alcohol use
Methamphetamines	A psychoactive drug derived from amphetamine that acts like a strong stimulant to produce increasing alertness and wakefulness
Motivation for Change	A motivational factor for quitting drugs that ranges from willfully contemplating change to preparing for it, acting on it, and maintaining it
Naltrexone	A neurotransmitter antagonist that reduces the reinforcing effects of a variety of psychoactive drugs. It is used to treat addiction by curbing drug craving and pleasure

continued . . .

GLOSSARY Continued

Term	Definition
Negative Addictions	An addiction in reference to psychoactive drugs that because of their use leads to long-term negative consequences
Negative Reinforcement	The removal of an unpleasant feeling by a response. For example, drugs remove the unpleasantness or agony of drug withdrawal symptoms
Negative Repercussions	The consequences of excessive or addictive Internet use characterized by social isolation, lying, arguing, low achievement, and fatigue
Neurotransmitter	A chemical substance whose action in the synapse between two neurons allows for the sending neuron to stimulate the next or receiving neuron
Opiates	A psychoactive drug (morphine, codeine, heroin) derived from the opium poppy that produces euphoria and reduces anxiety
Opponent-Process Theory	According to this theory, the initial pleasurable reaction to a drug is countered by an opponent process or drug-opposite effect that results in dysphoria and withdrawal when the drug wears off
Paradoxical Conditioning	This occurs in classical conditioning when the conditioned response occurs in the opposite direction to the unconditioned response
Positive Addiction	An addiction in reference to exercise (running) that leads to positive health consequences
Positive Reinforcement	A positive experience that results from a response. For example, drugs produce pleasure and euphoria
Priming	The reinstatement or increase in drug craving by a small dose of the drug or by stimuli associated with the drug
Psychoactive Drugs	Any chemical substance that alters a person's mood and behavior as a result of the drug's effect on the brain and can lead to dependence on the drug
Psychotherapeutics	A drug obtained by prescription for legitimate medical use as a pain reliever, tranquilizer, or sedative but now used for its euphoric effects only
Reuptake	Once a neurotransmitter has done its job of stimulating the next neuron, it is absorbed (taken up) by the sending neuron
Salience	Characteristic of addictive behavior that refers to the activity or the drug being the most prominent part of a person's life
Self-Control	The ability to override cravings and impulses that disrupt goal achievement. Drugs cause people to lose self-control. They use drugs compulsively, with lowered foresight of the consequences
Sensation-Seeking	A personality trait associated with seeking varied, intense, and novel sensations and the willingness to take risks to experience those sensations
Substance Use Disorder	The medical term for drug addiction, which is characterized by compulsive drug use, drug tolerance, and negative withdrawal symptoms when not using
Tolerance	When a person habituates to the stimulus effects of a psychoactive drug
Transcranial Magnetic Stimulation	A coil is placed near a person's head to send a small electric current into the adjacent region of the brain. The current reduces the activity of the brain's neurons in the stimulated area

continued ...

Continued

Term	Definition
Withdrawal Syndrome	The negative feelings of a drug-opposite effect (dysphoria) that results when addicted individuals abstain from using the psychoactive drug they are addicted to

REFERENCES

Aboujaoude, E., Koran, L. M., Gamel, N., Large, M. D., & Serpe, R. T. (2006). Potential markers for problematic internet use: A telephone survey of 2,513 adults. *CNS Spectrums, 11*, 750–755.

Adams, J., & Kirby, R. J. (2002). Excessive exercise as an addiction: A review. *Addiction Research and Theory, 10*, 415–437.

Agrawal, A., & Lynskey, M. T. (2008). Are there genetic influences on addiction: Evidence from family, adoption and twin studies. *Addiction, 103*, 1069–1081.

American Psychiatric Association (APA). (2013). *Diagnostic and statistical manual of mental disorders* (5th ed.). Arlington, VA: American Psychiatric Association.

American Society of Addiction Medicine (ASAM). (2017). Retrieved January 5, 2017, from www.asam.org/docs/default-source/advocacy/opioid-addiction-disease-facts-figures.pdf.

Badger, G. J., Bickel, W. K., Giordano, L. A., Jacobs, E. A., Loewenstein, G., & Marsch, L. (2007). Altered states: The impact of immediate craving on the valuation of current and future opioids. *Journal of Health Economics, 26*, 865–876.

Baker, T. B., Piper, M. E., McCarthy, D. E., Majeskie, M. R., & Fiore, M. C. (2004). Addiction motivation reformulated: An affective processing model of negative reinforcement. *Psychological Review, 111*, 33–51.

Ball, S. A. (2005). Personality traits, problems, and disorders: Clinical applications to substance use disorders. *Journal of Research in Personality, 39*, 84–102.

Bandura, A. (2006). Toward a psychology of human agency. *Perspectives on Psychological Science, 1*, 164–180.

Baumann, S. B., & Sayette, M. A. (2006). Smoking cues in a virtual world provoke craving in cigarette smokers. *Psychology of Addictive Behaviors, 20*, 484–489.

Berridge, K. C. (2007). The debate over dopamine's role in reward: The case for incentive salience. *Psychopharmacology, 191*, 391–431.

Berridge, K. C., Robinson, T. E., & Aldridge, J. W. (2009). Dissecting components of reward: "Liking", "wanting", and learning. *Current Opinions in Pharmacology, 9*, 65–73.

Black, A. H. (1965). Cardiac conditioning in curarized dogs: The relationship between heart rate and skeletal behaviour. In W. F. Prokasy (Ed.), *Classical conditioning: A symposium* (pp. 20–47). New York, NY: Appleton-Century-Crofts.

Blanchard, C. M., Rodgers, W. M., Courneya, K. S., & Spence, J. C. (2002). Moderators of the exercise/feeling-state relationship: The influence of self-efficacy, baseline, and in-task feeling states at moderate- and high-intensity exercise. *Journal of Applied Social Psychology, 32*, 1379–1395.

Block, J. J. (2008). Issues for DSM-V: Internet addiction. *American Journal of Psychiatry, 165*, 306–307.

Blum, K., Braverman, E. R., Holder, J. M., Lubar, J. F., Monastra, V. J., Miller, D., . . . Comings, D. E. (2000). Reward deficiency syndrome: A biogenetic model for the diagnosis and treatment of impulsive, addictive, and compulsive behaviors. *Journal of Psychoactive Drugs, 32* (supplement), 1–68.

Boecker, H., Sprenger, T., Spilker, M. E., Henriksen, G., Koppenhoefer, M., Wagner, K. J., . . . Tolle, T. R. (2008). The runner's high: Opioidergic mechanisms in the human brain. *Cerebral Cortex, 18*, 2523–2531.

Bohn, M. J., Krahn, D. D., & Staehler, B. A. (1995). Development and initial validation of a measure of drinking urges in abstinent alcoholics. *Alcoholism: Clinical and Experimental Research, 19*, 600–606.

Boileau, I., Dagher, A., Leyton, M., Krzysztof, W., Booij, L., Diksic, M., & Chawki, B. (2007). Conditioned dopamine release in humans: A positron emission tomography [^{11}C]Raclopride study with amphetamine. *The Journal of Neuroscience, 27*, 3998–4003.

Brandon, T. H., Tiffany, S. T., Obremski, K. M., & Baker, T. B. (1990). Postcessation cigarette use: The process of relapse. *Addictive Behaviors, 15,* 105–114.

Broms, U., Silventoinen, K., Madden, P. A. F., Heath, A. C., & Kaprio, J. (2006). Genetic architecture of smoking behavior: A study of Finnish adult twins. *Twin Research and Human Genetics, 9,* 64–72.

Carmack, M. A., & Martens, R. (1979). Measuring commitment to running: A survey of runners' attitudes and mental states. *Journal of Sport Psychology, 1,* 25–42.

Childress, A. R., Ehrman, R., Rohsenow, D. J., Robbins, S. J., & O'Brien, C. P. (1992). Classically conditioned factors in drug dependence. In J. H. Lowinson, P. Ruiz, R. B. Millman, & J. G. Langrod (Eds.), *Substance abuse: A comprehensive textbook* (2nd ed., pp. 56–69). Baltimore, MD: Williams & Wilkins.

Cockerill, I. M., & Riddington, M. E. (1996). Exercise dependence and associated disorders: A review. *Counseling Psychology Quarterly, 9,* 119–129.

Comer, S. D., Sullivan, M. A., Yu, E., Rothenberg, J. L., Kleber, H. D., Kampman, K., . . . O'Brien, C. P. (2006). Injectable, sustained-release naltrexone for the treatment of opioid dependence: A randomized, placebo-controlled trial. *Archives of General Psychiatry, 63,* 210–218.

Cox, R. H., Thomas, T. R., Hinton, P. S., & Donahue, O. M. (2006). Effects of acute bouts of aerobic exercise of varied intensity on subjective mood experiences in women of different age groups across time. *Journal of Sport Behavior, 29,* 40–59.

Cox, S. M. L., Benkelfat, C., Dagher, A., Delaney, J. S., Durand, F., McKenzie, S. A., . . . Leyton, M. (2009). Striatal Dopamine Responses to Intranasal Cocaine Self-Administration in Humans. *Biological Psychiatry, 65,* 846–850.

Dawe, S., Gullo, M. J., & Loxton, N. J. (2004). Reward drive and rash impulsiveness as dimensions of impulsivity: Implications for substance misuse. *Addictive Behaviors, 29,* 1389–1405.

de Wit, H. (2008). Impulsivity as a determinant and consequence of drug use: A review of underlying processes. *Addiction Biology, 14,* 22–31.

DeCaria, C. M., Hollander, E., Grossman, R., Wong, C. M., Mosovich, S. A., & Cherkasky, S. (1996). Diagnosis, neurobiology, and treatment of pathological gambling. *Journal of Clinical Psychiatry, 57* (supplement 8), 80–84.

DiClemente, C. (1999). Motivation for change: Implications for substance abuse treatment. *Psychological Science, 10,* 209–213.

DiClemente, C. C., Schlundt, D., & Gemmell, L. (2004). Readiness and stages of change in addiction treatment. *The American Journal on Addictions, 13,* 103–119.

DiFranza, J. R., Savageau, J. A., Fletcher, K., O'Loughlin, J., Pbert, L., Ockene, J. K., . . . Wellman, R. J. (2007). Symptoms of tobacco dependence after brief intermittent use: The development and assessment of nicotine dependence in youth-2 study. *Archives of Pediatrics & Adolescent Medicine, 161,* 704–710.

Dixon, M. J., Harrigan, K. A., Sandhu, R., Collins, K., & Fugelsang, J. A. (2010). Losses disguised as wins in modern multi-line video slot machines. *Addiction, 105,* 1819–1824.

Dom, G., D'haene, P., Hulstijn, W., & Sabbe, B. (2006). Impulsivity in abstinent early- and late-onset alcoholics: Differences in self-report measures and a discounting task. *Addiction, 101,* 50–59.

Doran, N., McChargue, D., & Cohen, L. (2007). Impulsivity and the reinforcing value of cigarette smoking. *Addictive Behaviors, 32,* 90–98.

Doubeni, C. A., Reed, G., & DiFranza, J. R. (2010). Early course of nicotine dependence in adolescent smokers. *Pediatrics, 125,* 1127–1133.

Garrett, B. E., & Griffiths, R. R. (2001). Intravenous nicotine and caffeine: Subjective and physiological effects in cocaine abusers. *The Journal of Pharmacology and Experimental Therapeutics, 296,* 486–494.

George, O., & Koob, G. F. (2013). Control of craving by the prefrontal cortex. *Proceedings of the National Academy of Sciences, 110,* 4165–4166.

Glasser, W. (1976). *Positive addiction.* New York, NY: Harper & Row.

Goeders, N. E. (2004). Stress, motivation, and drug addiction. *Current Directions in Psychological Science, 13,* 33–35.

Goldman, D., Oroszi, G., & Ducci, F. (2005). The genetics of addictions: Uncovering the genes. *Nature Reviews Genetics, 6,* 521–532.

Goldstein, R. Z., & Volkow, N. D. (2011). Dysfunction of the prefrontal cortex in addiction: Neuroimaging findings and clinical implications. *Nature Reviews Neuroscience, 12,* 652–669.

Grant, J. E., & Kim, S. W. (2001). Demographic and clinical features of 131 adult pathological gamblers. *Journal of Clinical Psychiatry, 62,* 957–962.

Grant, J. E., Suck, W. K., & Hartman, B. K. (2008). A double-blind, placebo-controlled study of the opiate antagonist Naltrexone in the treatment of pathological gambling urges. *Journal of Clinical Psychiatry, 69,* 783–789.

Griffiths, M. (1997). Exercise addiction: A case study. *Addiction Research, 5,* 161–168.

Griffiths, R. R., Bigelow, G. E., & Heningfield, J. E. (1980). Similarities in animal and human drug-taking behavior. In N. K. Mello (Ed.), *Advances in substance abuse: Behavioral and biological research* (pp. 1–90). Greenwich, CT: JAI.

Harris, A. C., & Gewirtz, J. D. (2005). Acute opioid dependence: Characterizing the early adaptations underlying drug withdrawal. *Psychopharmacology, 178,* 353–366.

Harte, J. L., Eifert, G. H., & Smith, R. (1995). The effects of running and meditation on beta-endorphin, corticotropin-releasing hormone and cortisol in plasma, and on mood. *Biological Psychology, 40,* 251–265.

Hausenblas, H. A., & Downs, D. S. (2002). How much is too much? The development and validation of the exercise dependence scale. *Psychology and Health, 17,* 387–404.

Hayashi, T., Ko, J. H., Strafella, A. P., & Dagher, A. (2013). Dorsolateral prefrontal and orbitofrontal cortex interactions during self-control of cigarette craving. *Proceedings of the National Academy of Sciences, 110,* 4422–4427.

Hittner, J. B., & Swickert, R. (2006). Sensation seeking and alcohol use: A meta-analytic review. *Addictive Behaviors, 31,* 1383–1401.

Hur, Y-M., & Bouchard, Jr., T. J. (1997). The genetic correlation between impulsivity and sensation-seeking traits. *Behavior Genetics, 27,* 455–463.

Hyman, S. E., Malenka, R. C., & Nestler, E. J. (2006). Neural mechanisms of addiction: The role of reward-related learning and memory. *Annual Review of Neuroscience, 29,* 565–598.

Jaffe, J. H., & Anthony, J. C. (2005). Substance-related disorders. In B. J. Sadock & V. A. Sadock (Eds.), *Comprehensive textbook of psychiatry: Volume I* (8th ed., pp. 1137–1168). Philadelphia, PA: Lippincott Williams & Wilkins.

Jayaram-Lindström, N., Hammarberg, A., Beck, O., & Franck, J. (2008). Naltrexone for the treatment of amphetamine dependence: A randomized, placebo-controlled trial. *The American Journal of Psychiatry, 165,* 1442–1448.

Johansson, B. A., Berglund, M., & Lindgren, A. (2006). Efficacy of maintenance treatment with naltrexone for opioid dependence: A meta-analytical review. *Addiction, 101,* 491–503.

Kendler, K. S., Jacobson, K. C., Prescott, C. A., & Neale, M. C. (2003). Specificity of genetic and environmental risk factors for use and abuse/dependence of cannabis, cocaine, hallucinogens, sedatives, stimulants, and opiates in male twins. *American Journal of Psychiatry, 160,* 687–695.

Kendler, K. S., Thornton, L. M., & Pedersen, N. L. (2000). Tobacco consumption in Swedish twins reared apart and reared together. *Archives of General Psychiatry, 57,* 886–892.

Kim, S. W., Grant, J. E., Adson, D. E., & Shin, Y. C. (2001). Double-blind naltrexone and placebo comparison study in the treatment of pathological gambling. *Biological Psychiatry, 49,* 914–921.

Kirk, J. M., & de Wit, H. (2000). Individual differences in the priming effect of ethanol in social drinkers. *Journal of Studies on Alcohol, 61,* 64–71.

Koob, G. F., & Le Moal, M. (2008). Addiction and the brain antireward system. *Annual Review of Psychology, 59,* 29–53.

Lessov, C. N., Swan, G. E., Ring, H. Z., Khroyan, T. V., & Lerman, C. (2004). Genetics and drug use as a complex phenotype. *Substance Use and Misuse, 39,* 1515–1569.

Lister-Landman, K. M., Domoff, S. E., & Dubow, E. F. (2015). The role of compulsive texting in adolescents' academic functioning. *Psychology of Popular Media Culture,* 1–15. http://dx.doi.org/10.1037/ppm0000100.

Maes, H. H., Neale, M. C., Kendler, K. K., Martin, N. G., Heath, A. C., & Eaves, L. J. (2006). Genetic and cultural transmission of smoking initiation: An extended twin kinship model. *Behavior Genetics, 36,* 795–808

McGue, M. (1999). The behavioral genetics of alcoholism. *Current Directions in Psychological Science, 8,* 109–115.

Meerkerk, G. J., Van Den Eijnden, R. J. J. M., Vermulst, A. A., & Garretsen, H. F. L. (2009). The Compulsive Internet Use Scale (CIUS): Some psychometric properties. *CyberPsychology and Behavior, 12,* 1–6.

Mondin, G. W., Morgan, W. P., Piering, P. N., Stegner, A. J., Stotesbery, C. L., Trine, M. R., & Wu, M. Y. (1996). Psychological consequences of exercise deprivation in habitual exercisers. *Medicine and Science in Sports and Exercise, 29,* 1199–1203.

Morgan, W. P. (1979). Negative addiction in runners. *Physician and Sports Medicine, 7,* 57–70.

Morris, M., Steinberg, H., Sykes, E. A., & Salmon, P. (1990). Effects of temporary withdrawal from regular running. *Journal of Psychosomatic Research, 34,* 493–500.

Nestler, F. I. (2005). Is there a common molecular pathway for addiction? *Nature Neuroscience, 8,* 1445–1449.

Nowak, D. E., & Aloe, A. M. (2014). The prevalence of pathological gambling among college students: A meta-analytic synthesis, 2005–2013. *Journal of Gambling Studies, 30,* 819–843.

O'Brien, C. P. (2005). Anticraving medications for relapse prevention: A possible new class of psychoactive medications. *The American Journal of Psychiatry, 162,* 1423–1431.

Ogden, J., Veale, D., & Summers, Z. (1997). The development and validation of the exercise dependence questionnaire. *Addiction Research, 5,* 343–355.

O'Malley, S. S., Krishnan-Sarin, S., Farren, C., Sinha, R., & Kreek, M. J. (2002). Naltrexone decreases craving and alcohol self-administration in alcohol-dependent subjects and activates the hypothalamo-pituitary-adrenocortical axis. *Psychopharmacology, 160,* 19–29.

Ostafin, B. D., Marlatt, G. A., & Troop-Gordon, W. (2010). Testing the incentive-sensitization theory with at-risk drinkers: Wanting, liking, and alcohol consumption. *Psychology of Addictive Behaviors, 24,* 157–162.

Patton, J. H., Stanford, M. S., & Barratt, E. S. (1995). Factor structure of the Barratt Impulsiveness Scale. *Journal of Clinical Psychology, 51,* 768–774.

Pavlov, I. P. (1927). *Conditioned reflexes.* New York, NY: Dover.

Perkins, K. A., Gerlach, D., Broge, M., Grobe, J. E., & Wilson, A. (2000). Greater sensitivity to subjective effects of nicotine in nonsmokers high in sensation seeking. *Experimental and Clinical Psychopharmacology, 8,* 462–471.

Pierce, R. C., & Kumaresan, V. (2006). The mesolimbic dopamine system: The final common pathway for the reinforcing effect of drugs of abuse? *Neuroscience and Biobehavioral Reviews, 30,* 215–238.

Plomin, R., DeFries, J. C., Knopik, V. S., & Neiderhiser, J. M. (2013). *Behavioral genetics* (6th ed.). New York, NY: Worth.

Robinson, T. E., & Berridge, K. C. (1993). The neural basis of drug craving: An incentive-sensitization theory of addiction. *Brain Research Reviews, 18,* 247–291.

Robinson, T. E., & Berridge, K. C. (2003). Addiction. *Annual Review of Psychology, 54,* 25–53.

Robinson, T. E., & Berridge, K. C. (2008). The incentive sensitization theory of addiction: Some current issues. *Philosophical Transactions of the Royal Society, 363,* 3137–3146.

Shaffer, H. J., Hall, M. N., & Vander Bilt, J. (1999). Estimating the prevalence of disordered gambling behavior in the United States and Canada: A research synthesis. *American Journal of Public Health, 89,* 1369–1374.

Sharpe, L. (2002). A reformulated cognitive-behavioral model of problem gambling: A biopsychosocial perspective. *Clinical Psychology Review, 22,* 1–25.

Siegel, S. (2005). Drug tolerance, drug addiction, and drug anticipation. *Current Directions in Psychological Science, 14,* 296–300.

Siegel, S. (2016). The heroin overdose mystery. *Current Directions in Psychological Science, 25,* 375–379.

Sigvardsson, S., Bohman, M., & Cloninger, C. R. (1996). Replication of the Stockholm adoption study of alcoholism. *Archives of General Psychiatry, 53,* 681–687.

Sinha, R. (2008). Chronic stress, drug use, and vulnerability to addiction. *Annals of the New York Academy of Sciences, 1141,* 105–130.

Sinha, R., Fox, H. C., Hong, K. A., Bergquist, K., Bhagwagar, Z., & Siedlarz, K. M. (2009). Enhanced negative emotion and alcohol craving, and altered physiological responses following stress and cue exposure in alcohol dependent individuals. *Neuropsychopharmacology, 34,* 1198–1208.

Sinha, R., Garicia, M., Paliwal, P., Kreek, M. J., & Rounsaville, B. J. (2006). Stress-induced cocaine craving and hypothalamic-pituitary-adrenal responses are predictive of cocaine relapse outcomes. *Archives of General Psychiatry, 63,* 324–331.

Smith, K. S., Mahler, S. V., Peciña, S., & Berridge, K. C. (2010). Hedonic hotspots: Generating sensory pleasure in the brain. In M. L. Kringelbach & K. C. Berridge (Eds.), *Pleasures of the brain* (pp. 27–49). New York, NY: Oxford University Press.

Solomon, R. L. (1980). The opponent-process theory of acquired motivation: The costs of pleasure and the benefits of pain. *American Psychologist, 35,* 691–712.

Solomon, R. L., & Corbit, J. D. (1974). An opponent-process theory of motivation: 1. Temporal dynamics of affect. *Psychological Review, 81,* 119–145.

Spencer, H. (1881/1977). *The principles of psychology.* Boston, MA: Longwood.

Stacy, A. W., & Wiers, R. W. (2010). Implicit cognition and addiction: A tool for explaining paradoxical behavior. *Annual Review of Clinical Psychology, 6,* 551–575.

Stewart, J., de Wit, H., & Eikelboom, R. (1984). Role of unconditioned and conditioned drug effects in the self-administration of opiates and stimulants. *Psychological Review, 91,* 251–268.

Summers, J. J., Machin, V. J., & Sargent, G. I. (1983). Psychosocial factors related to marathon running. *Journal of Sport Psychology, 5,* 314–331.

Summers, J. J., Sargent, G. I., Levey, A. J., & Murray, K. D. (1982). Middle-aged, nonelite marathon runners: A profile. *Perceptual and Motor Skills, 54,* 963–969.

Tangney, J. P., Baumeister, R. F., & Boone, A. L. (2004). High self-control predicts good adjustment, less pathology, better grades, and interpersonal success. *Journal of Personality, 72,* 271–324.

Tao, R., Huang, X., Wang, J., Zhang, H., Zhang, Y., & Li, M. (2010). Proposed diagnostic criteria for internet addiction. *Addiction, 105,* 556–564.

Widyanto, L., & Griffiths, M. (2006). Internet addiction: A critical review. *International Journal of Mental Health and Addiction, 4,* 31–51.

Widyanto, L., & McMurran, M. (2004). The psychometric properties of the Internet Addiction Test. *CyberPsychology and Behavior, 7,* 443–450.

Wildmann, J., Kruger, A., Schmole, M., Niemann, J., & Matthaei, H. (1986). Increase of circulating beta-endorphin-like immunoreactivity correlates with the changes in feeling of pleasantness after running. *Life Sciences, 38,* 997–1003.

Wulfert, E., Maxson, J., & Bianca, J. (2009). Cue-specific reactivity in experienced gamblers. *Psychology of Addictive Behaviors, 23,* 731–735.

Young, M. M., & Wohl, M. J. A. (2009). The Gambling Craving Scale: Psychometric validation and behavioral outcomes. *Psychology of Addictive Behaviors, 23,* 512–522.

Zuckerman, M. (1994). *Behavioral expressions and biosocial bases of sensation seeking.* Cambridge: Cambridge University Press.

Zuckerman, M. (2002). Genetics of sensation seeking. In J. Benjamin, R. P. Ebstein, & R. H. Belmaker (Eds.), *Molecular genetics and the human personality* (pp. 193–210). Washington, DC: American Psychiatric Publishing.

Zuckerman, M., Ball, S., & Black, J. (1990). Influence of sensation seeking, gender, risk appraisal, and situational motivation on smoking. *Addictive Behaviors, 15,* 209–220.

CHAPTER 5

Homeostasis: Temperature, Thirst, Hunger, and Eating

A hungry stomach will not allow its owner to forget it, whatever his cares and sorrows.

Homer, 800 B.C.

Hunger is the first course of a good dinner.

A French proverb

The body is a well-functioning machine that requires energy for motivation. But what is the source of this energy? This question and the following serve as guides for this chapter:

1. What internal physiological changes motivate humans to adjust their body temperature, fluid balance, and energy levels?
2. How do the psychological sensations of being cold, hot, thirsty, or hungry motivate behavior toward temperature regulation, drinking, and eating?
3. Is hunger the only motivation for eating, or do food characteristics also determine what and how much people eat?
4. Are there individual differences among people and their situations that determine what and how much they eat?

INTERNAL FACTORS OF BODY REGULATION

Individual accounts of extreme food or water deprivation provide insights into hunger and thirst motivation. In the late 1800s, for example, the explorer Sven Hedin suffered the tortures of thirst on a journey across a desert during which men and camels died from lack of water. What follows is his emotional reaction when he finally discovers a pool of water:

> I stood on the brink of a little pool filled with fresh, cool water—beautiful water! It would be vain for me to try to describe the feelings which now overpowered me. They may be imagined; they cannot be described. Before drinking I counted my pulse: it was forty-nine. Then I took the tin box out of my pocket, filled it, and drank. How sweet that water tasted! Nobody can conceive it who has not been within an ace of dying of thirst. I lifted the tin to my lips, calmly, slowly, deliberately, and drank, drank, drank, time after time. How delicious! What exquisite pleasure! The noblest wine pressed out of the grape, the divinest nectar ever made, was never half so sweet. My hopes had not deceived me. The star of my fortunes shone as brightly as ever it did. . . . I felt how that cold, clear, delicious water infused new energy into me. Every blood-vessel and tissue of my body sucked up the life-giving liquid like a sponge. My pulse, which had been so feeble, now beat strong again. . . . In a word, I felt my body was imbibing fresh life and fresh strength. It was a solemn, an awe-inspiring moment.

(Wolf, 1958, p. 144)

Hedin's strong pleasurable reaction to finding and drinking water indicates the interplay between his physiological and psychological demand for water, on the one hand, and the satisfaction that water can provide, on the other. In addition to the effects of water, how do physiological changes and psychological sensations motivate temperature regulation, hunger, and eating?

Homeostasis and Allostasis

The belief that internal demands of the body serve as a source of motivation begins with an idea formulated by the French physiologist Claude Bernard (1878/1961). He hypothesized a stable *milieu interieur* (internal environment) of fluids that bathe the body's 60 to 100 trillion cells. Walter Cannon (1939), a Harvard physiologist, expanded the work of Bernard and coined the term **homeostasis** (*stasis* meaning staying and *homeo* meaning the same) to describe the constant conditions maintained in the body. Disturbances from both inside and outside the body, such as fluid loss by sweating or environmental temperature change, are counteracted by body processes in order to maintain a stable internal environment. A similar concept **allostasis** (*allo* meaning variable) refers to maintaining internal stability by making changes that promote coping with anticipated environmental demands that can disrupt homeostasis (Ramsay & Woods, 2014).

Negative Feedback System

How is a stable internal environment maintained, such as a stable indoor temperature? Homeostasis depends on a **negative feedback system**, which is a self-correcting process that reduces the discrepancy between a desired state and an actual state. A desired state or *set point* is a condition crucial for life, comfort, or safety. The actual state of the system is compared to the set point. If a difference (discrepancy) is detected, a self-correction is made. The self-correction stops when the discrepancy reaches zero. A household furnace and air conditioner are common examples of a negative feedback system. The set point is the desired room temperature—for instance, 70°F. A comparator in the thermostat compares actual room temperature to the set point temperature. The room temperature is discrepant when it is either above or below the set point temperature. If above, self-correction occurs when the air conditioner turns on to cool the air back down to the set point temperature. If below, self-correction occurs when the furnace turns on to heat the air back up to the set point temperature. In either case, when the discrepancy reaches zero the comparator turns off the air conditioner or furnace.

A description of homeostasis and a negative feedback system illustrated for body temperature control is describe in a YouTube video titled "Introduction to Homeostasis" here: www.youtube. com/watch?v=-W7kAyUQT0E.

Allostasis works a bit differently to maintain a stable house temperature. First, the set point can change to anticipate future external temperatures that exist during winter and summer. So, the winter thermostat setting may change to 68°F and the summer setting to 75°F. The negative feedback system now operates around whichever set point temperature is in effect. In other words, set points can change and serve as new references for homeostasis. However, it is possible that the set point becomes misaligned with the season, such as high in winter and low in summer. In that case, the air conditioner or furnace operates around an inappropriate or inefficient set point.

Effects of Deviation from Set Point

How does the negative feedback system apply to homeostasis or allostasis? Humans have set points for different physiological states such as body temperature, fluid levels, energy, and various nutrients. A discrepancy between the set point and the actual physiological state defines a **physiological need**. For example, humans have a physiological need to maintain a constant or set point of body temperature, salt concentration, fluid level, and blood glucose level.

Incentives that reduce a physiological need or restore homeostasis increase pleasure. Cabanac (1971, 2010) discovered that whether temperature, odor, and taste stimuli produced pleasant or painful sensations depends on the person's internal state or physiological need. Stimulus sensations are judged pleasant if they decrease deviations from homeostasis—that is, reduce a physiological need. However, they are judged unpleasant if they increase the deviation from homeostasis—that is, increase the physiological need. Cabanac coined the term **alliesthesia** (*allios* meaning changed and *ethesia* meaning sensation) to refer to changes in a person's *milieu interieur* that determine whether a stimulus is judged pleasant or unpleasant. Hedin's description of drinking water as "delicious" and as "exquisite pleasure" illustrates how his strong physiological need for water— that is, his changed internal state—caused water to have this sensation. Alliesthesia motivated him to drink to restore his body's water level. Similarly, food is delicious to a hungry person and induces eating to restore the body's energy supply.

Thermoregulation

During the summer an individual is more likely to feel hot and in winter to feel cold. When skin temperature rises, the body makes a series of involuntary reactions, such as dilating blood vessels, sweating, and feeling warm. When skin temperature drops the body makes an opposite set of reactions, constricting blood vessels, shivering, and feeling cold. Feeling warm or cold motivates voluntary behavior to reduce the discomfort of those sensations before any involuntary changes become intense (Schlader et al., 2013). When feeling cold, a person voluntarily puts on a sweater to reduce the cold sensation, or because "it feels good" to warm up. When feeling hot, a person voluntarily takes off a sweater to reduce the hot sensation, or because "it feels good" to become less hot. Whether the sweater feels good on or off depends on the person's internal state. Thus, alliesthesia is responsible for motivating body temperature regulation by humans. To illustrate with an experiment, Mower (1976) made male participants hypothermic (cold) by placing them up to their shoulders in a bath of cool (15 to 18°C) water or hyperthermic (warm) by placing them in a bath of warm (41 to 43°C) water. This procedure resulted in the participants' core body temperatures decreasing or increasing by at least 1°C. Other participants were kept at normal body temperature. Next, participants dipped their hands into baths ranging from cool to warm and rated these baths on an *unpleasantness–pleasantness* scale. Ratings of the water baths depended on the participants' core body temperature (see Figure 5.1). When

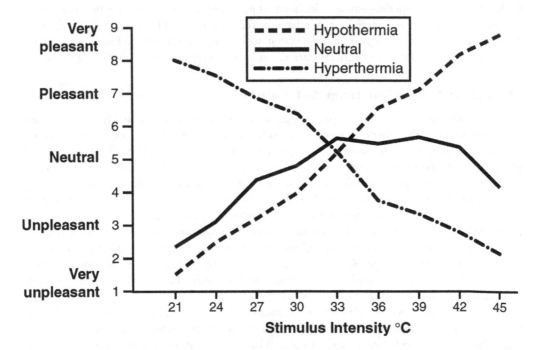

FIGURE 5.1 Core Body Temperature and Thermal Pleasantness. The unpleasantness or pleasantness of a water bath depends on a person's internal body temperature. When hypothermic (low internal temperature), cool water feels unpleasant and warm water feels pleasant. On the other hand, when hyperthermic (high internal body temperature), cool water feels pleasant and warm water feels unpleasant.

Source: From "Perceived Intensity of Peripheral Thermal Stimuli Is Independent of Internal Body Temperature" by G. D. Mower, 1976, *Journal of Comparative and Physiological Psychology, 90,* Figure 2a, p. 1154. Copyright 1976 by American Psychological Association.

participants were hypothermic (cold), they judged cooler baths as unpleasant and warmer baths as pleasant. When participants were hyperthermic (warm), however, they judged cooler baths as pleasant and warmer baths as unpleasant. Participants with normal core temperatures judged a water bath as unpleasant only when it deviated greatly from normal skin temperature. Baths that restore body temperature to homeostasis are those that feel pleasant (Cabanac, 1971). Baths are felt to be unpleasant if they cause actual body temperature to deviate further from set point temperature.

Thirst and Drinking

Exercising on a hot day or eating salty foods soon reminds a person of the need for water. The sensation of thirst may drive an individual to drink more water.

Thirst sensations. A cell is the smallest structure of the body capable of carrying out the functions necessary for life. In order for the trillions of cells composing the body to work properly, the amount of fluid they lose must be replaced by an equal amount. Water replaces lost fluids and is obtained through drinking and eating. The body's need for water is registered as thirst, which regulates drinking. To investigate thirst sensations, Engell and associates (1987) dehydrated male participants by forcing them to lose 3, 5, or 7 percent of their body water weight. The researchers accomplished this by restricting the men's drinking and eating and having them do light exercise in a hot, dry environment. Participants' ratings of the intensity of their local sensations (dry mouth and throat, scratchy throat) and general sensations (thirsty, tired, weary, dizzy) increased from the restrictions and exercise. In other words, thirst sensations and the inducement to drink became stronger and stronger. Early researchers thought that thirst resulted from a dry mouth and throat (Wolf, 1958) and that sensory loss to that area would eliminate thirst sensations. However, even when their larynx (the upper part of the windpipe containing vocal cords) is surgically removed, people still experience thirst as a general sensation (Miyaoka et al., 1987).

Water deprivation and the hedonics of drinking. Research has shown that the pleasure of replenishing fluids depends on the amount of fluid loss and on the temperature of the water. Hedin's experience of drinking as "exquisite pleasure" resulted from having suffered severe dehydration in the desert and because the water was cool. Sandick and associates (1984) had army personnel exercise on some days and rest on other days (the control). Following exercise or rest, participants were presented with water samples for drinking that ranged from cool to room temperature to warm. On exercise days participants preferred the cooler temperature more than the warmer temperature, whereas on control (rest) days these differences in preference were less pronounced. Participants also drank significantly more of the cooler water following exercise than following a rest day, although this difference disappeared with warmer water samples. Preference or hedonic ratings of the water (how much the water was liked) decreased as the temperature increased. The amount of water all participants drank followed their preference ratings, meaning that, as preference decreased, the amount of water participants drank decreased. Additional research on the relationship between exercise and water intake has shown that cool water temperatures are rated as more pleasurable, reduce thirst better, and are drunk in greater amounts either during or after exercise (Burdon et al., 2012). Cool water reduces core body temperature sooner than warm water and so is preferred based on alliesthesia.

Inhibitors of thirst. The quenching of thirst from drinking occurs several minutes before water replenishes the cells. This observation implies that, whatever physiological mechanism starts drinking, a different mechanism stops it, since water has not yet arrived where it is needed. Drinking is triggered by thirst and stopped by feedback from the mouth, throat, stomach, and eventually the absorption of water into the cells. Besides physiological signals of satiety, there are psychological ones that change with drinking (Engell et al., 1987). After being dehydrated (made thirsty) to different degrees, participants were given one hour to consume as much of a fruit-flavored drink as they wanted. The amount participants drank increased with the amount of dehydration but stopped before they were fully rehydrated. The disappearance of a dry mouth, chalk-like taste, and thirst inhibited drinking. For participants who had been the most severely dehydrated, the feeling of a full stomach also inhibited further drinking. Sandick and associates (1984) had US Army personnel exercise for about 30 minutes and then allowed them to drink as much water as they wanted. Drinking stopped when the sensations that begin and maintain drinking were alleviated. For example, there was a tendency to quit drinking with the disappearance of a dry mouth, feeling warm, and sweating. Finally, as Hedin's description in the opening paragraph implies, as the deliciousness of water diminishes, drinking stops.

The Body's Energy Requirements

I have, on rare occasions, discovered the consequences of failing to attend to the gasoline gauge. As the fuel indicator plummets below E, the car stutters and then stops. I have also discovered that feelings of fatigue follow the failure to attend to lunch. The analogy here is that the human body, like a car, also requires fuel. Furthermore, feelings of hunger, like the fuel gauge, are indications that energy reserves are running low and that it is time to eat. This analogy between a car's fuel requirements and the body's energy requirements will help in understanding hunger motivation. The body's energy requirements can be divided into three components: resting metabolism, thermic effects, and physical activity. Energy used for resting (basal) metabolism is analogous to using gasoline to keep the engine idling while the car is in neutral. *Resting metabolism* refers to the use of energy for body maintenance, the pumping of blood by the heart, oxygen utilization, the work of individual cells, and neural activity in the brain. Resting metabolic rate is measured by the body's heat production or oxygen consumption while a person is inactive and has not eaten for at least 12 hours. The *thermic effect* is analogous to the heat produced by running the car's engine. It refers to the energy cost of digesting, storing, and absorbing food. Thermic or heat production can continue for several hours after a meal. The energy used for physical activity is analogous to the energy used in moving the car. *Physical activity* involves voluntary movement, which includes behaviors from studying to running. As individuals become more physically active, they expend more energy. Also included is spontaneous activity, such as fidgeting and the maintenance of body posture (Levine et al., 1999). The motivation of behavior is really the motivation of physical activity.

Energy Homeostasis

Energy must be available to motivate behavior. Food provides this energy in the form of carbohydrates, fat, and protein (Hall, 2012). Energy must always be available because, in addition to behavior, our brain, heart, lungs, and cells are constantly working even during sleep. Food energy is stored primarily as fat, then protein, and temporarily as glycogen. Food energy is stored by its incorporation into the stomach, intestines, liver, and muscles and as fat storehouses (Hall, 2012). Energy intake (eating) and energy expenditure (behavior) vary considerably from day to day, yet the balance between intake and expenditure remains stable over the long-term (Speakman et al., 2011). This balance is known as **energy homeostasis** (Keesey & Powley, 2008; Sandoval et al., 2008; Woods et al., 2000). This is the balance between energy derived from carbohydrates, fat, and protein minus the energy used for resting metabolism, the thermic effect, and physical activity. This balance equals zero and is reflected in the constancy of an individual's weight over many years. The body's energy stores are out of balance when energy intake exceeds energy expenditure. In this case, a person gains weight. On the other hand, when energy intake falls below the required amount for energy expenditure, then a person loses weight. When an imbalance between intake and expenditure occurs corrective physiological, psychological, and behavior changes occur to restore the balance.

Set point for energy homeostasis. The negative feedback system describes energy homeostasis. Figure 5.2 shows the negative feedback system in operation for a low-weight, ideal-weight, and overweight individual. The set point of body weight refers to the amount of stored body fat, since it is the primary source of energy followed by protein (Hall, 2012). The brain compares information about the body's fat level with the set point fat level. Different outcomes may result from this comparison. One outcome, as indicated in the center of Figure 5.2, occurs when actual body fat matches the set point. In this case, the current rate of energy intake and expenditure is maintained. When there is a mismatch or discrepancy between actual body fat and the set point amount, then an adjustment is made. When body fat is below the set point level, food intake increases and energy expenditure decreases (Figure 5.2, left). But when body fat is above the set point food intake decreases and energy expenditure increases (Figure 5.2, right).

Monitoring the body's available energy. How is energy homeostasis maintained? This work is conducted by the brain and the results emerge in our consciousness as feelings of hunger or satiety. Energy levels are monitored by a part of the brain known as the **hypothalamus**, much like a car's gasoline gauge monitors how much fuel is in the tank. Glucose is one source of energy that the brain monitors (Sandoval et al., 2008). It is a simple sugar that is obtained from food carbohydrates. Glucose is immediately available from the stomach and intestines for energy. But if not used immediately glucose is converted so that it can be stored in the liver and muscles for later use. Glucose can also be converted to fat plus fat from other food sources can be stored in adipose (fat) cells. After several hours, however, a person runs out of available glucose energy from the stomach and intestines and begins to rely on the energy stores in the muscles and liver. During longer periods of not eating or famine, the body converts its stored fat to fatty acids for energy use (McArdle et al., 1996).

As a short-term energy source, the amount of glucose in our blood is associated with eating, and only small fluctuations in glucose are needed by the brain to govern eating behavior (Woods et al., 2000). For instance, Pittas and coresearchers (2005) continuously measured glucose levels in eight healthy women for three days. The researchers also measured the participants' degrees of hunger and desire for a meal. The results indicated that as hunger and desire for a meal increased, the amount of food eaten also increased. Furthermore, lower levels of blood glucose as well as a drop in glucose were associated with eating more food during meals. Conversely,

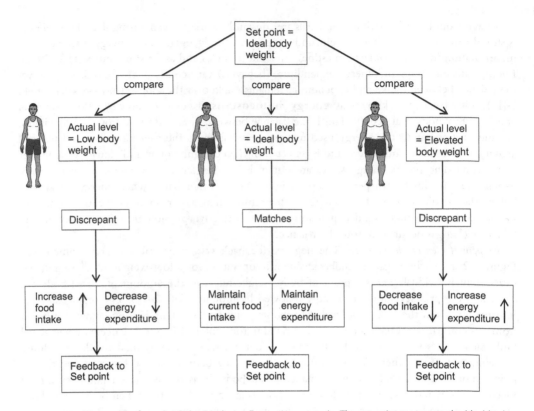

FIGURE 5.2 Discrepancy from Set Point Motivates Energy Homeostasis. The set point represents the ideal body weight. Actual body weight is compared to the set point body weight. If discrepant, then behavior changes so that actual body weight eventually matches the set point weight. On left, a discrepant low weight motivates an increase in food intake and a decrease in energy expenditure. On right, a discrepant high weight motivates a decrease in food intake and an increase in energy expenditure. In the center, actual body weight matches the set point weight. Here energy intake and energy expenditure balance; there is no discrepancy.

research has also shown that feeling full declines as an individual's glucose level falls (Lemmens et al., 2011).

Brain monitors energy-relevant hormones. The hypothalamus monitors the body's energy levels by means of signals received from various hormones. These include two inhibitory (like brakes) hormones, cholecystokinin (CCK) and leptin, and one excitatory (like an accelerator) hormone, ghrelin. The information they provide about the status of the body's energy level leads the brain to take corrective action to maintain body fat at the set point.

CCK is a hormone released in the upper part of the small intestine after food intake and acts as a temporary inhibitor of hunger and eating. Higher levels of CCK in the bloodstream are associated with higher degrees of satiety (Holt et al., 1992). CCK interacts with the amount of food to inhibit hunger and eating. Muurahainen and associates (1991) had male participants eat either 100 or 500 grams of soup followed by either an infusion of CCK or saline as a control substance. Next, the participants were allowed to eat as much as they wanted of a test meal of macaroni and beef. The amount participants ate depended both on CCK and on the size of the premeal soup. The CCK significantly inhibited eating of the test meal for those participants who had preloaded with the larger portion of premeal soup. The CCK, however, did not inhibit eating of the test meal for those participants who had the smaller amount of premeal soup. Thus, CCK has an inhibitory effect on hunger but perhaps only when coupled with other satiety cues, such as feeling full.

Leptin is involved in long-term energy homeostasis (see Figure 5.2). It is an inhibitory hormone for hunger and eating. Leptin is released by adipose tissue and circulates in the blood stream to provide information about the amount of body fat energy. The amount of circulating leptin is positively related to the amount of fat tissue. For instance, overeating increases the amount of circulating leptin but declines as individuals lose weight, so obese individuals have greater levels of leptin than lean individuals. An increase in leptin is associated with changes designed to increase energy expenditure by increasing basal metabolism, decreasing hunger, and decreasing food intake. A decrease in leptin, on the other hand, is associated with changes designed to conserve energy, such as a decrease in basal metabolism and an increase in appetite (Klok et al., 2007).

Ghrelin is a fast-acting excitatory hormone that stimulates hunger, eating, and mental images of food (Geary, 2004; Klok et al., 2007). Ghrelin is released by the stomach and rises to its highest point just prior to breakfast, lunch, and dinner. It then declines rapidly after eating, only to begin rising again until prior to the next meal. Thus, increases in the level of circulating ghrelin informs the hypothalamus about low levels of energy. For instance, when humans receive an injection of ghrelin they report greater hunger and eat more (Schmid et al., 2005). Furthermore, when individuals were asked to rate changes in their degree of hunger after eating, it was discovered that as ghrelin levels declined so did the accompanying degree of hunger that individuals experienced (Lemmens et al., 2011).

In summary, these three hormones have various effects. CCK and leptin inhibit hunger and eating, while ghrelin stimulates hunger and eating. CCK is a temporary signal indicating that our stomachs are full and suppresses further eating. Leptin signals an oversupply of energy and stimulates weight loss by inhibiting eating. Ghrelin, however, signals an undersupply of energy and stimulates hunger and eating. Ghrelin helps provide the motivation in Figure 5.2 for individuals to eat more. CCK and leptin, on the other hand, provide the motivation for individuals to eat less.

Defending the set point. What other changes occur in reaction to an oversupply or undersupply of energy? Change in resting metabolism is one adjustment the body makes to maintain a set point for energy homeostasis. To illustrate, Leibel and coresearchers (1995) increased or decreased by 10 percent the weight of both normal-weight and obese subjects. What happens to an individual's metabolism when weight is gained or lost? Figure 5.3 provides the answer. When subjects were made to increase their body weight, their total energy expenditure increased also. This increase was true for their resting metabolism, physical activity, and thermic effect. When subjects were made to lose weight, their metabolism decreased. In addition, with weight loss, individuals also used their muscles more efficiently and used less energy during mild exercise (Goldsmith et al., 2010).

In addition, the change in energy expenditure was greater for obese than for nonobese subjects (Leibel et al., 1995). One reason for this difference is the notion of **carrying cost**, which refers

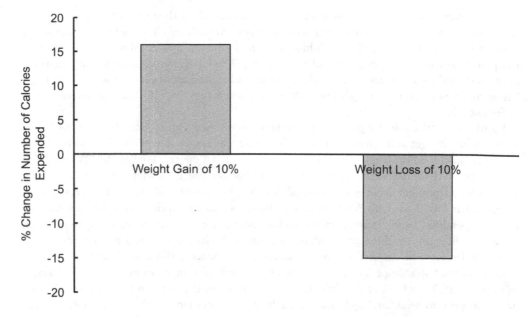

FIGURE 5.3 Changes in Energy Expenditure Following Weight Gain or Loss. A weight gain of 10 percent increased total energy expenditure (measured in calories) by both nonobese and obese subjects. A weight loss of 10 percent decreased total energy expenditure (measured in calories) by both nonobese and obese subjects. Total energy expenditure included resting metabolism plus physical energy. The changes in energy expenditure were greater for obese than for nonobese subjects.

Source: Adapted from "Changes in Energy Expenditure Resulting from Altered Body Weight" by R. L. Leibel et al., 1995, *New England Journal of Medicine, 332*, pp. 623, 624.

to the amount of energy required to carry one's weight. Greater carrying cost occurs with more weight (Van Itallie & Kissileff, 1983). Carrying cost levels off for an individual's weight because the amount of energy required to carry the excess weight equals the amount of food energy that is consumed. Whether jogging, bicycling, swimming, or walking, a heavier person will burn more calories doing these activities than will a lighter person (McArdle et al., 1996). The *Activity Calorie Calculator* verifies that heavier individuals burn more calories for physical activities than lighter individuals do—that is, they have greater carrying costs.

To calculate the number of calories you burn based on the activity, its duration, and your weight, use the calculator titled "Fitness Partner: Activity Calorie Calculator" here: www.primusweb.com/cgi-bin/fpc/actcalc.pl.

Hunger Sensations

The dashboard gauge monitors the amount of gasoline in the car's tank. When there is a low amount of gasoline, the gauge tilts toward E (empty). Similarly, the brain monitors the hormones regarding the status of the body's energy supply. This information then registers in consciousness as hunger sensations.

Sensations indicating energy depletion. Subjective sensations of hunger inform us that we are running low on energy. These sensations, although differing in intensity, are not located in one place but instead have varied locations (Friedman et al., 1999). Friedman and coresearchers (1999) devised intensity ratings for sensations related to hunger and appetite, such as the ones in Table 5.1. They also devised intensity ratings for sensations that are associated with hunger, such as anxiety, dizziness, dry mouth, headache, stomachache, stomach growling, and weakness. Do the intensities of these sensations change with hours of food deprivation? To answer this question, the researchers recruited male and female participants to go without food for 22 hours from 6:00 p.m. to 4:00 p.m. the following day. At six different times during the 22 hours, participants rated the intensity of their sensations as listed in Table 5.1 and the intensity of other hunger-associated sensations. Participants rated their sensations twice at 4:00 p.m., just before and right after their meal. Figure 5.4 shows that sensations of hunger, the desire to eat, and the amount

TABLE 5.1 Ratings of Hunger and Related Sensations

Rate the intensity of your hunger and related sensations that you feel right now:

Hunger: Not at all hungry	= 0 1 2 3 4 5 6 7 8 9 =	As hungry as I have ever felt
Desire to eat: Very weak	= 0 1 2 3 4 5 6 7 8 9 =	Very strong
How much could you eat: Nothing at all	= 0 1 2 3 4 5 6 7 8 9 =	A large amount
How full is your stomach: Not at all	= 0 1 2 3 4 5 6 7 8 9 =	Very full

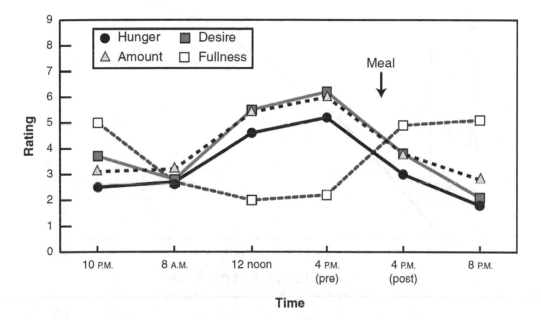

FIGURE 5.4 Hunger and Related Ratings. Ratings of hunger, desire to eat, and amount expected to eat increased with hours of deprivation and decreased with eating. Ratings of stomach fullness showed the reverse trend. *Note:* Values are means + *SEM* of 14 subjects.

Source: From "A Figurative Measure of Subjective Hunger Sensations" by M. I. Friedman et al., 1999, *Appetite, 32,* Figure 3, p. 399. Copyright 1999 by Elsevier. Reprinted by permission.

expected to eat all increased with hours of food deprivation and decreased after the meal. Ratings of stomach fullness showed the reverse pattern. Ratings of hunger-associated sensations showed similar patterns. For example, weakness, headache, dizziness, and stomach growl and ache increased with deprivation and then decreased after the meal.

Hunger predicts energy intake. It seems reasonable to assume that sensations of hunger indicate an energy deficit. Does the intensity of the sensation predict the amount of food energy a person will eat? In other words, as the body's energy supply declines, will individuals eat more to counteract the decline—that is, to return to energy homeostasis? To answer this question, Sadoul and coresearchers (2014) examined 23 studies that used 549 different participants to determine the nature of this relationship. The hunger scale ranged from *not at all hungry* = 0 to *very hungry* = 100 and the amount of energy consumed was measured in calories. One of their findings in Figure 5.5 shows that, as hunger ratings increase, the number of calories eaten also increases.

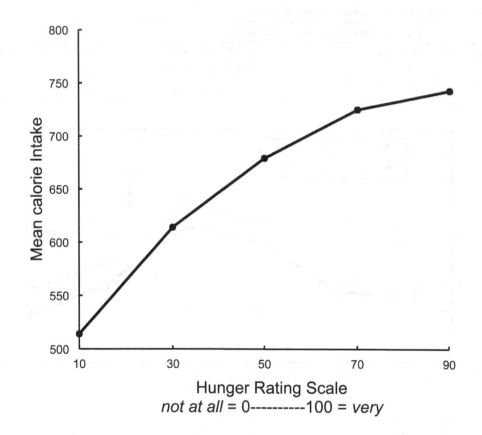

FIGURE 5.5 Amount Eaten Increases with Hunger. The number of food calories people eat increases with their hunger ratings prior to a meal. Numbers along horizontal axis indicate midpoint of hunger rating intervals: 0–20, 20–40, 40–60, 60–80, 80–100.

Source: Adapted from "The Relationship between Appetite Scores and Subsequent Energy Intake: An Analysis Based on 23 Randomized Controlled Studies" by B. C. Sadoul et al., 2014, *Appetite, 83,* Figure 3C, p. 157.

However, in addition to hunger ratings other factors determined the caloric value of a person's meal. For example, energy intake increased with resting metabolism. Heavier individuals have a greater resting metabolism than lean people and so eat more. Also, women eat less than men and older people eat less than younger people (Sadoul et al., 2014). The link between hunger and the need for calories, however, breaks down for long periods of fasting. People who go for days or weeks without food (Wolf, 1958) report that hunger sensations do not become more intense but instead disappear. As in a car, once the fuel tank is empty the gas gauge is not going to fall further past the empty mark.

Feedback Mechanisms for Satiety

If hunger motivates us to eat, then what motivates us to stop? One answer is *satiety*, which refers to having gratified hunger, feeling content, and having replenished energy stores. Other factors include feeling full and a decline in the pleasure food provides. Based on Figure 5.4 and energy homeostasis, would the quantity of food or quantity of food energy determine satiety and when a person stops eating? The quantity of food and the energy density of food determine the amount of energy a person consumes. Energy density refers to the number of calories per gram of food. Low-energy density foods provide fewer calories per gram than high-energy density food does. For example, cheese has a higher energy density than chicken, which has a higher energy density than vegetables. Eating is based on the quantity or weight of food rather than on the energy content. To illustrate Bell and coresearchers (1998) provided women with lunch, dinner, and an evening snack for two consecutive days. The meals consisted of either low-, medium-, or high-energy density food. Participants were free to eat as much food as they wanted at each meal. The results showed that the women ate an equal amount of each type of food. However, more calories (energy) were consumed during the high-energy density meal than during the low-energy density meal. Although, when energy density is high, people do eat a bit less of the high density food (Kral et al., 2004). Thus, people are also sensitive to the amount of food energy they consume. Another explanation for satiety is based on receptors in the stomach and intestines (Rolls et al., 1998). The stomach is sensitive to the amount of food it contains and stomach distension inhibits eating. In a series of surveys asking college students why they usually stop eating a meal, the most common answer given was when "I feel full" (Mook & Votaw, 1992, p 72). Finally, food may begin to taste less pleasant toward the end of the meal and so eating declines (Kral et al., 2004).

Dual Intervention Point Model

The energy set point model presented in Figure 5.2 implies that people's weight should remain constant over their lifetime. However, several lines of evidence indicate that is not the case. First, there is an increasing trend for people to become overweight (BMI = 25.0–29.9), then obese (BMI = 30.00–39.0), and eventually extremely obese (BMI ≥ 40) (BMI refers to body mass index. BMI = weight (kilograms)/height (meters)^2). As weight increases, BMI increases, since an individual's height remains constant. National Health and Nutrition Examination Surveys conducted between 1960 and 2010 found an increase in the percentage of adults who were either obese or very obese (Fryar et al., 2012). Second, people gain weight because of a combination of eating more and exercising less. In one longitudinal study, 121 thousand adult men and women gained an average of 3.35 pounds over a four-year period. Over that time, they increased their eating of potato chips, meats, candy, and desserts and drank more sugared beverages. They also ate fewer vegetables, nuts, whole grains, and fruits. In addition, they decreased their physical activity over that period (Mozaffarian et al., 2011).

The fact that people's weight creeps up over their lifetime is a problem for the set point concept. It implies that our weight should remain constant. An alternative explanation is the **dual intervention point model**. It proposes that body weight or amount of fat settles between an upper and lower boundary, as shown in Figure 5.6 (Speakman, 2013; Speakman et al., 2011). The lower boundary represents the minimum weight for survival. Body weight approaches the lower boundary as a result of prolonged low energy intake and high energy expenditure. As described earlier, the body's basal metabolism now slows to conserve energy, as shown in Figure 5.2 (left

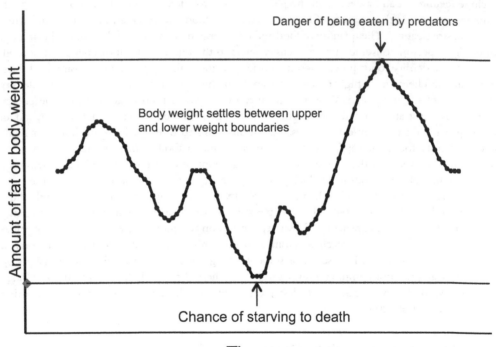

FIGURE 5.6 Body Weight Settles between Upper and Lower Boundaries. When body weight falls too low, physiological corrections drive body weight up. When too low, a person could starve to death. When body weight rises too high, physiological corrections drive body weight down. When too high, a person may not be fast enough to escape predators.

Source: Adapted from "Evolutionary Perspectives on the Obesity Epidemic: Adaptive, Maladaptive, and Neutral Viewpoints" by J. R. Speakman, 2013, *Annual Review of Nutrition, 33*, Figure 4, p. 305, and from "Set Points, Settling Points and Some Alternative Models: Theoretical Options to Understand How Genes and Environments Combine to Regulate Body Adiposity" by J. R. Speakman et al., 2011, *Disease Models and Mechanisms, 4*, Figure 5, p. 750.

side). In addition, people's muscles also work more efficiently in order to use less energy. Body weight approaches the upper boundary as a result of prolonged high energy intake and reduced energy expenditure. Approaching the upper boundary reflects the rise in obesity as a result of an overabundance of palatable food and energy-saving machinery. People do not exceed their individual upper boundary for several reasons. One idea is that over 2.5 million years ago the upper boundary was determined by the risk of predation—that is, being eaten by a carnivore (Speakman, 2013; Speakman et al., 2011). In other words, a person had to be agile, quick, and a fast runner to escape from a predator. Being overweight made a person less able to escape. The risk of predation is not a factor today and thus has allowed some people's weight to settle at the upper boundary. Weight levels off eventually at the upper boundary for several reasons. First, heavier people burn more calories because they have a higher resting metabolism. In addition, heavier people expend more calories during physical activity (carrying cost) and also have a higher thermic effect after eating. All of these factors contribute to burning more caloric energy (Hall, 2012).

Section Recap

The body attempts to maintain a stable internal environment, or *homeostasis*, which is accomplished with the aid of the *negative feedback system*. This system is the body's self-correcting process that reduces the discrepancy between a desired state (set point) and an actual state of the body. *Allostasis* resembles homeostasis but has varying set points, such as a different room temperature in winter and summer. In either homeostasis or allostasis, deviations from a set point define a *physiological need* for the incentive that will restore homeostasis or allostasis. Changes in a person's physiological interior alter sensations (*alliesthesia*) to stimuli that are relevant for restoring homeostasis or allostasis. According to the alliesthesia concept, incentives and behaviors that restore homeostasis are pleasant, while those that disrupt homeostasis further are unpleasant. Different physiological systems are maintained under homeostasis. A drop in body temperature below set point produces involuntary shivering and blood vessel constrict to raise temperature. A rise in body temperature produces involuntary sweating and blood vessel dilate to lower temperature. In addition, the accompanying sensations of feeling cold and hot can result in voluntary actions such as putting on or removing layers of clothing.

The sensation of thirst results from a loss of fluids. Specific and global thirst sensations intensify with water loss and cease with drinking even though fluids have not been completely replaced. Greater water deprivation results in stronger thirst sensations and promotes more drinking. Cooler water is deemed more pleasurable because it reduces body temperature more quickly.

Food provides energy for the body to function, which is measured in calories and comes primarily from glucose. Energy is used during resting metabolism for maintaining the body, during thermic effects for digesting and storing food energy, and for physical activity or behavior. *Energy homeostasis* refers to the enduring balance between energy intake from food, energy storage, and energy expenditure. When ideal weight is below set point, food intake increases and energy expenditure decreases. When ideal weight is above set point, food intake decreases and energy expenditure increases. Energy homeostasis is possible because the brain monitors the body's energy and stores excess energy in the liver and muscles or as fat in adipose tissue. Low amounts of energy emerge as hunger sensations in consciousness and are felt in the stomach and abdomen but also as dizziness, headache, and weakness. Hunger motivates eating, as shown by the finding that people eat more food when hungrier. Other factors that affect eating are a drop in blood glucose, monitoring the supply of calories, and variation in the amount of the hormones *cholecystokinin (CCK)*, *leptin*, and *ghrelin*. Satiety stems from feeling full and from the volume of food that was consumed. According to the *dual intervention point model*, body weight fluctuates between an upper and lower boundary. The lower boundary is the minimal for survival and triggers energy-saving strategies. The upper boundary is linked to being overweight and is associated with burning more calories because the *carrying cost* of one's weight is greater. The upper boundary was also linked to a threat of predation in our evolutionary past.

FOOD CHARACTERISTICS AND EATING

By perusing photos in cookbooks, a person realizes that food must also be pleasing to the eye as well as to the taste buds. Restaurant chefs do not slop food into a bucket to give to their patrons. Instead, they arrange food on a plate and add garnish to make the meal look attractive to diners. The whole practice of meal planning emphasizes the importance of color, form, variety, texture, temperature, and flavor of food. These considerations to the details of food make it apparent that there is more to eating than just reaching satiety. People often eat beyond satiety, especially when it involves their favorite food or dessert. What food characteristics determine what and how much you eat?

Cephalic Responses

Food has the power to make us eat. It can evoke a set of physiological responses that are preparatory to eating, digesting, metabolizing, and storing food (Nederkoorn et al., 2000). **Cephalic responses** to the smell and taste of food involve the secretion of saliva, gastric juices, and insulin from the pancreas (Powley, 1977). In addition, food can also evoke hunger sensations and the desire to eat. To illustrate, Bruce and associates (1987) evoked a cephalic response in their participants following an overnight fast. They presented them with a combination of sweetened gum, sweetened water, and the sight and smell of an appetizing breakfast. Ingesting the sweet stimuli plus the sight and smell of food raised the participants' insulin and lowered their level of blood glucose. Furthermore, the more their glucose levels dropped, the more appetizing they rated the anticipated breakfast. Nederkoorn and associates (2000) exposed their participants to their favorite foods and measured the cephalic response. As a result of the exposure, participants' hunger ratings and cravings increased along with their heart rate, blood pressure, salivation, and gastric activity. Marcelino and colleagues (2001) had participants visually inspect and smell four pizzas that differed in visual quality. Another group was not exposed to the pizzas. Appetite ratings were higher for individuals who saw and smelled the pizzas. Furthermore, the desire to eat a pizza also increased with its visual quality and the participant's degree of hunger.

Palatability and Amount of Food

Both the quality and amount of food determine the urge to eat and the amount that is eaten. The **palatability** of food refers to its hedonic value as determined by variety, texture, temperature, aroma, and flavor (Young, 1961). Highly palatable food is appetizing, delicious, and a pleasure to eat. For example, Moskowitz and associates (1974) showed that palatability depends on flavor intensity. In their experiment, they varied the sucrose concentration, or sweetness intensity, of vanilla pudding, yellow cake, and a cherry-flavored beverage. Pleasantness ratings of these foods at first increased but then decreased as they became sweeter and sweeter. In other words, people like their desserts to be sweet but not too sweet.

Not only does sugar enhance palatability, but fat does also. Drewnowski and colleagues (1983, 1985) determined the contribution that sweet and fat make to palatability for both fed and fasted participants. They had participants taste 20 different substances by a sip-and-spit technique, followed each time by rinsing the mouth. The 20 substances varied in five levels of fat (ranging from skim milk to heavy cream blended with safflower oil) and four levels of sweetness. Participants rated each substance for sweetness, fatness, creaminess, and liking. Ratings of sweetness, fatness, and creaminess increased as fat and sugar content increased, demonstrating that participants were sensitive to these factors. Liking ratings, however, increased and then decreased as the sugar and fat content of the substances increased. The best-liked substance consisted of about 21 percent fat and about 8 percent sugar (Drewnowski et al., 1985). Thus, people like things sweet and fat but not too sweet and not too fat. Not only do we have a "sweet tooth"; we also have a "fat tooth."

In addition to palatability, quantity also factors into the motivating effects of food. One observation is that, as the size of food portions increases, the amount eaten increases correspondingly. For instance, Rolls and coresearchers (2002) presented their male and female participants a lunch of macaroni and cheese in one of four different portions: 500, 625, 750, or 1,000 grams. Participants were instructed to eat as little or as much as they wanted. Prior to eating, the four groups did not differ in their hunger, thirst, and the amount they thought they could eat. Portion size, however, determined the amount they did eat. The results show that amount consumed increased as portion sizes increased. This increase occurred equally for both men and women although men ate significantly more than women for all portion sizes. Increased portion sizes of meals provided in restaurants or in packaged foods have been blamed for the increase in the percentage of overweight and obese individuals in our society (Harnack et al., 2000).

Plate size also determines the amount of food people select, eat, and waste as discovered from observing diners at a buffet. Wansink and van Ittersum (2013) observed diners in four different all-you-can-eat Chinese buffets. The restaurants offered two buffet lines: one with smaller and the other with larger plates. Diners could choose plates from either line. The researchers unobtrusively observed how much food diners put on their plates. Next, they calculated the serving size measured in square centimeters. Diners with the larger plates took more food, ate more of it, but also wasted more as shown in Figure 5.7.

The **Delbouef illusion** serves as an interpretation for the findings in Figure 5.7. The illusion (next to Figure 5.7) shows that the size of the outer circle influences the perceived size of the solid inner circle. The inner circle is perceived as larger when the outer circle is smaller. Generalizing to plates, an equal amount of food should appear larger on a smaller plate compared to a larger plate. Thus, diners place more food on larger plates than smaller ones, since larger plates do not appear as full as smaller ones for the same amount of food. Consequently, people select more and eat more food from larger than smaller plates (Wansink & van Ittersum, 2013).

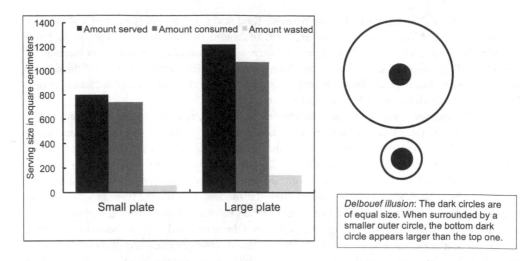

Delbouef illusion: The dark circles are of equal size. When surrounded by a smaller outer circle, the bottom dark circle appears larger than the top one.

FIGURE 5.7 Plate Size Determines Food Consumption. Diners who selected larger plates served themselves more food, ate more food, and wasted more food compared to diners who selected smaller plates. Those diners served themselves less food, ate less food, and wasted less.

Source: Adapted from "Portion Size Me: Plate-Size Induced Consumption Norms and Win-Win Solutions for Reducing Food Intake and Waste" by B. Wansink & K. Van Ittersum, 2013, *Journal of Experimental Psychology: Applied, 19*, Figure 2, p. 323.

Sensory-Specific Satiety

Quantity interacts with food variety to determine eating. As suggested in many cookbooks, eating will be a more pleasurable experience if a variety of palatable foods are served in a fashion appealing to the eye (Crocker, 1961). Serving only one dish or eating the same food repeatedly is enough to blunt anyone's appetite, which is the result of a process known as **sensory-specific satiety**. This process refers to a decreased liking and consumption of a particular food based on sensory characteristics, such as flavor, texture, and appearance (Raynor & Epstein, 2001). In an early experiment conducted by Rolls and associates (1981), participants tasted and then rated their liking of a number of foods, among which was cheese on crackers or sausage. Half of the participants had a lunch of cheese on crackers, while the other half had a lunch of sausage. Two minutes after the meal, participants were unexpectedly given a second course, which was either the same as the first course (cheese on crackers or sausage) or different (sausage or cheese on crackers). Participants also rated the liking of these foods during their second course. The ratings showed that the same food was liked less compared to a different food. In addition, if participants ate the same food during the second course as they did during the first, they tended to eat less than if the food was different between courses. For example, participants liked sausage less during the second course and ate less of it if they had also eaten sausage during the first course. Sensory-specific satiety means that satiety is specific to a food and does not generalize to other foods. Thus, although a person may quit eating one food, she will eat other foods, thereby ensuring that several varieties are eaten during a meal. A greater variety at meals provides greater enjoyment and increases the likelihood that a nutritionally balanced meal is eaten.

Food Preferences

Your innate dispositions toward food and the eating environment your parents provided jointly determined your current food likes and dislikes. In other words, food preferences result from the interaction between innate dispositions and environmental experiences (Birch, 1999).

Innate food preferences. As described in Chapter 3, humans are born liking certain tastes and foods and not others. For instance, Mennella and Beauchamp (1998) and Steiner (1977) showed that infants innately prefer sweet substances and reject bitter and sour substances. Thus, humans appear innately ready to eat sweet-tasting foods, which are relatively high in calories, and reject bitter or sour-tasting foods, which are associated with poison and being spoiled. Rats show different facial gestures depending on their being exposed to sweet or bitter stimuli (Grill & Norgren, 1978). Rats also show an innate preference for salt (Schulkin, 1991). The same is true for humans. Leshem and colleagues (1999) induced salt loss through perspiration in one group with exercise, compared to a control group who did not exercise. When allowed to flavor a cup of tomato soup to their liking, exercisers preferred more than a 50 percent increase in salt (NaCl) compared to what non-exercisers preferred. These results support the notion that salt preference increases as salt level in the body decreases. Young infants, however, are indifferent to the taste of salt, while infants four to 24 months of age prefer salt solutions over plain water. Children three to six years old, although rejecting salty fluids, prefer salted soups (Beauchamp et al., 1986). Rats and humans appear sensitive to and prefer food substances, like salt, that are necessary for body growth, maintenance, and repair.

Mere exposure to foods. The recommendation that a variety of foods promotes appetite should not detract from the contribution that familiarity makes in liking certain foods. People often prefer the foods they ate while growing up simply because of their exposure to them. According to Zajonc's (1968) **mere exposure effect**, people increase their positive evaluation of a stimulus because of repeated exposures. To illustrate this concept, Pliner (1982) had participants taste and swallow four different tropical fruit juices from zero to 20 times, each time rating their bitterness. Following the tasting, participants rated the juices for liking (from *dislike* to *like*). The rating outcomes were in accord with the mere exposure effect such that liking increased with the number of times a juice had been tasted. However, this effect did not last longer than one week. In another experiment, Birch and Marlin (1982) presented preschool children with three novel foods that consisted of sweet, salty, or plain tofu (soybean curd). The children tasted the foods up to 20 times over a series of days and each time rated how much they preferred them. Again, in accord with the mere exposure effect, as the number of food tastings increased, preference ratings increased.

The mere exposure effect has practical applications for getting children to like and eat their vegetables. To investigate this possibility, Lakkakula and coresearchers (2010, 2011) had elementary school children taste a variety of fruits and vegetables in the school's cafeteria. Apricots, bell peppers, cantaloupe, carrots, peaches, pears, peas, and tomatoes were tasted eight to 10 times over a period of eight to 10 weeks. The researchers examined changes in the liking for vegetables that were initially rated by the children as "I did not like it" (Lakkakula et al., 2010, p. 228; 2011, p. 300). The repeated tastings resulted in an increase in liking for all fruits and vegetables. This increased liking was still in effect during four-month and 10-month follow-ups (Lakkakula et al., 2011). Thus, in this practical demonstration repeatedly tasting fruits and vegetables increases the liking of those food items. One unresolved issue in this research is coaxing children to eat vegetables, which they judge unpalatable based on appearance.

Conditioned food preferences. Liking a particular food can also be enhanced by associating it with a hedonically pleasant taste. Zellner and associates (1983) likened this association to a classical conditioning procedure. In their experiment, the flavor of tea served as a conditioned stimulus for either the presence or absence of sugar in the tea. Sugar was the unconditioned stimulus, which evoked an unconditioned response of a hedonically pleasant taste. After drinking either the sweetened or unsweetened teas, the participants rated the teas, now without any sugar, for how much they liked them. The flavors of the teas that had been sweetened were liked more than those teas that had not been sweetened. This effect was still present one week later. The fact that sugar enhances the liking for food has not been lost on parents. In many different cultures, sugar is added to the food of infants so that they will eat it more readily (Jerome, 1977).

Conditioning with sugar is also a way of motivating children to eat their vegetables. Havermans and Jansen (2007) asked children to taste and then rank their preference for six vegetables from liked least to liked most: broccoli, carrots, cauliflower, peas, pumpkin, and zucchinis. Vegetables that received the middle ranks (3, 4) were then subjected to conditioning. Each vegetable was pureed with water and then dextrose (a sugar) was added to one of the vegetables. Thus, the taste (conditioned stimulus) of one vegetable was paired with sweetness (unconditioned stimulus), while the taste of the other vegetable was not paired with sweetness. During conditioning, the children tasted both the sweetened and unsweetened vegetables six times over two consecutive days. At the conclusion of the conditioning session, the children were asked again to rank order their liking of the six vegetables. All vegetables were now unsweetened. Did the ranking improve for the vegetable paired with sweetness compared to the unsweetened vegetable? Yes, according to the results presented in Figure 5.8. The vegetables paired with sweetness of dextrose increased in liking, while the unsweetened vegetable showed no change. Notice that the increased preference for the conditioned vegetable occurred after only six experiences with the sweet sensation.

It is also common, however, for a person not to eat a particular food because of a strong **taste aversion**. This refers to a strong dislike of a food because of its association with nausea, which resulted from spoiled food or illness (Bernstein, 1978; Garcia et al., 1966). Taste aversion in humans has several characteristics (Logue et al., 1981). First, the taste and smell of food and drink rather than their texture or appearance generally have more of an influence on taste aversion. Second, an aversion is more likely to develop to an unfamiliar or less-preferred food. Third, it does not matter whether nausea was the result of spoiled food or stomach flu. Even if individuals do not know why they became ill, an aversion still develops. Aversion may also result from overindulgence, as in the case of alcohol. In a sample of university students, Logue and associates (1981) found that approximately one-fourth had developed an aversion to alcohol. Of these aversions, approximately 69 percent were to hard liquor while 17 percent and 14 percent were to wine and beer, respectively. Lastly, once developed, an aversion can last for years. Although most prevalent in children, conditioned taste aversion does not last forever and declines with age (Garb & Stunkard, 1974). Eating the aversive food is a quicker way to overcome the aversion rather than just waiting for the passage of time (Logue et al., 1981).

Food stimuli determine food choices. Our food choices are not random. They are often anticipated by odor stimuli. Each food has a signature odor, which leads a diner to expect a similar food and not some other. For example, spicy odors lead a person to expect, say, a main course of

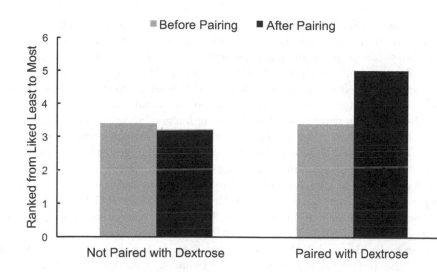

FIGURE 5.8 Pairing a Vegetable with Sugar Increases Its Liking. When a liquid mash of a vegetable was paired with dextrose sugar the liking for that vegetable increased compared to a vegetable that was not paired with dextrose. The rankings were reverse scored so that the increased liking is associated with the higher bar.

Source: Adapted from "Increasing Children's Liking of Vegetables through Flavour-Flavour Learning" by R. C. Havermans & A. Jansen, 2007, *Appetite, 48*, p. 261.

lasagna, while sweet odors lead a person to expect dessert. But odors do more than produce expectations; they also increase an individual's appetite for a similar food. Zoon and coresearchers (2016) had female participants, at different times, smell three different odors: sweet (chocolate), savory (beef) or neutral (odorless liquid). Following this procedure, participants rated their appetite for sweets such as cake or a caramel syrup waffle and for savory foods such as cheese cubes and chips. Appetite ratings were on a 100-millimeter (four-inch) line. Appetite ratings for sweet foods were higher when following sweet odors compared to savory odors. Similarly, appetite ratings for savory foods were higher following savory odors than following sweet odors.

Furthermore, individuals need not be cognitively aware of the odor stimuli. For instance, Gaillet-Torrent and coresearchers (2014) unobtrusively exposed one group of participants to the odor of pears for 15 minutes, while a control group was not exposed to this odor. The pear odor was barely perceptible and none of the participants had noticed the odor. Afterwards participants were escorted to another room where they could choose various foods to eat for lunch. They could choose from among appetizers, main courses, and a dessert of either a brownie or apple compote (apple stewed in syrup). The researchers reasoned that the odor of pears should prime their participants to choose other fruits such as the apple compote for dessert. The pear odor would not dispose participants toward other foods that did not contain fruity odors. The results showed that the two groups did not differ in their choices of appetizers and the main course. However, the participants exposed to the pear odor chose the apple compote more often for dessert, while the control group chose the apple compote less often. They were more likely to choose the brownie for dessert.

Restoring homeostasis. The degree that food restores energy homeostasis also determines how much it is liked. For instance, humans learn to prefer the flavors of foods that are associated with restoring the body's energy. Appleton and coresearchers (2006) had one group of individuals report to the laboratory immediately after breakfast or lunch. This group was defined as having low-energy requirements—that is, they were not hungry. Another group of individuals reported to the laboratory immediately prior to lunch or prior to the evening meal. They were defined as having high-energy requirements—that is, they were hungry. In the laboratory, participants ate one of four novel-flavored yogurts that had either a low- or high-energy content. This procedure was repeated over a five-day period, during which nonhungry or hungry participants ate a low- or a high-energy yogurt. Prior and during conditioning, participants rated the yogurts for liking and pleasantness of taste. An analysis of these ratings showed that all flavors received higher liking and pleasantness ratings when they had been consumed under high-energy (hungry) compared to low-energy (not hungry) requirements. Thus, hunger determines the liking of novel foods. This finding was especially true for yogurt with a high-energy content.

Other research also shows that the mere energy content of food is important for the development of taste preferences. In one illustrative experiment, Brunstrom and Mitchell (2007) had female participants eat two novel and distinctly flavored desserts, one with a high energy content and the other with a low-energy content. The desserts were eaten on alternate days over a six-day period. After eating a dessert, participants rated it for liking, desire, and enjoyment. Following the taste experiences, participants then tasted each dessert again. Both now had an intermediate level of energy. Did the preference for a particular dessert depend on its former energy content? Yes, the high-energy dessert was preferred. Initially, there were no differences in dessert preferences as shown by ratings collected on the first day. However, by the test day participants liked, enjoyed, and desired the high-energy flavored dessert more than the low-energy one. The pairing of a flavor with a high-energy content resulted in a preference for that flavor. The results of these experiments imply that people's preferences develop as a result of a food's ability to restore energy, which occurs when a hungry person eats high-energy food.

According to evolutionary psychology, food preferences for sweets and fats provided survival advantages because these foods contain more energy. Consequently, of two identical foods, the one with higher energy content should be preferred even if their flavors are identical. For instance, Zandstra and El-Deredy (2011) had hungry participants eat three-fourths of a cup of either a low- or high-energy yogurt drink on alternate days over a 10-day period. The yogurts differed in neither taste nor sweetness and were only identified by either a pink or blue sticker. The high-energy yogurt, however, was perceived as less creamy. On days 11–15, participants were asked to select the yogurt they preferred. The results indicated that the high-energy yogurt was preferred for 58 percent of the choices, while the low-energy yogurt was preferred for 42 percent of the choices. One implication of these results is that energy content can serve as an unconditioned stimulus for flavor conditioning. Food associated with high energy come to be preferred to food associated with low energy.

Section Recap

This section addressed the question whether there are factors besides hunger that determine how much people eat. The answer is a definite "yes." First, food has the power to make us eat, which is reflected in the *cephalic response*, such as salivation and gastric secretions. Tastier food and hunger increase the intensity of this response. The *palatability* of food is a key factor, and refers to its appearance, texture, aroma, and flavor in creating a pleasurable taste experience. In addition to palatability, increases in the amount of food presented to individuals also increase the amount they eat. According to the *Delbouef illusion*, equal amounts of food appear smaller on a large plate than on a small plate. Hence, people eat more of the food on a large plate because there appears to be less. In addition, people habituate to the sensory nature and flavor of a particular food and thus eat less and less of it. This decline in preference is known *as sensory-specific satiety*. Humans have innate preferences, especially for sweet and fat but also for salt, which becomes apparent when they are deprived of salt. The *mere exposure effect*, in contrast to innate food preferences, refers to the finding that the liking of foods stems from merely eating a particular food repeatedly. In addition, some foods are enjoyed because of a classical conditioning process. The food is associated with a particular pleasant flavor, such as adding a light sweetener to a vegetable. Some foods are strongly avoided because of *taste aversion*, an extreme dislike for a particular food because of the association of its aroma and taste with nausea. Furthermore, food odors can dispose individuals to choose foods that have similar odors even if the prior odors have not been noticed. People also learn to prefer the novel flavor of foods that restore energy homeostasis—that is, foods that have higher energy content or foods that are eaten while hungry.

PERSON CHARACTERISTICS AND EATING

> When I eat something fattening it is easier to eat at night. So I look forward to eating a cookie, my one cookie, late at night—I eat it really slow, and I have to eat by myself. I wait until the night after I have eaten a big dinner. I am not hungry for the cookie, I'm still thinking about it: "Oh, that is the time when I get to eat my cookie, even if I'm not hungry for it." . . . I get my only happiness from eating that cookie. Then I think I'm going to start eating to be happy. That gives me the fear that I will be unhappy about everything, and be happy about eating a cookie. Then it makes me afraid that I'm going to cure all my unhappiness by eating and eating cookies all the time, because my greatest fear is to lose control and to become fat.

> (Bruch, 1988, pp. 151–152)

These are the fears expressed by a young woman who suffers from anorexia nervosa, which is a disease characterized by emaciation because of extreme dieting. What differences among people and situations determine how much is eaten?

Boundary Model of Eating

The set point in the negative feedback system is located between two boundaries that define a comfort zone. For example, when the house temperature drops below the lower boundary in winter, the furnace heats the house. When the temperature goes above the upper boundary in summer, the air conditioner cools the house. Between these two boundaries there exists a comfort zone. Herman and Polivy (1984) used this zone idea in their **boundary model** of hunger (lower boundary) and satiety (upper boundary). According to this model, if a person drops below the lower boundary then she experiences aversive feelings of hunger, weakness, and an empty stomach; the further below the lower boundary, the greater the impetus to eat. Above the satiety (upper) boundary, a person stops eating when aversive physiological conditions begin to prevail, such as a full stomach. In between upper and lower boundaries is the *zone of biological indifference*, where instead of physiological reasons, social factors and the palatability of food determine how much is eaten.

The zone of biological indifference is different for normal eaters, dieters, binge eaters, and people with anorexia nervosa. Physiological factors largely govern when normal eaters start and stop eating. Dieters, however, have a wider zone of biological indifference. They strive to rely on a cognitively imposed diet boundary that determines how much they eat, often falling short of their satiety boundary (Herman & Polivy, 1984). For them, trying to lose weight, fitting into clothes, or achieving society's ideal body image are factors that also control their eating.

A number of psychological scales measure the extent that people voluntarily restrain their eating plus measure the characteristics of that restraint (Williamson et al., 2007). Table 5.2 presents some examples of the various concerns that dieters encounter when cognitively restraining the urge to eat. The *Revised Restraint Scale* is a specific example of such a survey that is used frequently to measure the extent that people restrain their eating (Herman & Polivy, 1980). Individuals who score high on the *Revised Restraint Scale* are defined as restrained eaters. They constantly think about what and how much they eat and then feel guilty when they have exceeded their diet. People who score low on the scale, however, are unrestrained. They eat when and however much they want. Restrained eaters are described as having lower hunger boundaries and higher satiety boundaries than unrestrained eaters. For example, it takes a greater amount of food deprivation for them to admit being hungry, and they eat less food after equivalent periods of deprivation. Perhaps

TABLE 5.2 Dieters' Concerns Measured by Various Eating Restraint Scales

Are you currently dieting?		
Not at all	= 0 1 2 3 4 5 6 7 8 9 =	Very much so
How frequently during the day are you aware of being hungry?		
Never	= 0 1 2 3 4 5 6 7 8 9 =	Frequently
How frequently during the day do you think of food?		
Never	= 0 1 2 3 4 5 6 7 8 9 =	Often
How much do you think your weight fluctuated over the past month?		
None at all	= 0 1 2 3 4 5 6 7 8 9 =	A great deal
To what extent do you cognitively control or watch how much you eat?		
No cognitive control	= 0 1 2 3 4 5 6 7 8 9 =	A great deal of cognitive control
Are you susceptible to bingeing or greatly overeating when you are alone?		
Not at all susceptible	= 0 1 2 3 4 5 6 7 8 9 =	Very susceptible
Do you feel guilty when you break your diet?		
Not at all	= 0 1 2 3 4 5 6 7 8 9 =	Very much so

dieters become accustomed to experiencing hunger and to eating less than unrestrained eaters (Herman & Polivy, 1984).

Some dieters also binge on occasion and thus are described as having a wider zone of biological indifference than normal eaters do. These individuals usually have an all-or-nothing view of their diet so that, when they break it, bingeing results. Binge eating refers to the inability to stop eating, only doing so when running out of food, being interrupted, or reaching physiological capacity (Wilson et al., 1996). Polivy and Herman (1985) claim that bingeing is a likely consequence of dieting because of the possibility that dieting makes a person chronically hungry.

Release of Diet Restraint

Are your boundaries for hunger and satiety well defined? Do you know the difference between hunger sensations, feeling full, and feelings of distress? Is your mind pushing your "start eating" boundary in one direction only to be opposed by your body pushing it in the other direction?

Food stimuli release of diet restraint. Restrained eaters set their diet boundary cognitively rather than physiologically. Consequently, they frequently struggle between physiological pressures to eat and their cognitively placed diet boundary. Dieting makes this struggle more intense, since it makes an individual even more susceptible to eating, especially when faced with palatable foods. Furthermore, when the cognitive boundary or restraint is lifted, the result is overeating or bingeing for some previously restrained eaters (Herman & Polivy, 1984; Polivy & Herman, 1985; Ruderman, 1986). For instance, Klajner and associates (1981) had dieters and nondieters go without eating for five hours and then presented them with freshly baked chocolate chip cookies. For half the participants, the cookies were made unpalatable from being colored green. Dieters salivated more to the palatable cookies than to the unpalatable ones, while nondieters salivated the same amount to both types of cookies.

When their cognitive restraint is lifted, dieters eat more. They experience stronger cephalic responses to palatable food, making them more susceptible to eating. To illustrate, Fedoroff and coworkers (1997) divided individuals into unrestrained and restrained eaters based on their scores on the *Revised Restraint Scale*. Participants were informed that the study was about food preferences and that they would be asked to taste and to give their opinion on various foods. Prior to tasting and rating pizzas, half of the restrained and unrestrained eaters were exposed to the odor of baking pizza for 10 minutes, or were told to think about pizza for 10 minutes. The other half of the restrained and unrestrained eaters were not exposed to the pizza odors and could think about whatever they chose. Afterward, all participants were asked to taste and rate the quality of the pizza. As you might imagine, both the odor of the baking pizza and thinking about pizza increased pizza consumption, but this was only true for restrained eaters. The restrained eaters also reported an increased liking, craving, and desire to eat pizza as a result of the pizza cues. The unrestrained eaters were not affected by these temptations. Additional research shows a definite inverse relationship between the degree of restraint and eating when that restraint is released. When directly exposed to food, individuals with increasing levels of restraint consume increasing amounts of food (Coelho et al., 2009).

Stress releases diet restraint. In the paragraph opening this section, the young woman expressed her fears that eating cookies would be her only source of happiness. For some people, eating is a way to relieve stress. What stress seems to do is to remove the diet boundary and cause eating, especially in restrained eaters, regardless of whether they are of normal weight or obese (Greeno & Wing, 1994; Ruderman, 1986). In a representative investigation, Ruderman (1985) tested whether failure-induced stress would inhibit dietary restraint. First, she measured the degree of dietary restraint in her female participants using the *Revised Restraint Scale*. During the experimental phase, half of her participants succeeded or failed at a concept-formation task. In the next phase, participants rated crackers for saltiness, knowing that afterward they could help themselves to any remaining crackers. The effects of failure and the degree of restraint affected the number of crackers eaten. The high-restraint participants in the failure group ate more crackers. Low- and high-restraint participants in the success group, however, did not differ in the number of crackers they ate.

Although distress can remove diet boundaries, positive mood can also remove the diet boundary, at least in female restrained eaters. In one interesting experiment, Cools and associates (1992) had women watch a 20-minute film that was either neutral, comic, or a horror genre to induce a neutral, positive, or negative mood. The researchers provided popcorn, since many people eat popcorn while at the movies. The real purpose in providing the popcorn was to determine how much of it would be eaten based on the type of film that was being watched. Figure 5.9 shows the amount of popcorn eaten during each film type by restrained or unrestrained eaters. Restrained eaters ate the most popcorn while viewing the horror film and the least while viewing the neutral film. They also ate more popcorn than unrestrained eaters during the comedy film and even more during the horror film. Unrestrained eaters, however, ate a similar amount of popcorn during each type of film.

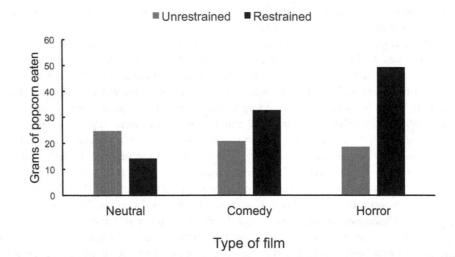

FIGURE 5.9 Stress and Eating Behavior. Restrained eaters ate less popcorn than unrestrained eaters did while watching the neutral film. However, restrained eaters ate more than unrestrained eaters during the comedy film and ate even more during the horror film.

Source: Adapted from "Emotional Arousal and Overeating in Restrained Eaters" by J. Cools et al., 1992, *Journal of Abnormal Psychology, 101,* p. 349.

Anorexia Nervosa

Individuals who impose extremely rigid diet boundaries on themselves are perhaps most puzzling for understanding the motivation for eating. An extreme eating restriction can result in a disorder known as **anorexia nervosa**. Diagnostic features consist of a "persistent energy intake restriction; intense fear of gaining weight or of becoming fat, or persistent behavior that interferes with weight gain; and a disturbance in self-perceived weight or shape" (p. 339, DSM-V; APA, 2013). The fear of weight gain is maintained in spite of weight loss and may even increase with a decline in weight. The self-esteem of these individuals relies almost exclusively on the shape and weight of their bodies. An anorexia nervosa diagnosis is given when individuals are willing to maintain a body weight that is significantly low or less than expected for what is normal for their age and height (APA, 2013). In a national survey involving face-to-face interviews, researchers discovered the prevalence of anorexia nervosa was 0.9 percent for women and 0.3 percent for men. The mean age of onset was 19 years, although that could range from 15 to 25 years (Hudson et al., 2007).

Anorexia nervosa does not occur at random. There are personality traits that make an individual susceptible. In a review of the literature, Kaye (2008) notes that personality traits of anxiety, perfectionism, and obsessive-compulsiveness existed before the development of anorexia nervosa. Such personality traits increase an individual's vulnerability toward anorexia nervosa when dieting begins. External factors also contribute to the onset of anorexia nervosa (Polivy & Herman, 2002; Stice, 2001). First, there are societal pressures that promote being thin and disparage being fat. This pressure comes from the media but may also come from parents and peers. Second, to the extent that thinness is accepted as a personal ideal, young individuals often develop dissatisfaction with their bodies. This dissatisfaction can lead to dieting and, in more extreme cases, also purging. In addition, anorexia nervosa is associated with excessive exercise, such that patients with developing symptoms do so compulsively (Davis, 1997).

If hunger and delicious foods are powerful motivators to eat, then what is the motivation to not eat? One theory maintains that the success of weight loss is more reinforcing than eating (Selby et al., 2014). For example, an individual's goal, say, of losing several pounds is reinforced by positive feelings, such as pride when this goal is accomplished. This positive reinforcement, in turn, strengthens further weight loss behavior. According to Selby and coresearchers (2014), the feeling of pride, however, is likely to trigger other positive emotions such as happiness, self-confidence, and vitality. These additional positive emotions further strengthen weight loss behavior. This trend, however, is more likely to occur in individuals with a low ability to differentiate among their positive emotions. Differentiation refers to the ability to distinguish among different positive emotions, such as pride versus glad versus enthusiastic. Thus, successful weight loss results in positive feelings among anorexics, especially those with low positive emotion differentiation. These individuals also engage in more weight loss behaviors, such as vomiting, laxative use, and low food intake (Selby et al., 2014).

Patients with anorexia nervosa are also confused about their internal body sensations in alleviating negative emotions (Bruch, 1988). For example, they might confuse anxiety or distress with hunger and respond with eating (Rebert et al., 1991). Women with anorexia nervosa who only restrict their food intake and those anorexics who also binge and purge are not sensitive to internal signals of hunger and satiety. To illustrate, Halmi and Sunday (1991) examined the course of hunger and fullness during a meal for patients with eating disorders and for normal individuals. Following a 10-hour fast, these individuals rated how hungry and full they were immediately before, during, and after drinking a liquid breakfast meal. For normal eaters, as the meal progressed, they became full and less and less hungry. Anorexic patients who restricted their diet rated themselves as full and not hungry at the start, during, and at the end of the meal. It was as if neither the 10-hour fast nor eating the liquid breakfast had any effect on their sense of hunger or satiety. Anorexic patients who also binged and purged showed an up-and-down hunger–fullness pattern during and after the meal. It was as if they also had trouble detecting when they were hungry or full. Patients who specifically exhibited these abnormal hunger–fullness patterns also ate less of the liquid meal than individuals who showed normal hunger–fullness patterns.

Patients with anorexia nervosa also develop adverse reactions to eating food, a condition known as the **refeeding syndrome**. As a result of extreme food deprivation, the body loses its ability to digest and absorb food. For example, food deprivation produces a sharp decline in phosphorous, which is an essential mineral within the body's cells. With refeeding, there is a sudden uptake of phosphorous, which can set off a cascade of life-threatening complications, such as heart failure, coma, and breathing problems. In addition, because of food deprivation, the intestines become intolerant to food, which can result in nausea and diarrhea when food is eaten (Solomon & Kirby, 1990). These adverse reactions mean eating food has a very low incentive value. However, food can have a positive incentive value when it comes to manipulating, handling, and preparing it but not for eating it. The incentive value for eating food may be so low that an anorexic individual is unable to become motivated enough to eat (Pinel et al., 2000).

The Office on Women's Health, U.S. Department of Health & Human Services Office, provides information about eating disorders here: http://womenshealth.gov/body-image/eating-disorders.

Section Recap

People differ in the extent they limit their eating. The *boundary model* defines the zone of biological indifference as situated between a hunger boundary and satiety boundary. Dieters and individuals suffering from anorexia nervosa have a hunger boundary that is lower and a satiety boundary that is higher than that of normal eaters. Dieters or restrained eaters also place a cognitive restraint, or diet boundary, on themselves, which is lower than their physiological hunger boundary. Unrestrained eaters, by contrast, rely on a higher physiological boundary for when to eat. Cognitive restraint can be released by making individuals break their diet boundary. The result is overeating. Both positive and negative stress can release diet restraints and lead to overeating in restrained individuals. In addition, dieting makes individuals more susceptible to eating palatable foods.

A puzzle for the motivation of eating occurs in individuals who suffer from *anorexia nervosa*, which is characterized by extreme weight loss and a distorted body image. Individuals with anorexia nervosa discover that not eating and extensive exercise contribute to weight loss. Not eating is more reinforcing than eating, since it is reinforced by the achievement of weight loss goals and accompanying positive feelings. After the illness develops they have confused internal body sensations and have trouble distinguishing when they are hungry or full. As a result of extreme food deprivation, anorexics develop a negative reaction to eating food known as the *refeeding syndrome*. In addition, eating food attains a very low incentive value, so an individual is not motivated to eat.

GLOSSARY

Term	Definition
Adipose	Fat cells in the body where fat from food is stored
Alliesthesia	Changes in a person's *milieu intérieur* or body that determine whether a stimulus is experienced as pleasant or unpleasant
Allostasis	*Allo* means variable. It is a way of maintaining internal stability by making changes in set points to cope with anticipated environmental demands that can disrupt homeostasis
Anorexia Nervosa	Diagnosis of a person unwilling to maintain at least 85 percent of normal body weight; strong fear of becoming fat or gaining weight even when emaciated
Binge Eating	Consequence of breaking a diet and involves the inability to stop eating and only doing so when out of food or reaching physiological capacity
Boundary Model	A dimension that shows when eating begins (hunger) and when eating stops (satiety)
Carrying Cost	The amount of energy that is required to carry one's weight; heavier people have greater carrying costs
Cephalic Response	A physiological reaction to the smell and taste of food. It consists of secreting saliva, gastric juices, and insulin from the pancreas
Cholecystokinin (CCK)	A hormone released in the upper part of the small intestine after food intake and is related to the inhibition of further eating
Dehydrated	The result of a procedure that is designed to make a person lose water, such as exercise, being in a hot place, or eating salted nuts
Delbouef Illusion	The size of the outer circle influences the perceived size of a solid inner circle. The solid inner circle is perceived as larger when the outer circle is smaller
Diet Boundary	Cognitively imposed boundaries of when to eat and when to stop eating; cognitive boundaries associated with greater hunger and stop short of satiety
Dual Intervention Point Model	Body weight settles between a lower and upper boundary. The lower boundary represents one's minimum weight. The upper represents one's maximum weight while remaining agile
Energy Homeostasis	The attempt to maintain a balance between energy intake from food and various forms of energy expenditure (rest to exercise)
Ghrelin	A hormone released by the stomach that stimulates hunger, eating, and mental images of food
Hedonic Ratings	Ratings of how much something is liked or enjoyed; ratings range from unpleasant or dislike to neutral to pleasant or like
Homeostasis	Constant stable internal environment that the body tries to maintain with various negative feedback systems

continued . . .

GLOSSARY Continued

Term	Definition
Hyperthermic	When actual body temperature is above the body's set point temperature; the person feels warm
Hypothalamus	A small section of the brain that monitors the body's energy levels from signals received from various hormones: cholecystokinin (CCK), leptin, and ghrelin
Hypothermic	When actual body temperature is below the body's set point temperature; the person feels cold
Leptin	A hormone released from adipose tissue that is involved in the long-term regulation of food energy located in fat cells
Mere Exposure Effect	Being repeatedly exposed to a stimulus leads to increased preferences for that stimulus; repeatedly eating a food increases one's liking of it
Milieu Interieur	The interior of the body responsible for the metabolism, growth, repair, and reproduction of the body's cells
Negative Feedback System	The body's self-correcting process that reduces the discrepancy between a desired state (set point) and an actual state of the body
Palatability	Hedonic value of food as determined by variety, texture, temperature, aroma, and flavor
Physical Activity	Voluntary movements that range from studying to running. Its energy use is compared to resting metabolism and the thermic effect
Physiological Need	A discrepancy between a bodily or physiological set point and an actual physiological state, e.g., a low amount of glucose
Refeeding Syndrome	Aversive reaction to eating following anorexia nervosa because body lost its ability to absorb and digest food; intestines intolerant of food
Resting Metabolism	Energy use (while a person is at rest) for body maintenance, pumping of blood, oxygen utilization, work of the cells, and neural activity of the brain
Satiety	A feeling that refers to having gratified hunger, feeling content, and having replenished energy stores
Sensory-Specific Satiety	Habituation or decline in preference for the sensory characteristics of a particular food, such as flavor, texture, and appearance
Set Point	A desired state of the body that is crucial for life, comfort, and safety, e.g., a set point body temperature
Taste Aversion	A strong dislike (nausea reaction) for a food because of a prior association of that food with nausea or upset stomach
Thermic Effect	The energy cost for digesting, storing, and absorbing food
Thirst Sensations	These reflect the body's need for water and manifest themselves locally (dry mouth and throat) and generally (thirsty, tired, weary, dizzy)
Zone of Biological Indifference	Middle portion or zone of the boundary model of eating in which a person is not motivated to eat; neutral zone regarding eating

REFERENCES

American Psychiatric Association (APA). (2013). *Diagnostic and statistical manual of mental disorders* (5th ed.). Arlington, VA: American Psychiatric Association.

Appleton, K. M., Gentry, R. C., & Shepherd, R. (2006). Evidence of a role for conditioning in the development of liking for flavours in humans in everyday life. *Physiology and Behavior, 87*, 478–486.

Beauchamp, G. K., Cowart, B. J., & Moran, M. (1986). Developmental changes in salt acceptability in human infants. *Developmental Psychobiology, 19*, 17–25.

Bell, E. A., Castellanos, V. H., Pelkman, C. L., Thorwart, M. L., & Rolls, B. J. (1998). Energy density of foods affects energy intake in normal-weight women. *The American Journal of Clinical Nutrition, 67*, 412–420.

Bernard, C. (1878/1961). *An introduction to the study of experimental medicine* (H. C. Green, trans.). New York, NY: Collier.

Bernstein, I. L. (1978). Learned taste aversions in children receiving chemotherapy. *Science, 200*, 1302–1303.

Birch, L. L. (1999). Development of food preferences. *Annual Review of Nutrition, 19*, 41–62.

Birch, L. L., & Marlin, D. W. (1982). I don't like it; I never tried it: Effect of exposure on two-year-old children's food preferences. *Appetite, 3*, 353–360.

Bruce, D. G., Storlien, L. H., Furler, S. M., & Chisholm, D. J. (1987). Cephalic phase metabolic responses in normal weight adults. *Metabolism, 36*, 721–725.

Bruch, H. (1988). *Conversation with anorexics* (D. Czyzewski & M. A. Suhr, Eds.). New York, NY: Basic.

Brunstrom, J. M., & Mitchell, G. L. (2007). Flavor-nutrient learning in restrained and unrestrained eaters. *Physiology and Behavior, 90*, 133–141.

Burdon, C. A., Johnson, N. A., Chapman, P. G., & O'Connor, H. T. (2012). Influence of beverage temperature on palatability and fluid ingestion during endurance exercise: A systematic review. *International Journal of Sport Nutrition and Exercise Metabolism, 22*, 199–211.

Cabanac, M. (1971). Physiological role of pleasure. *Science, 173*, 1103–1107.

Cabanac, M. (2010). The dialectics of pleasure. In M. L. Kringelbach & K. C. Berridge (Eds.), *Pleasures of the brain* (pp. 113–124). New York, NY: Oxford University Press.

Cannon, W. B. (1939). *The wisdom of the body* (2nd ed.). New York, NY: W. W. Norton.

Coelho, J. S., Jansen, A., Roefs, A., & Nederkoorn, C. (2009). Eating behavior in response to food-cue exposure: Examining the cue-reactivity and counteractive-control models. *Psychology of Addictive Behaviors, 23*, 131.

Cools, J., Schotte, D. E., & McNally, R. J. (1992). Emotional arousal and overeating in restrained eaters. *Journal of Abnormal Psychology, 101*, 348–351.

Crocker, B. (1961). *Betty Crocker's new picture cook book* (6th ed.). New York, NY: McGraw-Hill.

Davis, C. (1997). Eating disorders and hyperactivity: A psychobiological perspective. *The Canadian Journal of Psychiatry, 42*, 168–175.

Drewnowski, A., Brunzell, J. D., Sande, K., Iverius, P. H., & Greenwood, M. R. C. (1985). Sweet tooth reconsidered. Taste responsiveness in human obesity. *Physiology and Behavior, 35*, 617–622.

Drewnowski, A., & Greenwood, M. R. (1983). Cream and sugar: Human preferences for high fat foods. *Physiology and Behavior, 30*, 629–633.

Engell, D. B., Maller, O., Sawka, M. N., Francesconi, R. N., Drolet, L., & Young, A. J. (1987). Thirst and fluid intake following graded hypohydration levels in humans. *Physiology and Behavior, 40*, 229–236.

Fedoroff, I. C., Polivy, J., & Herman, C. P. (1997). The effect of pre-exposure to food cues on the eating behavior of restrained and unrestrained eaters. *Appetite, 28*, 33–47.

Friedman, M. I., Ulrich, P., & Mattes, R. D. (1999). A figurative measure of subjective hunger sensations. *Appetite, 32*, 395–404.

Fryar, C. D., Carroll, M. D., & Ogden, C. L. (2012). Prevalence of overweight, obesity, and extreme obesity among adults: United States, 1960–1962 through 2009–2010. *CDC National Center for Health Statistics*.

Gaillet-Torrent, M., Sulmont-Rossé, C., Issanchou, S., Chabanet, C., & Chambaron, S. (2014). Impact of a non-attentively perceived odour on subsequent food choices. *Appetite, 76*, 17–22.

Garb, J. L., & Stunkard, A. J. (1974). Taste aversion in man. *American Journal of Psychiatry, 131*, 1204–1207.

Garcia, J., Ervin, F., & Koelling, R. A. (1966). Learning with prolonged delay of reinforcement. *Psychonomic Science, 5*, 121–122.

Geary, N. (2004). Endocrine controls of eating: CCK, leptin, and ghrelin. *Physiology and Behavior, 81,* 719–733.

Goldsmith, R., Joanisse, D. R., Gallagher, D., Pavlovich, K., Shamoon, E., Leibel, R. L., & Rosenbaum, M. (2010). Effects of experimental weight perturbation on skeletal muscle work efficiency, fuel utilization, and biochemistry in human subjects. *American Journal of Physiology: Regulatory, Integrative and Comparative Physiology, 298,* R79-R88.

Greeno, C. G., & Wing, R. R. (1994). Stress-induced eating. *Psychological Bulletin, 115,* 444–464.

Grill, H. J., & Norgren, R. (1978). The taste reactivity test. I. Mimetic responses to gustatory stimuli in neurologically normal rats. *Brain Research, 143,* 263–279.

Hall, K. D. (2012). Modeling metabolic adaptations and energy regulation in humans. *Annual Review of Nutrition, 32,* 35–54.

Halmi, K. A., & Sunday, S. R. (1991). Temporal patterns of hunger and fullness ratings and related cognitions in anorexia and bulimia. *Appetite, 16,* 219–237.

Harnack, L. J., Jeffery, R. W., & Boutelle, K. N. (2000). Temporal trends in energy intake in the United States: An ecologic perspective. *American Journal of Clinical Nutrition, 71,* 1478–1484.

Havermans, R. C., & Jansen, A. (2007). Increasing children's liking of vegetables through flavour-flavour learning. *Appetite, 48,* 259–262.

Herman, C. P., & Polivy, J. (1980). Restrained eating. In A. J. Stunkard (Ed.), *Obesity* (pp. 208–225). Philadelphia, PA: W. B. Saunders.

Herman, C. P., & Polivy, J. (1984). A boundary model for the regulation of eating. In A. J. Stunkard & E. Stellar (Eds.), *Eating and its disorders* (pp. 141–156). New York, NY: Raven.

Holt, S., Brand, J. C., Soveny, C., & Hansky, J. (1992). Relationship of satiety to postprandial glycemic, insulin and cholecystokinin responses. *Appetite, 18,* 129–141.

Hudson, J. I., Hiripi, E., Pope Jr., H. G., & Kessler, R. C. (2007). The prevalence and correlates of eating disorders in the national comorbidity survey replication. *Biological Psychiatry, 61,* 348–358.

Jerome, N. W. (1977). Taste experience and the development of a dietary preference for sweet in humans: Ethnic and cultural variations in early taste experience. In J. M. Weiffenbach (Ed.), *Taste and development* (pp. 235–248). Bethesda, MD: U.S. Department of Health, Education, and Welfare.

Kaye, W. (2008). Neurobiology of anorexia and bulimia nervosa. *Physiology and Behavior, 94,* 121–135.

Keesey, R. E., & Powley, T. L. (2008). Body energy homeostasis. *Appetite, 51,* 442–445.

Klajner, F., Herman, C. P., Polivy, J., & Chabra, R. (1981). Human obesity, dieting, and anticipatory salivation to food. *Physiology and Behavior, 27,* 195–198.

Klok, M. D., Jakobsdottir, S., & Drent, M. L. (2007). The role of leptin and ghrelin in the regulation of food intake and body weight in humans: A review. *Obesity Reviews, 8,* 21–34.

Kral, T. V. E., Roe, L. S., & Rolls, B. J. (2004). Combined effects of energy density and portion size on energy intake in women. *The American Journal of Clinical Nutrition, 79,* 962–968.

Lakkakula, A., Geaghan, J. P., Wong, W-P., Zanovec, M., Pierce, S. H., & Tuuri, G. (2011). A cafeteria-based tasting program increased liking of fruits and vegetables by lower, middle and upper elementary school-age children. *Appetite, 57,* 299–302.

Lakkakula, A., Geaghan, J., Zanovec, M., Pierce, S. H., & Tuuri, G. (2010). Repeated taste exposure increases the liking for vegetables by low-income elementary school children. *Appetite, 55,* 226–231.

Leibel, R. L., Rosenbaum, M., & Hirsch, J. (1995). Changes in energy expenditure resulting from altered body weight. *New England Journal of Medicine, 332,* 621–628.

Lemmens, S. G., Martens, E. A., Kester, A. D., & Westerterp-Plantenga, M. S. (2011). Changes in gut hormone and glucose concentrations in relation to hunger and fullness. *American Journal of Clinical Nutrition, 94,* 717–725.

Leshem, M., Abutbul, A., & Eilon, R. (1999). Exercise increases the preference for salt in humans. *Appetite, 32,* 251–260.

Levine, J. A., Eberhardt, N. L., & Jensen, M. D. (1999). Role of nonexercise activity thermogenesis in resistance to fat gain in humans. *Science, 283,* 212–214.

Logue, A. W., Ophir, I., & Strauss, K. E. (1981). The acquisition of taste aversions in humans. *Behavior Research and Therapy, 19,* 319–333.

Marcelino, A. S., Adam, A. S., Couronne, T., Köster, E. P., & Sieffermann, J. M. (2001). Internal and external determinants of eating initiation in humans. *Appetite, 36*, 9–14.

McArdle, W. D., Katch, F. I., & Katch, V. L. (1996). *Exercise physiology: Energy, nutrition and human performance* (4th ed.). Baltimore, MD: Williams & Wilkins.

Mennella, J. A., & Beauchamp, G. K. (1998). Early flavor experiences: Research update. *Nutrition Reviews, 56*, 205–211.

Miyaoka, Y., Sawada, M., Sakaguchi, T., & Shingai, T. (1987). Sensation of thirst in normal and laryngectomized man. *Perceptual and Motor Skills, 64*, 239–242.

Mook, D. G., & Votaw, M. C. (1992). How important is hedonism? Reasons given by college students for ending a meal. *Appetite, 18*, 69–75.

Moskowitz, H. R., Kluter, R. A., Westerling, J., & Jacobs, H. L. (1974). Sugar sweetness and pleasantness: Evidence for different psychological laws. *Science, 184*, 583–585.

Mower, G. D. (1976). Perceived intensity of peripheral thermal stimuli is independent of internal body temperature. *Journal of Comparative and Physiological Psychology, 90*, 1152–1155.

Mozaffarian, D., Hao, T., Rimm, E. B., Willett, W. C., & Hu, F. B. (2011). Changes in diet and lifestyle and long-term weight gain in women and men. *New England Journal of Medicine, 364*, 2392–2404.

Muurahainen, N. E., Kissileff, H. R., Lachaussee, J., & Pi-Sunyer, F. X. (1991). Effect of a soup preload on reduction of food intake by cholecystokinin in humans. *American Journal of Physiology, 260*, R672–R680.

Nederkoorn, C., Smulders, F. T. Y., & Jansen, A. (2000). Cephalic phase responses, craving and food intake in normal subjects. *Appetite, 35*, 45–55.

Pinel, J. P. J., Assanand, S., & Lehman, D. R. (2000). Hunger, eating, and ill health. *American Psychologist, 55*, 1105–1116.

Pittas, A. G., Hariharan, R., Stark, P. C., Hajduk, C. L., Greenberg, A. S., & Roberts, S. B. (2005). Interstitial glucose level is a significant predictor of energy intake in free-living women with healthy body weight. *The Journal of nutrition, 135*, 1070–1074.

Pliner, P. (1982). The effects of mere exposure on liking for edible substances. *Appetite, 3*, 283–290.

Polivy, J., & Herman, C. P. (1985). Dieting and bingeing: A causal analysis. *American Psychologist, 40*, 193–201.

Polivy, J., & Herman, C. P. (2002). Causes of eating disorders. *Annual Review of Psychology, 53*, 187–213.

Powley, T. L. (1977). The ventromedial hypothalamus syndrome, satiety and a cephalic phase hypothesis. *Psychological Review, 84*, 89–126.

Ramsay, D. S., & Woods, S. C. (2014). Clarifying the roles of homeostasis and allostasis in physiological regulation. *Psychological Review, 121*, 225.

Raynor, H. A., & Epstein, L. H. (2001). Dietary variety, energy regulation, and obesity. *Psychological Bulletin, 127*, 325–341.

Rebert, W. M., Stanton, A. L., & Schwarz, R. M. (1991). Influence of personality attributes and daily moods on bulimic eating patterns. *Addictive Behaviors, 16*, 497–505.

Rolls, B. J., Castellanos, V. H., Halford, J. C., Kilara, A., Panyam, D., Pelkman, C. L., . . . Thorwart, M. L. (1998). Volume of food consumed affects satiety in men. *The American Journal of Clinical Nutrition, 67*, 1170–1177.

Rolls, B. J., Morris, E. L., & Roe, L. S. (2002). Portion size of food affects energy intake in normal-weight and overweight men and women. *American Journal of Clinical Nutrition, 76*, 1207–1213.

Rolls, B. J., Rolls, E. T., Rowe, E. A., & Sweeney, K. (1981). Sensory specific satiety in man. *Physiology and Behavior, 27*, 137–142.

Ruderman, A. J. (1985). Dysphoric mood and overeating: A test of restraint theory's disinhibition hypothesis. *Journal of Abnormal Psychology, 94*, 78–85.

Ruderman, A. J. (1986). Dietary restraint: A theoretical and empirical review. *Psychological Bulletin, 99*, 247–262.

Sadoul, B. C., Schuring, E. A. H., Mela, D. J., & Peters, H. P. F. (2014). The relationship between appetite scores and subsequent energy intake: An analysis based on 23 randomized controlled studies. *Appetite, 83*, 153–159.

Sandick, B. L., Engell, D. B., & Maller, O. (1984). Perception of drinking water temperature and effects for humans after exercise. *Physiology and Behavior, 32*, 851–855.

Sandoval, D., Cota, D., & Seeley, R. J. (2008). The integrative role of CNS fuel-sensing mechanisms in energy balance and glucose regulation. *Annual Review of Physiology, 70,* 513–535.

Schlader, Z. J., Perry, B. G., Jusoh, M. R. C., Hodges, L. D., Stannard, S. R., & Mündel, T. (2013). Human temperature regulation when given the opportunity to behave. *European Journal of Applied Physiology, 113,* 1291–1301.

Schmid, D. A., Held, K., Ising, M., Uhr, M., Weike, J. C., & Steiger, A. (2005). Ghrelin stimulates appetite, imagination of food, GH, ACTH, and cortisol, but does not affect leptin in normal controls. *Neuropsychopharmacology, 30,* 1187–1192.

Schulkin, J. (1991). Hedonic consequences of salt hunger. In R. C. Bolles (Ed.), *The hedonics of taste* (pp. 89–105). Hillsdale, NJ: Lawrence Erlbaum.

Selby, E. A., Wonderlich, S. A., Crosby, R. D., Engel, S. G., Panza, E., Mitchell, J. E., . . . Le Grange, D. (2014). Nothing tastes as good as thin feels: Low positive emotion differentiation and weight-loss activities in anorexia nervosa. *Clinical Psychological Science, 2,* 514–531.

Solomon, S. M., & Kirby, D. F. (1990). The refeeding syndrome: A review. *Journal of Parenteral and Enteral Nutrition, 14,* 90–96.

Speakman, J. R. (2013). Evolutionary perspectives on the obesity epidemic: Adaptive, maladaptive, and neutral viewpoints. *Annual Review of Nutrition, 33,* 289–317.

Speakman, J. R., Levitsky, D. A., Allison, D. B., Bray, M. S., de Castro, J. M., Clegg, D. J., . . . Westerterp-Plantenga, M. S. (2011). Set points, settling points and some alternative models: Theoretical options to understand how genes and environments combine to regulate body adiposity. *Disease Models and Mechanisms, 4,* 733–745.

Steiner, J. E. (1977). Facial expressions of the neonate infant indicating the hedonics of food-related chemical stimuli. In J. M. Weiffenbach (Ed.), *Taste and development* (pp. 173–189). Bethesda, MD: U.S. Department of Health, Education, and Welfare.

Stice, E. (2001). A prospective test of the dual-pathway of bulimic pathology: Mediating effects of dieting and negative affect. *Journal of Abnormal Psychology, 110,* 124–135.

Van Itallie, T. B., & Kissileff, H. R. (1983). The physiological control of energy intake: An econometric perspective. *American Journal of Clinical Nutrition, 38,* 978–988.

Wansink, B., & van Ittersum, K. (2013). Portion size me: Plate-size induced consumption norms and win-win solutions for reducing food intake and waste. *Journal of Experimental Psychology: Applied, 19,* 320–332.

Williamson, D. A., Martin, C. K., York-Crowe, E., Anton, S. D., Redman, L. M., Han, H., & Ravussin, E. (2007). Measurement of dietary restraint: Validity tests of four questionnaires. *Appetite, 48,* 183–192.

Wilson, G. T., Nathan, P. E., O'Leary, K. D., & Clark, L. A. (1996). *Abnormal psychology: Integrating perspectives.* Boston, MA: Allyn and Bacon.

Wolf, A. V. (1958). *Thirst: Physiology of the urge to drink and problems of water lack.* Springfield, IL: Charles C. Thomas.

Woods, S. C., Schwartz, M. W., Baskin, D. G., & Seeley, R. J. (2000). Food intake and the regulation of body weight. *Annual Review of Psychology, 51,* 255–277.

Young, P. T. (1961). *Motivation and emotion.* New York, NY: John Wiley.

Zajonc, R. B. (1968). Attitudinal effects of mere exposure. *Journal of Personality and Social Psychology Monograph Supplement, 9,* 1–27.

Zandstra, E. H., & El-Deredy, W. (2011). Effects of energy conditioning on food preferences and choice. *Appetite, 57,* 45–49.

Zellner, D. A., Rozin, P., Aron, M., & Kulish, C. (1983). Conditioned enhancement of human's liking for flavor by pairing with sweetness. *Learning and Motivation, 14,* 338–350.

Zoon, H. F., de Graaf, C., & Boesveldt, S. (2016). Food odours direct specific appetite. *Foods, 5,* 12.

CHAPTER 6

Behavior, Arousal, and Affective Valence

The body of man is a machine which winds its own spring.

J. O. De La Mettrie, 1748

Music hath charms to soothe a savage beast,
To soften rocks, or bend a knotted oak.

William Congreve, 1697

While taking an exam, a student is unable to retrieve an answer from memory. However, as soon as she exits the classroom the answer comes to mind. Could the anxiety aroused by the exam have interfered with recall of the answer? This question along with the following will guide your reading of this chapter:

1. In what ways is arousal similar and different from motivation?
2. What produces arousal?
3. Does arousal affect how well a person performs a task? If so, how?
4. Is arousal linked to the quality of our feelings? If so, what is the nature of this link?
5. How do incongruous events produce arousal? Do their resolutions contribute to our preferences and enjoyment of humor, and music?

AROUSAL AND PERFORMANCE

Whether pushed by a motive or pulled by an incentive, physiological and psychological arousal accompanies behavior. In one case, arousal is in the background and affects the efficiency of behavior. In the other case, arousal is in the foreground and is felt as an affective experience that people are motivated to experience in a positive manner. The following two quotes of people's experiences help clarify this distinction. The first quote illustrates the effects of arousal on behavioral competence.

> My math anxiety started because of a teacher that I had for math in the third grade. We were learning our times tables, and she didn't have any sympathy for the kids that were a little slower than the others. We would play a flash card game in front of the class, and if you got it wrong, she made you look like an idiot. So my anxiety comes from being afraid of being wrong in front of a group, and looking stupid.
>
> (Perry, 2004, p. 322)

This next quote illustrates how arousal serves as an affective experience.

> To her, the tension-and-release cycle that accompanies cinematic terror brings about something like a gambler's high. "It's not that I'm a self-mutilator," she [Ms. Gauh] said, "but it's just a powerful rush when you can overcome some pain." . . . "It's the adrenaline," said Sarah Stark, a movie theater manager in Lima, Ohio, explaining her long time interest in gory movies. For her, she said, violent horror movies amount to something of a personal endurance test, a bit like white-water rafting—the sheer terror of which clears the mind and, briefly, seems to reduce all of life down to a single exhilarating moment.
>
> (Williams, 2006, ¶ 12, 28)

The first quote by a student with math anxiety typifies the relationship between arousal and performance on a task. When arousal is high, as in the case of math anxiety, a student's performance is low. If only math anxiety could be reduced, but not totally, then a student might perform better when solving math problems or taking a math test. The second quote is from individuals who enjoy watching horror movies. For them, movie scenes create a level of arousal that is optimal for creating a sense of pleasure, like a rush or moment of exhilaration.

How do these two functions of arousal help us to understand motivation? But first, what is arousal, what causes it, and how does it affect behavior?

Categories of Arousal

Arousal refers to the mobilization or activation of energy that occurs in preparation or during actual behavior. "My heart is pounding" implies physiological arousal, while "I feel tense and anxious" implies psychological arousal.

Physiological arousal. If you raced through your presentation during speech class with clammy hands, pounding heart, and dry throat, then you were physiologically aroused. **Physiological arousal** refers to those bodily changes that correspond to our feelings of being energized, such as sweaty palms and increased muscle tension, breathing, and heart rate. These changes indicate that the body is getting ready for action, much like starting a car's engine means that it is ready to move. The *autonomic nervous system* controls physiological arousal and is divided into two branches: the sympathetic nervous system and the parasympathetic nervous system. The sympathetic nervous system is responsible for arousing or preparing the body for action. It stimulates the heart to pump blood more effectively. It causes glucose, epinephrine (adrenaline), and norepinephrine (noradrenaline) to be released in the bloodstream. The sympathetic nervous system also makes rapid breathing possible, which increases oxygen intake. The parasympathetic nervous system, however, is concerned with conserving the body's energy. It is active during quiet periods and tends to counteract the arousing effects of the sympathetic system.

TutorVista presents a YouTube video describing the autonomic nervous system titled "Autonomic Nervous System" here: www.youtube.com/watch?v=YFYRosjcVuU.

Psychological arousal. Is the anticipation you feel when receiving your exam results the same as the anticipation you feel when opening your birthday present? **Psychological arousal** refers to how subjectively aroused an individual feels. An alternative to relying on physiological arousal is to ask individuals how subjectively aroused they feel. "I'm full of pep," "I'm all psyched up," or "I'm tired and have no energy" are verbal reports of subjective arousal or activation. In researching subjective arousal, Thayer (1989) developed a theory of arousal that involves two dimensions: energetic arousal and tense arousal. **Energetic arousal** is a dimension characterized by a range of feelings from tiredness and sleepiness at the low end to alert and awake at the high end. High levels of energetic arousal are associated with a positive affective tone and optimism. For instance, energetic arousal could be associated with planning a vacation trip. **Tense arousal** is a dimension characterized by a range of feelings from calmness and stillness at the low end to tension and anxiety at the high end. High levels of tense arousal are associated with a negative affective tone. The student's description of math anxiety in the opening example is a case of tense arousal, while the report from the horror movie-goers suggests their experience is a mixture of tense and energetic arousal.

The *Scale Measuring Energetic Arousal and Tense Arousal* in Table 6.1 provides a way of determining the intensity of each type of arousal that a person is momentarily experiencing. The items in Table 6.1 indicate that energetic arousal is associated with positivity and pleasantness while tense arousal is associated with negativity and unpleasantness (Schimmack & Reisenzein, 2002). In validating these two types of arousal, Thayer (1978) found that students rated themselves more jittery and fearful (high tense arousal) on the day of an exam compared to a typical class day. Conversely, they were more likely to rate themselves as being more placid and calm (low tense arousal) on a typical class day than on an exam day. Thayer also found that taking a brisk 10-minute walk elevated energetic arousal compared to sitting restfully for a similar amount of time. Resting, however, reduced an individual's level of tense arousal compared to walking.

Trait vs. state anxiety. **Anxiety** is a widely accepted example of tense arousal. Anxiety is not a single entity but instead consists of two parts: trait and state. *Trait anxiety* is an individual difference measure of the disposition to perceive environmental events as threatening and to respond anxiously. *State anxiety* refers to the actual feelings of apprehension, worry, and sympathetic nervous system arousal that are evoked by threatening situations (Spielberger, 1975). In other words, trait anxiety is the propensity to react with state anxiety in threatening situations. For example, trait anxiety is the disposition to become anxious (state anxiety) during a math test. In general, state anxiety is damaging to performance especially on tasks that are complex (Zeidner & Matthews, 2005). But how does anxiety affect performance? Math anxiety, sport competition

TABLE 6.1   Scale Measuring Energetic Arousal and Tense Arousal

The six dimensions below describe arousal, energy, or activation levels. Please circle the number of each dimension that indicates how you feel at this moment

Energetic Arousal

sleepy	= 0 1 2 3 4 5 6 7 8 9 =	awake
tired	= 0 1 2 3 4 5 6 7 8 9 =	alert
drowsy	= 0 1 2 3 4 5 6 7 8 9 =	wakeful

Tense Arousal

at rest	= 0 1 2 3 4 5 6 7 8 9 =	restless
relaxed	= 0 1 2 3 4 5 6 7 8 9 =	tense
calm	= 0 1 2 3 4 5 6 7 8 9 =	jittery

Note: Sum all of your energetic arousal and tense arousal scores separately. The value of each score indicates the amount of each type of arousal that a person experiences at the moment

Source: Based on "Experiencing Activation: Energetic Arousal and Tense Arousal Are Not Mixtures of Valence and Activation" by U. Schimmack and R. Reisenzein, 2002, *Emotion, 2,* p. 414.

anxiety, and music performance anxiety are specific examples of state anxiety. As their names imply, anxiety can be raised when a student works on math, an athlete is ready to participate in sports, and a musician is ready to play for an audience.

Sources of Arousal

Does loud music, being evaluated, or playing a game energize you? These are examples of stimuli, situations, and behavior that all contribute to arousal and energization.

Someone calls out your name and you orient yourself toward the source of the sound. The sound of your name has both a cue function and an arousing function (Hebb, 1955). The cue function determines the type of response, and the arousing function determines the intensity of the response. The arousal function of a stimulus is apparent from the energizing properties of music, which are described later in this chapter.

In addition to arousal from a specific stimulus, background stimuli also affect a person's level of arousal. These stimuli, not the focus of an individual's attention, consist of time of day, caffeine, and being evaluated. Time of day effects are most obvious from people's sleep–wake cycles: low arousal during sleep and high arousal when awake. Clements and associates (1976) had students in university classes that met at various times of the day fill out a scale that measured energetic arousal. The results showed that energetic arousal followed an inverted-U relationship with time of day. Arousal began low for 8:00 a.m. classes, rose to its highest levels for noon and 2:00 p.m. classes, and then declined to its lowest value for evening classes. Other studies have also shown that psychological arousal increases from shortly after 8:00 a.m. to noon and 2:00 p.m. and then declines, reaching its lowest point prior to bedtime (Thayer, 1967, 1978). More subtle are changes in body temperature, which increases from 8:00 a.m. to 8:00 p.m. and then declines, as do changes in subjective alertness, which increases from 8:00 a.m. to around noon (Monk & Folkard, 1983). Caffeine from a cup of coffee boosts many people's energetic arousal in the morning. As described in Chapter 4, the arousing effects of caffeine are considered pleasurable. Finally, we live in an age when many

TABLE 6.2 Illustrations of Collative Variables

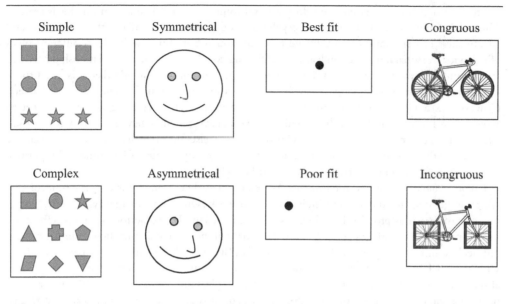

people suffer from evaluation anxiety, which occurs during exams, sports competition, and social situations (Zeidner & Matthews, 2005). Perhaps most pertinent to the reader is test anxiety and math anxiety, which are aroused by exams during statistics courses. Finally, the presence of others can arouse an individual, for example the arousal created by classmates when a student gives a speech or the arousal created by the audience during a music recital.

Besides stimulus intensity, other variables also affect arousal. Berlyne (1960) proposed the term **collative variables** to refer collectively to stimulus characteristics that include novelty, complexity, and incongruity. Some examples are in Table 6.2. A *novel* stimulus is one that is new and different from the stimuli to which a person has become accustomed. For instance, given a choice between two stimuli that differ in novelty, grade school children are more likely to choose the novel one. It is assumed that a more novel stimulus is also more arousing (Comerford & Witryol, 1993). The *complexity* variable is determined by the number of elements and the dissimilarity of those elements in a stimulus array. The *incongruity* variable refers to the disparity between a single element in the stimulus array and other accompanying stimulus elements or previous elements. Collative variables also affect an individual's curiosity. Looking time increases as complexity of various stimuli increases, such as drawings, photographs, and works of art (Faw, 1970; Nicki & Moss, 1975).

Arousal and Behavior

Does your test anxiety affect your exam performance? Are you nervous when speaking in front of the class? For many individuals, the answer is yes. But can arousal also help on occasion? So what is the relationship between arousal and behavior?

Arousal–performance relationships. You want to give a good speech, to make the basket, and to ace the statistics test. Sometimes you do great and sometimes not. The reason for this is arousal. There has long been an interest in psychology of how arousal affects the efficiency and effectiveness of behavior, not only in the types of arousal but also how it affects different types of behavior. Personal introspection leads to conflicting conclusions about the relationship between arousal and performance efficiency. For example, a person might conclude that it is good to be somewhat aroused while giving a speech, although too much arousal results in poor delivery. However, extreme arousal is necessary in some situations such as running across the street to avoid being hit by a car. But is there evidence that behavioral efficiency increases with arousal? This would be a positive relationship. Conversely, is it also possible that behavioral efficiency decreases with arousal? This would be a negative relationship. Figure 6.1 illustrates the positive and negative relationships between arousal and behavior.

Positive arousal–performance relationships. As described earlier, arousal varies with time of day, which is apparent to students and individuals who work swing shifts or graveyard shifts. Simple mental tasks such as proofreading for misspellings, for example, are performed more efficiently during midday than early morning or evening. More complex mental tasks show a similar pattern but decline in performance much earlier in the day. But in each case, higher arousal is associated with greater behavioral efficiency (Valdez et al., 2008). Simple and complex reaction times are also affected by arousal owing to time of day. For example, Childs and de Wit (2008) had participants rate their level of psychological arousal with adjectives such as vigor on a scale that ranged

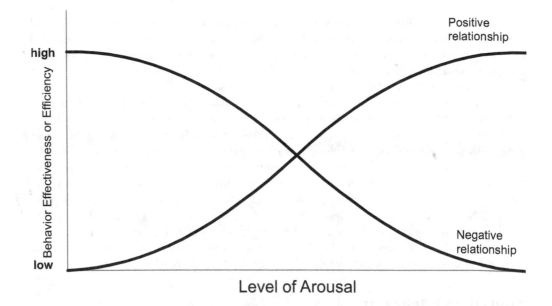

FIGURE 6.1 Positive and Negative Arousal–Performance Relationships. The upward sloping line shows a positive relationship: as arousal increases, behavioral effectiveness and behavioral efficiency increase also. The downward sloping line shows a negative relationship: as arousal increases, behavioral effectiveness and behavioral efficiency decrease.

from 0 = *not at all* to 4 = *extremely*. Ratings were collected at 3:00 a.m. and again at 5:00 p.m., along with measures of reaction time. For the reaction time tasks, participants had to press a mouse key as quickly as possible when an asterisk appeared on the screen. The results indicated quicker reaction times at 5:00 p.m., when felt vigor was higher, and slower at 3:00 a.m., when felt vigor was lower.

Coffee as a source of arousal also increases behavioral efficiency. Smith and coresearchers (2005) manipulated arousal with varying amounts of caffeine. On different days and in the space of 90 minutes, participants drank two beverages either both without caffeine, one with and one without caffeine, or both with caffeine. The simple reaction time task consisted of participants pressing a key as soon as they saw a square appear on the computer screen. The results showed that a greater amount of caffeine produced faster reaction times. In other words, as caffeine-induced arousal increased, reaction time became faster.

Some complex behaviors also benefit from caffeine-induced arousal. Brunyé and coresearchers (2012) had their participants consume 0, 100, 200, or 400 milligrams of caffeine in capsule form. The larger amount of caffeine is usually contained in a 20-ounce cup of coffee. Participants next engaged in a proofreading and grammar correction task. For example, find and correct the grammatical error in the sentence: "billionaire inventor Tony Stark enjoy a lavish life style" (p. 100). To measure the arousing effects of caffeine, participants rated the extent they felt active, calm, peppy and tired. This measurement showed caffeine was effective in increasing psychological arousal. Furthermore, as shown in Figure 6.2, grammatical error detection rate was higher for 400 milligrams of caffeine compared to no caffeine. Thus, error detection proficiency increased with increases in caffeine-induced arousal.

Negative arousal–performance relationships. Yet, sometimes behavioral efficiency and effectiveness decrease as arousal increases, such as public speaking or choking during athletic competition. In the case of basketball free-throw behavior, Wang and coresearchers (2004) had participants shoot 20 free throws in low- and high-pressure conditions designed to produce low and high arousal. First, participants shot free throws in the low-pressure condition, during which only one person was present who scored the shots and returned the ball. Next, in the high-pressure condition, participants shot their free throws while being videotaped in the presence of student spectators. In addition, participants received $1 for every shot they made plus an additional $4 was added or subtracted for every shot that exceeded or fell short of the number made in the low-pressure condition. In order to determine if all of these manipulations increased arousal, participants completed a scale that measured their cognitive anxiety and somatic (body) anxiety. *Cognitive anxiety* refers to negative expectations and mental concerns about performance in a competitive situation. *Somatic anxiety* refers to a person's perception of his or her physiological arousal that is associated with nervousness and tension. The high-pressure manipulations had the intended effect: both cognitive and body anxiety were greater in the high-pressure than in the low-pressure condition. How was free-throw performance affected? Negatively! Participants made significantly fewer free throws while they were more highly anxious. Thus, as arousal (anxiety) increased, free-throw effectiveness declined.

More complex behaviors are also affected by changes in anxiety as in the case of *music performance anxiety*. This anxiety refers to the anticipated distress that occurs while playing music in front of a critical audience. The distress has psychological and physiological characteristics that may actually impair musical performance. In short, music performance anxiety is akin to stage

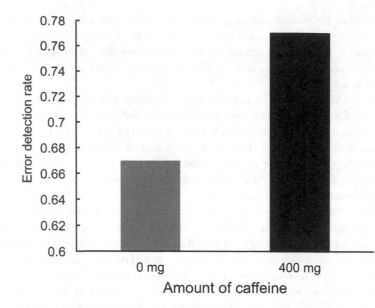

FIGURE 6.2 Caffeine Improves Proofreading. The arousal produced by caffeine improved proofreading proficiency. Participants who consumed caffeine were more efficient at detecting grammatical errors during a proofreading task.

Source: Adapted from "Caffeine Enhances Real-World Language Processing: Evidence from a Proofreading Task" by T. T. Brunyé et al., 2012, *Journal of Experimental Psychology: Applied, 18,* estimated from Figure 1(A), p. 100. Copyright 2012 by American Psychological Association.

fright. Yoshie and coresearchers (2009) created anxiety by having highly trained pianists play individually in a practice room or in front of an audience. In the audience condition, the performers received applause and could win $50, $100, or $200. Physiological and psychological measures of anxiety were taken in both conditions. Playing in front of an audience produced higher anxiety—that is, higher heart rate, more perspiration, and higher subjective ratings of anxiety. Five judges evaluated the players' performance in the practice room and in front of the audience. Anxiety had a negative effect on performance. The judges gave higher technical and artistic scores for pieces played in the practice room than those played in front of the audience. Thus, even though the pianists were motivated to play well, state anxiety created by the audience reduced their piano performance compared to solo playing.

A logical follow-up is that by lowering music performance anxiety the quality of musical performance should increase. Hoffman and Hanrahan (2012) measured music performance anxiety with the *Performance Anxiety Inventory.* The inventory requires musicians to rate themselves on various symptoms such as dread, physiological arousal, and performance-related behaviors. Higher ratings define higher music performance anxiety. The participants consisted of string, brass, woodwind players, pianists, and singers. The musicians were randomly divided into two groups. The cognitive restructuring group received three psychoeducational workshops designed to reduce their anxiety. A control group did not participate but were promised later participation in the work shop. Participants then played a piece of music of their choosing and two judges evaluated the quality of their performance. Compared to the control group, training in cognitive restructuring was effective. It lowered music performance anxiety and heart rate and raised musical performance. Thus, lowering performance anxiety improves music performance.

The detrimental effects of arousal also occur for cognitive tasks. A unique technique for inducing tense arousal is inhaling air enriched with 7.5 percent carbon dioxide for 20 minutes. Attwood and coresearchers (2013) employed this technique to create anxiety to determine if it influenced the accuracy of face matching. An example of face matching occurs when a police officer or bartender tries to match your driver's license photo to your face. In the experiment, participants inhaled carbon dioxide or plain air for 20 minutes each time. Next, participants were shown pairs of front-facing faces that had been photographed with different cameras. Participants indicated if the faces were the same or different. Inhaling carbon dioxide increased physiological arousal in the form of raised blood pressure and increased heart rate compared to the effects of plain air. In addition, carbon dioxide increased state anxiety ratings. As shown in Figure 6.3, compared to inhaling air, carbon dioxide reduced the ability to correctly match faces. Thus, in this experiment increased arousal in the form of anxiety decreased face matching accuracy.

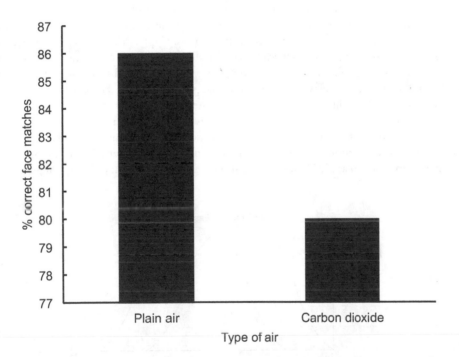

FIGURE 6.3 Anxiety Reduces Ability to Match Faces. Participants who breathed carbon dioxide-enriched air experienced acute anxiety compared to breathing plain air. As a result of the anxiety, participants performed worse on a face matching task—that is identifying two faces as the same or different.

Source: Adapted from "Acute Anxiety Impairs Accuracy in Identifying Photographed Faces" by A. S. Attwood et al., 2013, *Psychological Science, 24*, table 1, p. 1593.

Yerkes–Dodson law. Notice the experiments described previously provide different conclusions regarding the effects of arousal on performance. These differences were previewed in Figure 6.1. For example, in one case increases in arousal improve performance, as illustrated in Figure 6.2, while in another case arousal decreases performance, as illustrated in Figure 6.3. Two hypotheses suggest themselves for these results. First, some arousal helps performance but too much arousal hinders it. Second, how arousal affects performance depends on the nature of the task, such as free throws, face matching, and music playing versus reaction time and proofreading. The first hypothesis combines the positive and negative relationships described in Figure 6.1 and forms an **inverted-U arousal–performance relationship**: as arousal increases, performance increases, levels off, and then decreases (Hebb, 1955; Malmo, 1959). The two inverted-U curves in Figure 6.4 show that for each task an intermediate level of arousal is considered optimal—that is, the level that is associated with the best performance.

The second hypothesis suggests that the optimal level of arousal changes with the nature of the task being performed. In other words, the optimal level of arousal is not fixed but depends on the complexity or difficulty of the task being performed. This complication was an early discovery in the history of psychology by Yerkes and Dodson (1908). They trained mice to discriminate between a white box and a black box at three levels of difficulty. In the process of learning, if the mouse made the wrong choice it received an electric shock, which varied in intensity from weak to medium to strong. The strong electric shock "was decidedly disagreeable to the experimenters and the mice reacted to it vigorously" (pp. 467–468). The intensity of the shock has come to be equated with the level of arousal, although Yerkes and Dodson did not interpret their experiment in terms of arousal but in terms of the intensity of (electrical) stimulation. The results of their experiment show that performance on the discrimination problem depended on problem difficulty and on shock intensity. For easy discrimination problems, performance increased across all levels of shock intensity and almost never declined. For difficult discrimination problems, however, performance increased with shock intensity and then decreased. Medium-difficulty discriminations showed the most pronounced inverted-U relationship. These findings became known as the **Yerkes–Dodson law**: low arousal produces maximal performance

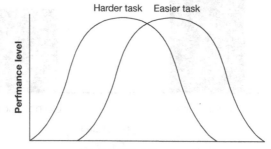

FIGURE 6.4 Yerkes–Dodson Law. Each curve shows the inverted-U arousal–performance relationship. As arousal increases, performance increases and levels off; further increases in arousal lead to decreases in performance. According to the Yerkes–Dodson law, the optimal level of arousal is lower for harder tasks than for easier tasks. The optimal level of arousal is associated with the best performance of a task.

on difficult tasks, and high arousal produces maximal performance on easy tasks. This law is diagrammed in Figure 6.4.

Few inverted-U relationships. Experiments showing inverted-U relationships between arousal and task performance have been scarce, however (Neiss, 1988). This is because creating a wide range of arousal conditions is difficult. However, some published studies do exist. Sjöberg (1975) had male participants pedal a stationary bicycle at workloads of 150, 300, 450, 600, and 750 kilopond meters per minute. A kilopond is a measure of force and the workloads refer to the amount of energy the participants use. Arousal as measured by heart rate increased with workload. While pedaling, participants performed a choice reaction time task by pressing one or the other of two buttons on the right handlebar. The experimenter measured how quickly the correct button was pushed in reaction to the appropriate signal. This reaction time was converted to how many times the participants could press the button accurately. An inverted-U relationship developed: as workload and heart rate increased, the number of button presses increased and then decreased.

Math problem-solving efficiency varies in an inverted-U relationship with math anxiety. However, like many relationships discovered in psychology, people do not show it equally. The inverted-U relationship between math anxiety and math problem-solving efficiency applies to students who have high math motivation (Wang et al., 2015). Wang and coresearchers measured math anxiety of university students with a brief version of the *Mathematics Anxiety Rating Scale*. With this scale, students answer questions about how much anxiety they feel in situations relevant to mathematics, such as studying for or taking a math exam. To measure the motivation for math, students rated the extent of their agreement with statements about their value and interest in math. Higher scores defined a greater motivation to learn mathematics. How does math anxiety and math motivation affect problem-solving proficiency? Math proficiency was measured with a problem verification task. Students were shown a problem and its solution for 10 seconds, during which time they had to indicate "right," "wrong," or "don't know." For example, they might be asked to verify the answers to problems such as 29 + 78 = 107? Two findings emerged about the relationship between levels of math anxiety and math proficiency. First, there was a negative relationship between the level of anxiety and problem-solving proficiency, but only for students who had low math motivation. For them, as their math anxiety increased problem-solving proficiency decreased. Second, there was an inverted-U shaped relationship for students who had high math motivation. For them, as math anxiety increased problem-solving proficiency increased, leveled off, but then decreased with further increases in math anxiety.

Zones of optimal functioning. Another reason for the shortage of evidence for an inverted-U relationship is that individuals have different optimal levels of arousal. In other words, the same general curve does not apply to everyone. The **zone of optimal functioning hypothesis** in sports psychology postulates individual inverted-U curves, each with a zone of optimal arousal where an athlete performs best (Hanin, 1989). Arousal below or above this zone leads to poorer performance. The effects of the zone have been tested most frequently with cognitive anxiety and somatic (body) anxiety. In a test of the hypothesis, Krane (1993) examined the relationship between cognitive anxiety and somatic anxiety and the performance of women players during soccer matches. Each player filled out the two anxiety scales about 20 minutes prior to each of the season's 12 soccer matches. A player's optimal zone for cognitive anxiety was defined as between one standard deviation below and above her season's cognitive anxiety mean. Her somatic anxiety zone was also defined as between one standard deviation below and above her season's somatic anxiety mean. At the end of the season, each player's soccer match performance was classified as below, within, or above her optimal zone for cognitive and for somatic anxiety. Krane found partial support for the hypothesis. A player performed best when she was within but also below her optimal zone and played worst when above her zone.

Section Recap

Arousal refers to energy mobilization and activation of a person prior to or while engaged in behavior. Arousal occurs in different modes. *Physiological arousal* refers to excitement of the body, as reflected by sweaty palms and increased muscle tension, breathing, and heart rate. The sympathetic nervous system is responsible for stimulating the heart to pump blood more effectively, the liver to release glucose, the release of epinephrine (adrenaline) and norepinephrine (noradrenaline), and increased oxygen uptake. Psychological arousal refers to how subjectively aroused an individual feels. Psychological arousal is composed of energetic and tense dimensions. *Energetic arousal* is associated with positive affect, while *tense arousal* is associated with anxiety and fearfulness. Tense arousal can be divided further into two types of *anxiety*. Trait anxiety refers to the degree a person is ready to respond negatively and with worry to the environment in general, while state anxiety refers to feelings of apprehension that actually occur in response to a particular situation.

Arousal itself stems from several sources. A stimulus, for example, has an arousing function and a cue function. In addition, background stimuli that do not capture a person's attention also increase arousal. Arousal varies with time of day, being highest around noon and lower in the morning and evening. Coffee boosts arousal, as does the process of being evaluated during exams, music performance, or sports competition. Arousal also depends on *collative variables*, which includes stimulus characteristics like novelty, complexity, and incongruity.

Sometimes arousal increases behavioral efficiency and in other instances decreases it. This inconsistency is handled by an inverted-U relationship and the Yerkes–Dodson law. According to the *inverted-U arousal–performance relationship*, as arousal increases performance on a task increases and then decreases. This relationship is refined by the *Yerkes–Dodson law*: the high point of the inverted-U or arousal–performance relationship depends on the complexity of the task being performed. Low arousal produces maximal performance on difficult tasks, and high arousal produces maximal performance on easy tasks. According to the *zone of optimal functioning hypothesis*, each individual has her preferred zone of arousal based on cognitive or somatic anxiety. Athletic performance is better within the zone and worse below and above it.

THEORIES ABOUT THE PERFORMANCE–AROUSAL RELATIONSHIP

Several theories have been proposed to explain the inverted-U arousal–performance relationship. The classic Hull–Spence drive theory emphasizes how arousal affects performance with little regard for any cognitive awareness by the individual. The cusp catastrophe model in sports psychology, arousal-biased competition theory, processing efficiency theory, and attentional control theory are more concerned with the cognitive aspects of arousal and how this affects behavioral efficiency. How well does each theory explain the effects of arousal on behavior?

Hull–Spence Drive Theory

According to the Yerkes–Dodson law in Figure 6.4, high arousal aids performance on an easy task but hinders it on a difficult task. The reason is that correct responses occur more readily with easy tasks, while incorrect responses are initially more likely with difficult tasks. To explain why this is so, Spence and coresearchers (1956a, 1956b) employed Hull's (1943, 1952) drive concept. For Hull, drive was a persistent internal stimulus or pushing action of a physiological need. The stronger the drive, the greater was the pushing action on all responses. Thus, for a simple task, as drive increases, the strength of the correct response increases. This push causes an increase in the difference between the correct and the wrong responses. In a complex task, however, the most dominant response is often not the correct one. As drive increases, the strength of wrong responses increases, as does the difference between these responses and the correct one. For the correct response to occur in these situations, the incorrect response must be weakened and the correct one strengthened.

To test this hypothesis, Spence and associates compared the learning of simple versus difficult paired associate tasks (Spence et al., 1956a, 1956b). In paired associate learning, a participant must learn to associate two words together, such that a stimulus word cues the participant to say the associated response word. The simple paired associate task involved such pairs of words as *complete–thorough* and *empty–vacant*. It is easy to learn the response *thorough* to the stimulus *complete*, since these words have similar meanings. With these pairs, an increase in drive should make the occurrence of the dominant but correct response more likely, and hence learning should be faster. The difficult task involved pairs such as *quiet–double* and *serene–headstrong*. These pairs are more difficult to learn because the responses *double* and *headstrong* are going to compete when the stimuli *quiet* or *serene* are presented. The reason is because *quiet* and *serene* are similar in meaning and thus will evoke the same response. An increase in drive in this case should also increase the likelihood of the dominant response, which is now the wrong response. This development should make learning more difficult. Drive or arousal in this experiment was defined by the participant's level of trait anxiety as measured by an anxiety scale. Participants with low trait anxiety were defined as low drive, and those with high trait anxiety were defined as high drive. The results confirmed the prediction: high-drive participants learned the easy paired associate task faster than did low-drive participants. High-drive participants, however, learned the difficult paired associate task slower than did low-drive participants (Spence et al., 1956a, 1956b). Notice that the results support the Yerkes–Dodson law in Figure 6.4: low drive benefitted the harder paired associate learning task, while high drive benefitted the easy paired associate learning task.

Cusp Catastrophe Model

Sport is one of those endeavors in which it is very important to control arousal in order to maximize performance. Arousal factors that determine athletic performance are addressed in the **cusp catastrophe model** from sports psychology. This model uses two types of arousal: cognitive anxiety and physiological or body arousal (somatic anxiety) (Hardy, 1996a, 1996b). At low physiological arousal, increases in cognitive anxiety produce a slight improvement in athletic performance, while, at high physiological arousal, increases in cognitive anxiety produce a decline in performance. Also, at lower levels of cognitive anxiety, increases in physiological arousal lead to small gradual increases and then decreases in athletic performance resembling a flattened inverted-U curve. However, at midrange or higher levels of cognitive anxiety, increases in physiological arousal lead to a cusp where performance is best. Here an athlete is described as a "clutch" player. Increases in physiological arousal beyond this cusp, however, result in a sudden and dramatic drop in performance. At this point the athlete "chokes" and performs very badly.

One implication of the cusp catastrophe model is that the drop in performance can be so drastic that it is manifested as paralysis—that is, the individual ceases all behavior. This behavioral paralysis is known as **tonic immobility**, which marks the final reaction to extremely stressful or dangerous circumstances. In reaction to danger, first an animal freezes, which involves stopping all movement and being extra alert for signs of more pronounced danger. Next are the flight/fight reactions. If an animal cannot flee successfully, then it will attempt to fight. The final step is tonic immobility, which is characterized by paralysis, the tendency to maintain the same posture, and unresponsiveness to pain as if the animal were scared stiff or was feigning death (Moskowitz, 2004; Ratner, 1967). Tonic immobility occurs in many animals but also in humans during highly stressful situations. It has been induced in a variety of birds, chickens, and rats by holding them on their backs for 15 to 30 seconds (Gallup et al., 1970; Ratner, 1967). When prey is immobile, predators lose interest and their attention lapses, which provides an opportunity for prey to escape. Hawks, for example, do not eat dead animals and would starve if not provided with moving prey to eat (Marks, 1987).

BBC Worldwide presents a YouTube video of tonic immobility titled "Animal hypnosis and trances" here: www.youtube.com/watch?v=SMZDieZoing&NR=1&feature=fvwp.

When tonic immobility occurs in humans, it is usually in emergency situations where people should be highly motivated to escape. Leach (2004) provides examples of the passenger ferry MV *Estonia*, which sank in September 1994 in the Baltic Sea. While sinking, passengers were seen standing still as if paralyzed, exhausted or in shock. Others were just sitting incapable of doing anything. In another case, a North Sea oil platform exploded as a result of natural gas accumulation in July 1988. Leach reports that many workers made no attempt to leave the platform and one worker just slumped down unable to move. Another emergency example is the case of an airplane that returned to the airport in Manchester, England, in 1985. Upon landing it was discovered that one of the engines was on fire. Unfortunately, there were delays in evacuating the plane because of the immobile behavior of many people: "several people were seen to remain in their seats until they became engulfed in flames" (Leach, 2004, p. 540). Tonic immobility also occurs during sexual abuse such as attempted and completed rape (Bovin et al., 2008; Heidt et al., 2005). In retrospective research, a sexually abused woman is asked to remember the intensity of the sexual assault perpetrated against her and her level of tonic immobility. To this end, psychologists have formulated the *Tonic Immobility Scale*, which contains items that assess the extent she felt frozen, unable to move, trembled, unable to vocalize, felt numb, cold, or fear, feared for her life, or felt self-detached (Fusé et al., 2007, p. 273). Greater tonic immobility is associated with more severe sexual abuse. Women have higher *Tonic Immobility Scale* scores as a result of attempted rape or rape versus sexual coercion or unwanted sexual contact (Bovin et al., 2008). Attempted and completed rape during childhood also resulted in greater tonic immobility compared to immobility that resulted from abusive sexual contact (Heidt et al., 2005).

According to evolutionary psychology, psychological mechanisms evolved because they had survival value. Are freezing and tonic immobility cases of psychological mechanisms or evolutionary old behaviors intruding into frightening emergency situations in the present? Yes, according to Moskowitz (2004), who wrote that tonic immobility in humans is a holdover from our evolutionary past, during which time humans were also prey. Just like animals today, who freeze and later show tonic immobility in order to increase their chances of survival, so did humans long ago. Thus, freezing, but especially tonic immobility that occurs in emergency situations such as sinking ships, burning airplanes, or sexual assault, are really remnants of this behavior, which once provided a survival advantage. Unfortunately, in such situations, these behaviors are incompatible with the actions that are required for escape.

Arousal-Biased Competition Theory

Another explanation of the inverted-U arousal–performance relationship is provided by Mather and Sutherland's (2011) **arousal-biased competition theory**. This theory holds that arousal biases information that is the focus of an individual's attention—that is, information that has high priority compared to information that has low priority. Furthermore, arousal increases the priority of processing significant information and decreases the priority of processing less important information. An interesting experiment by Kensinger and coresearchers (2007) provides evidence for this claim. The researchers briefly presented participants with a negative emotion stimulus or a neutral stimulus on a scenic background. For example, the negative emotion stimulus of a snake versus the neutral stimulus of chipmunk presented near a river background. After viewing the stimuli, participants were asked if they recognized each picture when it was presented individually—that is, the snake, chipmunk, or river by themselves. Compared to the neutral stimulus (chipmunk) and its background, participants recognized the emotion stimulus (snake) more while the river background was recognized less. This difference did not extend to the neutral stimulus and its background. In this case, the accuracy of recognition for the chipmunk and the river background were similar.

Based on arousal-biased competition theory, negative emotion stimuli have a higher priority for processing compared to neutral stimuli. After all, negative stimuli such as snakes and guns are potentially dangerous. As a consequence, they receive closer scrutiny and more processing but do so at the expense of background stimuli. The result is a greater contrast in the processing of the emotion stimulus versus its background. Consequently, the negative emotion stimulus is recognized more but its background is recognized less. This contrast is less for the neutral stimulus and its background. In this case, the neutral stimulus (chipmunk) is recognized less than the emotion stimulus (snake) but the chipmunk's background is recognized more (Mather & Sutherland, 2011). Thus, arousal improves the efficiency of behavior that concerns a crucial stimulus but does so at the expense of the background.

Memory Systems

Are there some events, such as violent crime or violent weather, so ingrained in our memories that we will never forget them, even if we want to? Is the memory for extremely emotional and arousing events somehow different than the memory for the more mundane things of life? One answer to these questions is based on a theory about the relationship between arousal and a shift in memory systems. This theory, by Metcalfe and Jacobs (1998), postulates the existence of two memory systems: a **cool memory system** and a **hot memory system**, each in a different area of the brain. The level of arousal determines which system is operating. The cool system, which is localized in the hippocampus, serves the memory of events occurring in space and time. For example, this system would help a person to remember the location of her residence and that her car is parked in a different spot today than yesterday. The hot system, which is localized in the amygdala, serves as the memory of events that occur under high arousal. The hot system is responsible for the intrusive memories of individuals who have experienced extremely traumatic events years earlier.

The level of activation of the cool and hot memory systems depends on the level of arousal (Metcalfe & Jacobs, 1998). The degree of activation or efficiency of the cool system follows the inverted-U curve shown in Figure 6.4. As arousal increases, activation of this memory system increases, levels off, and then decreases. The system is most efficient at intermediate levels of arousal but inefficient at very high levels. The hot memory system, however, shows increasing levels of activation with increasing amounts of arousal. This system is least efficient at low levels of arousal but most efficient at very high levels of arousal. Both systems interact to determine a person's total memory. Thus, where the cool system leaves off the hot system takes over. Metcalfe and Jacobs further theorize that the hot system is geared up for remembering the details of stimuli that predict the onset of highly stressful or arousing events, such as events that predict danger.

Anxiety Affects Cognitive Processing and Behavior

Evaluations occur in many facets of life, such as exams, sports competition, and social settings. These can become sources of anxiety (Zeidner & Matthews, 2005). However, the level of anxiety individuals experience in evaluative situations depends on their disposition to become anxious— that is, some people become anxious quicker than others. Recall that trait anxiety is the disposition to become anxious (state anxiety) during an evaluative situation. So, imagine being evaluated for speed and accuracy when attempting to solve "in your head" problems such as: 478 + 59 = ? Anxiety affects cognitive processing efficiency. But how?

Processing efficiency theory. According to **processing efficiency theory**, anxiety expresses itself as worry, which is a preoccupation with being evaluated and being concerned about one's performance. Worry, in turn, takes up working memory capacity and with less working memory available performance on cognitive tasks declines (Eysenck & Calvo, 1992). Anxiety and accompanying worry are especially telling in their effects on math problems. For instance, solving the problem 478 + 59 requires a person to retain intermediate solutions (7 and carry 1) in her working memory. According to processing efficiency theory, the capacity of working memory to retain an intermediate solution decreases because of the presence of intrusive thoughts of worry. In a relevant experiment, Ashcraft and Kirk (2001) compared low, medium, and high math anxiety students for accuracy in working math problems. Some problems did not require carrying operations (15 + 2) and other problems did (23 + 18). The effect of anxiety was only apparent with problems that required carrying operations. As math anxiety increases and uses more working memory space, problem-solving efficiency decreases for problems that require carrying operations.

Math anxiety appears to be unique. Ashcraft and Kirk (2001, exp. 3) hypothesized that math anxiety only affected the working memory capacity for numbers but not for letters. In their experiment, they compared the effects of anxiety on working memory capacity for numbers versus working memory capacity for letters. A participant's level of math anxiety was measured with a scale similar to the *Abbreviated Math Anxiety Scale*. With this scale, participants answer questions about how much anxiety is evoked in situations relevant to mathematics (Hopko et al., 2003). Examples may include using a table in a math book, listening to a lecture in math class, or being given a pop quiz in math class. During the actual experiment, the researchers used a listening span task to measure the working memory capacity for letters and used a computation span task to measure the working memory capacity for numbers. For the listening span, participants heard a number of simple sentences, answered a question about each, and were required to remember the last word of each sentence. For example, "It rained yesterday." When? "The dog sat on the porch." Where? After hearing and answering a number of such sentences, participants were asked to recall the last word in each sentence in the correct order (e.g., yesterday, porch). The mean number of words recalled correctly defined the letter-span size. The computation span task resembled the listening span task. The participant heard a series of simple problems, such as $7 - 3 = ?$ followed by $2 + 6 = ?$ They were required to solve each problem and also to remember the last number of each. At the recall, participants had to name the last number of each problem in the correct order (e.g., 3, 6). The amount recalled correctly defined the working memory capacity for numbers. Ashcraft and Kirk reasoned that on the basis of processing efficiency theory math anxiety should negatively influence working memory capacity for numbers but not for letters. Their results in Figure 6.5 show that, as anxiety increased, working memory capacity for numbers (computation span) decreased, while the capacity for letters (listening span) was affected slightly, although not significantly. If working memory is not used to capacity, then anxiety has little effect on math performance. However, when used to near capacity as in this experiment, anxiety has a detrimental effect on math performance because it takes up the remaining capacity.

Attentional control theory. This theory, an extension of processing efficiency theory, concentrates more on the effect of anxiety on attention (Eysenck & Derakshan, 2011). First, the overall effect of anxiety is to impair a person's ability to pay attention and decreases cognitive processing capacity. More specifically, anxiety weakens a person's ability to inhibit paying attention to extraneous stimuli and responses that are irrelevant to the goal at hand. In other words, a person is more prone to distractions. For example, a person is less able to ignore a text message while studying for a test. Second, anxiety weakens a person's ability to shift from one task to another when necessary. An example is the inability to shift your gaze from one stimulus to another, such as switching from looking at your smartphone to looking at your professor.

Anxiety, in the form of worry, influences attention and hinders behavior that involves connecting with a target (Wilson et al., 2009). Imagine visually aiming at the basketball hoop, the cup in golf, or the bull's-eye in archery and then acting to connect with the target. Whether your action was successful depends on the length of aim on the target immediately prior to executing the response, such as a basketball shot. This final aiming period is known as the quiet eye. It indicates the focus of attention. According to attentional control theory, anxiety inhibits a player's ability to disregard various sources of distraction. Feeling anxiety or worry interferes with the duration of the quiet eye and thus with the goal of hitting the target. Research supports this statement: the accuracy of hitting targets increases with the duration of the quiet eye (Vickers, 2007).

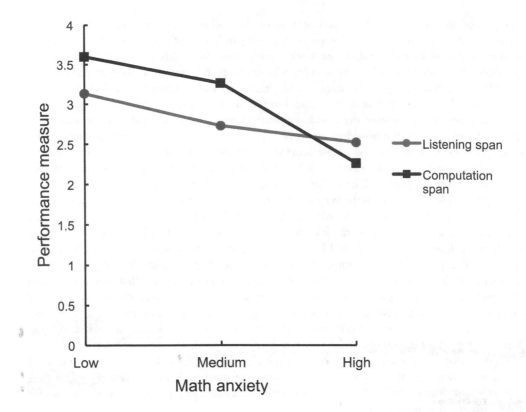

FIGURE 6.5 Math Anxiety and Performance. As math anxiety increased, working memory capacity for arithmetic decreased. Specifically, as math anxiety increased computation span with numbers decreased, while listening span for letters did not decrease significantly.

Source: Adapted from "The Relationships among Working Memory, Math Anxiety, and Performance" by M. H. Ashcraft and E. P. Kirk, 2001, *Journal of Experimental Psychology: General, 130*, Table 3, p. 233.

For instance, in their experiment, Wilson and coresearchers (2009) had basketball players shoot free throws in one of two conditions: a high-threat condition or a control condition. The high-threat condition was designed to create anxiety and worry. The researchers dramatically emphasized and warned the players to do their best in shooting their free throws. In the control condition, the players were simply told to try their best. To determine the effects of the threat instructions, the *Mental Readiness Form* was used to measure the players' current level of anxiety, especially worry. The researchers also used eye tracking equipment to measure the quiet eye duration of the basketball players just prior to beginning a free-throw. Figure 6.6 shows different aspects of the results. First, in the left graph, players in the high-threat condition exhibited more worry as measured by the *Mental Readiness Form*. Second, in the middle graph, the duration of the quiet eye was shorter in the high-threat condition than in the control condition. In other words, in the threat condition the players visually attended to the hoop for a shorter duration. Instead, they made a greater number of extraneous fixations on various areas of the rim and the

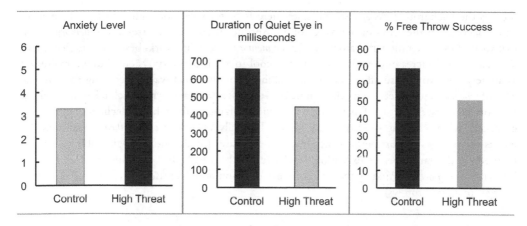

FIGURE 6.6 Anxiety Interferes with the Focus of Attention. Players were instructed to shoot free throws while in a threat condition to do their best or in a relaxed control condition. On the left, the threat treatment produced higher levels of anxiety. In the middle, the threat resulted in a shorter quiet eye—that is, shorter focus duration on the target. On the right, the threat treatment resulted in poorer free-throw performance.

Source: "The Influence of Anxiety on Visual Attentional Control in Basketball Free Throw Shooting" by M. R. Wilson et al., 2009, *Journal of Sport and Exercise Psychology, 31,* 152–168. Anxiety, p. 160; quiet eye, estimated from Figure 2, p. 161; free throw success, p. 160.

backboard. Third, in the right graph, longer quiet eye duration was accompanied by greater free-throw accuracy. Based on attention control theory, worry from the high-threat instructions interfered with the players' ability to not be distracted by extraneous stimuli. These are the very stimuli that interfere with their aim of making a basket.

Section Recap

Several theories explain the inverted–U arousal–performance relationship. According to the *Hull–Spence theory,* arousal magnifies the intensity of all responses. In a simple task, arousal magnifies the dominant response, which is usually the correct one. Arousal of the dominant response in complex tasks is most likely to be the incorrect response. Thus, arousal favors simple performance on simple tasks. According to the *cusp catastrophe model,* performance efficiency is based on the interaction between physiological (somatic) anxiety and cognitive anxiety. At low cognitive arousal, performance increases moderately but then decreases with increases in physiological arousal. At high cognitive arousal, however, performance increases and then drops catastrophically (steeply) as physiological arousal increases. During extremely arousing and dangerous situations a person may exhibit *tonic immobility,* which refers to behavioral paralysis, unresponsiveness to pain, and feigning death. This behavior was adaptive in our evolutionary past to escape predators but today that behavior interferes with escape from danger, as in the case of sinking ships, burning airplanes, or sexual assault.

For *arousal-biased competition theory,* arousal favors the processing of information on which the individual is focused. This is information that has high priority compared to low priority information, such as the background. As arousal increases there is better recall for high priority information and a decrease in the recall of the background. Another theory emphasizes a *cool memory system* that works best under moderate arousal and a *hot memory system* that works best under high arousal. Thus, as arousal increases there is a shift from a cool to a hot memory system. Arousal expressed as anxiety and worry also affects our mental abilities in additional ways. According to *processing efficiency theory*, state anxiety—especially in math—expresses itself as worry, which takes up working memory capacity. As a result of increasing state anxiety, solving math problems declines in efficiency, especially when carrying operations are involved. Finally, *attentional control theory* examines the effects of anxiety on sport performance. Anxiety decreases the duration of being able to remain focused on the target before executing a behavior, such as basketball free throws. This focus is known as the *quiet eye*. Anxiety reduces quiet eye duration and decreases the efficiency of hitting a target (e.g., free throws).

AROUSAL AND AFFECTIVE VALENCE

When considered an independent variable, arousal affects performance: some arousal aids performance but too little or too much hinders it. When considered a dependent variable, arousal depends on the collative variables of novelty, complexity, and incongruity. Humans are both pushed and pulled toward experiencing arousal at a certain intensity and valence. How does the intensity and valence of arousal motivate our behavior?

Variation in Affective Valence

Can a person be aroused or energized but still feel subjectively neutral? Or is arousal always accompanied by a positive or negative feeling (Thayer, 1989)? Simply relaxing, watching a suspenseful movie, or riding a roller coaster are pleasant experiences at varying levels of arousal. But being bored, being insulted, or witnessing a violent crime are unpleasant experiences also at varying levels of arousal. It may be difficult to separate affective valence from arousal (Neiss, 1988). Kuppens and associates (2013) conclude that "feelings of arousal are more likely to be accompanied by valenced feelings, positive or negative" (p. 932). In other words, there is a tendency for the intensity of positive and negative feelings to increase as arousal increases while neutral feelings are accompanied by very low arousal. Negative feelings vary from being blue and downcast to anxiety and stress. Positive feelings, on the other hand, range from contentment and relaxation to excitement and cheerfulness. Can a single explanation capture the relationship between the degree of arousal and the valence of feelings?

Optimal level of stimulation theory. What is the relationship between levels of arousal and affective valence? Zuckerman (1969) described the relationship as an inverted-U in his **optimal level of stimulation theory** (see Figure 6.7). One postulate of this theory is that every person has an optimal (best) level of stimulation or arousal that is associated with the highest positive affective valence. This optimal or preferred level of arousal is not fixed but changes with personality, age, time of day, and experience. Another postulate is that the optimal level of stimulation and arousal is usually at a moderate level—not too low and not too high. A third postulate is that deviations in either direction from this optimal level decrease positive affective valence. If arousal increases or decreases from the optimal level, then affective valence decreases. Finally, affective valence

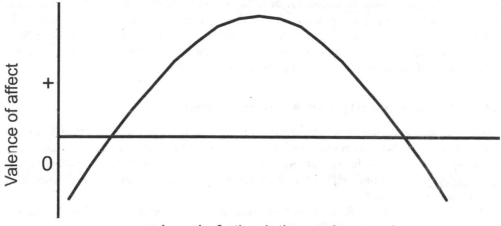

FIGURE 6.7 Graph of Optimal Level of Stimulation Theory. A person's affective valence depends on the level of stimulation and arousal. As the level of stimulation and subsequent arousal increases to a moderate level, affective valence increases. Further increases in the level of stimulation and arousal produce a decrease in affective valence. Very low and very high levels of arousal are associated with negative affective valence.

becomes negative when levels of stimulation and arousal are very low or very high (Zuckerman, 1969). According to Zuckerman (1969), people are motivated to position themselves at the intermediate level of stimulation that provides the highest positive affective valence. When arousal is low, increases in arousal are positively reinforcing. Thus, a person seeks stimulation, such as loud music with a beat, a party with friends, or an action TV program. When arousal is high, decreases in arousal are negatively reinforcing. Consequently, a person then seeks a decrease in stimulation, such as listening to soft music, being alone, or resting. Increases in arousal above the optimal level or decreases in arousal below the optimal level are punishing. Very low levels of arousal are associated with boredom and with a feeling that "there is nothing to do," while very high levels of arousal are associated with stress and a feeling that "I can't get everything done."

Benign masochism. At first glance, it might seem that optimal level of stimulation theory (Figure 6.7) applies only to stimuli that have a positive valence. As positive stimuli increase in intensity their pleasurable effects increase. Do negative stimuli show a reverse effect? As their intensity increases, is there an associated increase in unpleasantness? It appears that is not always the case. "**Benign masochism** refers to enjoying initially negative experiences that the body (brain) falsely interprets as threatening" (Rozin et al., 2013, p. 439). For example, people enjoy being scared at the movies or like sad movies. Using a scale 0 = *not at all* to 100 = *as much as I like anything*, rate yourself on activities such as eating spicy foods, watching sad movies, taking thrilling rides, and hearing disgusting jokes. At first glance, these seem like unpleasant experiences that people should not like and be motivated to avoid. However, this seems not to be the case. Many students enjoy thrill rides, spicy foods, disgusting jokes, sad music, and beer. In addition, the intensity of these experiences falls just short of what they can tolerate. In other words, a bit more intense and the experience would be painful. This is especially true for thrill rides, spicy foods, and disgusting jokes. People appear to enjoy the innate bodily responses that are defensive reactions against these negative stimuli. However, these defense reactions are of low intensity and are designed to prevent bodily harm (Rozin et al., 2013). As Rozin and his coresearchers (2013) speculate, perhaps the brain has been fooled into thinking there is danger when there is none. This mastery of danger is what provides pleasure.

Stimulus Complexity and Affective Valence

Have you ever seen a movie more than once because you did not understand it fully the first time? Do some websites seem too complex? Is some music too atonal or harsh for enjoyment? Each question addresses the role of stimulus collative variables, such as novelty, complexity, incongruity, and also symmetry. How do these variables contribute to arousal and valence, from which pleasure is derived?

Liking increases, decreases with complexity. Preferences for aesthetic stimuli depend on their arousal potential as determined by collative variables (Berlyne, 1970). Table 6.2 presents examples of collative variables. Optimal level of arousal theory states that stimulus preferences depend on their arousal potential produced by these collative variables. In the case of complexity, for example, increased complexity increases arousal. But as arousal becomes more intense preference changes in an inverted-U fashion (see Figure 6.7). Thus, moderately complex stimuli are preferred more, while stimuli of low and high complexity are preferred less. In presenting visual stimuli ranging from simple to complex and symmetric to asymmetric, Tinio and Leder (2009) found that individuals liked complex stimuli more than simple ones and symmetrical stimuli more than asymmetrical ones. Yet, as is often the case in psychology, an individual may not fit into the general rule. For instance, all individuals may not like the most symmetrical or moderately complex stimuli. Palmer and Griscom (2013) had participants rate different arrangements of five-dot patterns from simple to complex. Participants also rated for how well a single dot fit in a rectangle (see third column of Table 6.2) and how much they liked each stimulus arrangement. The results indicated that, on average, higher liking ratings were associated with higher complexity ratings and higher best-fit ratings. However, not all individuals liked the most symmetrical and best-fit stimuli the best. Some individuals liked the asymmetrical and worse-fit stimulus better. As the saying goes, "there's no accounting for taste" (Palmer & Griscom, 2013).

Complexity and symmetry also determine our interaction with web pages. Does the layout of a web page determine how enjoyable it is to navigate? In order to answer this question, Mai and coresearchers (2014) examined whether the complexity of web pages influenced the pleasure of examining a page. The researchers selected four actual corporate websites to represent low, medium, and high complexity. Next, a sample of Internet users browsed a single page for several minutes. Then the individuals rated the page on a seven-point scale for how complex they perceived it to be and how enjoyable their experience was. The ratings conformed to the inverted-U relationship shown in Figure 6.7. As perceived complexity increased, enjoyment ratings increased and then decreased. In addition, feelings of excitement, activation, and liveliness also changed in an inverted-U manner. Visual complexity as based on the number of graphics and animations was mainly responsible for changes in enjoyment (Mai et al., 2014). Additional research has shown that pleasure is also derived from the symmetry of web pages. Web pages that are symmetrical between the left and right sides are judged more beautiful and aesthetically pleasing than asymmetrical sites. This difference, however, has so far been demonstrated only for men (Tuch et al., 2010).

The effects of stimulus complexity also occur when listening to music in a natural setting. North and Hargreaves (1996) played short selections of low-, moderate-, or high-complexity New Age music in the cafeteria at a student union building. Diners rated the music on a scale ranging from *dislike very much* to *like very much*. Their ratings showed that they liked music of moderate complexity more than that of either low or high complexity. Furthermore, when asked "what they would like to change about the cafeteria" (p. 497), diners were more likely to recommend changing the music when it was of low or high complexity. In other words, moderately complex music was preferred most while eating lunch. People who are knowledgeable about music, such as music majors, also prefer music of moderate complexity. Burke and Gridley (1990) presented four piano compositions that covered a large range of perceived complexity as rated by music professors. The piano selection rated least complex was Bach's *Prelude and Fugue*, and Boulez's *Piano Sonata No. 1* was rated most complex. The four piano selections were played either to nonmusicians or to musicians, who were music majors. Analyses of the ratings indicated that as the complexity of the piano pieces increased both groups showed increases and then decreases in their liking.

Experiences, complexity, and liking. Perceived complexity is subject to stimulus habituation, which is a decline in response intensity from repeated exposure to the same stimulus. Consequently, preferred levels of complexity do not remain constant but instead change. This change in turn affects liking or preference for complex stimuli (see Figure 6.8). Specifically, repeated exposure decreases the perceived complexity of stimuli that are at or below optimal complexity. Thus, their appeal decreases, as indicated by the downward arrow in Figure 6.8. Repeated exposure also decreases the perceived complexity of stimuli that are above their optimal complexity. These stimuli have now shifted closer to the optimal level and hence their appeal increases, as indicated by the upward arrow in Figure 6.8. Thus, liking for a complex stimulus decreases if the stimulus moves away from the optimal level of complexity. On the other hand, liking increases if the stimulus moves toward the optimal level of complexity.

To illustrate, Smith and Dorfman (1975) exposed participants one, five, 10, or 20 times to visual stimuli of low, medium, or high complexity. Liking ratings decreased consistently for low-complexity stimuli and increased consistently for high-complexity stimuli over 20 exposures. However, liking ratings increased for medium-complexity stimuli during the first 10 exposures and then decreased with further exposures. Advertisements provide a real-world example of the effects of repeated exposures on visual complexity. The intent of an advertisement is to produce a favorable attitude toward a product and motivate people to buy. However, repeated advertisements of certain products can have the opposite effect. Cox and Cox (2002) presented participants with three different dresses that had either a simple design or a complex design. After one, two, or four exposures, participants rated the dresses for complexity and liking. Repeated exposures resulted in decreased complexity ratings. The simple-design dresses moved away and the complex-design dresses moved toward the optimal level of complexity. As a result, liking ratings decreased for simple-design dresses and increased for complex-design dresses. Thus, motivation toward or away from a stimulus changes with experience.

Preference for music also depends on level of complexity and amount of exposure. Specifically, listening experience determines what level of music complexity is most enjoyable

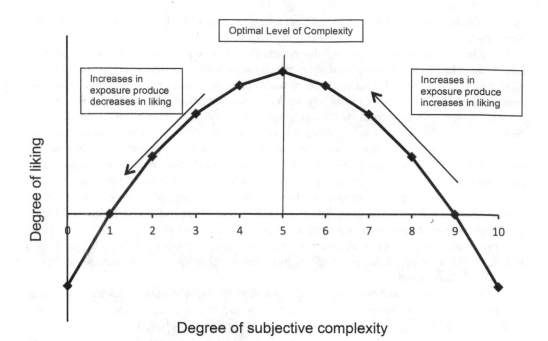

FIGURE 6.8 Liking Changes with Stimulus Exposures. With repeated exposure to a complex stimulus, its perceived or subjective complexity decreases. This decrease produces a corresponding decrease in liking (down arrow) if the stimulus began below the optimal level of stimulation. The stimulus is moving away from the optimal level of complexity where the most liking occurs. In contrast, this decrease produces a corresponding increase in liking (up arrow) if the stimulus began above the optimal level of stimulation. The stimulus is moving toward the optimal level of complexity where the most liking occurs.

(Steck & Machotka, 1975). To illustrate, Tan and coresearchers (2006) used short classical piano compositions that were initially near or above the listeners' perceived optimal level of complexity. Moderately complex were intact compositions, which consisted of one-minute selections from classical piano works. Highly complex were patchwork compositions, which were composed of 20-second segments from three different classical works. Two music professors independently rated the patchwork compositions as highly complex and the intact compositions as moderately complex. The research participants listened to the intact and patchwork compositions plus filler compositions up to four times: twice on Tuesday and twice on Thursday. After each listening, they rated the compositions on several dimensions, such as liking. The results indicated that liking ratings for the intact compositions overall declined slightly over the four listenings, while the ratings of the patchwork piece increased. Initially the patchwork compositions exceeded the optimal level of complexity, whereas the intact compositions were optimally complex. Repeated hearings reversed this difference. Patchwork compositions presumably approached the optimal level of complexity, while intact compositions decreased below that level. As a result, liking ratings increased for patchwork and decreased for intact compositions.

Processing fluency. But why does increased exposure lead to increased liking of stimuli that have high subjective complexity? One possibility relates to the ease with which stimuli are processed. According to the concept of **processing fluency**, from Chapter 3, if information is processed easily then it is felt as positive affect (Reber, 2012). In the case of perception, greater fluency would indicate faster recognition of an object, faster identification, and greater pleasure in doing so. In contrast, with lesser fluency objects are recognized slower, are more difficult to identify, and result in less pleasure. Objects that are easier to process, identify, or comprehend are perceived as more beautiful and liked, such as preferring symmetrical to asymmetrical objects, rounded compared to sharp-edged shapes, repeated stimuli compared to novel ones, and congruous to incongruous shapes (Reber, 2012). As Figure 6.8 implies, increases in stimulus exposure should lead to increased fluency and increased liking. To test this possibility, Forster and coresearchers (2013, exp. 2) presented their participants various images, such as an anchor, for 0.10 to 0.40 seconds. After each stimulus, participants were asked how much they liked that stimulus: 1 = *not at all* to 7 = *very much.* They were also asked about how fluent their perception of the stimulus felt. This felt fluency was also rated from 1 = *not at all* to 7 = *very much.* Ratings results indicated that with longer presentation times both felt fluency and liking increased. Also, liking strongly depended on felt fluency: as felt fluency ratings increased, liking ratings increased. Thus, processing fluency may be one explanation of why people enjoy listening to the same music. However, extreme fluency in processing may lead to boredom.

The concepts of stimulus habituation and extreme processing fluency imply that repeatedly listening to the same music should eventually reduce enjoyment. However, this decline does not happen often. On the contrary, people enjoy hearing their favorite piece of music over and over. For example, radio stations play music from the past (golden oldies), and people buy CDs in order to hear the same music repeatedly. So why doesn't your favorite piece of music get old? One possibility is that music is so complex that a person does not remember all of its attributes, such as changes in individual notes, chords, tempo, melody, rhythm, or loudness that occur with individual instruments. Hence, even after repeated listening enough complexity remains to enjoy the music (Salimpoor et al., 2015). Another possibility is that a part of our brain functions like a **musical grammar processor** (Jackendoff, 1992). This processor has a primitive understanding of basic musical grammar by which it comprehends musical notes. Regardless of whether the music is novel or highly familiar, the musical grammar processor works the same way each time to comprehend musical notes. Each rehearing brings pleasure because the processor is sealed off from long-term memory and so does not benefit from having heard the music before. It responds as if it has heard a familiar piece of music for the first time. Thus, each time it incorporates a novel or familiar musical note, enjoyment results.

Novelty and Incongruity in Music and Humor

Collative variables such as novelty and incongruity evoke arousal and determine the valence of a person's affective reaction. A novel stimulus is one that has not been experienced before. An incongruous stimulus is an unexpected outcome—that is, a specific stimulus was expected but something else occurred, such as a bicycle with square wheels (see Table 6.2). Events are incongruous because they do not fit or are not assimilated or integrated into knowledge structures known as **schemas**. These are mental representations of environmental regularities that an individual has experienced. They range from the abstract and general to the concrete and specific. Schemas can be thought of as scripts, recipes, maps, or concepts that help direct a person's attention, form hypotheses, develop expectations, and understand novel and incongruous events. For example, the musical grammar processor, described above, has primitive schema to represent basic sequences of musical notes.

The Pleasure of Music

The pleasures derived from listening to music are innate, although the evolutionary significance of music is unclear (McDermott & Hauser, 2005). However, one thing is clear. People the world over enjoy music. North and coresearchers (2004) found that enjoyment is the most frequently cited reason for listening to music, along with serving as a way to pass the time, being a habit, and helping to create the right atmosphere. Further research indicates that the pleasure derived from music comes from three main psychological functions, according to Schäfer and co-investigators (2013). They formulated a comprehensive list of music functions, from which they devised a 129-item rating scale of why people listen to music. For example, "I listen to music because it helps me think about myself" 0 = *not at all* to 6 = *fully agree*. A total of 834 people filled out the scale. The results were subjected to a statistical technique that allowed the investigators to place the ratings into three categories: mood regulation, self-awareness, and social relatedness. Figure 6.9 presents the importance of each category based on the 0–6 scale. *Mood regulation* was the most important reason for listening. It involves music as a form of distraction, elevating one's positive mood, enhancing relaxation, or increasing arousal. *Self-awareness* was rated next in importance. This means that music helps people think about themselves, their emotions, and their life's meaning. *Social relatedness* was rated as least important. It refers to feelings of belonging, being connected to friends, and understanding the social world.

Music produces chills. Music on occasion provides a unique source of physiological pleasure known as a **chill**. Goose bumps, shivers, and tingles characterize this physiological reaction. Chills are accompanied by electrodermal responses, which reflect sweating and blood flow (Grewe et al., 2007; Guhn et al., 2007). In one experiment regarding chills, participants listened to music that had been rated as either moderately or highly pleasurable or as creating a chill. Simultaneously, the participants' electrodermal, temperature, heart, and respiration responses were recorded. While listening, participants rated the music for the pleasure they were experiencing: 1 = *neutral*, 2 = *low pleasure*, 3 = *high pleasure* (Salimpoor et al., 2009). The results showed that feeling a chill was definitely associated with the intensity of their physiological responses. Electrodermal responses, heart rate, and respiration rate were highest when listeners experienced a chill and much lower at other times. Most interesting was that the intensity of chills correlated with the amount of pleasure derived from listening to the music—that is, more intense chills were associated with greater pleasure from listening (Salimpoor et al., 2009).

The intense psychological pleasure that accompanies chills correlates with events that occur in the pleasure circuit of the brain. The auditory cortex processes music and also connects with the nucleus accumbens, which is part of the pleasure circuit (Salimpoor et al., 2015). In the above experiment, Salimpoor and coresearchers (2011), using a PET scan and fMRI, discovered that dopamine was released in the nucleus accumbens while listening to pleasant music and especially during chills. In addition, the release of dopamine may also release opioids in hedonic hot spots

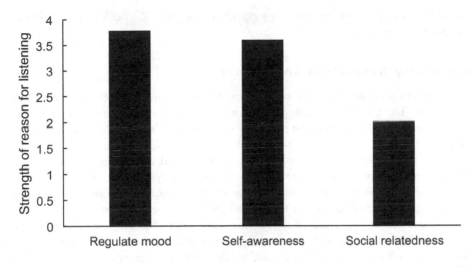

Function of listening to music

FIGURE 6.9 I Listen to Music Because. This graph shows how strongly people agreed with the reasons they listened to music. "I listen to music because" it regulates my mood, makes me aware of myself, or helps me connect with others: 0 = *not at all* to 6 = *completely agree*. At least 32 "I listen because . . ." statements covered each function. Mood regulation that included arousal was the strongest reason for listening, while social relatedness was the weakest reason.

Source: Adapted from "The Psychological Functions of Music Listening" by T. Schäfer et al., 2013, *Frontiers in Psychology, 4,* 2013, Figure 1 caption, p. 6.

located in the nucleus accumbens (Salimpoor et al., 2015). This release may be responsible for the heightened pleasure that accompanies chills. Remember from Chapter 4 that the release of dopamine in the nucleus accumbens was responsible for much of the pleasure that drugs produce. It is also responsible for the pleasure derived from eating, drinking, and sex, which are critical evolutionary behaviors.

Musical pleasure stems from anticipation. Music consists of patterned sound, which makes it possible to expect what notes will occur and when. Expectations develop because listening to music activates various schemas, such as the tempo, the progression of notes in a melody; the harmony, chords, or combination of tones; and the type of music, such as rock, blues, or symphonic (Gaver & Mandler, 1987). According to the **discrepancy hypothesis**, as stimuli deviate more and more from an expectation the pleasure that is evoked increases but then decreases (McClelland et al., 1953). These deviations are known as *prediction errors* regarding what musical notes are heard next. According to a discrepancy hypothesis, slight prediction errors (deviations) provide pleasure, while large prediction errors (deviations) produce much less so. However, when a musical note is confirmed, there is no prediction error. Yet, a feeling of pleasure still arises because correct predictions are critical to our survival (Gebauer et al., 2012). The pleasurable effects produced by prediction error in music have corresponding effects in the brain. These pleasures correspond to the release of dopamine in the brain's reward circuit especially the nucleus accumbens (Gebauer et al., 2012; Salimpoor et al., 2015).

Incongruity Resolution and Humor

Humor appreciation involves a two-state process. The detection of a discrepancy is followed by its resolution. The punchline contains the discrepancy, which must be resolved for the joke to be considered funny. In that case, the punchline of a good joke elicits smiles, laughs, and amused feelings.

Consider the following joke: "A mechanical engineer, an electrical engineer, and a computer software engineer were riding in a car when it broke down. 'It's probably a valve,' said the mechanical engineer. 'It's probably a spark plug,' said the electrical engineer. 'I know,' said the computer software engineer, 'let's all get out of the car and get back in again' " (Crossen, 1997). The stem of the joke activates a schema that aids the processing and comprehension of information contained therein. The stem constrains the reader to expect an ending such as the following: " 'The car's computer system has probably malfunctioned,' said the computer engineer." According to the actual punchline, however, the computer engineer suggests that everyone get out of the car and then get back in. In other words, the computer engineer's actual suggestion is incongruous with what one would expect to be the diagnosis of the car's problem. In a joke, the punchline disrupts cognitive processing of the stem material and produces surprise and arousal (Mandler, 1984). If the punchline is unresolved—that is, "I don't get it"—then the affective value of the incongruity remains puzzling and negative. The incongruity is resolved, however, by assimilating or integrating the punchline into an alternative, less obvious schema also residing in the stem. For example, the computer engineer's "computer solution" schema replaces the "car solution" schema. In this way, the punchline of "get out and get back in again" is assimilated into the "computer solution" schema. Thus, the punchline is understood when a person realizes that computer users occasionally fix their computers by turning them off and then on again (Deckers & Avery, 1994; Raskin, 1985). The resolution of the punchline results in amusement and feelings of mirth.

Expectancy violations in humor resemble those that occur in music. Small deviations are enjoyed but large deviations produce anxiety (Mandler, 1984). In the case of humor, a benign (small) deviation created by the punchline, for example, is considered more humorous than a severe deviation. McGraw and coresearchers (2012) showed that the *psychological distance* of the humor stimulus determines whether it is benign or severe. Psychological distance refers to the subjective impression of the nearness or farness of an event, such as time, physical distance, or social distance (friend versus stranger). In experiment 2, for example, McGraw and coresearchers varied severity by comparing being hit by a car versus stubbing your toe. Psychological distance varied from yesterday to five years ago. For example, what is more humorous: being hit by a car five years ago versus yesterday or stubbing your toe five years ago versus today (McGraw et al., 2012, p. 1218)? Of the participants, 99 percent chose being hit by a car five years ago to be more humorous than being hit yesterday. In contrast, only 18 percent chose stubbing your toe five years ago to be more humorous than stubbing it yesterday. Thus, the psychological distance of time made being hit by a car more benign (small deviation) and hence funnier. In contrast, time made stubbing a toe almost a nonviolation and hence not amusing. Thus, much like music, small deviations from expectations produce pleasure while large or nonexistent deviations do not.

Section Recap

Arousal is tinged with positive and negative affect. *Optimal level of stimulation theory* presents affective valence as changing with the level of arousal in an inverted-U relationship. As the level of stimulation and subsequent arousal increases, affective valence becomes more positive. But, with further increases, affective valence becomes less positive and more negative. Paradoxically, people also enjoy experiencing negative stimulation, short of bodily harm. This phenomenon of *benign masochism* results from a person preparing for the dangerous negative stimulation but none actually occurs.

The inverted-U curve describes the relationship between perceived stimulus complexity and how it influences the preference for visual stimuli, dresses, and music. However, repeated exposure decreases perceived stimulus complexity. The result is decreased liking of simple stimuli and moderately complex stimuli because they begin to fall below the optimal level of complexity. On the other hand, there is increased liking for complex stimuli because their level of complexity begins to rise toward the optimal level. Repeated stimulus exposure results in improved *processing fluency*, which refers to the ability to recognize, identify, and respond to novel stimuli. As processing fluency of stimuli increases, liking of those stimuli also increases. However, this increase contrasts with stimulus habituation; the decline in response intensity from repeated exposure to the same stimulus. Yet, repeatedly listening to the same music does not usually lead to a decline in enjoyment. One reason is that a piece of music contains varied sources of complexity, which makes habituation unlikely. Also, based on a *musical grammar processor*, people never tire of their favorite melody because the processor responsible for the resolution of musical notes has no memory. Thus, each time the music is novel.

Incongruity resolution provides the link between arousal and the enjoyment of music and humor. Musical notes and punchlines are enjoyed when elements from those domains are assimilated or incorporated into known *schemas*. These are representations of knowledge about regularities in the world, such as musical patterns, scripts, or concepts. An incongruous element is understood when it is resolved by fitting (assimilating) it into a prevailing schema. According to the *discrepancy hypothesis*, small deviations produce enjoyment, while larger deviations are enjoyed less. In the case of music, enjoyment stems from the listener's ability to assimilate the next note or musical phrase into an activated musical schema. However, if the next note is too discrepant, there is less enjoyment of the music. Some musical passages produce a *chill* (goose bumps, shivers), which are physiological reactions that occur when an incongruous or novel event occurs in the music. Jokes are enjoyed when the punchline is assimilated or resolved into an alternative schema inspired by the stem of the joke. Small deviations of the punchline from an expected ending produce amusement, while no deviations or large ones produce little amusement, if any.

GLOSSARY

Term	Definition
Affective Valence	Whether a feeling (affect) is negative (unpleasant) or positive (pleasant); its valence

continued . . .

GLOSSARY Continued

Term	Definition
Anxiety	A form of tense arousal that involves apprehension, worry, and nervousness about forthcoming or actual events
Arousal	Mobilization, activation, or energization of energy in a person that occurs in preparation to or during actual behavior
Arousal-Biased Competition Theory	Arousal biases the processing of information an individual is focused on. Information with high priority compared to low, such as background information
Arousing Function	A stimulus has the ability to activate or arouse behavior or determine the intensity of behavior
Assimilation	Cognitive process by which an incongruous event is resolved or understood when it fits into a person's schema
Attentional Control Theory	Anxiety and worry is to weaken a person's ability to inhibit paying attention to extraneous stimuli and responses that are irrelevant to the goal at hand
Benign Masochism	Enjoying initially negative experiences that the body (brain) falsely interprets as threatening. The negative experience stops short of being harmful
Chill	A physiological reaction to a music passage characterized by goose bumps, shivers, or tingles
Cognitive Anxiety	Negative expectations and mental concerns or worries about performance in a competitive situation
Collative Variables	Stimulus characteristics of novelty, complexity, and incongruity, which can affect arousal
Complexity Variable	Dimension regarding the number of elements and the dissimilarity among those elements in a stimulus array
Cool Memory System	Localized in the hippocampus and used for remembering things in space and time; works best during low arousal
Cue Function	A stimulus can evoke a specific response
Cusp Catastrophe Model	Model from sports psychology indicating that performance depends jointly on cognitive arousal and on physiological arousal (somatic anxiety)
Discrepancy Hypothesis	Stimuli that deviate from expectation are judged pleasant. However, large deviations are judged unpleasant
Energetic Arousal	Psychological arousal that ranges from tired, sleepy at the low end to alert and awake at the high end; positively felt arousal
Energization	Person is energized, aroused, or activated to behave, which determines the intensity of the behavior
Hot Memory System	Localized in the amygdala and serves for remembering events that occur during high arousal or remembering traumatic events
Hull-Spence Drive Theory	States that drive energizes both weak and strong responses so as to intensify behavior
Incongruity Resolution	When an incongruity is resolved or understood, such as resolving the incongruous punchline in a joke; when resolved amusement results

continued . . .

GLOSSARY Continued

Term	Definition
Incongruity Variable	Dimension regarding the disparity or discrepancy between a single element in a stimulus array and other accompanying elements or previous elements
Inverted-U Arousal–Performance Relationship	Changes in behavioral efficiency depend on degree of arousal; as arousal increases, performance increases, levels off, and then decreases
Musical Grammar Processor	A primitive mechanism that can anticipate and resolve or incorporate the next musical note, which results in enjoyment. It has no memory for music
Music Performance Anxiety	Similar to stage fright, it refers to physiological and psychological distress while playing music in front of an audience
Novel Stimulus	A stimulus that is new or different from stimuli to which a person has become accustomed or has habituated to
Optimal Level of Stimulation Theory	Theory that states positive valence is an inverted-U function of arousal: as arousal increases, valence increases, levels off, and then decreases
Paired Associate Learning	Learning task in which a person learns to associate a response word with a stimulus word, e.g., respond with *double* upon seeing the stimulus *quiet*
Physiological Arousal	Bodily changes that correspond to feelings of being energized or activated, e.g., increased heart rate, breathing, and muscle tension
Processing Efficiency Theory	Performance on a cognitive task depends on working memory. Efficiency declines when worry takes up the working memory space that is needed to perform the task
Processing Fluency	The ease with which a person can recognize, identify, and respond to novel stimuli. Enjoyment of stimuli, like music, increases with ease of processing of the stimuli
Psychological Arousal	Person's subjective feeling of being aroused, which can vary from feeling excited to feeling anxious
Psychological Distance	The subjective impression of the nearness or farness of an event, such as time, physical distance, or social distance as in friend versus stranger
Quiet Eye	Person's aim on the target immediately prior to executing the response, such as aim prior to basketball shot. The quiet eye indicates the focus of attention
Schemas	Mental representations of environmental regularities from the abstract to the specific, such as plans, scripts, recipes, maps, or concepts
Somatic (Body) Anxiety	Self-perception of physiological arousal that is associated with nervousness and tension
State Anxiety	Actual feelings of apprehension, worry, and sympathetic nervous system arousal that are evoked by a threatening situation
Stimuli	Discrete environmental event that arouses or energizes an individual and evokes a specific response
Sympathetic Nervous System	Division of the autonomic nervous system that is responsible for arousing and preparing the body for action
Tense Arousal	Psychological arousal that ranges from calm, still at the low end to tension, anxiety at the high end; negatively felt arousal

continued . . .

GLOSSARY Continued

Term	Definition
Tonic Immobility	Behavioral paralysis in times of extreme stress or danger and characterized by frozen posture and unresponsiveness to pain; feigning death
Trait Anxiety	An individual difference variable of the disposition or tendency to perceive events as threatening and to respond anxiously
Yerkes–Dodson Law	Behavioral efficiency depends on arousal and task complexity; low arousal is best for complex tasks but high arousal works best for easy tasks
Zone of Optimal Functioning Hypothesis	Location on the inverted-u arousal curve where an athlete performs best; each athlete has his or her own zone

REFERENCES

Ashcraft, M. H., & Kirk, E. P. (2001). The relationships among working memory, math anxiety, and performance. *Journal of Experimental Psychology: General, 130*, 224–237.

Attwood, A. S., Penton-Voak, I. S., Burton, A. M., & Munafò, M. R. (2013). Acute anxiety impairs accuracy in identifying photographed faces. *Psychological Science, 24*, 1591–1594.

Berlyne, D. E. (1960). *Conflict, arousal, and curiosity.* New York, NY: McGraw-Hill.

Berlyne, D. E. (1970). Novelty, complexity and hedonic value. *Perception and Psychophysics, 8*, 279–286.

Bovin, M. J., Jager-Hyman, S., Gold, S. D., Marx, B. P., & Sloan, D. M. (2008). Tonic immobility mediates the influence of peritraumatic fear and perceived inescapability on posttraumatic stress symptom severity among sexual assault survivors. *Journal of Traumatic Stress, 21*, 402–409.

Brunyé, T. T., Mahoney, C. R., Rapp, D. N., Ditman, T., & Taylor, H. A. (2012). Caffeine enhances real-world language processing: Evidence from a proofreading task. *Journal of Experimental Psychology: Applied, 18*, 95–108.

Burke, M. J., & Gridley, M. C. (1990). Musical preferences as a function of stimulus complexity and listeners' sophistication. *Perceptual and Motor Skills, 71*, 687–690.

Childs, E., & de Wit, H. (2008). Enhanced mood and psychomotor performance by a caffeine-containing energy capsule in fatigued individuals. *Experimental and Clinical Psychopharmacology, 16*, 13.

Clements, P. R., Hafer, M. D., & Vermillion, M. E. (1976). Psychometric, diurnal, and electrophysiological correlates of activation. *Journal of Personality and Social Psychology, 33*, 387–394.

Comerford, B., & Witryol, S. L. (1993). Information metrics for novelty level preference of first- and fifth-grade children. *Journal of Genetic Psychology, 154*, 155–165.

Cox, D., & Cox, A. D. (2002). Beyond first impressions: The effects of repeated exposure on consumer liking of visually complex and simple product designs. *Journal of the Academy of Marketing Science, 30*, 119–130.

Crossen, C. (1997, January 31). Funny business. *Wall Street Journal*, pp. A1, A6.

Deckers, L., & Avery, P. (1994). Altered joke endings and a joke structure schema. *Humor: International Journal of Humor Research, 7*, 313–321.

Eysenck, M. W., & Calvo, M. G. (1992). Anxiety and performance: The processing efficiency theory. *Cognition and Emotion, 6*, 409–434.

Eysenck, M. W., & Derakshan, N. (2011). New perspectives in attentional control theory. *Personality and Individual Differences, 50*, 955–960.

Faw, T. T. (1970). The effects of stimulus incongruity on free looking time of adults and children. *Psychonomic Science, 19*, 355–357.

Forster, M., Leder, H., & Ansorge, U. (2013). It felt fluent, and I liked it: Subjective feeling of fluency rather than objective fluency determines liking. *Emotion, 13*, 280–289.

Fusé, T., Forsyth, J. P., Marx, B., Gallup, G. G., & Weaver, S. (2007). Factor structure of the tonic immobility scale in female sexual assault survivors: An exploratory and confirmatory factor analysis. *Journal of Anxiety Disorders, 21*, 265–283.

Gallup, Jr., G. G., Nash, R. F., Potter, R. J., & Donegan, N. H. (1970). Effects of varying conditions of fear on immobility reactions in domestic chickens (*Gallus Gallus*). *Journal of Comparative and Physiological Psychology, 73*, 442–445.

Gaver, W. W., & Mandler, G. (1987). Play it again, Sam: On liking music. *Cognition and Emotion, 1*, 259–282.

Gebauer, L., Kringelbach, M. L., & Vuust, P. (2012). Ever-changing cycles of musical pleasure: The role of dopamine and anticipation. *Psychomusicology: Music, Mind, and Brain, 22*, 152.

Grewe, O., Nagel, F., Kopiez, R., & Altenmüller, E. (2007). Listening to music as a re-creative process: Physiological, psychological, and psychoacoustical correlates of chills and strong emotions. *Music Perception, 24*, 297–314.

Guhn, M., Hamm, A., & Zentner, M. (2007). Physiological and musico-acoustic correlates of the chill response. *Music Perception, 24*, 473–483.

Hanin, Y. L. (1989). Interpersonal and intragroup anxiety in sports. In D. Hackfort & C. D. Spielberger (Eds.), *Anxiety in sports: An international perspective* (pp. 19–28). New York, NY: Hemisphere.

Hardy, L. (1996a). A test of catastrophe models of anxiety and sports performance against multidimensional anxiety theory models using the method of dynamic differences. *Anxiety, Stress, and Coping, 9*, 69–86.

Hardy, L. (1996b). Testing the predictions of the cusp catastrophe model of anxiety and performance. *Sport Psychologist, 10*, 140–156.

Hebb, D. O. (1955). Drives and the C. N. S. [conceptual nervous system]. *Psychological Review, 62*, 243–254.

Heidt, J. M., Marx, B. P., & Forsyth, J. P. (2005). Tonic immobility and childhood sexual abuse: a preliminary report evaluating the sequela of rape-induced paralysis. *Behaviour Research and Therapy, 43*, 1157–1171.

Hoffman, S. L., & Hanrahan, S. J. (2012). Mental skills for musicians: Managing music performance anxiety and enhancing performance. *Sport, Exercise, and Performance Psychology, 1*, 17–28.

Hopko, D. R., Mahadevan, R., Bare, R. L., & Hunt, M. K. (2003). The abbreviated math anxiety scale (AMAS): Construction, validity, and reliability. *Assessment, 10*, 178–182.

Hull, C. L. (1943). *Principles of behavior*. New York, NY: Appleton-Century-Crofts.

Hull, C. L. (1952). *A behavior system*. New Haven, CT: Yale University Press.

Jackendoff, R. (1992). Musical processing and musical affect. In M. R. Jones & S. Holleran (Eds.), *Cognitive bases of musical communication* (pp. 51–68). Washington, DC: American Psychological Association.

Kensinger, E. A., Garoff-Eaton, R. J., & Schacter, D. L. (2007). Effects of emotion on memory specificity: Memory trade-offs elicited by negative visually arousing stimuli. *Journal of Memory and Language, 56*, 575–591.

Krane, V. (1993). A practical application of the anxiety-athletic performance relationship: The zone of optimal functioning hypothesis. *The Sport Psychologist, 7*, 113–126.

Kuppens, P., Tuerlinckx, F., Russell, J. A., & Barrett, L. F. (2013). The relation between valence and arousal in subjective experience. *Psychological Bulletin, 139*, 917–940.

Leach, J. (2004). Why people "freeze" in an emergency: Temporal and cognitive constraints on survival responses. *Aviation, Space, and Environmental Medicine, 75*, 539–542.

Mai, R., Hoffmann, S., Schwarz, U., Niemand, T., & Seidel, J. (2014). The shifting range of optimal web site complexity. *Journal of Interactive Marketing, 28*, 101–116.

Malmo, R. B. (1959). Activation: A neuropsychological dimension. *Psychological Review, 66*, 367–386.

Mandler, G. (1984). *Mind and body: Psychology of emotion and stress*. New York, NY: W. W. Norton.

Marks, I. M. (1987). *Fears, phobias, and rituals*. New York, NY: Oxford University Press.

Mather, M., & Sutherland, M. R. (2011). Arousal-biased competition in perception and memory. *Perspectives on Psychological Science, 6*, 114–133.

McClelland, D. C., Atkinson, J. W., Clark, R. A., & Lowell, E. L. (1953). *The achievement motive*. New York, NY: Appleton-Century-Crofts.

McDermott, J., & Hauser, M. (2005). The origins of music: Innateness, uniqueness, and evolution. *Music Perception, 23*, 29–59.

McGraw, A. P., Warren, C., Williams, L. E., & Leonard, B. (2012). Too close for comfort, or too far to care? Finding humor in distant tragedies and close mishaps. *Psychological Science, 23*, 1215–1223.

Metcalfe, J., & Jacobs, W. J. (1998). Emotional memory: The effects of stress on "cool" and "hot" memory systems. In D. L. Medin (Ed.), *The psychology of learning and motivation* (Vol. 38, pp. 187–222). New York, NY: Academic Press.

Monk, T., & Folkard, S. (1983). Circadian rhythms and shift work. In R. Hockey (Ed.), *Stress and fatigue in human performance* (pp. 97–121). Chichester: John Wiley.

Moskowitz, A. K. (2004). "Scared stiff": Catatonia as an evolutionary-based fear response. *Psychological Review, 111*, 894–1002.

Neiss, R. (1988). Reconceptualizing arousal: Psychobiological states in motor performance. *Psychological Bulletin, 103*, 345–366.

Nicki, R. M., & Moss, V. (1975). Preference for non-representational art as a function of various measures of complexity. *Canadian Journal of Psychology, 29*, 237–249.

North, A. C., & Hargreaves, D. J. (1996). Responses to music in a dining area. *Journal of Applied Social Psychology, 26*, 491–501.

North, A. C., Hargreaves, D. J., & Hargreaves, J. J. (2004). Uses of music in everyday life. *Music Perception, 22*, 41–77.

Palmer, S. E., & Griscom, W. S. (2013). Accounting for taste: Individual differences in preference for harmony. *Psychonomic Bulletin and Review, 20*, 453–461.

Perry, A. B. (2004). Decreasing math anxiety in college students. *College Student Journal, 38*, 321–324.

Raskin, V. (1985). *Semantic mechanisms of humor*. Dordrecht: D. Reidel.

Ratner, S. C. (1967). Comparative aspects of hypnosis. In J. E. Gordon (Ed.), *Handbook of clinical and experimental hypnosis* (pp. 550–587). New York, NY: Macmillan.

Reber, R. (2012). Processing fluency, aesthetic pleasure, and culturally shared tastes. In A. P. Shimamura & S. E. Palmer (Eds.), *Aesthetic science: Connecting minds, brains, and experience* (pp. 223–249). New York, NY: Oxford University Press.

Rozin, P., Guillot, L., Fincher, K., Rozin, A., & Tsukayama, E. (2013). Glad to be sad, and other examples of benign masochism. *Judgment and Decision Making, 8*, 439–447.

Salimpoor, V. N., Benovoy, M., Larcher, K., Dagher, A., & Zatorre, R. J. (2011). Anatomically distinct dopamine release during anticipation and experience of peak emotion to music. *Nature Neuroscience, 14*, 257–262.

Salimpoor, V. N., Benovoy, M., Longo, G., Cooperstock, J. R., & Zatorre, R. J. (2009). The rewarding aspects of music listening are related to degree of emotional arousal. *PLOS ONE, 4*, e7487.

Salimpoor, V. N., Zald, D. H., Zatorre, R. J., Dagher, A., & McIntosh, A. R. (2015). Predictions and the brain: How musical sounds become rewarding. *Trends in Cognitive Sciences, 19*, 86–91.

Schäfer, T., Sedlmeier, P., Städtler, C., & Huron, D. (2013). The psychological functions of music listening. *Frontiers in Psychology, 4*, 1–33.

Schimmack, U., & Reisenzein, R. (2002). Experiencing activation: Energetic arousal and tense arousal are not mixtures of valence and activation. *Emotion, 2*, 412–417.

Sjöberg, H. (1975). Relations between heart rate, reaction speed, and subjective effort at different work loads on a bicycle ergometer. *Journal of Human Stress, 1*, 21–27.

Smith, G. F., & Dorfman, D. D. (1975). The effect of stimulus uncertainty on the relationship between frequency of exposure and liking. *Journal of Personality and Social Psychology, 31*, 150–155.

Smith, S. A., Sutherland, D., & Christopher, G. (2005). Effects of repeated doses of caffeine on mood and performance of alert and fatigued volunteers. *Journal of Psychopharmacology, 19*, 620–626.

Spence, K. W., Farber, I. E., & McFann, H. H. (1956a). The relation of anxiety (drive) level to performance in competitive and non-competitive paired-associates learning. *Journal of Experimental Psychology, 52*, 296–305.

Spence, K. W., Taylor, J. A., & Ketchel, R. (1956b). Anxiety (drive) level and degree of competition in paired-associates learning. *Journal of Experimental Psychology, 52*, 303–310.

Spielberger, C. D. (1975). Anxiety: State-trait-process. In C. D. Spielberger & I. G. Saranson (Eds.), *Stress and anxiety: Volume 1* (pp. 115–143). New York, NY: John Wiley & Sons.

Steck, L., & Machotka, P. (1975). Preference for musical complexity: Effect of context. *Journal of Experimental Psychology, 104*, 170–174.

Tan, S-L., Spackman, M. P., & Peasle, C. L. (2006). The effects of repeated exposure on liking and judgments of musical unity of intact and patchwork compositions. *Music Perception, 23*, 407–421.

Thayer, R. E. (1967). Measurement of activation through self-report. *Psychological Reports, 20*, 663–678.

Thayer, R. E. (1978). Toward a psychological theory of multidimensional activation (arousal). *Motivation and Emotion, 2*, 1–34.

Thayer, R. E. (1989). *The biopsychology of mood and arousal*. New York, NY: Oxford University Press.

Tinio, P. P., & Leder, H. (2009). Just how stable are stable aesthetic features? Symmetry, complexity, and the jaws of massive familiarization. *Acta Psychologica, 130*, 241–250.

Tuch, A. N., Bargas-Avila, J. A., & Opwis, K. (2010). Symmetry and aesthetics in website design: It's a man's business. *Computers in Human Behavior, 26*(6), 1831–1837.

Valdez, P., Reilly, T., & Waterhouse, J. (2008). Rhythms of mental performance. *Mind, Brain, and Education, 2*, 7–16.

Vickers, J. (2007). *Perception, cognition, and decision training: The quiet eye in action*. Champaign, IL: Human Kinetics.

Wang, J., Marchant, D., & Morris, T. (2004). Coping style and susceptibility to choking. *Journal of Sport Behavior, 27*, 75–92.

Wang, Z., Lukowski, S. L., Hart, S. A., Lyons, I. M., Thompson, L. A., Kovas, Y., . . . Petrill, S. A. (2015). Is math anxiety always bad for math learning? The role of math motivation. *Psychological Science, 26*, 1863–1876.

Williams, A. (2006, April). Up to her eyes in gore, and loving it. *New York Times*. Retrieved July 14, 2008, from www.nytimes.com.

Wilson, M. R., Vine, S. J., & Wood, G. (2009). The influence of anxiety on visual attentional control in basketball free throw shooting. *Journal of Sport and Exercise Psychology, 31*, 152–168.

Yerkes, R. M., & Dodson, J. D. (1908). The relation of strength of stimulus to rapidity of habit formation. *Journal of Comparative Neurology and Psychology, 18*, 459–482.

Yoshie, M., Kudo, K., Murakoshi, T., & Ohtsuki, T. (2009). Music performance anxiety in skilled pianists: Effects of social-evaluative performance situation on subjective, autonomic, and electromyographic reactions. *Experimental Brain Research, 199*, 117–126.

Zeidner, M., & Matthews, G. (2005). Evaluation anxiety: Current theory and research. In A. J. Elliot & C. S. Dweck (Eds.), *Handbook of Competence and Motivation* (pp. 141–163). New York, NY: Guilford.

Zuckerman, M. (1969). Theoretical formulations: I. In J. P. Zubek (Ed.), *Sensory deprivation: Fifteen years of research* (pp. 407–432). New York, NY: Appleton-Century-Crofts.

CHAPTER 7

Stress, Coping, and Health

The blessings of life are not equal to its ills, though the number of the two may be equal; nor can any pleasure compensate for the least pain.

Pliny the Elder, A.D. 77

Life is not/merely being alive, but being well.

Martial, A.D. 95

Simply put, stress moves people into action. It motivates them to manipulate stressors so as to alter their impact. And it also motivates behavior aimed at diminishing or removing stress (Baum & Posluszny, 1999). This is the main theme of this chapter, and the following questions can help guide your understanding:

1. When are life events stressful, and when are they not?
2. How do stressors affect people physically, psychologically, and behaviorally?
3. Can the appraisal of life events alter their impact on a person's well-being?
4. How can a person cope with life events and the stress they evoke?
5. Is coping a process that involves planning, execution, and feedback?

RELATIONSHIP BETWEEN LIFE EVENTS AND STRESS

Occasionally, you may have a bad day. You oversleep because the alarm did not go off. Consequently, you are late for an important exam and so perform poorly. A friend borrowed a textbook and has not returned it. You wanted to study from it tonight. Of course this may not matter, since your boss says you need to fill in this evening for a sick coworker. You have no choice; you need the job, as you are chronically short of money. In addition, you've had this lingering cold and sore throat that seems unshakable. If only you had some time for yourself. This individual is confronted with a variety of events that make her or his life unhappy. Some of the events are distinct, while others are chronic; some are more intense than others; only some seem controllable; they appear to be accumulating; and all are negative. Nevertheless, these events motivate the individual into action in attempts at relief.

How and when do life events become stressors? How do they result in stress?

Demands, Coping, and Stress

The previous tale of woe illustrates how life events make demands on an individual's motivation and behavior. Completing projects, preparing for final exams, and considering career goals are examples of positive demands that motivate an individual to achieve them. A broken printer and a car that needs repair are negative events that motivate a person to remedy them. The death of a friend, a broken heart, or being in a bad traffic accident are severe negative events that require adjustment necessary for recovery. Background stimulation from noise, light, and overcrowding plus invisible germs motivate action that taxes the body's ability to cope. Action to meet the demands of life requires the appropriate resources. Does a person have enough time, tangible resources, and motivation? **Coping** refers to behavior that is motivated to adjust and to regulate those external demands and their consequences. What happens when an individual runs low on the resources needed to achieve positive events or to avoid or escape negative events? For instance, a student runs out of time before assignments are due and a low grade results. Fixing the printer or car strains a person's budget and means giving up buying other things. When family, friends, or counselors are not available for listening and advice, the student may be unable to dispel grief or make career decisions. Or, for example, what resources are required to maintain a romantic relationship, recover from an accident, or fight off germs? **Stress** results when life demands exceed coping resources either because the demands are too great or resources are inadequate. Stress is the interplay between environmental challenges and the body's attempt to maintain homeostatic regularity—that is, to remain in equilibrium or remain steadfast (Lazarus & Folkman, 1984; Monroe, 2008).

Characteristics of Stressors

Many demands in life motivate an individual to make adjustments. Passing university courses, fixing your car, and working are dealt with effectively by most people. Demands that are not dealt with effectively, however, become stressors; that is, they produce stress. Stressors have certain characteristics, as shown in Table 7.1 (Wheaton & Montazer, 2010). **Stressors** are conditions that are demanding, challenging, and threatening to the welfare of an individual. *Demand* means that the individual must deal or cope with the stressor, while *challenge* implies that greater effort than normal will be required. *Threat* means that stressors pose the possibility of being potentially harmful to the individual either psychologically or physically. There are a variety of different stressors, such as daily hassles, life demands, traumatic events, and nonevents. In addition, stressors vary in duration and magnitude plus predictability and controllability.

TABLE 7.1 Characteristics of Stressors

Characteristics	Description
Essentials of Stressors	
Challenge	Requires more than usual amount of effort to be managed or coped with
Demand	Must be managed or coped with in order for person to function well, ably
Threat	Potential to be psychologically or physically harmful
Features of Stressors	
Controllable	Range from uncontrollable (can do nothing) to controllable (can cope, manage)
Duration	Range from discrete with sudden onset and offset to chronic and long-lasting
Magnitude	Intensity or amount that a stressor is challenging, demanding, and enduring
Predictable	Likelihood or chance that the stressor will occur, which ranges from unlikely to certain
Types of Stressors	
Chronic	Stressors that develop gradually and deceptively; longer duration than life-change events
Daily hassles	Demands of daily life that are irritating, annoying, and distressing
Life-Change Events	Stressors that have clear, observable beginnings and ends
Nonevent	Desired anticipated or hoped-for event that fails to occur
Traumatic	Severe enough to threaten a person with death or injury; has long-lasting effects

Negative life events as stressors. Both positive and negative life events motivate coping actions. Repairing a printer, tolerating a neighbor's noisy stereo, or suffering disappointment are negative events a person would like to escape. Starting a romance, accepting new responsibilities at work, or planning a surprise birthday party are positive events that motivate a person to act. Early stress researchers often disregarded whether an event was positive or negative; both were considered stressful (Holmes & Rahe, 1967; Selye, 1976). Physiological arousal that resulted from positive events was called **eustress** (Selye, 1976), especially if the level of arousal was just right—not too low or not too high. **Distress**, in contrast, is the opposite of eustress and occurs when arousal is too low or too high. Moreover, distress has additional symptoms consisting of negative feelings, physical ailments, diseases, and maladaptive behavior. Thus, stress usually means distress.

In comparing positive and negative life events, Zautra and Reich (1983) found the **same domain effect**. Negative events produce distress and reduce the quality of life. Positive events, however, increase positive feelings and increase the quality of life. However, the same domain effect obscures the fact that people's reactions to negative events are stronger than their reactions to positive events. In other words, people react more strongly to bad events than to good events (Baumeister et al., 2001). Of course, positive and negative events may differ in many other ways as besides their valence. For example, do the following pairs of events differ only in valence: getting hired versus fired, getting married versus divorced, and passing a course versus failing? Even when positive and negative events are equated, negative events produce more distress than positive events produce eustress. A case in point is the scarcity of money, which is considered a source of chronic stress (Turner et al., 1995). What is the psychological effect of a raise in pay versus a reduction in pay? Boyce and coresearchers (2013) investigated how an increase versus decrease in household income affected people's subjective well-being. The researchers accessed survey data that covered at least two consecutive years from over 28,000 German households regarding their income and how satisfied they were with life on an 11-point scale ranging from 0 (*totally unhappy*) to 10 (*totally happy*). The researchers also obtained income data from over 20,000 British households along with the status of their general psychological well-being. The survey results showed that increases in income were associated with a rise in subjective well-being, while decreases were associated with a decline in subjective well-being. However, the decline in well-being was greater than the rise in well-being for correspondingly equal decreases and increases in income. In other words, people reacted more strongly to a decrease in income than to an increase.

Predictability and controllability of stressors. Would you like to know when an important exam is coming up, when a violent thunderstorm covers your campus, or when a terrorist will strike? Stressor magnitude, predictability, and controllability are three characteristics listed in Table 7.1 that determine the severity of stress. Psychologists have investigated these stressor characteristics with electric shock or breathing carbon dioxide as substitutes for stressors. First, in regards to the magnitude or intensity of stressor stimuli, an increase in intensity results in stronger stress responses. For instance, a startle reaction and anxiety are stronger to more intense aversive stimuli, such as to electric shock compared to an air blast onto the front of one's throat (Grillon et al., 2004). Second, in regards to predictability, individuals prefer to know when a stressor is coming rather than to be surprised. Lejuez and coworkers (2000) had participants breathe a 20 percent carbon dioxide mixture, which produces shortness of breath, anxiety, and hyperventilation. The researchers found that when given a choice between knowing and not knowing when the mixture would be administered, participants preferred to know. In other words, they preferred predictable to unpredictable stressors. Third, controllability of a stressor is another feature that contributes to stress. Can the individual do anything about the stressor? For instance, being unable to escape or terminate a threat is more distressing compared to being able to do so. Zvolensky and coresearchers (1999, 2001) found that their participants became more anxious when unable to terminate 20 percent carbon dioxide mixture compared to when they could terminate it.

Two hypotheses have been proposed to account for the preference of predictable and controllable stressors over unpredictable and uncontrollable stressors. The **preparatory response hypothesis** states that a signal preceding a biologically relevant event allows the organism to prepare for that event (Perkins, 1955). By knowing when the stressor is coming, a person can prepare and thus reduce its aversiveness. For instance, knowing when a shock or 20 percent carbon dioxide mixture would be delivered helps a person avoid it. By knowing when an exam or storm are coming a person can prepare for them and thus reduce any stress that may result. As an alternative, the **safety hypothesis** maintains that it is crucial to distinguish safe intervals when the stressor is absent from unsafe intervals when the stressor is present (Seligman, 1971). During safe intervals individuals can relax; they only need worry when the signal predicting the stressor is present. Thus, safe periods are those days when exams are not scheduled, when a tornado warning has not sounded, or when the all clear signal is given regarding any danger on campus. A person can relax during these safe times. Unsafe periods consist of those intervals signaling an exam, a tornado, or a campus-wide alert of danger. These intervals are times of stress and anxiety. In daily life, perhaps both hypotheses can explain human behavior. If we know when a negative life event is coming, then we can do something about it. Perhaps we can avoid it or reduce the negative impact it will have. And, according to the safety hypothesis, we can relax during those times when no negative life events are signaled.

Characteristics of Stress

Have you been troubled by the inability to sleep or slow down? Have you felt anxious or down? Are you trying to fight off a cold or the flu? Do you tend to eat junk food when under pressure? A "yes" to any of these questions may indicate stress. It manifests itself in physiological symptoms, psychological feelings, and maladaptive behaviors (see Table 7.2).

Physiological symptoms of stress. The physiological reactivity of an individual's body indicates stress, such as a headache, muscle tension, or an upset stomach. Furthermore, the feeling of stress will be greater the more frequent, intense, and lasting the symptoms. The *Hopkins Symptom Checklist* (Derogatis et al., 1974), the *Symptom Checklist* (Rosen et al., 2000), and the *Calgary Symptoms of Stress Inventory* (Carlson & Thomas, 2007), for instance, assess these physiological symptoms to determine a person's stress. In these scales, some attempt is made to quantify the level of stress based on intensity, frequency, or duration of the symptoms. For example, examine the physiological symptoms in Table 7.2 and then rate yourself on how intensely or long you have experienced them, say, in the past week: $0 = $ *not at all* to $4 = $ *extremely intensely (long)*. Now do the same for the frequency of these symptoms: $0 = $ *not at all* to $4 = $ *extremely frequently*. Higher scores indicate greater physiological stress.

Hormones are responsible for some of the physiological symptoms of stress, such as tense arousal or negative emotions. Hormones are chemical messengers that are released from various glands and travel in the blood stream to affect a particular organ. With the occurrence of a stressor such as an important exam or showdown with a roommate, the brain sends signals to the adrenal glands, which are located on top of one's kidneys. The adrenal glands release a surge of adrenaline (epinephrine) and cortisol, which in turn affect various organs. Adrenaline is a hormone that prepares the body for the fight-or-flight response. It causes the heart to pump faster, opens air passages to the lungs to provide more oxygen to the muscles, and shunt blood away from where it is not needed and into major muscle groups in preparation for action. Cortisol, known as the stress hormone, stimulates the release of glucose (sugar) into the bloodstream that provides the energy necessary for any fight-or-flight responses. It also stimulates one's appetite in order to restore the energy that was used for fleeing or fighting.

Healthhour describes the function of stress hormones in a YouTube video titled "Stress Response in Animation" here: www.youtube.com/watch?v=BIfK0L8xDP0

TABLE 7.2 Symptoms Indicating Stress

Physiological Symptoms	Psychological Symptoms	Maladaptive Behaviors
Colds	Feel hopeless, helpless	Drinking more alcohol
Gastrointestinal distress	Low self-esteem	Taking illicit drugs
Headaches	Low subjective well-being	Eating poorly, comfort foods
Nausea	Negative emotions (anger, anxiety, depression, sadness, fatigue)	
Psychophysiological disorders	Tense arousal	Resting or sleeping badly
Sickness behaviors	Worry	Filling time passively (too much Internet, sitting, staring)

A.D.A.M. describes the function of the adrenal glands during stress in a YouTube video, titled "Adrenal Glands Animation" here: www.youtube.com/watch?v=06jbq3bxKE0&feature=related.

Psychological feelings of stress. The psychological symptoms of stress have a negative valence— that is, they are experienced as being unpleasant or aversive. The psychologically stressed individual feels hopeless, anxious, fatigued, depressed, negative moods, and low subjective well-being. Again, scales are able to measure the frequency and intensity of various types of negative feelings that characterize distress. The *Perceived Stress Scale* measures the frequency with which a person has felt upset, stressed, nervous, irritated, for example, during the last month (Cohen et al., 1983). The *Perceived Stress Scale* extensively covers two features of stress: predictability and controllability. The first question asks if an event happened unexpectedly, while most of the remaining items measure the extent of being able to control problems or important events.

Mind Garden provides a copy of the Perceived Stress Scale here: www.mindgarden.com/docs/ PerceivedStressScale.pdf.

The *Perceived Stress Questionnaire* is another scale that measures psychological feelings of stress (Fliege et al., 2005). It contains 15 statements to assess three components of psychological stress. One component refers to worries such as anxiety about the future and feelings of desperation and frustration. A second refers to tension such as uneasiness, exhaustion, and a lack of relaxation. A final component refers to a lack of joy, as shown by the absence of energetic arousal and low feelings of security. Table 7.3 shows questions that are derived from statements in the *Perceived Stress Questionnaire*. In testing this questionnaire, Fliege and coresearchers (2005) found that hospital patients with psychosomatic disorders, such as affective, eating, and personality disorders, experienced the most stress, followed by patients who suffered from tinnitus (hearing a ringing or buzzing). Medical students experienced the next most stress, while healthy adults experienced the least stress. Finally, as the health of patients improved, their level of worries and tension decreased.

Behavioral symptoms of stress. Stress is an unpleasant, aversive internal state. Consequently, people engage in various behaviors to alleviate those feelings—that is, to reduce their stress. Wasting

TABLE 7.3 Psychological Components of the *Perceived Stress Questionnaire*

For each question use the adjacent scale to rate yourself on the stress dimension
Worry: How much do you worry?
Almost never = 1 2 3 4 5 = Usually
This refers to worrying about your future, your problems, and your goals being blocked
Tension: Do you feel any tension?
Almost never = 1 2 3 4 5 = Usually
This refers to feeling anxious or agitated or being mentally tired and being unable to unwind
Unhappiness: Do you feel any unhappiness?
Almost never = 1 2 3 4 5 = Usually
This refers to your lack of being happy, lack of being cheerful, lack of feeling secure, and being unable to take pleasure from different activities

Note: in the *Perceived Stress Questionnaire*, individuals sum their scores. Higher scores mean more psychological stress.

time, mindless TV watching, eating comfort foods, or drinking alcohol are examples of behaviors designed to reduce stress. In some instances, however, these behaviors can become stressful themselves.

Leisurely pursuits, such as playing computer games, are a way of avoiding the source of stress temporarily but can result in other types of stress. Wood and coresearchers (2007) had computer gamers (202 males, 78 females) complete an online survey regarding some reasons why they played and how they felt about time lost while playing. A large percentage (72 percent) stated that gaming helped them relieve stress or boredom. At the same time, many stated that gaming had negative aspects, such as missing other events (classes, appointments), losing sleep, feeling guilty about time wasted, and social conflict with others. Thus, although gaming helps relieve stress, it can also be a source of stress by interfering with other aspects of a person's life.

The **self-medication hypothesis** refers to using alcohol, nicotine, or illicit drugs to alleviate symptoms of stress. Self-medication is part of *comorbidity*, which refers to the association between psychological distress, on the one hand, and the use of alcohol or drugs on the other. Comorbidity occurs in individuals with mild chronic depression, for example (Bolton et al., 2009). It refers to the fact that such individuals are more likely to be alcohol and substance abusers than are members of the general population. This association is the result of sufferers being motivated to reduce their negative psychological feelings. Unfortunately, alcohol, nicotine, and illicit drug use bring about their own stress in the form of a withdrawal syndrome, which, you may remember, produces a drug-opposite effect. An individual experiences drug withdrawal in the form of headaches, lack of energy, depressed mood, and feelings of distress.

Stress affects eating. Psychologists have long known that stress affects eating. But why? One idea is that food acts as a negative reinforcer—that is, food reduces the unpleasant feelings of distress. For instance, when distressed many people attempt to cope by eating. Furthermore, when individuals feel stressed they do not eat just any kind of food. Zellner and coresearchers (2006) found that their respondents ate sweets (especially chocolate) and high-fat snack food because it reduced stress, relaxed them, and comforted them. In fact, the notion of **comfort food** is that it relieves our physiological and psychological distress. With this definition in mind, Wansink and coresearchers (2003) asked a random sample of 411 individuals aged 18 or older to list their favorite snack food. At the top of the list were potato chips, which were listed by 23 percent of their respondents, followed by ice cream, cookies, and candy (chocolate). In addition, the foods that people eat when stressed are the very foods that people try to avoid because those foods are high in sugar and fat and thus contain many calories.

Also, when stressed many people eat foods that they would normally avoid out of health and body weight concerns. Stress shifts people's preferences from wholesome food to high-calorie food that contains fat and sugar. To test this possibility, Zellner and coresearchers (2006) created stress by having participants try to solve anagrams that had no solution compared to anagrams that did. Participants who received the no-solution anagrams rated that experience much more stressful compared to participants who received solvable anagrams. During the anagram-solving phase of the experiment, participants were provided with 100 grams (3.53 ounces) of grapes and 100 grams of M&Ms to eat. Grapes are considered healthy, nutritious food, while M&Ms are considered less healthy. If M&Ms are a comfort food, compared to grapes, then will participants switch their food preference when they become stressed? This prediction was confirmed. The stressed participants ate more M&Ms than did the no-stress participants, who ate more grapes.

Stress motivated participants to shift their preferences from a healthy, low-calorie food to a less healthy, high-calorie sweet food. In addition, using questionnaire measures of stress, researchers have discovered that stress seems to promote hunger, a loss of control over eating, and a tendency to binge eat (Groesz et al., 2012). This relationship was stronger for tasty but nonhealthy food compared to less tasty but healthy food.

However, not everyone reacts to stress by overeating sweets. Thus, when stressed, (1) do you overeat, (2) do you undereat, or (3) are you unaffected? And, if you overeat, what foods do you most frequently overeat? Why do you eat these foods when stressed? Research shows that some individuals eat more and others eat less when stressed. For instance, Sproesser and coresearchers (2014) discovered that 56 percent of their respondents reported that stress consistently affected their eating. Of those, one-third ate more than normal and two-thirds ate less. Zellner and coresearchers (2006) found that the majority of women tended to overeat when stressed while the majority of men tended to undereat. However, there were also women who ate less and men who ate more when under stress. Thus, notice from these reports that a sizable number of people either overeat or undereat, which makes it difficult to generalize about the effects of stress on eating.

Although the emphasis is on how eating can alleviate distress, what about the other side of this relationship? Can eating that occurs in pleasant situations offset the eating behavior produced by distressing situations? In other words, do individuals who overeat when distressed eat less in pleasant situations? And do those who undereat when distressed eat more in pleasant situations? Sproesser and co-researchers (2014) conducted a laboratory experiment to answer this question by creating stress via social rejection. Participants were recruited for the experiment that purportedly concerned first impressions and taste. As part of the procedure, participants filled out a questionnaire about their views of first impressions. Next, participants made a video of themselves describing their career aspirations, which was to serve as an introduction to a potential partner for the next phase of the experiment. After supposedly viewing the participant's video, the potential partner indicated whether he or she was willing to meet with the participant. The potential partner provided three types of feedback to the participant: neutral, accepting, or rejection.

Neutral feedback: The potential partner had to cancel the meeting with them.
Accept feedback: The potential partner had viewed their video and looked forward to a meeting.
Reject feedback: The potential partner had viewed their video and decided not to meet them.

Participants rated their feelings regarding the three types of feedback. And, indeed, the reject feedback produced more negative feelings and a greater sense of social exclusion compared to the other two feedback conditions. In the next phase or taste phase of the experiment, participants were presented with three different types of ice cream, which they were to rate for taste, texture, and liking. During the ice cream evaluations, participants were told "to taste and eat as much as they liked" (p. 60). The experimenters measured the amount of ice cream consumed. After evaluating the ice cream, the experimenter asked the participants how they responded when colleagues, friends, partners, relatives caused them stress. Do you eat less than usual, the same amount, or more than usual? Based on their answers, participants were classified as undereaters or overeaters. The results in Figure 7.1 show that when rejected the overeaters ate more and the undereaters ate less compared to the neutral feedback condition. However, this trend reversed in

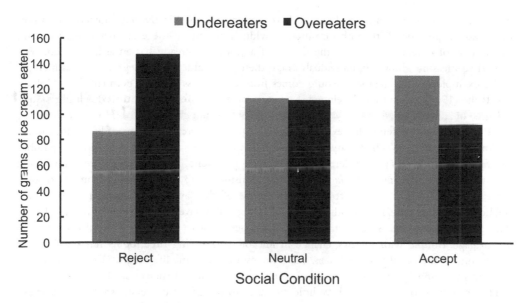

FIGURE 7.1 Effect of Inclusion/Exclusion on Eating. The effects on eating of being socially accepted or rejected depends on whether a person normally undereats or overeats in times of stress. When socially rejected, undereaters eat less than normal and overeaters eat more than normal. However, when socially accepted, undereaters eat more than normal and overeaters eat less than normal.

Source: Adapted from "The Bright Side of Stress-Induced Eating: Eating More When Stressed but Less When Pleased" by G. Sproesser et al., 2014, *Psychological Science, 25*, p. 60.

the accept feedback condition. When accepted, overeaters ate less and undereaters ate more. Thus, the motivating effects of negative and positive conditions on eating are complementary. In other words, overeating in one situation leads to undereating in the other situation and vice versa.

Stressor–Stress Relationship

What is the relationship between the types of stressors listed in Table 7.1 and the degree of distress? As chronic stressors, daily hassles, life change events, and traumatic stressors increase in magnitude, does distress increase? How do psychologists measure the magnitude of these various stressors?

Determining the impact of stressors. Life's demands motivate individuals to make adjustments. At what magnitude, however, do demands become so great that the required adjustments exceed a person's coping resources? A serious car accident versus a fender bender, flunking out of university versus flunking an exam, or the end of a long versus a brief romantic relationship illustrate demands that involve different levels of adjustment. One assumption is that greater demands require more adjustment and potentially more stress. In order to determine the shape of the stressor–stress relationship, it is necessary to quantify the impact of life demands and any subsequent stress. To this end, psychologists have employed both objective and subjective measures of stressor magnitude. With both measures, individuals indicate if the event happened to them. In the case of objective measures, the degree of adjustment already has an assigned value. For subjective measures, however, individuals assign their own value to the degree of adjustment.

An example of an objective measure comes from early stress research performed by Holmes and Rahe (1967), when they developed their concept of the **life change unit**. Each unit equals a degree of adjustment considered necessary to cope with a life change event (Holmes & Masuda, 1974). Adjusting to different life events, however, requires different numbers of life change units. Holmes and Rahe (1967) had a large sample of participants rate various life events for the number of life change units they considered necessary for adjustment. These ratings were summarized into the *Social Readjustment Rating Scale*, which consists of 43 items ranging from death of a spouse (100 adjustment units) to minor violations of the law (43 adjustment units). Since publication of this scale, several other life event rating scales have been developed (Miller, 1993). The *Social Readjustment Scale* contains many items pertinent to the general population, such as a mortgage, trouble with in-laws, change in line of work, being fired, or retirement. Another questionnaire, the *Social Stress Indicators,* asks 34 questions covering life events, 51 questions about chronic stress, and 19 questions about major traumatic events (Turner et al., 1995).

However, most of these items have little relevance to the life of university students. Life event items pertinent to university students can be found in the *Undergraduate Stress Questionnaire* (Crandall et al., 1992). It contains a number of items that have been rated for the severity of their stressfulness. Some example items, in order of decreasing stressfulness, are "had a lot of tests, had a class presentation, registration for classes, and got to class late." Objective ratings scales, however, imply that the same life event is equally severe or stressful for every person. Yet, one life event may require a great deal of adjustment on the part of one individual and little adjustment for another. Being interrupted from studying might be very annoying for one student but be judged a welcome relief by another. Other stress scales take into account the possibility that the same stressor does not impact everyone the same. For instance, the *College Students Life Events Scale* in Table 7.4 requires a student to assign a numerical value to both the degree and duration of tension created by a particular demand. The combination of tension and duration indicates the subjective impact a demand has on an individual. The accumulation of a greater score on this scale implies more life demands and thus a greater likelihood of stress. Finally, most stress questionnaires like the one in Table 7.4 make hardly any reference to positive events. Most stressors have a negative valence, which supports the idea described earlier that stressors are composed mainly of negative, not positive, events.

Stressor magnitude and stress. Random shootings and terrorist bombings are examples of very traumatic unpredictable and uncontrollable events. Both events have been responsible for a great deal of distress in both military and civilian populations. These events occur in seconds but have distressing and long-term consequences. In addition to shootings and bombings, other traumatic stressors such as sexual violence, severe injury, or threat of death produce a type of distress known as **post-traumatic stress disorder** (*PTSD*). A person can be a victim or witness of the event or learn that it happened to a loved one. Exposure to the event results in intrusive stressful memories and unpleasant dreams. In addition, people may experience flashbacks during which they act or feel as if the traumatic event has reoccurred. Stimuli associated with the trauma can later elicit physiological reactions and intense psychological distress that resemble the original

TABLE 7.4 College Students Life Events Scale

Instructions

Tension: indicate how much tension you felt while the most recent occurrence of the event was going on. By feelings of tension we mean feeling worried, anxious, irritable, or depressed. Such feelings may be accompanied by difficulty in sleeping or concentrating on other things. Use the following scale:

None	1
Slight	2
Some	3
Moderate	4
Significant	5
Severe	6
Almost Unendurable	7

Duration: if there was tension associated with the event, think about how long the tension associated with the event lasted (or has lasted if it is still going on). Use the following scale:

Less than 1 day	1
More than 1 day, but less than 1 week	2
More than 1 week, but less than 1 month	3
About 1 month	4
About 6 weeks	5
About 2 months	6
More than 2 months	7

Tension   *Duration*

Tension	Duration		
_____	_____	1.	Increase in normal academic course load (e.g., more academic work than previously, much harder work, etc.)
_____	_____	2.	Increased conflict in balancing time for academic and social activities
_____	_____	3.	Struggled with decision about major or career goal
_____	_____	4.	Inability to get desired courses or program
_____	_____	5.	Received much poorer grade than expected on a test or in a course
_____	_____	6.	Repeated arguments, hassles with cohabitants (e.g., racial, sexual, religious, personal idiosyncrasies, financial, etc.)
_____	_____	7.	Living arrangements consistently too noisy (to study, to sleep)
_____	_____	8.	Moved to new quarters on or off campus
_____	_____	9.	Realized that finances are increasingly inadequate to meet living expenses
_____	_____	10.	Significant increase in level of debt (e.g., took out large loan, charged more than can easily pay, gambling debts, etc.)
_____	_____	11.	Serious attempt to stop, decrease, or moderate use of drugs, alcohol, or smoking
_____	_____	12.	Significant increase in use of alcohol, resulting in problems in school, work, or other areas of life
_____	_____	13.	Increased attendance or participation in religious services or practices
_____	_____	14.	Decreased attendance or participation in religious services or practices
_____	_____	15.	Increased commitment or participation in political or social activism
_____	_____	16.	Began sexual unfaithfulness to a partner to whom you are not married
_____	_____	17.	Engaged in initial sexual intercourse
_____	_____	18.	Engaged in sex act without use of birth control measures (i.e., feared pregnancy)

continued . . .

TABLE 7.4 Continued

Tension	Duration		
_____	_____	19.	Became pregnant out of wedlock or partner became pregnant out of wedlock
_____	_____	20.	Experienced rejection of a more than casual sexual overture
_____	_____	21.	Unable to find a satisfactory sex partner
_____	_____	22.	Divorce or separation of parents
_____	_____	23.	Death of member of immediate family (e.g., parent, sibling, grandparent, etc.)
_____	_____	24.	Parental remarriage
_____	_____	25.	Decided for the first time not to go home for major holiday
_____	_____	26.	Increased conflict with parent (e.g., sex, drug use, dress, religious practices, lifestyle, sleeping out of home, etc.)
_____	_____	27.	Increased peer pressure to experiment with sex, drugs, etc.
_____	_____	28.	Lost a friend due to personal conflict
_____	_____	29.	Lost a good friend or friends because you or they moved, or transferred, etc.
_____	_____	30.	Realized necessity to make new friends
_____	_____	31.	Got married
_____	_____	32.	Entered new, serious relationship with boyfriend or girlfriend (e.g., engaged, living together, etc.)
_____	_____	33.	Boyfriend or girlfriend broke up your relationship
_____	_____	34.	You broke up with boyfriend or girlfriend
_____	_____	35.	Increased conflict with boyfriend or girlfriend (e.g., over sex, drugs, alcohol, independence, recreation, division of responsibilities, etc.)
_____	_____	36.	Deeply attracted to someone who showed no interest in you
_____	_____	37.	Important date was disappointing
_____	_____	38.	Your friend went out with someone you were interested in
_____	_____	39.	Struggled with decision to break up with boyfriend or girlfriend
_____	_____	40.	Increased job responsibilities
_____	_____	41.	Increased hassles on the job with boss or supervisor
_____	_____	42.	Quit job
_____	_____	43.	Realized job responsibilities interfered with academic work
_____	_____	44.	Victim of assault
_____	_____	45.	Busted for drug-related activity
_____	_____	46.	Victim of robbery or burglary
_____	_____	47.	Involved in auto accident as driver, without injury
_____	_____	48.	Involved in auto accident as passenger, without injury
_____	_____	49.	Illness or injury kept you out of school for one week or more
_____	_____	50.	Car broke down
_____	_____	51.	Activity run by your group was a flop (e.g., play, team lost game, no one came to your party, etc.)
_____	_____	52.	Realized responsibilities in extracurricular activities interfered with school work
_____	_____	53.	Unable to find adequate recreational or athletic outlets

Source: Adapted from "College Students Life Events Scale" by Murray Levine, University at Buffalo, and David Perkins, Ball State University. Printed with their permission.

traumatic experience. In the future, the individual tries to avoid associated stimuli, reminders, thoughts, or feelings that are connected with the traumatic event. Finally, a victim appears more aroused and reactive, such as being irritable, extremely vigilant, or easily startled, and have problems concentrating and sleeping. In order to be diagnosed as post-traumatic, the symptoms must persist longer than one month (American Psychiatric Association, 2013).

The degree of exposure to traumatic events determines the degree of PTSD. As an example, consider experiencing or witnessing the consequences of the terrorist attacks perpetrated against the United States on September 11, 2001. Two airplanes crashed into the World Trade Center in New York City, a third airplane crashed into the Pentagon, and a fourth crashed in a Pennsylvania field. The combined terrorist attacks killed an estimated 3,000 people and destroyed billions of dollars in property.

Five to eight weeks after the attack, a random telephone survey of New York City adults living within eight miles of the World Trade Center showed that, overall, 7.5 percent of the respondents experienced PTSD. Survey results show that the likelihood of suffering PTSD increased with being close (< 2 miles) to the attack site, directly witnessing the attack, and losing one's possessions or job (Galea et al., 2002). Also, as exposure intensity increases the likelihood of PTSD increases even two to three years later. For instance, DiGrande and coresearchers (2011) measured the degree of exposure of individuals who were actually in the World Trade Center towers when the airplanes hit. For example, was the person above or below the point of impact, did they sustain an injury, or were they exposed to the dust created by the impact? The *PTSD CheckList Stressor Specific Version* was used to measure the level of PTSD. The results showed that the severity of PTSD symptoms increased with the degree of exposure to the impact of the airplanes. The degree of exposure to a terrorist bombing also determines the likelihood of PTSD. On March 11, 2004, 10 terrorist bombs exploded on four commuter trains traveling toward downtown Madrid, Spain. Over 1,400 people were taken to the emergency room, 192 people died, and 335 police officers helped with the rescue. Does the likelihood of developing PTSD from this terrorist attack depend on being a victim, a police officer, or resident of the area where the bombings occurred? In order to answer this question, Gabriel and coresearchers (2007) used the Spanish version of the *Davidson Trauma Scale* to measure incidence of PTSD in these three populations. Their results showed that the likelihood of PTSD was 44.1 percent in victims, 12.3 percent in the residents, and 1.3 percent in police officers (Gabriel et al., 2007, Table 2). Usually, the incidence of PTSD is more like 5 to 20 percent for first responders such as the police. Nevertheless, their results support previous findings that the degree of trauma exposure determines the likelihood of PTSD.

PTSD motivates experiential avoidance. Individuals with PTSD are dominated by avoidance motivation. This becomes apparent in two questions from the *PTSD CheckList Stressor Specific Version*. One asks whether you avoid talking, thinking, and feeling about past stressful events. The second asks whether you avoid activities and situations that are reminders of past stressful events. This tendency is known as **experiential avoidance**—that is, the reluctance to endure painful sensations, memories, or thoughts (Chawla & Ostafin, 2007). My mother, even 55 years later, would not speak of her experiences in a Japanese concentration camp, as if unwilling to reexperience those memories. War veterans with PTSD exhibit experiential avoidance more than do veterans without PTSD. Kashdan and coresearchers (2010) asked veterans to list eight personal trivings, such as being a good role model or trying to avoid feeling inferior. Positive strivings or goals are approached, obtained, or achieved while negative strivings (also goals) are avoided, escaped, or rejected. The strivings concerned emotion regulation when they involved enhancing positive moods or happiness and avoiding unhappiness, anxiety, and stress. Veterans with and without PTSD differed in their strivings and emotion regulation. Veterans with PTSD reported spending more effort on emotion regulation and more effort in avoiding negative strivings. Veterans without PTSD spent more effort on positive strivings and less effort on emotion regulation. Thus, PTSD motivates individuals to avoid and escape the distress that can occur from environmental triggers and memories (Kashdan et al., 2010).

Cumulative effects of stressors. Do demands pile up at the end of the semester? Does something need repair the same time you are low on money? In order to determine the cumulative effects of stressors, Holmes and Masuda (1974) tabulated life changes for a large group of physicians and recorded the occurrence of illness or health changes that occurred within a two-year period following a cluster of such changes. Their results show that, as life change units increase, health changes increase also. In a prospective study, life change scores of resident physicians covering the previous 18 months were correlated with illnesses occurring in the next nine months. The relationship was positive: the percentage of individuals getting ill was greater for those with a larger number of life change units (Holmes & Masuda, 1974).

In addition to affecting illness, life changes can also depress behavior such as academic performance and GPA. Lloyd and colleagues (1980) assessed life changes among college students by having them indicate what changes had occurred in their lives. For instance, students were asked if they had experienced changes in sleeping, eating, recreation and family get-togethers, living conditions, or moving; or injury, illness, or the death of a friend or family member. Students were also asked to subjectively weigh each life change in regard to the amount of adjustment each required. Two measures were of interest: the total number of events that occurred in the previous year and the subjective weighted event total, which involved the subjective impact of a change. The life change measures were associated with a declining GPA: as life change scores went up, GPA went down. This finding was especially true for the subjective weighted event total. In addition, life changes in recreation, in work responsibilities, and in changing to a new line of work had a greater impact on students with lower GPAs.

In addition to the cumulative effects, stressors can also be chronic. These have an enduring nature, such as a consistently high likelihood of threat, an overload of demands from others, unresolved conflicts in relationships, and an imbalance between amount of effort and amount of reward (Wheaton and Montazer, 2010). The effort/reward ratio is an interesting measure of chronic stressors. An imbalance between effort and reward results when perceived effort increased and perceived reward decreased. For example, the reward/effort imbalance is greater if workers earn the minimum federal wage of $7.25 per hour compared to, say, $10 per hour or if students feel that their GPA is less than expected based on their weekly class preparation time. These examples are chronic stressors because work and attending college are long-term, not one-time, events. The *Effort-Reward Imbalance Questionnaire* measures effort and reward (Siegrist et al., 2004). Effort questions concern time pressure, interruptions, degree of demand, and number of responsibilities at work. Reward questions concern promotion opportunities, job security, degree of self-esteem, and salary. Thus, one would expect that as the imbalance increases—that is, high effort coupled with low reward—distress would also increase along with decreased health. How would you rate your current general health on the scale 1 = *bad* to 5 = *good*? Would your rating as a student or worker to this query depend on your level of perceived effort/reward imbalance? Siegrist and coworkers (2004) examined the rating of this question by employees in Belgium, England, France, and Germany. Their findings indicated that effort/reward ratios greater than 1 were associated with lower health scores. In other words, the chronic feeling that high effort produced low reward seemed to negatively affect the general health of the workers.

Racism as a stressor. Racism refers to attitudes and behaviors of one group that disparage and put down members of another (minority) group based usually on the physical appearance of the minority group members. Racial discrimination refers to treating a person differently by withholding benefits, services, or opportunities based on the individual's physical appearance, such as their skin color or facial features. Thus, as a member of a minority group, individuals often experience the stressors of racism and discrimination.

What are some indicators of discrimination and what are their consequences? One way is to list a wide variety of race-related stressors such as those described in the *Everyday Discrimination Scale*, the *Index of Race-Related Stress*, the *Race-Related Events Scale*, and the *Schedule of Racist Events* (Williams et al., 1997; Utsey & Ponterotto, 1996; Waelde et al., 2010; Landrine & Klonoff, 1996, respectively). Because of your race or ethnicity, have any of the events listed in Table 7.5 happened to you? For example, has someone ignored, insulted, dissed, verbally or physically abused you, or thought you were dishonest? The number of statements checked off signify the magnitude of racism as a stressor.

Racism causes stress. For instance, cultural and individual racism scores on the *Index of Race-Related Stress* correlated positively with scores obtained with the *Perceived Stress Scale* (Cohen & Hoberman, 1983). The *Schedule of Racist Events* scores correlate positively with stress-related psychiatric symptoms obtained from the *Hopkins Symptoms Checklist* (Derogatis et al., 1974), such as obsessive-compulsive disorders, depression, anxiety, and physical symptoms. In addition, people who were more stressed from racist events, as measured by the *Schedule*, were also more likely to use smoking as a stress reducer.

Racism also has physiological effects, especially in terms of high blood pressure (hypertension). High blood pressure results from excessive force on the walls of blood vessels, is responsible for heart attacks and kidney disease, and can interrupt the blood supply to the brain (stroke).

TABLE 7.5   Statements Illustrating Race-Related Stressors

---

1. You were treated unfairly in a store, restaurant, or place of business
2. You were ignored by clerks in stores, servers in restaurants, or business people
3. You were shown a lack of respect (dissed) by a clerk, boss, or teacher
4. You were not extended common courtesies such as a thank you, apology, or greeting
5. People treat you as if you are dishonest
6. You have been verbally harassed or insulted by other people
7. You have been refused housing
8. You have been physically threatened or harmed by other people
9. Although well-qualified, you were not offered the job or promotion
10. You feel the police treat you unfairly and look on you with suspicion

---

A greater frequency indicates a greater number of experienced stressors

Blood pressure dipping is a concept related to hypertension. Dipping refers to a decrease in blood pressure at night when a person is asleep. The lack of dipping has been associated with heart disease and early death (Ben-Dov et al., 2007; Ohkubo et al., 2002). Is racism involved in increasing blood pressure and in preventing a dip in blood pressure at night? In order to answer this question, Brondolo and coresearchers (2008) recruited African-Americans and Hispanic Americans, aged 24 to 65, to participate in a study testing this possibility. Participants' perception of their racist experiences was measured by how frequently they experienced events similar to those listed in Table 7.5. The participants were also outfitted with blood pressure monitors to measure their blood pressure while they were awake and asleep. The results showed that, as perceived racism increased, blood pressure increased while the individual was asleep but not when awake. The researchers also found that as perceived stress increased, blood pressure dipping decreased. Both higher blood pressure and the lack of nighttime dipping, as signs of stress, appear strongly linked to racism.

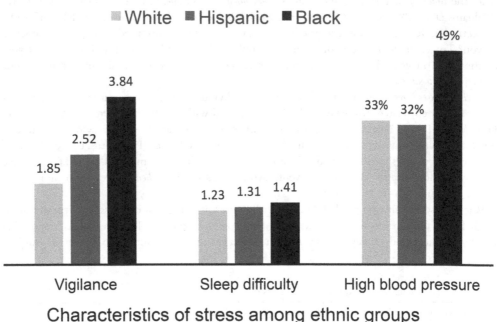

Characteristics of stress among ethnic groups

FIGURE 7.2 Vigilance, Sleep Difficulty, and High Blood Pressure by Ethnic Group. Ethnic groups differ in their degree of vigilance because of racial discrimination and consequently differ in the sleep difficulties and incidence of high blood pressure. African-Americans experienced the highest level of vigilance and consequently had the greatest sleep difficulties and highest percentage of high blood pressure compared to Whites and Hispanics.

Source: Adapted from "'Every Shut Eye, Ain't Sleep': The Role of Racism-Related Vigilance in Racial/Ethnic Disparities in Sleep Difficulty." by M. T. Hicken et al., 2013 *Race and Social Problems, 5,* Table 1, 107.

"Racial/Ethnic Disparities in Hypertension Prevalence: Reconsidering the Role of Chronic Stress" by M. T. Hicken et al., 2014, *American Journal of Public Health, 104,* high blood pressure, Table 1, p. 120.

Racism and vigilance. What behavior does racial discrimination motivate? **Race-related vigilance** refers to "preparation for and anticipation of discrimination" (Hicken et al., 2013, p. 101). Thus, individuals constantly attend their social environment for signs of perceived racism in order to reduce or avoid it. Researchers have hypothesized that this vigilance contributes to chronic stress in the form of sleep disturbance and hypertension. Hicken and coresearchers (2013, 2014) relied on survey responses provided by over 3,000 adults living in Chicago. The individuals filled out several questionnaires: (1) Two questionnaires asked about the extent the respondents suffered from discrimination during their daily lives but also about major experiences of discrimination; (2) a brief racism vigilance scale that asks individuals if they prepare for insults, if they try to look their best in order to receive good service and to avoid harassment, and if they avoid certain social situations; (3) sleep disturbance questions that ask how frequently, in the last four weeks, they had trouble falling asleep, waking at night or early in the morning, and had trouble going back to sleep. (4) Qualified technicians also measured the participants' blood pressure. Blacks displayed higher discrimination scores, both daily and major, compared to Whites or Hispanics. Furthermore, as Figure 7.2 shows that, compared to Whites and Hispanics, Blacks have the highest vigilance scores, have the greatest sleep difficulty, and have the largest percentage of individuals who suffer from high blood pressure. Discrimination motivates vigilance to be on the lookout for discrimination. But the cost of vigilance is stress in the form of sleep disturbances and high blood pressure (Hicken et al., 2013, 2014).

Section Recap

At times, individuals are motivated to do too many things at once because of the many demands life places on them. *Coping* is behavior that is motivated to adjust and to regulate those life demands and their consequences. *Stress* is the negative consequence when the demands are too great and the coping resources too few. *Stressors* are demanding, challenging, and threatening to one's well-being. When not coped with effectively, they produce stress. While negative life events produce stress, positive life events produce a type of arousal known as *eustress*, especially if the level of arousal is optimal. Stress usually means distress and is the opposite of eustress. According to the *same domain effect*, negative events produce distress, while positive events produce positive feelings and increase the quality of life and eustress. Stressors of sufficient magnitude that are unpredictable and uncontrollable produce distress. People prefer to know when a stressor is predictable. According to the *preparatory response hypothesis*, knowing when a stressor is coming allows the person to prepare for it. According to the *safety hypothesis*, it is important to distinguish stressor from stressor-free intervals, since a stressor-free interval allows the person to relax and feel safe. Stress shows as physiological arousal, psychological distress, and maladaptive behaviors. These are behaviors designed to reduce stress but become sources of stress themselves, such as self-medication. The *self-medication hypothesis* refers to the use of alcohol, nicotine, or illicit drugs to alleviate symptoms of stress. Self-medication occurs in individuals who suffer a psychological disorder, such as chronic mild depression.

People vary in their eating for coping with stress. Some undereat or overeat during stress. Eating comfort foods, such as chocolate or ice cream, can reduce stress but can also become a stressor if individuals feel guilty about breaking their diet. However, people who overeat during stress undereat in positive social situations, while those who undereat during stress overeat in positive social situations. Stress promotes eating, especially carbohydrates, in order to restore energy.

In general, as the magnitude of stressors increases and as stressors accumulate, stress increases. Scales have been developed to measure the impact of various stressors and the amount of adjustment they require. Some scales measure stress in terms of *life change units*, which refer to the amount of adjustment a stressor requires. Extremely traumatic events, such as terrorist attacks, result in an enduring stress disorder diagnosed as *post-traumatic stress disorder (PTSD)*. More traumatic experiences produce stronger PTSD symptoms. *Experiential avoidance* is a characteristic of PTSD and refers to the reluctance to reexperience painful sensations, memories, or thoughts. Stressors can also be chronic as in a high effort/reward ratio. In this case, stress results when a person works hard for a small return as in working for a minimum wage. Finally, several stressor/stress scales measure the experience of racism, which is experienced by African-Americans and other minority groups. Racism is associated with stress and higher levels of psychiatric symptoms. It results in *race-related vigilance*, which refers to being alert for discrimination in order to avoid it. The consequence of vigilance is stress in the form of sleep disturbances and high blood pressure.

STRESSORS AFFECT THE BODY

Have you ever been sick along with feeling awful, having little energy, and being socially withdrawn? Feeling sick results from an invasion of germs (bacteria, virus) and a weak immune system that was not up to the task of defending against these invaders. Do stressors weaken a person's immune system, increase the likelihood of getting sick, and make symptoms worse?

Psychophysiological Disorders

Stress has psychological, physiological, and medical effects. Psychological effects are highlighted in the *Perceived Stress Questionnaire* (see Table 7.3), which shows that stressors produce worry, tension, and a lack of joy. Some stressors when severe can produce PTSD, as described in the previous section. Physiological effects imply that stressors can physically arouse healthy individuals with increased heart rate, blood pressure, and muscle tension. Medical effects imply that stressors can worsen the medical condition of someone who is already sick. The *Diagnostic and Statistical Manual of Mental Disorders* (DSM-V) states that "Psychological Factors Affecting Other Medical Conditions" are psychological or behavioral factors that negatively affect a person's medical disorders (APA, 2013). This negative effect may take the form of interfering with a medical treatment, cause added health risks, or give rise to or worsen current medical symptoms. **Psychophysiological** or **psychosomatic disorders** are other names given to these medical conditions, including such classic examples as asthma, headaches, hypertension, and heart disease. How can stressors worsen or cause distress that is experienced as bodily symptoms. How do stressors trigger headaches, negatively affect the body's immune system, and worsen flu symptoms?

Headaches. Probably every person has experienced a headache at some time. These could consist of *migraine headaches*, which are long-lasting and so painful that a person longs for a quiet and dark spot to lie down. Migraine headaches can be accompanied by nausea and vomiting and are sometimes preceded by auras, such as halos around objects, light flashes, and tingling sensations.

Of lesser intensity are *tension headaches*, characterized by a dull aching pain and tightness of the forehead, sides, and back of the head. Do stressors play a role in triggering or causing a headache? Stressors can definitely trigger headaches (Nash & Thebarge, 2006). Retrospective investigations involve asking headache patients to recall events that triggered their headaches. For instance, Kelman (2007) asked 1,750 migraine patients to recall what and how often some event triggered a migraine headache. Patients reported that stress was the leading or second-leading migraine trigger. However, faulty memory and untangling stressors from stress are problems with retrospectively recalling what events triggered a headache. In addition to being unable to recall a trigger, a headache can be a stressor in its own right, since it leads to not fully participating or missing rewarding activities (Nash & Thebarge, 2006). These problems can be solved with prospective research, which involves measuring a person's headache intensity both before and after the onset of a suspected stressor. In one prospective study covering 90 days of diary keeping, for example, researchers found that prior experiences, such as psychic tension, private stress, and noise had some effect in triggering the onset of either a tension headache or migraine (Wöber et al., 2007).

The effect of a stressor is selective, however, and targets headache-prone individuals rather than causing a headache in everyone. Researchers have turned to the psychology laboratory to definitely ascertain whether stressors can induce headaches and if they only do so in headache-prone individuals. Cathcart and coresearchers (2010) examined the effects of a laboratory stressor on headache-prone individuals versus healthy control individuals. Headache-prone individuals were identified as having experienced many more headaches during the prior six months compared to the healthy control individuals. The experiment (see Table 7.6) involved three conditions: (1) in the control condition, a group of tension headache-prone participants engaged in a nonstressful reading task. (2) Another group of headache-prone participants engaged in a stressful problem-solving task. (3) A group of healthy (not headache-prone) participants also engaged in a stressful problem-solving task. The stressful task consisted of sitting in front of a computer screen and mentally solving both subtraction problems and anagrams for one hour. Participants in the nonstressor condition read magazines and newspapers for one hour. Every 10 minutes all participants rated the intensity of their headache (if any) on the scale: "0 = no headache, 1 = pain but easily ignored; 2 = can be ignored at times; 3 = painful but able to work; 4 = painful, work very difficult; and 5 = very painful, unable to work" (p. 287). Participants also rated their negative affect—that is, how stressed, anxious, angry, or depressed they were on the scale 0 (*not at all*) to 10 (*extremely*).

The stressful problem-solving task was effective in increasing negative affect for both the headache-prone and healthy participants. The stressful task also triggered headaches but only in the headache-prone participants, not in the healthy participants. Table 7.6 shows the percentage of participants who developed a headache after either the one-hour stressful or nonstressful period. Clearly, the laboratory stressor produced headaches but almost exclusively for individuals who are prone to get headaches.

Stressors, immune system, and disease. When you catch a cold or flu, does it happen at a time when there are many demands in your life? Are you more likely to be ill at the end of the semester than at the beginning? If so, this may not be your imagination. The field of **psycho-neuroimmunology** is the science that studies the relationship among stressors, the body's immune system, and disease. Scientists working in this field examine the manner in which stressors affect the immune system and whether this increases an individual's susceptibility to various diseases.

TABLE 7.6 An Experiment Featuring the Effects of Stressors on Headaches

Participant Type, Sex	Mean # Headaches Last Six Months	Treatment Condition	Effect Of Treatment	% Getting Headaches
Headache prone 34% M, 66% F	20.2	Nonstressful reading	Negative affect not increased	17%
Headache prone 34% M, 66% F	19.2	Stressful problem solving	Negative affect increased	91%
Healthy 36% M, 64% F	0	Stressful problem solving	Negative affect increased	4%

Source: Adapted from "Central Mechanisms of Stress-Induced Headache" by S. Cathcart et al., 2010, *Cephalalgia*, *30*, Table 1, pp. 288 and 289.

Bacteria and virus are *pathogens* that invade the human body to produce diseases, such as tuberculosis, cold, and flu. The job of the immune system is to identify and then destroy pathogens (Abbas et al., 2016). Cells that make up the immune system develop mainly in bone marrow and the thymus gland but do much of their work in the blood and lymph (clear fluid in the cells). The manner by which the immune system operates is relevant for understanding how stressors can contribute to disease. First, there are two components to the immune system: innate and adaptive. The innate immune system common to all humans uses a nonspecific approach to destroy pathogens. The adaptive immune system, in contrast, employs cells that have developed specifically to combat a distinctive population of pathogens. Second, in terms of duration, the innate immune system begins its attack within minutes, while the adaptive immune system may not be ready until days later to destroy any invading pathogens. Third, some immune cells identify pathogens and communicate this to other cells, who are the ones that actually destroy the pathogens. Finally, some cells in the immune system, known as **cytokines**, communicate the presence of pathogens to the brain.

Do stressors and stress impact the immune system? Many investigations have demonstrated that psychological stressors can downgrade the immune system (Segerstrom & Miller, 2004). Furthermore, the phrase "Psychological Factors Affecting Other Medical Conditions" implies that stressors can contribute to disease by weakening the immune system. However, only a few experiments have shown that disease is the outcome. One such investigation by Cohen and coresearchers (1999) showed that stress alters cytokine levels, which in turn are related to the severity of flu symptoms. In their research, they quarantined 55 healthy volunteers in a hotel. Following exposure to a flu virus, participants were evaluated daily for the next seven days for the severity of their flu symptoms. The researchers measured both the amount of mucus secreted into tissues and measured cytokine levels. Participants rated their symptoms (0 = *none* to 3 = *severe*) of chill, cough, headache, sneezing, sore throat, and nasal congestion and discharge. These ratings were summed for a total symptom score. The *Perceived Stress scale* was used to measure stress (Cohen et al., 1983). Individuals who scored above the median were classified as experiencing high stress and those who scored below were classified as experiencing low stress. The results showed that high-stress individuals, compared to low-stress, had higher levels of flu symptoms, secreted more mucus, and had higher levels of cytokines on all seven days of the investigation. The greatest difference occurred on the second day.

A lack of sleep as a symptom of stress may also weaken the immune system. To test this possibility, Prather and coresearchers (2015) measured sleep duration in 164 individuals for seven consecutive days. Next, the individuals were infected with a cold virus and monitored for cold symptoms for the next five days. The likelihood of developing a cold from the virus increased with a decrease in sleep duration. Most susceptible were individuals who slept five hours or less per night. Most protected were individuals who slept seven hours or more per night. Both the stress and sleep investigations illustrate how stress can weaken the immune system, which in turn increases one's susceptibility to disease.

Sickness Behavior

When sick, you may have felt down, lethargic, and uncommunicative. These traits characterize sickness behavior, which results when cytokines communicate the presence of pathogens to the brain (Chang et al., 2009). More precisely, **sickness behavior** is felt as fatigue, fever, mild depression, lack of appetite, lack of pleasure, sleepiness, slowed cognitions, and social withdrawal (Maes et al., 2012; Shattuck & Muehlenbein, 2015). This lack of motivation appears to be the result of low energy. But, actually, an individual's energy is directed to the immune system where it is needed. When pathogens invade, an individual's well-being is threatened. Consequently, the immune system needs energy to attack the pathogens. This energy trade-off from behavior to the immune system occurs because the activity of the immune system is momentarily more important for a person's survival than are goal pursuits, social interactions, and pleasurable activities (Maes et al., 2012; Shattuck & Muehlenbein, 2015).

Endotoxin has been used to produce traces of sickness behavior in healthy individuals. This substance challenges the immune system, produces mild physical symptoms, and raises the level of cytokines in the blood. Eisenberger and coresearchers (2010) hypothesized that endotoxin would produce an aspect of sickness behavior, known as social withdrawal, along with a depressed mood. The researchers administered endotoxin to healthy women and a placebo solution to control participants. The researchers measured the participants' body temperature as well as their self-reported physical symptoms, such as muscle pain, shivering, or fatigue. Also, measured were the participants' preference for social connectedness and their degree of negative mood. Compared to the placebo, the endotoxin increased the level of cytokines, body temperature, and physical symptoms in the participants. In addition, endotoxin increased feelings of being socially disconnected and feelings of negative mood. In related research, Reichenberg and coresearchers (2001, 2002) demonstrated that endotoxin also increased cytokine levels in the blood along with other changes in sickness behavior. For example, the researchers found that food consumption decreased, anxiety increased, and memory performance decreased all as a result of increased cytokines. Sickness behavior is an interesting challenge for the study of motivation. On the one hand, sickness behavior implies a lack of motivation; on the other, it indicates an immune system motivated to ensure the survival of the individual.

Section Recap

In addition to psychological effects, stressors affect the body physiologically and medically. Diseases caused or worsened by stressors have been referred to as *psychophysiological (psychosomatic) disorders.*

Headaches are examples. People who are prone to headaches are more likely to develop them as a result of stressful activities. *Psychoneuroimmunology* is a field that examines how psychological stressors degrade the immune system, making disease more likely. The body's immune system defends against invading pathogens, such as bacteria and viruses, which are responsible for various diseases. Psychological stressors, when of sufficient magnitude, can degrade the immune system, thereby increasing the likelihood of becoming ill from invading pathogens. The immune system also releases *cytokines* that communicate the presence of pathogens to the brain. The result is *sickness behavior* (fever, tired, no appetite), which is the body's way of combating pathogens. Lethargy is the result of the body directing energy toward the immune system to combat the pathogens.

VARIABLES MODERATING THE IMPACT OF LIFE EVENTS

When life hands you a lemon, do you turn sour or do you make lemonade? In a letter to an advice columnist, one distraught reader wrote that her husband left her for another woman. The writer claimed that as a result she suffered a heart attack even though she was only in her 40s. She went on to write:

> Since then my life has taken a 360-degree turn. I no longer smoke. I joined [a weight loss organization] and lost 58 pounds. I watch my salt, cholesterol and fat intake and exercise daily. How do I feel? Wonderful! . . . It's tough to admit, but I owe this newfound happiness to my ex-husband who dumped me. What I thought was the worst tragedy of my life turned out to be a blessing.

The advice columnist responded by writing, "When life hands you a lemon, make lemonade." The idea of making lemonade out of life's lemons illustrates the fact that people's reactions to life change demands are not fixed but variable. Stress depends on the appraisal of the life event.

Appraisal and Coping with Life Events and Stress

Do different features of a stressor motivate different coping strategies? And do the coping strategies people employ determine how well they alleviate their stress? Stressor controllability and magnitude (intensity), in Table 7.1, are two features that influence what coping strategies are employed. For instance, imagine the end of a romantic relationship from the view of the person who initiates the breakup and of the recipient. The breakup process is a stressor that leads to negative emotions, such as guilt, remorse, or anxiety from initiating the breakup and grief, fear, despair, or anger from being the recipient of that process. The negative emotions may be less intense for the person wanting to end the relationship. The emotions are probably more severe for the other individual, who may have been happy with the relationship. Also, the breakup process is controllable by the initiator but much less so by the recipient of the process. What type of coping behaviors are motivated by intensity and controllability? Do the individuals possess an efficient repertoire of coping strategies for this situation? And are they sensitive to feedback regarding the effectiveness of their coping strategies?

Appraisal. Coping with stressors and stress is a process that involves a sequence of three components: planning, execution, and feedback (Bonanno & Burton, 2013; Cheng et al., 2014). This sequence is shown in Figure 7.3. The first component, or planning stage, involves appraising the life demand and how to deal with it. The second component involves executing a coping strategy. The third component involves feedback. Is the strategy working and should the person

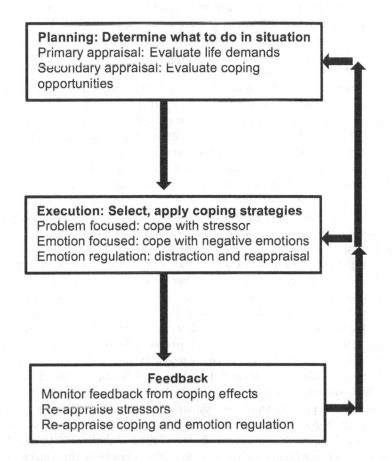

FIGURE 7.3 Flexibility in Coping. Flexibility in coping requires essential abilities at the planning, execution, and feedback stages. For the planning stage, an individual needs to be sensitive to the context in which a stressful life demand occurs and to the coping and emotion regulation opportunities that could be used. Next, an individual must select the most effective coping strategy or emotion regulation strategy from a broad and well-balanced repertoire to deal with the life demand. Finally, the individual must be sensitive to any feedback in order to revise their appraisal of stressors and stress in the situation or to revise their coping and emotion regulation strategies if necessary.

Source: Adapted from "Regulatory Flexibility: An Individual Differences Perspective on Coping and Emotion Regulation" by G. A. Bonanno & C. L. Burton, 2013, *Perspectives on Psychological Science, 8,* Figure 1, p. 595, and from "Coping Flexibility and Psychological Adjustment to Stressful Life Changes: A Meta-Analytic Review" by C. Cheng et al., 2014, *Psychological Bulletin, 140,* Figure 3, p. 1598.

make any changes? In the first component, a person appraises the situation and its effects. Appraisal alters the meaning of a life change event and consequently how an individual reacts (Folkman & Lazarus, 1985; Lazarus & Folkman, 1984). Does the rejected lover dwell on what might have been or view the end of the romantic relationship as a new beginning? In **primary appraisal** an event is evaluated as to whether it is relevant, benign, positive, or stressful. During the breakup, one person thinks "I am rejecting this individual," while the other thinks "I am being rejected." If the event is judged irrelevant, then a person may have little reaction to it. Benign or positive events produce little reaction or result in positive emotions but provide little if any stress. An event is appraised as stressful, however, if it implies a challenge, demand, or threat. Assessing what strategies can meet the demands of life events illustrates **secondary appraisal** (Folkman & Lazarus, 1985; Lazarus & Folkman, 1984). What resources does each individual possess to cope with the stress brought on by the breakup? First, each individual can establish if they have the appropriate resources to cope with the event. They can decide what coping strategy to employ and evaluate the likelihood that it will succeed. For example, are there friends to talk to or other people to date? How can I restructure my life? Will running override my distressing emotional feelings? All of these considerations are part of secondary appraisal.

Are individuals flexible in their appraisal of life demands and of their coping resources? In the breaking-up scenario, is the instigator aware of how controllable the process will be and what coping strategies will be effective? Does the rejected individual realize the breakup is imminent and is not controllable but may be amenable to distraction or reappraisal? Flexibility is important in the planning stage (Bonanno & Burton, 2013; Cheng et al., 2014). It means to be open minded to various possibilities. A flexible individual is able to appraise a life demand accurately and take inventory of any coping strategies. Flexibility also implies that person selects the appropriate strategy and is sensitive to feedback about the effectiveness of the strategy.

Coping. The second component in the coping sequence involves execution (see Figure 7.3). How can each person cope with the aftermath of the breakup? Coping has two functions: trying to deal with a life change demand and with any distress the demand produces (Folkman & Lazarus, 1985; Lazarus & Folkman, 1984). In Figure 7.3, **problem-focused coping** involves trying to identify the problem more clearly and to consider and try potential solutions. Just what does it mean that my romantic relationship has ended and how should I deal with that? **Emotion-focused coping** involves managing the negative reactions of the accompanying stress. There are a number of emotion-focused coping strategies. *Wishful thinking* is the desire that the problem would somehow go away or that the person would feel differently about it. *Distancing* refers to biding one's time before doing anything or trying to forget about the problem. Coping by *reappraisal* means reinterpreting the problem usually in a positive light. For example, the initiator of the breakup could emphasize the positive, such as thinking the breakup is for the best. *Self-blame* as a way of coping refers to the realization that you are responsible for your actions and their consequences. The recipient of the breakup might use self-blame by thinking they could have been kinder to their romantic partner. Smoking, drinking, drug-taking, eating, and running are tension reduction coping strategies that make the person feel better. Finally, some people employ *self-isolation*, in which they keep other people ignorant of their problems or avoid people in general (Folkman & Lazarus, 1985). *Distraction* means to prevent negative emotions by diverting attention away from the stressor, such as thinking about an exciting weekend activity (Bonanno & Burton, 2013). **Emotion regulation** is a specific type of coping that refers to the control of our emotions—that is, which to experience and when, how intensely, and how to express them. It refers to more than just reducing negative feelings of distress. Emotion regulation can involve both decreasing and increasing positive emotions but also negative ones (Gross, 1999). In regulation, positive emotions can mask negative feelings. Also, stronger negative emotions can serve to promote a particular goal. For example, increased anger motivates the jilted lover to "tell off" the former partner.

Flexibility in the execution phase means that people have an adequate repertoire of coping and regulation strategies to choose from. Flexibility also implies being able to choose the strategy that best fits a particular life demand. People have greater flexibility if they possess a broad range of strategies, have a balanced set of strategies, and are able to fit the strategy to the stressful situation (Cheng et al., 2014). In turn, greater coping flexibility allows for a more efficient alleviation of stress and to better psychological adjustment (Cheng et al., 2014).

For example, Sheppes and coresearchers (2014) had their participants look at a series of unpleasant stressful pictures. One series depicted low-intensity unpleasantness and the other high-intensity unpleasantness, for example, a woman crying versus a burn victim. Participants were instructed to view the pictures with one of two emotion regulation strategies: distraction and reappraisal. For distraction, the participants were instructed to "Try your best to feel less negative about the picture by thinking of something that is completely unrelated to the picture" (p. 167). For reappraisal, the participants were instructed to "Try your best to feel less negative about the pictures by attending to the picture and trying to change the meaning of it" (p. 167). Thus, when viewing the stressful picture, participants had a choice of which emotion regulation strategy to use: distraction or reappraisal. The results showed that the choice of strategy depended on the intensity of the unpleasantness of the picture. When the pictures were of low intensity, participants preferred to use reappraisal. But, when the pictures were of high intensity, participants preferred to use distraction. When applied to the breakup example, the initiator for whom the experience was less intense could reappraise the breakup as the opportunity to begin anew rather than as the end of a romance. If the breakup experience was more distressing for the recipient, then this individual selects distraction as a means of coping. For example, the person watches TV in order not to think about the breakup.

Stressor Controllability

Controllability is an important feature of stressors. As described in Table 7.1, a controllable stressor is one an individual can manage or cope with compared to an uncontrollable stressor, about which a person can do very little. Examples of controllable stressors are university exams, being stopped for drunk driving, and the end of a romance. Examples of uncontrollable stressors are weather disasters, terrorist attacks, and random shootings.

Controllability impacts coping. The benefits of flexibility also become apparent for stressors that are controllable. Controllability is a feature that increases the choice of coping strategies. In the breakup example, the instigator has control over how to end the relationship in order to alleviate feelings of guilt or remorse. The rejected individual has less control. Neither denying the breakup is occurring nor trying for a reconciliation are likely to work, especially if the other person wants to end it. Does each individual use a different coping strategy? In other words, does stressor controllability determine whether problem-focused or emotion-focused coping will be used?

Yes! People are more likely to use problem-focused coping when confronted with controllable stressors, but are more likely to use emotion-focused coping with less controllable stressors. Thus, if a stressor is not very controllable, then people are more likely to regulate their negative emotions. On the other hand, if they are controllable, then people are more likely to focus on the problem (Zakowski et al., 2001). In the breakup scenario, the instigator has more control to alleviate any unpleasant feelings. The individual could send a blunt text message, such as "we're through." The individual could also have a face-to-face conversation about the matter or simply quit replying to all communication. The rejected individual with less control will rely more on emotion-focused coping or emotion regulation.

Which coping strategy is more effective? And does that depend on the match between the degree of controllability and the type of coping or emotion regulation strategy? To answer this question, Forsythe and Compas (1987) asked their university participants to list the most stressful event they experienced in the last six months. These consisted of events such as moving from home, illness, or a death in the family. The participants next rated their degree of control over the event: very little or a great deal. For coping, participants reported using both problem-focused and emotion-focused coping. The researchers then determined which strategy a participant used relatively more: problem or emotion-focused coping. Finally, the *Hopkins Symptoms Checklist* measured the participants' level of stress. The results showed that the severity of the stress symptoms depended on stressor controllability and coping type. Symptoms were lower when problem-focused coping was used for controllable stressors. Symptoms were also lower when emotion-focused coping was used for uncontrollable stressors. Much less effective is using emotion-focused coping for controllable stressors and using problem-focused coping for uncontrollable stressors. Thus, in the breakup scenario, the instigator's feelings of guilt will be reduced more effectively with problem-focused coping. For the rejected individual, emotion-focused coping will be more effective in reducing feelings of grief, fear, despair, and anger.

Controllability impacts reappraisal. Reappraisal of a stressor is an emotion regulation strategy that involves changing the perception of a life event. Reappraisal is possible because, in Figure 7.3, coping is a process that changes in the light of feedback about its effectiveness. So appraisal and then reappraisal based on feedback can redefine the nature of a life event. Is it still stressful? For example, after being jilted and grieving for a while, you reappraise your busted romance as the opportunity for a new beginning. As a result, your mood improves. However, what if you controlled the breakup? Is reappraisal still useful? In both cases, flexibility in the execution phase becomes important, since it means determining when to use reappraisal: for controllable or uncontrollable stressors? To answer this question, Troy and coresearchers (2013) investigated whether the effectiveness of reappraisal depended on the controllability of the stressor. Specifically, the researchers examined three variables: amount of accumulated stress, cognitive reappraisal ability, and level of depression. Reappraisal ability refers to how well a person can view a negative stimulus more positively so as to reduce the negative emotion. For example, how much can you reduce the negative impact of a sad film through the use of reappraisal? The researchers used a *Life Experience Survey* to measure the accumulation of negative life events in their participants over the last 18 months. The researchers also measured the level of depression in their participants on a 0 to 3 scale, with higher numbers indicating more depression. A different group of participants rated these negative life events for controllability: 1 = *very uncontrollable* to 4 = *very controllable*. The controllability ratings indicated how much control participants could be expected to exercise over the negative life events.

The results showed that depression scores depended on the accumulation of negative life events. In other words, as stressful experiences accumulated individuals became more depressed. However, does an individual's appraisal ability affect the level of depression? Yes, but it depends on the controllability of the stressor. For stressors that are uncontrollable, high appraisal ability is beneficial; depression is lower. However, for stressors that are controllable, this ability was actually detrimental; depression was slightly higher. Thus, the effectiveness of an emotion regulation strategy depends on the degree a stressor is controllable. Applied to the breakup scenario, the jilted lover had less control. This individual will benefit more from any ability to reappraise the breakup and thus feel less distress. Reappraisal ability will not be helpful to the initiator of the breakup, who has control.

In Figure 7.3, during the execution stage, an individual decides what coping or emotion regulation strategies to employ. For example, if the stressor is controllable, then use problem-focused coping. On the other hand, if not controllable, then use emotion-focused coping. Furthermore, when a stressor is less controllable it is better to use reappraisal as an emotion regulation strategy. However, reappraisal is not helpful when the stressor is controllable. Intensity also determines what strategy is more effective. If the stressor is intense and enduring, then use the emotion regulation of distraction. For less intense stressors, a person can use the emotion regulation strategy of reappraisal.

Feedback

Figure 7.3 shows feedback as the third component in the coping sequence. Coping and emotion regulation may alter the nature of the stressor. However, are these strategies working? To determine if this is so, an individual needs to be sensitive to any feedback about their effectiveness. Information about effectiveness is fed back to the planning stage. Here an individual can reengage in the primary appraisal process. Has the nature of the stressor changed? The individual also reengages in the secondary appraisal process. What coping strategies are available to deal with the reappraised stressor? A reappraised stressor may be handled more effectively with different coping strategies. In addition, information about effectiveness is also fed back to the execution component. Should current coping strategies be kept, stopped, or changed? For example, the jilted lover discovers that TV watching serves as a distraction and lowers negative feelings of grief and despair. For the time being, the individual should keep this emotion regulation strategy. Reappraisal, on the other hand, is not working. For example, the jilted lover is unable to find an alternative meaning to the breakup. The person should stop this strategy and try it at a later date. Finally, some strategies need to be changed. For example, the jilted lover enjoys spending time with friends provided that there is no longer any discussion of the former lover.

Section Recap

Coping with stressors and stress involves planning, execution, and feedback. During the planning component, an individual appraises life change events. In *primary appraisal* an event is analyzed for whether it is positive, negative, or irrelevant for the individual's well-being. If appraised as negative, then an individual uses *secondary appraisal* to inventory the resources that can be used to manage the event. During the execution component, an individual determines how to cope with either the original stressor or with the stress. *Problem-focused coping* involves clarifying and trying to solve the stressor, while *emotion-focused coping* involves alleviating the accompanying distress. *Emotion regulation* is a type of coping that refers to the control of emotions, such as how intensely to experience them. For both appraisal and coping, being flexible helps. Stressor intensity determines the likelihood of whether distraction or reappraisal is the more effective emotion regulation strategy. When the stressor is of low intensity, reappraisal is a better strategy, but when of high intensity distraction is more effective. Stressor controllability impacts coping strategies. When controllable, problem-focused coping is best but when uncontrollable, emotion-focused coping is superior. During the feedback component, an individual is sensitive to feedback regarding the effectiveness of coping processes. Feedback can be used to reappraise the stressor and accompanying stress and to alter coping and emotion regulation strategies, if necessary.

The American Institute of Stress hosts a website that has helpful information about stressors, stress, and coping here: www.stress.org.

HELPGUIDE.ORG, a trusted guide to mental and emotional health, hosts a website about various aspects of stress here: www.helpguide.org/mental/stress_signs.htm.

GLOSSARY

Term	Definition
Adrenaline	A stress hormone that prepares the body for fight or flight by increasing heart rate, breathing capacity, and sending blood to the muscles
Comfort Food	Foods such as ice cream, chocolate, or potato chips that are eaten in order to reduce stress or to feel better
Comorbidity	When two negative states are associated together as when a person uses psychoactive drugs to alleviate stress, such as PTSD
Controllability	The extent to which a person can alter, change, or reduce the effects of a stressor
Coping	Behavior that is motivated to meet life's demands as in solving, managing, or dealing with those events (potential stressors) satisfactorily
Cortisol	A stress hormone that prepares the body for fight or flight by releasing glucose into the blood stream
Cytokines	Specialized cells of the body's immune system that communicate the presence of pathogens to the brain, which produce sickness behavior
Distancing	An emotion-focused coping strategy that involves biding one's time before doing anything or trying to forget about the problem
Distraction	A coping method to prevent negative emotions by diverting one's attention away from the stressor toward a more pleasant event
Distress	Term that emphasizes stress as being psychologically negative, i.e., negative stress
Effort/Reward Ratio	An indication of a chronic stressor. The imbalance results when an individual's efforts are much greater than the rewards received for that effort
Emotion-Focused Coping	It involves managing the negative reactions that accompany stress; to alleviate the symptoms of distress but not dealing with the source or stressor

continued ...

GLOSSARY Continued

Term	Definition
Emotion Regulation	A coping strategy for the control of both positive and negative emotions, such as which ones to experience, when, how intensely, and their expression
Endotoxin	A substance that produces indications of sickness behavior in a person
Eustress	Physiological arousal that results from positive events; considered positive stress and is the opposite of distress
Experiential Avoidance	A component of PTSD that refers to the reluctance to endure painful sensations, memories, or thoughts about an experienced traumatic event
Hormones	Chemical messengers released by glands in order to affect a particular organ. Certain hormones are released as part of stress; stress hormones
Immune System	A system of the body that is designed to attack and destroy pathogens and thus protect humans from disease
Life Change Unit	Arbitrary measure that indicates the degree of adjustment necessary to cope with a life change event
Migraine Headaches	Extremely painful, long-lasting headaches, which may be accompanied by nausea and may require a person to lie down in a dark room
Objective Measures	Preassigned number assigned to a stressor to indicate the stressor's impact or the degree of adjustment required to cope with it
Pathogens	Bacteria and virus that invade the human body to produce diseases, such as tuberculosis, cold, and flu
Post-traumatic Stress Disorder (PTSD)	A long-lasting source of distress from experiencing or witnessing very traumatic events such as shootings, bombings, sexual violence, severe injury, or death threats
Predictability	Likelihood or chance that a stressor will occur. It allows a person to anticipate the stressor
Preparatory Response Hypothesis	Signals that predict a biologically significant event allow the organism to prepare or be ready to cope with that event
Primary Appraisal	An event is evaluated as to whether it is relevant, benign, positive, or stressful for a person's well-being
Problem-Focused Coping	Trying to identify the problem or stressor and to consider potential solutions to deal with the stressor and then doing so
Psychoneuroimmunology	The science that studies the relationship among stressors, the body's immune system, and diseases
Psychophysiological or Psychosomatic Disorders	Medical conditions like asthma, headaches, and hypertension that are a consequence of or are made worse by stressors
Race-Related Vigilance	Anticipating and being prepared for racial discrimination. Individuals attend their social environment for signs of perceived racism in order to avoid or escape it
Racism	Attitudes and behaviors of one group that disparage members of another (minority) group based usually on the physical appearance of the latter
Reappraisal	A coping strategy that involves reinterpreting a stressor, usually in a positive light

continued . . .

GLOSSARY Continued

Term	Definition
Safety Hypothesis	Signals that predict the nonoccurrence of an aversive event, in contrast to signals that predict danger, to allow the organism to relax
Same Domain Effect	Valence of event and reaction to it are of the same dimension; negative events produce distress and positive events produce eustress
Secondary Appraisal	An inventory of coping resources that can be used to manage the event or manage the life change event
Self-Blame	An emotion-focused coping strategy that involves accepting responsibility for one's actions and the consequences
Self-Isolation	An emotion-focused coping strategy in which people keep others ignorant of their problems or avoid people in general
Self-Medication Hypothesis	When a person uses alcohol, nicotine, or other drugs in order to alleviate symptoms of stress
Sickness Behavior	Behavior exhibited when ill. It is felt as fatigue, fever, mild depression, lack of appetite, lack of pleasure, sleepiness, slowed cognitions, and social withdrawal
Stress	Negative physiological or psychological reactions that results when life's demands (stressors) exceed coping resources for dealing with the stressors
Stressors	Environmental demands that produce stress because the person could not cope with them adequately
Subjective Measures	Number assigned to a stressor by an individual to indicate the stressor's effect on the person or degree of adjustment required to cope with it
Tension Headaches	Dull aching pain and tightness of the forehead, sides, and back of head
Tension Reduction	An emotion-focused coping strategy that may involve smoking, drinking, eating, and jogging in order to feel better
Wishful Thinking	A coping strategy that focuses on the desire that the stressor would somehow go away or that the person would feel differently about it

REFERENCES

Abbas, A. K., Lichtman, A. H., & Shiv, P. (2016). *Basic immunology: Functions and disorders of the immune system* (5th ed.). St. Louis, MO: Elsevier.

American Psychiatric Association (APA). (2013). *Diagnostic and statistical manual of mental disorders* (5th ed.). Arlington, VA: American Psychiatric Association.

Baum, A., & Posluszny, D. M. (1999). Health psychology: Mapping biobehavioral contributions to health and illness. *Annual Review of Psychology, 50,* 137–163.

Baumeister, R. F., Bratslavsky, E., Finkenauer, C., & Vohs, K. D. (2001). Bad is stronger than good. *Review of General Psychology, 5,* 323–370.

Ben-Dov, I. Z., Kark, J. D., Ben-Ishay, D., Mekler, J., Ben-Arie, L., & Bursztyn, M. (2007). Predictors of all-cause mortality in clinical ambulatory monitoring: Unique aspects of blood pressure during sleep. *Hypertension, 49,* 1235–1241.

Bolton, J. M., Robinson, J., & Sareen, J. (2009). Self-medication of mood disorders with alcohol and drugs in the National Epidemiologic Survey on Alcohol and Related Conditions. *Journal of Affective Disorders, 115,* 367–375.

Bonanno, G. A., & Burton, C. L. (2013). Regulatory flexibility: An individual differences perspective on coping and emotion regulation. *Perspectives on Psychological Science, 8*, 591–612.

Boyce, C. J., Wood, A. M., Banks, J., Clark, A. E., & Brown, G. D. (2013). Money, well-being, and loss aversion: Does an income loss have a greater effect on well-being than an equivalent income gain? *Psychological Science, 24*, 2557–2562.

Brondolo, E., Libby, D. J., Denton, E., Thompson, S., Beatty, D. L., Schwartz, J., . . . Gerin, W. (2008). Racism and ambulatory blood pressure in a community sample. *Psychosomatic Medicine, 70*, 49–56.

Carlson, L. E., & Thomas, B. C. (2007). Development of the Calgary symptoms of stress inventory (C-SOSI). *International Journal of Behavioral Medicine, 14*, 249–256.

Cathcart, S., Petkov, J., Winefield, A. H., Lushington, K., & Rolan, P. (2010). Central mechanisms of stress-induced headache. *Cephalalgia, 30*, 285–295.

Chang, Q., Szegedi, S. S., O'Connor, I. C., Dantzer, R., & Kelley, K. W. (2009). Cytokine-induced sickness behavior and depression. In A. Siegel & S. S. Zalcman (Eds.), *The neuroimmunological basis of behavior and mental disorders* (pp. 145–182). New York, NY: Springer.

Chawla, N., & Ostafin, B. (2007). Experiential avoidance as a functional dimensional approach to psychopathology: An empirical review. *Journal of Clinical Psychology, 63*, 871–890.

Cheng, C., Lau, H. P. B., & Chan, M. P. S. (2014). Coping flexibility and psychological adjustment to stressful life changes: A meta-analytic review. *Psychological Bulletin, 140*, 1582–1607.

Cohen, S., Doyle, W. J., & Skoner, D. P. (1999). Psychological stress, cytokine production, and severity of upper respiratory illness. *Psychosomatic Medicine, 61*, 175–180.

Cohen, S., & Hoberman, H. M. (1983). Positive events and social supports as buffers of life change stress. *Journal of Applied Social Psychology, 13*, 99–125.

Cohen, S., Kamarck, T., & Mermelstein, R. (1983). A global measure of perceived stress. *Journal of Health and Social Behavior, 24*, 386–396.

Crandall, C. S., Preisler, J. J., & Aussprung, J. (1992). Measuring life event stress in the lives of college students: The Undergraduate Stress Questionnaire (USQ). *Journal of Behavioral Medicine, 15*, 627–662.

Derogatis, L. R., Lipman, R. S., Rickels, K., Uhllenhuth, E. H., & Covi, L. (1974). The Hopkins Symptom Checklist (HSCL): A self-report symptom inventory. *Behavioral Science, 19*, 1–15.

DiGrande, L., Neria, Y., Brackbill, R. M., Pulliam, P., & Galea, S. (2011). Long-term posttraumatic stress symptoms among 3,271 civilian survivors of the September 11, 2001, terrorist attacks on the World Trade Center. *American Journal of Epidemiology, 173*, 271–281.

Eisenberger, N. I., Inagaki, T. K., Mashal, N. M., & Irwin, M. R. (2010). Inflammation and social experience: An inflammatory challenge induces feelings of social disconnection in addition to depressed mood. *Brain, Behavior, and Immunity, 24*, 558–563.

Fliege, H., Rose, M., Arck, P., Walter, O. B., Kocalevent, R.-D., Weber, C., & Klapp, B. F. (2005). The perceived stress questionnaire (PSQ) reconsidered: Validation and reference values from different clinical and healthy adult samples. *Psychosomatic Medicine, 67*, 78–88.

Folkman, S., & Lazarus, R. S. (1985). If it changes it must be a process: Study of emotion and coping during three stages of a college examination. *Journal of Personality and Social Psychology, 48*, 150–170.

Forsythe, C. J., & Compas, B. E. (1987). Interaction of cognitive appraisals of stressful events and coping: Testing the goodness of fit hypothesis. *Cognitive Therapy and Research, 11*, 473–485.

Gabriel, R., Ferrando, L., Cortón, E. S., Mingote, C., García-Camba, E., Liria, A. F., & Galea, S. (2007). Psychopathological consequences after a terrorist attack: An epidemiological study among victims, the general population, and police officers. *European Psychiatry, 22*, 339–346.

Galea, S., Ahern, J., Resnick, H., Kilpatrick, D., Bucuvalas, M., Gold, J., & Vlahov, D. (2002). Psychological sequelae of the September 11 terrorist attacks in New York City. *New England Journal of Medicine, 346*, 982–987.

Grillon, C., Baas, J. P., Lissek, S., Smith, K., & Milstein, J. (2004). Anxious responses to predictable and unpredictable aversive events. *Behavioral Neuroscience, 2004*, 118, 916–924.

Groesz, L. M., McCoy, S., Carl, J., Saslow, L., Stewart, J., Adler, N., . . . Epel, E. (2012). What is eating you? Stress and the drive to eat. *Appetite, 58*, 717–721.

Gross, J. J. (1999). Emotion regulation: Past, present, future. *Cognition and Emotion, 13*, 551–573.

Hicken, M. T., Lee, H., Ailshire, J., Burgard, S. A., & Williams, D. R. (2013). "Every shut eye, ain't sleep": The role of racism-related vigilance in racial/ethnic disparities in sleep difficulty. *Race and Social Problems, 5,* 100–112.

Hicken, M. T., Lee, H., Morenoff, J., House, J. S., & Williams, D. R. (2014). Racial/ethnic disparities in hypertension prevalence: Reconsidering the role of chronic stress. *American Journal of Public Health, 104,* 117–123.

Holmes, T. H., & Masuda, M. (1974). Life change and illness susceptibility. In B. S. Dohrenwend & B. P. Dohrenwend (Eds.), *Stressful life events: Their nature and effects* (pp. 45–72). New York, NY: John Wiley.

Holmes, T. H., & Rahe, R. H. (1967). The Social Readjustment Rating Scale. *Journal of Psychosomatic Research, 11,* 213–218.

Kashdan, T. B., Breen, W. E., & Julian, T. (2010). Everyday strivings in war veterans with posttraumatic stress disorder: Suffering from a hyper-focus on avoidance and emotion regulation. *Behavior Therapy, 41,* 350–363.

Kelman, I. (2007). The triggers or precipitants of the acute migraine attack. *Cephalalgia, 27,* 394–402.

Landrine, H., & Klonoff, E. A. (1996). The schedule of racist events: A measure of racial discrimination and a study of its negative and physical and mental health consequences. *Journal of Black Psychology, 22,* 144–168.

Lazarus, R. S., & Folkman, S. (1984). *Stress, appraisal, and coping.* New York, NY: Springer.

Lejuez, C. W., Eifert, G. H., Zvolensky, M. J., & Richards, J. B. (2000). Preference between onset predictable and unpredictable administrations of 20 percent carbon-dioxide-enriched air: Implications for better understanding the etiology and treatment of panic disorder. *Journal of Experimental Psychology: Applied, 6,* 349–358.

Lloyd, C., Alexander, A. A., Rice, D. G., & Greenfield, N. S. (1980). Life events as predictors of academic performance. *Journal of Human Stress, 6,* 15–25.

Maes, M., Berk, M., Goehler, L., Song, C., Anderson, G., Gałecki, P., & Leonard, B. (2012). Depression and sickness behavior are Janus-faced responses to shared inflammatory pathways. *BMC Medicine, 10,* 66, 1–19.

Miller, T. W. (1993). The assessment of stressful life events. In L. Goldberger & S. Breznitz (Eds.), *Handbook of stress: Theoretical and clinical aspects* (2nd ed., pp. 161–173). New York, NY: Free Press.

Monroe, S. M. (2008). Modern approaches to conceptualizing and measuring human life stress. *Annual Review of Clinical Psychology, 4,* 33–52.

Nash, J. M., & Thebarge, R. W. (2006). Understanding psychological stress, its biological processes, and impact on primary headache. *Headache, 46,* 1377–1386.

Ohkubo, T., Hozawa, A., Yamaguchi, J., Kikuya, M., Ohmori, K., Michimata, M., . . . Imai, Y. (2002). Prognostic significance of the nocturnal decline in blood pressure in individuals with and without high 24-h blood pressure: The Ohasama study. *Journal of Hypertension, 20,* 2183–2189.

Perkins, C. C. (1955). The stimulus conditions which follow learned responses. *Psychological Review, 62,* 341–348.

Prather, A. A., Janicki-Deverts, D., Hall, M. H., & Cohen, S. (2015). Behaviorally assessed sleep and susceptibility to the common cold. *Sleep, 38,* 1353–1359.

Reichenberg, A., Kraus, T., Haack, M., Schuld, A., Pollmächer, T., & Yirmiya, R. (2002). Endotoxin-induced changes in food consumption in healthy volunteers are associated with TNF-α and IL-6 secretion. *Psychoneuroendocrinology, 27,* 945–956.

Reichenberg, A., Yirmiya, R., Schuld, A., Kraus, T., Haack, M., Morag, A., & Pollmächer, T. (2001). Cytokine-associated emotional and cognitive disturbances in humans. *Archives of General Psychiatry, 58,* 445–452.

Rosen, C. S., Drescher, K. D., Moos, R. H., Finney, J. W., Murphy, R. T., & Gusman, F. (2000). Six- and ten-item indexes of psychological distress based on the symptom checklist-90. *Assessment, 7,* 103–111.

Segerstrom, S. C., & Miller, G. E. (2004). Psychological stress and the human immune system: A meta-analytic study of 30 years of inquiry. *Psychological Bulletin, 130,* 601–630.

Seligman, M. E. P. (1971). Phobias and preparedness. *Behavior Therapy, 2,* 307–320.

Selye, H. (1976). *The stress of life* (rev ed.). New York, NY: McGraw-Hill.

Shattuck, E. C., & Muehlenbein, M. P. (2015). Human sickness behavior: Ultimate and proximate explanations. *American Journal of Physical Anthropology*, *157*, 1–18.

Sheppes, G., Scheibe, S., Suri, G., Radu, P., Blechert, J., & Gross, J. J. (2014). Emotion regulation choice: A conceptual framework and supporting evidence. *Journal of Experimental Psychology: General*, *143*, 163–181.

Siegrist, J., Starke, D., Chandola, T., Godin, I., Marmot, M., Niedhammer, I., & Peter, R. (2004). The measurement of effort-reward imbalance at work: European comparisons. *Social Science and Medicine*, *58*, 1483–1499.

Sproesser, G., Schupp, H. T., & Renner, B. (2014). The bright side of stress-induced eating: Eating more when stressed but less when pleased. *Psychological Science*, *25*, 58–65.

Troy, A. S., Shallcross, A. J., & Mauss, I. B. (2013). A person-by-situation approach to emotion regulation cognitive reappraisal can either help or hurt, depending on the context. *Psychological Science*, *24*, 2505–2514.

Turner, R. J., Wheaton, B., & Lloyd, D. A. (1995). The epidemiology of stress. *American Sociological Review*, *60*, 104–125.

Utsey, S. O., & Ponterotto, J. G. (1996). Development and validation of the Index of Race-Related Stress (IRRS). *Journal of Counseling Psychology*, *43*, 490–501.

Waelde, L. C., Pennington, D., Mahan, C., Mahan, R., Kabour, M., & Marquett, R. (2010). Psychometric properties of the Race-Related Events Scale. *Psychological Trauma: Theory, Research, Practice, and Policy*, *2*, 4–11.

Wansink, B., Cheney, M. M., & Chan, N. (2003). Exploring comfort food preferences across age and gender. *Physiology and Behavior*, *79*, 739–747.

Wheaton, B., & Montazer, M. (2010). Stressors, stress, and distress. In T. I. Scheid & T. N. Brown (Eds.), *A handbook for the study of mental health* (2nd ed., pp. 171–199). Cambridge: Cambridge University Press.

Williams, D. R., Yu, Y., Jackson, J. S., & Anderson, N. B. (1997). Racial differences in physical and mental health socio-economic status, stress and discrimination. *Journal of Health Psychology*, *2*, 335–351.

Wöber, C., Brannath, W., Schmidt, K., Kapitan, M., Rudel, E., Wessely, P., Wöber-Bingöl, C., & the PAMINA Study Group. (2007). Prospective analysis of factors related to migraine attacks: The PAMINA study. *Cephalalgia*, *27*, 304–314.

Wood, R. T. A., Griffiths, M. D., & Parke, A. (2007). Experiences of time loss among videogame players: An empirical study. *CyberPsychology and Behavior*, *10*, 38–44.

Zakowski, S. G., Hall, M. H., Klein, L. C., & Baum, A. (2001). Appraised control, coping, and stress in a community sample: A test of the goodness-of-fit hypothesis. *Annals of Behavioral Medicine*, *23*, 158–165.

Zautra, A. J., & Reich, J. W. (1983). Life events and perceptions of life quality: Developments in a two-factor approach. *Journal of Community Psychology*, *11*, 121–132.

Zellner, D. A., Loaiza, S., Gonzalez, Z., Pita, J., Morales, J., Pecora, D., & Wolf, A. (2006). Food selection changes under stress. *Physiology and Behavior*, *87*, 789–793.

Zvolensky M. J., Eifert, G. H., & Lejuez, C. W. (2001). Offset control during recurrent 20 percent carbon dioxide-enriched air induction: Relation to individual difference variables. *Emotion*, *1*, 148–165.

Zvolensky M. J., Eifert, G. H., Lejuez, C. W., & McNeil, D.W (1999). The effects of offset control over 20 percent carbon-dioxide-enriched air on anxious responding. *Journal of Abnormal Psychology*, *108*, 624–632.

CHAPTER 8

Psychological Needs and Motives

By annihilating desires you annihilate the mind. Every man without passions has within him no principle of action, nor motive to act.

Claude Adrien Helvetius, 1715–1771

Home is the place where, when you have to go there
They have to take you in.

The Death of the Hired Man by Robert Frost, 1914

The focus of this chapter is on motives—that is, the internal source of motivation. Keep that idea in mind as you consider the following questions:

1. What are the similarities and differences among physiological needs, drives, and psychological needs?
2. What is necessary to show that needs motivate behavior?
3. Can needs be categorized and ranked for their potential to motivate behavior?
4. What are the major psychological needs that motivate behavior?

DRIVES AND NEEDS AS INTERNAL SOURCES OF MOTIVATION

Why are some people labeled as driven, overachievers, and highly dedicated, while others are termed slackers, idlers, and loafers? Do the former possess some internal drive that the latter don't? How do internal sources of motivation such as drives and physiological and psychological needs differ from external sources of motivation?

Interaction of Push and Pull Motivation

As emphasized in Chapter 1, motivation comes from internal sources that push and from external sources that pull an individual. Internal motivation refers to drives and physiological and psychological needs, while external motivation concerns incentives and goals. The combined push and pull effects of internal and external sources must exceed some threshold for behavior to occur (see Table 8.1). When above the threshold, behavior occurs; when below, it does not (Kimble, 1990). Behavior can result from little external motivation, provided that there is a lot of internal motivation. For example, the food may not be very tasty but a hungry person will eat it. Or behavior can occur with little internal motivation, provided there is a lot of external motivation. For example, even though a person may not be very hungry, he will still eat a bowl of delicious ice cream. Internal motivation is the disposition to perform a particular action. It can be created through depriving an organism of an incentive such as food, water, or visual stimulation. In other instances, the disposition to respond is dormant, and a situational stimulus will arouse it. For instance, a psychological need such as the need for power could be activated by being a member of the police force, which allows for the legitimate exercise of power.

Physiological Needs, Drives, and Psychological Needs

There is a very important difference between physiological and psychological needs that is anchored in the distinction between materialism and mentalism. **Physiological needs** refer to deficits that exist in the material body or brain. **Psychological needs**, however, do not have any material existence and are mental or psychological in nature. There is reference to a deficit of some psychological entity; a discrepancy between a desired level and a current amount. In some cases, psychological needs are assumed to emerge into consciousness from physiological needs. Murray (1938), for instance, assumed that psychological needs emerged from processes that occurred in the brain. However, the possible physiological origin of psychological needs is usually ignored.

TABLE 8.1 Internal and External Motivation and Likelihood of Behavior

Strength of External Incentive	Strength of Internal Motive	
	Weak	Strong
Weak	Behavior not likely	Behavior likely
Strong	Behavior likely	Behavior very likely

Note: The combined effects of internal and external sources of motivation must be strong enough to exceed the threshold in order for behavior to occur. For example, eating depends on the palatability of food (external) and the degree of hunger (internal).

Need as the physiological basis for motivation. Homeostasis (see Chapter 5) describes the maintenance of constant conditions within the body in order to aid survival. Physiological needs are specifiable deviations from these homeostatic conditions that are detrimental to the person's physical well-being. For example, the need for food felt as hunger corresponds to a drop in glucose below a specific set point. The need for water felt as thirst occurs when the amount of fluid within and surrounding the body's cells is below the amount necessary for those cells to function properly. The need for iron exists when the amount is so low that the blood's capacity to carry oxygen is reduced. This condition results in feeling tired and lethargic and being unable to perform manual work without extensive feelings of fatigue. Another category of physiological need refers to sensory stimulation that exceeds a set point intensity, which is felt as discomfort or pain. Excessive sensory stimulation occurs when the french fries are too hot, the volume on the stereo is too loud, and the light in one's eyes is too bright. How do physiological needs motivate behavior? The answer is that the need is felt as unpleasant and thus motivates individuals to reduce this unpleasantness. From where did the idea of psychological needs arise?

Drives and psychological needs. According to Hull's theory described in Chapter 2, **drive** was the motivational construct that results when an animal is deprived of a needed substance, such as food, water, or environmental stimulation (Hull, 1943, 1951). Researchers created drives through incentive deprivation. Thus, food deprivation, water deprivation, and sensory deprivation produced hunger, thirst, and boredom drives, respectively. These different drives have one characteristic in common. They motivate the animal to seek out stimuli or experiences that reduce drive intensity. Thus, animals seek food, water, or novel stimuli for purposes of drive reduction.

Psychological needs motivate behavior in a similar manner, although there are some important differences. One difference is that psychological needs are only loosely linked to physiological needs and, in fact, there is a tendency to ignore their physiological basis. In the case of a psychological need, there is a deficit in a person's set point level of some incentive, activity, or experience. For example, the person's level of affiliation with others is less than hoped for. Second, psychological needs are not clearly tied to prior experimental manipulations, such as food deprivation. Rather, psychological needs already exist as a result of an individual's evolutionary or personal history. However, drives and psychological needs can be considered transitory, which means that they come and go. For example, the need for food only becomes apparent when an individual experiences hunger or feels weak, otherwise the need is nonexistent. Similarly, psychological needs become apparent when they are unfulfilled. For example, loneliness stems from not satisfying the need to belong, which then leads to seeking out others (Mellor et al., 2008). Both drives and needs can also be activated by environmental stimuli. The sight of food, for instance, increases people's hunger and their desire to eat (Nederkoorn et al., 2000). The process by which the environment activates a psychological need is known as **redintegration** (Murray, 1938). When aroused, a psychological need reminds individuals of the discrepancy between their current situation and a final desired state. Stimuli activate, redintegrate, or reinstate psychological needs because these stimuli have been associated with the arousal characteristics of needs in the past (McClelland et al., 1953).

Motivation by Psychological Needs

Psychological needs have several important functions according to Sheldon's (2011) **two-process model of psychological needs**. The most obvious is that needs motivate behavior to reduce or satisfy a need: a case of negative reinforcement. The behavior also results in positive psychological experiences necessary for well-being: a case of positive reinforcement. Thus, behavior that reduces a need is negatively reinforced because it removes the unpleasant feeling of a need, much like eating reduces the unpleasantness of hunger. However, behavior is also positively reinforced by the feelings added at the end of need reduction, much like the pleasure of eating dessert even when a person is no longer hungry.

To illustrate, negative and positive reinforcement motivate behaviors that are associated with the need to affiliate and belong. As a source of negative reinforcement, a belonging or affiliation motive may reflect an anxiety or fear of rejection. People are motivated to affiliate or connect with others to reduce this anxiety or fear. On the other hand, as a source of positive reinforcement, a type of affiliation motive called the **intimacy motive** emphasizes the pleasant feelings that exist between individuals in a social relationship. This motive refers to a "readiness for experiences of warm, close, and communicative interactions with other persons" (McAdams, 1992, p. 224). Does the intensity of an individual's intimacy motive determine the level of her social interaction, connection, and affiliation with others? In order to answer this question, McAdams and Constantian (1983) categorized students according to the strengths of their intimacy motive and then contacted the students seven times a day for a week using a beeper. Each time the students recorded what they were thinking and doing. They also rated their degree of affect in connection with other people, such as being alert, carefree, content, friendly, happy, and sociable. Students with a high intimacy motive thought more about other people, had a greater number of conversations, and were more likely to be writing letters (texting did not yet exist). Students with a high intimacy motive experienced greater positive affect during their social interactions compared to those with a low intimacy motive. It is important to note also that, when not interacting with others, low and high intimacy motive students did not differ in their affective feelings. People with a high intimacy motive enjoy their social interactions more than people with a low intimacy motive.

Negative and positive reinforcement also occur when Facebook is used to satisfy an affiliation need. In a series of studies, Sheldon and coresearchers (2011) measured how connected and disconnected university students felt to others and how this related to their use of Facebook. Connectedness was measured by items such as "I felt a sense of contact with people who care for me . . ." and disconnectedness was measured by "I was lonely" (p. 768). The students also rated the extent they used Facebook to cope, such as "when I am feeling lonely . . . I typically go on to Facebook" (p. 769). The results indicated that increases in feeling both connected and disconnected increased Facebook use. Facebook use from increased feelings of being connected is an instance of positive reinforcement—that is, a person feels even more connected. Second, when feeling disconnected, lonely, or out of touch students were more likely to use Facebook for coping: an instance of negative reinforcement. The researchers also asked the participants not to use Facebook for 48 hours. These 48-hours reduced feelings of being connected. Students who became more disconnected from deprivation increased their use of Facebook at the end of the 48-hour deprivation period: an instance of negative reinforcement.

Characteristics of Psychological Needs

Further elaboration is necessary to understand more fully the motivational properties of psychological needs. They exist in two different forms: traits and states. These two forms are illustrated by using the need for calories in Table 8.2. First, as a **trait**, psychological needs refer to how much of an incentive or activity is required for a person to function best. The body's need for energy from food is an example of a trait that varies among people. An average woman needs to consume 1,900 calories per day to meet her energy requirements, while an average man needs 2,300 calories (Table 8.2). Thus, a man has a greater need for calories than a woman does. Presumably, a man is motivated to eat more during a typical day. Second, as a **state**, a need refers to a temporary deficit, which refers to the discrepancy between the current versus the desired level of some incentive, activity, or experience. For example, hunger is the discrepancy between a current level of energy and a desired level of energy. Thus, hunger as a need for energy motivates searching, finding, and eating food. Once the need for energy has been satisfied, motivation ceases (Table 8.2).

Thus, psychological needs may occur as enduring traits and as temporary states or deficits. The nine psychological needs listed in Table 8.3 can be viewed both ways. For example, people can vary in their need to belong as a trait. Or an individual can be isolated from others and experience the need to belong as a state. The nine needs listed in Table 8.3 have captured the recent attention of psychologists. Table 8.3 gives a definition of each need along with the negative psychological consequences that result when the need is not met.

TABLE 8.2   Need for Energy as Trait and State

Need as stable **trait:** Example: Individuals vary in daily calorie requirements	Woman needs 1,900 calories daily to satisfy energy requirements	Man needs 2,300 calories daily to satisfy energy requirements
Need as a temporary **state:** Example: Person is hungry before eating meal but not hungry afterwards	Hunger: Person is hungry before meal	No hunger: Person is not hungry after meal

TABLE 8.3 Psychological Needs, Definitions, and Effects of Unfulfilled Needs

Need	Definition	Psychological Deficit from Unmet Need
Achievement	To engage in achievement behavior, do better than before, and with high standard of excellence	Negative emotions, such as sadness, frustration, and shame
Autonomy	To feel your free will is the cause of your own actions rather than to feel that external forces cause your actions. On website below: self-determination theory*	Lower psychological well-being, depressive feelings
Belong (relate, affiliate)	To seek others who care about you in order to experience feelings of affiliation, belonging, and intimacy. On website below: self-determination theory and Leary*	Loneliness, hurt feelings, homesickness, numbing of feelings, depressive feelings
Closure	To desire a definite answer or conclusion to a question or topic in contrast to an ambiguous or confusing conclusion. On website below: Kruglanski*	Mental fatigue
Cognition	To engage in and enjoy thinking in order to organize, summarize, and evaluate information. On website below: need for cognition*	Boredom
Competence	To feel capable and effective in your actions rather than being incapable and ineffective. On website below: self-determination theory*	Subjective and physical well-being declines, depressive feelings
Meaning	To determine how the self relates significantly to one's geographical, cultural, and social environments. On website below: meaning of life*	Psychological distress, depression and anxiety
Power	To exert influence over others, to be in charge, to be noticed, and to emotionally affect others	Higher sympathetic nervous system activation leads to lower immune function and illness
Self-Esteem	To feel you are a worthy and confident person, as good as anyone, and that you deserve the respect of others. On website below: Crocker* and Rosenberg**	Aggression and antisocial behavior

Notes:

* The above scales and many others are available at the following web address: www.webpages.ttu.edu/areifman/qic.htm.

** The Rosenberg Self-Esteem Scale is available at www.wwnorton.com/college/psych/psychsci/media/rosenberg.htm.

Implicit and explicit psychological needs. Psychological needs also differ in other ways. In order to understand these differences, consider your relationships with food. One relationship refers to the bodily pleasure of eating, which is especially acute when a person is hungry. In other words, the need (hunger) provides the basis for the pleasure of eating. A second relationship refers to the value that food has for a person—that is, an incentive value. In this case, palatable food is valued more than unpalatable food. These examples express the two different views of psychological needs, which are also referred to as motives: implicit and explicit (McClelland et al., 1989; Schultheiss et al., 2008; Stanton et al., 2010). An **implicit motive** is the capacity of individuals to maximize satisfaction from engaging in need-relevant activities. Put another way, McClelland and others (1989) "conceive of the [implicit] motive as leading to an activity that is the incentive for that motive" (p. 698) In other words, without the implicit motive, interaction with the incentive would not be rewarding, much like eating would not be rewarding without hunger. Thus, individuals with a strong need to achieve (achievement motive) derive pleasure from mastering a challenging task, while those with a strong need to affiliate attain satisfaction from starting, sustaining, or reinstating social relationships. Likewise, individuals with a strong need for power derive gratification from their influence over others (Schultheiss et al., 2008; Stanton et al., 2010). Based on experience, individuals naturally orient and seek incentives and activities that will maximize their satisfaction. Furthermore, those activities and incentives act as stimuli that elicit anticipated pleasure (Schultheiss et al., 2008; Stanton et al., 2010). For example, a person with a high need to affiliate is disposed to interact with people because the anticipated experience signals enjoyable social interactions. A person with a strong need for power is disposed to hold a position in an organization because of the anticipated satisfaction derived from the opportunity to influence others.

An **explicit motive**, on the other hand, resembles the conscious value a person places on a stimulus, activity, or experience. A distinction between the two types of motives is that individuals are much more aware of their explicit motive compared to their implicit motives (McClelland et al., 1989; Schultheiss et al., 2008; Stanton et al., 2010). In fact, an explicit motive resembles incentive value. An explicit motive related to the need to achieve is feedback regarding a person's group standing on an achievement task. For instance, did a student earn an A or C grade in a course? An explicit motive related to the need for affiliation concerns the value placed on joining a social organization. An explicit motive related to a need for power is the prestige value of being president compared to that of vice-president.

Consequences of unfulfilled needs. Not only do psychological needs motivate behavior; the failure to do so has negative consequences. As described earlier, unfulfilled physiological needs are detrimental to a person's physical well-being. For example, an unfulfilled need for vitamin C results in a disease known as scurvy. This disease is characterized by an inflammation of the gums and anemia, which is felt as weakness and fatigue. Similarly, each unsatisfied psychological need is accompanied by a particular set of symptoms of psychological ill health or low psychological well-being (Table 8.3). This is especially true for the needs of autonomy, relatedness, and competence (Chen et al., 2015; Deci & Ryan, 2000). Reis and coresearchers (2000) examined whether increased satisfaction of the needs of autonomy, competence, and relatedness during daily activities was associated with increased daily well-being. Satisfaction of the need for autonomy was analyzed from ratings that concerned whether an activity was done out of free choice or was imposed on the individual by external factors. Satisfaction of the need for competence was based on how capable a person felt in doing an activity. Fulfillment of the need for relatedness came from analyzing social interactions during the day. The extent a person felt "close and connected" to others during social interactions indexed the degree of need satisfaction. How do these measures of need satisfaction relate to well-being? To answer this question, students were asked to rate their positive affect (happy, fun), negative affect (depressed, worried), and vitality (feeling alive, energized). They also filled out a symptom checklist about ailments such as a runny nose, breathing difficulties and soreness. In general, the results supported the hypothesis that as need satisfaction increased, indicators of well-being also increased. Favorable changes in the satisfaction of autonomy and competence needs were accompanied by favorable changes in well-being. Increases in satisfying the relatedness need was associated with increases in positive affect and vitality but unassociated with changes in negative affect and symptoms.

When needs are unfulfilled, well-being decreases. The negative consequences of failing to satisfy the needs of affiliation, autonomy, and competence are universal (Chen et al., 2015). University students in Belgium, China, Peru, and the United States were assessed for how much each need was satisfied, but also the extent that need satisfaction was frustrated. Psychological health was measured with a *Satisfaction with Life Scale* and the *Subjective Vitality Scale*. "I feel alive and vital" illustrates a measure of subjective vitality (p. 224). Questions regarding feeling blue, depressed, lonely, and sadness measured depressive symptoms. The results showed that in all four countries increases in need satisfaction were associated with increases in vitality and life satisfaction. Conversely, increased frustration of need satisfaction was associated with increases in depressive symptoms. Chen and coresearchers (2015) conclude that the needs of affiliation, autonomy, and competence act like vitamins that are necessary for all people to function at their best.

Other examples from Table 8.3 show that unfulfilled needs of power, achievement, and affiliation result in unhappiness and symptoms of depression (Schultheiss et al., 2008), whereas failure to satisfy the need for esteem may result in aggression (Donnellan et al., 2005). Moreover,

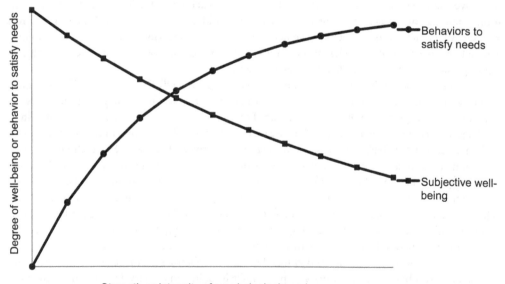

FIGURE 8.1 Motivation and Subjective Well-Being Depend on Need Intensity. The upward sloping curve shows that, as the intensity of a psychological need increases, behaviors designed to alleviate the need also increase. The downward sloping curve shows that, as the intensity of a psychological need increases, there are associated decreases in subjective well-being.

low self-esteem also predicts negative feelings, such as being sad or depressed (Orth et al., 2008). Failure to satisfy the need for closure is associated with prolonged mental fatigue (Webster et al., 1996). In contrast, a high need for cognition can stave off boredom, since such individuals are able to provide their own mental stimulation rather than rely on external events (Watt & Blanchard, 1994). Finally, the failure to find meaning in life is associated with psychological distress and anxiety and can also lead to depression (Debats et al., 1993; Mascaro & Rosen, 2008). Figure 8.1 summarizes the expected relationship between need intensity and motivation. As need intensity increases, the motivation of need satisfaction behaviors increases correspondingly. Figure 8.1 also shows that as need intensity increases, there are accompanying decreases in subjective well-being, such as more unhappiness, depression, boredom, and aggression.

Demonstrating that Psychological Needs Motivate Behavior

How do psychologists demonstrate that psychological needs motivate the behaviors that provide for need satisfaction? Behavior in service to need satisfaction cannot be used as evidence for the presence of a psychological need. The behavior may have resulted from other factors. For example, if a person's residence hall room is neat and tidy, does that mean she had a high need for order (Murray, 1938)? Or could it be that she is expecting company, whom she wants to impress?

Measuring psychological needs. Two steps are necessary to show that psychological needs motivate need reduction behavior. The first step is to measure the extent of a psychological need. An **operational definition** refers to the procedure that is used to measure or create the existence of a psychological construct, such as a need. However, the distinction between implicit and explicit motives has led to two distinct methods of measurement: projective measures for implicit motives and objective questionnaires for explicit motives. The use of projective measures is based on the following assumptions. If the psychological need is assumed to be dormant, then the measurement procedure must also activate it. Thus, the measuring device must contain such stimuli, especially stimuli that have been associated with need satisfaction in the past. This line of reasoning led to the development of the **projective test**. In such a test, a person verbally responds to an unstructured stimulus, such as an inkblot, in a manner that is presumably consistent with her activated motives. In researching the need to achieve, McClelland and associates (1953) adapted a projective test procedure pioneered by Murray (1938) known as the *Thematic Apperception Test* (TAT). The TAT consists of a series of pictures of people in ambiguous but potential achievement settings. The respondent is instructed to tell a story, which the picture may hint at but does not contain. Figure 8.2 resembles the TAT picture of two women in lab coats (McClelland, 1975, p. 387). To a series of such pictures, participants are asked the following questions:

1. "What is happening? Who are the persons?"
2. "What has led up to this situation? That is, what has happened in the past?"
3. "What is being thought? What is wanted? By whom?"
4. "What will happen? What will be done?" (McClelland et al., 1953, p. 98)

In answering the questions, an individual could have elaborated on the achievement behavior of the two women, on their friendship, or on the power or relationship status between the two. But what determines whether an individual responds with achievement, affiliation, or power?

The analyses in Table 8.1 provide the basis for the answer. Whether a story indicates an achievement, affiliation, or power motive depends on the strength of the respondent's dormant motive and the instigating force of the TAT card. In the case of need for achievement, for example, if either motive strength or TAT card force increases, then the likelihood of an achievement story increases (Tuerlinckx et al., 2002). An individual with a strong need to achieve, however, is more likely to respond with achievement imagery regardless of the force of the TAT card. Answers to the TAT-relevant questions are scored for achievement motivation based on references to competition with a standard of excellence, a unique accomplishment, or long-term involvement. For example, a protocol might state that the two women in lab coats have been working for many years (long-term involvement) developing a vaccine that has no negative side effects (high standard of excellence), which no one has ever accomplished before (unique accomplishment).

The TAT as a measure of the achievement motive has not escaped criticism. Entwisle (1972) challenged the reliability of the TAT pictures used to measure the need to achieve. The TAT has low reliability, which means that each picture is not measuring the need to achieve consistently.

FIGURE 8.2 Picture Resembling One from Thematic Apperception Test. The picture shows two women in lab coats and resembles one of the actual TAT pictures. Need to achieve is measured by evaluating respondents' answers to questions about this and other pictures in the test.

Source: Photo © iStock/AlexRaths

However, this is to be expected, since not every picture is equally forceful in evoking achievement imagery (Tuerlinckx et al., 2002). Also, answers to the questions seem to vary over time, which means that from one week to the next, for example, individuals' scores for need to achieve seem to fluctuate. This is an important point because the need to achieve is assumed to be a stable motive. Additional criticism comes from Klinger (1966), who questioned the validity of TAT measures. He found many studies showing no relationship between TAT measures and achievement-relevant behavior such as school grades. However, more recent analyses by Spangler (1992) indicate that a large number of studies found a positive correlation between TAT measures of achievement motivation and achievement behavior. Furthermore, many psychologists researching the area maintain that the TAT is a valid measure not only of the need to achieve but also of the need for affiliation and the need for power (Smith, 1992).

The operational definition or measurement of explicit motives, on the other hand, is straightforward. It involves objective questionnaires, which reduces the problem of reliability and validity found in projective tests. However, these questionnaires are also based on a different interpretation of psychological needs. It assumes that the need is not dormant but is a value system of which an individual is aware. The measurement procedure involves questions or scales that ask how much individuals value an activity or incentive. For instance, the needs for autonomy, competence, and belonging are measured—that is, operationally defined—by an individual's answers to the questions listed in the *Basic Psychological Needs Scale*. For instance, this **scale** measures the need for autonomy with a question about the extent an individual feels free to decide how to live her life. A need for competence is reflected in a question about the extent that one feels capable. A question tapping the need to affiliate inquires how much a person likes to interact with people (Deci & Ryan, 2000). Higher scores reflect stronger need intensities and thus greater motivation to satisfy those needs. A second type of operational definition is the experimental process by which a need-state or motive is induced. This technique employs redintegration by which a stimulus in the environment activates a psychological need. For example, the sight of your textbook evokes the need to achieve.

A website devoted to self-determination theory provides a link to the *Basic Psychological Needs Scale* here: www.selfdeterminationtheory.org/questionnaires.

Various psychological scales measure all the needs listed in Table 8.3. In the case of the need to achieve, the *Achievement Motives Scale* is a short questionnaire, revised by Lang and Fries (2006), that was designed to measure both the motive to achieve success and the motive to avoid failure. For example, to what extent do you agree with the statements: "I am attracted to tasks in which I can test my abilities" and "If I do not understand a problem immediately, I start to feel anxious" (p. 221)? The first statement measures the motive to achieve success, while the second statement measures the motive to avoid failure. The need for cognition is measured with the *Need for Cognition Scale*, which contains statements regarding a person's enjoyment in thinking and solving complex problems (Cacioppo & Petty, 1982; Cacioppo et al., 1996). For example, to what extent does a person enjoy thinking abstractly, coming up with new solutions to problems, putting forth mental effort, or watching educational programs? Both the presence and search for meaning are measured with a 10-item scale known as the *Meaning in Life Questionnaire* (Steger et al., 2006). This questionnaire contains statements about whether you understand the meaning of your life but also the extent you are looking for something to make it so. The need for self-esteem can be measured with the *Rosenberg Self-Esteem Scale* (Rosenberg, 1965).

A web page titled "Social-Personality Psychology: Questionnaire Instrument Compendium (QIC)," maintained by Alan Reifman of Texas Tech University, provides links to scales in Table 8.3 and others here: www.webpages.ttu.edu/areifmanSan/qic.htm.

A copy of the Rosenberg Self-Esteem Scale is available here: www.yorku.ca/rokada/psyctest/rosenbrg.pdf.

The relationship between needs and behavior. The second step in showing that psychological needs motivate behavior involves finding that need intensity scores are positively associated with need-satisfying behavior or negatively associated with psychological well-being. Thus, when need is high, there must be a great amount of need-satisfying behavior and low subjective well-being. An investigation between the need to belong and homesickness illustrates the two-step process. When you arrived at your university, your new country, town, or place of work, did you become homesick? Did you grieve, become depressed, and long for your old friends and family? What did you do to alleviate your homesickness? Many people have experienced this feeling, which not surprisingly is linked with the need to belong. Watt and Badger (2009) examined how the need to belong was associated with homesickness and with attempts to alleviate it. In their first study, they measured the need to belong with the *Need to Belong Scale*. In a second study, they induced the need to belong by presenting subjects with descriptions of articles about the need to belong. For example, " 'Where to turn?'—This article highlights the importance of having someone to turn to, for support or advice" (p. 529). In both studies, the investigators measured the degree of homesickness with the *Utrecht Homesickness Scale*. The researchers used the number of telephone calls home as an indicator of an attempt to alleviate homesickness. The findings of both investigations paralleled the relationships presented in Figure 8.2. First, more intense levels of the need to belong were associated with greater homesickness. Second, more intense levels of the need to belong were associated with more telephone calls home.

The website titled "Measurement Instrument Data Base for the Social Sciences" provides access to a copy of the *Need to Belong Scale* here: www.midss.org. The scale is also available here: www.midss.org/sites/default/files/ntb.pdf.

Maslow's Hierarchy of Needs Revised

Physiological needs are universal. For example, every human needs sufficient vitamin C and iron because without them physiological functioning declines. Psychological needs are also presumed to be universal according to evolutionary thinking (Schaller et al., 2010). The universal nature of human needs was hinted at by Abraham Maslow over 70 years ago, long before evolutionary psychology became a way of interpreting behavior. Maslow (1943, 1970) viewed his classification of needs as universal, compared to superficial desires and behaviors. He also formed a classification scheme cast as a hierarchy of needs: physiological, safety, belongingness, esteem, and self-actualization. Within this hierarchy, physiological needs in the lower tier are acted on first followed by needs at higher tiers. Although Maslow's theory has prevailed for 70 years, concepts from evolutionary psychology led to a revision shown in Figure 8.4 (Kenrick et al., 2010; Kesebir et al., 2010; Lyubomirsky & Boehm, 2010). In this revision, the need categories have evolutionary significance because they are crucial for the survival of the individual and for successful passing on of one's genes (Schaller et al., 2010). As in Maslow's original theory, a lower order need takes motivational precedence over a need higher up in the hierarchy. However, the needs are represented as overlapping triangles in order to indicate that lower order needs may become dominant again at any time (Kenrick et al., 2010). A person's stage in life and current circumstances determine what need is most potent. For example, mothers satisfy the physiological needs of their infants, while infants satisfy the belonging needs of their mothers. Thus, as infants early in

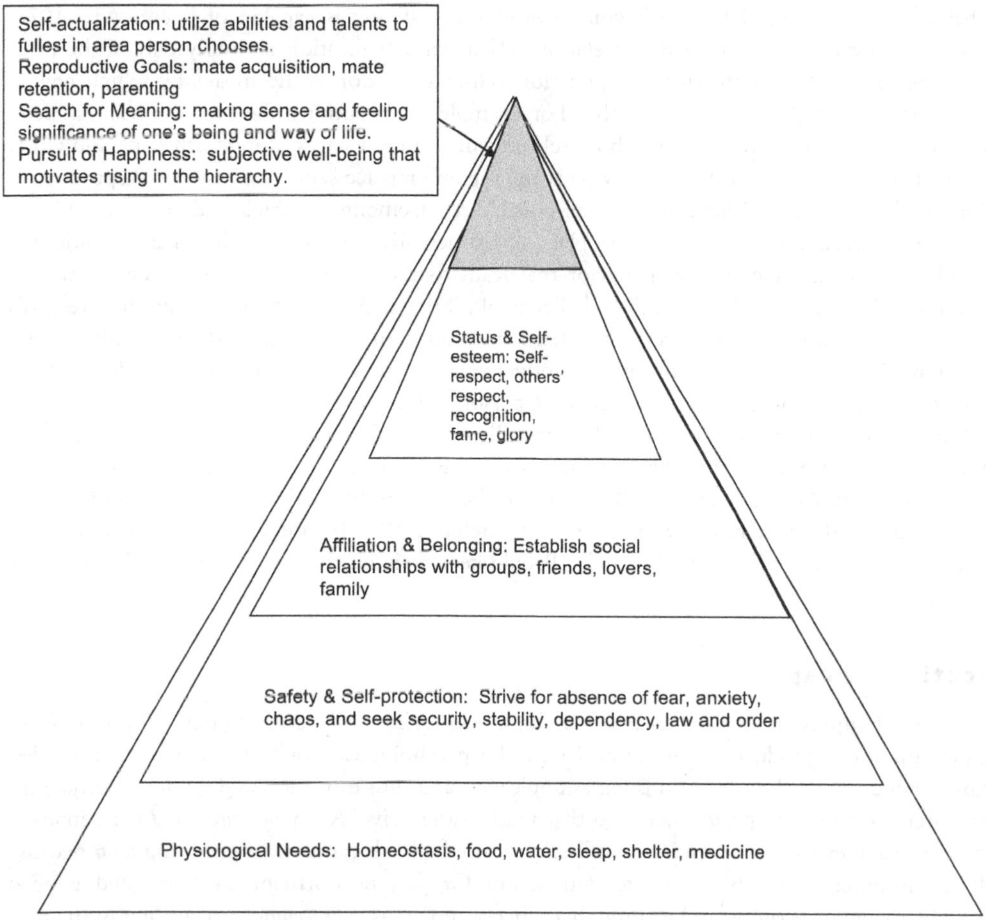

Self-actualization: utilize abilities and talents to fullest in area person chooses.
Reproductive Goals: mate acquisition, mate retention, parenting
Search for Meaning: making sense and feeling significance of one's being and way of life.
Pursuit of Happiness: subjective well-being that motivates rising in the hierarchy.

Status & Self-esteem: Self-respect, others' respect, recognition, fame, glory

Affiliation & Belonging: Establish social relationships with groups, friends, lovers, family

Safety & Self-protection: Strive for absence of fear, anxiety, chaos, and seek security, stability, dependency, law and order

Physiological Needs: Homeostasis, food, water, sleep, shelter, medicine

FIGURE 8.3   Maslow's Revised Hierarchy of Needs. People are motivated to satisfy their needs in a hierarchical fashion beginning with their physiological needs and working up. Although arranged hierarchically, the overlapping triangles indicate that a specific need can become dominant at any time. Several possibilities exist regarding an individual's final need, located at the peak of the hierarchy.

Source: Adapted from "Renovating the Pyramid of Needs: Contemporary Extensions Built upon Ancient Foundations" by D. T. Kenrick et al., 2010, *Perspectives on Psychological Science, 5,* 292–314 (see p. 293), and from "A Theory of Human Needs Should Be Human-Centered, Not Animal-Centered: Commentary on Kenrick et al. (2010)" by S. Kesebir et al., 2010, *Perspectives on Psychological Science, 5,* 315–319 (see p. 316), and from "Human Motives, Happiness, and the Puzzle of Parenthood: Commentary on Kenrick et al. (2010)" by S. Lyubormirsky & J. K. Boehm, 2010, *Perspectives on Psychological Science, 5,* 327–334.

life, physiological needs prevail but later in life as parents, belonging needs prevail. Later still, a need for meaning may gain dominance.

The first four overlapping triangles in Figure 8.3 follow Maslow's theory, with physiological needs at the bottom. However, what psychological need prevails when the four lower tiers are satisfied? For Maslow (1943, 1970), self-actualization was the next need to become active and thus was at the top of the hierarchy. Self-actualization is "the desire to become more and more what one idiosyncratically is, to become everything that one is capable of becoming" (1970, p. 46). However, an alternative interpretation is that self-actualization is simply part of the need for status and esteem. With this interpretation, self-actualization is the means by which people fulfill these needs (Kenrick et al., 2010). For example, by becoming the best musician, athlete, or actor possible an individual gains both self-esteem and high status, along with fame and glory.

What other psychological need may be at the top and replace self-actualization? Reproductive goals, life's meaning, and happiness are all possible replacements. Kenrick and coauthors (2010) placed reproductive goals at the top in place of self-actualization. The evolutionary significance of this goal is that it motivates behavior that leads to the "replication of our genes into our children's children [grandchildren]" (Schaller et al., 2010, p. 336). Achieving reproductive goals begins with acquiring a mate, retaining that mate, and then producing and successfully raising children. However, what happens once reproductive goals are met? Kesebir and coauthors (2010) believe that finding meaning in life may be a person's ultimate goal. Individuals may have mates and grandchildren and be well respected but still lack meaning in their lives. Meaning involves having a sense of purpose and direction and being able to relate to other individuals and events. Finally, happiness or subjective well-being may be responsible for both pushing and pulling individuals up the hierarchy (Lyubomirsky & Boehm, 2010). In other words, long-term well-being is at the top of the need hierarchy. People keep striving for this goal even after all other goals have been achieved.

Section Recap

The body requires an ideal set of internal conditions for its well-being, and any deviation from these conditions produces a *physiological need*, the psychological counterpart of which is *drive*. This form of internal motivation is felt as unpleasant and thus motivates and guides the organism to search for the appropriate incentive that reduces the drive. A *psychological need* is an internal motive to achieve a desired end-state of being satisfied. Needs can exist as enduring *traits* because the environment lacks the means for satisfaction. Or they lie dormant until activated as need *states* by the appropriate stimulus through a process known as *redintegration*. According to the *two-process model of psychological needs*, when needs are satisfied unpleasant feelings are reduced: a case of negative reinforcement. But need satisfaction can also be positively reinforced because of the added pleasure that results from need-reducing behavior. The need to affiliate is motivated by the reduction of unpleasant feelings associated with this need: a case of negative reinforcement. However, the *intimacy motive* emphasizes the addition of shared positive feelings between two individuals: a case of positive reinforcement. Psychological needs act both as traits and states. Needs as *traits* refer to long-term, consistent requirements for an incentive or activity for a person to function best. Needs as *states* refers to temporary deficits or discrepancies between the current and desired levels of some incentive, activity, or experience. In both cases, behavior is motivated to satisfy a need. As *implicit motives*, needs refer to the capability to experience pleasure when an individual interacts with a need-relevant incentive. As *explicit motives*, needs resemble a value system that a person places on a category of incentives. As need intensity increases, motivation for need satisfaction increases, as do increases in psychological ill health or low subjective well-being.

Two requirements are necessary for using psychological needs to explain behavior. One is to *operationally define* the need, which means to measure its intensity with a psychological scale or a projective test. In this test, a person verbally responds to an unstructured stimulus in a manner that is presumably consistent with her psychological needs. One type of projective test is the TAT, which consists of a series of pictures of people in ambiguous settings. The second requirement is to show that this need intensity correlates with the magnitude of need-satisfying behavior. A very influential theory is Abraham Maslow's hierarchy of needs, which includes physiological, safety, belongingness, esteem, and self-actualization. Needs must be satisfied from the lowest tier (physiological) on up to self-actualization. However, rather than self-actualization, the top need instead may consist of parenting, meaning of life, or pursuit of happiness.

SOME IMPORTANT PSYCHOLOGICAL NEEDS

As described in Chapter 2, from Georges Le Roy in 1764 to Henry Murray in 1938, students of human motivation have speculated on the existence of a wide variety of needs. Of these, the nine listed in Table 8.3 have become important for understanding the motivation of behavior: achievement, autonomy, belonging, closure, cognition, competence, meaning, power, and self-esteem. The purpose of this section is to describe each need in more detail.

Achievement Motivation

The motive or need to achieve has been a theme in popular literature. In a long series of books described as rags-to-riches stories, the nineteenth-century author Horatio Alger, Jr. implied that the road to success is by way of persistence and hard work. The main theme of all of Alger's stories is the motive to achieve or need to achieve (Tebel, 1963). Beginning with Murray (1938), the need to achieve has also been a popular theme with researchers and has probably received more attention from psychologists than any other psychological need.

The need to achieve or **motive to achieve success** (Ms) is a disposition to engage in task-oriented behavior or achievement behavior. It is characterized by doing things better than before or surpassing a high external or internal standard of excellence. The standards can be defined on the job, in sports, or in school and are based on the performance of others or on the person's own standards. The achievement motive is assumed to be dormant until activated by an associated achievement cue (McClelland et al., 1953), such as the sight of textbooks, instruments, or tools.

Do all individuals concentrate on achievement, or do some simply want to avoid failure? In addition to Ms, people also vary in their motivation to avoid failure. The **motive to avoid failure** (Maf) is the opposite of the need to achieve and inhibits a person from attempting achievement tasks (Atkinson, 1957/1983). Maf is characterized by anxiety and fear about failing a task. The strength of Ms and Maf combine to determine the tendency to attempt an achievement task (Atkinson, 1974). On the one hand, Ms motivates an individual to engage in the task, while on the other Maf motivates the individual to avoid tackling the task. Individuals in whom Ms is greater than Maf (Ms > Maf) are more likely to pursue achievement tasks, while individuals in whom Maf is greater than Ms (Maf > Ms) are more likely to avoid them (Atkinson, 1958/1983). Thus, individuals are attracted to and repelled from achieving a task to a degree consistent with the strength of these two motives. For example, in selecting a major or a final career goal, students are driven toward their choices by their Ms but at the same time are inhibited from pursuing those choices by their Maf. For instance, if a student has a career goal to become a marriage and family counselor, then her Ms pushes her toward that goal while at the same time her Maf pushes her away from it.

Factors that Affect Achievement Motivation

Individuals high in Ms or Maf show their differences in three important aspects of achievement behavior: probability of achieving the task, incentive value of the task, and persistence in trying to achieve the task.

Probability and incentive value of task success. Whether a person pursues an achievement task also depends on estimates of the probability of success and on the incentive value of that success. In other words: "What are the chances I can do it, and what is the value of doing it?" The probability and incentive value of success can be portrayed as opposite sides of the same coin. Atkinson (1957/1983, 1974) assumed that the incentive value of a task is inversely related to how difficult it is to achieve. The greater the difficulty of succeeding at a task, the higher its incentive value. The difficulty of a task is based on a person's subjective estimate of the probability of successfully achieving it. To illustrate, imagine a course that has a reputation of being very easy; almost everyone earns an A. Students might rate the probability of earning an A to be very high, and so the incentive value of earning an A is quite low. Imagine a different course that has the reputation of being tough; very few students earn an A. Students might rate the subjective probability of earning an A to be very low, and so the incentive value of earning an A is quite high. Thus, in general, as the subjective probability of success (Ps) decreases, the incentive value of success (Is) increases according to the formula $Is = 1 - Ps$

The incentive value of failure, however, is just the opposite. Imagine that you do not earn an A in a course where just about everyone else does. The negative incentive to avoid this outcome is quite high. However, it is not so bad if a student did not earn an A in the course where most other students also did not earn an A. The negative incentive to avoid this outcome is not so high. Thus, as the subjective probability of failure (Pf) increases, the negative incentive value of failure (−If) decreases according to the formula $-If = Pf$. (The minus [−] sign means that failure [f] has negative incentive value.) Consequently, whether an individual approaches or avoids an achievement task is based on both the probability and incentive value of either success or failure. Furthermore, Ms > Maf and Maf > Ms individuals are affected differently by these factors such that they act in opposite ways.

The outcomes of various research investigations show that tasks having a medium probability of success (around P = 0.50) are preferred by individuals for whom Ms > Maf but avoided by individuals for whom Maf > Ms. Atkinson and Litwin (1960) had male students stand any distance from the peg in a ringtoss game. It was assumed that intermediate distances should approximate a probability of 0.50 for successfully making a ringtoss. The results indicated that Ms > Maf students selected the intermediate distances more than Maf > Ms students did. In another relevant investigation, Karabenick and Youssef (1968) examined learning performance in participants who were both low and high in Ms and Maf. Participants for whom Ms > Maf performed better on a learning task of intermediate difficulty (P = 0.50) than did participants for whom Maf > Ms. The Ms > Maf and Maf > Ms students, however, did not differ in their learning of a task that was either very easy or very difficult. Vocational choice or aspiration is also governed by the variables in achievement motivation theory. Mahone (1960) found that Ms > Maf students were more realistic in their vocational choices when they were based on their interests and abilities. Students with Maf > Ms, however, were more likely to make unrealistic choices. Similarly, Morris (1966) examined the preferences for easy and difficult occupations of high school seniors as a function of the strength of their Ms and Maf. Seniors with high achievement motivation preferred occupations at an intermediate probability of success; those with low achievement motivation, however, preferred occupations that had either a low or high probability of success. In validating the *Achievement Motives Scale*, Lang and Fries (2006) found that higher achievement motive scores were associated with setting high but realistic goals—that is, ones that were still achievable.

Achievement motivation and behavioral persistence. Success at a task, project, or job depends on how long an individual persists. Individuals high in achievement motivation are expected to be more persistent, which is more likely to lead to success. In an early investigation of the need to achieve, Lowell (1952) found that high-Ms participants solved more anagrams during a 20-minute period than did low-Ms participants. When using addition problems, Lowell (1952) again found that high-Ms participants solved more problems than low-Ms participants. Sherwood (1966) had male and female students take the TAT for achievement motivation early in the semester and then participate in achievement tasks near the end of the semester. The achievement tasks required solving anagrams and addition problems. The results for both the male and female students showed that their output of solutions increased with their need to achieve. In another study, Atkinson and Litwin (1960) timed how long students spent taking their final exam in a psychology course. Students for whom Ms > Maf spent more time working on their final exams and earned higher scores than did students for whom Maf > Ms. Lang and Fries (2006), using the *Achievement Motives Scale*, also showed that motive for success scores correlated positively with goal performance, digit substitution, and reasoning-task performances, and most importantly with persistence. Fear of failure, however, correlated negatively with goal setting and reasoning-task performance.

Needs for Autonomy and Competence

Autonomy and competence are two needs that serve as the foundation of **self-determination theory** (Deci & Ryan, 2000, 2008). According to this theory, motivation stems from autonomous sources (within the person) and from external sources, such as those imposed by others like grades and money. However, autonomous motivation is more effective and produces greater well-being. Autonomous motivation "involves behaving with a full sense of volition [free will] and choice" (Deci & Ryan, 2008, p. 14), rather than motivation being imposed from the outside.

Need for autonomy. In its simplest form, the **need for autonomy** refers to doing what you want. Individuals prefer choosing their own goals and the means by which to accomplish them. The need for autonomy becomes salient when contrasted with external control of an individual's behavior. For example, a person's behavior could be dictated by someone else, fulfill someone else's expectations, and not fulfill an individual's personal desires. Behavior that satisfies the need for autonomy, however, is motivated more than behavior that is motivated by external sources. For instance, Pelletier and coresearchers (2001) investigated the contribution of autonomous motivation versus external motivation on the persistence of competitive swimmers to remain active over a two-year period. The researchers asked the swimmers to rate their coaches for perceived support for autonomy versus control. For example, a question about autonomy is 'My coach provides me with opportunity to make personal decisions' (p. 288). A question about control is 'My coach pressures me to do what he/she wants' (p. 288). The results showed that swimmers who remained in the competitive swim program rated their coaches as being more supportive of autonomy and less insistent on external control. In other words, autonomous motivation was more effective than external motivation for persistence in swimming.

Need for competence. The **need for competence** refers to feeling capable and successful in dealing with one's social and physical environment. It provides the means to experience pleasure when succeeding at a demanding task. The need for competence gains importance when contrasted to feeling unable, incompetent, and ineffectual. Satisfying the need for competence increases well-being (Reis et al., 2000) but it also motivates behavior to satisfy that need. An illustration of this motivating effect comes from an investigation tracking people's adherence to an exercise program (Vlachopoulos & Neikou, 2007). Men and women aged 18–49 years were tracked for their attendance at a fitness center to determine who was still active after six months. At the beginning of the investigation, participants filled out the *Basic Psychological Needs in Exercise Scale*, designed to measure their needs for autonomy, relatedness, and competence. A question that measured the need for competence read as "I feel I have been making huge progress with regard to the end result I pursue" (p. 477). Competence was the only predictor for exercise adherence. Individuals with a higher need for competence were more likely to continue their visits to the fitness center. The researchers concluded that the need for competence imparts the pleasure that results from the sense of accomplishment that exercise provides (Vlachopoulos & Neikou, 2007).

Need to Affiliate/Belong

The need to affiliate or belong is the third need that forms the foundation of self-determination theory. The need to affiliate and to belong may be considered different ends of a continuum. At one end is affiliation, which refers to frequent contacts with others who are accepting but yet tend toward indifference. For example, a person affiliates with class mates, team mates, and acquaintances. Belonging, on the other hand, refers to regular and intimate contact with others for whom one has deep feelings and a sense of attachment, for example, feelings that occur between people in committed relationships, in married couples, and between parents and children. According to the **belongingness hypothesis**, "humans have a pervasive drive to form and maintain at least a minimum quantity of lasting, positive, and significant interpersonal relationships" (Baumeister & Leary, 1995, p. 497). The relationships are stable and enduring and consist of frequent and pleasant interactions with others.

How did the need to belong arise? The need to belong is innate and results from natural selection, wrote Charles Darwin (1871) in his book *The Descent of Man*. Darwin reasoned that humans are social animals, who wish to live in societies and dislike solitude. The preference for group living results from natural selection because membership provided the survival advantage of safety, mutual aid and concern, a common defense, and the care of children. A conclusion from Darwin's view is that the need to affiliate and to belong is universal and is necessary in all cultures (Baumeister & Leary, 1995; Deci & Ryan, 2008). This section examines two of Darwin's (1871) contentions that humans, like animals, "are unhappy if long separated from them [fellow humans], and always happy to be in their company" (p. 86).

Need to belong as a trait. One prediction from the belongingness hypothesis and Darwin's writings is that humans are motivated to be included in groups and to form social connections with others. The extent of this motivation for inclusion depends on the strength of the need to belong. In this case, the need to belong is considered a trait, as shown in Table 8.2. Presumably, individuals with a greater need to belong should be more motivated to establish and maintain social relationships. The extent this is achieved may depend on how well people interpret the social cues that signal inclusion or exclusion from a group. Individuals with a higher need to belong are hypothesized to be more accurate at interpreting such social cues. In order to test this hypothesis, Pickett and coresearchers (2004) used the *Need to Belong Scale* to select participants who varied in the amount of this need. Next, the participants were tested for their accuracy in identifying facial expressions of anger, fear, happiness, and sadness. The results of the research supported the hypothesis. Individuals with a higher need to belong were more accurate in their identification of emotional expressions than were individuals with a lower level of this need.

Need to belong as a state. You were not invited to the party, not chosen to be on the team, and were not asked to dance—that is, you were excluded or rejected. Did it hurt? The consequences of rejection illustrate the power of an unfulfilled need to belong. In this case, the need to belong is considered a state, as shown in Table 8.2. The rejection results in several negative consequences (Gerber & Wheeler, 2009). First, being rejected makes a person feel bad—that is, it lowers positive mood and raises negative mood. Second, being rejected feels like a loss of control in the situation and consequently people behave in order to regain control or their sense of autonomy. Third, rejection also lowers a person's self-esteem. A fourth consequence suggested by Baumeister and coresearchers (2007) is numbness—that is, the rejected individual becomes emotionally insensitive and lacks feelings.

Does rejection make a person feel bad? Does it also motivate them to reestablish social contact? Yes, based on the results of experiments in which a feeling of rejection or belonging are created in the laboratory. Participants are informed that they will have either lonely or relationship-filled futures. Imagine being a participant in such an experiment (Maner et al., 2007, exp. 2). As part of the procedure, you complete a personality questionnaire. Based on the results, you are provided with accurate information about your personality. However, you are also provided with bogus feedback regarding your future social relationships. The false feedback is an elaboration that one of three types of future will dominate your life. Future alone feedback: "You're the type who will end up alone later in life" (p. 45). Future belonging feedback: "You're the type who has rewarding relationships throughout life" (p. 45). Misfortune control feedback: "You're likely to be accident-prone later in life" (p. 45). Following this feedback, participants completed the *Positive and Negative Affect Scale* to measure how their feelings were influenced by the types of feedback. In the next phase of the experiment, participants were asked to complete another task either alone or, if they wished, with others. In order to measure their preference, participants were asked: "To what extent would you prefer doing the experimental task with a few other social partners?" (0 = *not at all* to 11 = *extremely*; p. 45). The purpose of this question was to gauge the strength of the motive to socially reconnect with other individuals.

The results of the experiment are shown in Figure 8.4. First, the thought of future rejection described in the future alone condition increased negative affect compared with the feedback about a future filled with meaningful relationships or filled with accidents. In other words, the thought of a future alone makes the participants feel worse. Second, the desire to socially reconnect was also stronger for individuals who received future alone feedback compared to the other two types of feedback. Thus, the threat of an unfulfilled need to belong also increased the motivation to connect with others.

If being rejected feels like a loss of autonomy, then do people attempt to regain their autonomy? One way would be to prevent further rejection. Thus, one might hypothesize that rejection makes people more sensitive to identifying phony smiles, which may signal further rejection. To test this hypothesis, Bernstein and coresearchers (2008) created feelings of exclusion (rejection), feelings of inclusion (acceptance), and neutral feelings. Participants were asked to write about a time they felt "rejected or excluded" (rejection) or "accepted or included" (inclusion) or about yesterday morning (neutral condition). In the next phase of the experiment, participants watched 20 brief videos of models portraying either an authentic or phony smile. Participants had to indicate whether the smile was authentic or phony. Would participants in the rejected condition be more accurate, since they are more sensitive either to further rejection or to the possibility of inclusion? The results showed that rejected participants were more accurate in classifying the

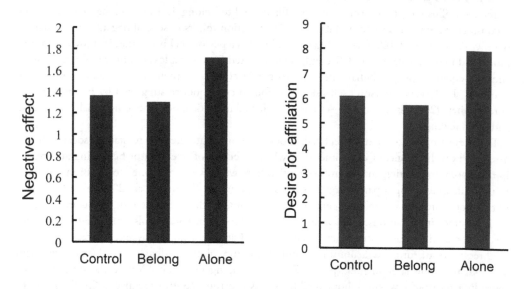

FIGURE 8.4 Effects of Belonging vs. Alone Forecasting. Participants who were informed that their future would be lonely experienced more negative affect (left) and expressed a greater desire to affiliate (right). Less negative affect and desire for affiliation was experienced by control participants for whom an accident-prone life was predicted and by belonging participants for whom lifelong meaningful relationships were predicted.

Source: Adapted from "Does Social Exclusion Motivate Interpersonal Reconnection? Resolving the 'Porcupine Problem'" by J. K. Maner et al., 2007, *Journal of Personality and Social Psychology, 92*, p. 45.

smiles than were either the inclusion participants or the control participants. The last two groups were equally accurate. Thus, increases in the need to belong, whether preexisting or activated, result in greater awareness of opportunities for inclusion and warnings of further exclusion. A high need to belong as either a trait or a state increases the ability to recognize facial expressions of emotion (Pickett et al., 2004; Bernstein et al., 2008, respectively).

Does being excluded dull an individual's physical and emotional feelings? Dewall and Baumeister (2006) show that this dulling can happen in different ways. These experimenters employed the use of false feedback described previously. Participants in the future alone condition were led to believe that they would be socially excluded and isolated. Participants in the future belonging condition were led to believe that they would develop lasting and meaningful relationships. Participants in the misfortune condition were led to believe that they were accident-prone. Pain tolerance was measured by applying pressure to the participants' index fingers. How much pressure is required to report "pain" and how long can pain be tolerated? The results showed that future alone participants reported a higher pain threshold and could tolerate pain longer than participants in the other conditions. The conclusion is that rejection is physically numbing and reduces a person's sensitivity to pain. In addition to physically numbing, social exclusion also numbs emotional feelings. Social exclusion makes individuals feel emotionally flat in response to both positive and negative events (DeWall & Baumeister, 2006).

Need for Closure and Need for Cognition

Do you prefer immediate and unambiguous conclusions or can you tolerate indecision and the necessity of evaluating additional possibilities before making a decision? This question addresses differences in need for closure. Do you prefer organizing, evaluating, and engaging in analytical thinking about problems or do you dislike this type of mental effort? This question addresses the need for cognition. Both the need for closure and need for cognition affect the frequency and reason that people use the Internet.

Need for closure and Internet use. The **need for closure** refers to the tendency to desire "a firm answer to a question and an aversion toward ambiguity" (Kruglanski & Webster, 1996, p. 264). The desire for closure is a continuum, which is anchored by a high and low closure at each end. A high need for closure motivates behaviors that promote attaining definite knowledge as opposed to ambiguity, forming immediate conclusions, and promoting impulsivity. The low need for closure, at the other end, favors being inconclusive and being reluctant to commit to a conclusion. Also, for individuals high in the need for closure, there is a tendency to seize and freeze. Seize refers to the urgency to attain closure and reach a conclusion or decision quickly. Freeze refers the tendency to make the closure permanent, since seeking and considering additional information or options is aversive and unpleasant (Kruglanski & Webster, 1996).

The need for closure has been examined for how it influences people's perusal of websites. What website features interact with the need for closure? To answer this question, researchers prepared two different mock websites that advertised a product (Amichai-Hamburger et al., 2004). One website was simple, while the other was more complex and provided multiple links to further information about the advertised product. Prior to the experiment, participants were classified as having either a high or low need for closure based on the *Need for Closure Questionnaire* (see Kruglanski in Table 8.3). The participants interacted and then reported on their attitudes about the site. When provided with unlimited time pressure, participants with a high need for closure were less willing to spend time and to seek information in order to make decisions. They preferred the noninteractive web, since it allowed for faster decisions and little opportunity for additional information. In other words, they demonstrated seize and freeze. In contrast, participants with a low need for closure preferred the interactive site, spent more time on it, and used more hyperlinks searching for information about the product. In other words, they showed the opposite of seize and freeze.

Need for cognition and Internet use. The **need for cognition** has been defined as "a need to structure relevant situations in meaningful, integrated ways. It is a need to understand and make reasonable the experiential world" (Cohen et al., 1955, p. 291). Cacioppo and Petty (1982) expanded on this meaning and developed the *Need for Cognition Scale*, which contains statements measuring a person's enjoyment in thinking and solving complex problems (Cacioppo et al., 1996). For example, to what extent does a person enjoy thinking abstractly, coming up with new solutions to problems, putting forth mental effort, or watching educational programs?

A high need for cognition describes individuals who are disposed to engage in and enjoy analytical thinking. Thus, these individuals should pay closer attention to messages designed to change attitudes. To illustrate, imagine a situation in which you are asked to read and evaluate the proposal that "seniors be required to pass a comprehensive exam in their major as a requirement for graduation" (Cacioppo et al., 1983, p. 807). This proposal was presented to students as an editorial written by a journalism student. One version presented a weak set of arguments, and the other version a strong set of arguments. Students either low or high in the need for cognition read either the weak or strong editorial version and evaluated it for effectiveness, liking, and convincingness. The students also rated themselves for how much cognitive effort they put into evaluating the editorial and were asked to recall as many arguments as they could remember. The results showed that students with a high need for cognition were affected more by the strength of the editorial than were those with a low need for cognition. They evaluated the strong argument more positively and the weak argument more negatively. They also reported expending more effort thinking about the editorial and recalled more messages than did students with a low need for cognition.

Differences in the need for cognition have implications for the field of advertising on the Internet. Individuals high, compared to low, in the need for cognition are expected to process information in an advertisement more deeply and enjoyably. However, processing differences may depend on the complexity of the web page advertisement. Thus, what type of advertising web page should be designed? Martin and coresearchers (2005) created two websites that differed in visual and verbal complexity. One site was visually more complex, since it used animated images rather than static ones. Also, one site was verbally more complex, since it had more text and required scrolling in order to read all of the information. The simple site had all verbal information on one page. For the research, participants were classified as having either a low or high need for cognition based on their scores on the *Need for Cognition Scale* (see Table 8.3). Next, participants interacted with the web pages and then evaluated their reactions to each page. Martin and coresearchers (2005) discovered that, for a page with low verbal complexity, participants with a low need for cognition had more favorable attitudes toward it. However, for a page with high verbal complexity, participants with a high need for cognition had more favorable attitudes. Individuals with a low need for cognition prefer a simpler page because it requires less cognitive processing. However, individuals with a high need for cognition prefer the complex page because they enjoy the more extensive cognitive processing. Low and high need for cognition participants did not differ in their preference for low versus high visual complexity.

Need for Meaning

The **need for meaning** refers to motivation aimed at restoring expected and predictable relationships between individuals and their physical and social environments. It provides the motivation by which individuals try to make sense of their lives (Heine et al., 2006; Park, 2010; Steger et al., 2006). Striving to fulfill one's need for meaning can occur in two different ways. First, the lives of individuals may be meaningful but they still search for new, additional, and deeper sources of meaning. In other words, they simply want their lives to be more meaningful than they currently are (Steger et al., 2006). Second, an individual may experience a deficit in meaning as a result of some crucial life event. These events conflict in significant ways with people's current beliefs, important goals, and personal sense of meaning. In this case, individuals are motivated to restore meaning—that is, to make their current situation meaningful (Heine et al., 2006; Park, 2010).

According to the **meaning-making model**, when an event occurs that makes no sense, individuals are motivated to restore meaning (Park, 2010). This process takes several steps. First, an individual must appraise the meaning of the current disruptive event. An example is trying to understand the death of a close friend. Next, the outcome of this appraisal is compared to an individual's global sense of meaning, which consists of beliefs about a person's role in the world, personal goals, and a person's purpose in life. For example, how does the death affect an individual's sense of fairness? If the appraised event is discrepant or does not make sense—that is, has no meaning—then the individual is motivated to restore meaning. This motivation can take the form of acceptance or changes in how one perceives the meaning of life.

Catastrophic events in a country's history illustrate the motivation to restore meaning. One familiar event is the September 11, 2001, terrorist attack on the United States, when two hijacked airplanes crashed into the World Trade Center's towers in New York City. The attack on home soil destroys people's global belief in a just, coherent, and predictable world. Would people try to make sense of that attack and succeed in doing so? Updegraff and coresearchers (2008) examined whether people's attempts to find meaning were successful and what the benefits were. The researchers used a web-based survey of individuals at two months, one year, and two years following the September 11 attack. The results showed that, two months after the attack, about two-thirds of the respondents reported searching for meaning but only 40 percent of them succeeded in finding at least a little meaning in the attack and 60 percent could find none. However, finding meaning had psychological benefits. First, respondents who found meaning were less fearful of future terrorist attacks. Second, those who found meaning also reported less stress at follow-ups one and two years later.

Personal tragedies also motivate people's search for meaning. Park (2008) investigated whether the motivation to regain meaning after a personal loss helped individuals adjust psychologically. University students involved in this research had experienced a personal loss, such as the death of a dear relative, friend, or pet or the end of a romantic relationship or friendship. Students reported that these events caused them to experience a reduction in the meaning of their lives— that is, it increased their need for meaning. Six weeks after these reports, Park measured the extent that thoughts about the loss intruded into their consciousness, the extent participants attempted to make sense of that loss, and any subsequent improvement in psychological health. A greater loss of meaning was associated with more distress and lower feelings of psychological well-being. It also produced more intrusive thoughts about the event and motivated attempts at restoring meaning. When restoration was partially successful, negative affect and symptoms of depression decreased.

How individuals should restore meaning is not as apparent as it is for other psychological needs. For instance, the need for belonging is satisfied by establishing relationships with other people. The need for achievement is satisfied by accomplishing challenging tasks and satisfying the need for power involves being in charge of an organization. One method that restores meaning is the use of **counterfactual thinking**, which refers to considering alternatives to the current situation. In other words, what might a person's life have been like if some other (counterfactual) event had occurred. An assumption is that counterfactual thinking will enhance the meaningfulness of one's life (Kray et al., 2010). For example, consider the counterfactual thought of having decided not to attend your current university or the counterfactual thought of not having met your best friend. How does considering such counterfactuals affect the meaning of your life in those areas? Kray and coresearchers (2010) asked those questions in an experiment summarized in Table 8.4. Participants dwelt on an event in their lives, such as attending their current university or about meeting their best friend. Then they wrote counterfactual essays about having chosen not to attend their current university or how things would have turned out differently had they not met their best friend. As a control condition, participants did not write further about their university or wrote about how events developed after meeting their friend. Following this, participants rated how meaningful their college choice or their friendship was in their lives. These ratings in Figure 8.5 show that counterfactual thoughts made these

TABLE 8.4 Effects of Counterfactuals on Personal Meaning

First Phase of Experiment	Second Phase of Experiment	Third Phase of Experiment
Experiment 1 All participants wrote a brief essay about the sequence of events they considered led to their decision to attend their university	Counterfactual thinking: half wrote about how events could have turned out differently Control condition: no further thinking or writing for other half of participants	Rate the following: Decision to attend defines who I am Decision added meaning to my life Decision was one of the most significant choices in my life 1 = *not at all* to 7 = *extremely*
Experiment 2 All participants wrote about a close friend, how they met, and the sequence of events that led to their meeting	Counterfactual thinking: half wrote about ways that they might not have met their friend and how things could have been different Factual thinking: other half wrote additional details about that meeting that determined the final outcome	Rate the following: Meeting my friend defines who I am Meeting added meaning to my life Meeting was one of the most significant events in my life 1 = *not at all* to 7 = *most definitely*

Source: Experimental design adapted from "From What *Might* Have Been to What *Must* Have Been: Counterfactual Thinking Creates Meaning" by L. J. Kray et al., 2010, *Journal of Personality and Social Psychology, 98*, p. 108.

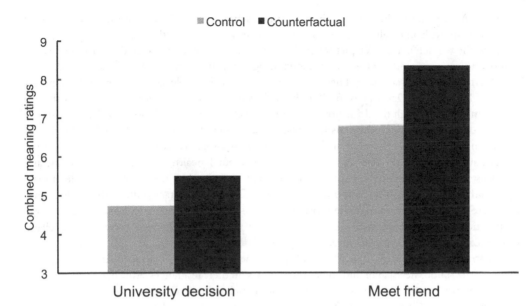

FIGURE 8.5 Counterfactual Thought Increases Personal Meaning. Need for meaning is satisfied by thinking counterfactual thoughts—that is, what might have been. Individuals' sense of personal meaning (meaning ratings) increased when counterfactual thoughts involved not attending their university. Sense of meaning (meaning ratings) also increased when counterfactual thought involved not having met their best friend.

Source: Adapted from "From What *Might* Have Been to What *Must* Have Been: Counterfactual Thinking Creates Meaning" by L. J. Kray et al., 2010, *Journal of Personality and Social Psychology, 98,* pp. 108, 109.

events more meaningful. Counterfactual thinking made students' choice of university more meaningful and their relationship with their best friends more meaningful.

Need for Power

Why would anyone want to be president of the United States, of your university, or of a university club? Is it for the money or the fame or to satisfy some inner drive or need? Consider the following "get ahead or get along scenario": A worker is offered a promotion to manager that will require supervising former coworkers, who are friends. By declining the promotion, she can remain in a situation that provides the opportunity for interacting with her friends. By accepting the promotion, however, she gains the opportunity to exercise authority. Would a person with a strong need for power accept this promotion?

Measuring need for power. To exert influence over other people, to be in charge, to be noticed, and to have high status are all characteristics of the **power motive** (Winter, 1988, 1992). Look again at the picture of the two women in lab coats (see Figure 8.2). A story written in response to this resemblance of a TAT picture is scored for the power motive if the response contains phrases related to power, giving unsolicited help, or trying to influence or impress people. Another power motive characteristic is a reference that the person's actions produce a strong emotional response in others. A character in the story might perform an action that produces gratitude on the part of the helped individual. Finally, a power motive involves a concern with reputation or image. For example, the women in the TAT picture might be described as having graduated from a top medical school and are now working for a well-known drug company (Veroff, 1992; Winter, 1992).

Characteristics of need for power. There are various ways that people satisfy their need for power (Winter, 1988, 1992). One way is to place themselves in legitimate positions of power. Both men and women with a high need for power are more likely to be office holders or be in positions to make decisions affecting others. As students, they are more likely to be residence hall counselors or student government officers. A high power motive is associated with entering power-related careers, such as being teachers, business executives, mental health workers, psychologists, and journalists. The power motive is satisfied in these occupations because the person has the legitimate right and duty to direct the behavior of the people she is in contact with. Individuals with a moderate to high power motive are more likely to succeed as managers and executives of large corporations, especially when this motive is coupled with a low affiliation motive (McClelland & Boyatzis, 1982). Since power means being visible to others, individuals with a high need for power strive to be so. Students with a high power need are more likely to write letters to the editor of the school newspaper and to put their names on their residences. Another demonstration of a high power motive is owning trappings of power, such as high-tech stereo equipment, expensive wines, elite credit cards, fancy cars, or valuable pictures or wall hangings. Power-motivated women, more than men, are interested in using clothing as a show of power (Winter, 1988, 1992). Finally, men and women with a high need for power place greater importance on status and wealth than do those with a low need for power (Parker & Chusmir, 1991).

Expressing need for power. Psychological needs may be interpreted as categories of incentives. Thus, a person who seemingly has a need for power is really one who prefers power-related incentives. If this is the case, then individuals with a need for power should enter and remain in situations that provide those incentives. Jenkins (1994) investigated this possibility in a longitudinal study tracking the career development of women who varied in need for power. Power motive scores were collected from these women when they were college seniors and then correlated with various aspects of their professional careers at age 35. Several of Jenkins's findings showed that women with a high need for power were sensitive to situations that allowed for expression of their power motives. First, they were more likely to have entered and remained in power-relevant careers (teacher, psychotherapist, business executive, journalist) than women with a low need for power had. Second, their degree of job satisfaction was related to the opportunity to exercise interpersonal power. Third, they were more likely to progress professionally provided they were in power-relevant jobs. When in non-power-relevant jobs, however, professional progress seemed absent. A conclusion of this study is that people with various needs are sensitive to the incentives that satisfy those needs. Consequently, we should not be surprised that they enter situations or professions that satisfy their needs. In the "get ahead or get along" scenario, a person with a high need for power probably would accept the promotion to manager.

Need for Self-Esteem

What does it mean to feel good about yourself? If individuals feel bad about themselves, then how does it motivate their behavior to feel better?

Defining self-esteem. **Self-esteem** is a case of *I* evaluating *me*, which results in either a positive or negative judgment (James, 1892). Thus, a person feels good about herself (positive self-esteem) if her current self compares well against possible selves, or she feels bad about herself (negative self-esteem) if the comparison is unfavorable. An insightful way of defining self-esteem was provided by James (1892, p. 187) through his formula:

$$\text{Self-esteem} = \frac{\text{Success}}{\text{Pretensions}}$$

In this context, pretensions could be thought of as imagined possible selves: to earn a 4.00 GPA, to become a rock star, to become rich, to receive a $60,000-a-year starting salary, or to become immensely successful as a motivational speaker. Success is defined through achieving these possible selves or pretensions. For example, success means a student earned a 4.00 GPA and received a $60,000-a-year job offer on graduation. Lack of success, however, means most people considered the student's guitar playing and singing awful, and his motivational speeches put people to sleep. According to James, an individual can raise her level of self-esteem by either reducing the number of possible selves (pretensions) or by increasing the number of successes. Self-esteem is lowered, however, by decreasing the number of successes or increasing the number of possible selves (pretensions).

Self-esteem depends on the contingency of self-worth. The current concept of **contingencies of self-worth** refers to specific domains in people's lives that they consider essential for their self-esteem (Crocker et al., 2003). In these domains people also formulate possible selves. High self-esteem or self-worth depends on success in those self-defined domains, while low self-esteem is associated with failures. A person's endeavors that fall outside of those domains of contingency have no effect on self-worth. Crocker and coresearchers (2003) hypothesized seven domains of contingencies of self-worth: others' approval, appearance, competition, academic competence, family support, virtue, and God's love (see Table 8.5). The 35-item *Contingencies of Self-Worth Scale* measures an individual's level of contingent self-worth in each domain (Crocker et al., 2003). A higher score indicates a greater level of contingent self-worth in a particular domain.

TABLE 8.5 Domains of Contingencies of Self-Worth

Contingency	Self-Esteem Depends on These Characteristics
Others' approval	The opinion, approval, or acceptance by other people in general
Appearance	A person's physical appearance of face and body
Competition	Outperforming or doing better than others in competitive tasks
Academic Competence	Academic performance, high grades, doing well in school, or high on teachers' evaluations
Family Support	Approval, acceptance, care, and love of family members
Virtue	Follow ethical principles or abide by a moral code
God's Love	Belief that one is loved and valued by God; feeling of religiosity

Source: Adapted from "Contingencies of Self-Worth in College Students: Theory and Measurement" by J. Crocker et al., 2003, *Journal of Personality and Social Psychology, 85*, pp. 895, 896, and Table 2, p. 899.

The website titled "Measurement Instrument Data Base for the Social Sciences" provides access to a copy of the *Contingencies of Self-Worth Scale* here: www.midss.org. The scale is also here: http://faculty.psy.ohio-state.edu/crocker/lab/documents/CSWscale.pdf.

Self-esteem depends on the domain of contingent self-worth in which a person experiences success or failure. Crocker and coresearchers (2002, 2005) tested this hypothesis in the domain of academic competence. They measured the level of students' contingent self-worth with items from the *Contingencies of Self-Worth Scale*. A sample item from this domain is "My self-esteem is influenced by my academic performance" (Crocker et al., 2003, p. 899). Students rated themselves on this and similar items with the scale 1 = *strongly disagree* to 7 = *strongly agree*. Students one standard deviation below and above the mean on the scale were defined as low and high in contingent academic self-worth, respectively. An important indicator of achievement in this domain is whether students are accepted to graduate schools. Does the rise or fall of a student's self-esteem depend on receiving a letter of acceptance or rejection? And does it also depend on whether they have high compared to low contingent self-worth in the domain of academic competence? In order to answer these questions, college seniors filled out a measure of self-esteem on days that a letter of acceptance or rejection was received and twice per week on regularly scheduled days when no news was received. The *Rosenberg Self-Esteem Inventory* was used to measure the level of self-esteem on all days.

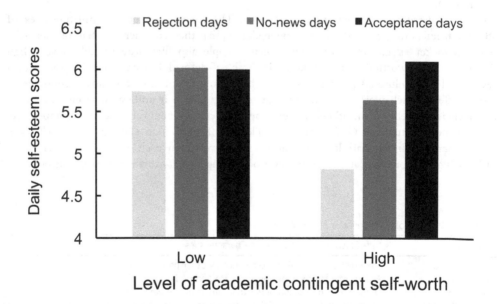

FIGURE 8.6 Self-Esteem Depends on Academic Contingent Self-Worth. Students low and high in academic contingent self-worth were affected differently by rejection from or acceptance to graduate school. Self-esteem dropped more with rejection and rose more with acceptance for students with a high academic contingent self-worth.

Source: Adapted from "Hopes Dashed and Dreams Fulfilled: Contingencies of Self-Worth and Graduate School Admissions" by J. Crocker et al., 2002, *Personality and Social Psychology Bulletin, 28*, p. 1280.

Measured self-esteem on a particular day depended on the type of letter received and on the level of contingent self-worth, as shown in Figure 8.6. For students with high contingent self-worth, a letter of rejection lowered their self-esteem, while a letter of acceptance raised their self-esteem compared to no-news days. For students with low contingent self-worth, letters of acceptance had no effect on self-esteem and a letter of rejection had a small negative effect on self-esteem compared to no-news days (Crocker et al., 2002; Crocker & Knight, 2005). These results and others suggest that people's self-esteem rises and falls with successes and failures but only in those domains that they consider important.

Section Recap

This section described how various psychological needs motivate behavior. Achievement motivation is guided by two internal sources: the need to achieve, or *motive to achieve success*, and the motive to avoid failure. The need to achieve is characterized by wanting to do things well, being persistent, and having a high standard of excellence. In contrast, the *motive to avoid failure* is characterized by fear and anxiety about failing at a task. Achievement motivation theory has been extended to include additional determinants of achievement behavior, such as the probability of success and failure and the incentive value of success and failure. *Self-determination theory* views individuals as the source, cause, or origin of their own freely chosen behavior, which is necessary for the satisfaction of *autonomy* (self-determination), *competence* (capability and effectiveness), and *affiliation* (relatedness, belonging) *needs*. Affiliation needs range from association at one end to belonging at the other. According to the *belongingness hypothesis*, people are motivated to form long-lasting positive relationships with others. Several factors can hamper this development. Social exclusion results in unpleasant feelings, a loss of autonomy, and numbness. In addition, the rejected individual is motivated to reestablish social connections. Other important needs include the *need for closure*, the motive to avoid ambiguities and to arrive at a firm conclusion, while the *need for cognition* refers to a desire to understand one's experiences and things in the world through thinking. The *need for meaning* is the motive to understand how the self relates to one's geographical, cultural, and social environments. According to the *meaning-making model*, individuals are motivated to restore meaning following catastrophic events or personal tragedies. One method is to employ *counterfactual thinking*, which means to consider alternatives that contrast sharply with an individual's current situation or friendships. The *power motive* is the wish to influence the lives of other individuals, to be in command, to have high status, and to be noticed. People with a power motive are more likely to be successful in occupations that allow for the legitimate exercise of power. *Self-esteem* refers to the evaluative feeling a person has about the self. According to James, self-esteem depends on how many possible selves (pretensions) a person has achieved or become. A contemporary view is that self-esteem rests on a *contingency of self-worth*, which can occur in various domains, such as academic competence. Successes in a domain boost self-esteem and failures lower self-esteem provided the individual has a high degree of contingent self-worth in that domain. Successes or failures in domains of low contingent self-worth have little effect on self-esteem.

GLOSSARY

Term	Definition
Belongingness Hypothesis	Motive for people to form long-lasting, positive, meaningful interpersonal relationships with others
Contingencies of Self-Worth	Specific domains in people's lives that they consider important for their self-esteem
Counterfactual Thinking	Thought process in which a person considers alternatives to the current situation; what would your life be like if some other event had occurred?
Drive	Drive emerges from a physiological (bodily) need as a result of being deprived of a required substance. Drive pushes or motivates behavior
Explicit Motive	It resembles a value a person places on a stimulus or activity
Implicit Motive	The capacity of a person to experience pleasure when the individual interacts with a need-relevant incentive
Intimacy Motive	People are motivated to form warm, close, or communicative social relationships with others because of the positive feelings that this brings
Incentive Value of Success	In achievement motivation theory, the incentive value of success = 1− probability of success. Difficult tasks have higher incentive value than easy ones
Maslow's Hierarchy of Needs	Theory that postulates a hierarchical order of needs from physiology, safety, belongingness, and esteem, to self-actualization. Needs are satisfied in that order
Meaning-Making Model	Hypothesis that people are motivated to restore meaning or to make sense of events following personal tragedies or catastrophic events
Motive to Achieve Success	Identical to need to achieve. It is the disposition to engage in task-oriented behavior or achievement behavior to surpass a high standard of excellence
Motive to Avoid Failure	Opposite of the need to achieve. It is the disposition to experience fear or anxiety about failing an achievement task
Need for Autonomy	Motive to freely choose your own goals and means to accomplish them; need to feel that people are the cause of their own actions
Need for Closure	Motive to desire a firm answer to a question or puzzle and a dislike of ambiguity
Need for Cognition	Motive or desire to understand one's experiences and things in the world through thinking
Need for Competence	Motive to feel capable and successful in dealing with one's social and physical environment
Need for Meaning	Motive to understand how the self relates to one's geographical, cultural, and social environment
Need to Achieve	Also known as the motive for success; a disposition to engage in task-oriented behavior or achievement behavior to surpass a high standard of excellence
Negative Affect	An unpleasant subjective feeling, such as sadness or worry; also the unpleasant subjective component of emotion

continued . . .

GLOSSARY Continued

Term	Definition
Operational Definition	The procedure that is used to measure or create the existence of a psychological construct, such as a psychological need
Physiological Need	Refers to a specifiable deviation from a set point of homeostatic conditions that are detrimental to the person's physical well-being, e.g., need for iron or glucose
Positive Affect	A pleasant subjective feeling, such as happy or glad; also the pleasant subjective component of emotion
Power Motive	The wish to influence the lives of other individuals, to be in command, to have high status, and to be noticed
Projective Test	An unstructured stimulus (Inkblot) that a person describes in terms of personal meaning that is consistent with any activated motives or needs
Psychological Needs	An internal motive defined as the discrepancy between a person's set point and some incentive or activity. It motivates a person to reduce this discrepancy
Redintegration	Process whereby an environmental stimulus activates a psychological need
Self-Determination Theory	Motivation stems from within individuals; they are the source, cause, or origin of their own freely chosen behavior; motivation is not external
Self-Esteem	Emotional outcome of a self-evaluation as in *I evaluate me*, which is based on the number of your successes in domains that are important to you
State, Need as a	As a state, need refers to a temporary deficit or discrepancy between the current versus desired level of some incentive, activity, or experience
Trait, Need as a	As a trait, psychological needs refer to long-term, consistent requirements for an incentive or activity for a person to function best
Two-Process Model of Psychological Needs	Needs motivate behavior because the behavior (1) satisfies the need. But also, because the behavior also (2) provides pleasant psychological experiences
Vitality	The subjective feeling of being alive or being energized

REFERENCES

Amichai-Hamburger, Y., Fine, A., & Goldstein, A. (2004). The impact of Internet interactivity and need for closure on consumer preference. *Computers and Human Behavior, 20*, 103–117.

Atkinson, J. W. (1957/1983). Motivational determinants of risk-taking behavior. In J. Atkinson (Ed.), *Personality, motivation, and action: Selected papers* (pp. 101–119). New York, NY: Praeger.

Atkinson, J. W. (1958/1983). Towards experimental analysis of human motivation in terms of motives, expectancies, and incentives. In J. W. Atkinson (Ed.), *Personality, motivation, and action: Selected papers* (pp. 81–97). New York, NY: Praeger.

Atkinson, J. W. (1974). The mainspring of achievement-oriented activity. In J. W. Atkinson & J. O. Raynor (Eds.), *Personality, motivation, and achievement* (pp. 13–41). Washington, DC: Hemisphere.

Atkinson, J. W., & Litwin, G. W. (1960). Achievement motive and test anxiety conceived as motive to approach success and motive to avoid failure. *Journal of Abnormal and Social Psychology, 60*, 52–63.

Baumeister, R. F., Brewer, L. E., Tice, D. M., & Twenge, J. M. (2007). Thwarting the need to belong: Understanding the interpersonal and inner effects of social exclusion. *Social and Personality Psychology Compass, 1*, 506–520.

Baumeister, R. F., & Leary, M. R. (1995). The need to belong: Desire for interpersonal attachments as a fundamental human motivation. *Psychological Bulletin, 117*, 497–529.

Bernstein, M. J., Young, S. G., Brown, C. M., Sacco, D. F., & Claypool, H. M. (2008). Adaptive responses to social exclusion: Social rejection improves detection of real and fake smiles. *Psychological Science, 19*, 981–983.

Cacioppo, J. T., & Petty, R. E. (1982). The need for cognition. *Journal of Personality and Social Psychology, 42*, 116–131.

Cacioppo, J. T., Petty, R. E., Feinstein, J. A., & Jarvis, W. B. G. (1996). Dispositional differences in cognitive motivation: The life and times of individuals varying in need for cognition. *Psychological Bulletin, 119*, 197–253.

Cacioppo, J. T., Petty, R. E., & Morris, K. J. (1983). Effects of need for cognition on message evaluation, recall, and persuasion. *Journal of Personality and Social Psychology, 45*, 805–818.

Chen, B., Vansteenkiste, M., Beyers, W., Boone, L., Deci, E. L., Van der Kaap-Deeder, J., . . . Ryan, R. M. (2015). Basic psychological need satisfaction, need frustration, and need strength across four cultures. *Motivation and Emotion, 39*, 216–236.

Cohen, A. R., Stotland, E., & Wolfe, D. M. (1955). An experimental investigation of need for cognition. *Journal of Abnormal and Social Psychology, 51*, 291–294.

Crocker, J., & Knight, K. M. (2005). Contingencies of self-worth. *Current Directions in Psychological Science, 14*, 200–203.

Crocker, J., Luhtanen, R. K., Cooper, M. L., & Bouvrette, A. (2003). Contingencies of self-worth in college students: Theory and measurement. *Journal of Personality and Social Psychology, 85*, 894–908.

Crocker, J., Sommers, S. R., & Luhtanen, R. K. (2002). Hopes dashed and dreams fulfilled: Contingencies of self-worth and graduate school admissions. *Personality and Social Psychology Bulletin, 28*, 1275–1286.

Darwin, C. (1871). *The descent of man.* New York, NY: D. Appleton.

Debats, D. L., van der Lubbe, P. M., Wezeman, F. R. A. (1993). On the psychometric properties of the life regard index (LRI): A measure of meaningful life. *Personality and Individual Differences, 14*, 337–345.

Deci, E. L., & Ryan, R. M. (2000). The "what" and "why" of goal pursuits: Human needs and the self-determination of behavior. *Psychological Inquiry, 11*, 227–268.

Deci, E. L., & Ryan, R. M. (2008). Facilitating optimal motivation and psychological well-being across life's domains. *Canadian Psychology, 49*, 14–23.

DeWall, C. N., & Baumeister, R. F. (2006). Alone but feeling no pain: Effects of social exclusion on physical pain tolerance and pain threshold, affective forecasting, and interpersonal empathy. *Journal of Personality and Social Psychology, 91*, 1–15.

Donnellan, M. B., Trzesniewski, K. H., Robins, R. W., Moffitt, T. E., & Caspi, A. (2005). Low self-esteem is related to aggression, antisocial behavior, and delinquency. *Psychological Science, 16*, 328–335.

Entwisle, D. R. (1972). To dispel fantasies about fantasy-based measures of achievement motivation. *Psychological Bulletin, 77*, 377–391.

Gerber, J., & Wheeler, L. (2009). On being rejected: A meta-analysis of experimental research on rejection. *Perspectives on Psychological Science, 4*, 468–488.

Heine, S. J., Proulx, T., & Vohs, K. D. (2006). The meaning maintenance model: On the coherence of social motivations. *Personality and Social Psychology Review, 10*, 88–110.

Hull, C. L. (1943). *Principles of behavior.* New York, NY: Appleton-Century-Crofts.

Hull, C. L. (1951). *Essentials of behavior.* New Haven, CT: Yale University Press.

James, W. (1892). *Psychology.* New York, NY: Henry Holt.

Jenkins, S. R. (1994). Need for power and women's careers over 14 years: Structural power, job satisfaction, and motive change. *Journal of Personality and Social Psychology, 66*, 155–165.

Karabenick, S. A., & Youssef, Z. I. (1968). Performance as a function of achievement motive level and perceived difficulty. *Journal of Personality and Social Psychology, 10*, 414–419.

Kenrick, D. T., Griskevicius, V., Neuberg, S. L., & Schaller, M. (2010). Renovating the pyramid of needs: Contemporary extensions built upon ancient foundations. *Perspectives on Psychological Science, 5*, 292–314.

Kesebir, S., Graham, J., & Oishi, S. (2010). A theory of human needs should be human-centered, not animal-centered: Commentary on Kenrick et al. (2010). *Perspectives on Psychological Science, 5,* 315–319.

Kimble, G. A. (1990). Mother nature's bag of tricks is small. *Psychological Science, 1,* 36–41.

Klinger, E. (1966). Fantasy need achievement as a motivational construct. *Psychological Bulletin, 66,* 291–308.

Kray, L. J., George, L. G., Liljenquist, K. A., Galaniski, A. D., & Tetlock, P. E. (2010). From what *might* have been to what *must* have been: Counterfactual thinking creates meaning. *Journal of Personality and Social Psychology, 98,*106–118.

Kruglanski, A. W., & Webster, D. M. (1996). Motivated closing of the mind: "Seizing" and "freezing." *Psychological Review, 103,* 263–283.

Lang, J. W. B., & Fries, S. (2006). A revised 10-item version of the achievement motive scale. *European Journal of Psychological Assessment, 22,* 216–224.

Lowell, E. L. (1952). The effect of need for achievement on learning and speed of performance. *Journal of Psychology, 33,* 31–40.

Lyubomirsky, S., & Boehm, J. K. (2010). Human motives, happiness, and the puzzle of parenthood: Commentary on Kenrick et al. (2010). *Perspectives on Psychological Science, 5,* 327–334.

Mahone, C. H. (1960). Fear of failure and unrealistic vocational aspiration. *Journal of Abnormal and Social Psychology, 60,* 253–261.

Maner, J. K., DeWall, N., Baumeister, R. F., & Schaller, M. (2007). Does social exclusion motivate interpersonal reconnection? Resolving the "porcupine problem." *Journal of Personality and Social Psychology, 92,* 42–55.

Martin, B. A. S., Sherrard, M. J., & Wentzel, D. (2005). The role of sensation seeking and need for cognition on web-site evaluations: A resource-matching perspective. *Psychology and Marketing, 22,* 109–124.

Mascaro, N., & Rosen, D. H. (2008). Assessment of existential meaning and its longitudinal relations with depressive symptoms. *Journal of Social and Clinical Psychology, 27,* 576–599.

Maslow, A. H. (1943). A theory of human motivation. *Psychological Review, 50,* 370–396.

Maslow, A. H. (1970). *Motivation and personality* (2nd ed.). New York, NY: Harper & Row.

McAdams, D. P. (1992). The intimacy motive. In C. P. Smith, J. W. Atkinson, D. C. McClelland, & J. Veroff (Eds.), *Motivation and personality: Handbook of thematic content analysis* (pp. 224–228). New York, NY: Cambridge University Press.

McAdams, D. P., & Constantian, C. A. (1983). Intimacy and affiliation motives in daily living: An experience sampling analysis. *Journal of Personality and Social Psychology, 45,* 851–861.

McClelland, D. C. (1975). *Power: The inner experience.* New York, NY: Irvington (Halsted Press, John Wiley).

McClelland, D. C., Atkinson, J. W., Clark, R. A., & Lowell, E. L. (1953). *The achievement motive.* New York, NY: Appleton-Century-Crofts.

McClelland, D. C., & Boyatzis, R. E. (1982). Leadership motive pattern and long-term success in management. *Journal of Applied Psychology, 67,* 737–743.

McClelland, D. C., Koestner, R., & Weinberger, J. (1989). How do self-attributed and implicit motives differ? *Psychological Review, 95,* 690–702.

Mellor, D., Stokes, M., Firth, L., Hayashi, Y., & Cummins, R. (2008). Need for belonging, relationship satisfaction, loneliness, and life satisfaction. *Personality and Individual Differences, 45,* 213–218.

Morris, J. L. (1966). Propensity for risk taking as a determinant of vocational choice: An extension of the theory of achievement motivation. *Journal of Personality and Social Psychology, 3,* 328–335.

Murray, H. A. (1938). *Explorations in personality.* New York, NY: Oxford University Press.

Nederkoorn, C., Smulders, F. T. Y., & Jansen, A. (2000). Cephalic phase responses, craving and food intake in normal subjects. *Appetite, 35,* 45–55.

Orth, U., Robins, R. W., & Roberts, B. W. (2008). Low self-esteem prospectively predicts depression in adolescence and young adulthood. *Journal of Personality and Social Psychology, 95,* 695–708.

Park, C. L. (2008). Testing the meaning making model of coping with loss. *Journal of Social and Clinical Psychology, 27,* 970–994.

Park, C. L. (2010). Making sense of the meaning literature: An integrative review of meaning making and its effects on adjustment to stressful life events. *Psychological Bulletin, 136,* 257–301.

Parker, B., & Chusmir, L. H. (1991). Motivation needs and their relationship to life success. *Human Relations, 44,* 1301–1312.

Pelletier, L. G., Fortier, M. S., Vallerand, R. J., & Briére, N. M. (2001). Associations among perceived autonomy support, forms of self-regulation, and persistence: A prospective study. *Motivation and Emotion, 25,* 279–306.

Pickett, C. L., Gardner, W. I., & Knowles, M. (2004). Getting a cue: The need to belong and enhanced sensitivity to social cues. *Personality and Social Psychology Bulletin, 30,* 1095–1107.

Reis, H. T., Sheldon, K. M., Gable, S. L., Roscoe, J., & Ryan, R. M. (2000). Daily well-being: The role of autonomy, competence, and relatedness. *Personality and Social Psychology Bulletin, 26,* 419–435.

Rosenberg, M. (1965). *Society and the adolescent self-image.* Princeton, NJ: Princeton University Press.

Schaller, M., Neuberg, S. L., Griskevicius, V., & Kenrick, D. T. (2010). Pyramid power: A reply to commentaries. *Perspectives on Psychological Science, 5,* 335–337.

Schultheiss, O. C., Jones, N. M., Davis, A. Q., & Kley, C. (2008). The role of implicit motivation in hot and cold goal pursuit: Effects on goal progress, goal rumination, and emotional well-being. *Journal of Research in Personality, 42,* 971–987.

Sheldon, K. M. (2011). Integrating behavioral-motive and experiential-requirement perspectives on psychological needs: A two process model. *Psychological Review, 118,* 552–569.

Sheldon, K. M., Abad, N., & Hinsch, C. (2011). A two-process view of Facebook use and relatedness need-satisfaction: Disconnection drives use, and connection rewards it. *Journal of Personality and Social Psychology, 100,* 766–775.

Sherwood, J. J. (1966). Self-report and projective measures of achievement and affiliation. *Journal of Consulting Psychology, 30,* 329–337.

Smith, C. P. (1992). *Motivation and personality: Handbook of thematic content analysis.* New York, NY: Cambridge University Press.

Spangler, W. D. (1992). Validity of questionnaire and TAT measures of need for achievement: Two meta-analyses. *Psychological Bulletin, 112,* 140–154.

Stanton, S. J., Hall, J. L., Schultheiss, O. C. (2010). Properties of motive-specific incentives. In O. C. Schultheiss & J. C. Brunstein (Eds.), *Implicit motives* (pp. 245–278). New York, NY: Oxford University Press.

Steger, M. F., Frazier, P., Oishi, S., & Kaler, M. (2006). The Meaning in Life Questionnaire: Assessing the presence of and search for meaning in life. *Journal of Counseling Psychology, 53,* 80–93.

Tebel, J. (1963). *From rags to riches.* New York, NY: Macmillan.

Tuerlinckx, F., De Boeck, P., & Lens, W. (2002). Measuring needs with the Thematic Apperception Test: A psychometric study. *Journal of Personality and Social Psychology, 82,* 448–461.

Updegraff, J. A., Silver, R. C., & Holman, E. A. (2008). Searching for and finding meaning in collective trauma: Results from a national longitudinal study of the 9/11 terrorist attack. *Journal of Personality and Social Psychology, 95,* 709–722.

Veroff, J. (1992). A scoring manual for the power motive. In C. P. Smith (Ed.), *Motivation and personality: Handbook of thematic content analysis* (pp. 286–300). New York, NY: Cambridge University Press.

Vlachopoulos, S. P., & Neikou, E. (2007). A prospective study of the relationships of autonomy, competence, and relatedness with exercise attendance, adherence, and dropout. *The Journal of Sports Medicine and Physical Fitness, 47,* 475–482.

Watt, J. D., & Blanchard, M. J. (1994). Boredom proneness and the need for cognition. *Journal of Research in Personality, 28,* 44–51.

Watt, S. E., & Badger, A. J. (2009). Effects of social belonging on homesickness: An application of the belongingness hypothesis. *Personality and Social Psychology Bulletin, 35,* 516–530.

Webster, D. M., Richter, L., & Kruglanski, A. W. (1996). On leaping to conclusions when feeling tired: Mental fatigue effects on impressional primacy. *Journal of Experimental Social Psychology, 32,* 181–195.

Winter, D. G. (1988). The power motive in women—and men. *Journal of Personality and Social Psychology, 54,* 510–519.

Winter, D. G. (1992). Power motivation revisited. In C. P. Smith (Ed.), *Motivation and personality: Handbook of thematic content analysis* (pp. 301–310). New York, NY: Cambridge University Press.

CHAPTER 9

Personality and Motivation

Fierce eagles do not produce timorous doves.

Horace, 13 B.C.

With a good heredity, nature deals you a fine hand at cards; and with a good environment, you learn to play the hand well.

Walter C. Alvarez, M.D.

Different things motivate different people. The last chapter showed that different motivators could be organized according to various psychological needs. This chapter examines whether different motivators can be grouped according to people's personalities. Do people who differ in personality have different motives, incentives, and goals? This chapter presents possible answers to this and the following questions:

1. Are personality traits real?
2. Do personality traits determine what motivates people?
3. Do personality traits affect a person's reaction, selection, and manipulation of a situation?
4. Do personality traits influence the manner in which psychological needs are satisfied?

PERSONALITY ASSOCIATED WITH MOTIVATION

After being separated since infancy for 39 years, identical twins Jim Springer and Jim Lewis were reunited. Even though they were adopted and reared by different families, there were some uncanny similarities between the twins. Each had been married twice, had a son named James, and had a dog named Toy during childhood. In regards to personal habits, both smoked and drank lite beer, bit their fingernails, and vacationed in the same beach area in Florida. Both twins had worked part-time as sheriffs, owned light blue Chevrolets, and wrote love notes to their wives (Segal, 1999, pp. 116–118). How can two individuals reared in different environments be so similar? Is it due to chance or due to their similar personalities, which were shaped by their genes?

Are personality traits real? Were the twins' personalities alike and thus they were motivated similarly? If people's personalities are not alike, then are they motivated differently?

Personality Traits as Categories or Causes of Behavior

Do people show consistency in their behavior from one time to the next or from one similar situation to another? **Personality traits** refer to the consistency in a specific set of behaviors across time and across relevant situations. A trait is also defined by the relationship among different behavioral habits. The trait of sociability, for example, consists of such behaviors as going to parties, liking to talk, preferring listening to reading, and being bored when alone (Eysenck, 1990). Sociability indicates that a person shows these behavioral characteristics from one time to the next and from one social situation to the other.

Personality traits help answer two important questions. First, why do people react differently to the same situation? Second, why do people differ in the situations they approach or avoid? Consider the physical trait of being left-handed versus right-handed. Left-handed individuals find it more awkward to use right-handed scissors, to swing golf clubs designed for right-handers, and take notes sitting in classroom desk chairs designed for right-handed people. They are also more likely to be bumped by the right-handed individual when seated in the middle of a crowded dinner table. In all of these situations, left-handed individuals might feel less comfortable and efficient than right-handed persons. And, if given a choice, a left-handed person might prefer a left-handed desk chair or left-handed golf clubs, and sitting on the far left of the dinner table.

Being left- or right-handed illustrates that differences among people are associated with differences in their reaction to and preferences for different situations. Similarly, people with different personality traits also react to situations differently and prefer to be in different situations. For example, the extravert may look forward to a large party, while it makes the introvert anxious. The high-sensation seeker may explore a new restaurant in town, while the low-sensation seeker will stay with her familiar eating place. However, to use personality traits as an explanation of why people differ in what motivates them, some assumptions are necessary. Are traits categories of behavior only, or can they also serve as causes of behavior? Revelle (1987) and John and Robins (1993) describe traits as categories of behavior and also as causes of behavior. People can be categorized as left- or right-handed, but handedness also causes people to prefer different situations.

Personality Traits for Motivation

Five-factor model. Personality dimensions have the capacity to motivate different behaviors. One set of critical dimensions comes from the **five-factor model** of personality: openness-to-experience, conscientiousness, extraversion, agreeableness, and neuroticism (John, 1989, 1990; McCrae, 1989; McCrae & Costa, 1987). These five factors spell the acronym OCEAN, which helps us to remember them. Each factor can be considered a dimension, which ranges from low to high. Table 9.1 lists some trait descriptors that help define each end of the five personality dimensions (John, 1989). Extraversion and neuroticism have been studied the most extensively in their relationship to motivation. Personality dimensions are important for motivation because they help explain why people are motivated by different incentives, situations, and activities. Individuals at one end of a dimension may be motivated differently than individuals at the other end. For example, a person high in the trait of agreeableness is more motivated to grant you a favor than a person low in agreeableness. An individual high in neuroticism may be easier to induce into a bad mood, while an individual low in neuroticism is not.

The Department of Psychology, University of Oregon supports a web page by Sanjay Srivastava with information about the five-factor model of personality here: www.uoregon.edu/~sanjay/bigfive.html.

Sensation-seeking. This is another personality trait linked to differences in motivation. It is usually considered separately from the five-factor model. **Sensation-seeking** "is a trait defined by the seeking of varied, novel, complex, and intense sensations and experiences, and the willingness to take physical, social, legal, and financial risks for the sake of such experience" (Zuckerman, 1994, p. 27). Risk-taking is an accompaniment of sensation-seeking, since it is the consequence of the rewarding sensation or experience. For example, people may experiment with drugs to obtain a certain sensation or experience. The consequence, however, is that the drug may kill them (physical risk) or may cause them to get arrested (legal risk) or fined (financial risk). In addition, they may have their names published in the local paper for all to read (social risk). Yet, high-sensation seekers are willing to take greater risks only because of the rewards provided by the sensation-seeking activities and experiences. Low-sensation seekers, however, are not willing to take such risks because those same sensation-seeking activities are not rewarding to them.

Sensation-seeking is not one large trait, however, but instead consists of four factors. *Thrill-and-adventure-seeking* is the desire for sensations induced by participating in risky activities, such as sky diving and fast driving. Although people may not have participated in these activities, they

TABLE 9.1 Dimension Descriptors of Personality

Openness	
Shallow, simple, unintelligent——————————Artistic, clever, curious	
Conscientiousness	
Careless, disorderly, forgetful——————————Cautious, deliberate, dependable	
Extraversion	
Quiet, reserved, shy——————————Active, assertive, dominant	
Agreeableness	
Cold, cruel, unfriendly——————————Affectionate, cooperative, friendly	
Neuroticism	
Calm, contented, unemotional——————————Anxious, emotional, moody	

Source: Adapted from "Towards a Taxonomy of Personality Descriptors" by O. P. John, 1989, in D. M. Buss & N. Cantor (Eds.), *Personality Psychology: Recent Trends and Emerging Directions*, Table 19.2, p. 265. New York, NY: Springer Verlag.

express a desire to do so. *Experience-seeking* is the desire for mental and sensory stimulation from art, travel, drugs, and music. These individuals are characterized by desiring a more unconventional lifestyle. *Disinhibition* reflects the desire for variety attained by drinking, partying, gambling, sexual activity, and other hedonic pursuits. These people can be characterized as extraverted sensation seekers in that they seek other individuals as a source of stimulation. Finally, *boredom susceptibility* is an aversion to boredom resulting from repetitive experiences and the absence of stimulation from activities and other people. Individuals with this factor have a low tolerance for boredom and become restless in such situations (Zuckerman, 1979).

Biological Reality of Traits

Are personality traits real? Imagine people who have large feet versus those who have small feet. One could almost say that having large feet motivates a person to buy large shoes and that having small feet motivates a person to buy small shoes. These individuals are doing nothing more than buying shoes that fit. After all, good-fitting shoes allow the wearer to walk comfortably and efficiently, while poor-fitting shoes make this difficult. The point is that the foot is a real biological entity and not some hypothetical construct postulated to account for differences in shoe behavior among people. Applying this reasoning to personality traits, it is assumed that personality traits are real entities that account for differences in motivation among people.

The reality of personality traits is verified in several ways. First, **operational definitions** of personality traits refer to the procedures by which the traits are measured. This usually involves a valid psychological paper-and-pencil scale. Second, other people's appraisal externally validates the existence of a personality trait. For example, if you rate yourself as an extravert and a sensation seeker, then another person, such as a good friend, will agree with your assessment. Third, personality traits have biological correlates. Neural activity in the brain correlates or corresponds with operational measures of personality traits. Finally, the biological correlates of personality traits are genetically transmitted—that is, traits run in families. How do these trait-verification procedures work?

Operational definitions of personality traits. It is important to separate measures of a personality trait from the behavior the trait is supposed to explain. To reason that a person frequently attends parties because she is an extravert and then use frequent party attendance as evidence for extraversion provides little understanding about the motivation for party attendance. Frequent party attendance cannot serve both as evidence for the trait of extraversion and as the behavior to be explained by extraversion. Instead, it is necessary to measure a personality trait independently of the behavior that is to be explained. The existence of a personality trait is validated by how it is measured—that is, its operational definition (see Chapter 8). The *NEO Personality Inventory* measures the five personality factors presented in Table 9.1 (Costa & McCrae, 1985, 2001). The inventory consists of 243 items that a person rates on a five-point scale, which ranges from strongly disagree to strongly agree. The *Mini-Marker Set* is a much briefer scale, which involves a list of 40 adjective markers that are descriptive of the big five personality factors (see Table 9.2; Saucier, 1994, 2003). Individuals endorse each adjective in the set according to how accurately it reflects their personality. The more accurate an adjective is rated, the more indicative it is of a person's personality trait. Thompson (2008) has revised the *Mini-Marker Set* to include terms more familiar to speakers for whom English is their second language.

TABLE 9.2 The 40-Item *Mini-Marker Set*: How Accurately Can You Describe Yourself?

Please use this list of common human traits to describe yourself as accurately as possible. Describe yourself as you see yourself at the present time, not as you wish to be in the future. Describe yourself as you are generally or typically, as compared with other persons you know of the same sex and of roughly your same age. Before each trait, please write a number indicating how accurately that trait describes you, using the following rating scale:

1	2	3	4	5	6	7	8	9
Extremely Inaccurate	Very Inaccurate	Moderately Inaccurate	Slightly Inaccurate	Neither Inaccurate nor Accurate	Slightly Accurate	Moderately Accurate	Very Accurate	Extremely Accurate

The eight words underneath each of the big five personality traits are descriptive markers of that trait.

Openness	Conscientiousness	Extraversion	Agreeableness	Neuroticism
Uncreative–	Careless–	Bashful–	Cold–	Relaxed–
Unintellectual–	Disorganized–	Quiet–	Harsh–	Unenvious–
Philosophical	Inefficient–	Shy–	Rude–	Envious
Complex	Sloppy–	Withdrawn–	Unsympathetic–	Fretful
Creative	Efficient	Bold	Cooperative	Jealous
Deep	Organized	Energetic	Kind	Moody
Imaginative	Practical	Extraverted	Sympathetic	Temperamental
Intellectual	Systematic	Talkative	Warm	Touchy

Note: A negative sign after a word indicates reverse scoring: 1 = 9, 2 = 8, 3 = 7, 4 = 6, 5 = 5, etc. Sum the scores for each personality trait. A higher score indicates a greater degree of that personality trait.

Source: Adapted from The 40-Item *Mini-Marker Set* by G. Saucier, available at www.uoregon.edu/~gsaucier/gsau41.pdf.

The *Sensation Seeking Scale* was developed to measure the four factors of the sensation-seeking trait (Zuckerman, 1978, 1979, 1994). A person receives one score for each factor, ranging from zero to 10, and a total score equal to the sum of the four factors. The *Sensation Seeking Scale* assesses the thrill-and-adventure-seeking component with preferences for activities such as sky diving, mountain climbing, or motorcycle riding and assesses the experience-seeking component with whether a person would like to be hypnotized, try new foods, or experiment with drugs. The disinhibition component is measured by one's preference for emotionally expressive individuals, liking to get high, or observing sex scenes in movies. Finally, the boredom susceptibility component is measured by whether one gets bored seeing the same old faces, watching the same movie again, and preferring unpredictable friends.

The BBC Science Home Page provides a link to a complete version of the *Sensation Seeking Scale* developed by Zuckerman (1979, 1994) here: www.bbc.co.uk/science. The scale is directly available here: www.bbc.co.uk/science/humanbody/mind/surveys/sensation/index.shtml.

Traits manifested as states. Do the descriptors listed in the *Mini-Marker Set* (Table 9.2) show themselves in a person's behavior? Imagine being sent a text that asks what you have been doing for the last half-hour? Answer by rating yourself on some of the descriptors in the *Mini-Marker Set* from (1) *not at all* to (7) *very much*. Your answer shows the extent your personality traits express themselves as actual behaviors. For example, are people with trait extraversion talkative and are people with trait conscientiousness organized? A **personality state** is identical to a personality trait but consists of actual behavior for a short duration, such as a couple of hours or less. Thus, a state is the behavior that represents the trait, such as talking a lot this past half-hour signifies the trait of extraversion. In research that investigated this trait–state relationship, Fleeson and Gallagher (2009) discovered two main findings. One is that traits do express themselves as states— that is, as actual behavior typical for that trait. Second, although behavior may be typical of a trait, individuals still show great variability in how they act. For example, extraverted individuals act extraverted more frequently than introverted individuals do. However, an extravert may also act introverted in many situations and an introverted individual may act extraverted on occasion.

Personality neuroscience. Another method by which to validate personality traits is to examine their correlation with brain structures and functions. Carl Jung (1924), a one-time collaborator with Freud, was one of the first to propose that a personality trait was real in the sense that it had a biological basis. In regard to the particular disposition of a person, "It may well be that physiological causes, inaccessible to our knowledge, play a part in this" (p. 416). Gordon Allport (1937, 1966), one of the originators of the trait theory of personality, also believed that traits are real, meaning that they have direct counterparts in the brain.

Personality neuroscience studies the relationship between different personality traits and their counterparts in the brain from which the traits emerge (Allen & DeYoung, 2015). Thus, differences among personality traits should correlate with differences in the neural functioning of the brain. DeYoung and coresearchers (2010) hypothesized that brain volume might have that function. In other words, the more of a trait behavior a person exhibits, the larger should be the brain portion responsible for that behavior. In order to test this idea, the researchers measured the big five personality traits of university students with the *NEO Personality Inventory*. They also measured the volume of various regions of the students' brains using magnetic resonance imaging (MRI). Was there a correspondence between a dominant personality trait and the volume of a particular brain region that carried out the function of that trait? Indeed, this was the case for extraversion, neuroticism, agreeableness, and conscientiousness but not for openness-to-experience. The researchers discovered that those four traits were each associated with a larger volume of unique corresponding brain regions.

The trait of extraversion has received special attention for how it relates to brain volume. Specifically, how it relates to characteristics of brain neurons known as gray matter and white matter. As described in Chapter 4, the brain is composed of billions of neurons. The cell body of a neuron is where the nerve impulse originates. It tends to be a pinkish gray. A large concentration of these cell bodies is termed gray matter. The middle segment of the neuron is responsible for transmitting the neural impulse. This segment tends to be white. An assembly of neurons that project out from their cell bodies are known as white matter because of their white appearance. Does the volume of gray versus white matter help account for the distinction between introverts and extraverts? In order to find out, Forsman and coresearchers (2012) used MRI to measure volume (amount of space) taken up by gray matter and white matter in the brains of individuals who differed in the degree of extraversion. They found a negative correlation between level of extraversion and the volume of gray matter and white matter. This negative correlation means that introverts, compared to extraverts, had a greater volume of neurons in various areas of the brain. This negative relationship occurred in brain regions involved in the inhibition of behavior, which may be why introverts are more socially withdrawn than extraverts. Future brain imaging research will yield more precise correlations between brain activity and personality traits. Currently, the major conclusion is that differences in the levels of personality traits emerge from differences in corresponding brain regions.

Sensation-seeking also varies with brain function. Cservenka and coresearchers (2013), for instance, compared the brain function of low- and high-sensation seekers as they were playing a computer game. In the game, the 12- to 16-year-old participants had to choose between two choices of winning money. After making a choice, participants were informed if they won or lost. The researchers used an fMRI to examine the brain activity in response to the won and lost outcomes. Brain responses to wins and losses were different for the low- and high-sensation seekers. High-sensation seekers showed differences in activity in areas of the prefrontal cortex while low-sensation seekers showed no difference. The prefrontal cortex is the front part of the brain located behind your forehead. The brain response of high-sensation seekers was weaker to losing the bet as if they were less sensitive to negative outcomes. The low sensitivity to negative outcomes makes high-sensation seekers more willing to take risks for the sake of experiencing intense sensation. The different brain reactions of low- and high-sensation seekers indicates further that personality traits are real—that is, they correspond to differently formed structures in the brain.

Behavioral genetics. Another method of demonstrating the reality of traits is through **behavioral genetics**. This is the science of the genetic inheritance of biological traits relevant to behavior and personality. The use of this method is based on the assumption that the intricate structures and components of the brain and nervous system are genetically transmitted. Furthermore, greater genetic similarity between two individuals is associated with greater similarity in their brains and nervous systems, which, in turn, is associated with corresponding resemblances in their personality traits (Plomin et al., 2013). For instance, identical, or monozygotic (MZ), twins come from a single fertilized egg that splits in half, resulting in two genetically identical individuals who have 100 percent of their genes in common. Fraternal, or dizygotic (DZ), twins and siblings represent two different eggs fertilized by two different sperm, resulting in two individuals who share an average of 50 percent of their genes. Parents and their biological children share 50 percent of their genes, while grandparents and grandchildren share 25 percent. Parents and their adopted children have no genes in common. In regards to the similarity of personality traits, identical twins should be more similar than fraternal twins and siblings. In addition, fraternal twins, siblings, and parents with biological children should be more similar in personality traits than grandparents and grandchildren, who are more similar than two unrelated individuals. For example, twins should be more alike in extraversion (sociable, outgoing) and sensation-seeking (daring, adventure-some) than siblings, who should be more alike on those traits than unrelated children.

A YouTube video titled "What are 'twin studies'?" compares identical twins and fraternal twins to determine the effects of genes (nature) and the environment (nurture) here: www.youtube. com/watch?v=BTYCv1ObZrI.

Evidence for genetic influences on the big five personality dimensions comes from Hahn and coresearchers (2012) in Germany. Using a German version of a big five personality inventory, they measured the personality traits of pairs of identical twins, pairs of siblings, and pairs of grandparents and grandchildren. Figure 9.1 shows correlations between these three sets of individuals on the five dimensions. Identical twins with 100 percent of their genes in common were more alike than siblings, who share 50 percent of their genes. They, in turn, were more

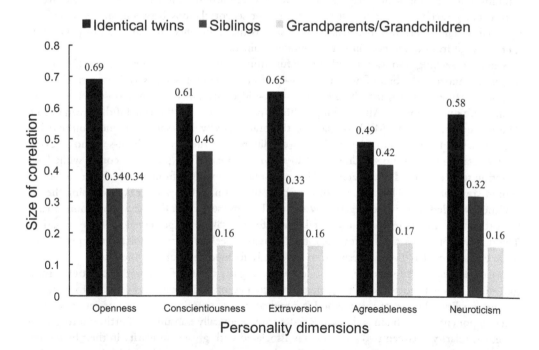

FIGURE 9.1 Personality Traits and Genetic Relatedness. Correlations between family members for the big five personality factors depend on their degree of genetic relatedness. Identical twins have 100 percent genetic relatedness, siblings have 50 percent relatedness, and grandparents and grandchildren are 25 percent related.

Source: Adapted from "The Complexity of Personality: Advantages of a Genetically Sensitive Multi-Group Design" by E. Hahn et al., 2012, *Behavior Genetics, 42*; correlation values printed in Figure 3, p. 227.

alike than grandparents and their grandchildren, who share only 25 percent of their genes. Riemann and coworkers (1997), also in Germany, used *NEO Personality Inventory* scores obtained from identical and fraternal twins. They found higher correlations for identical twins than for same-sex fraternal twins on all five personality dimensions. Notice that, in both investigations, the more alike people were genetically, the greater their similarity in personality.

One could make the argument, however, that this greater similarity between identical twins is the result of rearing practices. Perhaps identical twins are treated more alike than are fraternal twins, which results in greater behavioral similarities. Also, grandparents and grandchildren differ widely in age and most likely live in separate homes, which accounts for their personality differences. One answer to this criticism is to compare twins who have been reared together with those who have been reared in separate homes. If the environment has an effect, then twins reared together should be more alike than twins reared separately. This comparison is possible when twins are adopted by different families and reunite years later, as was true for the Jim twins in the case that opened this chapter. Loehlin (1992) summarizes the similarity in extraversion and neuroticism of twins reared together or separately in Finland, Sweden, the United States, and Great Britain. These analyses show that the correlations for both extraversion and neuroticism are greater for identical twins (MZ) than for fraternal twins (DZ), regardless of whether the twins were reared together or apart. Thus, even when rearing environments differ, greater genetic similarity corresponds to greater similarity in extraversion and neuroticism. Also, identical twins reared together were more similar than identical twins reared apart, which implies that rearing conditions have some effect on extraversion and neuroticism.

There is also strong evidence for a genetic contribution to sensation-seeking (Zuckerman, 2002). The closer the genetic relationship between individuals, the greater their similarity in sensation-seeking. Stoel and coresearchers (2006) used sensation-seeking scores available from the Netherlands twin register. Sensation-seeking had been measured with a Dutch translation of Zuckerman's *Sensation Seeking Scale*. The correlations between twins on the four sensation-seeking components was approximately twice as strong for identical twins as it was for fraternal twins. It is unlikely that the greater similarity between identical twins is the result of rearing environments. Hur and Bouchard (1997) examined the correlation between separated MZ and DZ twins on the four traits that comprise sensation-seeking. The correlations, shown in Figure 9.2, indicate greater similarities between MZ twins than DZ twins on all traits of sensation-seeking except thrill-and-adventure-seeking. Even when identical twins were reared separately in different environments, they were still similar on all four sensation-seeking traits.

The results of these behavioral genetic investigations indicate that similarity in the big five personality traits and in sensation-seeking is more the result of genetic similarity among pairs of twins than it is the result of environmental similarity, such as where the twins were reared. Bear in mind, however, that "personality traits are not inherited as such; only the biological structures coded in the DNA are inherited" (Zuckerman, 1994, p. 295). Also, as stated in Chapter 3, genes are recipes for proteins to build brains, which as we have seen account for personality traits.

Section Recap

A *personality trait* refers to consistency in a specific set of behaviors across similar situations from one time to the next. A trait can serve as a category for similar behaviors but also as a cause of

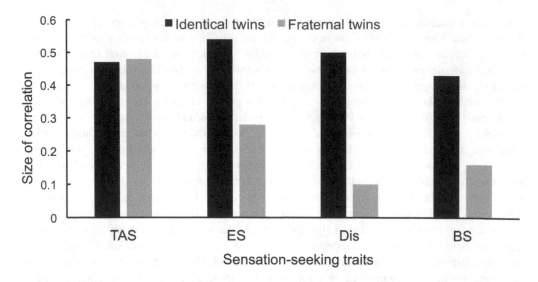

FIGURE 9.2 Sensation-Seeking of Separated Identical and Fraternal Twins. Correlations are presented between identical (MZ) and fraternal (DZ) twins for the four traits that comprise sensation-seeking: TAS = thrill-and-adventure-seeking, ES = experience-seeking, Dis = disinhibition, BS = boredom susceptibility. Correlations were higher for MZ twins than for DZ twins on all sensation-seeking factors except for thrill-and-adventure-seeking.

Source: Adapted from "The Genetic Correlation between Impulsivity and Sensation-Seeking Traits" by Y-M Hur and T. J. Bouchard, Jr., 1997, *Behavior Genetics*, 27, Table III, p. 460.

why people differ in their reactions to, and in their approach and avoidance of, different situations. Traits that form the *five-factor model* are important for motivation. They are represented by the acronym OCEAN: openness (shallow–curious), conscientiousness (careless–dependable), extraversion (quiet–active), agreeableness (unfriendly–friendly), and neuroticism (calm–moody). Another trait important for understanding motivation is *sensation-seeking*. This trait is characterized by seeking intense sensations and experiences and the willingness to take risks and incur costs for the sake of such experiences.

Several procedures help validate the reality of personality traits. First, *operational definitions* refer to the use of psychological scales to measure the extent of personality traits in a person. The *NEO Personality Inventory* and the *Mini-Marker Set* are two ways to measure the big five personality factors. Second, the appraisal of traits by other individuals correlates with a person's self-assessment of those traits. Also, a *personality state* consists of temporary behaviors that are representative of the personality trait. People still show great differences in their traits depending on the situation. Third, personality traits have biological correlates. Brain imaging techniques are used to study differences in brain structure, chemistry, and function to determine how these relate to personality and behavior. For instance, dominant personality traits are associated with greater brain areas for those traits. High-sensation seekers, compared to low-sensation seekers, show greater reactivity in their prefrontal cortex to wins versus losses. Fourth, *behavioral genetics* is the science of the inheritance of behavioral characteristics. The degree of trait similarity between two individuals increases with their genetic relatedness. Identical twins, whether reared together or apart, are more alike than fraternal twins on all big five personality traits and on sensation-seeking. The personality traits of parents and children are more alike than that of grandparents and grandchildren.

PERSONALITY TRAITS AFFECT MOTIVATION

Personality traits have a real existence. Their counterparts are in our brains. But how do personality traits affect motivation?

Personality and Environment

Two concepts from behavioral genetics—gene–environment interaction and gene–environment correlation (Loehlin, 1992; Plomin et al., 2013)—will help us understand the influence of personality traits on motivation. These two concepts will be used with personality to form trait–environment interaction and trait–environment correlation. **Trait–environment interaction** means that how individuals react to an environmental situation depends on the amount of a particular trait they possess. Individuals with different levels of a personality trait react differently. For example, an extravert enjoys a large party, while an introvert does not. An individual high in neuroticism may be more upset by unfavorable weather than an individual who is low in neuroticism. Finally, a high-sensation seeker enjoys the latest scary movie, while the low-sensation seeker feels frightened. A **trait–environment correlation** means that traits and environments are associated in their effects on behavior, because personality traits determine the situations a person chooses or alters (Plomin et al., 2013). Trait–environment correlation has three forms. A *passive correlation* occurs when the biological parents create their children's environment. For example, extraverted parents enjoy socializing and so provide a home environment for their children in which there are frequent guests. This social environment contributes to the development of the child's extraversion. Introverted parents, on the other hand, provide a home life for their children in which there are few visitors. An *evocative correlation* occurs when the individual's personality trait determines the type of reaction she or he evokes from others. For example, adults react differently to extraverted children compared to introverted children. At a school social function, individuals are more likely to speak to extraverted children and their parents compared to speaking to introverted children. An *active correlation* refers to individuals seeking and creating environments that match their personality traits (Plomin et al., 2013). For example, individuals who have a high level of openness-to-experience are more likely to visit museums than those with a low amount of this trait. Or, when given the opportunity to ride a scary roller coaster, a high-sensation seeker gives a definite yes, while a low-sensation seeker bows out. As Snyder (1983) suggests, people "may choose to enter and spend time in situations that facilitate behavior expressions of their characteristic dispositions" (p. 502). These situations allow for the satisfaction of motives that are characteristic of those personality traits. In other words, when trait levels are different, choices are different. But when trait levels are similar, choices are similar. The Jim twins, presumably having similar personality traits, selected the same vacation spots, cars, cigarettes, and part-time law enforcement work.

Cybernetic Big Five Theory

It is a given that goals motivate behavior. The first step in the goal motivation process is the selection of and commitment to a goal. For example, a high school senior selects the goal of

TABLE 9.3 Personality Traits Determine Goal Selection

Big Five Trait	Type of Goal	Example
Openness-to-Experience	Approach cognitive goals that visualize possibilities and advance creative achievement in the arts and sciences	A person visits art museums, enjoys abstract art, listens to non-Western music, and ponders literary quotations
Conscientiousness	Approach and commit to socially respected long-term goals instead of more immediate short-term alternative goals	Socially respected goal of being students: be organized, not lazy, control impulses, and be responsible for their grades
Extraversion	Approach goals that provide rewards, such as winning a lottery or cooperating with others to achieve a task	Mirror (mimic) your partner's actions to meet the goal of establishing rapport that will lead to group success
Agreeableness	Approach social goals that benefit the group and cooperate with others to achieve goals; avoid more selfish goals	A person does volunteer work, donates money to charitable causes, and helps others
Neuroticism	Approach visceral goals that relieve negative feelings; avoid goals that lead to negative affect, threat or punishment	A person engages in behaviors with the goal of relieving distress, e.g., smoking, drinking, drug use, and risky sex

earning a university degree and commits by applying for admission. Do any of the big five personality traits influence the type of goal an individual favors? For example, does a dominant personality trait favor one type of career over another? Yes, according to **cybernetic big five theory**, which proposes that the big five personality traits influence what type of goals individuals choose (DeYoung, 2015). The selection of a goal illustrates trait–environment correlation. In other words, the environment offers goal opportunities, but the individual's dominant personality trait determines the nature of selected goal. Table 9.3 describes how a dominant personality trait favors the selection and approach to a particular goal. All people may entertain the goals in Table 9.3 at some time. However, a particular personality may give that goal greater emphasis.

Furthermore, the pursuit of a selected goal gives rise to personality state relevant behaviors (McCabe & Fleeson, 2016). For instance, suppose you are assigned either a social goal or a work goal. For the social goal, you are to connect with other people and make them laugh. The trait of extraversion is relevant for this goal. For the work goal, you are to get things done and use your time effectively. The trait of conscientiousness is relevant for this goal. After trying to achieve these goals, participants filled out a state personality inventory that measured extraversion and conscientiousness. The state ratings indicated that participants acted more extraverted when trying to connect with people and to make them laugh. On the other hand, participants acted more conscientiously when their goal was to accomplish things and make effective use of their time. Thus, the nature of the goal can motivate a set of personality state behaviors that are effective for achieving that goal (McCabe & Fleeson, 2016).

Effects of Openness-to-Experience on Motivation

Would you be motivated to visit an art museum, attend a concert of non-Western (Asian, Oriental) music, and afterwards eat some escargots? The extent of your motivation for these activities depends on your level of openness-to-experience. A question that illustrates a trait–environment interaction asks whether liking art depends on a person's level of openness-to-experience? An answer comes from a massive correlational study of over 90,000 individuals, who participated in an Internet study in the United Kingdom. The participants filled out a personality questionnaire and also rated how much they liked 24 paintings that represented Renaissance, Impressionist, Japanese, and Cubist styles. The results clearly showed that openness predicts liking for art. Individuals who were higher in openness-to-experience liked all forms of art more (Chamorro-Premuzic et al., 2009). Similar to art appreciation is interest in and understanding of literary sayings, such as those at the top of each chapter in this book. Fayn and coresearchers (2015) measured the level of openness-to-experience in nearly 100 university students and then had them rate seven literary quotations for interest and understanding. Their results showed that openness correlated with students' interest and understanding of the quotations.

If people are interested in art and literature, then does this translate into establishing goals relevant to those areas? As indicated in Table 9.3, individuals high on openness-to-experience pursue cognitive goals that allow them to be creative in the arts and sciences. To determine the validity of this claim, Kaufman and coresearchers (2015) questioned over 1,000 individuals in four different samples regarding their level of openness-to-experience and their achievements in the arts and sciences. The *Creative Achievement Questionnaire* was used to measure people's achievements in these areas. A sample question is "my work [creative writing] has won an award or prize." The results of this correlational study showed that higher levels of openness-to-experience were associated with greater achievements in the arts and sciences. Thus, this instance of trait–environment correlation shows that individuals high in openness-to-experience are motivated to select and achieve goals related to creative achievements.

Effects of Extraversion on Motivation

The following questions illustrate the relationship between extraversion and motivation. (1) Trait–environment interaction: how would you react at a party where you did not know most of the guests? (2) Trait–environment correlation: on Saturday night would you prefer to attend a large party or watch a movie with a few friends? The answer to each question depends on a person's degree of extraversion. Extraverts would react and choose one way, and introverts another.

Extraversion–environment interaction. The differences between introverts and extraverts account for the variation in their reactions to the same situation. To illustrate, extraverts are easier to put into a good mood than introverts. Larsen and Ketelaar (1989, 1991) had extraverts and introverts imagine as vividly as possible either a pleasant or unpleasant experience happening to them. The pleasant experience consisted of imagining that they had won a $50,000 lottery and were vacationing in Hawaii. The unpleasant experience consisted of imagining being expelled from school in an embarrassing manner and also having a close friend die. A control group of introverts and extraverts were asked to imagine visiting a supermarket and taking a car trip on the highway. Following this, participants were asked to rate their level of positive mood and their level of negative mood. Extraverts developed a greater positive mood than did introverts as a result of imagining the pleasant experience. The result of imagining the unpleasant experience, however, did not necessarily put introverts in a more negative mood than it did extraverts.

This susceptibility toward positive moods may result from the relationship between extraversion and **reward sensitivity**. This sensitivity refers to extraverts reacting more positively to rewards that put them in a good mood. But what is a good or positive mood composed of? Can it have a quality of activation or excitement such as being excited, elated, and euphoric? But can it also have a pure hedonic quality but of low activation, such as being happy, cheerful, and content? Thus, are extraverts more susceptible toward energetic arousal, such as being excited or elated, or are they more susceptible to a more positive hedonic tone, such as being happy or content? Smillie and coresearchers (2012) attempted to answer this question by exposing introverts and extraverts to one of three mood induction procedures. Based on their personality test scores, participants who scored one standard deviation below the mean (bottom 16 percent) were defined as introverts and those one standard deviation above the mean (top 16 percent) were defined as extraverts. Next, the introverted and extraverted participants were randomly assigned to one of three conditions. In the neutral condition, participants imagined shopping at a supermarket while listening to neutral music. In the pleasant mood condition, participants imagined lying on a beach in the warm sun while listening to relaxing happy music. In the appetitive reward condition, participants imagined having won a lottery for over $1,000 while listening to exciting waltz music. Following the mood induction procedure, participants rated themselves on their level of hedonic tone and energetic arousal. Adjectives such as cheerful and happy reflected hedonic tone, while adjectives such as alert and vigorous reflected energetic arousal. The results showed that introverts and extraverts did not differ in hedonic tone in any of the three conditions. However, as Figure 9.3 shows, extraverts (compared to introverts) showed greater energetic arousal as a result of the appetitive reward condition but not as a result of the pleasant mood and neutral conditions. The greater energetic arousal of extraverts indicates that they are more sensitive to and react more strongly to rewarding stimuli such as winning a lottery. These results are an instance of trait–environment interaction: how individuals react depends on their level of extraversion. If introverted, react one way; if extraverted, react another way.

Extraversion–environment correlation. The results in Figure 9.3 show that extraverts (compared to introverts) experience more energetic arousal in reaction to rewarding activities such as imagining winning a lottery or seeing an exciting chase scene where the hero catches the villain. In addition to reacting positively to rewarding activities, extraverts are more motivated to spend time in such activities. To illustrate, Oerlemans and Bakker (2014) hypothesized that extraverts enjoy and spend more time on reward pursuit activities. These activities are "work related activities with financial rewards" and contrast with merely pleasurable activities, such as "watching TV, reading a book, listening to music, shopping and relaxing" (p. 14). To test their hypothesis, they had over 1,300 Dutch participants keep a daily diary in which they described their activities and the duration of those activities, the involvement of others, and the experienced happiness during the activity. Happiness was rated with the scale 0 = *extremely unhappy* to 10 = *extremely happy*. The participants also filled out the extraversion portion of the *NEO Personality Inventory* (see Table 9.2). The results confirmed the researchers' hypotheses. First, extraverts (compared to introverts) spent more time on reward pursuit activities and more time on activities with other people. They did not differ from introverts in pursuit of pleasurable activities. Second, extraverts

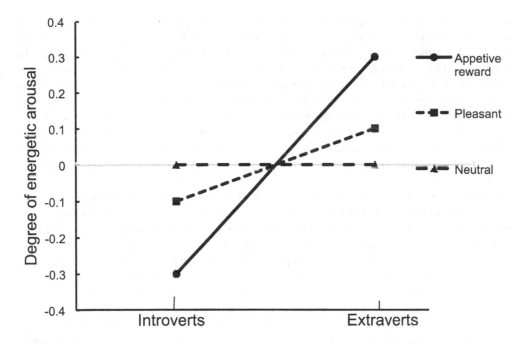

FIGURE 9.3 Energetic Arousal in Extraverts. Introverted and extraverted participants imagined grocery shopping (neutral), lying on a beach (pleasant), or winning a lottery (appetitive reward) while also listening to music that matched the imagined situations. Afterwards, the participants rated themselves on energetic arousal, such as being active, energetic, and alert. In the appetitive reward condition, imagining winning a lottery produced higher energetic arousal in extraverts compared to introverts. The other two imaginary scenes did not affect the energetic arousal of introverts and extraverts differently. The horizontal line represents the mean energetic arousal of both groups combined.

Source: From "Do Extraverts Get More Bang for the Buck? Refining the Affective-Reactivity Hypothesis of Extraversion" by L. D. Smillie et al., 2012, *Journal of Personality and Social Psychology, 103,* Figure 2, p. 316. Copyright 2012 by American Psychological Association.

also enjoyed reward pursuit activities and being with others more than introverts did. Extraverts and introverts, however, did not differ in their enjoyment of pleasurable activities. As an instance of trait–environment correlation, extraverts are more motivated to pursue reward activities. They are also more motivated to spend time with others because of the greater amounts of happiness that those activities provide (Oerlemans & Bakker, 2014).

In addition to spending more time on reward pursuit activities, extraverts are also more motivated than introverts to achieve a goal that involves other individuals. Extraverts are motivated to work harder to achieve a social goal. To illustrate, Duffy and Chartrand (2015) had pairs of participants work on a goal of describing photographs of faces or listing words from a specific category. Prior to this task, participants were randomly assigned to either an affiliation goal condition or nonaffiliation goal condition. For the nonaffiliation goal, participants were simply given task instructions about describing faces or listing words. But for the affiliation goal condition, participant were also told that "the next task had the best results when both people got along well" (p. 1797). One way people get along is for them to mimic (mirror) one another's behavior. In this experiment, one of the participants had been instructed to continuously touch her face and hair. The other participants' motivation to build rapport (to get along well) would show by how much they mimicked—that is, also touched their face and hair. To measure extraversion, participants filled out the extraversion portion of the 40-item *Mini-Marker Set* (see Table 9.2). The results showed that in the affiliation goal condition, extraverts (compared to introverts) showed more mimicry—that is, they touched their hair and face more than introverts did. The mimicry by introverts and extraverts did not differ in the nonaffiliation goal condition. Thus, in this instance of trait–environment correlation, extraverts were more motivated to do well on these tasks by engaging in mimicry, since that would lead to rapport and better goal performance (Duffy & Chartrand, 2015).

Extraversion and the channeling of motives. The last chapter showed that psychological needs are stable individual differences that have motivational properties. They push individuals into action. Personality traits are also stable individual differences in behavior but have no motivational properties. However, as Table 9.3 indicates, traits determine the preferences that people have for various goals. Differences in the degree of psychological needs produce differences in behavior. Differences in personality traits are also associated with differences in behavior.

A reason for the motivational distinction between needs and traits is that their studies have separate histories in psychology. However, there are attempts to link the effects of needs and traits for the motivation of behavior. An example is to link extraversion to the need for affiliation and to the need for power. Winter and associates (1998) express this idea in their **channeling hypothesis**, which states that personality traits channel or convey how psychological motives are represented and satisfied. To support their theory, they used the results of important longitudinal studies to illustrate how extraversion channels the expression of the affiliation motive and the power motive. The use of longitudinal data makes it possible to show how over a long period of time extraversion channels motive expression.

How would introverts and extraverts differ in their attempts to satisfy their affiliation motives? Winter and associates (1998) hypothesized that extraverts would channel the expression of their affiliation motive by doing volunteer work. Such activity would provide the means for satisfying their affiliation motive along with the opportunity for meeting new people. Introverts with a high affiliation motive, however, would shy away from volunteer work as a way of satisfying their need for affiliation, since they do not particularly enjoy meeting new people. A low need for affiliation also would not motivate introverted or extraverted women to do volunteer work. In studies consulted by these researchers, Mills College women had their need for affiliation and for power measured with the TAT at age 21 and their level of extraversion measured at age 43. Radcliffe College women had their need for affiliation and for power measured with the TAT at age 18 and their level of extraversion measured at age 43. The results confirmed the predictions for both the Mills and Radcliffe samples. Extraverted women with a high affiliation motive sought to do volunteer work at age 43, while introverted women with a high affiliation motive shied away from it.

How would an extravert and an introvert differ in their attempts to satisfy the power motive? Entering an impact career such as business, education, psychotherapy, or journalism is a way of expressing one's power motive (Jenkins, 1994). Winter and associates (1998) hypothesized that extraverts with a high power motive would enter high-impact careers, since these provided opportunities for interacting with other individuals. Introverts with a high power motive, however, would shy away from such careers and would channel their power motive in some alternative career direction. The results show that extraverted Radcliffe graduates with a high need for power selected high-impact careers. Introverted Radcliffe graduates did not use high-impact careers to satisfy their power motives. For Mills women graduates, however, impact careers were selected by both introverts and extraverts to satisfy their power motives. One reason for this difference between the two college samples is that Radcliffe women entered more traditionally male impact careers (psychiatrist, professor), while Mills women entered more traditionally female careers (social worker, elementary school teacher) (Winter et al., 1998).

The channeling hypothesis is an instance of trait–environment correlation. A woman's level of extraversion determined the manner in which she chose to satisfy her affiliation motive and her power motive. For instance, for the affiliation motive, if extraverted, then do volunteer work but if introverted, do something else. In satisfying the power motive of Radcliffe graduates, if extraverted, then pursue a high-impact career, but if introverted select a different career.

Effects of Neuroticism on Motivation

Neuroticism refers to a complex of trait dimensions that ranges from being characteristically nonemotional (calm, contented) at the low end to being emotional (anxious, quickly aroused) at the high end. What types of situations produce different reactions in individuals low versus high in neuroticism? How do those individuals differ in the situations they select or modify?

Neuroticism–environment interaction. Individuals high in neuroticism are easier to put in a negative mood than those low in neuroticism. Rusting and Larsen (1997) had participants imagine pleasant scenes, such as winning the lottery, or unpleasant scenes, such as having a friend die of cancer. Follow-up mood measures showed a greater degree of negative mood in high- compared to low-neuroticism individuals. Neuroticism did not correlate with the degree of positive mood that had been induced in the participants. Suls and associates (1998) had male participants who resided in the community record the occurrence of problems and moods several times per day over eight days. The degree of negative mood depended both on daily problems and on the level of neuroticism. Daily problems put everyone in a negative mood, but the level of negative mood was greater for the more neurotic men. For relationship satisfaction, Watson and colleagues (2000) found that, at least for women, neuroticism correlated negatively with satisfaction. Women high in neuroticism were less satisfied with their married or dating relationship than were women low in neuroticism. However, neuroticism had no effect on men's satisfaction. Neuroticism also has a negative impact on career satisfaction. Employees high in neuroticism tended to evaluate their careers more negatively than employees low in neuroticism (Seibert & Kraimer, 2001).

Neuroticism–environment correlation. People's level of neuroticism determines the extent they choose to engage in risky behavior to enhance their positive feelings or lessen their negative feelings. For instance, Mohr and coresearchers (2001) examined the link between negative interpersonal exchanges and drinking over a 30-day period in a community sample of adults. Negative exchanges were measured by the answers to such questions as: did anyone yell at you, take advantage of you, or prevent you from working on your goals today? If any of these negative social events happened, then how likely is an individual to have a drink alone that evening? The results showed that individuals high in neuroticism coped with negative events by drinking alone more frequently than individuals low in neuroticism. Figure 9.4 provides a clear indication of a trait–environment correlation. High-neuroticism individuals chose to increase their number of solitary drinks in response to an increase in the number of negative interpersonal exchanges they experienced. Low-neuroticism individuals did not show this increase.

As indicated in Table 9.3, individuals high in neuroticism try to avoid goals that are linked to negative affect, threat, or punishment. The possibility of goal failure suggests an instance of negative affect in the form of disappointment, for example, avoiding certain courses or majors because of the disappointment that failure in those areas will bring. However, there are instances when individuals high in neuroticism are willing to experience negative affect to help motivate them to achieve difficult goals. Tamir (2005) induced either positive or negative affect in her participants by having them imagine and then write about a truly happy event or a truly worrisome event in their lives. Afterwards, participants were asked to solve as many of 45 anagrams as possible in five minutes. Does a participant's happy or worried mood affect anagram solutions? There was no difference for participants low in neuroticism. However, participants high in neuroticism solved approximately 10 more anagrams when in a worried compared to a happy mood. Worry as an instance of state neuroticism enhanced performance. Worry increases the motivation of individuals high in neuroticism to do well or in this case to avoid doing poorly on the anagram task.

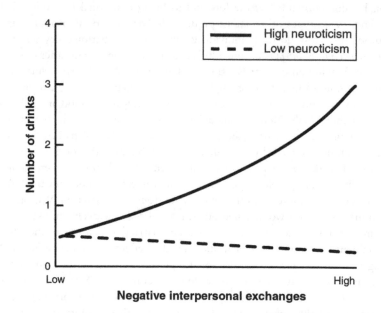

FIGURE 9.4 Neuroticism and Drinking Alone. The impact of negative interpersonal exchanges is different for individuals high in neuroticism compared to those low in neuroticism. High-neuroticism individuals choose to increase their solitary drinking as the number of negative interpersonal exchanges increases. Low-neuroticism individuals are unaffected.

Source: From "Daily Interpersonal Experiences, Context, and Alcohol Consumption: Crying in Your Beer and Toasting Good Times" by C. D. Mohr et al., 2001, *Journal of Personality and Social Psychology, 80,* Figure 2, p. 496. Copyright 2001 by American Psychological Association.

Effects of Conscientiousness on Motivation

A person with a high level of conscientiousness is competent, orderly, dutiful, achievement-striving, self-disciplined, and deliberate in her actions. The effects of this personality trait are often seen in goals that require long-term commitment (see Table 9.3). Commitment to long-term goals is reflected in various behaviors, such as academic work and health-related activities. In the case of academic work, Noftle and Robins (2007) examined the relationship between conscientiousness and GPA at two different University of California campuses. The major finding in all cases was that conscientiousness correlated with GPA even after indicators of scholastic aptitude were factored out. Simply put, more-conscientious students earned higher grades! Furthermore, students who became more conscientious as their academic careers progressed over the four years were also inclined to earn higher grades. The increase in grades with conscientiousness was the result of what the researchers termed academic effort. For example, students were asked, "on average, how many hours a week (outside of class time) have you spent on school work the current semester [quarter]?" (p. 121). More-conscientious students reported that they put in more academic effort, which was associated with earning higher grades (Noftle & Robins, 2007).

A goal of good health requires a lifetime commitment. Conscientiousness is associated with lifestyle behaviors that promote healthful living and disassociated with unhealthy lifestyle choices. Bogg and Roberts (2004) examined numerous studies that covered the relationship between conscientiousness and health-related behaviors. On the whole, the authors found that increases in the level of conscientiousness were associated with decreases in excessive alcohol use, illicit drug use, unhealthy eating, risky driving, risky sex, and tobacco use. Individuals lower in conscientiousness were more likely to engage in these health-threatening behaviors. Conversely, individuals higher in conscientiousness were more likely to engage in health-promoting behaviors. Being motivated to engage in such behaviors resulted in high-conscientiousness people having better health in general (Atherton et al., 2014).

Effects of Agreeableness on Motivation

Individuals high in agreeableness tend to be trusting, compliant, and helpful. They are oriented toward goals that will allow cooperation with others at the expense of forgoing their own personal goals. So would they be more likely to help individuals in distress? Consider the following common scenario: Imagine driving and seeing an individual whose car has broken down along the side of the road. How likely is it that you will risk being late somewhere in order to help this individual if he or she was a stranger, a friend, or one of your siblings? Consider the following extraordinary scenario: how likely would you enter a burning house at the risk of death in order to save the life of the occupant if that person were a stranger, a friend, or one of your siblings? Are individuals high, compared to low, in the trait of agreeableness more or less likely to help? Graziano and coresearchers (2007) presented these two scenarios to university students in order to answer this question. Based on a personality questionnaire, participants were divided into two groups: low agreeableness and high agreeableness. The results for the first scenario are shown in Figure 9.5. Individuals high in agreeableness reported a greater willingness to be late in order to help a stranded motorist provided that individual was a friend or sibling. There was no difference in the likelihood of helping a stranger. However, when it came to saving strangers from a burning house, high-agreeable people were a bit more likely to do so than low-agreeable

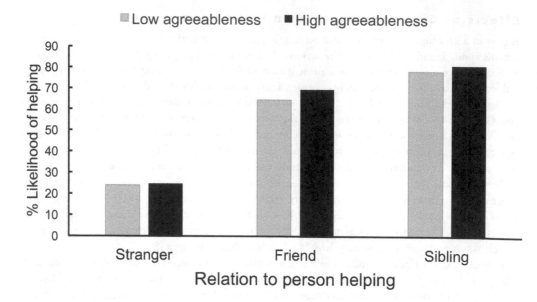

FIGURE 9.5 Agreeableness and Helping. Participants high in agreeableness were more likely to help a stranded motorist when that person was a friend or sibling. There was no difference between low and high agreeableness in the likelihood of helping strangers.

Source: Adapted from "Agreeableness, Empathy, and Helping: A Person × Situation Perspective" by W. G. Graziano et al., 2007, *Journal of Personality and Social Psychology, 93*, p. 586.

people were. Low- and high-agreeable individuals were equally likely to save friends and siblings from burning buildings. Thus, agreeable people are more likely to help individuals who are in distress. However, helping also depends on the situation and on the relationship between the helper and the person helped. Individuals in grave danger are helped nearly equally by low- and high-agreeable people. However, when helping creates an inconvenience, such as being late, highly agreeable people are more likely to help.

Effects of Multiple Traits on Motivation

The concept of trait–environment correlation emphasizes that an individual's dominant personality trait determines her choice of situations and activities. However, rather than operating separately, traits can also operate together to motivate behavior. In such cases, the combined effect of several personality traits would determine choice. Furthermore, since personality traits are enduring characteristics, their effects accumulate over the life of an individual. Thus, a particular combination of traits might have a quite noticeable effect over the lifetime of an individual. What are some of the cumulative effects of combined personality traits on behaviors regarding Internet usage, prejudice, subjective well-being, coping, and body weight?

Internet usage. Does the extent of Internet usage correlate with an individual's personality traits? This question was examined in university students by Landers and Lounsbury (2006). Students could indicate their Internet usage along eight incremental steps that ranged from less than one hour per week to more than 10 hours per day. Internet usage could involve communication (e-mail or chat), leisure (music, shopping, games), and academics (research, course participation). Agreeableness, conscientiousness, and extraversion correlated negatively with Internet usage. However, in the case of conscientiousness, Internet usage for academic purposes increased. Overall, the researchers concluded that "more introverted, less agreeable, and less conscientious students engaged in higher levels of Internet usage" (p. 288). Perhaps less agreeable students find that fewer demands for cooperation are placed on them when they use the Internet. High conscientiousness may discourage use of the Internet for leisure because these individuals spend more time in structured student activities such as sports or clubs. In addition, being high in conscientiousness increases the motivation to use the Internet for academic purposes. Finally, extraverted students may enjoy real social encounters in place of the more solitary encounters that the Internet provides (Landers & Lounsbury, 2006).

Prejudice. What is your attitude to groups or individuals who are different from you? This question taps into an individual's prejudices. The definition of prejudice usually involves negative attitudes and feelings about a social group or its members. Jackson and Poulsen (2005) reasoned that prejudice could be tempered by the amount of favorable contact that a person has with another group or individual. This contact, however, may depend on the strength of certain personality traits. Based on the **selection hypothesis**, an individual's personality determines the type of contact sought with members of other groups. The selection hypothesis is an instance of trait–environment correlation, since personality is associated with the amount of group contact. Jackson and Poulsen (2005) hypothesized that individuals high on openness-to-experience would be more likely to seek contact with minority group members, such as African-Americans or Asian-Americans. Furthermore, they reasoned that the quality of contact should be greater with increases in openness-to-experience but also with agreeableness. In their investigation, after the big five personality traits were assessed, students described the amount of their contact experiences with either African-Americans or Asian-Americans, followed by an assessment of their level of prejudice toward those groups. The results indicated that, as the trait of openness increased, the frequency of group contact increased. In addition, as openness and agreeableness increased, the quality of contact also increased. Individuals high in openness and high in agreeableness had lower negative attitudes and higher positive attitudes toward those groups as a result of their contact experiences (Jackson & Poulsen, 2005). It is important to note that individuals high in openness-to-experience are more willing to initiate contact with members of other groups. As a result, they, along with people high in agreeableness, report those experiences as positive, friendly, and pleasant.

Subjective well-being. Happiness or subjective well-being is captured by answers to such questions as: how much control do you have over your life, how satisfied are you with life currently, and overall? How free are individuals to determine their level of happiness? As described earlier, personality is partly under genetic control. The effects of genes, over which an individual has little control, imply that people's personality traits are determined and so is their level of happiness, which stems from personality. Evidence for this conclusion comes from examining subjective well-being in twins. Weiss and coresearchers (2008) measured the five personality traits (see Table 9.1) and levels of subjective well-being of 365 pairs of identical twins and 688 pairs of fraternal twins. First, in regards to personality, identical twins were more similar than fraternal twins were, which replicates the results in Figure 9.1. Second, in regards to subjective well-being, identical twins were also more alike than fraternal twins were. In this case, greater genetic similarity corresponded to greater similarity in subjective well-being. Third, neuroticism correlated negatively and extraversion correlated positively with subjective well-being. In other words, increases in neuroticism were associated with decreases in subjective well-being whereas increases in extraversion went with increases in subjective well-being. To a lesser extent, increases in conscientiousness were also associated with greater subjective well-being. A conclusion is that people's happiness depends partly on their genetically determined personality traits (Weiss et al., 2008).

Another way of examining the relationship between personality traits and happiness is to compare individuals at the extreme of the happiness dimensions (low to high). Diener and Seligman (2002) identified 22 (top 10 percent) very happy and 24 (bottom 10 percent) very unhappy university students out of an initial sample of 222. The classification of whether one is happy or unhappy depended on a screening procedure that involved four psychological scales, memory for positive and negative events, and an evaluation by people who knew the students. The results in Figure 9.6 clearly show that very happy and unhappy individuals differ on three of the personality factors. Very happy students were significantly lower on neuroticism and higher on extraversion and agreeableness. They did not differ in conscientiousness and openness-to-experience. Figure 9.6 shows that neuroticism and extraversion appear to be the most influential personality factors governing happiness. Hayes and Joseph (2003) also found that high neuroticism was associated with lower subjective well-being. High extraversion and conscientiousness, on the other hand, went along with high subjective well-being. Weiss and coresearchers (2008) raise the possibility that how well a person can recover from events that made them unhappy depends on the individual's dominant traits. Perhaps extraverts and individuals low in neuroticism can recover more easily from stressful events compared to individuals high in neuroticism.

Personality effects during coping. Imagine that an important project involving an oral presentation is due in one of your classes. As described in Chapter 7, individuals can cope with the potential stressors directly (problem-focused coping) to reduce their negative impact. For example, a student could cope by rehearsing her presentation in front of friends prior to the due date. Individuals can also employ emotion-focused coping, which involves reducing the negative impact of a potential stressor by avoiding, escaping, or withdrawing from it. In other words, the stressor is not dealt with directly. For example, the student could procrastinate and not begin work until the night before the due date. In this manner, she reduces the distress of the forthcoming assignment for a while by neither dealing nor thinking about it.

Does an individual's dominant personality trait determine exposure to stressors and the selection of a coping strategy? This question concerns trait–environment correlation. It turns out that the exposure to stressors and the selection of a coping strategy do indeed depend on the levels of an individual's personality traits (Carver & Connor-Smith, 2010). First, Carver and Connor-Smith note that personality traits help determine the degree of exposure to stressors. For instance, individuals high in conscientiousness plan their futures better and formulate long-term goals (see Table 9.3), which results in a decreased likelihood of unforeseen stressors. For example, they are more likely to make time in order to rehearse their oral presentation for class. Individuals high in agreeableness experience fewer stressors from interpersonal conflict because they are more cooperative and emphasize social goals (see Table 9.3). Individuals high in neuroticism, on the

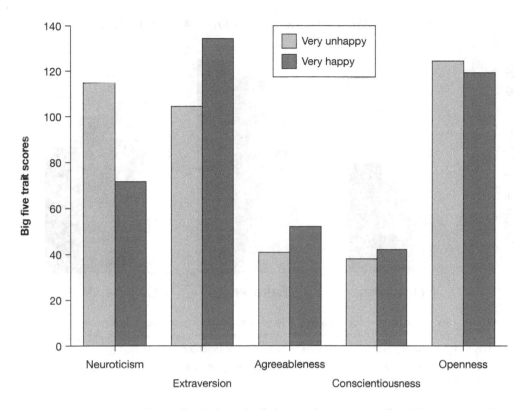

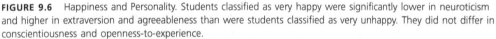

FIGURE 9.6 Happiness and Personality. Students classified as very happy were significantly lower in neuroticism and higher in extraversion and agreeableness than were students classified as very unhappy. They did not differ in conscientiousness and openness-to-experience.

Source: Adapted from "Very Happy People" by E. Diener and M. E. P. Seligman, 2002, *Psychological Science, 13*, Table 3, p. 84.

other hand, experience higher levels of interpersonal conflict. Consequently, they experience greater levels of stress. Second, Carver and Connor-Smith note that the manner of coping with stressors and stress also varies with personality traits. For instance, individuals high in conscientiousness, extraversion, and openness-to-experience are more likely to cope by direct engagement with stressors, such as reinterpreting the problem, seeking assistance, or solving it directly. Individuals high in neuroticism, on the other hand, evaluate stressors more negatively. In addition, they are more likely to cope by disengaging from the stressor, such as escaping from it and engaging in wishful thinking, which is the desire that the stressor will vanish or that the individual would feel differently about it. Individuals high in conscientiousness and agreeableness, on the other hand, are less likely to use disengagement.

Personality and weight gain across the life-span. Trait–environment correlation can refer to the association between specific personality traits and the choices people make continuously. The cumulative effects of such choices become apparent, for example, in people's weight changes over

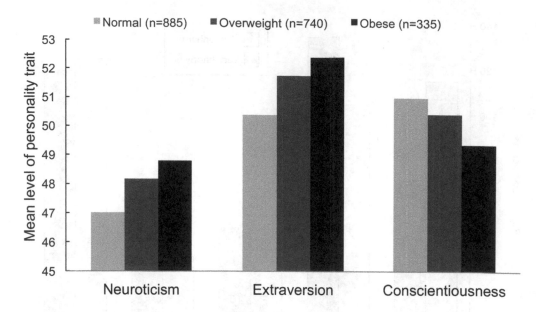

FIGURE 9.7 Association between Weight Gain and Personality. The amount of weight people gain over their lifetime depends on their dominant personality traits. Greater weight gain is associated with higher levels of neuroticism, higher levels of extraversion, and lower levels of conscientiousness.

Source: Adapted from "Personality and Obesity Across the Adult Life Span" by A. R. Sutin et al., 2011, *Journal of Personality and Social Psychology, 101*, Table 1, p. 583.

their lifetime. The accumulation of daily choices of how much to eat, drink, and exercise becomes apparent in a person's weight, body fat, waist, and hip size. Do people's personalities determine the likelihood of how much to eat, drink, and exercise? To answer this question, Sutin and coresearchers (2011) examined weight changes over a 50-year period of 1,960 individuals as a function of their personality. At age 57, measurements were taken of their big five personality traits and their body mass index (BMI) (BMI = weight (kilograms)/height (meters)^2). The researchers categorized people into three weight categories: normal (BMI < 24.99), overweight (BMI = 25–29.99), and obese (BMI ≥ 30). The results in Figure 9.7 indicate that the three weight categories were associated with the level of neuroticism, extraversion, and conscientiousness. Overweight and obese, as compared to normal-weight, individuals were higher in neuroticism and extraversion and lower in conscientiousness.

Specific aspects of personality traits determine weight gain (Sutin et al., 2011). One aspect of neuroticism is impulsiveness, which refers to the tendency to choose small immediate rewards in contrast to a large delayed reward. For example, consider a choice between the immediate reward of delicious dessert versus a delayed reward of keeping a trim figure. Individuals high in neuroticism are more impulsive and are thus likely over the years to choose dessert at the cost of weight gain—that is, the loss of being trim. Excitement-seeking is an aspect of extraversion that was strongly associated with weight gain over the years. Sutin and coresearchers speculate that excitement-seeking disposes an individual to seek food and alcohol at the cost of weight gain. A low level of conscientiousness is associated with a lack of self-discipline. Such an individual is more likely to forgo a healthy diet when faced with the temptation of sweets and alcohol. Again, the effects of such choices accumulate over the years. Being cynical, aggressive, and arrogant are characteristic of individuals who are low in agreeableness. Sutin and coresearchers discovered that such individuals are more likely to gain weight over their lifetime compared to individuals high in agreeableness. Again, a person's dominant personality traits help determine their motivation regarding eating and drinking.

Effects of Sensation-Seeking on Motivation

What are your sensation-seeking tendencies like? Would you like to sample some raw oysters or frog legs? Would you enjoy the newest roller coaster ride at an amusement park? Do you consider tattoos and body piercings attractive? How people answer these questions depends on their level of sensation-seeking.

Differences in motivation can stem from differences in sensation-seeking. The sensation-seeking–environment interaction implies that the sensation experienced as pleasurable by a high-sensation seeker is aversive to a low-sensation seeker. And a pleasurable sensation for a low-sensation seeker may be aversive for a high-sensation seeker. Also, since sensations result from activities, high- and low-sensation seekers engage in different activities in order to attain their most pleasurable level of sensation. In addition, different behaviors are selected, depending on whether the person is seeking sensation from thrill-and-adventure-seeking, experience-seeking, disinhibition, or boredom susceptibility. Zuckerman (1994) has provided a rich source of evidence indicating that, in comparison to low-sensation seekers, high-sensation seekers have engaged in a wide variety of behaviors that provide intense sensations and experiences. Many high-sensation behaviors, however, are illicit, such as substance abuse, reckless driving, theft, vandalism, and risky sexual behavior (Wagner, 2001).

The sensation-seeking–environment correlation implies a difference in the choice of activity between high- and low-sensation seekers. For instance, individuals who participate in high-risk sports are more likely to be high- rather than low-sensation seekers. Freixanet (1991) compared alpinists (those who had participated in several expeditions to the Himalayas), mountaineers (mountain climbers and skiers), other sportsmen (scuba divers, water skiers, white-water canoeists, sky divers, race car drivers), and a control group of individuals who did not participate in any sports. All three sports groups scored higher on thrill-and-adventure-seeking and experience-seeking and had higher total sensation-seeking scores than did the control group. A major finding of this study was that the biggest difference was between sports groups and the controls; also, there was little difference among the sports groups. In comparing hang gliders, auto-racers, and bowlers, Straub (1982) found that hang gliders and auto-racers scored higher on all components of the sensation-seeking scale. Men and women who canoe and kayak white-water rivers involving long rapids and moderate waves have higher thrill-and-adventure-seeking scores than the general population. Higher thrill-and-adventure-seeking scores also are associated with lower anxiety levels prior to launching into the river (Campbell et al., 1993).

Sensation-seeking is associated with stimulus preference. For instance, high- and low-sensation seekers differ in the type of humor they prefer. Using factor analysis, Ruch has classified humor into three factors: incongruity resolution, nonsense, and sex (see Ruch & Hehl, 1998). Incongruity resolution humor involves jokes and cartoons in which the incongruity is completely resolvable. Nonsense humor contains incongruities that are either not or only partially resolvable or create new incongruities on resolution. The sex factor refers to jokes and cartoons having a sexual theme. Ruch (1988) found that participants high in experience-seeking and boredom suscept-ibility prefer nonsense humor over incongruity resolution humor. Participants high in disinhibition preferred humor based on sexual content more than did participants low in disinhibition. High- and low-sensation seekers also differ in their preference for eroticism. For example, Zuckerman (1978) found that high-disinhibition and experience-seeking participants prefer viewing erotic films more than low-disinhibition and experience-seeking participants do.

Section Recap

Realizing that people differ in personality traits helps us understand why they are motivated by different incentives, goals, and activities. First, individuals with a high level of a particular trait act as the trait name implies: open to experience, conscientious, extraverted, agreeable, and neurotic. Sensation seekers are individuals willing to take risks in order to experience varied, novel, complex, and intense sensations and experiences. Individuals with different levels of traits react differently but also choose to be in different situations. Based on the *trait–environment interaction*, individuals at one end of a personality dimension react differently to various situations than do individuals at the other end. Thus, for each of the big five personality traits and sensation-seeking, people with high levels of each trait react or respond differently to a situation than do those with low levels of each trait. According to the *trait–environment correlation*, individuals at one end of a personality dimension seek out, create, or modify situations differently than do individuals at the other end. In this case, for each big five trait and sensation-seeking, high trait levels are associated with seeking, creating, or modifying situations in ways that are different from those of individuals with low levels of each trait. The task of psychology is to determine what those situations and behaviors are. According to *cybernetic big five theory*, personality traits determine what type of goal an individual chooses. Furthermore, the type of goal motivates personality state behaviors that are effective for achieving that goal.

In some representative findings, extraverts and introverts react similarly to stimuli designed to put them in a pleasant hedonic mood. However, extraverts have greater *reward sensitivity*, which means they react with greater energetic arousal in response to the pursuit of rewards. Extraverts are more likely than introverts to seek social stimulation in a variety of situations. According to the *channeling hypothesis*, extraversion channels or conveys how psychological motives such as power and affiliation are expressed and satisfied. Extraverts are more likely than introverts to do volunteer work to satisfy their affiliation motive and to enter high-impact careers to satisfy their power motive.

Other traits have also been examined for how people react and select or modify different situa-tions. Individuals high in neuroticism are easier to put in a bad mood and are less satisfied with their relationships and careers. They are also more likely to choose to drink in solitude following negative social exchanges. Individuals high in conscientiousness earn higher grades and are more likely to engage in health-enhancing behaviors. High agreeableness is associated with a greater likelihood of helping friends and siblings in distress. Frequently a composite of trait levels is associ-ated with a particular behavior. For instance, students low in extraversion, agreeableness, and conscientiousness spend more time using the Internet. According to the *selection hypothesis*, individuals high in openness-to-experience sought out minority contact more and reported less prejudice as a result than did individuals high in agreeableness. Happiness is associated with high levels of extraversion and agreeableness and low levels of neuroticism. Coping styles also vary with personality traits. Individuals high in conscientiousness experience fewer stressors because of planning. Individuals high in agreeableness experience fewer interpersonal stressors because they are more cooperative while those high in neuroticism experience more interpersonal stressors. In addition, individuals high in conscientiousness, extraversion, and openness-to-experience cope through direct engagement with stressors while those high in neuroticism cope through disengagement, such as escaping from a stressor or not thinking about it. Weight gain over people's lifetimes is greater when their neuroticism and extraversion traits are high and their conscientiousness trait is low. Aspects of low agreeableness also contribute to weight gain. High-sensation seekers respond positively to risky events, drugs, and unusual experiences, while low-sensation seekers respond negatively. High-sensation seekers are more likely to seek out and engage in risky sports, prefer unusual stimuli and situations, and experiment with things out of the ordinary. Different components of sensation-seeking are associated with a preference for nonsense humor or sexual humor content.

GLOSSARY

Term	Definition
Active Correlation	Part of trait–environment correlation: individuals seek and create environments that match their personality traits
Agreeableness	One of the five-factor model personal dimensions that ranges from cold, hard, and rude to kind, sympathetic, and warm
Behavioral Genetics	Science of the genetic inheritance of biological traits relevant to behavior and personality traits
Boredom Susceptibility	Component of sensation-seeking that is an aversion to boredom resulting from repetitive experiences and the absence of stimulation
Channeling Hypothesis	Personality traits channel or convey how psychological motives are represented and satisfied
Conscientiousness	One of the five-factor model personality dimensions that ranges from careless and disorganized to cautious, deliberate
Cybernetic Big Five Theory	Theory that proposes that the big five personality traits determine what type of goal an individual chooses
Disinhibition	Component of sensation-seeking that through the release of inhibition reflects the desire for variety attained by drinking, partying, gambling, and sexual activity
Evocative Correlation	Trait–environment correlation wherein an individual's personality trait determines the type of reaction she or he evokes from others
Experience-Seeking	Component of sensation-seeking characterized by the desire for mental and sensory stimulation from art, travel, drugs, and music

continued . . .

GLOSSARY Continued

Term	Definition
Extraversion	A personality trait (dimension) that ranges from quiet, reserved, and shy to active, assertive, and dominant
Extraverts	People at upper end of the extraversion dimension and characterized as bold, energetic, and talkative
Five-Factor Model	Theory that postulates five major personality traits (OCEAN): openness-to-experience, conscientiousness, extraversion, agreeableness, neuroticism
Introverts	Lower end of the extraversion dimension and characterized as bashful, quiet, shy, and withdrawn
Neuroticism	One of the five-factor model personality dimensions that ranges from relaxed and unenvious to moody, temperamental, and touchy
Openness-to-Experience	Personality trait (dimension) that ranges from shallow, simple, and unintelligent to artistic, clever, and curious
Operational Definitions	Personality traits are defined by the procedures used to measure them. Operational definitions involve valid psychological paper-and-pencil scales
Passive Correlation	Trait–environment correlation wherein the biological parents create their children's environment
Personality	Consistent ways of behaving in different situations as a result of the interaction between temperament and social experiences
Personality Neuroscience	Studies the relationship between different personality traits and their counterparts in the brain from which traits emerge
Personality States	Behavioral manifestation of a trait. State consists of temporary behaviors that are representative of the personality trait
Personality Traits	Consistency in a specific set of behaviors across time and across relevant situations from one time to the next
Prejudice	Negative attitude or feeling about a social group or its members
Reward Sensitivity	A person reacts with greater energetic arousal in response to rewards or the pursuit of rewards
Selection Hypothesis	An individual's personality trait determines the type of contact sought with members of other groups
Sensation-Seeking	Personality trait characterized by seeking intense sensations and experiences and the willingness to take risks and incur costs for the sake of such experiences
Subjective Well-Being	A term for happiness that indicates a person has control over her life and is satisfied with life overall; low incidence of negative moods
Thrill-and-Adventure-Seeking	Component of sensation-seeking characterized by the desire for sensations from participating in risky activities, e.g., sky diving and fast driving
Trait–Environment Correlation	Personality traits and environments are associated in their effects on behavior because traits determine the situations a person chooses or alters
Trait–Environment Interaction	A person's reaction to the environment depends on the amount of a personality trait he or she possesses

REFERENCES

Allen, T. A., & DeYoung, C. G. (2015). Personality neuroscience and the five factor model. *Oxford handbook of the five factor model*. New York, NY: Oxford University Press.

Allport, G. W. (1937). *Personality: A psychological interpretation*. New York, NY: Holt.

Allport, G. W. (1966). Traits revisited. *American Psychologist, 21*, 1–10.

Atherton, O. E., Robins, R. W., Rentfrow, P. J., & Lamb, M. E. (2014). Personality correlates of risky health outcomes: Findings from a large Internet study. *Journal of Research in Personality, 50*, 56–60.

Bogg, T., & Roberts, B. W. (2004). Conscientiousness and health-related behaviors: A meta-analysis of the leading behavioral contributors to mortality. *Psychological Bulletin, 130*, 887–919.

Campbell, J. B., Tyrrell, D. J., & Zingaro, M. (1993). Sensation seeking among whitewater canoe and kayak paddlers. *Personality and Individual Differences, 14*, 489–491.

Carver, C. S., & Connor-Smith, J. (2010). Personality and coping. *Annual Review of Psychology, 61*, 679–704.

Chamorro-Premuzic, T., Reimers, S., Hsu, A., & Ahmetoglu, G. (2009). Who art thou? Personality predictors of artistic preferences in a large UK sample: The importance of openness. *British Journal of Psychology, 100*, 501–516.

Costa, P. T., Jr., & McCrae, R. R. (1985). *The NEO Personality Inventory Manual*. Odessa, FL: Psychological Assessment Resources.

Costa, P. T., Jr., & McCrae, R. R. (2001). *The NEO Personality Inventory*. Retrieved August 9, 2003, from www.rpp.on.ca/neopir.htm.

Cservenka, A., Herting, M. M., Seghete, K. L. M., Hudson, K. A., & Nagel, B. J. (2013). High and low sensation seeking adolescents show distinct patterns of brain activity during reward processing. *Neuroimage, 66*, 184–193.

DeYoung, C. G. (2015). Cybernetic big five theory. *Journal of Research in Personality, 56*, 33–58.

DeYoung, C. G., Hirsh, J. B., Shane, M. S., Papademetris, X., Rajeevan, N., & Gray, J. R. (2010). Testing predictions from personality neuroscience brain structure and the big five. *Psychological Science, 21*, 820–828.

Diener, E., & Seligman, M. E. P. (2002). Very happy people. *Psychological Science, 13*, 81–84.

Duffy, K. A., & Chartrand, T. L. (2015). The extravert advantage: How and when extraverts build rapport with other people. *Psychological Science, 26*, 1795–1802.

Eysenck, H. J. (1990). Biological dimensions of personality. In L. A. Pervin (Ed.), *Handbook of personality, theory and research* (pp. 244–276). New York, NY: Guilford.

Fayn, K., Tiliopoulos, N., & MacCann, C. (2015). Interest in truth versus beauty: Intellect and openness reflect different pathways towards interest. *Personality and Individual Differences, 81*, 47–52.

Fleeson, W., & Gallagher, P. (2009). The implications of Big Five standing for the distribution of trait manifestation in behavior: Fifteen experience-sampling studies and a meta-analysis. *Journal of Personality and Social Psychology, 97*, 1097.

Forsman, L. J., de Manzano, O., Karabanov, A., Madison, G., & Ullén, F. (2012). Differences in regional brain volume related to the extraversion-introversion dimension—A voxel based morphometry study. *Neuroscience Research, 72*, 59–67.

Freixanet, M. G. I. (1991). Personality profile of subjects engaged in high physical risk sports. *Personality and Individual Differences, 12*, 1087–1093.

Graziano, W. G., Habashi, M. M., Sheese, B. E., & Tobin, R. M. (2007). Agreeableness, empathy, and helping: A person × situation perspective. *Journal of Personality and Social Psychology, 93*, 583–599.

Hahn, E., Spinath, F. M., Siedler, T., Wagner, G. G., Schupp, J., & Kandler, C. (2012). The complexity of personality: Advantages of a genetically sensitive multi-group design. *Behavior Genetics, 42*, 221–233.

Hayes, N., & Joseph, S. (2003). Big 5 correlates of three measures of subjective well-being. *Personality and Individual Differences, 34*, 723–727.

Hur, Y-M., & Bouchard, Jr., T. J. (1997). The genetic correlation between impulsivity and sensation-seeking traits. *Behavior Genetics, 27*, 455–463.

Jackson, J. W., & Poulsen, J. R. (2005). Contact experiences mediate the relationship between five-factor model personality traits and ethnic prejudice. *Journal of Applied Social Psychology, 35*, 667–685.

Jenkins, S. R. (1994). Need for power and women's careers over 14 years: Structural power, job satisfaction, and motive change. *Journal of Personality and Social Psychology, 66*, 155–165.

John, O. P. (1989). Towards a taxonomy of personality descriptors. In D. M. Buss & N. Cantor (Eds.), *Personality psychology: Recent trends and emerging directions*. New York, NY: Springer Verlag.

John, O. P. (1990). The "big five" taxonomy: Dimensions of personality in the natural language and in questionnaires. In L. Pervin (Ed.), *Handbook of personality theory and research*. New York, NY: Guilford.

John, O. P., & Robins, R. W. (1993). Gordon Allport: Father and critic of the five-factor model. In K. H. Craik, R. Hogan, & R. N. Wolfe (Eds.), *Fifty years of personality psychology* (pp. 215–236). New York, NY: Plenum.

Jung, C. G. (1924). *Psychological types* (H. G. Baynes, trans.). New York, NY: Harcourt, Brace.

Kaufman, S. B., Quilty, L. C., Grazioplene, R. G., Hirsh, J. B., Gray, J. R., Peterson, J. B., & DeYoung, C. G. (2015). Openness to experience and intellect differentially predict creative achievement in the arts and sciences. *Journal of Personality, 82*, 248–258.

Landers, R. N., & Lounsbury, J. W. (2006). An investigation of Big Five and narrow personality traits in relation to Internet usage. *Computers in Human Behavior, 22*, 283–293.

Larsen, R. J., & Ketelaar, T. (1989). Extraversion, neuroticism and susceptibility to positive and negative mood induction procedures. *Personality and Individual Differences, 10*, 1221–1228.

Larsen, R. J., & Ketelaar, T. (1991). Personality and susceptibility to positive and negative emotional states. *Journal of Personality and Social Psychology, 61*, 132–140.

Loehlin, J. C. (1992). *Genes and the environment in personality development*. Newbury Park, CA: Sage.

McCabe, K. O., & Fleeson, W. (2016). Are traits useful? Explaining trait manifestations as tools in the pursuit of goals. *Journal of Personality and Social Psychology, 110*, 287–301.

McCrae, R. R. (1989). Why I advocate the five-factor model: Joint factor analyses of the NEO-PI with other instruments. In D. M. Buss & N. Cantor (Eds.), *Personality psychology: Recent trends and emerging directions* (pp. 237–245). New York, NY: Springer Verlag.

McCrae, R. R., & Costa, Jr., P. T. (1987). Validation of the five-factor model of personality across instruments and observers. *Journal of Personality and Social Psychology, 52*, 81–90.

Mohr, C. D., Armeli, S., Tennen, H., Carney, M. A., Affleck, G., & Hromi, A. (2001). Daily interpersonal experiences, context, and alcohol consumption: Crying in your beer and toasting good times. *Journal of Personality and Social Psychology, 80*, 489–500.

Noftle, E. E., & Robins, R. W. (2007). Personality predictors of academic outcomes: Big five correlates of GPA and SAT scores. *Journal of Personality and Social Psychology, 93*, 116–130.

Oerlemans, W. G., & Bakker, A. B. (2014). Why extraverts are happier: A day reconstruction study. *Journal of Research in Personality, 50*, 11–22.

Plomin, R., DeFries, J. C., Knopik, V. S., & Neiderhiser, J. M. (2013). *Behavioral genetics* (6th ed.). New York, NY: Worth.

Revelle, W. (1987). Personality and motivation: Sources of inefficiency in cognitive performance. *Journal of Research in Personality, 21*, 436–452.

Riemann, R., Angleitner, A., & Strelau, J. (1997). Genetic and environmental influences on personality: A study of twins reared together using the self- and peer report NEO-FFI scales. *Journal of Personality, 65*, 449–476.

Ruch, W. (1988). Sensation seeking and the enjoyment of structure and content of humour: Stability of findings across four samples. *Personality and Individual Differences, 9*, 861–871.

Ruch, W., & Hehl, F.-J. (1998). A two-mode model of humor appreciation: Its relation to aesthetic appreciation and simplicity-complexity of personality. In W. Ruch (Ed.), *The sense of humor: Explorations of a personality characteristic* (pp. 109–142). New York, NY: Mouton de Gruyter.

Rusting, C. L., & Larsen, R. J. (1997). Extraversion, neuroticism, and susceptibility to positive and negative affect: A test of two theoretical models. *Personality and Individual Differences, 22*, 607–612.

Saucier, G. (1994). Mini-markers: A brief version of Goldberg's unipolar big-five markers. *Journal of Personality Assessment, 63*, 506–516.

Saucier, G. (2003). Mini-markers. Retrieved September 8, 2003, from http://darkwing.uoregon.edu/~gsaucier/gsau41.htm.

Segal, N. L. (1999). *Entwined lives*. New York, NY: Dutton.

Seibert, S. E., & Kraimer, M. L. (2001). The five-factor model of personality and career success. *Journal of Vocational Behavior, 58*, 1–21.

Smillie, L. D., Cooper, A. J., Wilt, J., & Revelle, W. (2012). Do extraverts get more bang for the buck? Refining the affective-reactivity hypothesis of extraversion. *Journal of Personality and Social Psychology, 103*, 306–326.

Snyder, M. (1983). The influence of individuals on situations: Implications for understanding the links between personality and social behavior. *Journal of Personality, 51*, 497–516.

Stoel, R. D., De Geus, E. J., & Boomsma, D. I. (2006). Genetic analysis of sensation seeking with an extended twin design. *Behavior Genetics, 36*, 229–237.

Straub, W. F. (1982). Sensation seeking among high- and low-risk male athletes. *Journal of Sports Psychology, 4*, 246–253.

Suls, J., Green, P., & Hillis, S. (1998). Emotional reactivity to everyday problems, affective inertia, and neuroticism. *Personality and Social Psychology Bulletin, 24*, 127–136.

Sutin, A. R., Ferrucci, L., Zonderman, A. B., & Terracciano, A. (2011). Personality and obesity across the adult life span. *Journal of Personality and Social Psychology, 101*, 579–592.

Tamir, M. (2005). Don't worry, be happy? Neuroticism, trait-consistent affect regulation, and performance. *Journal of Personality and Social Psychology, 89*, 449–461.

Thompson, E. R. (2008). Development and validation of an international English big-five mini-markers. *Personality and Individual Differences, 45*, 542–548.

Wagner, M. K. (2001). Behavioral characteristics related to substance abuse and risk-taking, sensation-seeking, anxiety sensitivity, and self-reinforcement. *Addictive Behaviors, 26*, 115–120.

Watson, D., Hubbard, B., & Wiese, D. (2000). General traits of personality and affectivity as predictors of satisfaction in intimate relationships: Evidence from self- and partner ratings. *Journal of Personality, 68*, 413–449.

Weiss, A., Bates, T. C., & Luciano, M. (2008). Happiness is a personal(ity) thing: The genetics of personality and well-being in a representative sample. *Psychological Science, 19*, 205–210.

Winter, D. G., John, O. P., Stewart, A. J., Klohnen, E. C., & Duncan, L. E. (1998). Traits and motives: Toward an integration of two traditions in personality research. *Psychological Review, 105*, 230–250.

Zuckerman, M. (1978). The search for high sensation. *Psychology Today, 11*, 38–46, 96–99.

Zuckerman, M. (1979). *Sensation seeking: Beyond the optimal level of arousal*. Hillsdale, NJ: Lawrence Erlbaum.

Zuckerman, M. (1994). *Behavioral expressions and biosocial bases of sensation seeking*. Cambridge: Cambridge University Press.

Zuckerman, M. (2002). Genetics of sensation seeking. In J. Benjamin, R. P. Ebstein, & R. H. Belmaker (Eds.), *Molecular genetics and the human personality* (pp. 193–210). Washington, DC: American Psychiatric Publishing.

CHAPTER 10

Extrinsic and Intrinsic Motivation

A thing is worth whatever the buyer will pay for it.

Publius Syrus, 50 B.C.

Let not the enjoyment of pleasure now within our grasp be carried to such excess as to incapacitate you from future repetition.

Seneca, 4 B.C.–A.D. 65

In the push/pull metaphor of motivation, incentives and goals are outside the person and either pull or repel. What qualities determine their strength of pull or repulsion? How does this strength wane with temporal distance to when the incentive or goal becomes available? These questions along with the following are for your consideration:

1. How do incentives differ from reinforcers and punishers in motivating behavior?
2. What characteristics influence the value of an incentive?
3. How does incentive value affect the motivation of behavior?
4. Can behavior be motivating in its own right—that is, be intrinsically motivating?
5. How do extrinsic and intrinsic sources interact to motivate behavior?

EXTRINSIC MOTIVATION AND INCENTIVE VALUE

According to the familiar axiom of "wanting more," to have something desirable is good, and to have more of it is better, and to have still more is better yet; to have less is worse. One corollary of the axiom of wanting more is that the more frequently a desirable event occurs, the better it is, and the less frequently it occurs the worse it is. A second corollary is that the sooner a desirable event occurs the better it is, and the later it occurs the worse it is. The reverse, then, is likely to be true: to have something undesirable is bad, to have more of it is worse, and to have still more is worse yet; to have less is better. A corollary of this axiom is that the more frequently an undesirable event occurs, the worse it is, and the less frequently it occurs the better it is. A second corollary is that the sooner an unpleasant event occurs, the worse it is and the later it occurs the better it is.

These axioms, or self-evident truths, describe some major features of extrinsic motivation: more and larger incentives are preferred—though not in the case of negative incentives—and are more motivating than fewer and smaller incentives. But, what characteristics determine the value of an incentive and how does this affect a person's choices and behavior?

Reinforcers and Punishers versus Incentives

How does a student know which behaviors result in good grades? How does a worker know how to earn a year-end bonus? Why does the prospect of good grades or a bonus motivate certain behaviors and not others? These questions address the difference between reinforcers and punishers, on the one hand, and positive and negative incentives, on the other. The difference is based on the effects of past events versus the anticipation of future events. In the past, attending class, studying, or working diligently resulted in a good grade or a year-end bonus. When anticipating the future, a good grade or year-end bonus motivate behavior.

Selecting versus motivating behavior. Learning what to do and actually doing it illustrate the separate effects of reinforcers and incentives (Cofer & Appley, 1964; Tolman, 1955; Tolman & Honzik, 1930). Learning what to do results from the action of **reinforcers**. These are stimuli that select appropriate behaviors and make them more likely to occur in a situation (see Skinner, 1938, 1953; Staddon & Simmelhag, 1971). Learning what not to do results from the action of **punishers** that select against behaviors and make them less likely to occur (Skinner, 1953). Thus, attending class and studying are selected for by good grades (reinforcers), while skipping classes and not studying are selected against by failing exams and courses (punishers). **Incentives** are the external stimuli that motivate or induce behavior to occur (Bolles, 1975; Logan & Wagner, 1965). A positive incentive motivates the behavior that is instrumental in attaining the incentive. For example, the incentive of a good grade motivates studying. A negative incentive motivates avoidance behavior, which is instrumental in averting or preventing the incentives from happening. For example, the negative incentive of failing a course motivates a student to avoid skipping classes.

Past versus future. Reinforcers and punishers are the actual consequences of behavior, whereas positive and negative incentives are the anticipated consequences. Incentives influence behavior based on their anticipation (Bolles, 1975; Karniol & Ross, 1996). Both mechanistic and cognitive accounts have provided explanations. According to one mechanistic explanation, anticipation of an incentive consists of minuscule responses that resemble the final consummatory response of the incentive (Hull, 1952). For instance, a person salivates driving to a restaurant and then, when there, he salivates more intensely while eating. Or a student smiles in anticipation of receiving congratulations from family members at graduation. According to a cognitive explanation, people visualize themselves in a future incentive situation (Markus & Nurius, 1986). For instance, a student cognitively represents the incentive of a university degree as "my earning a B.A. or B.S." The cognitive representation bridges the present to the future and motivates a person's behavior. Thus, a student may form a mental image of her professor giving an exam, which in turn motivates the student to study for the exam.

Some incentives are derived from their association with reinforcement and punishment. If a response consistently results in a reinforcer, then that reinforcer becomes a positive incentive; it will be sought out or approached. If a response consistently results in a punisher, then that punisher becomes a negative incentive; it will be avoided (Bolles, 1975; Logan, 1960). In some instances, however, prior experience seems unnecessary for a stimulus to act as an incentive. A new car, for example, serves as an incentive to save money even if an individual has never owned a new car. A person also avoids touching a hot stove even if she has never been burned by one before. Table 10.1 summarizes the distinctions between reinforcers and punishers and positive and negative incentives.

Progress through a university illustrates the distinctions in Table 10.1. Studying and attending class produce passing grades, parental approval, and a feeling of pride. These consequences are reinforcers, provided they increase or maintain those behaviors. As anticipated consequences these outcomes serve as positive incentives that motivate a student to attend class and study. Not attending class and not studying produce failing grades, parental disapproval, and perhaps a feeling of shame. These consequences are classified as punishers, provided they decrease those behaviors. As anticipated consequences these outcomes are negative incentives if they motivate a student to avoid them by not missing class and not neglecting to study (see Table 10.1).

TABLE 10.1 Distinction between Reinforcers and Punishers versus Positive and Negative Incentives

	Outcomes of Behavior: Past Events	Anticipated Outcomes of Behavior: Future Events
Positive Stimulus	Reinforcer:	Positive Incentive:
	Behavior is selected for and becomes more likely.	Motivates approach behavior to attain the incentive.
	Example: past passing grade, parental approval, and pride	Example: anticipated passing grade, parental approval, and pride
Negative Stimulus	Punisher:	Negative Incentive:
	Behavior is selected against and becomes less likely.	Motivates avoidance behaviors to prevent occurrence of incentive.
	Example: past failing grade, parental disapproval, and shame	Example: anticipated failing grade, parental disapproval, and shame

Objective and Subjective Incentive Value

An incentive refers to the motivational properties of a reinforcer. The value of an incentive determines its preference and motivational strength. Terms such as more, bigger, and better usually indicate increased value of a positive incentive, while less, smaller, and worse usually indicate decreased value. **Incentive value** refers to the attractiveness of an incentive and is based on objective properties such as the number or the amount. In contrast, subjective incentive value refers to an individual's appraisal of the objective value. The distinction between the objective and subjective value of economic goods serves as a case in point. According to economists, subjective value is synonymous with **utility**, which refers to the satisfaction, pleasure, or usefulness of an economic good. A pen has a certain objective value based, say, on how much it costs, but it also has a great deal of utility. It is a very useful instrument (try attending school without one) but it also provides satisfaction when writing. Utility rather than objective value provides a better understanding of why economic goods such as cars, clothes, and computers are satisfying.

What is the nature of the relationship between the objective and subjective value or utility of an incentive? Fechner (1860/1966) provided one answer when he explored the relationship between stimulus intensities and corresponding psychological sensations. Fechner showed that equal increases in stimulus intensity produce smaller and smaller increases in sensations. For instance, equal increases in a tone's loudness produce increases in the sensation of loudness but in diminishing amounts. This relationship became known as **Fechner's law**. Several economists in the late 1800s noted that the relationship between an amount of money and its utility followed Fechner's law (Stigler, 1950). Even earlier, in 1738, the French mathematician Bernoulli made a similar proposal about money and its utility (Stevens, 1972). Figure 10.1 shows such a relationship: As the number of dollars increases, the utility of those dollars increases but in diminishing amounts. Utility is measured in *utils*, units employed at one time by economists to indicate the utility of

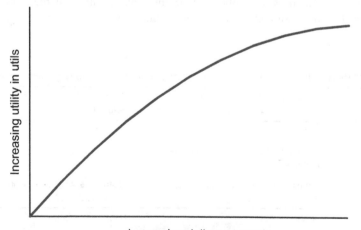

FIGURE 10.1 Dollars and Utility. The relationship between the number of dollars and their utility is such that as the dollar amount increases, utility increases, but in smaller and smaller amounts. The graph is only an approximation of the true dollar–utility relationship.

economic goods. For example, a person's first $10 corresponds to 10 utils of satisfaction, whereas an additional $10 corresponds to approximately nine more utils of satisfaction. Although $20 is twice as much as $10, $20 does not have twice as much utility as $10. Equal increments in dollar value lead to smaller and smaller increases in utility. Perhaps the most general statement we can make about money and its utility is that more is better.

Positive and Negative Incentives

Suppose there is very little time remaining in a very exciting game and your team has the ball. Will your team score and win or not score and lose? The outcome of any game ends with a change in status for each team. One team attains a positive incentive or win, while the other team fails to prevent a negative incentive or loss. Which outcome has the greater psychological effect? The win or the loss? Unpleasant anticipated outcomes serve as negative incentives and pleasant ones as positive incentives. When experienced, negative incentives feel unpleasant to painful and positive incentives feel pleasant to euphoric. In addition to producing opposite feelings, negative incentives are experienced more intensely than positive incentives are experienced. In other words, the losing fan's disappointment is greater than the winning fan's joy. But what is the evidence for this difference in the intensity of negative and positive feelings?

Bad is stronger than good. Many examples confirm that negative outcomes are felt more intensely than positive outcomes are (Baumeister et al., 2001; Rozin & Royzman, 2001). In the area of interpersonal relationships, negative interactions are more destructive than are positive interactions. When forming impressions about others, negative information about a person has a stronger impact than does positive information. Moods and emotions are also weighted toward the unpleasant. Negative moods impact people more strongly than positive moods. The greater number of negative emotion words in language attests to its greater impact on people's behavior. In their interaction with the environment, people focus more on negative than on positive stimuli. We search the environment more for information about potentially harmful stimuli than about beneficial stimuli. Finally, when coming nearer to a goal, the strength of negative goal features become stronger than those of positive goal features. From all of these examples, Baumeister and coauthors (2001) conclude that "bad is stronger than good" (p. 354). If this is so, then the motivation to avoid bad should be stronger than the motivation to attain good.

To demonstrate that the effects of bad are stronger than those of good, it is necessary that the bad and good stimuli are identical and of the same intensity. Otherwise, the difference between stimuli may result from some factor other than bad versus good. The stimuli could differ in intensity, duration, or their combination rather than the quality of bad or good. One solution to this problem is to consider the gain of a positive stimulus as good but the loss of that same stimulus as bad, much like winning the game is good and losing it is bad. In this case, the stimuli are identical. In other examples, compare the gain of a romantic partner at the beginning of a relationship versus the loss of that partner from a breakup. Or compare your reaction to the acquisition of your new smartphone versus its loss when stolen. Finally, consider the rise of your GPA by 0.1 units rather than its fall by the same amount at semester's end.

Buyer and seller experiments. Money is a good way to measure the effects of identical losses versus gains. Money reflects how much a person pays to gain (buy) an item and how much a person receives for the loss (sale) of an item. Using this approach, Kahneman and associates (1990) conducted a marketing experiment during which they randomly gave half the students in a class some attractive coffee mugs imprinted with the name of the university. The new owners were informed that the mugs were theirs to keep or they could sell them. The nonowners were told to examine their neighbors' mugs and that they could offer them any price to buy one. Owners (potential sellers) had to decide at what price they were willing to sell their mugs. Nonowners (potential buyers) had to decide how much they were willing to pay. The purpose of the individual price setting was to determine the subjective value of the loss of a mug when sold and the subjective value of the gain of a mug when bought. To summarize:

Subjective value of loss = Willingness-to-accept price for mug
Subjective value of gain = Willingness-to-pay price for mug

If losses are more dissatisfying than gains are satisfying, then the willingness-to-accept prices should be higher than the willingness-to-pay prices. In other words, the decrease in value from losing (selling) a mug would be greater than the increase in value from gaining (buying) a mug. To make these experiments as realistic as possible, Kahneman and associates (1990) also let students barter for pens and folding binoculars. Students had been told to bring their own money to class in order to make any purchases, and provisions were made for extending credit and for making change. For all commodities, a typical seller's willingness-to-accept price exceeded a typical prospective buyer's willingness-to-pay price (Kahneman et al., 1990). Thus, greater compensation was required to offset dissatisfaction from the loss of an item compared to compensation for the gain in satisfaction from the same item. This difference in price indicates that the loss of a particular item was more dissatisfying than the gain of the same item was satisfying.

Prospect theory. This theory integrates the difference in the subjective value of gains and losses. First, it views positive and negative incentives as gains and losses from a neutral reference point. Second, it recognizes that losses are felt more intensely than gains are felt. The ***value function curve*** in Figure 10.2 illustrates these two views (Kahneman, 2011; Kahneman & Tversky, 1979, 1982). The curve shows how the amount of a loss or gain on the horizontal axis translates into a psychological value on the vertical axis. The neutral reference point, designated 0, is located where the curve crosses the horizontal axis. The curve is steeper below the horizontal axis than it is above. This steepness indicates that the negative psychological intensity of a loss develops more quickly than the positive psychological intensity for an identical gain. For instance, consider the loss versus gain of $100 as shown in Figure 10.2. Even though the change is objectively equal in both directions, a $100 loss produces a greater increase in dissatisfaction than a $100 gain produces an increase in satisfaction. The curve in Figure 10.2 explains the results of the buyer/seller experiment. In that experiment, the loss and gain are identical: one mug in each case. Subjectively, on the other hand, the loss of a mug was felt more strongly than the gain of a mug. This difference was reflected in the sale price being higher than the buy price. The greater psychological intensity of an incentive loss compared to a gain is known as **losses loom larger than gains**. This phrase simply means that losses are more dissatisfying than identical gains are satisfying (Kahneman, 2011; Kahneman & Tversky, 1979, 1982).

Gains and losses conditioning. The value function curve of Figure 10.2 also implies that individuals are more motivated to prevent losses than to acquire gains. In one illustrative experiment, researchers required participants to solve six anagrams (jumbled words), such as etkbas solved as

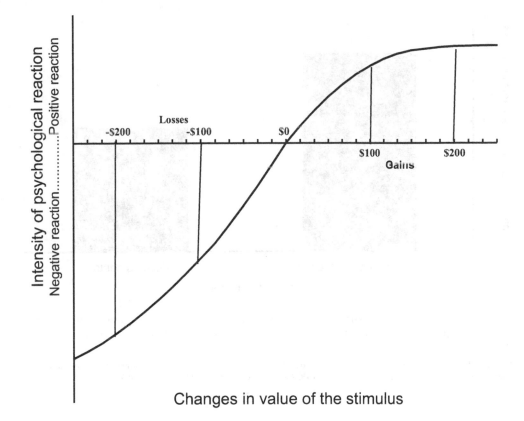

FIGURE 10.2 Value Function Curve of Prospect Theory. The horizontal axis locates losses of $100 and $200 and gains of $100 and $200 at equal distances to the left and right of the neutral reference point of $0. However, the vertical axis shows that the negative psychological reaction to the loss of these amounts of money is more intense than the positive psychological reaction to the gain of those amounts. For example, the loss of $100 is felt more intensely than the gain of $100 is felt.

basket (Goldsmith & Dhar, 2013). Participants in the gain condition received 25¢ for each anagram solved correctly for a possible total of $1.50. Those in the avoid loss condition received an initial $1.50 in quarters and would have 25¢ deducted for each anagram not solved. There was no time limit and participants could inform the experimenter when finished. Two anagrams were unsolvable so that participants would not quit because they had solved all six anagrams (Goldsmith & Dhar, 2013). Would participants in the gain or the avoid loss condition persist longer in attempting to solve the anagrams? If the loss of 25¢ is more dissatisfying than the gain of 25¢ is satisfying, then participants in the avoid loss condition should persist longer than those in the gain condition. In other words, the loss of 25¢ is a greater negative incentive than the gain of 25¢ is a positive incentive. And indeed, the results came out as predicted (see Figure 10.3). Participants persisted nearly six minutes longer to avoid a 25¢ loss per unsolved anagram compared to a 25¢ gain per solved anagram.

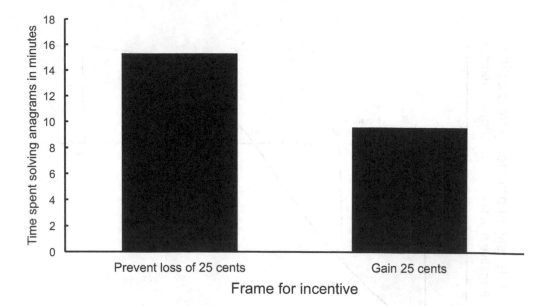

FIGURE 10.3 Motivational Persistence to Prevent a Loss versus to Acquire a Gain. Participants persisted longer at solving anagrams in order to prevent the loss of 25¢ per unsolved anagram compared to the gain of 25¢ per solved anagram.

Source: Adapted from "Negativity Bias and Task Motivation: Testing the Effectiveness of Positively Versus Negatively Framed Incentives" by K. Goldsmith & R. Dhar, 2013, *Journal of Experimental Psychology: Applied, 19,* p. 360.

Section Recap

Prior reinforcers and punishers provide the knowledge, and anticipated incentives provide the motivation for what behavior to carry out in a particular situation. *Reinforcers* select a particular behavior, making it more likely to occur in the appropriate situation. *Punishers*, however, select against a particular behavior, making it less likely to occur. *Incentives* are external stimuli that induce or motivate the behavior to occur in a particular situation. People are motivated toward positive and away from negative incentives. The degree an incentive motivates behavior depends on its *incentive value*, which is based on objective properties such as number or quantity. Subjective value or *utility* is based on the pleasure, satisfaction, or usefulness of the incentive. As objective incentive value increases, subjective value or utility increases but in smaller and smaller amounts, as described by *Fechner's law*. According to *prospect theory*, positive incentives can be interpreted as gains and negative incentives as losses. In addition, the psychological impact of a loss is stronger than the impact of a gain. This is expressed in the phrase *losses loom larger than gains*, which means that the loss of an incentive is more dissatisfying than the gain of an incentive is satisfying. A *value function curve* expresses these two ideas. The curve declines steeply for losses and rises slightly for gains. When applied to motivation, individuals are more persistent to prevent the loss of an incentive compared to the gain of an incentive of equal value.

FACTORS THAT AFFECT INCENTIVE VALUE

The axiom that opened this chapter implied that we are always motivated to have things in greater quantity, quality, frequency, and sooner. As a general rule, this is true. The greater the quantity or quality of incentives, the more people are motivated to attain them. People are also more motivated by incentives that are available more frequently and sooner. However, there are complications and exceptions. For example, can a person be paid too much? Is the quantity and quality of an incentive in the eye of the beholder? Can an external incentive, such as money or grades, demotivate behavior? This section provides some answers.

Amount

Whether incentives motivate behavior depends on several factors. First, there are differences among people in their personality traits and stable psychological needs. These differences give weight to the saying "one person's junk is another person's treasure." Second, individuals differ from one time to the next as in food motivates eating when hungry but not when full. Both sets of differences can be surmounted by using money as an incentive. Money is an extremely powerful incentive for humans and probably motivates most individuals in the world (Lea & Webley, 2006). Third, incentive effectiveness depends on whether or not the behavior is performed willingly. An incentive can motivate a behavior that a person does not perform willingly. For example, incentives may motivate studying for a boring course or doing a menial job. Will an incentive increase the motivation for behavior that is performed willingly out of personal choice? In other words, if the behavior is already occurring, then will an incentive increase the intensity, duration, or quality of that behavior? Here the answer is less clear, since sometimes incentives help but may also harm.

Incentives motivate behavior or thoughts about behavior. This action of incentives causes a person to work both harder and smarter (Condly et al., 2003). If incentives motivate behavior, then will larger incentives motivate behavior more? Incentive amount refers to the quantity, number, or duration of incentives. One generalization is that increases in pay increases work performance. Condly and coresearchers (2003), in summarizing 45 studies, found that monetary incentives increased both mental work and manual labor. Financial incentives also show some success in education. For example, incentives increase school attendance, which increases the likelihood of graduation. Financial incentives also produce modest gains in academic performance (Gneezy et al., 2011). Surprisingly, adding larger and larger incentives can increase, decrease, or have no effect on behavior (Camerer & Hogarth, 1999; Frey & Jegen, 2001). For instance, Gneezy and Rustichini (2000) asked their participants to answer 50 questions from an IQ test. The likelihood of a correct answer depended on the degree of effort expended. One group was simply requested to answer the questions, a second received an additional 0.10 Israeli shekels per correct answer, and a third and fourth group received one or three shekels extra per correct answer. (An Israeli shekel is worth $0.27). Surprisingly, receiving 0.10 shekels per solution decreased effort below that of answering the questions for free. However, the larger payment of one or three shekels per answer raised effort above doing the task for free. Thus, compared to no incentive, a small incentive actually reduced motivation while larger incentives increased motivation. It was as if the small incentive crowded out the motivation of doing the task for free (Frey & Jegen, 2001).

How incentives affect behavior also depends on the nature of the task, such as a cognitive (thinking) task versus a motor manual task. For the cognitive task, Ariely and coresearchers (2009) presented students with a 3×3 matrix of nine three-digit numbers. Students were instructed to identify the two numbers that would sum to 10. For example, 3.58 and 6.42 were the two numbers out of nine that summed to 10. For the manual task, students had to alternate between pressing the v and n keys as rapidly as possible. Performance was measured by the number of matrices solved or the number of v–n alternations in four minutes. Students could earn $30 in the low incentive condition and up to $300 in the high incentive condition. Increasing the amount of the monetary incentive affected the two tasks differently. Increases in the monetary incentives increased the number of v–n alternations but actually resulted in fewer solutions in the cognitive addition task. Thus, greater incentives increased the motivation of simple motor tasks but decreased the motivation of more complex cognitive tasks.

Incentive value also affects the motivation for behavior not to occur—that is, behaviors to avoid. In other words, think of being rewarded for behaviors that you avoid, such as skipping class, texting while driving, and procrastinating. As a research example, incentives have been used to reduce smoking among university students. Correia and Benson (2006) recruited smokers in order to examine the motivating effects of incentive amount on smoking abstinence. Smokers reported to the laboratory twice per day for one week and were paid in cash if their carbon monoxide level was below the criterion amount. Carbon monoxide is obtained from a person's breath and indicates the amount a person has smoked recently. The researchers also recorded the number of cigarettes participants had smoked and the number of hours of not smoking. The amount paid defined the incentive value for not smoking: up to $40 versus $80 for the week. The results indicated that the larger incentive was more effective in reducing smoking than the smaller incentive. Carbon monoxide levels and the number of cigarettes smoked were lower for smokers who received the larger incentive. In addition, the larger incentive resulted in a greater number of hours of not smoking.

Internal States Determine Incentive Value

The value of an incentive does not remain constant. It changes with a person's internal disposition or state that reflects the degree of incentive deprivation. A hot state occurs when a person is deprived and a cold state when the person is satiated (Fisher & Rangel, 2014; Loewenstein, 1996). For instance, drug craving is a hot state that results from abstinence. The subjective value of drugs increases as cravings increase. Hunger is a hot state that increases the subjective value of food. Psychological needs also influence incentive value. Incentives that satisfy needs are valued more than alternatives that do not. Incentive value also depends on personality traits. For example, the opportunity to volunteer has greater value for a person high, compared to low, in conscientiousness.

Are people aware of how much they value a particular incentive when in a hot state compared to a cold state and vice versa? For instance, can hungry individuals judge how much they would value food when satiated? And, conversely, can satiated individuals judge how much they would value food when hungry? To answer this question, Fisher and Rangel (2014) had students report to their psychology laboratory on two separate days. Prior to each day's session, students had fasted for four hours (hungry) or had eaten a large snack (satiated). At each session participants were shown snack foods such as candy bars, potato chips, crackers, and berries. To measure the incentive value of food, the participants were given $4 to bid "for the right to eat each of the foods at the end of the second day" (p. 121). Participants could keep any money not spent bidding on snacks.

Would satiated versus hunger affect the amount bid for snacks? Yes! When hungry, participants bid more for the snacks they would eat the next time when they were satiated. Conversely, when satiated, participants bid less for the snacks they would eat the next time when hungry. In other words, when hungry, participants overestimated how much they would value food when they were not hungry (satiated). Conversely, when satiated, participants underestimated how much they would value food when hungry. The amount of over- and underestimation was the same in each direction—that is, from hunger to satiation and from satiation to hunger. The lesson here is that hot versus cold states influence incentive value. Furthermore, those values may not be the same when a person is in a different state later (Fisher & Rangel, 2014; Loewenstein, 1996). For example, a person may underestimate the value of an incentive when satiated compared to its value when in a state of withdrawal.

Rate of Reinforcement

The frequency of an incentive or reinforcer also affects motivation. Rate of reinforcement is studied in situations where an animal is given a choice between two responses, one of which is reinforced more frequently. For example, pigeons are presented with two response keys to peck. Pecking one key yields 30 reinforcers per hour, while pecking the other key yields 15 or 45 reinforcers per hour. If reinforcement rate affects motivation, then the pigeon should peck whatever key produces the higher rate. To verify this prediction, Herrnstein (1961) varied the rate of reinforcement between the left and right response keys. For example, pecking the left response key yielded 27 reinforcers per hour, while the right key yielded 13 reinforcers per hour. The results showed that pigeons chose the left response key more than the right one, since the former provided a higher rate of reinforcement. Humans are also affected by the rate of reinforcement. Neef and associates (1992) reinforced special education students for working on math problems from one of two stacks situated on the students' right and left. When students worked on one stack of problems they were reinforced with a nickel or token every 30 seconds, on average, compared to every 120 seconds from the other stack. The rate of reinforcement affected their choice. Students spent more time working math problems from the stack that provided a higher rate of reinforcement. Thus, animals and humans shift to activities that provide higher rates of reinforcement (de Villiers, 1977).

People seek higher rates of reinforcement when possible—that is, they meliorate. **Melioration** refers to a shift toward an activity that is more lucrative or provides a greater rate of reinforcement (Herrnstein, 1990). For example, if the rate of reinforcement declines for one activity, then a person switches to another activity that provides a higher rate. To illustrate, a person may switch credit cards to one that offers a lower interest rate or go to another restaurant because the food is better. One implication of melioration is that a faster rate of responding will produce a faster rate of reinforcement. Imagine a hungry rat in a Skinner box that is reinforced with food each time it presses a lever. Faster rates of responding result in faster rates of reinforcement. A similar relationship exists in our daily lives between the amount of responding and the magnitude of the reinforcer. For example, enrolling in more courses results in quicker graduation, studying more results in higher grades, and working more hours produces larger paychecks. Lippman (2000) provided experimental demonstrations of this relationship. In order to earn points (reinforcers), participants pushed a button. All that was required for a fixed amount of reinforcement was to push the button once at the conclusion of a 15-second interval. However, additional button presses during the 15 seconds increased the size of the reinforcer in one condition, while it decreased the size of the reinforcer in another condition. As might be expected, response rate increased when it provided for a larger reinforcer and decreased when it produced smaller reinforcers. Lippman's experiments showed that the amount of the anticipated incentive determines the rate of responding. The anticipation of a larger incentive increased responding, but the anticipation of a smaller incentive decreased responding.

Contrast Effects

Incentive contrast refers to a change in the psychological value of an incentive based on the value of prior similar incentives. *Positive incentive contrast* refers to an upward shift in incentive quantity or quality. The upward shift increases behavior above its previous intensity or frequency. *Negative incentive contrast* refers to a downward shift in incentive quantity or quality. This downward shift decreases behavior below its prior level. For example, imagine two workers, both of whom earn $10 per hour. However, this hourly rate resulted from positive incentive contrast for one: a raise from $8 to $10 per hour. For the other worker, the hourly rate resulted from negative incentive contrast: a decline from $12 to $10 per hour. They now both earn $10 per hour, but who will temporarily work harder and who will be happier?

Quantity and quality. A store may advertise: buy two, get one free; 30 percent off the original price; or every car, truck, or van in stock marked down. Such sale notices bring customers into stores and motivate them to buy. Shoes advertised at $40 are considered a bargain (more value) when contrasted with their original $60 price, as in the example: $60 shoes marked down to $40. Without this contrast provided by the $60, however, the same shoes at $40 would be less attractive to a buyer. In other words, $40 by itself would not be considered a good bargain. However, even when there is no accompanying contrasting stimulus, comparisons are still made with one's adaptation level—that is, a person's shoe pricing experiences (Helson, 1964). Thus, whether the $40 shoes are considered good value depends on a shopper's shoe-adaptation level. Nevertheless, when a contrast between prices is observed, as in the sign "$60 shoes, now $40," shoppers consider the sale price to be a greater bargain and are more motivated to buy (Compeau & Grewal, 1998, Krishna et al., 2002).

The quality of incentives is also affected by contrast. The effects of contrasts in incentive quality are captured by the **law of hedonic contrast**, which Beebe-Center (1932/1965) attributed to the German psychophysicist Fechner (1876). According to this law, the pleasure a stimulus provides will be greater if it contrasts with sources of lesser pleasure or displeasure. Similarly, the displeasure a stimulus provides will be greater if it contrasts with sources of greater pleasure or less displeasure. For instance, does the pleasure derived from gazing on attractive faces depend on viewers' experience with other faces? Yes! The attractiveness of a face will be enhanced if the viewer had viewed slightly less attractive faces earlier. Conversely, perceived attractiveness will be reduced if prior faces were slightly more attractive (Cogan et al., 2013). My advice to romantic couples is only look at people who you consider less attractive than your partner. As a result, your partner's looks and mate value will increase.

Contrast effects, however, also depend on how those other sources are categorized. Are they from the same or a different category? Zellner and coresearchers (2003) investigated the effects that category membership had on the hedonic evaluation of fruit drinks. Three groups of participants evaluated the pleasantness of eight fruit-flavored drinks followed by two diluted test drinks. The test drinks were either from the same or a different category than the prior eight. One group was told that all 10 solutions were commercial drinks from England—that is, the two test drinks were from the same category as the first eight drinks. Another group was informed that only the last two solutions were drinks from England—that is, the last two drinks were from a different category. A control group only evaluated the two diluted test drinks.

Contrast effects were apparent in two ways. First, the two diluted drinks were rated lower in pleasantness when they followed the eight full-strength solutions as compared to being the only two drinks. In addition, the test drinks were rated as more unpleasant when they were labeled as being from the same category compared to a different category. Zellner and coresearchers (2002) found similar results for coffee and beer. The contrast effect of ordinary coffee compared to gourmet coffee was greater when all coffees were labeled as belonging to the same compared to different categories. Contrast effects were also greater for beers from the same category than from different categories. These category effects imply that people's stimulus preferences can be manipulated through comparison with other stimuli. The contrast effects will be greater if people are told the comparison stimuli are from the same category rather than a different category. In the prior face example, the rated attractiveness of a face is unaffected by prior faces that are extremely attractive, as if those extremely attractive faces belonged to a different category (Cogan et al., 2013).

Contrast effects also depend on a person's expectations. For instance, students have experienced changes in their feelings as a result of the contrast between the exam grade they expected and the grade they received (Shepperd & McNulty, 2002). Imagine a class where you have taken an exam for which you expected an A. When the professor returned the exam, you found that you earned an A (or C). How does that make you feel? Or, imagine that you expected a C on the exam and found that you earned a C (or A). How does that make you feel? More precisely, how unhappy or happy would you feel about expecting an A and receiving an A or C and expecting a C and receiving a C or A? Use the following scale: 1 = *very unhappy* to 7 = *very happy*. The hedonic contrast effects found in such an experiment are presented in Figure 10.4 (Shepperd & McNulty, 2002). An A grade produces the greatest happiness if contrasted with an expected C rather than an expected A. And a C grade produces the least happiness if contrasted with an expected A rather than an expected C.

Contrast between behavior and incentive. You earned an A in a course where almost every student earned an A versus a course where hardly anyone did. Which A do you value more? Notice that, objectively, both As affect a student's GPA equally, count equally toward graduation, and count equally on graduate school applications. However, most likely, students will value an A more in the course in which few others earned As. Subjectively, the A is not valued equally in both courses because of how that grade contrasted with the value of academic work necessary to achieve it. Presumably academic work has a negative value but it is necessary to earn an A. And, as the amount of academic work increases, its negative value increases also. Thus, academic

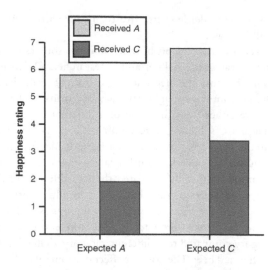

FIGURE 10.4 Happiness and Expected Grades. Happiness ratings were highest when the received grade was higher than the expected grade (expected C, received A). Happiness ratings were lowest when the received grade was lower than the expected grade (expected A, received C). Ratings were intermediate when the received grade matched the expected grade, although an A produced greater happiness than a C.

Source: Adapted from "The Affective Consequences of Expected and Unexpected Outcomes" by J. A. Shepperd and J. K. McNulty, 2002, *Psychological Science, 13,* Table 1, p. 86.

work has a more negative value in a difficult course than in an easy course. The difference (contrast) between the negative value of academic work and the positive value of an A is greater in the difficult course. This greater contrast is what is responsible for the greater value placed on the A in the difficult course. The conclusion is that contrast between the value of behavior and subsequent rewards determines the value of that reward (Zentall, 2010).

For experimental evidence for the above hypothesis, imagine participating in an experiment resembling one described in Figure 10.5 (Alessandri et al., 2008; Klein et al., 2005). In step one of the experiment, participants are required to press a key so that two stimuli will appear on the screen. Half of the time they are required to press a key with little effort—that is, little force, short duration, or few push responses. The other half of the time they are required to use much effort—that is, much force, long duration, or many push responses. Low-effort responses produce one stimulus pair and the high-effort responses produce a different stimulus pair (see Figure 10.5). In step 2, participants learn which stimulus of a pair is labeled correct (S+) and which is labeled wrong (S−). Participants' responses are reinforced with appearance of the word "correct" when selecting S+ or punished with the word "wrong" when selecting S−. In step 3, participants are asked to pick which of the two S+ stimuli they prefer. Results show that participants tend to prefer the S+ stimulus that had been associated with the greater effort required to produce it (Alessandri et al., 2008; Klein et al., 2005). Greater effort has greater negative value and thus forms a greater contrast with the positive value of S+. This greater contrast is responsible for the bigger subjective value placed on that stimulus—that is, on the preferred stimulus.

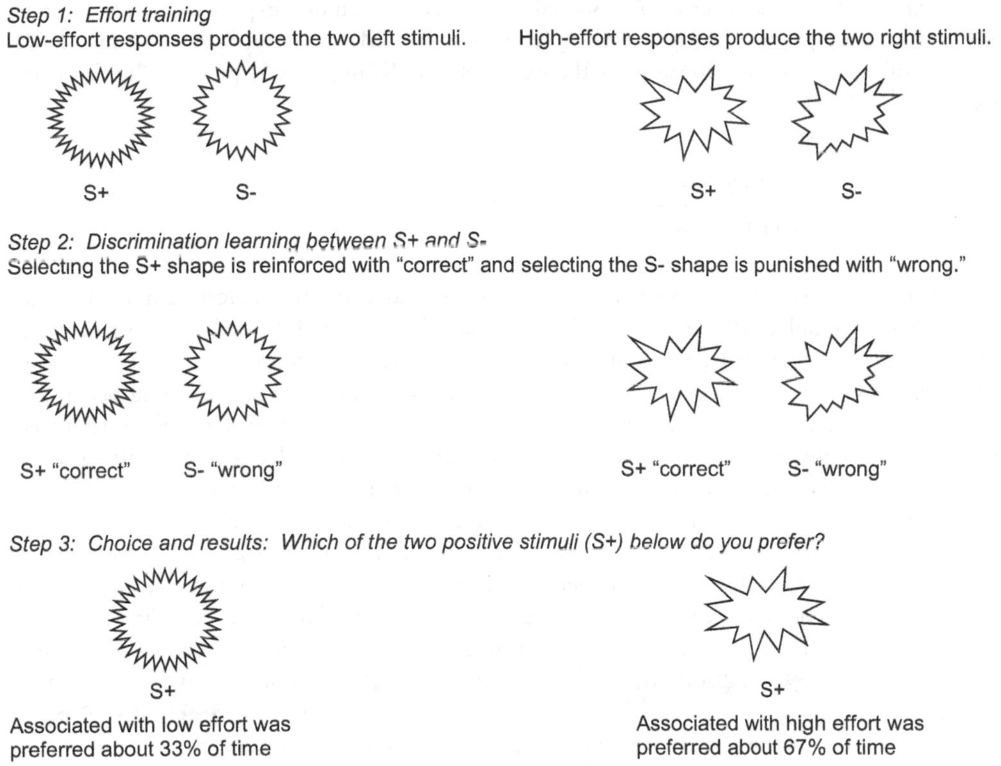

Step 1: Effort training
Low-effort responses produce the two left stimuli.   High-effort responses produce the two right stimuli.

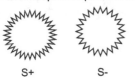

S+   S-   S+   S-

Step 2: Discrimination learning between S+ and S-
Selecting the S+ shape is reinforced with "correct" and selecting the S- shape is punished with "wrong."

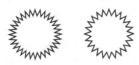   

S+ "correct"   S- "wrong"   S+ "correct"   S- "wrong"

Step 3: Choice and results: Which of the two positive stimuli (S+) below do you prefer?

S+   S+

Associated with low effort was   Associated with high effort was
preferred about 33% of time   preferred about 67% of time

FIGURE 10.5   Contrast between Degree of Effort and Stimulus Preference. Individuals prefer the positive stimulus that stemmed from much effort compared to the positive stimulus that stemmed from little effort.

Source: Adapted from "Preferences for Rewards that Follow Greater Effort and Greater Delay" by J. Alessandri et al., 2008, *Learning and Behavior, 36,* pp. 352–358, and "Contrast and the Justification of Effort" by E. D. Klein et al., 2005, *Psychonomic Bulletin and Review, 12,* pp. 335–339.

Temporal Motivation Theory

You have known for two weeks that there will be an exam on this material but you have not started studying in earnest until two days before. Why is that? One answer is that incentives are based in the future. This feature has tremendous negative impact on incentive value. Although incentive value increases with amount, it decreases with delay. How do these two features combine to determine the value or utility of a future incentive? Remember that value refers to the amount of an incentive while utility refers to its usefulness and ability to provide satisfaction. Thus, $50 has greater value than $10 but also has greater utility, since more goods and services can be purchased with $50.

Incentive utility from value and delay. Several mathematical formulas express how the utility of an incentive changes with delay (Green & Myerson, 2004; Mazur, 1987; Steel & König, 2006). As part of their temporal motivation theory, Steel and König (2006) provide the following formula:

$$\text{Utility} = \frac{\text{Expected incentive value}}{(1+ \text{Delay interval})}$$

Temporal motivation theory integrates how incentive utility changes temporally (with time) (Steel & König, 2006). Utility in this formula refers to the ability of a positive incentive to motivate approach behavior and a negative incentive to motivate avoidance behavior. The term "expected" in the formula refers to the likelihood that the incentive will occur. The expectation is that the incentive is promised or likely to happen despite not being guaranteed. For example, a job interview may result in a job and diligent studying may result in an A. However, the job or the A are not guaranteed. Finally, the denominator of the formula represents the temporal distance to the incentive—that is, the incentive delay interval.

This interval refers to the time between current behavior and the availability of a future incentive. For example, there is a delay between a telephone call or text message for a date and the actual date or between studying and taking an exam. The Saturday night date (the incentive) occurs after (the delay) the telephone call or message. The exam is scheduled some time after a student has studied. As a consequence of this delay, incentives are lower in value. A future incentive is represented in the present at a marked-down value by a process known as **delay discounting** or temporal discounting (Green & Myerson, 2004; Myerson & Green, 1995). The amount of discounting increases with the length of the delay interval. For instance, the value of a Saturday night date or an exam depends on how far in the future they are. The later they occur, the lower their value in the present. However, as their due time approaches, their value increases. As Saturday night approaches, the value of the date increases, and as exam time approaches the value of the exam increases.

To clarify how incentive value changes with delay discounting, decide between each of the following six choices:

Choice 1. $25 now	versus	$50 now (0 delay)
Choice 2. $25 now	versus	$50 in 2 weeks
Choice 3. $25 now	versus	$50 in 4 weeks
Choice 4. $25 now	versus	$50 in 6 weeks
Choice 5. $25 now	versus	$50 in 8 weeks
Choice 6. $25 now	versus	$50 in 10 weeks

Assume that a hypothetical individual preferred $50 on choice 1 and also preferred $50 on choices 2 through 4—that is, he preferred the larger delayed reward over the smaller immediate reward. But then, on choices 5 and 6, he preferred $25 now (0 delay). What happened? As the delay interval increased from 0 delay to 10 weeks, the expected value of $50 was subjected to delay discounting—that is, its value decreased more and more. Eventually, the discounted value of $50 fell below that of $25. Consequently, on choice 5 the individual chose $25 with no delay.

Because of delay discounting, as the incentive delay interval decreases (approaches 0), the utility of positive and negative incentive increases. However, the change in delay discounting is steeper for negative incentives than for positive incentives. Consequently, as the delay interval shortens the unpleasantness of a negative incentive increases faster than does the pleasantness of a positive incentive (Knetsch & Sinden, 1984; Miller, 1959). Finally, when the incentive is reached (delay interval = 0), then the incentive value equals the amount of the incentive. At this point, a positive incentive becomes a reinforcer, and a negative incentive becomes a punisher (Rachlin, 1989). However, their values are not equal. The absolute subjective value of a negative incentive (e.g., $100 loss) is greater than the absolute subjective value of an identical positive incentive (e.g., $100 gain). The reason for this is shown in Figure 10.2: a loss has a greater psychological impact than does a corresponding gain.

Preference reversal. Do these changes in preference occur in daily life? Have you ever planned to do one thing only to change your mind later? For example, this morning you planned to work on an important project this evening. But, when evening arrived, you decided to socialize instead. What happened? Generally, students prefer large rewards such as a good grade on an important project rather than small rewards such as socializing. But, also, individuals prefer their rewards sooner rather than later. In this case, socializing was available immediately in the evening but the grade on the project is not available until the end of the semester. A change from preferring a delayed large reward to preferring an immediate small reward is known as **preference reversal** (Green et al., 1994; Green & Myerson, 2004; Steel & König, 2006). For example, this morning you valued the larger delayed reward of a good grade on the project more than socializing. However, this evening you valued the immediate smaller reward of socializing more than a good grade. In other words, your preference reversed. Figure 10.6 illustrates preference reversal between time *x* and time *y*. During time *x*, the larger delayed incentive has a higher value, but, as the delay interval decreases, the smaller immediate incentive attains a higher value during time *y*.

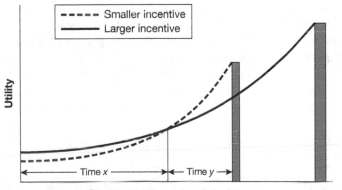

FIGURE 10.6   Changes in Utility over Time. During time *x*, the larger incentive has a greater value than the smaller incentive. As the delay interval decreases, the smaller incentive attains the higher value during time *y*.

Thus, preference reversal occurs because of the change in value between two incentives as their delay intervals decrease. In the prior demonstration of $25 now versus $50 after various delays, preference reversal occurred on choice 5. On choice 4, the individual preferred $50 in six weeks over $25 now. However, on choice 5 she reversed her preferences. On that choice, $25 now was preferred over $50 in eight weeks.

Intangible consequences of choice. Temporal motivation theory describes the process of deciding between outcomes that occur at different temporal distances, such as choosing between receiving $25 now versus receiving $50 four weeks later. Both monetary outcomes are concrete and tangible. However, often choices that involve delayed outcomes are intangible—that is, they are elusive, vague, or abstract (Rick & Loewenstein, 2008). If a student chooses to study the textbook, the immediate outcome is easy to imagine: survey, read, recall, and review each chapter. The same is true for making a purchase: select the item and then give money or credit card to the clerk. However, the alternative outcomes of, say, not studying or not buying are delayed but also intangible. By not studying, how will that affect a student's academic achievement? If a person does not purchase an item, then for what will the savings be used? In addition, the effects of delayed outcomes might be imperceptible, uncertain, and have a low likelihood of occurring (Rick & Loewenstein, 2008). The immediate outcome of indulging in dessert or alcohol is sensory pleasure while the long-term outcomes may imperceptibly produce weight gain or imperceptibly increase the likelihood of alcoholism. On the other hand, not indulging denies pleasure, while the long-term consequences of doing so are intangible. Table 10.2 summarizes the differences that occur between choices that bring immediate outcomes versus delayed outcomes (Rick & Loewenstein, 2008).

Choice based on a common currency. How then does an individual decide between two alternatives? For example, in the case of two different laptops with equal features, a person can base the decision on money: buy the less expensive computer. Or does one see the matinee or evening movie? Again, a decision based on money dictates going to the matinee, since the admission price is cheaper. Finally, does an individual purchase a pair of shoes or attend a rock concert? A decision based on price could help determine a person's choice. In each of these examples, money serves as the **common currency**, which is the shared dimension on which decisions are based. In other words, the value of all goods and services can be compared on the basis of their monetary value—that is, their common currency. However, what is the common currency for decisions about $25 now versus $50 later? One answer is that anticipated pleasure is the common currency. It serves as the collective basis for the final decision between two alternatives (Cabanac, 1992, 2010; Rick & Loewenstein, 2008). The common currency of pleasure operates algebraically by summing the anticipated negative and positive feelings produced by each alternative. The alternative with greatest predicted pleasure or least unpleasantness is chosen.

TABLE 10.2 Differences in Outcomes between Immediate and Delayed Incentives

Immediate Outcome	Delayed Outcome
Consequences are tangible	Consequences are intangible
Effects of choice are perceptible	Effects of choice are imperceptible
High probability of expected outcome	Low probability of expected outcome
Certain what outcomes will be	Uncertain what outcomes will be

Thus, an individual selects to receive $25 immediately rather than $50 in eight weeks because the wait reduces the anticipated pleasure of the $50 below that of the pleasure anticipated from an immediate $25. In other words, the pleasure of $25 now has greater currency than the pleasure of $50 in eight weeks.

Procrastination. Waiting until the last hour to file a federal tax return, not studying for an exam until the last opportunity, or finishing a paper late the night before it is due are examples of procrastination. However, is procrastination merely putting off until later what can be done now? One perspective is that "to procrastinate is to voluntarily delay an intended course of action despite expecting to be worse off for the delay" (Steel, 2007, p. 66). This definition indicates that procrastination depends on the temporal distance of the important activity and the state of being "worse off." For example, an essay that is due in one week has high positive utility (for the potential of a good grade) and being "worse off" is also high (because postponing writing can result in a bad grade and added stress). Not writing the essay in this case would be an instance of procrastination. Steel (2007) presents a hypothetical illustration of student procrastination (see Figure 10.7). A student is assigned an essay on September 15 that is due on December 16, a 92-day delay. The expected incentive value of the essay is based on its letter grade and the likelihood that the student's efforts will produce it. However, how high should the utility of the essay be so that a student will work on it compared to other activity-related utilities? In Figure 10.7, socializing is always available either down the hall, across the campus, with a text message, or with a phone call. So a student socializes because its utility is higher than essay writing. However,

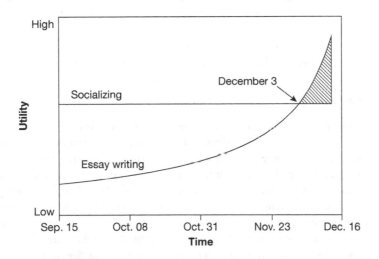

FIGURE 10.7 Changes in Utility of Socializing versus Essay Writing. This graph shows a student's utility estimation of socializing versus writing an essay over the course of the semester. The utility of socializing remains constant, since that activity is always available. The utility of writing an essay increases as the essay's due date approaches—that is, the delay interval decreases.

Source: From "The Nature of Procrastination: A Meta-Analytic and Theoretical Review of Quintessential Self-Regulatory Failure" by P. Steel, 2007, *Psychological Bulletin, 133,* Figure 1, p. 72. Copyright 2007 by American Psychological Association. Reprinted by permission.

on December 3, 12 days before the essay is due, its utility exceeds that of socializing and the student begins to work.

The formula [Utility = (Expected incentive value)/(1 + Delay interval)] helps show what factors will affect procrastination. First, the lower incentive value of a task, the more people will procrastinate on it. For example, students are more likely to procrastinate on assignments they consider less interesting (Ackerman & Gross, 2005). Second, as indicated in Figure 10.7, when procrastinating on a task individuals are doing something else, such as socializing. Thus, procrastination should increase for alternative activities that have greater value. For example, students procrastinate with activities that they consider more pleasant, less stressful, and less difficult than their assignments (Pychyl et al., 2000a). They procrastinate by watching TV, sleeping, talking, playing, eating, or working.

How can we identify procrastinators? One way is to use a psychological scale, such as Lay's (1986) *General Procrastination Scale*. Students identified as procrastinators, for example, tend to predict that they will study less for an exam and do so. In addition, they are more likely than nonprocrastinators to cram by squeezing more of their study time into the last three days (Pychyl et al., 2000b). In general, investigators have concluded that procrastination does make a person worse off. Rothblum and associates (1986) found that students identified as procrastinators had lower GPAs for the semester, delayed taking self-paced quizzes, and had more anxiety or anxiety-related symptoms that accompanied their procrastination. Tice and Baumeister (1997) also showed that procrastinators as defined by Lay's (1986) *General Procrastination Scale* turned in their papers later or late, earned lower scores on their papers, and earned lower exam scores in the course. In addition, procrastination took its toll on the procrastinators at the end of the semester. Procrastinators reported more stress, more symptoms, and more health center visits than did nonprocrastinators.

Lay's (1986) *General Procrastination Scale* is available here: www.yorku.ca/rokada/psyctest/prcrasts.pdf, or here: www.salisbury.edu/counseling/New/Procrastination_Assess.html.

Section Recap

This section covered incentive motivation. Incentive amount refers to the objective quantity or number of stimuli that serve as incentives. Usually, as incentive amount increases, indicators of motivation also increase. However, there are cases where an incentive can decrease motivation compared to no incentive. The motivating effects of an incentive depends on an individual's internal disposition, such as a food incentive being more valuable when one is hungry (hot state) than when satiated (cold state). Incentives also affect choice behavior, as shown by the fact that a person will shift to a better incentive if one is available. According to the concept of *melioration*, a person keeps shifting to alternatives that provide a higher rate of reinforcement than the current one. The phenomenon of *incentive contrast* means that the motivational effects of an incentive depend on the person's experience with prior incentives. Positive incentive contrast refers to a sudden increase in incentive amount that results in a sudden upward shift in motivation. Negative incentive contrast, however, refers to a sudden decrease in incentive amount that results in a sudden downward shift in motivation. The degree of contrast between behavioral effort and the subsequent earned incentive determines the value of that incentive. More difficult behavior will elevate the value of the subsequent incentive. The *law of hedonic contrast* refers to the subjective feelings that accompany incentive contrasts. Positive contrast produces pleasant feelings, while negative contrast produces unpleasant feelings.

According to *temporal motivation theory*, the utility (usefulness) of an incentive depends on the value of the expected incentive and when it becomes available in the future. This relationship is expressed in the formula: Utility = (Expected incentive value)/(1 + Delay interval). The incentive delay interval represents the time span between the present and the availability of the incentive in the future. *Delay discounting* is the process by which the future incentive is represented in the present but at a reduced (discounted) value. Thus, longer delays result in greater discounting, which can result in *preference reversal*. This means that initially an individual prefers a large delayed reward but, as the delay interval gets longer and longer, preferences reverse for a smaller immediate reward.

However, the choice between immediate and delayed incentives can be complicated, since the latter may be intangible, imperceptible, and uncertain. Choices between two incentives are made on the basis of a *common currency*, which refers to the degree of anticipated pleasure that each incentive provides. Pleasure is what both incentives share and serves as the common foundation for comparison. Procrastination means to delay work on an important task with the knowledge that a person is worse off as a consequence of this delay. Procrastination results from temporally discounting the task below that of an immediate alternative activity.

INTRINSIC MOTIVATION

Do you need an external reward for everything you do? Do you enjoy some activities in their own right regardless of whether they are rewarded? Probably. Not all behavior is done for extrinsic incentives. Many activities are done for other reasons. To illustrate, consider author John Irving's motivation for writing:

> The unspoken factor is love. The reason I can work so hard at my writing is that it's not work for me. Or, as I said before, work is pleasure to me. I work, and always have, quite obsessively. I can't just write for four or five hours and then turn the book off. I wake up in the middle of the night and I'm writing it.
>
> (Amabile, 1989, p. 56)

Consider the motivation for dancing to rock-and-roll music expressed by a dancer:

> When you feel [the music] resonating through you, it really helps. Cause when it's loud, like when you're dancing to a rock group, you can really feel yourself vibrate almost. And also, the louder it is, the more it blocks out other noises, so it's more of a total immersion in the music, which is also a very good sensation and is also conducive to just dancing and being part of the music—almost incorporating it.
>
> (Csíkszentmihályi, 1975, p. 105)

In these examples, the motivation for writing or dancing seems inherent in the activity. External rewards or incentives are not apparent. What are the differences between motivation for an activity that seems inherent or intrinsic to that activity and motivation that is external or extrinsic to the activity? How do these two types of motivation combine to influence behavior?

Differences between Extrinsic and Intrinsic Motivation

Are you reading these pages to reduce your anxiety about a forthcoming exam, to earn a good grade, to please your parents, or to feel good about yourself? Or are you reading to satisfy your curiosity, because the material is interesting, or to act in accord with your self-concept as a student? Whatever the reasons, the source of motivation defines whether behavior is extrinsically or intrinsically motivated. **Extrinsic motivation** comes from an external source, such as money, good grades, or the approval of others. **Intrinsic motivation**, in contrast, is inherent in the activity being performed. Extrinsically motivated behavior is coerced (forced) by environmental contingencies, while intrinsically motivated behavior is freely chosen (Deci & Ryan, 1985). Money forces a person to work. A passing grade on an exam forces a student to study. Intrinsically motivated behavior, however, is not forced but is performed because the person wants to experience the activity for its own sake. Thus, individuals may play tennis, bowl, or watch a movie simply for the sake of doing that activity and not because they were forced to do it in order to obtain something. Intrinsic motivation should also be separated from psychological needs. For instance, a person could be motivated to play tennis to satisfy needs of achievement, affiliation, and power. Tennis played for these reasons would be extrinsically motivated, however, since satisfying these psychological needs is external to playing the game. However, playing tennis for the enjoyment that the game provides would be an instance of intrinsic motivation.

Could a student who enrolled in a course because it was required end up liking it? Is it possible that although the original reason for doing an activity is no longer relevant the person still performs the activity anyway? Behavior that began for extrinsic reasons later can be performed for its own sake—that is, for intrinsic reasons. This shift in motivation describes Allport's (1937) concept of the **functional autonomy of motives**. Allport characterizes the idea as "what was a means to an end has become an end in itself" (Allport, 1937, p. 150). Allport uses the example of doing fine work. An individual may feel compelled to do an excellent job even though job security or pay is no longer dependent on performance as was originally the case. In the case of college work, a student may enroll in a course to please her parents or because it comes at a convenient hour. Yet the course may prove to be so interesting that the student decides to major in the field and make it her life's profession.

Purpose of Intrinsically Motivated Behavior

Is intrinsically motivated behavior an end in itself? Or is it linked to other sources of motivation? For instance, intrinsically motivated behavior may be in service to satisfying curiosity and developing competence and self-determination. Curiosity provides the motivation to learn about the environment (Woodworth, 1958), while motives for competence and self-determination provide reasons to control the environment (White, 1959).

Curiosity. Can you avoid eavesdropping on a conversation about someone's sexual escapades at the next table? Can you ignore an e-mail or a text or not bother to answer your phone? These questions illustrate the power of curiosity to intrinsically motivate behavior (Loewenstein, 1994). A stimulus situation can evoke an intense feeling of curiosity. For example, a suspenseful mystery novel is difficult to put down. Curiosity also makes people act impulsively in their desire to seek information, even against their better judgment. For example, a person might eavesdrop on the conversation at the next table at the risk of being rude and being embarrassed if caught.

Furthermore, curiosity can make people act against their own self-interest. For example, a person may experiment with an illegal and potentially dangerous drug. Although curiosity can be classified as an instance of intrinsic motivation, it is linked to a person's desire to know. Curiosity results when the amount of information that individuals want to know exceeds their current knowledge. A situation evokes curiosity to the extent it has the capacity to resolve this gap in knowledge (Loewenstein, 1994).

Is there evidence that people are motivated to satisfy their curiosity? For instance, are you curious to know the answer to the trivia question "what does 'SPF' mean on sunscreen containers?" To find out, Marvin and Shohamy (2016) presented university students 69 questions, one at a time. For each question, students stated how long they would be willing to wait for the answer. A willingness to wait indicates how motivated (persistent) individuals are to satisfy their curiosity. Following presentations of the questions, participants rated their level of curiosity for each with the scale 1 = *not at all curious* to 7 = *very curious*. They also rated how satisfied they were with the answers to each question with the scale 1 = *not at all satisfied* to 7 = *very satisfied*. Participants chose to wait longer for answers to questions that evoked greater curiosity. Furthermore, an answer could more than satisfy curiosity or fall short. Answers that satisfied curiosity were remembered better one week later. The results indicate that curiosity makes information valuable, much like hunger makes food valuable. Thus, satisfying one's curiosity motivates exploring and learning about the environment for answers.

Effectance motivation. A person plays games, pursues hobbies, or spends time with friends simply because these activities are pleasurable or intrinsically motivating. However, intrinsic motivation is also in service to the development of competence. Intrinsically motivated behavior guides an animal or child to act effectively on its surroundings—that is, to become competent (White, 1959). The increase in competence is gained from such activities as exploring novel objects, playing, crawling, walking, speaking, writing, and thinking. These activities result from **effectance motivation**, which is the motive to actively interact and control one's environment (White, 1959). For example, Piaget (1951/1976) refers to a child's mastery play resulting from the mere joy of conquering a particular behavior. A child plays to make things happen and gain control over those happenings.

A simple experiment illustrates effectance motivation in infants who were eight weeks old (Watson, 1972/1976). One thing the infants could do at that age was to press their heads back against their pillows, and so this response was used in the experiment. Watson (1972/1976) devised a mobile that was placed above the infants in their cribs at home. Some mobiles moved and others did not when the infants pressed their heads back against their pillows. In the contingent condition, pressing against the pillow caused the overhead mobile to turn. In the noncontingent condition, the pillow pressing response had no effect on turning the mobile. Although the mobile moved on occasion, it did so independent of any pillow pressing by the infant. In the stable condition, the mobile remained stationary regardless of what the infant did. Being able to have an effect on the mobiles motivated the infants. They increased their frequency of pillow pressing in the contingent condition but not in the noncontingent and stable conditions. In addition, infants in the contingent condition began cooing and smiling as if they were enjoying their mastery over the movements of their mobiles. Infants in the other conditions cooed and smiled much less at their mobiles. So, even at a very young age, infants are intrinsically motivated to have an effect on their environment.

Flow. Competence is also gained by pushing oneself successfully to the limits of one's capability. To illustrate, on more than one occasion I have heard a student say, "I work hard in a course I like." Couldn't the reverse also be true? That is, "I like a course because I work hard in it." The fit between a person's efforts and success at an activity produces **flow** (Csíkszentmihályi, 1975, 1988; Csíkszentmihályi & Rathunde, 1993). It refers to the desirable subjective state a person experiences when completely involved in some challenging activity that matches the individual's skills. The activity has a clear goal and provides immediate feedback regarding the caliber of one's performance. In addition, a person is concentrating all attention on the activity so that time, fatigue, and everything else are disregarded (Csíkszentmihályi, 1975, 1988; Csíkszentmihályi & Rathunde, 1993). Flow has also been used as a metaphor to describe the feelings experienced by artists, athletes, composers, dancers, scientists, and others when engaged in their favorite activities of doing something for the sake of doing: "They are in their flow."

What happens when personal capabilities exceed or fall below the demands of a task? The answer is that individuals are now out of their flow. People are aware of opportunities that challenge them as well as their capabilities of handling that challenge. When the challenges of the task exceed the person's capabilities, then stress is felt as anxiety and worry. However, when the challenges of the task are easily met, then a person feels bored. Flow, however, is experienced when the individual's skills fit with the demands of the task (Csíkszentmihályi, 1975, 1988; Csíkszentmihályi & Rathunde, 1993). To illustrate, canoeing, skiing, and playing chess can be performed at various levels of difficulty. However, whether any of these activities produce flow depends on the match between the difficulty level and the person's capability. If the water is too swift, the slope too steep, or the opponent too skilled, then the canoeist, skier, or chess player experiences stressful reactions such as anxiety and worry. However, when the water is too slow, the slope too flat, and one's opponent less skilled, then the person generally experiences boredom. These activities, however, will provide maximum enjoyment and flow when there is a match between the challenge of the activity and the person's capability level (Csíkszentmihályi, 1975, 1988; Csíkszentmihályi & Rathunde, 1993). Personality psychologist Gordon Allport (1937) also noted the positive relationship between ability and interest. He remarked, "A person likes to do what he can do well" (p. 150).

Interaction between Extrinsic and Intrinsic Motivation

What happens when extrinsic and intrinsic motivation combine? When amateur athletes become professionals, does money make them enjoy their sports more or less? Do retired professional athletes still play their sport for fun? The combination of extrinsic and intrinsic motivation affects the enjoyment and performance of behavior differently (Cerasoli et al., 2014; Tang & Hall, 1995; Wiersma, 1992).

Extrinsic reward and intrinsic motivation. One major league outfielder said, "I used to enjoy playing baseball until I started getting paid for it" (Arkes & Garske, 1977, p. 251). This quote previews some findings regarding the effects of extrinsic rewards on intrinsically motivated behavior. As the quote implies, extrinsic reward can undermine intrinsically motivated behavior. However, it is doubtful that the outfielder quit playing. Thus, both intrinsic and extrinsic motivation affect behavior simultaneously.

The decline in intrinsic motivation from extrinsic rewards comes from experiments in which a person is given a choice at the end of a paid behavior session: to continue the intrinsically motivated behavior for no payment or stop. Individuals often choose to stop or reduce their efforts as if the reward had weakened the intrinsic motivation for the behavior. So, when the reward is removed, the behavior ceases (Cerasoli et al., 2014; Tang & Hall, 1995; Wiersma, 1992). However, besides choice, motivation is also reflected in performance measures of behavior. Although extrinsic reward undermines intrinsic interest, it facilitates performance measures of motivation (Wiersma, 1992). For example, what would happen to performance on an intrinsically motivated task if the person started receiving contingent pay—that is, pay based on behavior? Such a question was asked by Harackiewicz and associates (1984, study 2) in their investigation of students who engaged in the intrinsically motivated behavior of playing pinball. The expected-reward group was offered and received a reward (movie pass) if its pinball playing performance was at the 80th percentile level. The unexpected-reward group was not told anything about a reward (movie pass) and unexpectedly received it anyway at the end of the game. A no-reward group neither expected nor received any kind of reward for its playing. At the conclusion of one game of pinball, the experimenter informed each participant they had performed at the 80th percentile. The experimenter then left the room on some pretext. Before leaving, however, the experimenter suggested that participants play some more pinball or just relax while waiting. While gone, the number of balls that were played, the score achieved, and the enjoyment of any playing were recorded. The number of balls played and enjoyment measures are indicators of intrinsic interest, while the score achieved is a performance measure of motivation. Figure 10.8a shows that fewer balls were played in the expected-reward condition than in the unexpected-reward condition. Thus, being rewarded for playing decreased the intrinsic motivation for pinball. However, ratings indicating enjoyment did not differ among the three conditions. The performance measure of motivation in Figure 10.8b shows that participants in the expected-reward condition, however, achieved higher scores for playing than participants in the unexpected-reward and no-reward conditions. Thus, when a performance measure is used, extrinsic motivation can enhance performance that is based on intrinsic motivation (Wiersma, 1992). Similarly, regardless of what effect salaries have on the enjoyment of their sport, professional athletes still play extremely well when paid millions of dollars.

Quality versus quantity of behavior. Behavior varies in quantity and quality. Do intrinsic and extrinsic motivation differ in the type of behavior they affect: quantity versus quality (Cerasoli et al., 2014)? For example, students are motivated extrinsically by course grades but also intrinsically by exciting professors teaching interesting topics. The effects of extrinsic and intrinsic motivation differ for quantity versus quality. Quantity refers to how much a person does, while quality refers to how well she does it, for example, the excellence of a paper compared to its length or how well a piece of equipment is assembled at the factory versus the number of pieces assembled. Also, an incentive can be contingent or noncontingent on behavior. A contingent incentive is attained only after the behavior has been performed. For example, in the pinball playing experiment, participants were paid if they reached the 80th percentile of performance. A noncontingent incentive is not tied to performance on the task. For example, participants are paid unexpectedly at the end of the pinball session regardless of whether they reached the 80th percentile.

The interaction between extrinsic and intrinsic motivation are applicable to a student's assignment of writing a seven- to 10-page term paper. The paper can range in quantity from

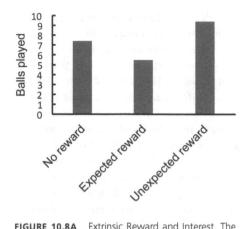

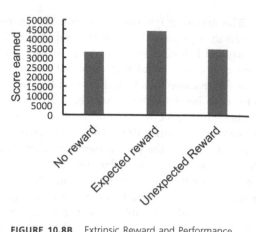

FIGURE 10.8A Extrinsic Reward and Interest. The graph shows the mean number of pinballs played during a free period. Fewer balls were played during the expected-reward condition, which indicates that extrinsic reward undermined intrinsic interest in the game.

Source: Adapted from "Rewarding Pinball Wizardry" by J. M. Harackiewicz et al., 1984, *Journal of Personality and Social Psychology, 47*, p. 294.

FIGURE 10.8B Extrinsic Reward and Performance. The graph shows scores earned playing pinball during a free period. Pinball performance was greatest in the expected-reward condition, which indicates that an extrinsic incentive can enhance performance based on intrinsic motivation.

Source: Adapted from "Rewarding Pinball Wizardry" by J. M. Harackiewicz et al., 1984, *Journal of Personality and Social Psychology, 47*, p. 294.

seven pages to 10 pages. It can also vary in quality by being interesting, well organized, and well written. Extrinsic and intrinsic motivation increase both the quantity and quality of behavior (Cerasoli et al., 2014). However, intrinsic motivation increases the quality of behavior more, while extrinsic motivation increases quantity more. For instance, assume that the paper could account for 20 percent or 40 percent of the course grade. This percentage is an example of a contingent incentive: a better paper earns a higher grade. In this case, a quantity measure of the paper will be affected more than its quality. Thus, students will write more words for 40 percent than for 20 percent of the course grade; the quality of the paper increases only slightly. One interpretation is that the contingent incentive crowds out the effect of intrinsic motivation (Frey & Jegen, 2001). The incentive of the 40 percent grade is more noticeable and seems to be the obvious factor that controls the student's behavior. The intrinsic motivation for researching and writing the paper has been crowded out. The student acknowledges that she is writing the paper because her course grade depends on it and not because she enjoys the writing process.

However, intrinsic motivation stems from a student being curious about her topic, enjoying her library research, and pleasure from putting her thoughts into words. The greater her intrinsic motivation in this case, the more the quality of the paper will improve, more so than quantity. Thus, greater intrinsic motivation translates into a more interesting, organized, and well-written paper although quantity will also increase slightly. In this case, the presence of a noncontingent incentive can increase the quality of the paper because the noncontingent incentive is not considered controlling—that is, it does not crowd out intrinsic motivation.

Cognitive evaluation theory provides another explanation of extrinsic rewards undermining or crowding out intrinsic interests (Deci & Ryan, 1985). According to this theory, a person's intrinsic motivation for a task depends on what is perceived to be the reason for the behavior. If the reason is perceived as external, as in the case of being paid, then a person perceives the reward as the basis for doing the task. Consequently, when payment ceases, the behavior ceases. In this case, intrinsic motivation declines, since the individual reasons that his behavior is externally rather than internally controlled. However, when no contingent external rewards are perceived, then the person concludes that her behavior is under self-control, which means that it is freely chosen and is intrinsically motivating.

Motivational Orientation

Activities such as schoolwork and employment are done for reasons of both extrinsic and intrinsic motivation. When performing such activities, individuals differ in their **motivational orientation,** which refers to being consistently directed toward an extrinsic or an intrinsic source of motivation (Amabile et al., 1994, 1995). A person is extrinsically oriented when studying is done solely for a grade or working is done solely for money. A person is intrinsically oriented when studying or working are done solely for their own sake. Of course, an individual could be motivated both intrinsically and extrinsically to various degrees. Both types of motivation are present at school and work. But do extrinsic and intrinsic motivations sum to increase behavior in those situations? Or do extrinsic rewards such as grades and money actually weaken behavior? A person's motivational orientation may help determine how these two sources of motivation interact over the long run. Does the likelihood of graduation depend on grades or on students enjoying their coursework? Does how long a worker remains on the job depend on pay or on the pleasure the job provides? In an answer to these questions, Wrzesniewski and coresearchers (2014) followed the careers of over 10,000 students (cadets) who entered the United States Military Academy at West Point, New York. The academy functions like a university. On graduation, the cadets are commissioned as officers in the United States Army for a minimum commitment of five years. Over a nine-year period, each entering class answered a series of questions regarding their intrinsic and extrinsic motivation for selecting the academy, being commissioned, and subsequent military advancement. Intrinsic motivation questions included the importance of leadership training, desire to be an army officer, and personal development. Extrinsic motivation questions included importance of the quality and reputation of the academic program, being able to get a better job, and being able to make more money.

A greater emphasis in orienting toward intrinsic motivation resulted in more success than did an emphasis on orienting toward extrinsic motivation. The two types of motivation did not sum to increase behavior. Rather, the greater emphasis on extrinsic motivation crowded out intrinsic motivation. The results showed that cadets who emphasized intrinsic reasons over extrinsic reasons were more likely to be commissioned, more likely to remain in the army, and more likely to be considered for early promotion. Cadets who emphasized extrinsic over intrinsic reasons, on the other hand, showed the reverse pattern. They were less likely to be commissioned, less likely to remain in the army, and less likely to be considered for early promotion (Wrzesniewski et al., 2014). These results show the effects of different degrees of emphasis on intrinsic versus extrinsic motivation.

Section Recap

Motivation can come from sources external to behavior or from the satisfaction that the behavior itself provides. *Extrinsic motivation* is coerced by an external incentive, such as praise, money, or good grades, while *intrinsic motivation* is freely chosen and is inherent in the activity. Intrinsic motivation may be in service to curiosity and the evolution of competence. In some instances behavior that is performed for extrinsic reasons is eventually maintained by intrinsic motivation, as described by the concept of *functional autonomy of motives*. People are motivated to satisfy their curiosity. In fact, curiosity provides the motivation for learning about one's environment to find answers that satisfy curiosity. Competence results from *effectance motivation*, which provides the impetus for children to interact effectively with their environment so that they can learn to control it. Another feature of intrinsic motivation is *flow*, which is the desirable subjective feeling that results from being involved in a challenging activity that matches one's skills. Adding extrinsic motivation to an intrinsically motivated activity has two effects. On the one hand, extrinsic motivation decreases the intrinsic value of the activity, but, on the other, extrinsic motivation enhances the performance of the intrinsic activity. Furthermore, intrinsic motivation affects the quality of behavior more, such as school work, while extrinsic motivation influences the quantity of behavior more. Extrinsic incentives can reduce intrinsic motivation as if the incentives crowds out the effects of intrinsic motivation. According to *cognitive evaluation theory*, the reason for the decline in intrinsic interest is that motivation for a task depends on the perceived reason for the behavior. If the reason is perceived as external, as in the case of an external incentive, then removal of the incentive leads to a decline in motivation. Finally, individuals differ in their consistent *motivational orientation* toward extrinsic and intrinsic motivation. A person can be high or low on either type of motivational orientation. When extrinsically oriented, a person works for grades or money, but when intrinsically oriented, a person works for the inherent satisfaction the activity provides. In regards to long-term goals, a dominance of intrinsic motivation leads to greater success than does a dominance of extrinsic motivation.

GLOSSARY

Term	Definition
Cognitive Evaluation Theory	A person evaluates the reason for her behavior. If the reason is external, then this results in a decline in intrinsic interest in the task
Common Currency	The shared dimension of anticipated pleasure on which decisions are made regarding different immediate versus delayed incentives
Curiosity	An intrinsic motive that serves as the basis for learning about the environment and is linked to the desire to know
Delay Discounting	Also known as temporal discounting, this is a process by which a future incentive is represented in the present at a marked-down value
Effectance Motivation	The motive to actively interact and control one's environment; to want to make things happen
Extrinsic Motivation	Source of motivation is external to the person; behavior is coerced by external incentives, such as money, grades, or the approval of others

continued . . .

GLOSSARY Continued

Term	Definition
Fechner's Law	Stimulus–response relationship characterized by equal increases in stimulus intensity produces smaller and smaller increases in sensations
Flow	Desirable subjective state a person experiences when completely involved in some challenging activity that matches the individual's skills
Functional Autonomy of Motives	Behavior that began for extrinsic reasons (motivation) later can be performed for its own sake, that is, for intrinsic reasons (motivation)
Incentive	An external stimulus that motivates or induces behavior to occur, such as a promise
Incentive Amount	The quantity of or number of incentives, e.g., $20 is a larger incentive than $10
Incentive Contrast	A shift in incentive value (amount or quality). The ability of an incentive to motivate depends on how it differs (contrasts) from prior incentives
Incentive Value	The attractiveness of an incentive that is based on objective properties such as number or amount
Intrinsic Motivation	Source of motivation is inherent in the activity being performed; the activity is freely chosen
Law of Hedonic Contrast	The pleasure a stimulus provides depends on if it contrasts with sources of lesser pleasure (displeasure) or sources of greater pleasure (less displeasure)
Losses Loom Larger than Gains	The loss of an incentive is more dissatisfying than the gain of an incentive is satisfying
Melioration	A shift toward an activity or behavior that is more lucrative or provides a greater rate of reinforcement
Motivational Orientation	Being consistently directed toward an extrinsic or intrinsic source of motivation, e.g., studying for grades (extrinsic) or studying for pleasure (intrinsic)
Negative Incentive Contrast	A downward shift in incentive value, which decreases behavior below what it was previously
Positive Incentive Contrast	An upward shift in incentive value, which increases behavior above what it was previously
Preference Reversal	A shift in preference from a large delayed incentive to a small immediate incentive, which occurs when the delay for the larger incentive increases
Procrastination	To voluntarily postpone or delay an intended course of action despite anticipating that you will be worse off because of that delay
Prospect Theory	It views positive incentives as gains and negative incentives as losses. Also, the psychological impact of a loss is stronger than the impact of a gain
Punishers	A consequence of behavior that selects against the behavior or decreases the frequency or likelihood of that behavior
Reinforcers	A consequence of behavior that selects or increases the frequency or likelihood of that behavior
Temporal Motivation Theory	It maintains that the utility (usefulness) of an incentive depends on the value of the expected incentive and when it becomes available in the future

continued . . .

GLOSSARY Continued

Term	Definition
Utility	Usefulness of an incentive based on its ability to produce satisfaction or happiness; usually refers to an economic good
Utils	A measure of the utility of an economic good or service. It is no longer used but was at one time by economists
Value Function Curve	A curve of the relationship between the objective amount of a loss or gain and the value or intensity of the consequent psychological reaction

REFERENCES

Ackerman, D. S., & Gross, B. L. (2005). My instructor made me do it: Task characteristics of procrastination. *Journal of Marketing Education, 27*, 5–13.

Alessandri, J., Darcheville, J.-C., & Delevoye-Turrell,Y. (2008). Preference for rewards that follow greater effort and greater delay. *Learning & Behavior, 36*, 352–358.

Allport, G. W. (1937). The functional autonomy of motives. *American Journal of Psychology, 50*, 141–156.

Amabile, T. M. (1989). *Growing up creative: Nurturing a lifetime of creativity*. New York, NY: Crown.

Amabile, T. M., Hill, K. G., Hennessey, B. A., & Tighe, E. M. (1994). The Work Preference Inventory: Assessing intrinsic and extrinsic motivational orientations. *Journal of Personality and Social Psychology, 66*, 950–967.

Amabile, T. M., Hill, K. G., Hennessey, B. A., & Tighe, E. M. (1995). The Work Preference Inventory: Assessing intrinsic and extrinsic motivational orientations: Correction. *Journal of Personality and Social Psychology, 68*, 580.

Ariely, D., Gneezy, U., Loewenstein, G., & Mazar, N. (2009). Large stakes and big mistakes. *The Review of Economic Studies, 76*, 451–469.

Arkes, H. R., & Garske, J. P. (1977). *Psychological theories of motivation*. Monterey, CA: Brooks/Cole.

Baumeister, R. F., Bratslavsky, E., Finkenauer, C., & Vohs, K. D. (2001). Bad is stronger than good. *Review of General Psychology, 5*, 323–370.

Beebe-Center, J. G. (1932/1965). *The psychology of pleasantness and unpleasantness*. New York, NY: Van Nostrand.

Bolles, R. C. (1975). *Theory of motivation* (2nd ed.). New York, NY: Harper & Row.

Cabanac, M. (1992). Pleasure: The common currency. *Journal of Theoretical Biology, 155*, 173–200.

Cabanac, M. (2010). The dialectics of pleasure. In M. L. Kringelbach & K. C. Berridge (Eds.), *Pleasures of the brain* (pp. 113–124). New York, NY: Oxford University Press.

Camerer, C. F., & Hogarth, R. M. (1999). The effects of financial incentives in experiments: A review and capital-labor-production framework. *Journal of Risk and Uncertainty, 19*, 7–42.

Cerasoli, C. P., Nicklin, J. M., & Ford, M. T. (2014). Intrinsic motivation and extrinsic incentives jointly predict performance: A 40-year meta-analysis. *Psychological Bulletin, 140*, 980–1008.

Cofer, C. N., & Appley, M. H. (1964). *Motivation: Theory and research*. New York, NY: Wiley.

Cogan, E., Parker, S., & Zellner, D. A. (2013). Beauty beyond compare: Effects of context extremity and categorization on hedonic contrast. *Journal of Experimental Psychology: Human Perception and Performance, 39*, 16–22.

Compeau, L. D., & Grewal, D. (1998). Comparative price advertising: An integrative review. *Journal of Public Policy and Marketing, 17*, 257–273.

Condly, S. J., Clark, R. E., & Stolovitch, H. D. (2003). The effects of incentives on workplace performance: A meta-analytic review of research studies. *Performance Improvement Quarterly, 16*, 46–63.

Correia, C. J., & Benson, T. A. (2006). The use of contingency management to reduce cigarette smoking among college students. *Experimental and Clinical Psychopharmacology, 14*, 171–179.

Csíkszentmihályi, M. (1975). *Beyond boredom and anxiety*. San Francisco, CA: Jossey-Bass.

Csíkszentmihályi, M. (1988). The flow experience and its significance for human psychology. In M. Csíkszentmihályi & I. S. Csíkszentmihályi (Eds.), *Optimal experience: Psychological studies of flow in consciousness* (pp. 15–35). New York, NY: Cambridge University Press.

Csíkszentmihályi, M., & Rathunde, K. (1993). The measurement of flow in everyday life: Toward a theory of emergent motivation. In R. Dienstbier (Series Ed.) & J. E. Jacobs (Vol. Ed.), *Nebraska Symposium on Motivation: Vol. 40. Developmental perspectives on motivation* (pp. 57–97). Lincoln, NE: University of Nebraska Press.

de Villiers, P. (1977). Choice in concurrent schedules and a quantitative formulation of the law of effect. In W. K. Honig & J. E. R. Staddon (Eds.), *Handbook of operant behavior* (pp. 233–287). Englewood Cliffs, NJ: Prentice Hall.

Deci, E. L., & Ryan, R. M. (1985). *Intrinsic motivation and self-determination in human behavior*. New York, NY: Plenum.

Fechner, G. T. (1860/1966). *Elements of psychophysics*. New York, NY: Holt, Rinehart and Winston.

Fechner, G. T. (1876). *Vorschule der aesthetik* [Introduction to aesthetics]. Leipzig: Breitkopf & Härtel.

Fisher, G., & Rangel, A. (2014). Symmetry in cold-to-hot and hot-to-cold valuation gaps. *Psychological Science, 25*, 120–127.

Frey, B. S., & Jegen, R. (2001). Motivation crowding theory. *Journal of Economic Surveys, 15*, 589–611.

Gneezy, U., Meier, S., & Rey-Biel, P. (2011). When and why incentives (don't) work to modify behavior. *The Journal of Economic Perspectives, 25*, 191–209.

Gneezy, U., & Rustichini, A. (2000). Pay enough or don't pay at all. *The Quarterly Journal of Economics, 15*, 791–810.

Goldsmith, K., & Dhar, R. (2013). Negativity bias and task motivation: Testing the effectiveness of positively versus negatively framed incentives. *Journal of Experimental Psychology: Applied, 19*, 358–366.

Green, L., Fry, A. F., & Myerson, J. (1994). Discounting of delayed rewards: A life span comparison. *Psychological Science, 5*, 33–36.

Green, L., & Myerson, J. (2004). A discounting framework for choice with delayed and probabilistic rewards. *Psychological Bulletin, 130*, 769–792.

Harackiewicz, J. M., Manderlink, G., & Sansone, C. (1984). Rewarding pinball wizardry: Effects of evaluation and cue value on intrinsic interest. *Journal of Personality and Social Psychology, 47*, 287–300.

Helson, H. (1964). *Adaptation-Level Theory: An experimental and systematic approach to behavior*. New York, NY: Harper & Row.

Herrnstein, R. J. (1961). Relative and absolute strength of response as a function of frequency of reinforcement. *Journal of the Experimental Analysis of Behavior, 4*, 267–272.

Herrnstein, R. J. (1990). Rational choice theory: Necessary but not sufficient. *American Psychologist, 45*, 356–367.

Hull, C. L. (1952). *A behavior system*. New Haven, CT: Yale University Press.

Kahneman, D. (2011). *Thinking, fast and slow*. New York, NY: Farrar, Straus and Giroux.

Kahneman, D., Knetsch, J. L., & Thaler, R. H. (1990). Experimental tests of the endowment effect and the Coase theorem. *Journal of Political Economy, 98*, 1325–1348.

Kahneman, D., & Tversky, A. (1979). Prospect theory: An analysis of decision under risk. *Econometrica, 47*, 263–291.

Kahneman, D., & Tversky, A. (1982). The psychology of preferences. *Scientific American, 246*, 160–173.

Karniol, R., & Ross, M. (1996). The motivational impact of temporal focus: Thinking about the future and the past. *Annual Review of Psychology, 47*, 593–620.

Klein, E. D., Bhatt, R. S., & Zentall, T. R. (2005). Contrast and the justification of effort. *Psychonomic Bulletin and Review, 12*, 335–339.

Knetsch, J. L., & Sinden, J. A. (1984). Willingness to pay and compensation demanded: Experimental evidence of an unexpected disparity in measures of value. *Quarterly Journal of Economics, August*, 507–521.

Krishna, A., Briesch, R., Lehmann, D. R., & Yuan, H. (2002). A meta-analysis of the impact of price presentation on perceived savings. *Journal of Retailing, 78*, 101–118.

Lay, C. (1986). At last, my research article on procrastination. *Journal of Research in Personality, 20*, 474–495.

Lea, S. E., & Webley, P. (2006). Money as tool, money as drug: The biological psychology of a strong incentive. *Behavioral and Brain Sciences, 29*, 161–209.

Lippman, L. G. (2000). Contingent incentive value in human operant performance. *The Psychological Record, 50*, 513–528.

Loewenstein, G. (1994). The psychology of curiosity: A review and reinterpretation. *Psychological Bulletin, 116*, 75–98.

Loewenstein, G. (1996). Out of control: Visceral influences on behavior. *Organizational Behavior and Human Decision Processes, 65*, 272–292.

Logan, F. A. (1960). *Incentive*. New Haven, CT: Yale University Press.

Logan, F. A., & Wagner, A. R. (1965). *Reward and punishment*. Boston, MA: Allyn and Bacon.

Markus, H., & Nurius, P. (1986). Possible selves. *American Psychologist, 41*, 954–969.

Marvin, C. B., & Shohamy, D. (2016). Curiosity and reward: Valence predicts choice and information prediction errors enhance learning. *Journal of Experimental Psychology: General, 145*, 266–272.

Mazur, J. E. (1987). An adjusting procedure for studying delayed reinforcement. In M. L. Commons, J. E. Mazur, J. A. Nevin, & H. Rachlin (Eds.), *Quantitative analyses of behavior: Vol. 5. The effect of delay and of intervening events on reinforcement value* (pp. 55–73). Hillsdale, NJ: Lawrence Erlbaum.

Miller, N. E. (1959). Liberalization of basic S-R concepts: Extensions to conflict behavior, motivation, and social learning. In S. Koch (Ed.), *Psychology: A study of a science* (Vol. 2, pp. 196–292). New York, NY: McGraw-Hill.

Myerson, J., & Green, L. (1995). Discounting of delayed rewards: Models of individual choice. *Journal of the Experimental Analysis of Behavior, 61*, 263–276.

Neef, N. A., Mace, F. C., Shea, M. C., & Shade, D. (1992). Effects of reinforcer rate and reinforcer quality on time allocation: Extensions of matching theory to educational settings. *Journal of Applied Behavior Analysis, 25*, 691–699.

Piaget, J. (1951/1976). Mastery play. In J. S. Bruner, A. Jolly, & K. Sylva (Eds.), *Play—its role in development and evolution* (pp. 166–171). New York, NY: Basic.

Pychyl, T. A., Lee, J. M., Thibodeau, R., & Blunt, A. (2000a). Five days of emotion: An experience sampling study of undergraduate student procrastination. *Journal of Social Behavior and Personality, 15*, 239–254.

Pychyl, T. A., Morin, R. W., & Salmon, B. R. (2000b). Procrastination and the planning fallacy: An examination of the study habits of university students. *Journal of Social Behavior and Personality, 15*, 135–150.

Rachlin, H. (1989). *Judgment, decision, and choice*. New York, NY: W. H. Freeman.

Rick, S., & Loewenstein, G. (2008). Intangibility in intertemporal choice. *Philosophical Transactions of the Royal Society, 363*, 3813–3824.

Rothblum, E. D., Solomon, L. J., & Murakami, J. (1986). Affective, cognitive, and behavioral differences between high and low procrastinators. *Journal of Counseling Psychology, 33*, 387–394.

Rozin, P., & Royzman, E. B. (2001). Negativity bias, negativity dominance, and contagion. *Personality and Social Psychology Review, 5*, 296–320.

Shepperd, J. A., & McNulty, J. K. (2002). The affective consequences of expected and unexpected outcomes. *Psychological Science, 13*, 85–88.

Skinner, B. F. (1938). *The behavior of organisms*. New York, NY: Appleton-Century-Crofts.

Skinner, B. F. (1953). *Science and human behavior*. New York, NY: Macmillan.

Staddon, J. E. R., & Simmelhag, V. L. (1971). The "superstition" experiment: A reexamination of its implications for the principles of adaptive behavior. *Psychological Review, 78*, 3–43.

Steel, P. (2007). The nature of procrastination: A meta-analytic and theoretical review of quintessential self-regulatory failure. *Psychological Bulletin, 133*, 65–94.

Steel, P., & König, C. J. (2006). Integrating theories of motivation. *Academy of Management Review, 31*, 889–913.

Stevens, S. S. (1972). *Psychophysics and scaling*. Morristown, NJ: General Learning Press.

Stigler, G. J. (1950). The development of utility theory. *Journal of Political Economy, 58*(4), 307–327; *58*(5), 373–396.

Tang, S.-H., & Hall, V. C. (1995). The overjustification effect: A meta-analysis. *Applied Cognitive Psychology, 9*, 365–404.

Tice, D. M., & Baumeister, R. F. (1997). Longitudinal study of procrastination, performance, stress, and health: The costs and benefits of dawdling. *Psychological Science, 8,* 454–458.

Tolman, E. C. (1955). Principles of performance. *Psychological Review, 62,* 315–326.

Tolman, E. C., & Honzik, C. H. (1930). Introduction and removal of reward, and maze performance in rats. *University of California Publications in Psychology, 4,* 257–275.

Watson, J. (1972/1976). Smiling, cooing and "the game." In J. S. Bruner, A. Jolly, & K. Sylva (Eds.), *Play—its role in development and evolution* (pp. 268–276). New York, NY: Basic.

White, R. W. (1959). Motivation reconsidered: The concept of competence. *Psychological Review, 66,* 297–333.

Wiersma, U. J. (1992). The effects of extrinsic rewards in intrinsic motivation: A meta-analysis. *Journal of Occupational and Organizational Psychology, 65,* 101–114.

Woodworth, R. S. (1958). *Dynamics of behavior.* New York, NY: Holt.

Wrzesniewski, A., Schwartz, B., Cong, X., Kane, M., Omar, A., & Kolditz, T. (2014). Multiple types of motives don't multiply the motivation of West Point cadets. *Proceedings of the National Academy of Sciences, 111,* 10990–10995.

Zellner, D. A., Kern, B. B., & Parker, S. (2002). Protection for the good: Subcategorization reduces hedonic contrast. *Appetite, 38,* 175–180.

Zellner, D. A., Rohm, E. A., Bassetti, T. L., & Parker, S. (2003). Compared to what? Effects of categorization on hedonic contrast. *Psychonomic Bulletin and Review, 10,* 468–473.

Zentall, T. R. (2010). Justification of effort by humans and pigeons: Cognitive dissonance or contrast. *Current Directions in Psychological Science, 19,* 296–300.

CHAPTER 11

Goal Motivation

In all human affairs there is always an end in view—of pleasure, or honor, or advantage.

Polybius, 125 B.C.

Our plans miscarry because they have no aim. When a man does not know what harbor he is making for, no wind is the right wind.

Seneca, 4 B.C.–A.D. 65

Goals focus motivation. Individuals concentrate their resources to achieve a goal, such as reading this chapter to answer the following questions:

1. From where do goals originate?
2. What goal characteristics are important for motivation?
3. What factors determine whether a goal should be pursued?
4. How do people commit to, plan, and achieve a goal?
5. What are the consequences of goal success and goal failure?

ORIGINS OF GOALS

Words from Steve Jobs provide a good introduction to this chapter. Jobs, who launched the Macintosh computer, the iPod, iTunes, the iPhone, the iPad, the iCloud, and the Apple company, stated:

My passion has been to build an enduring company where people were motivated to make great products. Everything else is secondary. Sure, it was great to make a profit, because that was what allowed you to make great products. But the products, not the profits, were the motivation.

(Isaacson, 2011, p. 567)

Jobs also commented that individuals must love and have a passion for their work because often it is very hard that a rational person might give up. This passion is necessary in order to persevere and work hard over a long period of time in order to achieve goal success. So what characterizes goals and where do goals come from?

From Possible End-States to Goals

As indicated in Chapter 1, motivation resembles a journey toward some destination or end-state. Of several end-states, which one does a person select, commit to, and attempt to achieve? **Mindset theory of action** provides a two-phase answer (Gollwitzer, 2012). Individuals set their minds to different phases of the goal achievement process. In the first phase, they mentally focus on goal selection. What criteria are critical? And what goal will be selected and committed to? In the second phase, individuals plan on what behaviors are available to achieve the selected goal.

Goal characteristics. A **goal** is the cognitive image of a future outcome. It can represent an object, behavior, or feeling. This image activates and guides behavior. However, the future outcome does not qualify as a goal until a person commits to achieving it (Austin & Vancouver, 1996; Elliot & Fryer, 2008; Klinger, 1977). Goals are assisted by the use of incentives to boost the motivation of goal achievement behavior. The focus remains on the goal but the incentive provides a boost. For example, in the Jobs quote, money was an incentive because it helped motivate work toward the goal of making great products.

Several dimensions characterize goals (see Table 11.1) (Austin & Vancouver, 1996). Goals differ in importance. They can range from Jobs's goal of making excellent electronic products to something minor like what to eat for dinner. Goals range from easy to difficult. For instance, developing a laptop computer is more difficult than preparing dinner. Goals range from vague to specific. Higher-level goals are usually vaguer, while lower-level goals are more specific. For example, the goal of establishing a career is vaguer than the subgoal of graduating from college. The temporal range of goals extends from the immediate to the delayed. Subgoals are immediate and serve as steps toward the final goal. They are like individual stairs for reaching the desired floor (final goal). To illustrate, passing a course is the subgoal for the final goal of graduation. Goals also differ in duration. Thus, launching a particular product, such as an iPhone, is of short duration, whereas maintaining a great enduring company lasts for decades. Goals differ in the degree to which a person is aware of them. For example, a student may be aware of trying to pass a course but does not dwell on the fact that this success is necessary for graduation. Finally, some goals are simple and some are complex. Complexity determines how many links there are to other goals and the number of subgoals. A career goal, for instance, is linked to many other goals, such as a student's major or a bachelor's degree. Dinner preparation, on the other hand, has fewer links and fewer subgoals.

TABLE 11.1 Dimensional Characteristics of Goals

Importance	Goal's attractiveness, intensity, relevance, priority, and sign (positive, negative)
Difficulty	Level of goal that determines how challenging it is to achieve
Specificity	Goal is qualitative and ranges from being vaguely to precisely stated
Temporal Range	Goals range from proximal (immediate) to distal (delayed) and of short to long duration
Level of Consciousness	Cognitive awareness of goals is greater for proximal goals than for distal goals
Connectedness/Complexity	With greater complexity, goals have more connections to behaviors, subgoals, and other goals

Selecting a goal. According to the mindset theory of action, students might put their minds to considering the following alternatives on a Saturday afternoon:

1. Wash dirty clothes. Clean clothes have a great utility.
2. Prepare for a psychology exam on Monday. An A in this class is important for achieving a desired career.
3. Decide whether to go to a party that evening and whom to ask as a date. Enjoying oneself and looking for a romantic partner are important to a sense of well-being.
4. Decide on a university major, since that determines the selection of courses.

What determines which available outcome is selected as a goal (Karniol & Ross, 1996)? In this example, what determine the student's choice: Clean clothes, an A on Monday's exam, the party, or a scholastic major? The choice of alternatives, however, depends on several factors. First, the value or utility of the outcome is important. Is the goal helpful for future endeavors? Is it useful? Does it provide satisfaction? Washing clothes competes with studying for the exam. Doing well on the exam may be more important than clean clothes, but clean clothes are needed immediately, while the exam is two days away. Second, all other things being equal, the outcome with the highest probability of success will be selected. The probabilities of getting a date or going alone determine whether the student decides to go to the party. The time and effort to achieve a goal are also factors in the decision. If the alternatives are valued equally, then the one requiring the least amount of time and effort is pursued (Hull, 1943; Tolman, 1932). Perhaps the student will choose to wash clothes, if that requires less time and effort than studying for the exam. Value or utility, probability, and effort are all factors that interact to determine what alternative is chosen as the goal. A person commits to and persists in trying to achieve a goal, however, until one of three things has occurred: the goal has been achieved, the original goal has been displaced by another goal, or the goal has been abandoned (Atkinson & Birch, 1970; Klinger, 1977). A person can also work toward one goal while at the same time think or plan on how to achieve another.

Future orientation of goals. Goals range from immediate to delayed (see Table 11.1). The seeming capacity of the future to motivate present behavior is a feature that goals share with incentives. This capacity is realized when a future positive goal is represented in the present as something a person is motivated to become or motivated to achieve. A negative goal, when visualized in the present, on the other hand, is something to be avoided and represents what a person does not want to become. Thus, the current representation becomes the occasion for achievement behaviors designed to accomplish a goal or avoid it (Karniol & Ross, 1996).

How does a goal that is in the future motivate behavior that is in the present? To illustrate, assume that it has become the goal of your psychology department to require a comprehensive exam of all graduating psychology majors. Two positive features of this goal are that the exam is an opportunity for self-evaluation and for departmental evaluation. Two negative features are your distress and the possibility that you may do poorly. How much in favor are you of this comprehensive exam if it were given two or four semesters from now? Goals, like incentives, are affected by their distance in the future (see Figure 11.1). The closer an individual comes to her goal, the stronger the motivation to approach its positive features and avoid its negative features (Markman & Brendl, 2000; Miller, 1959). When a long time away, the approach tendency is stronger, but as the goal gets nearer the avoidance tendency is stronger. In the case of the comprehensive exam, a student supports taking the exam when it is four semesters away because the approach features of this goal are strongest. When the exam is two semesters away, however, a student does not support the goal because now the avoidance features are strongest.

The change in strength of avoidance and approach features results from delay discounting (Chapter 10). Shelley (1994) demonstrated that losses or negative features of a goal are discounted more steeply than are gains or positive features. In other words, the value of the negative features declines more steeply than the value of the positive features. This difference in discount rates explains why the avoidance curve in Figure 11.1 is steeper than the approach curve. So, when

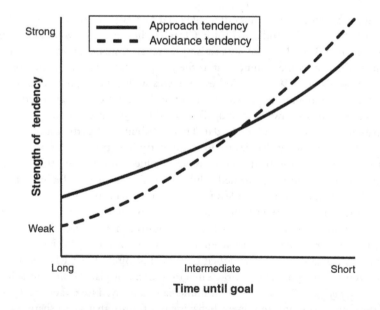

FIGURE 11.1 Goal-Approach and Goal-Avoidance Tendencies. The tendency to approach positive goal features and to avoid negative features increases as a goal draws closer. Changes in the strength of an approach tendency are slower than changes in an avoidance tendency. At distant intervals, the approach tendency is stronger, while at nearer intervals the avoidance tendency is stronger.

the exam is four semesters away its negative features are discounted more than its positive features. When two semesters away, however, the negative features are discounted less than the positive features. Discounted positive and negative features are equal where the two curves cross in Figure 11.1. The reader may get the impression that an individual is forever stuck where the two curves cross, a situation that resembles the donkey in Aesop's fable, who starved to death between two haystacks because it could not decide which one to eat from. But life does not resemble Figure 11.1. For instance, if the negative features are too strong an individual abandons the goal. Also, in life, the positive features of important goals outweigh the negative features; this maintains goal pursuit.

Sources of Goals

One question for students of motivation concerns the origin of goals. Where do goals come from?

Levels of aspiration. Traditionally, **levels of aspiration** referred to a person's desire to excel, to do better the next time, or to do better than others (Rotter, 1942). Research on the level of aspiration describes people's desires to strive for goals that exceed their current levels (Lewin et al., 1944). Our human nature drives us to want more or to improve, not to want less or get worse. Setting and pursuing goals is one way to achieve this. For instance, a promotion and raise in salary are likely to be goals, while a demotion and cut in salary are unlikely to be. Another indicator of level of aspiration is the idea of *future possible selves*. These can become goals to approach and also to avoid. Based on self-concept, individuals may visualize possible selves they would like to become and other possible selves they would like to avoid. For example, individuals may visualize themselves in meaningful careers, which is a goal to approach, but may also foresee being alone, which is a goal to avoid.

Association of goals with affect. Anticipating how we will feel, our affect, is another goal motivation mechanism. *Affective forecasting* resembles a weather forecast but concerns the individual's expected subjective feelings whether negative or positive. These feelings arise when the goal is achieved and from the accompanying consummatory behavior, such as the pride of accomplishment. For example, in asking someone for a date an individual may forecast positive feelings if the person accepts but negative feelings if the person declines. In this example, the goal of requesting a date may arise from its association with anticipated positive affect. Goals producing positive affect are approached, while those producing negative affect are avoided. This idea that goals are associated with affect can be traced back to Thomas Hobbes in his book *Human Nature* (1640/ 1962). In modern terminology, Hobbes reasoned that people pursue as goals those things they anticipate will give pleasure and avoid as goals those things they anticipate will bring displeasure or pain. Troland (1928/1967) also claimed the present anticipation of future pleasure is pleasant and the present anticipation of future pain is unpleasant. Thus, anticipating a positive goal is associated with pleasant feelings, while expecting a negative outcome is associated with unpleasant feelings.

Affect also influences goal motivation by influencing a person's estimate of the likelihood that the goal will be achieved. Outcomes with positive affect are estimated to be more likely to occur than outcomes with negative affect are (Shepperd et al., 2015). In other words, an individual thinks good things are more likely to happen and bad things are less likely to happen. In an illuminating experiment, Lench and coresearchers (2016) asked participants the likelihood that a positive or negative event would happen to them. For instance, what is the likelihood that you will work for a relative? For one group, the word relative attained a positive valence as a result of it being paired with positive words such as smile. For another group, the word relative gained negative valence as a result of it being paired with negative words such as loss. The valence manipulation was effective. Participants judged that it would be more pleasant to work for a relative when the word had positive valence compared to a negative valence. But, did valence influence likelihood estimates of working for a relative? It did! Participants thought it would be more likely for them to work for a relative when the word had accrued a positive valence compared to a negative valence.

Estimates of goal achievement also stem from its association with prior approach or avoidance behavior. Since positive goals motivate approach behavior, Lench and coresearchers investigated if likelihood estimates of a neutral event would be influenced by being associated with either approach or avoidance behavior. They discovered that an event associated with approach behavior was thought more likely to occur than an event associated with avoidance behavior (Lench et al., 2016). For instance, assume that the word relative had a neutral valence—that is, neither positive nor negative. Now, before estimating the likelihood of working for a relative, the participants performed one of two actions. The approach action required the participants to make a pulling action toward themselves. The avoidance action required the participants to make a pushing action away from themselves. Did these approach and avoidance actions influence the subsequent likelihood estimates that you will work for a relative? Yes! A prior approach action resulted in a higher likelihood estimate of working for a relative compared to the prior avoidance action. A conclusion of these findings is that goals associated with positive affect are estimated as more likely to be achieved but also goals that are associated with approach behavior are also considered more likely.

Goals that satisfy needs. Some substances become goals because they satisfy physiological needs. Feelings of hunger and thirst, for instance, are the reasons that attaining food and water become goals. How does an individual know what substance satisfies a particular physiological need? Several psychological concepts can answer this question. One is Warden's (1931) *drive–incentive link*, which maintains that the physiological drive automatically directs behavior toward the substance that will satisfy it (see Chapter 2). Thus, attaining that substance becomes the goal of the drive. Second is Tolman's (1959) theory of purposive behavior, which states that the subjective value, or *valence*, of a stimulus depends on a person's motivational or physiological state. According to the valence concept, a substance with the highest valence is selected as a goal, whereas those with a low or negative valence are avoided. Thus, for a hungry person food has a positive valence and becomes a goal, while watching television or reading a book has either a lower or a negative valence and is avoided. Third, Cabanac's (1971, 2010) *alliesthesia* concept refers to a person's interior physiological condition, which determines whether a stimulus is judged pleasant or unpleasant. In this case, pleasant stimuli are also the ones that restore homeostasis—that is, reduce the physiological need. Consequently, attaining these stimuli becomes an individual's goals (see Chapter 5).

Like a physiological need, a psychological need also influences the valence of anything that satisfies it. This becomes a goal. For instance, the goal of becoming a police officer satisfies the need for power and becoming a crossword puzzle developer satisfies the need for cognition. Our interactions with people become goals for the psychological needs of affiliation and belonging.

For instance, the goal of joining an organization satisfies the need for affiliation, while forming a romantic relationship satisfies the need to belong. In addition, the needs of self-esteem, competence, and mastery foster their own distinct set of goals. Achieving these goals helps satisfy those needs. As noted in Chapter 9, personality traits also determine what goals become important. The trait of conscientiousness, for example, may determine whether a person considers recycling to be a worthwhile goal. Finally, a person's value system can determine her goals. If a person places a high ethical value on the lives of animals, then being a vegetarian may become a goal.

Goal setting for evaluating self-efficacy. Do you think you can make the grade, pass the inspection, or get the job done? Goals serve as a standard for evaluating one's **self-efficacy** (Bandura, 1977, 1991). This is the belief that individuals have about how capable they are in performing the behavior necessary for achieving a specific goal. Self-efficacy is task-specific, which means individuals evaluate their capability of achieving the task at hand. For example, a professional musician might rate himself as having high self-efficacy for playing an instrument and low self-efficacy for working on plumbing. Indications of success and failure at particular tasks raise or lower self-efficacy, which in turn affects a person's future goal striving. Self-efficacy helps determine goal level settings in cognitive tasks such as problem-solving. Cervone and Peake (1986) manipulated self-efficacy by asking participants if they could solve more than, equal to, or less than a standard number of anagrams. The standard was either a high or low number. As a rating of their self-efficacy, participants were asked how many anagrams they thought they were capable of solving. Participants exposed to the high standard gave higher self-efficacy ratings than participants exposed to the low standard. Furthermore, during the anagram-solving task, high-self-efficacy participants persisted longer than low-self-efficacy participants. Thus, goal setting allows individuals to test their self-efficacy. Successes and failures can raise and lower self-efficacy, which in turn can raise and lower the motivation to achieve one's goal.

Environmentally activated goals. Goals may become associated with stimuli present in the situation in which goal achievement behavior occurs. If these associations happen frequently enough, then those stimuli may activate goals. Markman and Brendl (2000) provide an example of a person who notices the picture of a check as part of an advertisement displayed in the window of a bank. The check activates the goal that the rent must be paid, which is achieved when the person arrives home. Murray (1938) had a similar idea when he hypothesized that psychological needs can be evoked by environmental demands. Goal-relevant stimuli can activate goals from memory, as shown in an experiment by Patalano and Seifert (1997). In the learning phase, they presented participants with a set of goals and with relevant objects that could be used to accomplish those goals. In the recall phase, participants were more likely to recall a goal when a relevant object was presented as a cue. For example, when Vaseline rather than masking tape was presented as a cue, participants were more likely to recall the goal: remove stuck ring from finger.

Other people as sources for goals. A person's relationships with other people also determine his goals (Hollenbeck & Klein, 1987). For instance, role models can serve as goals (Morgenroth et al., 2015). First, role models are individuals who inspire us; second, they display what is possible to achieve; and, third, they model the behaviors necessary for goal achievement. These three attributes of a role model serve as a source of goals for an individual. Another social source of goals comes from comparing ourselves to others. According to social comparison theory, the level of the goal set by an individual is determined by her standing relative to members in the group (Lewin et al., 1944). For example, imagine a task in which some individuals perform better than the group's average, while others perform worse. In setting future goals, individuals who are above average tend to lower their performance goals, whereas those below average tend to raise theirs. As Locke and Latham (1990) note, the demands other individuals make on a person often become goals. Professors make demands on students. Coaches make demands on players. Children and parents make demands on one another. In addition, the goals of the group become the goals of the individual. To illustrate, the goal of the team is to win games, but this is also the goal of an individual player when she joins the team. In the case of a student, if the professor's goal is to give an exam on Monday, then as a member of the class the student accepts that goal.

Section Recap

According to the *mindset theory of action*, a person first examines potential end-states and then selects and commits to one as the goal. This decision is then followed by deciding how the goal will be achieved. The *goal* is the internal representation of the selected end-state. A goal motivates behavior, while an incentive has the function of helping to motivate goal achievement behavior. A goal can differ on a number of dimensions: importance, difficulty, specificity, temporal range, consciousness, and complexity. The motivational power of a goal decreases as its distance in the future increases as a result of delay discounting. Negative goal features are discounted more steeply than are positive features. People's *level of aspiration*, which refers to their desire to want more and do better, and possible selves serve as the motivation to set goals to accomplish that. Goals originate from their association with positive or negative affect, which is the emotional feeling the anticipated goal produces. Positive affect leads to approaching the goal, whereas negative affect leads to avoiding the goal. Also, goals associated with positive affect are considered more likely to occur than those with negative affect. Goals associated with approach behavior are also considered more likely than goals associated with avoidance behavior. Goals are the means for satisfying physiological and psychological needs. Obtaining food is the goal for satisfying hunger, and obtaining praise is the goal for satisfying a need for self-esteem. Goals provide the opportunity for the evaluation of *self-efficacy*, which refers to one's capability to perform the task at hand. Achieving a goal increases self-efficacy, while failing to achieve a goal decreases it. Stimuli can activate goals as a result of the repeated association between goal pursuits in situations that contain those stimuli. People are also sources of goals. For instance, people who serve as role models become sources of goals. Also, in the case of social comparisons, the goal to which a person aspires depends on how her performance compares to other members of the group. In addition, the goal of the group is also the goal of the individual members.

GOAL CHARACTERISTICS AND EXPECTATIONS

Table 11.1 summarized six goal characteristics. Of these, importance, difficulty, and specificity are crucial. A goal motivates behavior consistent with the importance and difficulty of a goal and guides behavior according to the specificity of a goal. But, before a person selects a goal, its value and likelihood of being achieved are estimated along with whether the goal is framed as achieving a gain or avoiding a loss.

Motivating Characteristics of Goals

What if a person were not committed to any goals? Is such an individual bored, listless, and without aim? A goal would eliminate that. But how does a goal lead to the planning, execution, and achievement behavior?

Goal level and goal difficulty. People set goals for themselves at various levels. **Goal level** refers to the rank of a goal in a hierarchy of potential goals. Higher-level goals have higher value and greater utility and provide greater benefits compared to lower-level ones. One person may have a goal to walk five miles per week, while another individual plans to run 10 miles per week. One student may have a GPA goal of 3.50, while another is satisfied with a GPA just high enough to graduate. Goal level is associated with **goal difficulty**, which means that some goals are harder to achieve than others (Lee et al., 1989; Locke & Latham, 1990). "While high goals may be harder to reach than easy goals, in life they are usually associated with better outcomes" (Locke & Latham, 1990, p. 121). In other words, as the value of a goal increases, the difficulty of achieving it also increases. In an attempt to determine the relationship between goal level and outcomes, Mento and associates (1992) told participants to assume that as undergraduate students their goal was to achieve a GPA close to an A (4.00), B (3.00), or C (2.00). Next, participants were asked to rate what benefits their GPA goal would bring, such as pride, respect, and confidence; job benefits; scholarship and graduate school benefits; and life and career benefits. The results showed a strong relationship between the GPA goal level and benefit ratings. Higher GPA goals were associated with greater benefits. Matsui and associates (1981) had students perform a clerical aptitude test that involved detecting a discrepancy between two lists of numbers. The goal set for the students varied between easy and hard. Prior to working on the clerical task, students were asked to rate the expected value of their goals for achievement, self-confidence, competence, persistence, and the ability to concentrate. The ratings showed that more difficult goals were rated as having higher value and greater benefits.

Goal specificity. How important is it for a person to be able to visualize a goal? Is it necessary for a student to visualize herself in her chosen career? One requirement of goal setting is that a person must be able to visualize the goal in some respect (Beach, 1990; Miller et al., 1960; Schank & Abelson, 1977). The clearer the image a person has of his goal, the better he will know if it has been achieved. "Vague goals make poor referent standards because there are many situations in which no discrepancy would be indicated and, therefore, there would be no need for corrective action" (Klein, 1989, p. 154). A goal with a vague image will more likely result in poorer performance, because feedback from a variety of behaviors may appear to have met the goal (Klein, 1989). In contrast is **goal specificity**, which refers to how precise the goal is in contrast to how vague or unspecified it is (Lee et al., 1989; Locke & Latham, 1990). For example, during one minute, list four, seven, or 12 uses for a coat hanger or as many uses as you can (Mento et al., 1992). Listing four, seven, or 12 uses is a specific goal, while "as many uses as you can" is a vague goal. In the former case, a person can determine whether the specific goal was met, while it is very difficult to determine whether the vague do-your-best goal was met.

An additional benefit of goal specificity is that it increases planning (Locke & Latham, 1990). To illustrate, Earley and associates (1987) required research participants to present an argument in favor of a certain advertising medium for products that ranged from household goods to business computers. In the do-your-best condition, participants had to present as many arguments as they could in 60 minutes. The goal for these participants was vague, since they did not know when they had done their best. In the assigned goal condition, participants had to present a minimum of four arguments per advertising medium. The goal for these participants was specific. They knew precisely if they had met their goal. Following the completion of the task, the experimenter asked how much planning and energy participants had expended. Participants assigned specific goals spent more time planning and expended more effort than participants who were given vague do-your-best goals.

Joint effect of goal level and goal specificity. Goal level affects the magnitude of performance, while goal specificity affects the variability of performance (Locke et al., 1989; Mento et al., 1992). Imagine students being asked for ways in which the psychology department at their university could be improved. The number of requested improvements could vary in specificity. For example, imagine being asked to suggest three improvements, which is a specific number, or to suggest several improvements, which is a vague number. The task could also differ in goal level. Students could be asked to suggest many improvements or could be asked to suggest very few. In the Locke and associates (1989) study, some of the students were given vague goals at different levels— for example, "List a small, medium, or large number of improvements." These categories are vague, since a small, medium, or large number is undefined. Other students were given moderately specific goals—for example, "List between one and three, two and four, or three and five ways of improving the department." Other students were provided with very specific goals at three different levels—for example, "Provide exactly two, three, or four ways of improving the department." In the actual study, Locke and associates (1989) asked students to list improvements for the undergraduate business and management programs. The number of proposed

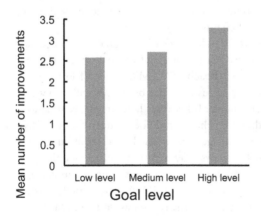

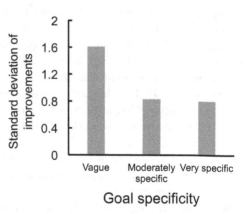

FIGURE 11.2A Performance and Goal Level. The mean number of suggested improvements increases with the level of the goal.

Source: Adapted from "Separating the Effects of Goal Specificity from Goal Level" by E. A. Locke et al., 1989, *Organizational Behavior and Human Decision Processes, 43,* Table 4, p. 280.

FIGURE 11.2B Performance and Goal Specificity. The standard deviation of the number of suggested improvements decreases as a goal becomes more specific.

Source: Adapted from "Separating the Effects of Goal Specificity from Goal Level" by E. A. Locke et al., 1989, *Organizational Behavior and Human Decision Processes, 43,* Table 4, p. 280.

improvements should depend on goal level, while variability of the number of improvements should depend on goal specificity. Greater variability is expected for vague goals, because a wider variety of improvements will be accepted as having met those goals. The results in Figure 11.2a show that higher-level, more difficult goals produce a greater number of recommended improvements. The results in Figure 11.2b indicate that variability (standard deviation) in the number of improvements decreases as the stated goal becomes more specific. In other words, as a goal becomes more precise, there is greater agreement on whether it has been achieved. In the coat hanger study described previously, the vague do-your-best goal produced low achievement as did the goal of four uses, with greater achievement resulting from the goal of listing seven or 12 coat hanger uses. In general, research has shown that both difficult and specific goals result in more achievement behavior than do vague goals or no goals (Locke et al., 1981; Mento et al., 1992).

In summary, goals have both energizing and directing functions (Locke et al., 1989). Goal level has an **energizing function**, since it motivates a person to expend effort to achieve a goal. Higher goals lead to greater expenditure of effort. Goal specificity has a **directing function**, since it informs the individual exactly what behavior is acceptable for goal achievement. The greater the specificity of a goal, the more precisely it directs behavior. Thus, one major conclusion is that specific, high-level goals lead to greater performance than do vague, low-level goals.

Expectancy Value Theory and Expected Utility Theory

What characteristics from Table 11.1 determine whether a person commits to a particular goal? Is it the importance of the goal, since those will have greater utility or greater value? A person, however, might be dissuaded from a goal that is difficult—that is, has a low probability of being achieved. For example, based on the quote by Steve Jobs, building an enduring company is more important than creating a single device (e.g., the iPhone) but it is also more difficult. The company goal has greater utility or value but also lower probability of being achieved compared to that of a single device.

Two theories attempt to explain how goal value or utility and probability of goal achievement determine goal selection. According to **expectancy value theory**, expectancy is an individual's belief in the likelihood that she can achieve a goal, while value is the worth or attractiveness of that goal. Goal value is based on its importance, intrinsic enjoyment, and usefulness minus the cost of attaining it (Wigfield et al., 2009). The Little Blue Engine's belief of "I think I can" in Chapter 1 illustrates expectancy and that reaching the next town represents goal value. Usually, high expectancy and high goal value motivate goal selection. In addition, the expected value, which is the multiplication of expectancy times value, also motivates goal selection (Nagengast et al., 2011). For instance, how much do you value the goal of a career in psychology? How likely do you expect to achieve this career goal? Nagengast and coresearchers (2011) asked similar questions regarding careers in science of nearly 400,000 high school students in 57 countries. As predicted from expectancy value theory, aspiring to a science career increased with the perceived value of such a career and with the expectancy of achieving such a career. Most critical, however, was that the interaction between expectancy and value also predicted career aspirations. In other words, increases in a student's expected value (expectancy × value) increased career aspirations in the sciences.

Expected utility theory states that goal choice is based on the utility and probability of being achieved. Utility is viewed differently than value. For instance, what has more value or utility: a necklace or pen? Goal utility refers to the usefulness in satisfying a person's wants or in providing satisfaction or happiness. People want to own possessions, to have experiences, and to have particular feelings. Utility describes how well a goal satisfies those wants. A goal with high utility will satisfy a person's wants much better than a goal with low utility. Thus, a person may have the goal of wanting to own a car, wanting to listen to music, or wanting to reduce hunger pangs. Whether a matching goal is selected, however, also depends on the subjective probability that it can be achieved. **Subjective probability** is a person's belief that a particular event will occur and is expressed as a number between 0.00 and 1.00 (Savage, 1954). According to expected utility theory, the utility of a goal is multiplied by its subjective probability of being achieved: Expected utility = utility $\times$ subjective probability (Arkes & Hammond, 1986; Edwards, 1961; Shoemaker, 1982). Thus, when faced with a choice among several end-states, a person determines the utility of each and also estimates the probability of achieving each. The end-state with the highest expected utility is selected as a goal. In this sense, expected value and expected utility are the same. However, in contrast to expectancy value theory, expected utility theory focuses more on the role of expected utility in motivating behavior than on examining value and probability separately.

Choice based on utility, probability, or expected utility. In the case of expected utility theory, how is it possible to separate the effects of utility, probability, and expected utility? Gray (1975) demonstrated a way in an experiment with elementary school children. She provided them with arithmetic problems that differed in utility and probability of a correct solution. A problem's difficulty level defined its probability of a solution. Level 1 problems were the easiest and level 6 problems were the most difficult to solve. The arithmetic problems were written on index cards and placed in six stacks according to their level of difficulty. The children attempted to solve problems from each level and were asked, "If you had to do 10 problems from this deck, and they were all pretty much like the one you tried first, how many do you think you could get right out of 10?" (p. 150). The children's answer to this question was their subjective probability estimate. The utility of correctly solving a problem was defined by the number of red poker chips associated with each difficulty level. If a child solved a problem correctly from the easiest deck, she received one red poker chip. The next easiest deck was worth two poker chips and so on up to six poker chips for the most difficult problem deck. However, if a child did not solve a problem correctly, he had to pay the experimenter the same number of poker chips as the deck's value. Since a child could go into debt, each child received 10 red poker chips at the start of the experiment. During the experiment, a child was given the opportunity to solve 15 arithmetic problems to earn as many red poker chips as possible.

The problems children selected to solve could be based on the utility, subjective probability, or expected utility of the solutions. First, the children could select a problem deck based on its utility as indicated by the number of red poker chips, since a higher number implies greater utility. Children might choose deck 6, since it would provide the most chips. Second, the children might select problems based on the estimated probability of success. Easier problems might be chosen, since more of them could be solved, thus earning more poker chips. Third, children could make their selections based on the expected utility of a problem. The expected utility would be the child's probability estimate of solving a problem multiplied by the utility of that

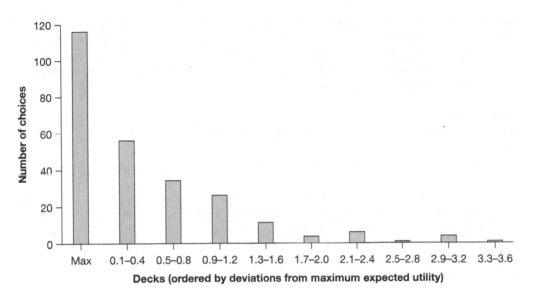

FIGURE 11.3 Choice and Expected Utility. Children made choices based on the expected utility of solving the problem.

Source: Reprinted from by C. A. Gray, 1975, *Organizational Behavior and Human Performance, 13,* "Factors in Students' Decisions to Attempt Academic Tasks" p. 153. Copyright 1975, with permission from Elsevier.

problem as indicated by the number of poker chips. Different children had different expected utilities for each deck because they gave different probability estimates. For example, one child might estimate deck 4 to have a probability of 0.70, while for another child the probability might be 0.60. Thus, the expected value or utility for deck 4 (worth four chips) for each child would be 2.80 and 2.40, respectively. Gray (1975) examined how the children distributed their choices according to the utility, subjective probability, and the expected utility of a problem deck. The children did not make their choices according to the utility of a deck. Their choices were spread fairly evenly over the different utilities of the decks. The subjective probability of a correct solution for a problem also had no effect. Their choices were spread fairly evenly over the six subjective probabilities of the decks. The expected utility of a problem deck was the main determiner of the children's choices. As shown in Figure 11.3, children distributed their choices based on the expected utility of solving the problems. Problem decks with the highest expected utility were chosen most often. As the problems deviated more and more from their expected utility, they were chosen less and less.

Framing

Is a glass half full or half empty? Is an exam the opportunity to earn an A or to avoid an F? Is a date the opportunity to have fun or a way to avoid a lonely Saturday night? Should a person focus on achieving gains or avoiding losses? **Framing** refers to the perspective from which a goal is viewed. A goal can be viewed as the opportunity for a gain or to avoid a loss. How a choice is framed coupled with the probability of achieving the outcome determines a person's decision.

Framing and the probability of gaining or losing money affects our choices, according to Kahneman and Tversky (1979). Imagine trying to decide between buying a lottery ticket for A or B. Which ticket would you buy?

Problem 1

Prospect A1: 90 percent chance of winning $3,000; expected utility = $2,700

or

Prospect B1: 45 percent chance of winning $6,000; expected utility = $2,700

Suppose you won the lottery and now have money to invest in a business venture. In this case, concentrate more on the prospects of losing the money during the first year of the business. In which of the two prospects would you invest your money?

Problem 2

Prospect A2: 90 percent chance of losing $3,000; expected utility = –$2,700

or

Prospect B2: 45 percent chance of losing $6,000; expected utility = –$2,700

What prediction would expected utility theory make for these two problems? It would predict no difference in the choices a person would make between the pairs of prospects. In problem 1, both prospects have an expected utility equal to $2,700. Therefore, 50 percent of the participants should choose prospect A1 and the other 50 percent should choose prospect B1. Similarly, in problem 2 the expected utility equals –$2,700 in both prospects. Again, participants should evenly split their choices. The actual results, however, are not in accord with predictions from expected utility theory (see Figure 11.4). In problem 1, 86 percent of Kahneman and Tversky's (1979) participants selected the prospect of a 90 percent chance of gaining $3,000. In problem 2, 92 percent of the participants chose the prospect of a 45 percent chance of losing $6,000. The two choices made in problems 1 and 2 are mirror images.

Prospect Theory

The results in Figure 11.4 show that people do not behave according to predictions derived from expected utility theory. They should have chosen each prospect equally, since their expected utilities were equal. An alternative, **prospect theory**, is more descriptive of what humans do in these choice situations (Kahneman & Tversky, 1979; Kahneman, 2011). First, for prospect theory, the psychological value of a loss is greater than the psychological value of an identical gain. This observation comes from Chapter 10 regarding losses loom larger than gains, as in the example that a $100 loss is more dissatisfying than a $100 gain is satisfying. Second, people prefer smaller gains that are highly likely over larger gains that are much less likely (see Figure 11.4). This preference reverses with losses. People prefer larger losses that are highly unlikely over smaller losses that are likely (see Figure 11.4). An explanation of this reversal from gains to losses rests on two opposing human characteristics: risk aversion and risk-seeking. **Risk aversion** applies

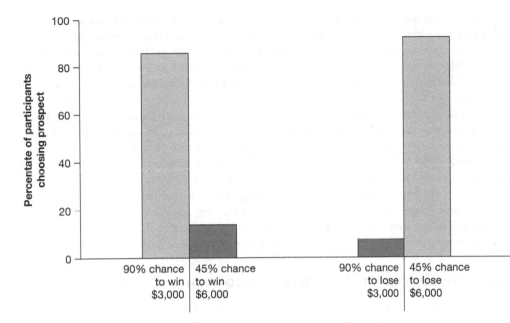

FIGURE 11.4 Expected Utility and Probability of Gain/Loss. People are risk averse in regard to winning money—that is, they do not like to take risks and prefer the more certain (90 percent) win, since it is less risky. People are risk-seeking in regard to losing money—that is, they prefer to take a risk. Thus, they choose the loss that is less likely, the riskier option. So they choose the 45 percent chance of losing money.

Source: Adapted from "Prospect Theory" by D. Kahneman and A. Tversky, 1979, *Econometrica, 47,* Table 1, p. 268.

to gains. It means that people are opposed, reluctant, or unwilling to take risks, since that may mean losing or failing to gain a valued item. Thus, in a choice between two gains the more likely prospect is preferred. For example, the 90 percent chance of gain was preferred because it was less risky, or more certain, than the 45 percent chance of a gain (see Figure 11.4, left). **Risk-seeking**, on the other hand, applies to losses. It means that people pursue or go after chancy or uncertain alternatives. Thus, in a choice between two losses, the riskier alternative is preferred—that is, the one less likely to occur. Thus, when given a choice between two potential losses, individuals seek the riskier option. The 45 percent chance of a loss was preferred because it was riskier—that is, less likely to occur than the 90 percent chance of a loss (see Figure 11.4, right).

Section Recap

Not all goals are of equal value. *Goal level* refers to the value or utility of a goal, with higher levels indicating higher values. As goal level increases, so does *goal difficulty*, which refers to how challenging it is to achieve a goal. *Goal specificity* refers to how precisely a goal is defined. Specific goals, in contrast to vague ones, provide a directive function. Specific, high-level goals lead to better achievement behavior than do vague, low-level goals. Goals have both an *energizing function* that motivates the person toward the goal and a *directing function* that informs the person what behaviors are necessary to achieve a goal. According to *expectancy value theory*, an individual pursues goals that have a high value, a high likelihood of being achieved, and the product of those two factors, e.g., expected value. According to *expected utility theory*, the goal an individual pursues is the one with the highest expected utility. Value refers to the worth of a goal, while utility refers to the usefulness of a goal. A person arrives at expected utility from judging the utility of a goal and multiplying that by *subjective probability*, which is a personal estimate of the likelihood that a goal can be achieved. Does the person see the goal as a potential gain or as avoiding a loss? This depends also on how the goal is *framed*, which means a goal can be viewed either positively as a gain or negatively as avoiding a loss. People prefer gains that have a higher likelihood of success, even if the value of the gain is low. This preference reverses for losses. People prefer losses that have a low likelihood of occurring even if the loss has a higher value. According to *prospect theory*, the explanation for these mirror image results is that people are both *risk averse* and *risk-seeking*. People are risk averse in the case of gains. They are reluctant to take risks because it may result in not gaining a valued item. People are risk-seeking in the case of losses. Thus, a risky loss is preferred since that means that a negative event is less likely to occur.

GOAL COMMITMENT, PLANNING, AND ACHIEVEMENT

According to the mindset theory of action, a person first selects a goal. The second phase involves goal achievement. But how does a person plan to achieve a goal? And what happens if the individual fails?

Committing to a Goal

Answer true or false: "I think I can graduate from this university." If true, then you are committed to a goal of graduation and are trying to achieve it.

Commitment as a factor in goal achievement. **Goal commitment** is the process whereby a person becomes set to achieve a goal (Klinger, 1977; Locke & Latham, 1990; Locke et al., 1981). It implies a person's willingness and persistent determination to expend time and effort in its pursuit (Locke et al., 1988). In fact, an analysis of a number of investigations supports the generalization that greater commitment means a greater expenditure of effort in trying to achieve a goal (Klein et al., 1999). For example, the more committed a student is to achieving a particular GPA goal, the more time the student will spend studying. The effects of commitment, however, are more apparent for difficult goals compared to easier ones. For instance, commitment becomes more important if a student's goal is to earn a 3.50 GPA compared to a 2.50 GPA. Finally, greater commitment is associated with a goal being more attractive and being considered more achievable (Klein et al., 1999). Continuing the GPA example, greater commitment is associated with more appreciation of the GPA goal's value and with its chances of being achieved.

How can goal commitment be measured? One way is to ask how committed an individual is to achieving a particular goal. A second and more precise way is to use the *Hollenbeck, Williams, and Klein Goal Commitment Items* (Hollenbeck et al., 1989a, 1989b; Klein et al., 2001). Table 11.2 presents these items as self-report statements that measure how dedicated or devoted individuals are to a particular goal (Klein et al., 2001). Do you have a GPA goal this semester and how committed are you to it? If this scale measures commitment, then students who score highly

TABLE 11.2   Goal Commitment Scale Items

1. It's hard to take this goal seriously. (R)
2. Quite frankly, I don't care if I achieve this goal or not. (R)
3. I am strongly committed to pursuing this goal.
4. It wouldn't take much to make me abandon this goal. (R)
5. I think this is a good goal to shoot for.

Note: Answer each item with this scale: Strongly disagree = 1 2 3 4 5 = Strongly agree.

Items followed by (R) are reverse scored; for example, 1 becomes 5 and 4 becomes 2. The higher the score, the higher the level of goal commitment.

Source: From "The Assessment of Goal Commitment: A Measurement Model Meta-Analysis" by H. J. Klein et al., 2001, *Organizational Behavior and Human Decision Processes, 85,* Table 1, p. 34. Copyright 2001 by Elsevier. Reprinted by permission.

should spend more time and effort trying to achieve their goal than students who score low. Hollenbeck and associates (1989b) conducted a study testing this predicted relationship. One group of students had voluntarily committed to the goal of a 0.25 increase in GPA, while another group was assigned this goal. Both the voluntary goal group and the assigned goal group had their level of commitment measured with an earlier version of the *Goal Commitment Items.* The GPA for that quarter improved slightly for students in both groups, but the amount of improvement also depended on the level of commitment. Students who scored higher on the *Goal Commitment Items* came closer to achieving their goal than students who scored lower.

People can increase their level of commitment by announcing their goals publicly (Salancik, 1977). Telling other significant people such as friends about the goal makes it more difficult to abandon. Hollenbeck and associates (1989b) also tested this possibility by having half of the students publicly announce their goal of a 0.25 increase in GPA. This announcement was made by distributing to all students a list of names containing each student's GPA goal. In addition, the publicly committed students had to send a statement of their goal to a significant other, usually a parent or sibling. The public commitment manipulation worked. Students who had publicly announced their goals earned higher GPAs than students who had not made a public announcement. Thus, one way you can perform better on the next exam is to announce your exam goal score to a friend. This announcement increases commitment and motivates you to study harder.

Commitment as goal shielding. On the way toward achieving a goal, many alternative goals and behaviors may get in the way of progress. Commitment helps prevent this from happening. In the case of the Apple company, Jobs felt that the goal of making good products had to be protected from a focus on profits. This focus would alter people's priorities away from making the best products. In other examples, the goal of studying for tomorrow's exam may be dislodged by several hours of pleasant television viewing. Or the goal of working out in the gym is replaced by a snack and a nap. **Goal shielding** refers to preventing other goals or behaviors from interfering with the pursuit of the current one. Goal shielding is accomplished by inhibiting the pulling power of alternative goals or nongoal behaviors (Shah, 2005). The necessity of shielding a goal from distractions increases in relevancy with a goal's importance. Thus, there should be fewer opportunities to be sidetracked when a goal is important. In one investigation, Shah and coresearchers (2002, study 1) had participants list a goal to which they were either strongly or weakly committed. Next, participants were asked about other goals and the manner in which they hoped to achieve them. For the strong-commitment goal, there were fewer other goals listed, while for the weak-commitment goal a greater number of other goals were listed. Thus, shielding was greater for the strong-commitment goal, since it was accompanied by fewer alternatives. In addition, the strong-commitment goal was accompanied by a longer list of means by which to achieve it.

Planning to Achieve a Goal

How does a person plan to achieve a goal? What knowledge is necessary and how does that guide the behavior instrumental for achieving a goal? According to Gollwitzer's (2012) mindset theory, following the choice of and commitment to a goal, an individual enters an implemental mindset. Here individuals are receptive to information about how to achieve their goals. During this phase, a person forms an **implementation intention**, which is an if–then plan. These consist of a cognitive link between a specific situation (if) and goal achievement behavior (then) (Gollwitzer & Sheeran, 2006). If–then plans specify when, where, and how the person will behave to achieve a goal. Thus, if the situation or time X occurs, then individuals perform the behavior necessary to achieve their goals. For example, earlier in the day a student formulates and commits to the plan that "when my TV program ends, I will work on my term paper." That evening, when the TV program ends, the student proceeds to work on her paper, as if the end of the TV program elicited her work.

The effects of if–then implementations were examined in a nonsense word-search experiment by Webb and Sheeran (2007). The task involved finding as quickly as possible a nonsense word (avenda) hidden in a 10×10 array of letters. Participants in the implementation condition were instructed to develop the following aim: "if I see avenda, then I will press the key as quickly as possible" (p. 297). Participants in the control condition "were asked to look at the item [avenda] on the screen and repeat it under their breath for 30s [seconds]" (p. 297). Does the if–then implementation intention lead to finding nonsense words faster compared to the control condition of merely repeating the word? Ye—participants in the implementation condition found the nonsense word faster. Thus, the implementation of intentions leads to faster goal attainment. The researchers also concluded that the instructions formed a link between the cue situation (array of letters) and the key press when the nonsense word was found. Participants are also more prepared to react to a goal cue. And their goal achievement behavior is more strongly linked to that cue (Webb & Sheeran, 2007). Consequently, implementation intentions aid goal achievement in two ways. First, individuals are more sensitive to any goal cues. Second, they are more ready to react with goal achievement behavior when such a cue occurs.

Progress toward Goal Achievement

A goal provides two sources of motivation (Locke & Latham, 1990). First, people set goals that exceed or improve upon their current state, level, or position. Second, people behave in order to achieve their goals—that is, to reduce the discrepancy between their current state and their goal (Locke, 1991).

Feedback. The negative feedback loop in Figure 11.5 represents the two sources of motivation: the goal and the discrepancy from the goal. A thermostat and house furnace illustrate the negative feedback loop (see Chapter 5). The set point temperature of the house thermostat informs the furnace to generate heat. Similarly, a goal motivates and informs people about what behavior to perform. The furnace ceases when the house temperature is compared to the set point temperature and is judged equal. Similarly, achievement behavior ceases when current progress is compared to the goal and is judged equal. This means the goal has been achieved. Progress toward achievement is possible because of the **feedback** individuals receive about their current state relative to the goal (Locke & Latham, 1990). As Figure 11.5 shows, information about a person's current state is fed back into the comparator to determine the degree of discrepancy from the goal. When this discrepancy is zero, the goal is achieved. However, without feedback goal achievement would not be possible. Bandura and Cervone (1983) demonstrated the joint effect of a goal plus feedback on motivation. They had participants perform an exercise task that required alternately pushing and pulling two arm levers on an exercise machine. The amount of effort expended on this task defined the participants' motivation. Following five minutes of exercise,

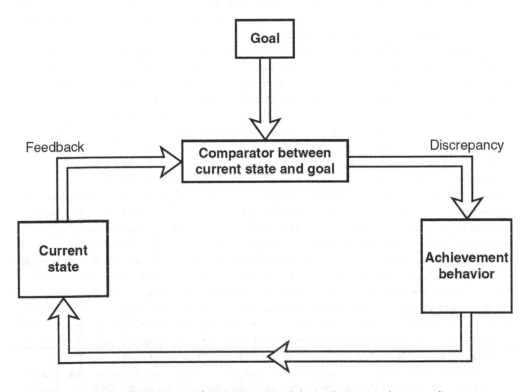

FIGURE 11.5 Negative Feedback Loop of Goal Achievement Behavior. Setting a goal creates a discrepancy between a current state and the goal state. The comparator detects this discrepancy, which then motivates goal achievement behavior. When the comparator no longer detects a discrepancy, goal achievement behavior ceases because zero discrepancy means the goal was achieved.

participants were divided into four experimental groups. The goal-plus-feedback group was to increase their effort by 40 percent over the next five minutes and was given feedback as to how well they had done. The goal group was given the same goal but was not provided with any feedback at the end of the five-minute period. Without feedback, participants in this group had no way of knowing how close they had come to achieving their goal. The feedback group was not given a goal but was given feedback at the end of the five-minute period. Their feedback was provided as if they had a goal of 40 percent increased effort. The feedback was meaningless for this group, since they did not know what the goal was. The control group was given neither a goal nor feedback. To determine the effects of a goal plus feedback, goal alone, feedback alone, or neither, participants were to exercise on the machine for an additional five minutes. During this third exercise period, the group that received a goal plus feedback put in twice as much effort compared to the groups that received only a goal or only feedback. These last two groups did no better than the control group, which received neither a goal nor feedback. Thus, for a goal to motivate behavior, it is necessary to receive feedback.

Perspectives of goal progress. Achievement toward a goal can proceed along two perspectives. In the **to-go perspective**, how much further does an individual have to progress before the goal is achieved? In this perspective, students look ahead to graduation, much like drivers look ahead while driving. Graduation is the reference point and progress is measured by the number of semesters remaining until then. The negative feedback loop in Figure 11.5 described the to-go perspective. In the **to-date perspective**, how much has an individual already accomplished toward achieving a goal? In this perspective, students determine how many semesters they have already completed, much like drivers look at the trip odometer to see how far they have traveled. In this case, a student's initial enrollment is the reference point and progress is measured by the accumulation of completed semesters (Bonezzi et al., 2011; Heath et al., 1999; Koo & Fishbach, 2008).

Motivation changes in opposite directions for each perspective (Bonezzi et al., 2011). Motivation increases with progress toward the goal in the to-go perspective but decreases in the to-date perspective. In the to-go perspective, with graduation as the reference point, each completed semester brings a student closer. Thus, motivation increases because each semester that remains becomes a larger percentage of what is left to be achieved. For example, a student's first semester represents only one-eighth of the distance toward graduation in eight semesters. But the seventh semester represents one-half of the two semesters that remain. In other words, in terms of percentage the seventh semester represents 50 percent of what remains to be achieved. So, the last two semesters are more motivating. In the to-date perspective, on the other hand, the initial enrollment is the reference point and each completed semester indicates the amount already accomplished. Motivation decreases because each additional semester of progress becomes a smaller percentage of those semesters completed already. For example, the first semester represents a 100 percent increase in achievement from the initial enrollment represented by zero semesters. The seventh semester, however, represents only an additional one-seventh of the seven semesters achieved toward graduation, which occurs at the conclusion of the eighth semester. The eighth semester is the least motivating and accounts for a student malady know as *senioritis.* However, this decrease in motivation to complete the remaining semesters does not mean a student is on the verge of quitting. In the to-date perspective, the completed semesters imply increased commitment, especially when commitment was initially low, which in turn signals that the goal is worthy. It also increases the likelihood that the goal will be achieved. In addition, each completed semester raises students' self-efficacy or belief that they can achieve their goal of graduation (Koo & Fishbach, 2010).

Subgoals as achievements toward final goals. Are there motivational strategies that can help an individual achieve her goals once implementation intentions are translated into goal achievement behaviors? One strategy is to achieve a series of subgoals along the way toward the final goal. If reaching the top of a ladder is the final or *distal* goal, then each individual rung is a **subgoal**, sometimes referred to as a *proximal* goal. A person must climb each individual rung in order to reach the top of the ladder. Likewise, goals are arranged in a hierarchical fashion, with the final goal at the top and subgoals below (Miller et al., 1960). To reach a final goal, subgoals must be achieved along the way.

Motivation for the final goal increases with the addition of subgoals that must be achieved along the way (Latham & Seijts, 1999; Locke & Latham, 1990; Weldon & Yun, 2000). For example, Latham and Seijts (1999) had university students participate in a complex simulated manufacturing task during which they were to buy material to build and sell toys. The experiment employed three different groups, each with a different goal regarding the amount of money to be earned. For the do-your-best goal condition, participants were urged to make as much money as possible. For the final goal condition, participants were told to earn more than a specific designated amount. In the subgoal-plus-final goal condition, specific subgoals were to be achieved along the way

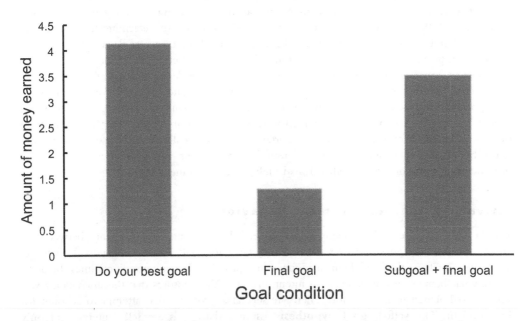

FIGURE 11.6 Subgoals Increase Motivation. The amount of money earned at the end of a simulated manufacturing task was greatest when participants were given subgoals along with a final goal. A final goal alone resulted in the least amount of money earned at the end of the task with the do-your-best goal falling in between.

Source: Adapted from "The Effects of Proximal and Distal Goals on Performance on a Moderately Complex Task" by G. P. Latham and G. H. Seijts, 1999, *Journal of Organizational Behavior, 20,* p. 426.

toward achievement of the final goal. The simulated manufacturing task consisted of six 10-minute sessions, during which prices changed for the purchase of materials and for sale of the toys. During the sessions, participants had to buy, manufacture, and sell toys while trying to make a profit according to the different goal criteria. Figure 11.6 shows the amount of money earned in each goal condition. The subgoals increased motivation toward the final goal, as shown in the subgoal-plus-final goal condition. Here participants earned the most money. Participants in the subgoal-plus-final goal condition also developed a greater sense of self-efficacy during the course of the six sessions, which helped them perform better—that is, earn a greater profit.

Subgoals provide several advantages for achievement of the final goal. First, they provide a more immediate source of motivation than that provided by the final goal. Second, subgoals serve as feedback about progress toward the final goal. Third, feedback from subgoals provides information about whether achievement strategies are effective or need to be modified. Fourth, the achievement of subgoals increases a person's sense of self-efficacy, which is associated with increased persistence and effort (Bandura, 1997).

The value of subgoals also depends on the extent they can help satisfy final goals (Markman & Brendl, 2000). A subgoal that is relevant for the achievement of a final goal should be more valuable than a similar one that is not relevant. For example, college courses that are directly relevant for a student's chosen career should be valued more than other courses. To illustrate the importance of subgoals, take out a sheet of paper. On the left, list all courses you have taken and next to each course indicate how important earning a good grade is for your career plans. Raynor (1970/1974) asked such questions of university students to determine how important they considered a particular course as a subgoal for their final career goal. He expected that the more important a course was for a student's career, the better the grade she earned in that course. Courses rated as very important or important were designated as having high career instrumentality—that is, fostered career development. Courses rated as fairly, not too, or not at all important were designated as having low career instrumentality. The ratings indicated that students earned higher grades in their high-instrumentality courses and lower grades in their low-instrumentality courses. Thus, as the importance of the subgoal increases, the effort to achieve that subgoal also increases. Raynor also found that students earned higher grades in an introductory psychology course when it had high career instrumentality.

Activating Goal Achievement Behavior

As indicated in Figure 11.5, achieving a goal proceeds by reducing the discrepancy between the current state and the goal. However, the necessary behaviors will not occur if individuals forget about their goals or think of them in inopportune places and at inconvenient times. In other words, what happens if implementation intentions fail? What ensures that the discrepancy will activate goal achievement behavior? There are several approaches that attempt to account for this problem. The **selfish goal hypothesis** assumes that goals are self-centered and only concerned with self-survival—that is, being achieved (Bargh & Huang, 2009). In order for this to happen, the goal operates according to Darwin's principle of selection. The goal selects stimuli and behaviors that ensure its achievement. Thus, a goal takes charge and focuses only on goal-relevant stimuli, shuns away from competing goals, and selects behaviors that will lead to goal success. As a result the goal is achieved.

There are two other hypotheses regarding the association between a goal and goal achievement behavior. First, according to Bargh and Williams (2006), the *perception–behavior link* refers to the idea that a goal elicits achievement behavior because goals and their achievement behaviors have been associated together many times in the past. Thus, the representation of a goal in consciousness automatically produces relevant achievement behavior. For example, the goal of writing a paper automatically elicits an image of a computer and its available word-processing program. Second, according to Cesario and coresearchers (2006), *motivated preparation* means that the aim of the behavior depends on a goal's valence—that is, whether the goal is negative or positive. Imagine that the concept of a social group has been automatically activated. The perception–behavior link hypothesis predicts that subsequent behavior toward a member of the group is based on the group's characteristics. For example, walk slowly in the presence of old people, since they walk slowly. The motivated preparation hypothesis, however, would maintain that behavior also depends on whether the group is evaluated negatively or positively. Negative evaluations might prompt avoidance behaviors, while positive evaluations prompt approach behaviors. Thus, how slow or fast a person walks may depend on whether the image of an old person was evaluated negatively or positively. If negative, then walk fast to escape; if positive, walk slow to maintain interaction (Cesario et al., 2006).

Goal Achievement and Goal Failure

Once a goal is achieved, a person receives both extrinsic and intrinsic satisfaction—that is, extrinsic from the goal itself and intrinsic from the feeling that results from having achieved the goal.

Achievement valence. While goal valence refers to the benefits derived from a goal, **achievement valence** refers to the satisfaction a person receives from achieving it. Higher benefits accompany more difficult goals, but the likelihood of attaining satisfaction actually decreases (Mento et al., 1992). A person is more likely to fail to achieve a difficult goal and thus be disappointed. Failure is less likely when trying to achieve an easy goal. In one experimental demonstration, students were first asked to assume that their personal GPA goal was 4.0, 3.0, or 2.0. Next, to ascertain achievement valence, they were asked how satisfied they would be with an A, B, or C average. For example, if your goal was a 3.0 GPA and you earned an A, B, or C average, then how satisfied would you be on a scale from incredibly dissatisfied to incredibly satisfied? The results showed that satisfaction ratings decreased as GPA goal increased (Mento et al., 1992, study 7). Satisfaction resulted from an earned GPA exceeding the goal GPA, while dissatisfaction resulted from an earned GPA falling below the goal GPA. A student with a goal of A would only be satisfied with an A and be dissatisfied with anything less. A student with a goal of B would be satisfied with a B but would be much more satisfied with an A and dissatisfied with a C. A student with a goal of C would be satisfied with a C but would be more satisfied with a B and incredibly satisfied with an A. Thus, as goal difficulty increases, the likelihood of achievement decreases and attaining satisfaction is less likely. People often set goals as high as possible but not so high that the likelihood of failure exceeds some acceptable level.

Consequences of success and failure. What happens when goals are not achieved was summarized humorously by the comedic actor W. C. Fields. "If at first you don't succeed, try, try, again. Then quit. There's no use being a damn fool about it." One consequence of not achieving a goal is to try, try, again. A second consequence is to quit that particular goal, scale it down, or seek an alternative goal.

The negative feedback loop in Figure 11.5 implies that a goal, once set, is forever fixed. However, just as a homeowner can alter the desired temperature setting on the thermostat, an individual can change her goals. Goals are altered based on the feedback an individual receives regarding goal achievement. If feedback indicates that a person is failing to meet her goal, then one choice is to reduce the level of the goal. Feedback indicating success might mean raising the level of a future goal. Furthermore, success and failure affect subgoals and consequently final goals, since the lowering or raising of subgoals will result in a lower or higher final goal, respectively. These possible effects were examined in male and female track and field athletes during one season of competition (Donovan & Williams, 2003). Subgoals referred to performance in an individual competition and final goals referred to performance over the entire eight-week season. Prior to each competition, the athletes were asked to indicate their goals for the next competition and for the entire season. How did their goals change when they failed, met, or exceeded their goals? The results showed that if athletes failed to achieve their goals, then there was a tendency to lower their goals for the next competition and for the season's final goal. However, if they met or exceeded their goals, then subsequent competition and season goals were revised upward. Furthermore, the greater the discrepancy between their stated goals and actual performance, the greater was the revision of all their future goals (Donovan & Williams, 2003).

Academic goals also change with success and failure feedback. Success and failure affect the level that students set for their subgoals of individual exams and for the final goal of the course grade. Campion and Lord (1982) asked university students to report their minimum satisfactory grade for an approaching exam and for the course. As would be expected from levels of aspiration, the minimum satisfactory grade goal was about one letter grade higher than performance on a previous exam. However, the level of this goal was also consistent with a student's ability and past performance. So, for example, if a student earned a D on the last exam, she might aspire to a C on the next one, while another student who previously earned a B might aspire to an A. In the Campion and Lord (1982) investigation, those students who exceeded their goals were more likely to raise them for the next exam. If a student's goal was a B and she earned an A, then for the next exam her goal would be raised to an A. Furthermore, consistent and repeated success in meeting exam grade goals led to raising course grade goals. Students who failed to reach their exam goals, however, were more likely to lower them for the next exam. If a student's goal was a B but he earned a C, then he was more likely to lower his goal to a C for the next exam. Repeated failures to meet exam grade goals also led to a lowering of course grade goals. Raising goals following achievement and lowering goals following failure was more apparent when examined over the entire academic quarter. Figure 11.7 shows that students were more likely to raise their exam grade and course grade goals following success on exams. However, when students consistently failed to meet their goals, they were more likely to lower their subsequent exam and course grade goals. An important conclusion from this research and that of the athletes is that goals are not static. Goals change as a result of success or failure of earlier goals.

There are exceptions to the preceding generalizations. Following success, a minority of students lowered their goals, while after failure another minority raised their goals (see Figure 11.7). Thus, success or failure is not the sole determiner of whether individuals raise or lower their goals.

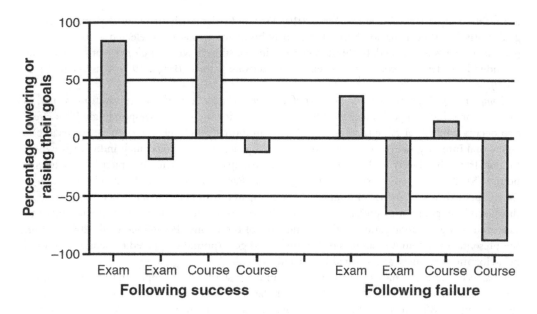

FIGURE 11.7 Effects of Goal Success or Failure. Students were more likely to increase their exam grade goals and their course grade goals following success in meeting a previous goal. They were more likely to lower goals following failure in meeting a previous goal. The data are averaged over four exams given during the academic quarter.

Source: Adapted from "A Control Systems Conceptualization of the Goal-Setting and Changing Process" by M. A. Campion and R. G. Lord, 1982, *Organizational Behavior and Human Performance, 30*, Table 4, p. 279, and Table 7, p. 283.

Raising or lowering a goal is mediated by self-efficacy, which is the belief about how capable a person feels about achieving a particular goal. Bandura and Cervone (1986) showed that, despite failure, a person with strong self-efficacy was more likely to try harder the next time, while a person with weak self-efficacy was more likely to decrease effort. Thus, high-self-efficacy individuals are more likely to increase their goal level following failure, while low-self-efficacy individuals are more likely to lower it. In addition, following success, individuals with low self-efficacy did not think they were able to achieve their goal a second time. These individuals were less likely to expend more effort the next time, especially when they had just expended a lot of effort to meet the goal.

Goal Achievement without Awareness

According to the ancient Roman poet Ovid (43 B.C.–A.D. 17), "[t]he cause is hidden but the effect is known." This statement could be interpreted to mean that humans may not be aware of some of the events that motivate their behavior. For instance, in not being aware of the motivational source, individuals may consider thought or intentions to be responsible for their behavior when in fact they were not. Two hypotheses describe how motivation without awareness is possible (Bargh, 1990; Custers & Aarts, 2010). First, individuals may be unaware that a particular goal motivated their behavior. Second, they may be unaware that they selected a goal or that a particular goal was activated. In this instance, subliminal stimuli, which are ones that occur below an individual's level of cognitive awareness, can activate a goal (Bargh, 1990; Custers & Aarts, 2010).

Comparing goals presented below the level of awareness. One effect of goal motivation is that, as the level or value of a goal increases, achievement behavior increases correspondingly. This effect also occurs when goal value is represented below an individual's level of awareness. For example, behavioral intensity, such as force used on a handgrip, depends on how much individuals expect to gain from that behavior. In one experiment, participants were shown a picture of a British pound ($1.29) or a penny prior to a handgrip task. Participants squeezed a handgrip harder if they expected to gain a British pound ($1.29) compared to a penny. Even when the picture of the pound or penny was presented subliminally (below cognitive awareness), participants still squeezed harder in anticipation of the pound than of the penny (Pessiglione et al., 2007). Thus, the presentation without awareness of a more valued goal (pound compared to penny) motivates behavior more strongly as measured by a handgrip task.

Goal value also depends on an individual's internal state. For example, the value of food is greater to hungry than to sated individuals. A similar claim can be made for the effects of sensory-specific satiety. With repeated bites, the sensory appeal of a food declines, making an alternative food more appealing. In a demonstration of the subliminal effects of sensory-specific satiety, Ziauddeen and coresearchers (2011) measured handgrip force that participants exerted in order to attain a food incentive of either pizza or cake. Participants were instructed that greater force would yield more of either food incentive. At the start of each trial a picture of the food incentive was presented above or below a participant's level of awareness. After a number of trials, participants received a piece of either pizza or cake to eat. Eating should produce sensory-specific satiety for the consumed item. Afterwards participants received additional trials with the same procedure. The researchers hypothesized that, based on sensory-specific satiety, the hedonic value of the eaten food would be less than that of the noneaten food. For example, eating pizza lowers its hedonic value and not eating cake keeps its hedonic value constant. Thus, participants should exert less force for the eaten food and more force for the alternative food. The effects of sensory-specific satiety occurred as predicted. Less force was used to earn the eaten food and more force was used to earn the noneaten food, even when the pictures of those foods were presented below a participant's level of awareness.

Activating goal value below the level of awareness. A goal can also be selected or activated without individuals being aware of it. The effects on behavior of this activation become apparent when comparing different goal values. In one demonstration, Bargh and coresearchers (2001) primed participants without their awareness for a high-performance goal—that is, a goal or motive to do well on a puzzle task. To prime this goal, participants worked on a word-search puzzle that required finding words embedded in a 10×10 matrix of letters. Words designed to prime a high-performance goal included *win, compete, succeed, strive, attain, achieve,* and *master.* When participants found these words, it was assumed that this would prime a high-performance motive. In the neutral prime control condition, participants solved a word-search puzzle that contained words such as *ranch, carpet, river, shampoo, robin, hat,* and *window.* A high-performance motive was assumed not to be activated in this condition. After completing one of these initial puzzles, participants were instructed to work on three additional puzzles that contained words related to foods, bugs, and colors. Performance on these puzzles during a 10-minute period served to measure the different effects produced by the prior high-performance versus neutral priming procedures. The results showed that participants primed for a high-performance goal discovered significantly more solution words than did the neutrally primed participants. Furthermore, in a post-experimental debriefing, no participant reported being aware of the relationship between the priming nature of the first puzzle and performance on the second set of puzzles. These results imply that a nonconsciously primed high-performance goal elevates achievement performance, at least in the case of puzzle-solving behavior.

The attractiveness of a goal can also be increased nonconsciously—that is, without individuals being aware that this has occurred even though their behavior increases as a consequence. To illustrate, imagine being required to squeeze a handgrip for 3.5 seconds when the word *squeeze* appears on the computer screen. How much force an individual exerts in order to achieve this goal activity depends on the task's affective value. As goal value increases, more force should be exerted even if that value was created without the individual's awareness. In such an experiment, Aarts and coresearchers (2008) presented words such as *exert* and *vigorous* very fast so that they were below the participant's level of awareness. These words are associated with the handgrip task. After presentation of the handgrip words, participants were shown positive adjectives such as *good* and *pleasant* for longer intervals so that participants were aware of seeing them. For a control, the researchers used neutral words such as *furthermore* and *around* also presented above the participants' level of awareness. The researchers' hypothesis was that the positive adjectives would add affective value to the goal of handgrip-squeezing as represented by the words *exert* and *vigorous*. Little, if any, value would be added by the neutral words. Indeed the results supported their hypothesis. When participants had positive adjectives paired with the nonconscious priming of exertion (*exert*, *vigorous*), they began squeezing the handgrip sooner and exerted more effort over the entire 3.5-second period compared to the squeezing of the control participants (Aarts et al., 2008).

Section Recap

Once a goal is selected, the process of *goal commitment* indicates that individuals declare a willingness to persist in expending time and effort to achieve their goal. Goal commitment increases the likelihood of goal achievement. It also produces *goal shielding*, which means preventing other goals and behaviors from interfering with current goal pursuit. Also when a person commits to a goal, *implementation intentions* become significant. Accordingly goal achievement behavior is the product of a cognitively prepared if–then plan. If an anticipated time or situation arises, then goal achievement automatically follows. The negative feedback loop is a model for goal achievement behavior. Progress toward a goal depends on *feedback*, which is information about the outcome of achievement behavior regarding changes in the discrepancy between the current state and the goal. Two different perspectives describe goal achievement progress. In a *to-go* perspective, the goal is the reference point, while in a *to-date* perspective the beginning of the achievement process is the reference point. The to-go perspective is identified by the negative feedback loop, in which achievement behavior is motivated to reduce the discrepancy between the current state and a person's goal. In the to-date perspective, motivation depends on how much a person has already achieved. Achievement of the final goal is aided by *subgoals*, which are like individual rungs of a ladder that must be climbed to reach the top or final goal.

Goal achievement behavior is obviously necessary for achieving a goal. There are different views of how goal achievement behavior occurs. According to the *selfish goal hypothesis*, the assumption is that goals are self-centered and in charge, which causes them to select stimuli and behaviors that will ensure their achievement. According to the perception–behavior link, a goal activates the appropriate achievement behavior because the two have been associated many times in the past. According to the concept of motivated preparation, goal valence determines the aim of achievement behavior. Positive goals spur approach behavior and negative goals spur avoidance behavior. Associated with goal value is *achievement valence*, which refers to the satisfaction attained from accomplishing a goal. Following success, a goal is usually scaled up, while following failure it is usually scaled down.

Goals can motivate behavior without awareness because the person is unaware that a goal is motivating her behavior or that a goal was activated. The value of a goal can be manipulated subliminally (below a person's cognitive awareness). These altered values influence behavior. Research has also shown that when a goal is activated without awareness, participants behave in a manner consistent with that goal, such as the activation of a high-performance goal yielding high-achievement behavior.

GLOSSARY

Term	Definition
Achievement Valence	The satisfaction a person achieves from accomplishing or achieving her or his goal
Directing Function	Ability of a goal to guide the exact behavior that is acceptable or necessary for achieving the goal
Energizing Function	Ability of a goal to motivate a person to expend effort in order to achieve that goal
Expectancy Value Theory	Goal value (V) multiplies with the expectancy (E) of achieving the goal. Theory examines effect of goal value and expectancy and their combination
Expected Utility Theory	Goal utility (U) multiplies with the probability or expectancy (E) of achieving the goal. The emphasis is on E×U product to determine goal selection
Feedback	Information provided to an individual regarding if progress is being made or if a person is getting closer to his or her goal
Framing	Perspective from which a goal is viewed, such as the opportunity of making a gain or avoiding a loss
Goal	The cognitive image of a future outcome that represents an object, behavior, or feeling. A person commits to the goal, which motivates and guides behavior
Goal Commitment	Process whereby a person becomes set to achieve a goal; a willingness and persistent determination to expend time and effort in goal pursuit
Goal Difficulty	Characteristic of the level of a goal and refers to how hard that goal is to achieve

continued ...

GLOSSARY Continued

Term	Definition
Goal Level	Rank of a goal in a hierarchy of potential goals. Higher-level goals have higher value and greater utility and provide greater benefits than do lower-level goals
Goal Shielding	To prevent other goals or behaviors from interfering with the pursuit of one's current goal
Goal Specificity	Characteristic of a goal that refers to how precisely a goal is stated in contrast to it being vague or unspecified
Implementation Intentions	If–then plans of a cognitive link between a specific situation and goal achievement behavior
Incentive–Drive Link	Warden's term that a physiological drive matches up with the appropriate incentive, such as hunger matches with food and curiosity with novel stimuli
Levels of Aspiration	A person's desire to excel, to do better the next time, or to do better than others
Mindset Theory of Action	Describes phases of focusing on goal selection and commitment and then focusing on relevant behaviors for achieving the goal
Motivated Preparation	Aim of behavior depends on the valence of the goal, i.e., whether the goal is evaluated negatively or positively
Negative Feedback Loop	It represents the negative discrepancy between the current state and the goal. Achievement behavior reduces this negative discrepancy to achieve the goal
Perception–Behavior Link	Idea that a goal elicits achievement behavior because goals and their achievement behaviors have been linked together in the past
Prospect Theory	Goal is viewed as a prospect that is appraised with a decision weight, which is analogous to the value or importance of the goal
Risk Aversion	People's reluctance to take risks or reluctance to take gambles in regards to gains; they prefer a likely positive event compared to an unlikely positive event
Risk-Seeking	People willingly take risks in regards to losses; they prefer an unlikely negative event compared to a likely negative event
Self-Efficacy	Person's belief about how capable she or he is in performing the behavior necessary for achieving a specific goal
Selfish Goal Hypothesis	Idea that goals are self-centered and only concerned with their own survival, i.e., with being achieved
Senioritis	Extremely low motivation of senior students to complete their final semester of study
Subgoals	Intermediate goals that must be achieved on the way toward achieving the final goal; they resemble rungs on a ladder before the top rung or goal
Subjective Probability	A person's personal belief that a particular event will occur or goal can be achieved, expressed as a number between 0.00 and 1.00
To-Date Perspective	How much individuals have accomplished on the way toward achieving their goal. The reference point is the beginning of the achievement process

continued . . .

GLOSSARY Continued

Term	Definition
To-Go Perspective	The amount of work that still needs to be accomplished to achieve one's goal. The reference point is the final goal
Utility	Refers to a goal's usefulness in satisfying a want, bringing satisfaction, or creating happiness
Valence	The subjective value of a goal that determines if a goal is selected to be achieved

REFERENCES

Aarts, H., Custers, R., & Marien, H. (2008). Preparing and motivating behavior outside of awareness. *Science*, *319*, 1639.

Arkes, H. R., & Hammond, K. R. (1986). General introduction. In H. R. Arkes & K. R. Hammond (Eds.), *Judgment and decision making: An interdisciplinary reader* (pp. 1–11). Cambridge: Cambridge University Press.

Atkinson, J. W., & Birch, D. (1970). *The dynamics of action*. New York, NY: Wiley.

Austin, J. T., & Vancouver, J. B. (1996). Goal constructs in psychology: Structure, process, and content. *Psychological Bulletin*, *120*, 338–375.

Bandura, A. (1977). Self-efficacy: Toward a unity theory of behavioral change. *Psychological Review*, *84*, 191–215.

Bandura, A. (1991). Self-regulation of motivation through anticipatory and self-reactive mechanisms. In R. Dienstbier (Series Ed.) & R. Dienstbier (Vol. Ed.), *Nebraska symposium on motivation: Vol. 38. Perspectives on motivation* (pp. 69–164). Lincoln, NE: University of Nebraska Press.

Bandura, A. (1997). *Self-efficacy: The exercise of control*. New York, NY: Freeman.

Bandura, A., & Cervone, D. (1983). Self-evaluative and self-efficacy mechanisms governing the motivational effects of goal systems. *Journal of Personality and Social Psychology*, *45*, 1017–1028.

Bandura, A., & Cervone, D. (1986). Differential engagement of self-reactive influences in cognitive motivation. *Organizational Behavior and Human Decision Processes*, *38*, 92–113.

Bargh, J. A. (1990). Auto-motives: Preconscious determinants of social interaction. In E. T. Higgins & R. J. Sorrentino (Eds.), *Handbook of motivation and cognition* (Vol. 2, pp. 93–111). New York, NY: Guilford.

Bargh, J. A., Gollwitzer, P. M., Lee-Chai, A., Barndollar, K., & Trötschel, R. (2001). The automated will: Nonconscious activation and pursuit of behavioral goals. *Journal of Personality and Social Psychology*, *81*, 1014–1027.

Bargh, J. A., & Huang, J. Y. (2009). The selfish goal. In G. B. Moskowitz & H. Grant (Eds.), *The Psychology of goals* (pp. 127–152). New York, NY: Guilford Press.

Bargh, J. A., & Williams, E. L. (2006). The automaticity of social life. *Current Directions in Psychological Science*, *15*, 1–4.

Beach, L. R. (1990). *Image theory: Decision making in personal and organizational contexts*. Chichester: Wiley.

Bonezzi, A., Brendl, C. M., & De Angelis, M. (2011). Stuck in the middle: The psychophysics of goal pursuit. *Psychological Science*, *22*(5), 607–612.

Cabanac, M. (1971). Physiological role of pleasure. *Science*, *173*, 1103–1107.

Cabanac, M. (2010). The dialectics of pleasure. In M. L. Kringelbach & K. C. Berridge (Eds.), *Pleasures of the brain* (pp. 113–124). New York, NY: Oxford University Press.

Campion, M. A., & Lord, R. G. (1982). A control systems conceptualization of the goal-setting and changing process. *Organizational Behavior and Human Performance*, *30*, 265–287.

Cervone, D., & Peake, P. K. (1986). Anchoring, efficacy, and action: The influence of judgmental heuristics on self-efficacy judgments and behavior. *Journal of Personality and Social Psychology*, *50*, 492–501.

Cesario, J., Plaks, J. E., & Higgins, E. T. (2006). Automatic social behavior as motivated preparation to interact. *Journal of Personality and Social Psychology*, *90*, 893–910.

Custers, R., & Aarts, H. (2010). The unconscious will: How the pursuit of goals operates outside of conscious awareness. *Science, 329*, 4750.

Donovan, J. J., & Williams, K. J. (2003). Missing the mark: Effects of time and causal attributions on goal revision in response to goal-performance discrepancies. *Journal of Applied Psychology, 88*, 379–390.

Earley, P. C., Wojnaroski, P., & Prest, W. (1987). Task planning and energy expended: Exploration of how goals influence performance. *Journal of Applied Psychology, 72*, 107–114.

Edwards, W. (1961). Behavioral decision theory. *Annual Review of Psychology, 12*, 473–498.

Elliot, A. J., & Fryer, J. W. (2008). The goal construct in psychology. In J. Y. Shah & W. L. Gardner (Eds.), *Handbook of motivation science* (pp. 235–250). New York, NY: Guilford.

Gollwitzer, P. M. (2012). Mindset theory of action phases. In P. A. M. Van Lange, A. W. Kruglanski, & E. T. Higgins (Eds.), *The handbook of theories of social psychology: Vol. 1* (pp. 526–545). Thousand Oaks, CA: Sage.

Gollwitzer, P. M., & Sheeran, P. (2006). Implementation intentions and goal achievement: A meta-analysis of effects and processes. *Advances in Experimental Social Psychology, 38*, 69–119.

Gray, C. A. (1975). Factors in students' decisions to attempt academic tasks. *Organizational Behavior and Human Performance, 13*, 147–164.

Heath, C., Larrick, R. P., & Wu, G. (1999). Goals as reference points. *Cognitive Psychology, 38*, 79–109.

Hobbes, T. (1640/1962). *Human nature*. Cleveland, OH: Bell & Howell.

Hollenbeck, J. R., & Klein, H. J. (1987). Goal commitment and the goal-setting process: Problems, prospects, and proposals for future research. *Journal of Applied Psychology, 72*, 212–220.

Hollenbeck, J. R., Klein, H. J., O'Leary, A. M., & Wright, P. M. (1989a). Investigation of the construct validity of a self-report measure of goal commitment. *Journal of Applied Psychology, 74*, 951–956.

Hollenbeck, J. R., Williams, C. R., & Klein, H. J. (1989b). An empirical examination of the antecedents of commitment to difficult goals. *Journal of Applied Psychology, 74*, 18–23.

Hull, C. L. (1943). *Principles of behavior*. New York, NY: Appleton-Century-Crofts.

Isaacson, W. (2011). *Steve Jobs*. New York, NY: Simon & Schuster.

Kahneman, D. (2011). *Thinking, fast and slow*. New York, NY: Farrar, Straus and Giroux.

Kahneman, D., & Tversky, A. (1979). Prospect theory: An analysis of decision under risk. *Econometrica, 47*, 263–291.

Karniol, R., & Ross, M. (1996). The motivational impact of temporal focus: Thinking about the future and the past. *Annual Review of Psychology, 47*, 593–620.

Klein, H. J. (1989). An integrated control theory model of work motivation. *Academy of Management Review, 14*, 150–172.

Klein, H. J., Wesson, M. J., Hollenbeck, J. R., & Alge, B. J. (1999). Goal commitment and the goal setting process: Conceptual clarification and empirical synthesis. *Journal of Applied Psychology, 84*, 885–896.

Klein, H. J., Wesson, M. J., Hollenbeck, J. R., Wright, P. M., & DeShon, R. P. (2001). The assessment of goal commitment: A measurement model meta-analysis. *Organizational Behavior and Human Decision Processes, 85*, 32–55.

Klinger, E. (1977). *Meaning and void: Inner experience and the incentives in people's lives*. Minneapolis, MN: University of Minnesota Press.

Koo, M., & Fishbach, A. (2008). Dynamics of self-regulation: How (un)accomplished goal actions affect motivation. *Journal of Personality and Social Psychology, 94*, 183–195.

Koo, M., & Fishbach, A. (2010). Climbing the goal ladder: How upcoming actions increase level of aspiration. *Journal of Personality and Social Psychology, 99*, 1–13.

Latham, G. P., & Seijts, G. H. (1999). The effects of proximal and distal goals on performance on a moderately complex task. *Journal of Organizational Behavior, 20*, 421–429.

Lee, T. W., Locke, E. A., & Latham, G. P. (1989). Goal setting theory and job performance. In L. E. Pervin (Ed.), *Goal concepts in personality and social psychology* (pp. 291–326). Hillsdale, NJ: Lawrence Erlbaum.

Lench, H. C., Smallman, R., & Berg, L. A. (2016). Moving toward a brighter future: The effects of desire on judgments about the likelihood of future events. *Motivation Science, 2*, 33–48.

Lewin, K., Dembo, T., Festinger, L., & Sears, P. S. (1944). Level of aspiration. In J. M. Hunt (Ed.), *Personality and the behavior disorders* (pp. 333–378). New York, NY: Ronald.

Locke, E. A. (1991). Goal theory vs. control theory: Contrasting approaches to understanding work motivation. *Motivation and Emotion, 15*, 9–28.

Locke, E. A., Chah, D.-O., Harrison, S., & Lustgarten, N. (1989). Separating the effects of goal specificity from goal level. *Organizational Behavior and Human Decision Processes, 43*, 270–287.

Locke, E. A., & Latham, G. P. (1990). *A theory of goal setting and task performance*. Englewood Cliffs, NJ: Prentice Hall.

Locke, E. A., Latham, G. P., & Erez, M. (1988). The determinants of goal commitment. *Academy of Management Review, 13*, 23–39.

Locke, E. A., Shaw, K. N., Saari, L. M., & Lathan, G. P. (1981). Goal setting and task performance: 1969–1980. *Psychological Bulletin, 90*, 125–152.

Markman, A. B., & Brendl, C. M. (2000). The influence of goals on value and choice. In D. L. Medin (Ed.), *The psychology of learning and motivation* (Vol. 39, pp. 97–128). San Diego, CA: Academic Press.

Matsui, T., Okada, A., & Mizuguchi, R. (1981). Expectancy theory prediction of the goal theory postulate, "the harder the goals, the higher the performance." *Journal of Applied Psychology, 66*, 54–58.

Mento, A. J., Locke, E. A., & Klein, H. J. (1992). Relationship of goal level to valence and instrumentality. *Journal of Applied Psychology, 77*, 395–405.

Miller, G. A., Galanter, E., & Pribram, K. H. (1960). *Plans and the structure of behavior*. New York, NY: Henry Holt.

Miller, N. E. (1959). Liberalization of basic S-R concepts: Extensions to conflict behavior, motivation, and social learning. In S. Koch (Ed.), *Psychology: A study of a science* (Vol. 2, pp. 196–292). New York, NY: McGraw-Hill.

Morgenroth, T., Ryan, M. K., & Peters, K. (2015). The motivational theory of role modeling: How role models influence role aspirants' goals. *Review of General Psychology, 19*, 465–483.

Murray, H. A. (1938). *Explorations in personality*. New York, NY: Oxford University Press.

Nagengast, B., Marsh, H. W., Scalas, L. F., Xu, M. K., Hau, K. T., & Trautwein, U. (2011). Who took the "×" out of expectancy-value theory? A psychological mystery, a substantive-methodological synergy, and a cross-national generalization. *Psychological Science, 22*, 1058–1066.

Patalano, A. L., & Seifert, C. M. (1997). Opportunistic planning: Being reminded of pending goals. *Cognitive Psychology, 34*, 1–36.

Pessiglione, M., Schmidt, L., Draganski, B., Kalisch, R., Lau, H., Dolan, R. J., & Frith, C. D. (2007). How the brain translates money into force: A neuroimaging study of subliminal motivation. *Science, 316*, 904–906.

Raynor, J. O. (1970/1974). Relationships between achievement-related motives, future orientation, and academic performance. *Journal of Personality and Social Psychology, 15*, 28–33. Reprinted with modifications in J. W. Atkinson & J. O. Raynor (Eds.), *Motivation and achievement* (pp. 173–180). Washington, DC: V. H. Winston.

Rotter, J. B. (1942). Levels of aspiration as a method of studying personality. I. A critical review of methodology. *Psychological Review, 49*, 463–474.

Salancik, G. R. (1977). Commitment and the control of organizational behavior and belief. In B. M. Staw & G. R. Salancik (Eds.), *New directions in organization behavior* (pp. 1–54). Chicago, IL: St. Clair Press.

Savage, L. J. (1954). *The foundations of statistics*. New York, NY: John Wiley.

Schank, R. C., & Abelson, R. P. (1977). *Scripts, plans, goals and understanding*. Hillsdale, NJ: Lawrence Erlbaum.

Shah, J. Y. (2005). The automatic pursuit and management of goals. *Current Directions in Psychological Science, 14*, 10–13.

Shah, J. Y., Friedman, R., & Kruglanski, A. W. (2002). Forgetting all else: On the antecedents and consequences of goal shielding. *Journal of Personality and Social Psychology, 83*, 1261–1280.

Shelley, M. K. (1994). Gain/loss asymmetry in risky intertemporal choice. *Organizational Behavior and Human Decision Processes, 59*, 124–159.

Shepperd, J. A., Waters, E. A., Weinstein, N. D., & Klein, W. M. (2015). A primer on unrealistic optimism. *Current Directions in Psychological Science, 24*, 232–237.

Shoemaker, P. J. H. (1982). The expected utility model: Its variants, purposes, evidence and limitations. *Journal of Economic Literature, 20*, 529–563.

Tolman, E. C. (1932). *Purposive behavior in animals and men*. New York, NY: Appleton-Century.

Tolman, E. C. (1959). The principles of purposive behavior. In S. Koch (Ed.), *Psychology: A study of a science: Vol. II. General systematic formulations, learning, and special processes* (pp. 92–157). New York, NY: McGraw-Hill.

Troland, L. T. (1928/1967). *The fundamentals of human motivation*. New York, NY: Hafner.

Warden, C. J. (1931). The Columbia Obstruction Method. In C. J. Warden (Ed.), *Animal motivation: Experimental studies on the albino rat* (pp. 3–16). New York, NY: Columbia University Press.

Webb, T. L., & Sheeran, P. (2007). How do implementation intentions promote goal attainment? A test of component processes. *Journal of Experimental Social Psychology, 43*, 295–302.

Weldon, E., & Yun, S. (2000). The effects of proximal and distal goals on goal level, strategy development, and group performance. *Journal of Applied Behavioral Science, 36*, 336–344.

Wigfield, A., Tonks, S., & Klauda, S. L. (2009). Expectancy-value theory. In K. R. Wentzel & A. Wigfield (Eds.), *Handbook of motivation at school* (pp. 55–75). New York, NY: Routledge.

Ziauddeen, H., Subramaniam, N., Gaillar, R., Burke, L. K., Farooqi, I. S., & Fletcher, P. C. (2011). Food images engage subliminal motivation to seek food. *International Journal of Obesity, 35*, 1–3.

CHAPTER 12

Economics of Motivation

Laziness travels so slowly that poverty soon overtakes him.

Benjamin Franklin, 1756

Work is the price you pay for money.

Anonymous

Goals are not free. People pay for them with achievement behavior. As costs, do these behaviors impede goal motivation? Consider how behavioral costs affect motivation along with the following questions:

1. How are the behavioral costs measured?
2. Do people have resources of motivation to pay for their goals?
3. Is goal achievement behavior governed by physical and mental fatigue?
4. Do behaviors that result in goal achievement resemble economic transactions?
5. Are the principle of least effort and the economic demand law widespread in motivation?

MOTIVATION COSTS AND RESOURCES

Once upon a time there was a king who on his deathbed promised his kingdom to the son who was the laziest. The eldest son proclaimed to be the laziest, since he would not bother to remove a drop of water from his eye in order to sleep. The second son claimed the kingdom, maintaining that he was too lazy to remove his burning heel from a fire. The third son exclaimed that the kingdom should be his because he indeed was the laziest: "If the hangman's noose were already around my neck, then I would be too lazy to cut it with a knife so that I could save myself." Guess who inherited the kingdom (Grimm, 1884/1968).

This fairy tale portrays a puzzling goal achievement scenario. Usually, higher-level or more difficult goals—like acquiring a kingdom—require more work. But in this story achievement was conditional on the least amount of effort. Push and pull motivation require effort. Whether a person is pushed to satisfy a physiological or psychological need, the expenditure of some type of effort is required. Similarly, if a person is pulled toward a goal, then this also requires effort. The paradox in motivation is that people value high-level goals that they hope to achieve with minimal effort. These two preferences are incompatible. Either select a high-level goal or select low effort. But, in life, high-level goals require high effort, while low-level goals require low effort. What is a person to do? What are the behavioral costs of achieving goals?

Costs of Motivated Behavior

Goal achievement depends on motivated behavior that brings the goal closer and closer until finally achieved. Various methods are used to measure the cost of this behavior. For example, if your goal is to type a 10-page paper, then it will cost you in terms of responses, time, physical energy, psychological energy, and lost opportunities. These costs are laid out in detail in Table 12.1. In general, as goal level increases, the cost of goal achievement increases also.

Response and time costs. Responses refer to discrete behavioral units that are required to achieve a goal. The typing example in Table 12.1 classifies keystrokes as responses. Response costs have been studied extensively with animals in a Skinner box. This box is a chamber in which a rat, for example, presses a lever in order to earn a pellet of food. The cost of food is set by the number of lever presses, which is controlled by a **fixed ratio (FR) schedule of reinforcement**. For this schedule, an experimenter establishes a ratio between the number of lever presses the rat must perform to earn one reinforcer. For instance, an FR 10 requires 10 lever presses for one reinforcer, while an FR 100 requires 100 lever presses for one reinforcer. Thus, a food pellet requiring 100 lever presses is more expensive than one requiring 10 lever presses.

A difficulty with the response-cost measure is quantifying the form and intensity of a response. Is it feasible to count the number of responses in any complex human activity, such as working

TABLE 12.1 The Motivational Costs of Typing a 10-Page Paper

Response Costs	Number of responses required to complete the task (e.g., keystrokes) Estimated 15,000 keystrokes for 3,000 words (10 pages)
Time Costs	Amount of time required to complete the task (e.g., minutes, hours) Estimated 1.5 hours of typing at 30 words per minute
Physical Energy Costs	Utilizing oxygen and glucose (e.g., calories burned) A 140-pound person burns 143 calories typing for 1.5 hours
Psychological Effort Costs	Self-control to keep on task toward goal and not give into temptations; to organize, remember information, to make decisions
Opportunity Costs	Activities person gave up to type paper (e.g., next best activities) Person gave up watching TV with friends to type paper

or studying? In the case of typing, are typing the letters q and z with the little finger equal to typing the letters t and b with the index finger? One way out of the difficulty of response measurement is to use time costs. Employers compensate workers for time spent working, such as per hour or per month. Thus, the cost of typing a 10-page paper can be measured by how much time was required rather than by how many keystrokes. Time spent working can be translated into an exact dollar amount. Thus, it is possible to translate the dollar costs of various goods and services into working-time costs. For instance, suppose a worker who earned the federal minimum wage of $7.25 per hour ordered a hamburger, French fries, and a cola drink, which cost $5.69. In terms of time spent working, this meal cost 47 minutes ($5.69/$7.25 × 60 minutes = 47 minutes).

Physical energy costs. The workings of our muscles and brain require the use of glucose for energy either with or without the aid of oxygen. Thus, both glucose and oxygen consumption may be used as cost measures of behavior. The calorie is a unit of physical energy that can serve as the cost measure for the duration and intensity of activities. For example, a 140-pound person burns 222 calories walking for one hour at 20 minutes per mile and burns 318 calories walking at 15 minutes per mile. The same individual would burn 143 calories typing a 10-page paper (Table 12.1). Lighter and heavier individuals burn fewer or more calories on these activities, respectively.

To calculate the number of calories you burn based on the activity, its duration, and your weight, use the calculator titled "Fitness Partner: Activity Calorie Calculator" here: www.primus web.com/cgi-bin/fpc/actcalc.pl.

Psychological effort costs. Terms such as cognitive or mental effort refer to the amount of attention given to a psychological task, such as remembering concepts, deciding among alternatives, or planning to achieve a goal. The energy used to motivate cognitive or mental effort has no physical basis. The energy is imaginary; it is not equivalent to glucose or glycogen. As an example of mental effort, do you devote none, some, or all of your attention to a professor's lecture? More effort is required to devote all your attention to the lecture than only some of it. Or consider note-taking during a lecture. This common student activity involves mental effort devoted to holding information in the memory so that what is important can be selected and recorded. Researchers measure mental effort in such tasks with a probe, such as sounding a tone. How rapidly do participants respond to a tone while engaged in a cognitive task? For example, while taking notes on your laptop during a lecture, how quickly can you press a key upon hearing a tone? Slower reaction times to the tone imply that greater mental effort was expended on taking notes. Note-taking during a lecture requires more mental effort, for example, than taking notes while reading or copying from a text (Piolat et al., 2005).

Opportunity costs. You gave up the opportunity to do something else so that you could read this chapter. According to economists, the **opportunity cost** for reading this chapter is the next preferred activity that you gave up. Any lesser preferred activities should not be counted. Perhaps you gave up the opportunity to watch TV, which was your most preferred alternative, while studying for another class was the next alternative. Studying should not be counted as an opportunity cost, since it was preferred less than TV watching. However, Schwartz (2004) points out that choosing one option may involve multiple opportunity costs—that is, forgoing several other alternatives. Perhaps you gave up watching TV with friends and so you also gave up the opportunity to socialize. Opportunity costs can have an effect in different ways (Schwartz, 2004).

First, the opportunity cost of a decision increases with the number of abandoned alternatives. For example, the opportunity cost of reading this chapter is greater if you abandoned watching TV with friends rather than watching TV alone. Second, the evaluation of lost opportunities produces regret, an unpleasant feeling brought on by a wrong decision. Regret is more likely from a greater number of abandoned opportunities.

Regret is likely to occur when a person's choice did not fulfill expectations or was a disappointment. Regret also depends on the value of the alternatives or opportunities that were rejected. Sagi and Friedland (2007) conducted a series of experiments showing that the intensity of regret is based on the combined values of the rejected alternatives. To understand how the value of rejected alternatives determine regret, consider being a participant in their second experiment. This experiment begins with this vignette:

> After a very busy week you had, at last, a free evening. Knowing that it would be a while before you get a free evening again, you wanted to make the most of it. You could go to the movies, go to bed early, go to a café, or read a book.
>
> (p. 518)

Now imagine that you chose to go to the movie, which turned out to be long and boring, a disappointment. How much do you regret your decision? It depends on the union or combination of values of the alternatives, which are listed in Table 12.2. Prior to the experiment a separate group of participants rank ordered the four activities in Table 12.2 according to their personal preferences. Watching a movie was preferred most, followed by going to a café, while going to bed early was preferred least (Table 12.2). In the main experiment, one group was asked how much they regretted their movie choice when compared to the alternatives in set 1 while a different group based their regret on the alternatives in set 2. Regret was measured with a scale of 1 = *not at all* to 7 = *very much*. Notice that for set 1 the alternatives were going to a café or reading a book, while in set 2 reading a book was replaced by going to bed early. The combined value of set 1 is higher than that of set 2 and so greater regret was predicted, which is what happened. The intensity of regret shown in the rightmost column of Table 12.2 is higher for set 1, where the combined value of the alternatives was greatest.

TABLE 12.2 Regret Depends on the Combined Value of the Alternative Opportunities

Value of the Rejected Alternatives					
Choices	Chose	Highest value	Medium value	Lowest value	Rate intensity of regret: 1–7
Set 1: Higher Valued Alternatives	Saw movie: disappointing	Go to local café	Read a book	—	Higher amount of regret = 5.13
Set 2: Lower Valued Alternatives	Saw movie: disappointing	Go to local café	—	Go to bed early	Lower amount of regret = 4.20

Source: Adapted from "The Cost of Richness: The Effect of the Size and Diversity of Decision Sets on Post-Decision Regret" by A. Sagi and N. Friedland, 2007, *Journal of Personality and Social Psychology, 93*, p. 518.

Effort Discounting

Chapter 10 contained a description of delay discounting: the process whereby a future goal is represented in the present but at a lower or discounted value. For example, $100 available in 10 weeks is discounted to be worth $10. **Effort discounting** is a similar process but the reduced value of a goal is due to effort, not time. Effort discounting means that the subjective value of an incentive or goal decreases with increases in the effort necessary to obtain them. Figure 12.1 represents the general relationship between effort and goal value. The curve shows that, as effort increases, the subjective value of a goal decreases. The required effort to achieve is a cost that subtracts from the goal's value so that it is worth less. But how does effort discounting occur?

Effort was a common theme in all of the behavioral costs described so far. How do these costs affect goal value and goal choice? For example, imagine the following choices in preparing for an exam and the resulting expected grade.

Choice 1: Only read the chapter summaries for a C.
Choice 2: Skim the chapters and read the summaries for a B.
Choice 3: Read the chapters and read the summaries for an A.

Notice that a greater amount of time, energy, or mental effort in preparing for the exam is expected to result in a higher grade. But does the amount of mental effort help determine your

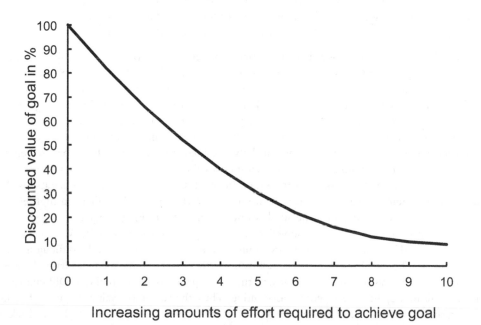

Increasing amounts of effort required to achieve goal

FIGURE 12.1 Effects of Effort Discounting on Goal Value. A goal that requires no effort to achieve has a value of 100 percent. Goals that require an effort to achieve are reduced in value as a result of that effort—that is, effort discounts the value of the goal. So as the effort required to achieve a goal increases, the subjective value of that goal is discounted more and more. As a result, the value of the goal decreases below the starting 100 percent value.

choice? You could decide on choice 1, since it requires the least effort but the lowest grade. Or decide on choice 3, since it results in the highest grade but for the most effort. Or does a person combine effort and value to decide on her choice? Research shows that effort and value combine to make choices. But, first, how can we measure mental effort?

One way is to measure the mental effort required for remembering information, such as that for an exam. This is possible with the *n-back memory task* (Westbrook et al., 2013). In this task, letters appear on the computer screen one after the other. A participant must remember if the current letter occurred 1, 2, 3, 4, 5 or 6 positions back. For example, in the case of n = 1 (back-1), the letters might be k, k, r, f, b, d, w; the person must remember that the second k also occurred one letter back. For n = 4 (back-4), the letters might be v, x, l, p, v, c, p; the person must remember that the second v also occurred four letters back. Thus, mental effort increases from remembering one letter to remembering six. And, indeed, participants who have performed these tasks rate them as more mentally demanding and effortful as the memory requirements increase (Westbrook et al., 2013).

Now, imagine individuals who are familiar with the effort involved in all six n-back memory tasks. They are offered a series of choices to perform various n-back memory tasks for different amounts of money. The money sets the value of the goal and the memory task is the cost of achieving that goal. For example,

Choice 1: $1 for doing the back-1 task versus $1 for doing the back-4 task
Choice 2: $1 for doing the back-1 task versus $1.40 for doing the back-4 task
Choice 3: $1 for doing the back-1 task versus $1.80 for doing the back-4 task

On the left, the cost of a $1 goal is to remember one letter back. But, on the right, the goals have increasingly higher values but at a greater cost. The cost of the $1.40 and $1.80 goals is to remember four letters back. Suppose on choice 1, a participant selects to perform the back-1 task for $1. The low mental effort for the back-1 task is worth the $1 benefit but the high effort for the back-4 task is not worth $1. Then suppose on choice 3 the participant switches. He selects to perform the back-4 task because it is worth $1.80 benefit. How do we account for this reversal? Does it mean that somewhere between these two choices, the effort to benefit ratios were equal? For example, on choice 2 an individual decides that the back-1 task is worth $1 but also that the back-4 task is worth $1.40. In other words, the effort/benefit ratio is the same for both choices—that is, low benefit from low effort and high benefit from high effort. For choice 2, an individual cannot decide because the options are judged equal.

Using the n-back memory tasks coupled with a variety of monetary benefits, Westbrook and coresearchers (2013) found that participants required more money to perform the difficult n-back memory tasks. The easy back-1 memory task was worth $1 but the harder memory tasks were not. More money was necessary to motivate the participants to perform them. Difficult tasks require more money because of effort discounting. Thus, the subjective value of the $1 for the back-1 task declines because of the greater mental effort required for the harder back-2 to back-6 tasks. From these results, the researchers determined the percentage that $1 was discounted for the more difficult back-2 to back-6 tasks. These results follow the pattern presented in Figure 12.1. The difficulty of the memory task was a cost that subtracted from the value of the money.

Effort discounting influences goal selection. The value of a goal is discounted according to how difficult the goal is to achieve. The selection of a goal, therefore, is based on this discounted value. To investigate the cost of effort discounting in an academic task, Ostaszewski and coresearchers (2013) presented participants with hypothetical options of receiving less than $1,200 for expending no effort or a payment equal to $1,200 for reading 100, 300, or 600 book pages. For example, do you choose a goal of $816 for doing nothing or a goal of $1,200 for reading 100 pages and do you choose $660 for doing nothing or $1,200 for reading 300 pages? Participants' choices showed they were willing to expend effort for the higher payment provided the page reading requirements were low. For example, they would choose to read 100 pages for $1,200 but not choose to read 300 pages for that amount. Generally, as the number of pages to read increased, participants would begin to choose the smaller reward for expending no effort. In other words, like the curve in Figure 12.1, the subjective value of the payments decreased as the associated page requirements increased. When applied to goal selection, increased effort discounting makes a goal less valuable. For instance, in the exam preparation example, the extra effort for an A could result in the value of that grade being discounted below the value of a B. In that case, a student chooses to work for the less costly B alternative.

Motivation Resources

When a couple enters a restaurant to enjoy a meal, one assumes they have the resources to pay. Similarly, when individuals are pushed to satisfy a need or pulled to achieve a goal, they must have the resources to cover the costs. Otherwise, they will fail. The costs listed in Table 12.1 also serve as categories of motivation resources. For example, a meal costs money but money is also a resource. Does the likelihood of satisfying a need or achieving a goal depend on a person's motivation resources?

Response resources. Instrumental behavior acts like money (Allison, 1993). Like an amount of money, an amount of behavior determines how much a person accomplishes. For instance, the concept of **reflex reserve** was proposed by Skinner (1938) as a hypothetical entity that refers to the total available activity for obtaining reinforcers. Available activity can refer to the number of lever press responses a rat has in reserve during an experimental session. According to Skinner (1938), reserves are built up during conditioning. Thus, each reinforcement builds up the reserve of lever presses to some maximum amount. Extinction and fatigue, however, reduce the size of the reserve. If lever press responses are no longer reinforced during an extinction session, then the rat eventually quits responding, as if its reserve of responses had run out. Applied to motivation, reflex reserve can indicate a person's persistence for achieving a goal. A greater reserve makes goal achievement more likely.

Can something akin to a reflex reserve be built up? Some people are more intelligent, which is a characteristic that helps them achieve their goals. Other people, regardless of their intelligence, are more persistent, determined, and tenacious in trying to achieve their goals. One example of this persistence is the construct of **learned industriousness**, which refers to the acquired ability to sustain effort or be persistent in spite of the buildup of subjective fatigue (Eisenberger, 1992). Sustained physical or mental effort produces fatigue, which is an aversive feeling that makes a person quit trying. Effort is qualitatively similar for different behaviors, and the resulting fatigue is similar for different activities. Thus, learning to respond in the presence of fatigue transfers from one behavior to another behavior. However, if effort is sustained in spite of physical or mental fatigue, the animal or individual is eventually reinforced by success (Eisenberger, 1992).

A prime example of this in animal learning is the *partial reinforcement in extinction effect*. This effect refers to the greater persistence in responding during extinction by animals who have received prior intermittent reinforcement rather than continuous reinforcement. For instance, Boren (1961) reinforced different groups of rats from once per response to once per 21 responses. Following the delivery of 60 reinforcers, an extinction procedure began during which no responses were reinforced. Responding during extinction was greatest for the group that had experienced the most nonreinforced responses (the group reinforced once per 21 responses). These infrequently reinforced rats persisted longer before giving up completely. According to Eisenberger's (1992) learned industriousness interpretation, a rat's effort during nonreinforced responding was eventually rewarded, which reduced the aversiveness of response-produced fatigue. Because effort is less aversive, an animal with such a reinforcement history is able to persist longer in the future than is an animal without such experience.

In humans, effort and persistence also occur in cognitive tasks and transfer across such tasks. In one experiment, children with learning disabilities were rewarded with a token every time they learned to spell or read a word, whereas other children were only rewarded after learning every fourth or fifth word. Nevertheless, the greater effort of the less frequently rewarded children was eventually reinforced. This experience made their effort more tolerable. Next, when working on a math test, the less frequently rewarded children worked longer on their problems and produced more correct answers than the other children (Eisenberger et al., 1979). The implication is that learned industriousness is a type of motivational resource. All other things being equal, more industrious individuals have more of this motivational capital to draw on. As a result they persist longer, work harder, and expend a greater effort toward completing their goals compared to less industrious individuals.

Grit. Another motivational resource and one that resembles learned industriousness is an individual difference variable labeled as **grit** (Duckworth et al., 2007). It refers to the "perseverance and passion for long-term goals" (p. 1087). Individuals with a lot of grit can work hard for years toward distant goals despite setbacks, failures, hardships, and intervals of little progress. The concept of grit is captured by a 1903 remark attributed to the inventor of the light bulb, Thomas Edison, who said that "Genius is one percent inspiration, ninety-nine percent perspiration." In other words, long, hard work is way more responsible for great achievements than brilliance. Duckworth and coresearchers (2007) have developed the *Grit Scale*, which attempts to measure an individual's degree of grit. The scale examines two major attributes of grit: consistency of interest and perseverance of effort. Individuals rate themselves to the extent they agree with each statement on a scale that ranges from 1 = *not at all like me* to 5 = *very much like me*. For example, consistency of interest is captured by statements such as "I often set a goal but later choose to pursue a different one" (p. 1090). A high rating on this statement would imply a small amount of grit. Perseverance of effort is reflected in statements such as "I have achieved a goal that took years of work" (p. 1090). A high score on this statement does reflect a large amount of grit.

The *Grit Scale* is on the web page of Angela Duckworth here: www.sas.upenn.edu/~duckwort.

Are people's scores on the *Grit Scale* indicative of consistent interest and long-term perseverance of effort? Yes, based on evidence from a study of participants in the 2006 Scripps National Spelling Bee (Duckworth et al., 2010). First, participants were surveyed for how much they enjoyed various types of practice for the spelling bee: deliberate practice, being quizzed, and leisure reading. Deliberate practice involved memorizing words alone, while being quizzed meant someone else helped by reporting whether the individual pronounced and spelled a word correctly. Leisure reading was reflected in the number of books that were read during the past week, month, or year. Second, participants filled out the *Grit Scale*, as a measure of their long-term commitment. Participants reported that they enjoyed deliberate practice the least, considered it the most effortful, but also considered it highly relevant for their success. Time spent in deliberate practice increased in preparation of the spelling bee, especially in the week prior to the competition. Grit acted like a motivational resource, with scores on the *Grit Scale* predicting the amount of time spent on deliberate practice (Duckworth et al., 2010). Increased deliberate practice resulted in reaching a higher round in the National Spelling Bee.

In addition to spelling bee performance, there are other benefits of having the motivation resource of grit (Duckworth et al., 2007). First, higher grit scores are associated with higher levels of education. For example, it takes more grit to complete four additional years of education to earn a college degree following high school graduation. Older individuals have more grit than younger individuals. This age effect indicates that your parents possess more grit than you do. Grit is also associated with GPA. Students with higher grit scores had higher GPAs even after the effects of SAT scores were eliminated statistically. Grit scores also predicted long-term achievements, such as for United States Military Academy cadets who successfully completed a demanding summer training program. Thus, grit is an important motivational resource especially for achieving arduous long-term goals.

Self-control as a resource. The way toward goal achievement is strewn with temptations that interfere with this process. These temptations provide immediate pleasures but interfere with progress toward a goal. For example, checking your Facebook page interferes with the goal of completing a course paper. The resolve to remain on track toward a goal is known as **self-control**. It is the ability to override desires, emotions, or impulses that disrupt goal achievement behavior. Thus, a person displaces the urge to nap with studying, forgoes dessert to maintain a healthy weight, or suppresses anger so as not to escalate an argument. According to the **strength model,** self-control relies on a psychological resource or energy. People expend this energy when they practice self-control. Baumeister and coresearchers (1998) showed that, when self-control energy was drawn on for one task, less energy was available for another task. For example, the experimenters concluded that participants used more self-control energy resisting the temptation to eat chocolate chip cookies than resisting the temptation to eat radishes. This conclusion was based on the finding that participants who had resisted cookies did not persist as long at a later puzzle-solving task because they were low in self-control energy. Self-control has been compared to muscle energy. It can be depleted with use and restored with rest, much like our muscles can (Muraven & Baumeister, 2000).

If self-control runs on energy, then it can be used currently but it can also be conserved for the future. One experiment tested this possibility by questioning whether people's ability to keep their hands in ice water depended on their self-control energy and on conserving that energy for future use. If some self-control energy is depleted, then this cold-water task should be more difficult. However, performance on the cold-water task should also depend on whether self-control is required for a future task. To test these two possibilities, Muraven and coresearchers (2006) reduced self-control strength in some participants by requiring them to "not think about a white bear." Once this instruction is given, it takes self-control to prevent pictures of bears from intruding into one's consciousness. Other participants did not perform the white bear suppression task and so they presumably had more available self-control energy. Furthermore, if

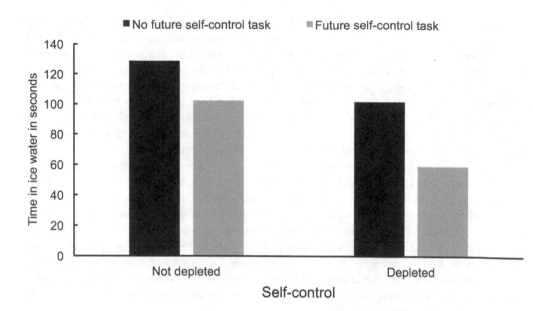

FIGURE 12.2 Depleting and Conserving Self-Control. Self-control energy was depleted in one group by "not thinking of a white bear." Consequently, depleted, participants shortened the time their hands remained in ice water. When a future self-control task was required, all participants shortened their time in ice water as if to conserve energy for the future self-control task.

Source: Adapted from "Conserving Self-Control Strength" by M. Muraven et al., 2006, *Journal of Personality and Social Psychology, 91*, Table 1, p. 527.

self-control is a resource, then a person might conserve some for future tasks. Half of the participants were led to expect a third self-control task after the cold-water task while the other half was not. The third task would require participants to inhibit their facial expressions of mirth while watching a video of an extremely funny stand-up comedian. Would participants conserve self-control energy for the third task by not keeping their hands in the ice water as long? Following the white bear suppression task, participants submerged their hands in ice water. The number of seconds their hands remained in ice water depended on the amount of available self-control energy and on the necessity of conserving energy for the third task (see Figure 12.2). First, when some self-control strength had been depleted by "not thinking of a white bear," participants shortened their time in ice water. Second, when expected to perform another (third) self-control task, participants conserved their self-control strength. How? By not keeping their hands in ice water as long as those participants who were not expected to perform the future self-control task. The results of this experiment imply that self-control strength is powered by mental energy and that the energy can be conserved.

Section Recap

There are costs for satisfying a motive or achieving a goal. These costs are classified as response and time costs, physical and psychological energy costs, and opportunity costs. Response costs are measurable in a Skinner box with a *fixed ratio (FR) schedule of reinforcement*, which details cost as the number of lever presses per reinforcer. Time costs refer to how long it takes to achieve a desired outcome. Behavior requires physical energy, which is derived from glucose and oxygen and is measured in terms of calories. Psychological energy has no material basis in glucose. It powers cognitive or mental effort, which is used for attention, memory, decision-making, and goal planning. *Opportunity costs* refer to those activities that a person rejected in favor of a more preferred one, such as rejecting the chance to watch TV in order to study. Regret results when a choice was disappointing and increases with the combined value of the rejected alternatives. In general, stronger motives and higher goals are more expensive in terms of motivational costs. Effort is the cost for achieving a goal. Effort subtracts from the value of the goal by a process known as *effort discounting*.

People also have motivation resources with which to satisfy their motives and achieve their goals. *Reflex reserve* is a resource that consists of a bank of stored responses that accumulated through reinforcement and are available for attaining future reinforcers. *Learned industriousness* refers to persistence that was acquired as a result of putting forth extended effort that eventually results in reinforcement. *Grit* is an individual difference variable that describes consistent interest in an activity and persistent effort in order to achieve success. *Self-control* is a resource that refers to a person's ability to remain on track toward achieving long-term goals. With self-control people are able to inhibit desires, emotions, or impulses, which derail goal progress. According to the *strength model*, psychological energy powers the exercise of self-control. The energy is depleted with use, restored with rest, and can be conserved for future use.

FUNCTION OF FATIGUE

Does running low on resources register as fatigue and lower motivation? My body is fatigued from physical effort such as running a half-marathon. My brain is fatigued from reading and writing. Both physical and mental fatigue reduce motivation. The half-marathoner is unwilling to run another step. The student is unwilling to read another page or write another sentence. How does fatigue occur and why does it reduce motivation?

Self-Control Strength

Mental fatigue can disturb a person's self-control. Do people falter in their self-control because they have run out of energy, as maintained by the strength model? Do they yield to temptation because their self-control energy was depleted, as implied by the results in Figure 12.2? Glucose is one candidate as the energy source for self-control (Gailliot et al., 2007). If that is the case, then engaging in a self-control task should reduce the motivation of subsequent tasks because of a decline in a person's glucose. To test this possibility, Molden and coresearchers (2012) devised a two part experiment: first, the ego-strength depletion task; second, the motivation task. The ego-strength depletion task required two groups. For one group, an easy procedure depleted self-control energy by a low amount. For the other group, a difficult procedure depleted self-control energy by a high amount. The low depletion procedure required participants to cancel every e on two pages of text. The high-depletion procedure required participants to cancel every e on the first page but on the second page they had to cancel an e provided it was more than two

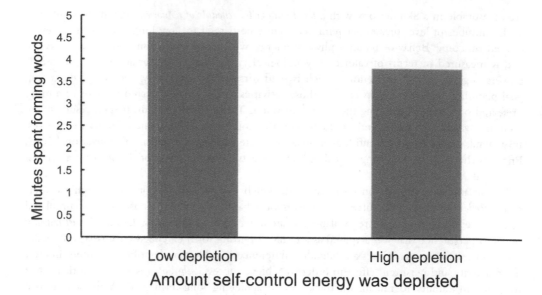

FIGURE 12.3 Depleted Self-Control Reduces Persistence. Participants had their self-control energy depleted by either a low or high amount. When depleted by a high amount, participants persisted less on a motivation task of forming words from a list of letters. However, blood glucose levels were neither related to the depletion of self-control nor to how long participants persisted on the word-forming task.

Source: Adapted from "Motivational Versus Metabolic Effects of Carbohydrates on Self-Control" by D. C. Molden et al., 2012, *Psychological Science, 23*, p. 1139.

letters away from another vowel. This second page required participants to focus more intently, which should deplete more of their glucose energy. Blood glucose level was measured in each participant both before and after the e cancellation task. The second part of the experiment involved the motivation task. Participants were to form as many words as possible from a set of seven letters. How long will participants persist at this task? According to the strength model, persistence should depend on the level of self-control energy as measured by the amount of available glucose. Self-control should be lower and blood glucose should be lower for participants who carried out the difficult e-cancelling procedure. They should persist less on the word-forming task. The results in Figure 12.3 showed that, indeed, lower levels of self-control resulted in less persistence on the word-forming task. However, the participants did not show a drop in blood glucose from before to after the e-cancelling procedure. Also, low- and high-depletion participants did not differ in their levels of blood glucose. If low- and high-depletion participants did not differ in their amount of glucose, then what accounts for their difference in persistence on the word-forming task?

Fatigue Motivates Alternative Behaviors

Many experiments, such as those in Figures 12.2 and 12.3, demonstrate that the exercise of self-control on one task results in poorer performance on a second task (Hagger et al., 2010). But this poorer performance does not result from a lower amount of glucose. However, mental fatigue does play a role. **Mental fatigue** involves feeling tired and exhausted and being reluctant to continue with the present course of action. When fatigued, individuals have difficulty planning, focusing their attention, and altering their behavior. Fatigue is the feeling your efforts are high and your benefits are low (Boksem & Tops, 2008).

Fatigue originates either from physical or mental effort. It feels like you have run out of energy. No energy means no motivation, much like a car quits running when out of gas. However, this view of fatigue is incorrect! The brain has plenty of energy in the form of glucose and glycogen, which is stored in special cells in the brain. The brain uses about 20 percent of the body's energy. Most of that energy is used to keep the brain running. Any added mental tasks, such as not thinking of a white bear, cancelling the letter e, or refraining from eating chocolate chip cookies, consume less than 5 percent of the brain's energy. In other words, plenty of brain energy is available for all tasks (Gibson, 2007; Raichle, 2010). The same is true for energy that resides in the body. People may be motivated to stop exercising, running, or bicycling but this occurs before they run out of energy. People stop strenuous activities before they have employed all of their muscle fibers, used all of their oxygen, or depleted all of their glucose and glycogen (Edwards & Polman, 2013; Noakes, 2011, 2012). So what is the function of physical fatigue? One idea is that fatigue resembles a brain emotion. This emotion functions to ensure that strenuous behavior ceases before bodily harm occurs or to maintain homeostasis of the body (Noakes, 2012). But what is the function of mental fatigue?

Fatigue stems from opportunity costs. As described earlier, an opportunity cost is the next best behavior a person could be performing. Eventually, the next best behavior provides a higher rate of reinforcement than your current behavior. For example, the opportunity cost for reading this page might be texting a friend. But, after reading many pages, texting might be more rewarding. But what determines that an individual should switch to this next best behavior? Why not keep reading until you fall asleep? To answer this question, imagine the mental effort required in researching and composing a course paper. Suppose that in various university courses the grade of B on a paper may require an average of 20, 40, or 60 minutes of mental effort per page. As the price of effort increases, a student's mental fatigue increases also. Opportunity costs are responsible for this rising fatigue. According to an **opportunity cost model**, a person is aware of the cost and benefits of her current behavior (Kurzban et al., 2013). She compares these costs and benefits to those expected from the next best alternative behavior—that is, of her opportunity costs. For example, a student compares her current costs/benefits of composing a course paper with the costs/benefits of texting a friend. The costs/benefits of the alternative behavior are felt as rising mental effort and eventually fatigue. In other words, the cost/benefit of the current behavior is declining in comparison to the alternative behavior. For example, the student's feeling of mental fatigue indicates that she should consider doing something else, such as texting, since that may provide greater benefits at a lower costs (Kurzban et al., 2013).

Other psychologists have suggested that fatigue results from extensive focus on goal achievement behavior. Fatigue slows or stops this behavior so that the person can consider alternative goals. The alternative may provide greater benefits for less effort. In that case, an individual can commit to that alternative goal instead (Hockey, 2011). A person does not consciously and deliberately perform a cost/benefit analysis of his activities. This analysis is performed below the level of conscious awareness. However, these deliberations reach awareness by being felt as mental effort and fatigue. They signal that costs are high and benefits are low (Kurzban et al., 2013). Thus, fatigue tells a person that her current behavior may not be the best strategy, especially if an individual's goal has not been achieved. Fatigue also serves as the motive to lessen one's effort, in order to conserve energy. The alternative goal of conserving energy means that energy is available to react in a potential crisis. Hence, this increases a person's chances of survival (Boksem & Tops, 2008).

Cost/benefit of self-control. Figure 12.3 shows persistence on a problem-solving task after participants' self-control had been depleted. Recall that depletion was accomplished with a difficult e cancellation task. Are the findings in Figure 12.3 a function of fatigue? Inzlicht and coresearchers (2014) reasoned that self-control tasks produce temporary mental fatigue. The fatigue results from the have-to goals imposed in self-control experiments, such as being asked to not eat chocolate chip cookies, not think of a white bear, or cancel the letter e on two pages of text. Participants feel they must perform these tasks at the request of the experimenter. Have-to goals are pursued out of duty, social convention, or shame and guilt if not performed. However, eventually participants prefer not to continue these have-to tasks because fatigue signals that the costs seem high and the benefits low. Following the have-to tasks, the subsequent problem-solving task demands more of the same. However, since participants are already mentally fatigued, alternative want-to tasks become salient. These tasks are more appealing, especially if they provide immediate gratification. Want-to tasks are intrinsically motivated and pursued for their inherent pleasure. Thus, rather than persist at a second have-to task, such as persisting at solving puzzles, participants choose a want-to task, such as a time-out or rest—that is, they quit the problem-solving task sooner than control participants, who are not fatigued (Inzlicht et al., 2014).

Section Recap

Mental fatigue means being tired, exhausted, not functioning effectively, and not wanting to proceed further with the current activity. It feels like the individual has run out of mental energy. However, that is not the case. Participants quit strenuous activities before they have run out of energy. Tasks designed to deplete self-control result in temporary mental fatigue, which leads individuals to perform worse on a subsequent motivation task. However, this decline is not the result of being depleted of glucose. Instead, fatigue actually functions as a signal that current behavior costs are high and benefits are low. Consequently, individuals should consider alternative activities that provide more benefits at lower costs. According to the *opportunity cost model*, tasks that deplete self-control tasks are akin to have-to goals. Participants become mentally fatigued from pursuing these goals. As a consequence, alternative want-to goals become salient and provide higher benefits and lower costs. As a result, participants cease their pursuit of have-to goals sooner so that they can pursue want-to goals, such as time-out or quitting.

SPENDING MOTIVATION RESOURCES

Which product do you prefer: (1) a state-of-the-art home entertainment system for audio and video or (2) a small TV and radio? Which payment do you prefer: (1) $6,000 or more or (2) $300 or less? The choices illustrate two extensive but incompatible motivational forces. On one hand, motivation is geared to obtain the most valuable incentive possible. On the other hand, humans are motivated to expend the least amount of time and effort necessary to attain these incentives. In other words, we want the most for the least. In economics, people spend their money to obtain goods and services. In motivation, people expend their motivation resources in order to satisfy their motives and achieve their goals. Are there principles of economics that can help in the understanding of motivation?

Demand Law

From Chapters 10 and 11, we learned that, as incentive value or goal level increases, motivation increases. Thus, an A grade is more motivating than a C, first place in a race is more motivating than second, and $100 is more motivating than $10. However, the ability of an incentive to motivate behavior also depends on the cost of attaining it. In the preceding examples, an A costs more study time than a C, first place requires more calories for faster running than second place does, and earning $100 requires more work than $10 requires. Thus, the likelihood of achieving a goal depends on its value but also on the cost of achievement. The effect of cost is described by the **demand law**, or demand schedule, which refers to the relationship between the quantity of goods a person is willing to purchase (demand) at various prices. When the price of economic goods is raised, less is bought; when the price of goods is lowered, more is bought. In the Skinner box, demand refers to the amount of reinforcement an animal demands or consumes at various lever press prices as set by an FR schedule of reinforcement (Hursh, 1980; Hursh & Bauman, 1987). Figure 12.4 provides two hypothetical curves that illustrate the demand law in a Skinner box. Notice that, as FR requirements increase, demand decreases.

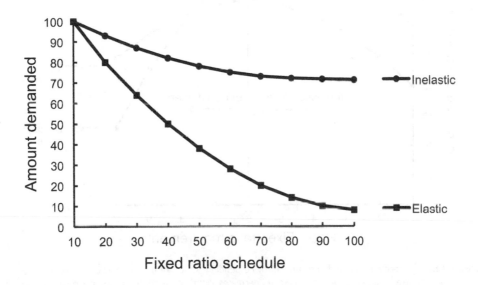

FIGURE 12.4 Demand Elasticity. As the cost of a reinforcer increases from FR 10 to FR 100, the demand for that reinforcer decreases. Decline in demand is shallow for the inelastic reinforcer and steep for the elastic reinforcer.

Elasticity

Is the demand for need satisfaction or goal attainment affected equally by price? Are there some needs and goals that humans will quickly abandon if the cost of their satisfaction becomes too high? Are there other needs and goals that humans will attempt to satisfy regardless of the cost?

Elasticity of demand. Demand changes as the price for a reinforcer changes but this change is not equal for all reinforcers. In Figure 12.4, notice that, as FR requirements increase from 10 to 100, the demand for a reinforcer could decline little (upper curve) or could decline a great deal (lower curve). The amount of decline depends on the type of reinforcer and if there are alternative reinforcers. When reinforcers decline greatly in demand as FR requirements increase, this is termed **elastic demand**. When reinforcers decline very little in demand as FR size increases, this is termed **inelastic demand**. The demand for inelastic reinforcers is much more resistant to price increases than is the demand for elastic reinforcers. The elasticity of reinforcers or goods is based on their utility. Goods with low utility are known as luxuries, such as soft drinks, movies, and CDs. Goods with high utility are known as necessities, such as food, computers, and gasoline.

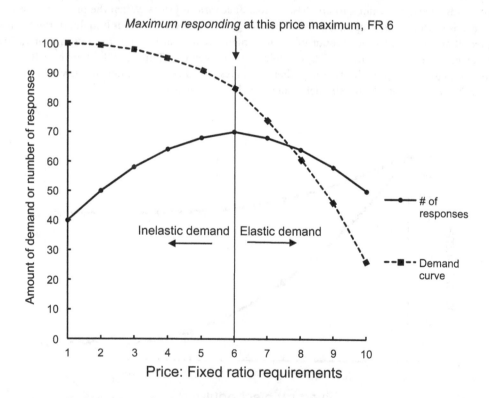

FIGURE 12.5 Elasticity of Demand and Amount of Responding. At left of *maximum responding*, demand is inelastic. As the fixed ratio price increases, demand decreases slightly because of an increase in responding, which offsets the increase in price. At the right of *maximum responding*, demand is elastic. As the fixed ratio price increases, demand decreases much more because there is a decrease in responding.

Elasticity and responses. Demand for elastic reinforcers declines more than for inelastic reinforcers with an increase in price. The smaller decline for an inelastic reinforcer occurs because the price increase is offset with an increase in responding. However, for elastic reinforcers, the decline in demand is greater because there is also a decline in responding (Hursh, 1980; Hursh & Bauman, 1987). In addition, a reinforcer may be inelastic at one range of price increases and elastic at another range (see Figure 12.5; Johnson & Bickel, 2006). For example in Figure 12.5, as price increases from FR 1 to FR 6, there is a slight decrease in demand but as price increases further from FR 6 to FR 10 the decline in demand is greater. This change reflects the transition from inelastic to elastic demand. Inelastic demand occurs because increases in price (FR 1 to FR 6) are offset by increases in responding (see # of responses curve in Figure 12.5). Elastic demand, on the other hand, occurs when price increases (FR 6 to FR 10) now produce decreases in responding (see # of responses curve in Figure 12.5). The maximum price is that point on the demand curve where demand changes from inelastic to elastic, which occurs at FR 6 (Figure 12.5). Here maximum responding occurs, which is tantamount to saying that here is the place of maximum motivation. At FR 6, individuals are motivated the most because they respond the most, they respond less at both lower and higher FR ratios. For example, the individual responds less at FR 5 and at FR 7 (Johnson & Bickel, 2006).

The relationship between demand elasticity and instrumental responding occurs for a variety of reinforcers and behaviors. For instance, research on smokers responding for puffs on a cigarette has revealed an overall demand curve showing both inelastic and elastic properties. In a series of 17 experiments involving 74 smokers, Bickel and Madden (1999) had smokers pull and reset a plunger at various FR prices in order to earn access to a cigarette to puff on. The initial decline in the demand for puffs on a cigarette was inelastic and decreased moderately. Smokers offset the increase in price up to FR 400 by making more responses in order to access a cigarette. Beyond FR 400, however, cigarette demand became elastic. The price of a puff became too high, demand declined steeply, and the number of responses to earn a cigarette declined also (Madden, 2000).

Elasticity and the Substitution Effect

When response requirements rise, reinforcer demand declines. Does this mean the individual ceases working for the reinforcer, or will she work for a substitute? The **substitution effect**, in economics, refers to the principle that an increase in the price of one economic good leads to increased demand for a different economic good. Reinforcers can serve as substitutes, complements, or independent commodities (Green & Freed, 1993). Substitutability means that one reinforcer can replace another, provided that both have the same function (for instance, exchanging one cola drink for another, one elective course for another, or one roommate for another). Complementary reinforcers are ones that have a joint function, such as toothbrush and toothpaste or paper and pencil. Independent reinforcers are ones that serve different and unrelated functions, such as colas and printers, elective courses and toothpaste, or roommates and paper. The function of substitutes is very important for determining the shape of demand curves. Increase the price of a reinforcer, and the demand for it decreases while the demand for its substitute increases. For example, if the price of pepperoni pizza increases, then its consumption decreases, while consumption of substitute mushroom pizza increases. Similarly, if the requirements for one elective course become too high, students will substitute another elective course in its place.

The substitution effect demonstrates how the motivation for an incentive depends on the behavioral cost of that incentive. At low costs, one incentive is preferred but as its cost rises a substitute is preferred. In an illustrative experiment with two groups, Goldfield and Epstein (2002) had participants press the button on a joy stick in order to make three symbols appear on the computer screen. When the symbols matched, the participant earned points, which they exchanged for snack foods, fruits and vegetables, or pleasurable sedentary activities. The researchers manipulated the price of the incentives by increasing the number of button presses required to earn the points. As shown in Table 12.3, group-1 participants could choose to earn points for

TABLE 12.3 Choices that Vary in Cost of the Reinforcers

Group 1				Group 2			
Choices	# responses required for snacks	or	# responses required for fruits and vegetables	Choices	# responses required for snacks	or	# responses required for sedentary activities
Choice 1	2	or	2	Choice 1	2	or	2
Choice 2	4	or	2	Choice 2	4	or	2
Choice 3	8	or	2	Choice 3	8	or	2
Choice 4	16	or	2	Choice 4	16	or	2
Choice 5	32	or	2	Choice 5	32	or	2

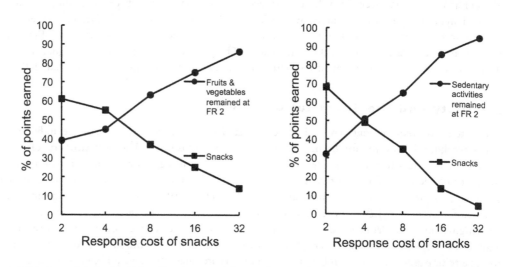

FIGURE 12.6 Substitution Effect. The cheaper reinforcer substitutes for the originally preferred reinforcer. As the original reinforcer becomes more expensive, participants substitute it with a cheaper reinforcer. At the cost of FR 2, snacks are preferred over fruits and vegetables and over sedentary activities. As the cost of snacks increases from FR 2 to FR 32, the preference for snacks decreases and the preference for fruits and vegetables and sedentary activities increases. The cost remained constant at FR 2 for the fruits and vegetables and sedentary activities.

Source: "Can Fruits And Vegetables and Activities Substitute For Snack Foods?" by G. S. Goldfield & L. H. Epstein, 2002, *Health Psychology, 21,* Figure 1, p. 301. Copyright 2002 by American Psychological Association.

snacks or for fruits and vegetables, while group-2 participants could choose to earn points for snacks or for sedentary activities. These activities consisted of playing computer games, solving puzzles, and watching TV or music videos. For each of their five choices, the cost of snacks rose from two to 16 button pushes, while the cost of the alternative remained constant at two button pushes. Does the rising cost of one reinforcer motivate participants to choose the other? Figure 12.6 shows how preferences for fruits and vegetables or for sedentary activities increase as the cost of snacks rises. When costs are equal at two responses per reinforcer, participants prefer snacks more than the alternatives. Thus, at this low price, snacks are more motivating. However, as the price of snacks increases, they are preferred less and fruits and vegetables or sedentary behaviors are preferred more. Thus, at a high price snacks are less motivating. The lesson here is that motivation for an incentive depends on the price a person has to pay for it. When cost is low, one incentive is preferred over another. When cost increases, however, preferences shift. Notice that the results in Figure 12.6 parallel effort discounting. The discounted values of the snacks decrease because more and more effort is required for them. Eventually their discounted values fall below that of the alternatives whose price has remained constant.

Substitutes can be independent as shown in Figure 12.6. The increase in the price of snacks led to an increase in the preference for various activities that are unrelated to food. Substitution also occurs for various other reinforcers, such as a visual stimulus serving as a substitute for auditory or social stimuli. To illustrate, Tustin (1994) had mentally disabled men push one of two buttons on a computer joystick to earn one of two reinforcers. In the case of one man, the choice was between computer-generated visual stimuli versus auditory stimuli or between visual stimuli versus social attention (smile, nod, and praise from a known person). For each choice, the price of the visual reinforcer remained constant at FR 5, while the price of the auditory or social reinforcer ranged from FR 1 to FR 20. Substitution occurred. As the price of the auditory reinforcer and the social reinforcer increased, the individual began to prefer the visual reinforcer. In other words, the visual reinforcer served as a substitute for either auditory or social reinforcers when their FR requirements became too high.

Section Recap

Principles from economics aid in understanding motivation. The number of goals achieved (goals demanded) depends on the price of doing so in terms of motivation resources. According to the *demand law*, when prices go up, demand goes down; when prices go down, demand goes up. For instance, in the Skinner box, demand would refer to the number of reinforcers that a rat obtains at a set price, which is the number of required lever presses. Elasticity of demand defines the amount of decrease in demand with increases in price. *Inelastic demand* means that demand decreases very little as price increases. In this case, the increase in price is offset by increased responding, thereby allowing little decline in demand. Incentives that have high utility (necessities) such as gasoline or required courses have inelastic demand. *Elastic demand* means that incentive demand decreases a great deal as price increases. In this case, the increase in price results in decreased responding, thereby producing a dramatic decline in demand. Incentives that have low utility (luxuries), such as soft drinks or elective courses, have elastic demand. A reinforcer may be inelastic for price increases at the low end of a price range but be elastic for price increases at the high end. Also, demand declines steeply if there are substitute reinforcers but declines slowly if there are no substitutes. The *substitution effect* means that, as price goes up, a person is more likely to obtain an alternative reinforcer.

MOTIVATION TOWARD LEAST EFFORT

There are two main aspects of motivation to keep in mind. First, humans are motivated more to satisfy strong rather than weak needs and to achieve high-level rather than low-level goals. Second, strong needs and high-level goals cost more in terms of motivation resources. The cost factor would not be an issue if everyone had unlimited motivation resources, such as time and energy. However, since resources are limited, there is a tendency to use them in the most efficient manner possible. How do we reconcile these two competing principles: inclination to spend the fewest motivation resources to satisfy the strongest motives and achieve the highest goals?

Early Views on Effort and Motivation

During the first half of the 1900s, psychologists recognized that effort and motivation were inversely related. Tolman (1932) described the relationship between effort and motivation in his **principle of least effort** as that

> which is found in numerous sciences under a variety of names, when applied to the study of behavior would assert that the final choices between alternative means–routes will always tend to occur in the direction of a minimum expenditure of physical energy.
>
> (p. 448)

In other words, given a choice between two incentives of equal value, the one requiring the least effort will be selected. In his research, Tolman provided hungry rats a choice of two routes to the goal box at the end of a complex maze. In this situation, the rats tended to choose the shorter and quicker route to the goal. Although Tolman was aware of this principle in the physical sciences, he lacked physiological indicators of effort that he could apply to behavior.

Hull (1943) formulated a similar principle, which he named the **law of less work**:

> If two or more behavior sequences, each involving a different amount of energy consumption or work (W), have been equally well reinforced an equal number of times, the organism will gradually learn to choose the less laborious behavior sequence leading to the attainment of the reinforcing state of affairs.
>
> (p. 294)

Hull arrived at this part of his theory by relying on an experiment performed by Mowrer and Jones (1943). In their experiment, hungry rats were required to press a lever in a Skinner box to earn a food reinforcer. After they had learned this task, the rats were divided into three groups, and extinction was carried out, during which time lever presses did not produce reinforcers. For one group, the lever had to be pressed with a force of five grams; for another group a force of 42.5 grams was required; and for a third, 80 grams. According to Hull (1943), 80 grams of force is more work than 42.5 grams, which is more work than five grams of force. The results showed that the number of lever presses decreased as their force requirements increased. When effort was slight, the rats made many more responses during extinction than when effort was hard.

Choices Based on Least Effort

How do economic principles such as the demand law, elasticity, and least effort affect the choices that people make?

Romantic love. How are romantic choices affected? Economic principles apply to sexual and dating behavior (McKenzie & Tullock, 1981). Sex, for example, can be considered a service that each member of a couple provides for and receives from the other. Dating and sex have both utility and costs. The opportunity cost of dating or spending time with one person means that you cannot be spending time with someone else. Thus, forgoing a date with one individual is your opportunity cost for going out with another. Dating and sex also involve energy costs and time costs of trying to please the other person. Finally, a person's willingness to be romantically involved with a particular individual depends on substitutes, such as other dating partners, friends, or family members.

Incentive value, demand, costs, and substitution effects describe why romantic relationships begin, endure, and end. With these concepts, Rusbult (1983) developed an **investment model** for describing people's commitment to each other in a relationship. Investment refers to things people have put into a relationship that they cannot get back if the relationship ends. Examples of investments are shared friends and shared material possessions (Rusbult, 1983). Commitment to a relationship depends on the rewards provided, the costs, the value of alternative relationships, and how much has been invested. To test the investment model, Rusbult recruited dating couples early in the academic year, when they had been together an average of about four weeks. Every 17 days over the course of the academic year, she asked one member of each couple a series of questions to determine the cost, rewards, alternatives, and investments in the relationship. Some of the questions were:

1. How rewarding is this relationship? (1 = *not at all*, 9 = *extremely*)
2. How costly is this relationship? (1 = *not at all*, 9 = *extremely*)
3. In general, how appealing are your alternatives (dating another person or other persons, or being without a romantic involvement)? (1 = *not at all appealing*, 9 = *extremely appealing*)
4. All things considered, are there objects/persons/activities associated with the relationship that you would lose (or value less) if the relationship were to end? (1 = *none*, 9 = *many*) (Rusbult, 1983, p. 106)

At the end of the academic year, members of the couples were placed into one of three categories. Stayers were partners who were still involved in their relationship. Leavers were persons who had ended their relationship. The abandoned were people whose partners had ended the relationship. The change in the reward value of the relationship, its costs, the value of a substitute relationship, and investment size were different for stayers, leavers, and the abandoned. Figure 12.7 shows that the reward value increased most for stayers but not at all for leavers. Changes in cost, however, showed the reverse pattern. Stayers' costs increased very little, while leavers' costs increased a great deal over the year. Perhaps it is not surprising that leavers ended their relationship. After all, their costs increased at a high rate, while their rewards remained practically

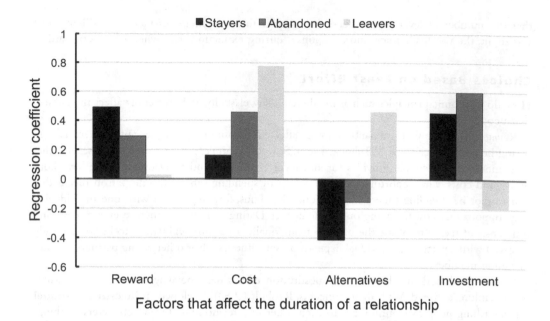

FIGURE 12.7 Investment Model and Relationships. Changes in magnitude of reward, cost, alternative, and investment values in a romantic relationship over the academic year are shown for stayers, the abandoned, and leavers.

Source: Adapted from "A Longitudinal Test of the Investment Model" by C. E. Rusbult, 1983, *Journal of Personality and Social Psychology, 45,* Table 6, p. 111.

constant over the duration of their relationships. The substitution effect was also apparent during the course of these relationships. For stayers and the abandoned, there was a decrease in the appeal of alternatives. In contrast, for leavers there was an increase in the appeal of their alternatives or substitutes. Leavers ended their relationship when costs increased, perhaps because they had highly attractive substitutes. The abandoned, however, appeared more willing to pay the costs of their relationship, since the attractiveness of substitutes for them had decreased over the year.

While there is a cost of staying in a relationship, there is also a cost of ending a relationship. This cost is reflected in investment size. The more people have invested in a relationship, the more it will cost them to end it. Figure 12.7 shows that the investment size for stayers and the abandoned became larger as the academic year progressed. Thus, for them a breakup would be more costly. The investment size for leavers was negligible and showed no change over the academic year. It was easier for leavers to terminate their romantic relationship, since they had very little invested and so very little to lose.

Body consequences of least effort. People frequently face such choices as walk or ride, stairs or elevator, and exercise or watch TV. Does the energy cost of each choice bias the decision toward the less exerting activity? As one might expect, the principle of least effort fosters a sedentary lifestyle rather than an active one. As a consequence, there is an increasing trend for people to become overweight (BMI = 25.0–29.9), then obese (BMI = 30.00—39.0), and eventually

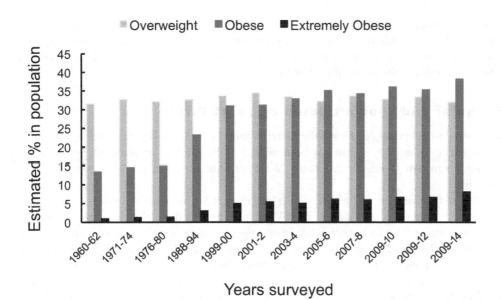

FIGURE 12.8 Trends in Overweight and Obesity. National Health and Nutrition Examination Surveys conducted from 1960–1962 to 2013–2014 in the United States show an increase over the years in the percentage of 20- to 74-year-old individuals who are overweight (BMI = 25.0–29.9), obese (BMI = 30.0 – 39.9), or extremely obese (BMI ≥ 40).) [Body Mass Index (BMI) = weight (kilograms)/height (meters)^2]. Survey results may be found in Table 1 at www.cdc.gov/nchs/data/hestat/obesity_adult_13_14/obesity_adult_13_14.htm.

extremely obese (BMI ≥ 40) (BMI refers to body mass index. BMI = weight (kilograms)/height (meters)^2). As weight increases BMI increases, since an individual's height remains constant. Obesity is accompanied by health problems that include diabetes, high blood pressure, cardiovascular disease, and various cancers. National Health and Nutrition Examination Surveys conducted between 1960 and 2014 found an increase in the percentage of adults who were either obese or very obese (see Figure 12.8). The percentage of people who are overweight remained constant because with further weight gain a person is placed in the obese category. One explanation for this increase in people becoming overweight and obese is that it results from a change in energy balance: people's energy intake has increased, and their energy expenditure has decreased over the years (Khan & Bowman, 1999).

The National Heart, Blood, and Lung Institute USAGov provides a formula for you to calculate your body mass index (BMI) here: www.nhlbi.nih.gov/health/educational/lose_wt/BMI/bmicalc.htm.

The principle of least effort contributes to this energy imbalance. For instance, the case has been made, at least in Britain (Prentice & Jebb, 1995), that the energy imbalance results from slothfulness (least effort). Humans evolved during a time that required a much greater expenditure of physical energy than is required today. Currently, we have many labor-saving conveniences that provide a choice between being active or being sedentary. It is now possible to replace physical labor with energy- and time-saving appliances, power equipment, power tools, and motorized transport (Prentice & Jebb, 1995). The principle of least effort motivates the use of these machines, which results in a decrease in energy expenditure. This decrease in energy expenditure, however, is not offset by a decrease in energy intake. Weight gain, obesity, and associated health problems are the consequences.

Behavior and Thought Based on Least Effort

In addition to the principle of least effort determining choice, it also determines people's behavior. Thus, whatever motive or goal has been chosen to be satisfied or achieved, people tend to economize in how to achieve those aims. What are some ways that people economize on their behavior?

Behavioral economizing. Why walk if you can drive, take the stairs if there is an elevator, or exercise for pleasure when a couch and TV are available? As these choices imply, opportunities for economizing time and effort occur frequently, such as meal preparation and path creation. For instance, fast-food restaurants, takeout meals, home food deliveries, and easily prepared meals are often the preferred modes of meal preparation. In fact, the term fast-food implies that the time cost for the meal is low. For another example, when people want to get from one place to another they try to use the least amount of effort possible, as can be seen by the development of paths on campuses. The campus landscape architect lays out a concrete walk from one building to another by going around a beautifully manicured lawn. However, some individual creates a shortcut, an alternative path that cuts across the lawn in order to save time, steps, and calories. Indeed, students often create paths across campus precisely to shorten distance and lessen effort. The results of actual wayfinding experiments have shown that participants prefer the shortest routes to their destinations, those that require the least expenditure of energy (Butler et al., 1993). Cattle are of a similar mind when it comes to developing trails from one place to another. With the aid of a global positioning satellite, Ganskopp and coworkers (2000) observed that cattle were more likely to develop the easiest trails possible over rugged terrain. The cattle tended to select a combination of the shortest routes with the shallowest slopes—that is, trails that required the least effort to walk from a watering hole to other pasture areas.

Economizing also governs the speed with which individuals reach their destination. Individuals can increase their speed of walking by combining an increase in the length and frequency of their strides. Walking or running at one's preferred stride length is the most economical. If either stride frequency or length increases beyond the person's preferred level, then energy costs will increase (Holt et al., 1995; Sparrow & Newell, 1998). However, it will be less costly to increase the frequency of one's strides than to lengthen them (Holt et al., 1991). Now imagine that you are in a great hurry to get to your destination and you begin to increase your walking speed. At some point, you will break into a run. The transition from walking to running occurs because of a reduction in energy costs—that is, less oxygen and glucose is used. Costs will be higher, however, if a person runs slower than her preferred walking speed (Hanna et al., 2000).

Avoidance of cognitive demand. Are there goals you rejected from consideration because it would be too demanding to achieve them? For example, was a major in computer science, pre-med, and biology rejected because of anticipated excessive cognitive demands from math, anatomy, and genetics courses? These rejections of potential majors may occur even though a person has no direct experience regarding the cognitive demands or amount of mental effort required in these courses. Dunn and coresearchers (2016) used a reading task to investigate the avoidance of cognitive demands. They manipulated the amount of cognitive demand or effort required for reading by changing the orientation of words on a page. The standard orientation consisted of a page on which words were parallel to the top of the page. In the second orientation, the page rotated 60 degrees to the left while the words remained stationary, while in the third orientation the page remained stationary but the words were rotated 60 degrees. In the fourth orientation, both the page and words rotated 60 degrees to the left. The researchers asked what orientation of words participants preferred to read. They also measured how long it took participants to read the words in that orientation and recorded the errors that were made. Participants chose the standard orientation most often and the fourth orientation least often. The standard orientation was read the fastest with the fewest errors and the fourth orientation was read the slowest with the most errors. In between, participants preferred to read the rotated page over the rotated words. However, reading time and number of errors did not differ between the fourth orientation and the rotated words rotation even though the fourth orientation was chosen least often. In other words, the choice of orientation was not based on an objective factor such as time to read or number of errors. Instead, participants made their reading selections based on a general cognitive awareness of the effort required in such tasks. They avoided tasks that required the greatest cognitive demand (Dunn et al., 2016).

Cognitive economizing. People appreciate having a choice of universities to attend, academic majors to pursue, and varieties of clothing styles, smartphones, and laptop computers to buy. These choices, however, might require an extensive expected utility analysis in order to make the best decision. In the case of computers, for example, it might involve comparing such features as the maker, size of hard drive, size of working memory, operating speed, screen size, game capabilities, and price. Imagine how exhaustive this process can become as the number of available computers to choose from increases from, say, two to 10.

The existence of too many alternatives can also result in **choice overload**. This phenomenon refers to the demotivating effect of too many choices on the decision-making process (Iyengar & Lepper, 2000). An individual is initially attracted to a large array of available choices yet is less likely to decide and is more dissatisfied when a decision is made. Iyengar and Lepper (2000) conducted three experiments in which individuals were presented with a limited-choice condition or an extensive-choice condition. In one experiment, shoppers at a grocery store had available for sampling a display of either six jams or 24 jams. More shoppers purchased a jar of jam after having visited the limited-choice display of six jams. In the second experiment, university students could write an essay for extra credit from a list of six versus 30 topics. More students wrote essays when they were presented with the limited choice of six topics rather than the extensive choice of 30 topics. In a third experiment, participants were led to believe that they were in a marketing study that investigated how people selected chocolates based on their names and flavors. They could also select one of the chocolates to eat. Participants either examined a limited-choice display of six chocolates or an extensive-choice display of 30 chocolates. The results showed that participants in the limited-choice conditions were more satisfied with their chocolate selection than those in the extensive-choice condition. In addition, as pay for their participation in the research, the participants were given an option of $5 or a box of chocolates ($5 value). More participants from the limited-choice condition chose the box of chocolates instead of $5. The authors note that people enjoy the decision-making process when provided with an extensive set of choices. However, they also feel more responsible for making the best decision and feel more regret when they have made an unsatisfactory decision. Perhaps the responsibility of choosing the best option demotivates people in those situations that provide so many options.

People prefer the availability of options, although too many produce various costs, such as choice overload. How is it possible that, as options increase, satisfaction increases and then decreases? One answer is based on changes in the degree of costs and benefits that arise from an increasing number of options (see Figure 12.9). First, benefits do increase but then begin to level off. Benefits from increased choice consist of a greater feeling of autonomy, greater possible utility, and greater potential happiness. Costs, however, also increase, at first moderately, but then they accelerate and subtract from the benefits. Costs involve greater expectations to be happy but also greater disappointment if expectations are not met. More options also mean greater opportunity costs, since a person will have rejected many more alternatives, which can lead to a greater likelihood of regret (Grant & Schwartz, 2011). Finally, more options means it takes more time to make a decision. Net satisfaction then is the result of benefits minus costs, which shows as an inverted-U shape in Figure 12.9 (Grant & Schwartz, 2011). In other words, as options

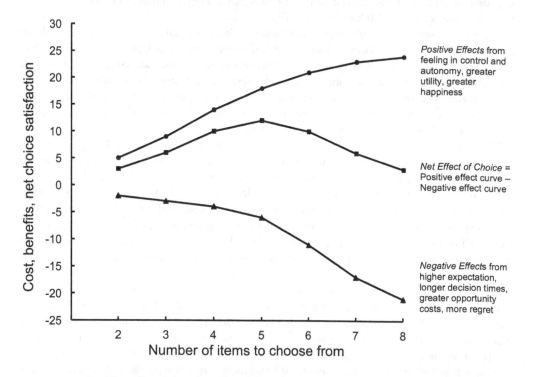

FIGURE 12.9 Net Effect of Increasing Alternatives. Potential positive outcomes increase with increases in the number of alternatives from which to choose. However, potential negative outcomes also increase with the number of alternatives. Positive and negative outcomes sum algebraically to yield net benefits represented by the inverted-U curve: as alternatives increase, net benefits increase but, with further increases in alternatives, net benefits decrease.

increase, net satisfaction increases but then decreases. Based on a large number of studies, it appears that three to five options produce the most satisfaction (Patall et al., 2008).

The net effect curve in Figure 12.9 implies that the best choice may require a great deal of time and energy and may be too costly. In other words, an extensive expected utility analysis to choose a laptop computer or smartphone may not be worth the effort. As an alternative, a person could employ **satisficing** (Simon, 1955/1979), which means to find an option that is satisfactory but not necessarily the best. Using shortcuts and energy-saving procedures, an individual arrives at an acceptable expected utility and bases her decision on that. Instead of comparing computers on all features, only some features are examined provided they have met some minimum standard. For example, a person only examines computers that are available at the local electronics store and that are priced below a certain amount.

Would you do an expected utility analysis of all computers or would you be more apt to satisfice? The *Maximization Scale* measures the extent of an individual's tendency to maximize in order to decide among options (Schwartz, 2004; Schwartz et al., 2002). For example, the extent individuals agree with the following statement indicates their tendency to maximize: "I never settle for second best" (Schwartz et al., 2002; p. 1182). Higher scores on the *Maximization Scale* indicate a greater tendency to maximize. Both satisficing and maximizing have costs and benefits (Schwartz, 2004; Schwartz et al., 2002). First, satisficing requires less time to make a decision. Second, satisficers consider fewer alternatives than maximizers and thus have lower opportunity costs. Third, satisficers have fewer feelings of regret as a result of their lower opportunity costs compared to the regrets of maximizers. Fourth, satisficers are less indecisive regarding a decision, whereas maximizers may feel powerless—that is, experience choice overload. Finally, however, maximizers make better choices than satisficers do (Iyengar et al., 2006).

The website titled "Measurement Instrument Data Base for the Social Sciences" provides access to a copy of the *Maximization Scale* here: www.midss.org. The scale is also here: www.pier rettedesrosiers.com/documents/quest_maximization_scale_web_001.pdf.

Section Recap

People try to achieve their goals by expending the least amount of time, responses, and energy according to Tolman's *principle of least effort* and Hull's *law of less work*. In addition to least effort, the demand law and elasticity explain the choices that people make, such as the choice of convenience foods and shortcuts. In the case of romance, according to the *investment model*, people put resources into a romantic relationship that they cannot get back; this investment determines whether the couple chooses to remain together. In addition, the likelihood of choosing to stay in a relationship depends on the reward, costs, and alternatives (substitutes) that are available to each partner. Our choice to embrace human energy-saving devices (elevator rather than stairs) has led to increases in weight, obesity, and associated health problems.

Economic principles also explain motivated behavior and cognition. Behavioral economizing occurs, for example, in the transition from walking to running. Beyond a certain speed, it takes less energy to run than to walk. In the case of cognitive economizing, the number of choices has an effect. First, too many choices can result in *choice overload*, which occurs when individuals have too many alternatives to choose from. In this case, people become demotivated and less likely to make a choice. Second, although many choices are preferred, it also increases decision time and increases the likelihood of regret because of the many rejected alternatives. Consequently, as the number of choices increases, net satisfaction increases and then decreases. Sometimes people do an elaborate expected utility analysis to maximize their likelihood of making the best choice. People's tendency to maximize is measured by the *Maximization Scale*. However, instead of maximizing, sometimes people employ *satisficing*, which means to make a decision on a "that is good enough" basis.

GLOSSARY

Term	Definition
Choice Overload	When an individual is faced with too many alternatives from which to choose, which has a demotivating effect on making a choice
Cognitive Demand	This refers to the amount of mental effort required for a task such as reading
Demand Law	Relationship between the quantity of goods a person is willing to purchase (demand) at various prices; price goes up, demand goes down
Effort Discounting	The subjective value of an incentive or goal is decreased or devalued based on the amount of effort necessary to obtain or achieve them
Elastic Demand	When demand is very responsive in changes to price; as price goes up, for example, demand declines steeply
Fast-Food	The time and behavioral cost necessary for obtaining a meal is low
Fixed Ratio (FR) Schedule of Reinforcement	The ratio between the number of responses (e.g., lever presses) required for a single reinforcer (e.g., a food pellet); ratio of responses per reinforcer
Grit	An individual difference variable that refers to consistent interest and passion for long-term goals and persisting in trying to achieve them
Inelastic Demand	When demand is not very responsive in changes to price; as price goes up, for example, demand declines only slightly
Investment Model	Commitment in a romantic relationship depends on things put into (invested in) the relationship that a person cannot get back if the relationship ends
Law of Less Work	Organisms will learn to choose the less laborious labor or response sequence that will lead to a reinforcing state of affairs
Learned Industriousness	Acquired ability to sustain physical or mental effort or to be persistent in spite of building up subjective fatigue
Luxuries	Goods with lower utilities, i.e., things people like but do not need, such as soft drinks, movies, and CDs
Mental Fatigue	Being tired, exhausted, not functioning effectively, and not wanting to proceed further with the current mental course of action; contrast with physical fatigue
N-back Memory Task	As a way to measure mental effort, letters are presented in succession and participants must remember if the current letter occurred one to six positions back
Necessities	Goods with higher utilities, i.e., things people need, such as food, computers, and gasoline

continued . . .

GLOSSARY Continued

Term	Definition
Opportunity Cost Model	People compare the cost and benefits of their current behavior with that of the best alternative. Fatigue occurs if current costs/benefits exceed the alternative
Opportunity Costs	This refers to those activities that a person rejected in favor of a current, more preferred one, such as rejecting the chance to watch TV in order to study
Principle of Least Effort	Given a choice between two incentives of equal value, the one requiring the least effort will be selected
Reflex Reserve	Skinner's concept of a hypothetical entity that refers to the total amount of activity or number of responses available for obtaining reinforcers
Satisficing	Finding a satisfactory option or satisfactory choice but not necessarily the best choice in a situation and basing a decision on that
Self-Control	It is the resolve to remain on track toward a goal based on the ability to override desires, emotions, or impulses that interrupt goal achievement behavior
Strength Model	Self-control relies on a psychological resource or energy. People use this energy to engage in self-control; more energy implies greater self-control
Substitution Effect	One reinforcer can replace another, e.g., the increases in price of one economic good (reinforcer) leads to increased demand for a replacement economic good

REFERENCES

Allison, J. (1993). Response deprivation, reinforcement, and economics. *Journal of the Experimental Analysis of Behavior, 60,* 129–140.

Baumeister, R. F., Bratslavsky, E., Muraven, M., & Tice, D. M. (1998). Ego depletion: Is the active self a limited resource? *Journal of Personality and Social Psychology, 74,* 1252–1265.

Bickel, W. K., & Madden, G. J. (1999). The behavioral economics of smoking. In F. J. Chaloupka, M. Grossman, W. K. Bickel, & H. Saffer (Eds.), *The economic analysis of substance use and abuse* (pp. 31–61). Chicago, IL: University of Chicago Press.

Boksem, M. A., & Tops, M. (2008). Mental fatigue: Costs and benefits. *Brain Research Reviews, 59,* 125–139.

Boren, J. J. (1961). Resistance to extinction as a function of the fixed ratio. *Journal of Experimental Psychology, 61,* 304–308.

Butler, D. L., Acquino, A. L., Hissong, A. A., & Scott, P. A. (1993). Wayfinding by newcomers in a complex building. *Human Factors, 35,* 159–173.

Duckworth, A. L., Kirby, T. A., Tsukayama, E., Berstein, H., & Ericsson, K. A. (2010). Deliberate practice spells success: Why grittier competitors triumph at the National Spelling Bee. *Social Psychological and Personality Science, 1,* 1–8.

Duckworth, A. L., Peterson, C., Matthews, M. D., & Kelly, D. R. (2007). Grit: Perserverance and passion for long term goals. *Journal of Personality and Social Psychology, 92,* 1087–1101.

Dunn, T. L., Lutes, D. J., & Risko, E. F. (2016). Metacognitive evaluation in the avoidance of demand. *Journal of Experimental Psychology: Human Perception and Performance, 42,* 1372–1387.

Edwards, A. M., & Polman, R. C. J. (2013). Pacing and awareness: Brain regulation of physical activity. *Sports Medicine, 43,* 1057–1064.

Eisenberger, R. (1992). Learned industriousness. *Psychological Review, 99,* 248–267.

Eisenberger, R., Heerdt, W. A., Hamdi, M., Zimet, S., & Bruckmeir, M. (1979). Transfer of persistence across behaviors. *Journal of Experimental Psychology: Human Learning and Memory, 5,* 522–530.

Gailliot, M. T., Baumeister, R. F., DeWall, C. N., Maner, J. K., Plant, E. A., Tice, D. M., Brewer, L. E., & Schmeichel, B. J. (2007). Self-control relies on glucose as a limited energy source: Willpower is more than a metaphor. *Journal of Personality and Social Psychology, 92*, 325–336.

Ganskopp, D., Cruz, R., & Johnson, D. E. (2000). Least-effort pathways? A GIS analysis of livestock trails in rugged terrain. *Applied Animal Behaviour Science, 68*, 179–190.

Gibson, E. L. (2007). Carbohydrates and mental function: Feeding or impeding the brain? *Nutrition Bulletin, 32* (Issue Supplement), 71–83.

Goldfield, G. S., & Epstein, L. H. (2002). Can fruits and vegetables and activities substitute for snack foods? *Health Psychology, 21*, 299–303.

Grant, A. M., & Schwartz, B. (2011). Too much of a good thing: The challenge and opportunity of the inverted U. *Perspectives on Psychological Science, 6*, 61–76.

Green, L., & Freed, D. E. (1993). The substitutability of reinforcers. *Journal of the Experimental Analysis of Behavior, 60*, 141–158.

Grimm, J. L. K. (1884/1968). *Grimm's household tales* (Vol. I-2; M. Hunt, Ed. and trans.). Detroit, MI: Singing Tree Press.

Hagger, M. S., Wood, C., Stiff, C., & Chatzisarantis, N. L. D. (2010). Ego depletion and the strength model of self-control: A meta-analysis. *Psychological Bulletin, 136*, 495–525.

Hanna, A., Abernethy, B., Neal, R. J., & Burgess-Limerick, R. (2000). Triggers for the transition between human walking and running. In W. A. Sparrow (Ed.), *Energetics of human activity* (pp. 124–164). Champaign, IL: Human Kinetics.

Hockey, G. R. J. (2011). A motivational control theory of cognitive fatigue. In P. L. Ackerman (Ed.), *Cognitive fatigue: Multidisciplinary perspectives on current research and future applications* (pp. 167–188). Washington, DC: American Psychological Association.

Holt, K. G., Hamill, J., & Andres, R. O. (1991). Predicting the minimal energy costs of human walking. *Medicine and Science in Sports and Exercise, 23*, 491–498.

Holt, K. G., Jeng, S. F., Ratcliffe, R., & Hamill, J. (1995). Energetic costs and stability during human walking at the preferred stride frequency. *Journal of Motor Behavior, 27*, 164–178.

Hull, C. L. (1943). *Principles of behavior*. New York, NY: Appleton-Century-Crofts.

Hursh, S. R. (1980). Economic concepts for the analysis of behavior. *Journal of the Experimental Analysis of Behavior, 34*, 219–238.

Hursh, S. R., & Bauman, R. A. (1987). The behavioral analysis of demand. In L. Green & J. H. Kagel (Eds.), *Advances in behavioral economics* (pp. 117–165). Norwood, NJ: Ablex.

Inzlicht, M., Schmeichel, B. J., & Macrae, C. N. (2014). Why self-control seems (but may not be) limited. *Trends in Cognitive Sciences, 18*, 127–133.

Iyengar, S. S., & Lepper, M. R. (2000). When choice is demotivating: Can one desire too much of a good thing? *Journal of Personality and Social Psychology, 79*, 995–1006.

Iyengar, S. S., Wells, R. E., & Schwartz, B. (2006). Doing better but feeling worse: Looking for the "best" job undermines satisfaction. *Psychological Science, 17*, 143–150.

Johnson, M. W., & Bickel, W. K. (2006). Replacing relative reinforcing efficacy with behavioral economic demand curves. *Journal of the Experimental Analysis of Behavior, 85*, 73–93.

Khan, L. K., & Bowman, B. A. (1999). Obesity: A major global public health problem. *Annual Review of Nutrition, 19*, xiii–xvii.

Kurzban, R., Duckworth, A., Kable, J. W., & Myers, J. (2013). An opportunity cost model of subjective effort and task performance. *Behavioral and Brain Sciences, 36*, 661–679.

Madden, G. J. (2000). A behavioral economics primer. In W. K. Bickel & R. E. Vuchinich (Eds.), *Reframing health behavior change with behavioral economics* (pp. 3–26). Mahwah, NJ: Lawrence Erlbaum.

McKenzie, R. B., & Tullock, G. (1981). *The new world of economics: Explorations into the human experience* (3rd ed.). Homewood, IL: Richard D. Irwin.

Molden, D. C., Hui, C. M., Scholer, A. A., Meier, B. P., Noreen, E. E., D'Agostino, P. R., & Martin, V. (2012). Motivational versus metabolic effects of carbohydrates on self-control. *Psychological Science, 23*, 1137–1144.

Mowrer, O. H., & Jones, H. M. (1943). Extinction and behavior variability as functions of effortfulness of task. *Journal of Experimental Psychology, 33*, 369–386.

Muraven, M., & Baumeister, R. F. (2000). Self-regulation and depletion of limited resources: Does self-control resemble a muscle? *Psychological Bulletin, 126*, 247–259.

Muraven, M., Shmueli, D., & Burkley, E. (2006). Conserving self-control strength. *Journal of Personality and Social Psychology, 91*, 524–537.

Noakes, T. D. (2011). Time to move beyond a brainless exercise physiology: The evidence for complex regulation of human exercise performance. *Applied Physiology, Nutrition, and Metabolism, 36*, 23–35.

Noakes, T. D. (2012). Fatigue is a brain-derived emotion that regulates the exercise behavior to ensure the protection of whole body homeostasis. *Frontiers of Physiology, 3*, 1–13.

Ostaszewski, P., Bąbel, P., & Swebodziński, B. (2013). Physical and cognitive effort discounting of hypothetical monetary rewards. *Japanese Psychological Research, 55*, 329–337.

Patall, E. A., Cooper, H., Robinson, J. C. (2008). The effects of choice on intrinsic motivation and related outcomes: A meta-analysis of research findings. *Psychological Bulletin, 134*, 270–300.

Piolat, A., Olive, T., & Kellogg, R. T. (2005). Cognitive effort during note taking. *Applied Cognitive Psychology, 19*(3), 291–312.

Prentice, A. M., & Jebb, S. A. (1995). Obesity in Britain: Gluttony or sloth? *British Medical Journal, 311*, 437–439.

Raichle, M. E. (2010). Two views of brain function. *Trends in Cognitive Sciences, 14*, 180–190.

Rusbult, C. E. (1983). A longitudinal test of the investment model: The development (and deterioration) of satisfaction and commitment in heterosexual involvements. *Journal of Personality and Social Psychology, 45*, 101–117.

Sagi, A., & Friedland, N. (2007). The cost of richness: The effect of the size and diversity of decision sets on post-decision regret. *Journal of Personality and Social Psychology, 93*, 515–524.

Schwartz, B. (2004). *The paradox of choice*. New York, NY: HarperCollins.

Schwartz, B., Ward, A., Monterosso, J., Lyubomirsky, S., White, K., & Lehman, D. R. (2002). Maximizing versus satisficing: Happiness is a matter of choice. *Journal of Personality and Social Psychology, 83*, 1178–1197.

Simon, H. (1955/1979). A behavioral model of rational choice. In H. Simon (Ed.), *Models of thought* (pp. 7–19). New Haven, CT: Yale University Press.

Skinner, B. F. (1938). *The behavior of organisms*. New York, NY: Appleton-Century-Crofts.

Sparrow, W. A., & Newell, K. M. (1998). Metabolic energy expenditure and the regulation of movement economy. *Psychonomic Bulletin and Review, 5*, 173–196.

Tolman, E. C. (1932). *Purposive behavior in animals and men*. New York, NY: Appleton-Century.

Tustin, R. D. (1994). Preference for reinforcers under varying schedule arrangements: A behavioral economic analysis. *Journal of Applied Behavior Analysis, 27*, 597–606.

Westbrook, A., Kester, D., & Braver, T. S. (2013). What is the subjective cost of cognitive effort? Load, trait, and aging effects revealed by economic preference. *PLOS ONE, 8*, e68210.

CHAPTER 13

Emotions and Moods

The advantage of the emotions is that they lead us astray.

Oscar Wilde, 1891

It is the hardest thing in the world to put feeling, and deep feeling, into words.

Jack London, 1899

Emotion is a process closely allied with motivation. Emotions serve as a unique source of motivation that both activates and guides behavior. But, first, what characterizes emotion from other sources of motivation? Consider this question, along with the following, when reading this chapter:

1. What is an emotion?
2. Is there a basic set of prototype emotions?
3. What are some characteristics of emotion?
4. How are subjective emotional experiences labeled in ourselves and described?
5. What is the function of physiological arousal for emotions?
6. What are moods, and how do they differ from emotions?

CHARACTERISTICS AND CATEGORIES OF EMOTIONS

Can you distinguish between feeling hungry and thirsty, hot and cold, or excited and sleepy? How about feeling the distinction between love and lust or guilt and shame? All of these distinctions concern sensing differences between internal states. The first two comparisons refer to internal feelings that are based on our body's homeostasis and usually arise gradually. The last comparison refers to emotional feelings that arise suddenly in reaction to stimulus changes. Both sets of feelings motivate behavior. Emotions, like sad and happy, are motives that can cause approach, withdrawal, or even inaction. An interesting characteristic about emotional feelings is that they are difficult to describe. Their descriptions are heard in song lyrics about a broken heart, feeling blue, and rain falling from your eyes. Lyrics are also more about negatively felt emotions than positively felt ones because, as Descartes noted long ago, there are more negative than positive emotions. So, what is an emotion? How did psychologists identify different emotions and how did they categorize them?

What Is an Emotion?

You became sad when your best friend moved away but happy when you attended graduation exercises. Sad feels the opposite of happy, like dejected and despondent feel the opposite of elated and cheerful. Furthermore, when sad your behavior was sluggish but when happy your behavior was energetic. These examples provide the introduction to what an emotion is. First, an **emotion** is a functional reaction to a stimulus event or change, such as an actual or anticipated loss or gain. For example, the loss of a friend but a gain in status at graduation. Second, an emotional reaction is channeled along psychological, physiological, and behavioral dimensions, for example, how you feel and act when sad versus when happy. Third, these channels operate in synchrony for the purpose of coping and adapting to these stimulus changes. For example, the feelings and behaviors of sadness form a cluster, which differs from the cluster formed for happiness (Keltner & Shiota, 2003). These channels, however, are external signs of emotion, as shown in Figure 13.1. Emotion is a psychological construct that represents the coherent relationship among these channels as they react and adapt to stimulus change.

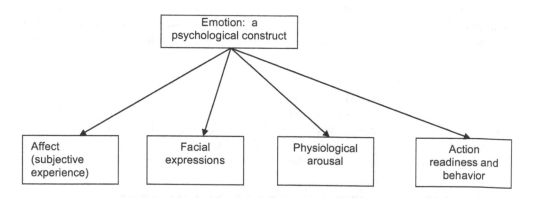

FIGURE 13.1 Emotion as a Psychological Construct. Emotion is an integrated reaction among behavioral channels to a critical environmental event. These channels consist of core affect, physiological arousal, facial expressions, action readiness, and behavior. The channels respond in unison to that event.

Emotion channels. The channels consist of affect, facial expressions, physiological arousal, action readiness, and behavior. *Affect* refers to the private subjective experience that floods consciousness. It is experienced directly by an individual but can be conveyed to others verbally. Language is rich with emotion words to convey a person's affective experiences. The words happiness, sadness, fear, and anger are descriptors of different affective states. Facial expressions are another channel for emotions and are associated with affect. For example, smiles coincide with happiness, scowls with anger, raised eyebrows with surprise, and tears with grief. Physiological arousal as a channel for emotions received credibility from the first American psychologist, William James (1884/1948), who asked what fear is without "the feelings either of quickened heart-beats nor of shallow breathing, neither trembling of lips nor of weakened limbs, neither of goose-flesh nor of visceral stirrings" (p. 295). Physiological responses are a salient channel for emotions and occur as changes in electrodermal responses, blood pressure, heart rate, respiration rate, skin temperature, and muscle activity (Chapter 6). Physiological arousal is important for *action readiness*, which refers to being prepared to engage in behaviors that will satisfy the aim of the emotion. The source of all of these channels is the brain. Our understanding of emotions will be enhanced if we can determine how neural events that occur in the brain are thought to underlie the other channels. Neuroscientists are currently describing how communication among various brain areas serves as the material basis from which emotions emerge. Like different routes on a map, diverse interconnections among various brain areas help to distinguish one emotion from another (Barrett, 2017; Raz et al., 2016; Wager et al., 2015).

Coherence among channels. In everyday parlance, emotion refers to a person's private subjective experience or affect that occurs in reaction to some meaningful life event, such as university graduation or job loss. However, psychologists view emotion as a *psychological construct* that serves as a label for the coherence among the various channels (see Figure 13.1). Each channel could react independently, rather than jointly, to an emotional event. Thus, affect, physiological reactions, and facial expressions may all be unrelated in their reaction to some emotion stimulus. However, if the reaction is to be termed emotional, then these channels should act in concert—that is, cohere. According to the **response coherence postulate** (Mauss et al., 2005), the channels that underlie emotions are associated together; they do not act independently.

Various emotion investigators have examined the response coherence postulate. Rosenberg and Ekman (1994) videotaped the facial expressions of female participants as they viewed emotional film clips. Afterwards the participants reported their affective feelings to those clips. The results showed coherence between affect and facial expressions. Participants jointly experienced affective feelings along with corresponding expressive reactions for disgust, sadness, fear, happiness, contempt, and anger. For example, feelings of disgust corresponded to expressions of disgust and feelings of happiness corresponded to smiles. Furthermore, the degree of coherence increased with greater facial or affective intensity. Ruch (1995) also found coherence in the domain of humor. He showed that, in response to jokes and cartoons, funniness ratings and facial expressions correlated—that is, as funniness ratings increased, associated facial expressions of humor increased also.

In a more extensive investigation of four emotion channels, Mauss and coresearchers (2005) exposed participants to sad and amusing stimuli. Specifically, women participants viewed a five-minute video composed of amusing and sad scenes. They continuously rated these segments for amusement and sadness while their facial expressions were videotaped. Measurements were also taken of their heart rate, electrodermal responses, and general activity by way of a sensor attached to the bottom of their chair. Evidence in favor of response coherence requires that the various measures correlate positively, which was definitely the case for amusement. Amusement ratings, heart activity, electrodermal responses, and general activity all correlated positively—that is, they all cohered in reaction to the amusing episodes. The case for sadness was mixed. Sadness ratings and facial expressions of sadness correlated positively but each correlated negatively with electrodermal responses. In other words, as feelings of sadness and facial expressions increased together, accompanying electrodermal responses decreased. Finally, as facial signs of sadness increased, participants tended to remain still. All in all, the results of the experiment provided some support for response coherence. However, how tightly emotion channels adhere may depend on the emotion (Mauss et al., 2005). For example, coupling might be tighter for arousing emotions such as anger and fear than for a dampening emotion such as sadness.

In addition, there may be several other reasons why the channels that represent emotion do not cohere tightly (Mauss & Robinson, 2009). First, other parts of the environment may affect each channel differently. For example, facial expressions of happiness may be amplified in the presence of one's favorite aunt, while the threat of retaliation may inhibit action readiness and the acting out of anger. Second, coherence may not occur if channels react with different intensities to an emotion stimulus, as is the case with amusement versus sadness. Finally, laboratory measurements of emotion channels are artificial and in a real situation the individual's behavior would correspond more closely with their affect. For instance, anger affect is accompanied by yelling, disgust affect by escape behavior, and fear affect by heightened vigilance while remaining still.

Theory of constructed emotion. Are individuals merely reacting to their environment when experiencing an emotion as the response coherence postulate implies? Or do individuals act on their environment in order to create an emotion? To illustrate acting on the environment consider the following: is there any commonality among activities such as sculling, paying, fishing, saving, swimming, and borrowing? As listed, they do not provide much meaning. Perhaps, if a person could categorize the words, they would become more meaningful, such as using the word bank. However, an individual is still in doubt, since it depends on the function of the word. Is it a building that holds money or is it the side of a river? Thus, how a person uses the word bank provides meaning to the activities. If river bank, then sculling, fishing, and swimming make sense, since these are activities that occur nearby. Similarly, if money bank, then paying, saving, and borrowing become meaningful activities. Thus, the collection of activities becomes meaningful when a person organizes them into functional categories.

The construction and purpose of an emotion works in a similar way. For instance, imagine a social situation when someone dissed (disrespected) you. Several things happened. One is your awareness of what the individual did in the situation. Almost simultaneously, you felt a mosaic of indistinguishable affective feelings; no one feeling was dominant. In addition, your face felt warm, your heart rate rose, your breathing increased, and your posture became rigid. At this instance your brain simulates what to expect next. Recall from Chapter 1 that simulation refers to an array of anticipated or predicted psychological experiences that occur as if the individual were actually experiencing what is going to happen next. In the case of emotion, the brain simulates an emotion concept, where the events are anticipated to fit best. In other words, your brain generates, in the moment, a concept that efficiently encompasses all the things that are happening. In this manner the brain has constructed an emotion according to the **theory of constructed emotion** (Barrett, 2014, 2017; Lindquist et al., 2012). Furthermore, being dissed becomes meaningful when the situation and reactions are perceived as instances of a category, which is the emotion. Not until the individual categorized the events as anger or fear did she or he experience the emotion. And, as an emotion, the concept gains a function, much like a financial bank functions for check cashing and a river bank functions for fishing.

Why are emotions constructed? One reason is that an emotion helps individuals simulate or predict what to do next. Through simulation, individuals make sense of the various outcomes that stem from the emotion situation. In other words, the constructed emotion provides that meaning. The alternative is confusion and uncertainty. From meaning an individual's affective experiences become differentiated—that is, the affect is now perceived as an instance of fear or anger. Second, the constructed emotion guides a person's interpretation of the situation. For example, a person thinks "I am angry because I was dissed." Third, the ability to generate emotions is based on what an individual simulates based on her knowledge and culture. For example, when individuals in a particular cultural milieu are dissed they feel anger but in another culture they may feel fear or be embarrassed. Whatever emotion concept is simulated to best fit the situation is the one experienced. Fourth, individuals label their array of outcomes to being dissed with an emotion word. With this label, individuals have a source of knowledge to further guide their actions in the emotion situation. For example, when categorized as fear, a person who has been dissed may withdraw from the situation to prevent further insults but if categorized as anger the person verbally retaliates.

Methods for Uncovering Basic Emotions

A strategy of science is to classify its subject matter into various categories. Chemists classify basic elements. Botanists classify plants. Zoologists classify animals. Psychologists have classified emotions into basic categories (see Table 13.1). Each category represents a basic emotion, and these cannot be grouped into larger categories without losing some defining characteristics. Basic emotions are assumed to actually exist and that this categorization is not just some convenient classification system that has no correspondence in nature (Ekman, 1992; Ortony & Turner, 1990; Russell, 1991). The emotion words within each category in Table 13.1 are listed in the order of decreasing intensity. For example, happiness ranges from being light-hearted or serene to ecstasy. The emotion categories were derived by various means, such as by making a semantic (meaning) analysis of emotion words, investigating how emotions may have evolved, and analyzing facial expressions.

Category analysis of emotion words. In analyzing the meaning of emotion words, psychologists assume that those words developed to describe people's inner experiences. In other words, the reason for words such as love, hate, sad, happy, afraid, and angry is because each labels a distinctly unique feeling in a particular situation. If people did not experience these distinctly unique feelings, then words designating emotion would not have been formed. Johnson-Laird and Oatley conducted an extensive analysis of 590 English words to determine the various ways they expressed emotions (1989; Oatley & Johnson-Laird, 1990). They then classified words into emotion categories, with words of similar meaning being classified together. Their semantic analysis produced five basic emotion categories: happiness, sadness, anger, fear, and disgust.

Each category is listed in decreasing intensity

TABLE 13.1 Basic Emotions Derived from Three Different Methods of Analysis

Category Analysis	Evolution Theory	Facial Expressions	Matching Photos Below
Happiness/Joy[a,b] ecstatic euphoric happy carefree light-hearted	Reproduction ecstasy *joy* delight cheerfulness serenity	Happiness (emotion intensity increases with facial expression intensity)	
Love[b] passion attraction liking fondness tenderness	Incorporation *love* liking trust tolerance acceptance		
Surprise[b] amazement surprise astonishment	Orientation astonishment *surprise* confusion distraction uncertainty	Surprise (emotion intensity increases with facial expression intensity)	
Sadness[a,b] wretched depressed melancholic gloomy wistful	Reintegration grief sorrow *sadness* dejection gloominess	Sadness (emotion intensity increases with facial reaction intensity)	
Fear[a,b] terror panicky fearful anxious timid	Fear terror panic *fear* apprehension wariness	Fear (emotion intensity increases with facial reaction intensity)	
Anger[a,b] fury irascible irritable touchy grouchy	Destruction fury rage *anger* exasperation hostility	Anger (emotion intensity increases with facial reaction intensity)	
Disgust[a] queasy nausea	Rejection revulsion *disgust* aversion dislike boredom	Disgust (emotion intensity increases with facial reaction intensity)	
	Exploration anticipation expectancy curiosity inquisitive mindfulness		

continued . . .

TABLE 13.1 Continued

Category Analysis	Evolution Theory	Facial Expressions	Matching Photos Below
		Self-conscious emotions[c] embarrassment (negative) shame (negative) guilt (negative) pride (positive)	

Notes:

a Johnson-Laird and Oatley, 1989.
b Shaver et al., 1987.
c Leary, 2007.

Sources: Photos © iStock/spfoto; iStock/CREATISTA; iStock/CherylCasey; iStock/Camrocker; iStock/bowie15; iStock/master1305; iStock/SIphotography

Another language-based method of discovering emotions is to ask people what words represent emotions. Imagine being asked "please list as many items of the category 'EMOTION' as come readily to mind" (Fehr & Russell, 1984, p. 468). If you were like at least 10 percent of the participants in this investigation, then you would have listed the following words: happiness, anger, sadness, love, fear, hate, joy, excitement, anxiety, depression, frustration, crying, feelings, jealousy, disgust, laughter, elation, caring, guilt, and embarrassment. Further insight can be obtained if this method is followed by asking people how they would categorize emotion words. Imagine participating in a study designed to answer this question (Shaver et al., 1987). As a participant, you would receive 135 cards, each containing an emotion word along with the following instructions:

> We'd like you to sort these cards into categories representing your best judgments about which emotions are similar to each other and which are different from each other. There is no one correct way to sort the cards—make as few or as many categories as you wish and put as few or as many cards in each group as you see fit.
>
> (Shaver et al., 1987, p. 1065)

Participants classified the emotion words according to their own categorization schemes. However, the degree of agreement among participants showed how people in general categorize emotions. One participant put all 135 words into two categories of positive and negative emotions. For example, contentment and desire would be placed in the positive category, while fury, worry, and disappointment would be placed in the negative category. Another participant employed 64 different categories. A statistical analysis, however, indicated that six categories provided the best summary of the participants' classification efforts. These categories were labeled: *happiness/joy, love, surprise, sadness, fear,* and *anger.* Each label represents an **emotion prototype**, which suggests the average or typical meaning that all words in the emotion category have in common (Shaver et al., 1987). The prototype is really an abstract image that contains a set of features that is representative of the category members. The prototype does not exist by itself; it is only a mental abstraction. Specific emotions within a category in Table 13.1 are like individual family members who bear a resemblance to one another. A specific emotion attains category membership based on the degree it matches the mental prototype. As a note of caution, however, a variation of this sorting procedure has resulted in different category names, such as excitement, lust, melancholy, hate, extreme pain, pain, and low-level hostility (Alvarado, 1998). Nevertheless, evidence for the universal development of emotion categories has also been found. Hupka and associates (1999) looked at 64 different languages for emotion words under the major categories of joy, love, surprise, sadness, fear, and anger. They found that most languages had all of the emotion words. This led them to conclude that these emotion categories, based on English terms, were relatively similar across languages. The results of Johnson-Laird and Oatley's (1989) semantic analysis and Shaver and associates' (1987) categorization are grouped together in Table 13.1 as seven basic or prototype emotions. Specific instances of an emotion prototype are listed in order of decreasing intensity within a category. Although the specific emotions vary in intensity, each bears a resemblance to its prototype. Table 13.1 also shows the role of evolution and facial expression in emotion, which are described next.

Evolution theory. Emotions have a purpose. They are not random agitations of body and mind. Instead emotions are assumed to promote the survival of individuals and their offspring (Nesse & Ellsworth, 2009; Plutchik, 1980). Specific emotions evolved because they increased the capacity of humans to solve specific persistent environmental threats to survival. Individuals with these emerging emotions had a survival advantage when they encountered situations that were detrimental to their existence and that of their offspring. In other words, emotions motivate specific behaviors that aid survival. For example, anger motivates attack, fear motivates escape, and sadness motivates cries for help, while joy motivates continued goal pursuits (Nesse & Ellsworth, 2009). In addition, social emotions evolved to promote survival of offspring and to promote harmonious social living. Thus, there evolved such emotions as love, guilt, and shame. For example, as described in Chapter 2, love evolved to solve the commitment problem, which refers to the need of two individuals to bond together for their mutual survival benefits (Buss, 2006; Frank, 1988). The eight emotions listed in Table 13.1 (middle column) correspond to eight functions necessary for survival. The eight functions are reproduction, incorporation, orientation, reintegration, fear, destruction, rejection, and exploration. Examples of emotion in the service of each function are listed in order of decreasing intensity (Plutchik, 1980, 1984).

Facial expressions. Another line of reasoning is that each basic emotion has a corresponding facial expression. If there is no distinctive facial expression, then the corresponding subjective state should not be considered an emotion (Ekman, 1984, 1994a; Izard, 1971). Both Ekman and Izard discovered that posed facial expressions of emotions were identified accurately by people of different cultures throughout the world (Ekman, 1984, 1994a; Ekman & Friesen, 1971; Izard, 1971). These findings led Ekman to propose the six basic emotions presented in the right column of Table 13.1, along with representative facial expressions. Ekman (1984) assumed that the intensity of a felt emotion and the intensity of its facial expression increase together. More defined facial expressions accompany more intense emotional feelings. However, the face expresses more than emotions. It shows a blend of emotions, intentions, social customs, and even an expression dialect. These aspects can make discerning emotions a challenging task; more on this in Chapter 14.

Happiness, surprise, sadness, fear, anger, and disgust have clearly identifiable facial expressions, as shown in Table 13.1. Nevertheless, Darwin (1873) noted that, in addition to facial expressions, humans can also signal emotions vocally and behaviorally through blushes, hiding the face, laughs, screams, and shrugs. It is through these modes of communication that humans can signal **self-conscious emotions** such as shame, guilt, embarrassment, and pride. The category of self-conscious emotions stems from the evaluation that people think others are making about them. This is an added category in Table 13.1. These emotions, in turn, help regulate people's interpersonal relationships (Leary, 2007). Self-conscious emotions are signaled in various ways. The sequence of signals that are involved in embarrassment, for example, involve a downward gaze followed by a closed lipped, inhibited smile and conclude with the head turning away and perhaps even blushing (Keltner & Anderson, 2000). Shame and guilt show similar expressions (Keltner, 1995). Pride, which results from a perceived positive evaluation, has distinct facial and behavioral features that involve a slight head tilt, a weak smile, and an expanded posture (Tracy & Robins, 2004, 2007). Finally, romantic love, which is considered an emotion in the minds of many people, has behavioral accompaniments. These include sincere smiles, leaning toward one's partner, affirmative head nods, and gesticulations (Gonzaga et al., 2001, 2006).

Characteristics of Emotion

We all experience emotions, and so we can use ourselves as a source of information. Verbal descriptions of another person's affect or conscious feelings should be verifiable by our own experiences. We have a feel or sense for what a person is experiencing when she says "I'm in love with," "People who litter anger me," or "I'm anxious about the upcoming exam." The reason we can understand these statements is that we have said similar things. In addition to the subjective feel, emotion words also provide other information about the intensity of the experience and the relation between the person experiencing the emotion and the cause of that emotion. There are also words describing complex emotions (Johnson-Laird & Oatley, 1989).

Private affective experience. Can you describe what it feels like to be happy, sad, angry, or afraid? **Affect** refers to those subjective feelings and is one of the channels of emotion (see Figure 13.1). Affect consists of two parts: core affect and emotion-specific feelings. Core affect refers to physiological feelings that stem from the autonomic nervous system that reach conscious awareness. When their intensity increases they are accompanied by valence—that is, they are felt either as negative or unpleasant versus positive or pleasant (Barrett & Bliss-Moreau, 2009; Russell, 2009). Thus, the core affect of happy and proud is positive or pleasant, while that of sad or angry is negative or unpleasant. The other component of affect refers to its emotion-specific feeling. It is that part of affect that uniquely characterizes each emotion listed in Table 13.1.

How well do words describe these unique feelings? In a semantic analysis of emotion words, Johnson-Laird and Oatley considered their emotion categories as representing the most primitive subjective experiences possible (1989; Oatley & Johnson-Laird, 1990). According to philosophers, primitive subjective experiences are known as **qualia**. This means that the emotion words that represent the affective experiences are not fully describable by other words. Describing a basic emotion is like trying to describe the flavor of a strawberry or mango. The same problem is encountered in trying to describe feelings of joy, sadness, fear, anger, and disgust. The problem of qualia becomes apparent if we were to describe our emotions to someone who is emotionally blind like a robot (Johnson-Laird & Oatley, 1989).

But how strongly is affect tied to the other components of emotion shown in Figure 13.1? An answer comes from Heavey and coresearchers (2012), who comment on the characteristics of affect. First, some individuals exhibit all the components of emotion yet claim not to feel affect. For example, a person can be provoked and act angry or sad yet not feel that way. Second, each prototype emotion has a distinct affect. Yet, feelings can be vague or individuals can be unsure if they are even experiencing an affect as a part of an emotion. Furthermore, some feelings occur but individuals are unaware of any accompanying physiological arousal as if the feeling occurred in the individual's head. Finally, a person can experience contradictory or complementary feelings simultaneously. Sport fans, for instance, might vacillate between hope and dread at the prospect of their team winning or losing a championship game. Feelings can also blend like cream blends into coffee. For example, the excitement of graduation is composed of a blend of eagerness and dread about the future. Eagerness for new opportunities but dread of the unknown. Finally, how does an individual integrate the feelings that compose an emotion and exclude those feelings that are irrelevant? In the case of anger, a person attends to tension, rapid breathing, a flushed face, and an urge to shout but ignores hunger pangs, a headache, and background music or voices. In the case of anxiety, on the other hand, a person attends to clammy hands and tightness in the stomach but ignores a flushed face or an urge to shout. Thus, although an individual may experience different feelings and sensations only certain ones combine to characterize an emotion (Heavey et al., 2012).

How then do we describe our emotional feelings? One method might be to describe the eliciting conditions for emotions. For example, joy is what you feel when someone accepts your proposal of marriage. Sadness is what you feel when the family dog dies. Anger is what you feel when someone insults you. These eliciting examples, however, would not help emotionally blind individuals understand these emotions, since they would not feel what we feel in those situations.

Emotion emerges from the brain. What is happening in the brain when we experience an emotion? How does an emotion emerge from the brain? One way to find out is to create different emotions in people and at the same time scan their brain using fMRI. So imagine your brain being scanned while you listen to a music clip or view a film clip designed to produce various emotions, such as amusement, surprise, sadness, fear, anger, or a neutral state as a control condition. The fMRI identifies brain regions that are using excessive energy (glucose, oxygen) indicating these regions are active for the specific emotion that is experienced (Barrett, 2017; Saarimäki et al., 2016; Wager et al., 2015). To understand how the brain responds to these emotion induction procedures, think of a map of your state as representing the brain. The map contains a network of towns connected by roads. The roads vary in how directly they connect to towns and vary in how frequently they are traveled. The towns represent brain regions and the roads represent connecting neurons. The neurons originate in one brain region and extend (connect) to another region. The neural connections can be direct or circuitous and vary in strength.

What have neuroscientists discovered (Barrett, 2017; Kragel & LaBar, 2015; Raz et al., 2016; Saarimäki et al., 2016; Wager et al., 2015)? One result is that emotions are not localized to one region of the brain. Using the map analogy, emotions X, Y, and Z are not represented by activity in corresponding cities A, B, and C. Activation of a specific brain area does not define an emotion, since the area may have additional functions. Instead, continuing with the map analogy, different networks of cities and their connecting roads represent different emotions. Thus, emotion X involves a road connecting cities A and B, emotion Y involves a road connecting cities B and

C, and emotion Z involves a road connecting all three cities. However, the networks are more complex and involve several regions (towns) connected by different neural paths (roads) both directly and circuitously. Thus, each prototype emotion consists of a neural network composed of various brain regions and their neural connections. Networks also change with the complexity of the emotion stimulus and with the intensity of the emotion. Networks are also extensive. Some of them are located in the cortex, which is a layer of neurons that covers the outer surface of the brain. Other networks occur in the more interior parts of the brain. Finally, the networks in these two locations also connect. Thus, an emotional experience emerges into consciousness when certain situations activate a specific emotion network and the connection among networks.

Of interest is the fact that neural networks for subjective emotional experiences may be laid down in the limbic system, which is located in the interior of the brain. Patients who suffer epileptic seizures that involve the limbic system also experience affect. An epileptic seizure is an excessive discharge of neurons in the brain that can result in rigidity, tremors, convulsions, loss of balance, and even loss of consciousness. Other seizures, however, might only involve subtle changes in thought, mood, or behavior. Persons with epilepsy may experience an **epileptic aura**, which consists of psychological changes preceding the occurrence of an actual seizure. The seizures, localized in the limbic system, are preceded by auras involving feelings of happiness, sadness, fear, anger, disgust, and depression and are often accompanied by facial expressions (Gloor et al., 1982; MacLean, 1986; Williams, 1956). Table 13.2 provides case reports of patients whose auras involved emotional experiences.

TABLE 13.2   Emotional Experiences during Epileptic Auras

Emotion	Description
Happiness	Reported by a 41-year-old housewife: "There is a sudden feeling of being lifted up, of elation, with satisfaction, a most pleasant sense. 'I am just about to find out knowledge no one else shares—something to do with the line between life and death.' Her heart pounds, and she is seen to be pale and trembling" (Williams, 1956, p. 57)
Sadness	Reported by a 34-year-old woman: "There would be a dramatic onset of depression, always with a thought, half remembered, about 'Death and the World,' and a compulsive urge to suicide; always the feeling about 'Death and the World' comes with a feeling like going under gas" (Williams, 1956, p. 52)
Fear	Reported about a 19-year-old woman: She "had seizures that started with a feeling of intense fear followed by loss of consciousness and automatism in which she acted as if she were in the grips of the most intense terror. She let out a terrifying scream and her facial expression and bodily gestures were those of someone having a horrifying experience" (Gloor et al., 1982, p. 132)
Anger	Reported by a male patient describing one of his auras: "I just get an electrical feeling, and it goes all the way through me; it starts in my head (I'd say both the stomach and head) and then it makes me do things I don't want to do—I get mad" (unpublished records of MacLean & Stevens, cited in MacLean, 1986, p. 76)
Disgust	Reported by an 18-year-old schoolgirl: "A very brief unpleasant throat sensation, a queer unpleasant feeling in the body, and an unpleasant emotional state without fear, which may lead to a major fit" (Williams, 1956, p. 58)

Emotion education. Although it is difficult to describe affect, people have learned to label their own feelings with emotion words through a process known as **emotion education** (Buck, 1988; Fulcher, 1942). Through this process a child learns from people and from situations to indirectly label his feelings. For example, consider the process by which a child learns that the name of a certain object is pencil, that the name of its color is yellow, and that it is used for writing. In this instance, the object is visible to both the child and her teacher. Thus, a teacher can point to the object and say, "This is a pencil, its color is yellow, and it is used for writing." A problem in emotion education, however, is that a subjective feeling is not open for public inspection like a pencil is. Instead, emotion education takes place by noting the situation in which the emotion presumably occurs, the facial expression of the child, and her behavior and that of other people who may be experiencing the emotion (Buck, 1988; Fulcher, 1942). For instance, a birthday party may produce happiness, or being denied a toy may produce anger. In these situations a parent may label the child's feelings by asking "Are you happy with your presents?" or "Are you angry because you can't have the toy?" Presumably, a child will use these emotion words to label her feelings in future situations that are similar. A parent also assumes that a recognizable facial expression of emotion is linked to a subjective feeling. A crying child versus a laughing child produces different behaviors in the parent. When a child is crying, the mother might ask "Did you hurt yourself?" or "Why are you so sad?" When a child is laughing, the father might ask "Why are you so happy?" Presumably, the child will use these emotion words to label her feelings associated with those facial expressions. Behavior may also indicate to a parent whether a child is feeling happy or angry. Jumping up and down may indicate happiness, while shouting "no" may indicate feelings of anger.

A child can observe the emotional behavior of other people. For example, a child might see the expression of fear on the face of another child as he runs to his father on seeing a large dog.

FIGURE 13.2 Triadic Relation for Emotion Education. The establishment of a shared affective experience requires (1) the child's reaction to (2) the dog. This reaction is shared with (3) the parent. Both child and parent share the emotion of anxiety or fear in reaction to the dog. The parent labels the child's affective reaction to the dog as anxiety or fear.

The child might hear the father say, "Don't be afraid. The dog won't bite you." The child learns in this instance that the feeling associated with the expression and the running away receives the label "fear" or "I'm afraid." By many such lessons, children eventually learn to use emotion words to label their internal subjective (affective) feelings (Buck, 1988; Fulcher, 1942).

Emotion education can also proceed from what is known as a *triadic relation*, in which internal states between two individuals are shared in their reactions to a referent stimulus (Echterhoff et al., 2009). This relationship is expressed in Figure 13.2, in which a child and parent share their affective reaction to a dog. The parent infers the child's inner state is in reaction to the dog because the child gazed at the dog, pointed at the dog, facially responded to the dog, or, as in Figure 13.2, runs away from the dog. In other words, the parent assumes that the child is anxious or afraid of the dog. In addition, the parent's reaction is similar to the child's, such as being concerned or anxious about the dog. Finally, parent and child share the reality about the dog but also share their affective reactions to it—that is, they both show some degree of concern (Echterhoff et al., 2009). This connectedness between the two individuals is another source of information that children can use to label their affect.

Intensity and Duration of Emotions

Positive and negative emotions vary in intensity and duration. The valence of the stimulus change produces the quality of the emotion. The onset of negative stimuli produces unpleasant emotions, while the onset of positive stimuli produces pleasant emotions. The intensity of stimulus changes produces the strength and duration of an emotion. According to the **law of change**, the "greater the [stimulus] change, the stronger the subsequent emotion" (Frijda, 2007, p. 11). Empirical evidence for the law of change comes from investigations in which participants were asked to recall various facets of their emotions. For example, each evening imagine being asked various versions of the following questions used by Verduyn and coresearchers (2009a, 2011):

1. How many times did you experience anger, fear, joy, gratitude, or sadness?
2. Rate the importance of the event that elicited the emotion: *not at all important* = 0 to 7 = *very important*.
3. Rate the intensity of the beginning of the emotion: *not at all intense* = 0 to 7 = *very intense*.
4. What was the duration of the emotion in minutes? 0–10, 11–20, 21–30, 31–40, 41–50, 51–60, 60+ minutes?
5. Did the actual physical emotion-eliciting stimulus reoccur during any of the intervals?
6. Did you think of or mentally reevaluate the emotion-eliciting stimulus during any of the intervals?

Figure 13.3 summarizes several of their findings. First, the importance or intensity of the initiating stimulus determines the strength of the emotion (Verduyn et al., 2009a; Verduyn et al., 2011). For instance, Bernat and coresearchers (2006) presented male participants with pictures with negative or positive themes, such as weapons and erotica. Other pictures contained neutral themes, such as unexpressive faces and household objects. Stimulus intensity was manipulated by picture content. For example, a pointed gun is a more intense theme than one not pointed, while a nude female is considered more intense than a clothed one. Participants rated the pictures for

[handwritten] ✗ Peak oF
Intensity is Shart.
● Overall emotion is longer

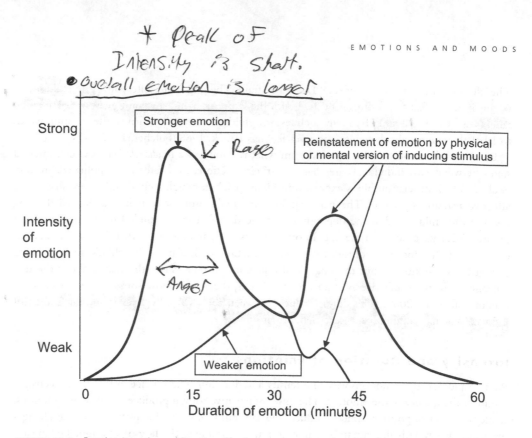

FIGURE 13.3 Emotion Intensity and Duration. The importance or intensity of the emotion-inducing stimulus and the steepness of the initial rise determine the duration of the emotion experience. The recurrence of the emotion-inducing stimulus, either physically or mentally, reinstates the emotion and prolongs its duration.

pleasantness and arousal intensity, while their frown muscles and skin conductance responses were also measured. Analysis of the results showed that positive pictures were rated more pleasant and negative pictures were rated more unpleasant compared to neutral pictures. In addition, arousal ratings of the positive and negative pictures were higher than those of the neutral pictures. The degree of emotion stimulus change across pictures also had an effect. For example, a pointed gun was rated more intense in unpleasantness than a side view of the same gun. Frowns and skin conductance were sensitive to the intensity of the pictures and theme content. Frowns became more intense as the pictures became more negative but less intense as the pictures became more positive. Skin conductance responses, however, increased as the picture-theme became either more negative or more positive.

Second, the results in Figure 13.3 show that emotions last in the order of minutes rather than hours. The median duration of an emotional episode ranged from 11 to 22 minutes for anger, 16 minutes for fear, 12 to 26 minutes for joy, and 15 to 20 minutes for sadness. Figure 13.3 also shows that emotional intensity fluctuates—that is, an emotion weakens and then strengthens, which contributes to duration (Verduyn et al., 2009a; Verduyn et al., 2011).

Third, Figure 13.3 shows that the steepness of the rise determines how long the emotion will last. Notice that the emotion that rises more steeply is the one with a longer duration. The steepness of onset also provides insight into the unfolding of emotions. Thus, abrupt and unexpected stimuli are more likely to produce an emotion with sudden rather than gradual onset. For example, joy and sadness have a more sudden onset compared to affection and anger (Verduyn et al., 2009b). The slower onset may depend on the accumulation of events, such as repeatedly thinking about the event or an escalation of insults, as in the case of anger. However, emotion intensity and duration are negatively related—that is, the more intense an emotion, the shorter its duration (Frijda et al., 1992; van Thriel & Ruch, 1994). For example, being ecstatic does not last as long as being cheerful, and being in a rage does not last as long as being hostile. The relationship between emotion intensity and duration was explored by van Thriel and Ruch (1994), who measured the intensity and duration of facial muscle activity that occurred before, during, and after the punchline of a joke. They found that at peak intensity the duration of facial muscle activity was shorter, while at a weaker intensity the duration was longer. Duration is a factor defining emotion, according to Ekman (1984), who reasoned that "the great majority of expressions of felt emotions last between 1/2 second and 4 seconds, and those that are shorter or longer are mock or other kinds of false expressions" (pp. 332–333). Yet each emotion may have its own window of time. Surprise may be an emotion of short duration, while sadness or fear may be of much longer duration.

Fourth, emotion duration also depends on the recurrence of the original stimulus or its mental counterpart (see second set of peaks in Figure 13.3; Verduyn et al., 2009a; Verduyn et al., 2011). These characteristics are captured by Frijda's (2007) **law of emotional momentum**, which states that an emotion stimulus can repeatedly elicit the same emotion provided that an individual has not habituated to the stimulus. Thus, each time a reminder of the original emotion stimulus intrudes into consciousness a person experiences a portion of the emotion all over again. For example, you might recall a joyous occasion spent with friends and as a result a happy smile appears on your face. Or you might recall an embarrassing moment and consequently become embarrassed all over again. Grief is the emotional reaction that occurs with the loss of a person or pet. Even though grief to the original loss has subsided, it can be evoked again by mental intrusions regarding the loss. For example, in one survey of 350 widows and widowers 13 months after the death of their spouses, 14 percent avoided looking at pictures or belongings of their deceased spouses and 16 percent found visiting the cemetery too painful. In addition, 20 percent cried whenever they thought of their spouses and 53 percent would cry whenever they spoke of their deceased spouse (Shuchter & Zisook, 1993). The researchers concluded that stimuli associated with former spouses acted as triggers for painful feelings of loss.

Emotional stimuli can lose their potency to evoke emotions, however, by the process of habituation, which occurs, for example, in the case of romantic love. Initially, one's beloved has the ability to intrude into a person's thoughts, to sexually and physiologically arouse the person, and to evoke the urge to touch. One way that habituation becomes evident is in the declining frequency of sexual intercourse over the years of marriage (Call et al., 1995). For example, from the data provided by a sample of 400 married women, Udry (1980) found that their frequency of sexual intercourse per month declined by about 32 percent over a four-year period. James (1981) examined the frequency of sexual intercourse for newlyweds over a 12-month period. He found that frequency declined from a median of 17.5 times during the first month to 8.8 times during the twelfth month of marriage. The high frequency of intercourse early in a marriage or relationship compared to later has been termed the **honeymoon effect** (James, 1981).

Section Recap

Emotion refers to a psychological construct that is represented by several channels: affect, facial expressions, physiological arousal, readiness to act, and behavior. According to the *response coherence postulate*, these channels all work in unison during an emotional experience in order to adapt to stimulus change. The *theory of constructed emotion* describes the process of categorizing the various reactions to an emotion stimulus into a bounded whole. This process provides the reactions with both meaning and function—that is, it forms an emotion. Various types of investigations have led to the formation of a set of basic emotions. For instance, semantic analyses, evolution theory, and facial expressions are methods that have led to the formulation of emotion categories. Emotions that are qualitatively similar are grouped into one of six to eight categories. The label of the category represents the *emotion prototype*, which is a summarized mental abstraction of the individual emotions in the category. Most emotion prototypes have a specific facial expression associated with them. However, expressions also show communication, a dialect, and social custom. Emotions within a category differ in intensity. Shame, guilt, embarrassment, and pride are *self-conscious emotions* that result from how we think other people are evaluating us. The subjective quality of an emotion, known as *affect*, has either a negative or positive valence coupled with an emotion-specific feeling. Affect is difficult to describe to others because of a property known as *qualia*. According to this concept, affective experiences have such basic and primitive qualities that words cannot describe them adequately. Some individuals may act emotional but yet not feel the emotion. Affect may be felt as vague or may occur as if there is no corresponding physiological arousal. Finally, different feelings can occur simultaneously, such as excitement and dread. A person must learn to determine which feelings are relevant for an emotion and which are not.

Emotions evolved to solve persistent environmental problems. Brain imaging techniques show that emotions resemble networks of neural connections among brain areas both in the cortex and in the brain's interior. In addition, *epileptic auras* occur before a seizure in the brain's limbic system and can involve an emotional experience of joy, sadness, fear, anger, or disgust. *Emotion education* is the process by which individuals learn to attach emotion labels to their subjective feelings. This process occurs when a child associates an internal feeling, facial expression, behavior, and situation with the emotion label provided by another individual or it is shared with another person. Whether an emotion is pleasant or unpleasant depends on whether the emotion stimulus had a positive or negative valence. The intensity and duration of an emotion depend on the strength of the emotion stimulus and whether stimulus reminders intrude into consciousness to induce the recurrence of the emotion. In addition, according to the *law of change*, the greater the stimulus change the stronger the emotion. The *law of emotional momentum* holds that an emotion stimulus evokes the same emotion provided a person has not habituated to the stimulus. Habituation occurs to some emotion stimuli as illustrated by the *honeymoon effect*, which means that the initial passion in a romantic relationship fades in intensity.

THE FUNCTION OF AROUSAL

Physiological arousal is one of the channels of emotion. But what is its function? Is the pattern of a person's physiological arousal synonymous with the emotional experience? Or does arousal represent a state of alertness for monitoring the environment? Could arousal indicate a readiness for action such as attacking, withdrawing, or perhaps doing nothing?

Changes in various physiological variables are indispensable accompaniments to affective feelings; without them a person might wonder whether an emotion was being experienced. Several possible connections exist between physiological arousal and subjective emotional feelings. First, arousal is the source of emotional feelings. If physiological arousal is absent, so is affect. What remains is a thought. Second, arousal is the impetus for attending to and interpreting the environment, with the emotional feeling occurring as a result. Third, arousal and subjective feelings occur together, with arousal providing a readiness for important activity, such as fight or flight. Finally, an individual categorizes various aspects of arousal in order to construct an emotion. As described in Chapter 2, philosophers such as Francis Bacon and René Descartes briefly described the correspondence between physiological responses and subjective experiences. Bacon, for example, described anger by paleness, blushing, and trembling, while Descartes described sadness as being accompanied by a feeble, slow pulse and a constriction around the heart. The attention paid to physiological arousal as a factor in emotional feelings attained increased significance in William James's (1884/1948) very influential article "What Is an Emotion?" published in the journal *Mind*.

To set the stage for understanding the relationship between arousal and affective experiences, imagine the following situation: You are in bed ready to doze off, when suddenly you hear the sound of breaking glass. What could this mean? Is someone attempting to break into your apartment, or has your careless roommate broken something? Will you experience fear of a would-be burglar or anger toward your roommate? What will be the nature of your physiological arousal and subjective experiences that could arise in this situation according to the James–Lange theory, cognitive arousal theory, Cannon's theory, and the construction of an emotion?

James–Lange Theory

One interpretation of the interaction between arousal and affective experience is derived from the writings of William James (1884) and Carl Lange (1885/1968). According to the **James–Lange theory**, each specific emotion is accompanied by a unique pattern of physiological responses. James reasoned that emotion occurs when we become aware of our body's physiological arousal and emotional behavior in reaction to an exciting stimulus. According to him, "The bodily changes follow directly the Perception of the exciting fact, and that our feeling of the same changes as they occur Is the emotion" (James, 1884/1948, p. 291; emphasis in original). Suppose you hear the sound of breaking glass. From a commonsense view, if this means someone is attempting to break into the apartment, then you become afraid, which produces trembling and a pounding heart. If the sound of breaking glass resulted from your roommate's carelessness, then you become angry, which produces a pounding heart and increased blood pressure. James felt, however, that this commonsense sequence was incorrect. According to him, a person's awareness of his own trembling and pounding heart is the basis for the emotional experience of fear of the would-be burglar, while a rise in blood pressure is the source of a person's subjective anger (Levenson, 1992). Thus, in the James–Lange theory, the sequence of events in experiencing an emotion is:

Emotion stimulus → Physiological response pattern → Affective experience

The James–Lange theory stimulated extensive research to determine the correspondence between affective experiences and unique physiological response patterns. For James, emotional behavior, such as fleeing from your apartment or setting your jaw tightly in anger, also serves as information. A paper by Lange published in 1885, however, placed great emphasis on autonomic nervous system arousal as the input for subjective affect. Thus, the James–Lange theory emphasizes physiological arousal to the exclusion of emotional behavior as the determiner of emotional feelings (Mandler, 1990).

Research on physiological response specificity of emotion. The James–Lange theory proposes that each emotional feeling has a unique pattern of physiological responses associated with it. To show this, various criteria must be met (Cacioppo et al., 1993). First, at least two emotions should be induced. The physiological response patterns should differ between them and also differ from the pattern produced by a nonemotional control condition. Second, the presence of any emotion should also be verified using other measures, such as facial expressions or verbal reports. For example, suppose that, in a hypothetical experiment, procedure H is used to create happiness, such as an unexpected monetary bonus for participating in the experiment, while procedure A is used to create anger by frustrating a participant with unsolvable puzzles. A nonemotional control procedure measures baseline levels of physiological responding in the absence of any emotional experience. Verbal reports or facial expressions would have to verify that participants undergoing procedure H were experiencing happiness, that participants undergoing procedure A were experiencing anger, and that control participants were not experiencing any emotion. During the procedure, two different physiological responses would be measured, such as heart rate and electrodermal responses. Hypothetical results that would support the James–Lange theory are presented in Figure 13.4. Procedure H (happiness) produced a heart rate–electrodermal response pattern that differed from the pattern produced by procedure A (anger). Furthermore, both patterns differ from the pattern accompanying the control procedure. Different patterns presumably provide participants with information for different subjective emotional experiences. If physiological response patterns are similar, then there would be no basis for feeling different emotional experiences, according to the James–Lange theory.

Is there evidence for the physiological specificity of emotions? Yes, but the evidence has been difficult to uncover. Initially, after a careful analysis of published experiments, researchers (Cacioppo et al., 2000; Larsen et al., 2008) found some specific physiological differences among discrete emotions. For example, heart rate was greater during anger and fear than during happiness and was also greater during fear than during sadness. Diastolic blood pressure was higher in anger than either fear, sadness, or happiness and was also higher during sadness than during happiness. Electrodermal responses increased more during fear than during sadness. However, there were also occasions when a physiological variable would not differentiate between two emotions. The researchers mainly concluded that there was not a unique physiological pattern for each basic emotion (Cacioppo et al., 2000; Larsen et al., 2008). The failure to find specific physiological patterns results from the nature of the autonomic nervous system. It responds in a global fashion rather than showing specific reactions in an emotion-inducing situation. People are only aware of general changes in their autonomic nervous system rather than of specific changes (Mandler,

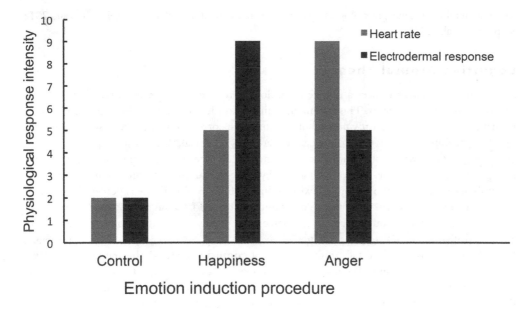

FIGURE 13.4 Physiological Response to Emotion. Hypothetical results of an experiment show a different physiological response pattern for each subjective emotional experience. The pattern for happiness is different from the pattern for anger, and both of these differ from the control pattern.

1984). Consequently, perception of our body's physiological reactions does not provide enough information to determine the subjective nature of an emotional experience.

TutorVista presents a YouTube video describing the autonomic nervous system titled "Autonomic Nervous System" here: www.youtube.com/watch?v=YFYRosjcVuU.

Physiological pattern specificity coincides with affect. However, further research has led to a different conclusion. A new research strategy known as **pattern classification analysis** allows researchers to detect patterning in physiological responding (Friedman et al., 2014; Kragel & LaBar, 2013; Stephens et al., 2010). The strategy is to determine if a recognizable pattern of physiological responses coincides with current affect. In the psychology laboratory, participants watch film clips designed to induce a specific emotion, such as amusement, anger, contentment, fear, sadness, surprise, or a neutral state. Simultaneously, a variety of cardiovascular, electrodermal, and respiratory responses are recorded, such as heart rate, blood pressure, skin conductance level or response, and breathing rate or variability. The researchers found that each emotion-inducing film clip tended to result in an identifiable corresponding physiological response pattern. Thus, the pattern for amusement was different from anger, which was different from sadness. However, there were also some similarities among the patterns. This similarity resulted in occasionally identifying the wrong emotion based on the physiological response pattern. For example, anger and fear might be confused with one another. However, successfully identifying an emotion based on its physiological response pattern supports James's idea of physiological specificity. A person's affect corresponds with a unique pattern of physiological arousal. This correspondence, however, has not resulted in 100 percent correspondence between affect and physiological response patterns. There is still some generality among physiological patterns (Friedman et al., 2014; Kragel & LaBar, 2013; Stephens et al., 2010).

Cognitive Arousal Theory

An emotion stimulus produces a unique physiological response pattern from which a particular affective experience emerges. This statement is the main idea of the James–Lange theory. Yet, as we have discovered, there is only partial but not complete correspondence. Is it possible to account for the remaining confusion that occurs between physiological patterns and specific affective experiences? One hypothesis is that when a physiological pattern is ambiguous different affective interpretations are possible. In describing this hypothesis, Larsen and coresearchers (2008) use the ambiguous figure of the young/old woman in Figure 13.5. The figure is perceivable as either the head of a young woman or that of an old woman but not both simultaneously. The researchers reason a similar process could occur in the perception of physiological response patterns. Thus, a pattern of physiological responses could serve as the basis for different affective experiences. How the pattern is perceived falls in the domain of **cognitive arousal theory** (Mandler, 1984; Reisenzein, 1983; Schachter & Singer, 1962). A specific affective experience results from the interpretation a person gives her physiological arousal, based on the information extracted from the situation. In this theory, arousal is important for several reasons (Mandler, 1984). First, the occurrence of arousal forces the person to focus her attention on the environmental events that may have been responsible. Thus, on hearing glass breaking, all your attention is focused on the source of the sound. Second, arousal leads a person to analyze the meaning of the sound. What could have made that noise: someone breaking in or a careless roommate? Third, arousal enables

FIGURE 13.5 Young Girl–Old Woman Ambiguous Figure. This figure is perceivable as a young girl or as an old woman depending on the observer's perspective. By analogy, a pattern of physiological responses could be perceived as representing different affective states depending on individuals' perspectives of their internal states (Larsen et al., 2008).

the person to respond to the environment more effectively. Perhaps you should dial 911; then again, maybe you should tiptoe into the kitchen to assess how much damage your roommate has done. Mandler (1984) refined the original cognitive arousal theory (Schachter & Singer, 1962) by emphasizing two dimensions of emotion: quality and intensity. The quality of an emotional experience depends on the evaluation and subsequent meaning given to the emotion-inducing event. The intensity of the emotional experience, however, depends on the degree of physiological arousal. For example, the subjective emotion produced by hearing the sound of breaking glass depends on the meaning assigned to the noise. Is someone breaking in, or has your careless roommate dropped a drinking glass? The first interpretation evokes fear, while the second evokes anger. The sound of breaking glass also produces physiological arousal in both cases. The intensity of that arousal, however, determines whether a person feels anxiety, fear, or terror of a would-be burglar or mild annoyance to intense anger toward a roommate.

In cognitive arousal theory, the emotion stimulus is the source of information for behavior but also the source of arousal. Recall that, according to the law of change, greater stimulus changes produce stronger emotions and hence greater physiological arousal. Thus, when participants are presented with arousing stimuli such as an aimed gun or snake compared to a flower or mushroom, their physiological arousal is greater to the former—that is, to the more arousing stimuli (Bernat et al., 2006; Greenwald et al., 1989).

However, whether the arousal comes from the original stimulus or from elsewhere does not seem to matter based on the findings from **excitation transfer** experiments. In these, physiological arousal induced from one source influences emotional experience and behavior induced by another source (Zillmann, 1978, 1984). For instance, physiological arousal induced by physical exercise or by viewing action-packed films influences emotion induced by another stimulus. To illustrate, consider how an unrelated source of arousal can influence someone's romantic attraction for a person. White and associates (1981) produced low and high levels of physiological arousal in male participants by having them run in place for 15 or 120 seconds, respectively. After 15 minutes of rest, participants viewed a five-minute videotape of a university coed. In one version, she was made up attractively and talked about herself in an energetic fashion. In another version, she was made up unattractively and talked about herself in a generally dull manner. Participants then rated the videotape model for romantic attraction: her physical attractiveness and how much they would like to date her and kiss her. They also rated her for general attraction: how similar they were to her and how much they would like to work with her, get to know her better, and get along with her.

The experiment contained the two features that were necessary for emotion, according to cognitive arousal theory. First, there was the emotional aspect of the model, who was made to look and sound either attractive or unattractive. In evaluating her, the male participants presumably experienced some degree of emotional reaction. Second, there was a low or high amount of arousal that transferred from another source, which was running in place for either 15 or 120 seconds. The interaction between these two features influenced romantic attraction and general attraction ratings of the models. Higher arousal increased the emotional attraction for the attractive model while at the same time decreasing the emotional attraction for the unattractive one. The emotional experience evoked by the model increased because additional arousal transferred from running in place. If the model was unappealing, the added arousal made her more unappealing. If she was appealing, the added arousal made her more appealing. A potential piece of advice for the lovelorn is to take your date to an exciting basketball game or movie. The arousal from the game or movie should transfer over to the arousal being produced by the person. As a consequence of the transferred arousal, a person should be even more attracted to his or her date.

Cannon's Theory of Arousal

The question opening this section implied that a particular emotion is linked to a certain part of the body (Nieuwenhuyse et al., 1987). For example, sadness is felt as a broken heart and disgust is felt as gagging. For Bacon, "The *Spirits*, in all *Passions*, resort most to the *Parts*, that labour most, or are most affected" (Bacon, 1627/1974, p. 525; italics in original). In other words, the affected part of the body is ready for action during a particular emotional experience. These insights of Bacon are forerunners of the emergency response concept, which is a major point of emphasis in **Cannon's theory** (Cannon, 1929/1953). Accordingly, physiological arousal is merely an indication that the organism is ready or prepared for an emergency response, such as fighting or fleeing. For example, the liver releases glucose for the muscles to use as fuel for running or fighting. The adrenal glands release adrenaline (epinephrine) to restore the vigor of fatigued muscles. In addition, blood is shifted to the heart, lungs, and skeletal muscles of the limbs to be of greater service in transporting oxygen. Blood clotting is also more likely during this time, since bleeding might occur in a fatal injury. According to Cannon (1927, 1929/1953), these **emergency responses** make the organism more capable of dealing with situations that produce fear, rage, and pain. Hearing the sound of breaking glass produces an emergency response. You may need to be prepared to flee from a burglar or to confront your roommate. The emergency response is similar to Frijda's (1986, 2007) **action readiness**, which is a state of preparedness to execute a particular kind of behavior. These states are felt as urges and impulses to act in a certain fashion depending on the emotional experience. Thus, when frustrated a person may have an urge to yell insults or when in love a person may have the impulse to touch another person. Emotions and action readiness are linked together. Fear readies you to flee the apartment from the would-be burglar, while anger readies you to yell at your roommate.

Action readiness implies that each discrete negative emotion is a motive for a different type of behavior. Consequently, each emotion requires a different pattern of physiological support. The basic emotion of anger, for example, produces a readiness to fight and act aggressively. Therefore, increased heart rate is necessary to distribute blood more efficiently to the muscles. Fear is also associated with increased heart rate, since that emotion is associated with a readiness to flee. Disgust, however, does not require any extensive activity on the part of a person other than the expulsion of sickening objects. As expected, Levenson (1994) has noted that a higher heart rate accompanies anger and fear, while a lower heart rate accompanies disgust. In reviews of research cited earlier, Cacioppo and others (2000; Larsen et al., 2008) found that the physiological pattern for disgust did not differ from a nonemotional control pattern. Furthermore, compared to anger, fear is associated with vasoconstriction, lower blood pressure, and less blood to peripheral vessels. Blood instead is redirected to the larger muscles in preparation for flight, which is consistent with the function of fear (Levenson, 1992). In other words, each negative emotion may have a somewhat different physiological profile, since each is linked to a readiness to perform different behaviors.

Arousal Helps Construct an Emotion

In the example of hearing the sound of breaking glass, the brain regulates the energy for behavior that will be employed in that emotion situation; energy such as glucose, adrenaline, the use of oxygen, and the stress hormone cortisol. An individual perceives the release of this energy by way of feedback from internal physiological changes—that is, physiological arousal. According to Barrett's (2017) theory of constructed emotions, an individual groups these internal sensations together based on their similarity to accomplish some goal function, based not on physical resemblance but on functional resemblance. In the breaking glass example, the changes are grouped one way when constructing the emotion of anger and another way when constructing the emotion of fear. In each case, the elements of the emotions can be highly variable. In other words, what is the specific function of an anger or fear encounter? When grouped one way, the brain constructs an anger emotion labeled miffed, vexed, annoyed, pissed, irritated, livid, or enraged. When grouped another way, the brain constructs a fear emotion labeled timid, anxious, afraid, scared, or terrified. Labeling the categorized grouping of physiological feelings constructs the emotion. In doing so, the emotion guides a person's thoughts and behaviors in the situation—that is, how I will confront my roommate or a burglar.

Section Recap

Four different theories attempted to account for the function that physiological arousal has for emotions. According to the *James–Lange theory*, each emotion has a specific physiological response profile. Research that uses *pattern classification analysis* of physiological profiles shows that there is some match with affective experiences. Yet some ambiguity remains in the physiological patterns, which may allow for different interpretations of affect. An analogy is the profile of seeing either an old or young woman in the ambiguous figure of the young/old woman. In other words, interpretation of the physiological profile determines a particular affective feeling. According to *cognitive arousal theory*, arousal forces a person to attend to and interpret the surrounding situation. The interpretation determines the valence of affective experience, while the intensity of the physiological arousal is associated with the intensity of the experience. *Excitation transfer* experiments show that arousal from one source transfers and influences the intensity of the emotional experience induced by another source. Research with excitation transfer experiments illustrates the importance of arousal for interpreting the situation. The intensity of arousal created by the emotion stimulus correlates with intensity of affect. The third theory, *Cannon's theory*, maintains that arousal prepares the person to make an *emergency response*. For example, physiological arousal associated with fear results from glucose and adrenaline (epinephrine) being released into the bloodstream so that an emergency response such as running away can be executed effectively. Similar to the emergency response is the concept of *action readiness*, which refers to an urge or impulse characteristic of the associated emotion. A conclusion regarding Cannon's theory is that different physiological arousal patterns are linked to different forms of fight-or-flight emergency responses for the benefit of the organism in an emotion-inducing situation. For the theory of constructed emotions, an individual categorizes internal physiological feelings according to their function to accomplish a goal.

MOODS

Are you cheerful, gloomy, grouchy, blue, or serious? These descriptors refer to mood states as in cheerful mood or serious mood. In the description of internal states, psychologists have borrowed from everyday language. Thus, they use terms such as emotion and mood without having empirically distinguished their difference, if any. What differentiates mood from emotion? What variables influences our mood?

Differences between Moods and Emotions

Mood is a subjective experience similar to emotion. First, according to Morris (1992), moods are usually considered to last longer than emotions, although there is no consensus on the duration. Usually, moods are considered to last on the order of hours and days, whereas emotions last for seconds or minutes (Ekman, 1994b; Goldsmith, 1994; Verduyn et al., 2011). Second, the intensity of moods is less than that of emotions. Moods are more global and diffuse. Watson and Clark (1994a) imply that moods may be milder versions of emotions. For example, gloomy is classified in the sadness category (see Table 13.1) and may be a better indicator of mood than of emotion. A person might say, "It is a gloomy day," meaning that the weather is producing a gloomy mood. Similarly, under the happiness/joy (or reproduction) category (see Table 13.1), being carefree and cheerful may be more indicative of moods rather than of low-intensity emotions. Third, a person is less likely to be aware of the stimulus that produced a mood and more aware of the stimulus that produced an emotion. Davidson (1994) claims that moods follow from stimulus events that occur slowly over time, while emotions follow stimuli that occur more quickly. For example, the seasons of the year change slowly, and people's moods change with the seasons (Smith, 1979). An emotion stimulus, however, has a more sudden onset, like the punchline of a joke or a friend failing to show up for a date.

Mood and emotion also differ in their consequences and physiology (Beedie et al., 2005). Emotions are thought of as being directed toward an intended consequence, as if there was an aim of the emotion. For example, the aim of jealousy is to protect your relationship with someone. Moods, on the other hand, appear without direction or without an intended outcome. Furthermore, physiological involvement is more salient for emotions than it is for moods. Individuals are more aware of their body's involvement during an emotional experience than during a mood experience.

Another distinction between mood and emotion relates to a dimension versus a category view of affect. Moods belong in either positively valenced or negatively valenced dimensions in contrast to membership in one of the six to eight categories of emotion presented in Table 13.1 (Watson, 2000; Watson & Clark, 1994a). The dimensional analysis means that moods have no specific affective feel or qualia, like prototypical emotions do. Instead, moods have either an unpleasant (negative) or pleasant (positive) feeling that can fluctuate somewhat in intensity.

Measurement of Moods

The measurement of mood valence, intensity, and duration is necessary in order to determine what factors determine those characteristics. Mood is measured by psychological scales, such as the *General*

Dimensions Scale of the Positive and Negative Affect Schedule (PANAS; Watson & Clark, 1994b). This portion of the *Schedule* contains 20 descriptive terms that measure affective valence—that is, negative or positive affect. The 10 descriptors for the positive dimension depict a tendency to approach and engage in situations and activities, while the 10 descriptors for the negative dimension depict the opposite. To illustrate: for positive affect, participants indicate the extent they have felt active, enthusiastic, and strong. For negative affect, participants indicate the extent they have felt afraid, irritable, or upset. This scale and an earlier version have been used extensively in examining the relationship between mood and other variables. The expanded version of the PANAS (PANAS-X) contains descriptors that can be used for all of the categories of emotions listed in Table 13.1, except for love and disgust.

The website titled "Measurement Instrument Data Base for the Social Sciences" provides access to a copy of the PANAS here: www.midss.org. The scale is also here: www2.psychology.uiowa. edu/Faculty/Clark/PANAS-X.pdf.

Factors that Affect Mood

Mood refers to low-intensity negative or positive affect that has no discernible stimulus. However, psychologists have observed that mood fluctuates with several environmental variables: time of day, day of week, seasons, weather, and sleep. How does mood change with these variables?

Time of day, day of week. Moods are linked to systematic changes in the environment, especially time of day (Hill & Hill, 1991). This last statement probably comes as no surprise to students with 8:00 a.m. classes. Clark and associates (1989) measured the positive and negative moods of college students every three hours from 6:00 a.m. to 3:00 a.m. (depending on whether the students were awake at that time). The results of their investigation showed that positive mood rose rapidly from 9:00 a.m. to noon and then remained stable until about 9:00 p.m., at which time it declined suddenly. Students were energetic and active during the middle of the day and less so in the morning and evening. Negative mood ratings, however, were low and remained relatively stable throughout the day.

In a replication study, Watson and colleagues (1999) had University of Iowa students rate their positive and negative affect and take their body temperature every two hours over a period of one week. Figure 13.6 plots their positive and negative affect scores and body temperature as a function of time of day. The graph has been standardized so that the scores represent the number of standard deviations below or above the mean. Zero (0) represents the mean. Positive affect and temperature show similar trends. They are both low early in the morning and late at night, although positive affect peaks between 11:00 a.m. and 1:00 p.m. while body temperature peaks between 5:00 and 7:00 p.m. Negative affect, however, remained relatively the same throughout the day. The temperature curve in Figure 13.6 is part of a person's *circadian rhythm*. This rhythm refers to the 24-hour cycle of biological processes, such as body temperature changes and a person's sleep/wake cycle.

Changes in positive affect with time of day (see Figure 13.6) are not the same for every individual but depend on a trait referred to as *morningness–eveningness*. This dimension refers to the time of day that a person functions best. Morning types prefer and work best earlier in the day, in contrast toward later in the day, which is preferred by evening types. The *Morningness–Eveningness Questionnaire* measures an individual's location on this dimension. Extreme morning-type individuals

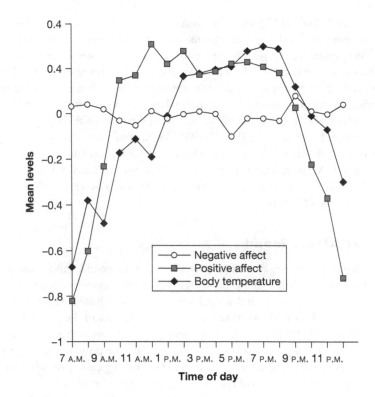

FIGURE 13.6 Mood, Body Temperature, and Time of Day. Positive affect and body temperature increase from morning to late afternoon, remain fairly constant, and then decline in early evening. Negative affect remains fairly constant throughout the day.

Source: From "The Two General Activation Systems of Affect: Structural Findings, Evolutionary Considerations, and Psychobiological Evidence" by D. Watson et al., 1999, *Journal of Personality and Social Psychology, 76,* Figure 6, p. 835. Copyright 1999 by American Psychological Association.

are more cheerful, active, alert, and happier during late morning compared to evening. In contrast, extreme evening-type individuals do not reach their peak mood until early evening (Jankowski & Ciarkowska, 2008).

The website titled Sleep Habits contains the *Morningness–Eveningness Questionnaire* here: https://sleephabits.net/morningness-eveningness-questionnaire.

In addition to time of day, mood also varies with the day of the week. Larsen and Kasimatis (1990) had university students rate themselves daily for 84 days on the extent they experienced a series of positive and negative mood adjectives. The researchers computed a single mood score as the average of pleasant adjectives such as happy, pleasant, and joyful minus unpleasant adjectives such as unhappy, depressed, and angry. A positive score indicates a dominance of positive affect and a negative score a dominance of negative affect. The researchers also measured each student's level of extraversion and based on the extraversion score formed one group of introverts and another group of extraverts. As shown in Figure 13.7, positive affect prevails over negative affect—that is, ratings of pleasant adjectives were higher than ratings of unpleasant adjectives. The graph shows that positive affect starts off low on Sunday and Monday and then proceeds to rise daily to its highest level on Saturday. Interestingly, daily positive affect was greater for extraverts than it was for introverts. These results confirm the findings in Figure 9.6 that in general extraverts are happier than introverts. In a similar investigation, Watson (2000) had students use the PANAS to rate their positive and negative affects over a 30-day period. The results showed that positive affect starts low on Sunday and rises through the week to its high point on Saturday. Negative affect shows a reverse trend. Although it rises from Sunday to Monday, it then declines for the rest of the week and reaches its lowest points on Friday and Saturday. From Thursday through Saturday, positive affect was higher than negative affect. These results led Watson (2000) to conclude that "the subjective weekend of college students seems to last from Thursday through Saturday" (p. 130).

Effects of seasonal weather variation and mood. The effect of weather or season of the year also affects mood. General changes in the weather such as temperature and amount of sunlight correspond to seasons of the year, especially in the southern and northern latitudes. However, within a season the weather can fluctuate daily within a geographical region. If moods are slow acting, then they may

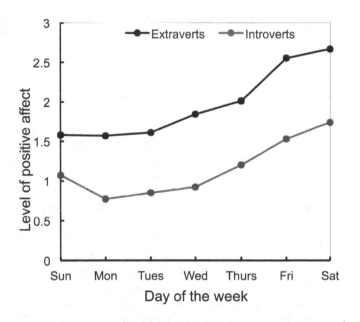

FIGURE 13.7 Mood and Day of the Week. Positive affect rises across the days of the week from Sunday to Saturday for both introverts and extraverts although the rise for introverts begins on Monday. Positive mood is highest on Friday and Saturday. For every day of the week, positive affect is greater for extraverts than it is for introverts.

Source: Adapted from "Individual Differences in Entrainment of Mood to the Weekly Calendar" by R. J. Larsen & M. Kasimatis, 1990, *Journal of Personality and Social Psychology, 58,* Table 1, p. 168. Copyright 1999 by American Psychological Association.

show changes more to the seasons than to daily fluctuations. For instance, when individuals are asked on the *Seasonal Pattern Assessment Questionnaire* what month they feel best and what month they feel worst, there is a consistent tendency to mark winter months as their least favorite (Murray et al., 2001). From this low point in winter, there is a revival of happiness the following spring as the weather warms, the vegetation greens, and the days lengthen (Smith, 1979). Some individuals, however, are extremely affected by changes in the seasons, especially decreased sunlight during the winter. These individuals have **seasonal affective disorder** (SAD), which is frequently characterized by sadness, decreased activity, anxiety, irritability, and daytime tiredness, especially in the winter (Magnusson & Partonen, 2005). However, symptoms of SAD decrease and positive affect increases when daylight lengthens or individuals travel to areas closer to the equator or are exposed to light therapy (Magnusson & Partonen, 2005; Westrin & Lam, 2007).

However, there is some question whether more severe forms of depression are linked to the change of seasons. Traffanstedt and coresearchers (2016) measured depression in over 34,000 adults with the eight-item *Patient Health Questionnaire*. The questionnaire asks individuals how many days in the last two weeks they felt down, depressed, hopeless, or tired and had little interest in doing things. Their findings showed that depression did not change with the number of days of winter, season of the year, amount of sunlight, or latitude. People in the north did not show more depression than those in the south. The authors conclude that "being depressed during winter is not evidence that one is depressed because of winter" (p. 832). Depression in winter seems rooted in folk psychology with little supporting empirical evidence (Traffanstedt et al., 2016).

The *Seasonal Pattern Assessment Questionnaire* is available here: www.ubcmood.ca/sad/SPAQ-SAD.pdf.

The website of the Stanford Patient Education Research Center provides a link to the eight-item *Patient Health Questionnaire* here: http://patienteducation.stanford.edu/research/phq.pdf.

Effects of daily weather variation on mood. Mood changes as a result of daily variation in the weather have been difficult to demonstrate. Denissen and coresearchers (2008) found small changes in negative affect with variation in temperature, wind speed, and amount of sunlight. People also differed in their sensitivity to changes in the weather. However, the influence of weather may depend on its daily variability. Thus, a clear day is enjoyed more when it follows many days of rain, a warm day is appreciated more when it follows a cold snap, and a cool day is enjoyed when it follows a heatwave. All of these instances are examples of the law of hedonic contrast (from Chapter 10): the positive effect of weather on a particular day depends on prior days being worse. For example, people enjoy spring because of the prior cold, dark, and dreary winter. In addition, Keller and coresearchers (2005) reasoned that the effects of weather depend on a person being outside rather than indoors. They found that for people who were outside more than 30 minutes, mood valence (positive–negative affect) increased with temperature and with amount of sunlight. Furthermore, mood improves when people are allowed outside on warm, clear days compared to being forced to remain indoors. Keller and coresearchers also discovered that temperature increases mood in the spring time but that further increases in temperature during the summer decreased mood especially in southern climates. In other words, positive mood tends to decrease when it gets too hot.

Sleep. Are you ever cranky because you did not get enough sleep? Probably so and there is evidence to support your experience. Talbot and coresearchers (2010) investigated the effects of

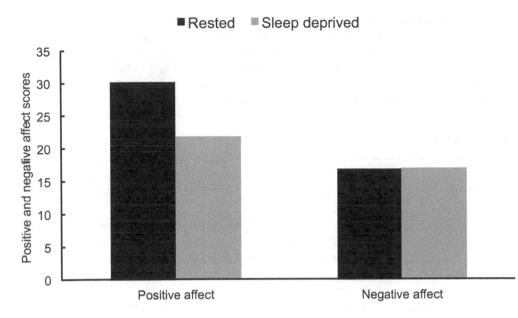

FIGURE 13.8 Effect of Sleep Deprivation on Affect. Sleep deprivation reduced positive affect but had no influence on negative affect. The PANAS was used to measure the level of affect after two nights of sleep deprivation and after two nights of plenty of sleep.

Source: Adapted from "Sleep Deprivation in Adolescents and Adults: Changes in Affect" by L. S. Talbot et al., 2010, *Emotion, 10*, Table 3, p. 837.

sleep deprivation on people's moods. The researchers allowed their participants no more than 6.5 hours of sleep one night. And on the following night the participants were only allowed two hours of sleep between 3:00 and 5:00 a.m. Afterwards, participants filled out the PANAS in order to measure their degree of positive and negative affect. Then, to make up for the effects of sleep deprivation, the participants slept 8.5 hours on the next two nights and then filled out the PANAS again. Figure 13.8 compares the degree of positive and negative mood when participants are fully rested versus when they are sleep deprived. As Figure 13.8 shows, sleep deprivation reduced positive affect but had no effect on the amount of negative effect.

Section Recap

Moods are a milder and longer form of emotional affect. Moods are classified as either positively valenced or negatively valenced affect. The PANAS-X can be used to measure the intensity of positive and negative affect. Stimuli producing mood changes appear to have a gradual and subtle beginning. For example, our moods are affected by hour of the day, day of the week, season of the year, and weather. Positive mood is highest during the middle of the day and lowest early morning or late evening. In general, positive mood is lowest Sunday and Monday and rises to a high on Saturday. *Morningness–eveningness* is the dimension during which an individual functions best; morning for some and evening for others. Positive mood is higher during spring and lower during the winter but also higher as a result of weather contrast, such as the pleasant effect of a sunny day is greater when it follows a cloudy day. Some individuals experience *seasonal affective disorder* (SAD), which is characterized most by mild depression in the winter owing to lack of sunlight, although depression can occur in summer owing to heat. However, more severe depression is unaffected by seasons, latitude, and amount of daylight. Finally, sleep deprivation lowers positive affect but has no effect on negative affect.

GLOSSARY

Term	Definition
Action Readiness	A state of preparedness, felt as an urge or impulse, to execute a particular behavior in the service of achieving the aim of an emotion
Affect	The subjective feeling part of an emotion and one of the channels of emotion
Cannon's Theory	Physiological arousal is an indication that the organism is ready or prepared for an emergency response, e.g., fight or flight
Circadian Rhythm	A person's internal clock that is in tandem with the day/night cycle and accounts for a person's sleep/wake cycle
Cognitive Arousal Theory	Affective experience results from the interpretation a person gives her physiological arousal pattern based on information available in the situation
Core Affect	Physiological feelings that stem from the autonomic nervous system and reach conscious awareness and are accompanied by a positive or negative valence
Emergency Response	An emotional response that occurs during an urgent situation or emergency, such as fighting or fleeing
Emotion	An evolved coordinated effort among physiological, psychological, and behavioral dimensions to cope with an environmental demand or problem
Emotion Channels	Dimensions along which emotions are expressed, e.g., affect, facial expressions, physiological arousal, action readiness, and behavior
Emotion Education	Process by which people learn to label their own emotional feelings with emotion words
Emotion Prototype	Label given to an emotion category, which suggests the average meaning that all emotion words in that category have in common
Epileptic Aura	Physiological changes that precede the occurrence of an actual epileptic seizure and are accompanied by emotion feelings
Evolution Theory of Emotion	Emotions evolved because they increased the capacity of humans to solve specific persistent environmental threats to survival of the individual
Excitation Transfer	Physiological arousal induced from one source influences emotional experience and behavior induced from another source
Honeymoon Effect	Decline in the frequency of sexual intercourse from early in the marriage or relationship compared to later in the relationship
James–Lange Theory	The theory that each specific emotional feeling is accompanied by a unique physiological response pattern specific to that feeling

continued . . .

GLOSSARY Continued

Term	Definition
Law of Change	The greater the change of the emotion stimulus, the stronger the subsequent emotion
Law of Emotional Momentum	An emotion stimulus can repeatedly elicit the same emotion provided that an individual has not habituated to the stimulus
Mood	A positive or negative subjective affective experience of lesser intensity than emotional affect, and of longer intensity, that is part of the background of consciousness
Morningness–Eveningness	A personality dimension that refers to the time of day that a person functions best, e.g., best in the morning or best in the evening
Pattern Classification Analysis	A research strategy by which researchers detect patterns of physiological responses to determine if they coincide with a person's current affect
Qualia	Emotion words that represent affect are not fully describable by other words, i.e., affect is difficult to describe
Physiological Response Specificity	A specific or unique pattern of physiological responses that corresponds to an emotional feeling
Response Coherence Postulate	The channels or dimensions that underlie emotions are associated and respond together uniformly; they do not act independently
Seasonal Affective Disorder (SAD)	Emotional affect changes with seasons of the year and is characterized by depression, sadness, anxiety, and daytime sleepiness in the winter
Self-Conscious Emotions	Emotions such as shame, guilt, embarrassment, and pride that result from the evaluation that people think others are making about them
Theory of Constructed Emotion	The brain generates, in the moment, a concept that efficiently encompasses the situation and body's reactions that have happened. This concept is the emotion
Triadic Relation	In the process of emotional education, it refers to emotional feelings being shared by two individuals in response to the same emotion stimulus

REFERENCES

Alvarado, N. (1998). A reconsideration of the structure of the emotion lexicon. *Motivation and Emotion, 22,* 329–344.

Bacon, F. (1627/1974). Sylva sylvarum. In S. Diamond (Ed.), *The roots of psychology* (pp. 523–525). New York, NY: Basic.

Barrett, L. F. (2014). The conceptual act theory: A précis. *Emotion Review, 6,* 292–297.

Barrett, L. F. (2017). *How emotions are made: The secret life of the brain.* Boston, MA: Houghton Mifflin.

Barrett, L. F., & Bliss-Moreau, E. (2009). Affect as a psychological primitive. In M. P. Zanna (Ed.), *Advances in experimental social psychology* (Vol. 41, pp. 167–218). Amsterdam: Academic Press.

Beedie, C. J., Terry, P. C., & Lane, A. M. (2005). Distinctions between emotion and mood. *Cognition and Emotion, 19,* 847–878.

Bernat, E., Patrick, C. J., Benning, S. D., & Tellegen, A. (2006). Effects of picture content and intensity on affective physiological response. *Psychophysiology, 43,* 93–103.

Buck, R. (1988). *Human motivation and emotion* (2nd ed.). New York, NY: Wiley.

Buss, D. M. (2006). The evolution of love. In R. J. Sternberg & K. Weis (Eds.), *The new psychology of love* (pp. 65–86). New Haven, CT, & London: Yale University Press.

Cacioppo, J. T., Berntson, G. G., Larsen, J. T., Poehlmann, K. M., & Ito, T. A. (2000). The psychophysiology of emotion. In M. Lewis & J. M. Haviland-Jones (Eds.), *Handbook of emotions* (2nd ed., pp. 173–191). New York, NY: Guilford.

Cacioppo, J. T., Klein, D. J., Berntson, G. G., & Hatfield, E. (1993). The psychophysiology of emotion. In M. Lewis & J. M. Haviland (Eds.), *Handbook of emotions* (pp. 119–142). New York, NY: Guilford.

Call, V., Sprecher, S., & Schwartz, P. (1995). The incidence and frequency of marital sex in a national sample. *Journal of Marriage and the Family, 57*, 639–652.

Cannon, W. B. (1927). The James–Lange theory of emotions: A critical examination and alternative theory. *American Journal of Psychology, 39*, 106–124.

Cannon, W. B. (1929/1953). *Bodily changes in pain, hunger, fear and rage.* Boston, MA: Charles T. Branford.

Clark, L. A., Watson, D., & Leeka, J. (1989). Diurnal variation in the positive affects. *Motivation and Emotion, 13*, 205–234.

Darwin, C. (1873). *The expression of the emotions in man and animals.* London: John Murray.

Davidson, R. J. (1994). On emotion, mood, and related affective constructs. In P. Ekman & R. J. Davidson (Eds.), *The nature of emotion* (pp. 51–55). New York, NY: Oxford University Press.

Denissen, J. J. A., Butalid, L., Penke, L., & van Aken, M. A. G. (2008). The effects of weather on daily mood: A multilevel approach. *Emotion, 8*, 662–667.

Echterhoff, G., Higgins, E. T., & Levine, J. M. (2009). Experiencing commonality with others' inner states about the world. *Perspectives on Psychological Science, 4*, 496–521.

Ekman, P. (1984). Expression and the nature of emotion. In K. R. Scherer & P. Ekman (Eds.), *Approaches to emotion* (pp. 319–344). Hillsdale, NJ: Lawrence Erlbaum.

Ekman, P. (1992). Are there basic emotions? *Psychological Review, 99*, 550–553.

Ekman, P. (1994a). Moods, emotions, and traits. In P. Ekman & R. J. Davidson (Eds.), *The nature of emotion* (pp. 56–58). New York, NY: Oxford University Press.

Ekman, P. (1994b). Strong evidence for universals in facial expressions: A reply to Russell's mistaken critique. *Psychological Bulletin, 115*, 268–287.

Ekman, P., & Friesen, W. V. (1971). Constants across cultures in the face and emotion. *Journal of Personality and Social Psychology, 17*, 124–129.

Fehr, B., & Russell, J. A. (1984). Concept of emotion viewed from a prototypes perspective. *Journal of Experimental Psychology: General, 113*, 464–468.

Frank, R. H. (1988). *Passions within reason.* New York, NY: W. W. Norton.

Friedman, B. H., Stephens, C. L., & Thayer, J. F. (2014). Redundancy analysis of autonomic and self-reported, responses to induced emotions. *Biological Psychology, 98*, 19–28.

Frijda, N. H. (1986). *The emotions.* Cambridge: Cambridge University Press.

Frijda, N. H. (2007). *The laws of emotion.* Mahwah, NJ: Lawrence Erlbaum.

Frijda, N. H., Ortony, A., Sonnemans, J., & Clore, G. L. (1992). The complexity of intensity: Issues concerning the structure of emotion intensity. In M. S. Clark (Ed.), *Review of personality and social psychology: Vol. 13. Emotion* (pp. 60–89). Newbury Park, CA: Sage.

Fulcher, J. S. (1942). "Voluntary" facial expression in blind and seeing children. *Archives of Psychology, 272*, 2–49.

Gloor, P., Olivier, A., Quesney, L. F., Andermann, F., & Horowitz, S. (1982). The role of the limbic system in experiential phenomena of temporal lobe epilepsy. *Annals of Neurology, 12*, 129–144.

Goldsmith, H. H. (1994). Parsing the emotional domain from a developmental perspective. In P. Ekman & R. J. Davidson (Eds.), *The nature of emotion* (pp. 68–73). New York, NY: Oxford University Press.

Gonzaga, G. C., Keltner, D., Londahl, E. A., & Smith, M. D. (2001). Love and the commitment problem in romantic relations and friendship. *Journal of Personality and Social Psychology, 81*, 247–262.

Gonzaga, G. C., Turner, R. A., Keltner, D., Campos, B., & Altemus, M. (2006). Romantic love and sexual desire in close relationships. *Emotion, 6*, 163–179.

Greenwald, M. K., Cook III, E. W., & Lang, P. J. (1989). Affective judgment and psychophysiological response: Dimensional covariation in the evaluation of pictorial stimuli. *Journal of Psychophysiology, 3*, 51–64.

Heavey, C. L., Hurlburt, R. T., & Lefforge, N. L. (2012). Toward a phenomenology of feelings. *Emotion, 12*, 763–777.

Hill, C. M., & Hill, D. W. (1991). Influence of time of day on responses to the Profile of Mood States. *Perceptual and Motor Skills, 72*, 434.

Hupka, R. B., Lenton, A. P., & Hutchinson, K. A. (1999). Universal development of emotion categories in natural language. *Journal of Personality and Social Psychology, 77*, 247–278.

Izard, C. E. (1971). *The face of emotion*. New York, NY: Appleton-Century-Crofts.

James, W. (1884/1948). What is an emotion? *Mind, 9*, 188–204. Reprinted in W. Dennis (Ed.), *Readings in the history of psychology* (pp. 290–303). New York, NY: Appleton-Century-Crofts.

James, W. H. (1981). The honeymoon effect on marital coitus. *Journal of Sex Research, 17*, 114–123.

Jankowski, K. S., & Ciarkowska, W. (2008). Diurnal variation in energetic arousal, tense arousal, and hedonic tone in extreme morning and evening types. *Chronobiology International, 25*, 577–595.

Johnson-Laird, P. N., & Oatley, K. (1989). The language of emotions: An analysis of a semantic field. *Cognition and Emotion, 3*, 81–123.

Keller, M. C., Fredrickson, B. L., Ybarra, O., Côté, S., Johnson, K., Mikels, J., . . . Wager, T. (2005). A warm heart and a clear head: The contingent effects of weather on mood and cognition. *Psychological Science, 16*, 724–731.

Keltner, D. (1995). Signs of appeasement: Evidence for the distinct displays of embarrassment, amusement, and shame. *Journal of Personality and Social Psychology, 68*, 441–454.

Keltner, D., & Anderson, C. (2000). Saving face for Darwin: The functions and uses of embarrassment. *Current Directions in Psychological Science, 9*, 187–192.

Keltner, D., & Shiota, M. N. (2003). New displays and emotions: A commentary on Rozin and Cohen (2003). *Emotion, 3*, 86–109.

Kragel, P. A., & LaBar, K. S. (2013). Multivariate pattern classification reveals autonomic and experiential representations of discrete emotions. *Emotion, 13*, 681–690. DOI: 10.1037/a0031820.

Kragel, P. A., & LaBar, K. S. (2015). Multivariate neural biomarkers of emotional states are categorically distinct. *Social Cognitive and Affective Neuroscience, 10*, 1437–1448.

Lange, C. (1885/1968). The emotions. In W. S. Sahakian (Ed.), *History of psychology: A source book in systematic psychology* (pp. 207–211). Itasca, IL: F. E. Peacock.

Larsen, J. T., Berntson, G. G., Poehlmann, K. M., Ito, T. A., & Cacioppo, J. T. (2008). The psychophysiology of emotion. In M. Lewis, J. M. Haviland-Jones, & L. F. Barrett (Eds.), *Handbook of emotions* (3rd ed., pp. 180–195). New York, NY: Guilford.

Larsen, R. J., & Kasimatis, M. (1990). Individual differences in entrainment of mood to the weekly calendar. *Journal of Personality and Social Psychology, 58*, 164–171.

Leary, M. R. (2007). Motivational and emotional aspects of the self. *Annual Review of Psychology, 58*, 317–344.

Levenson, R. W. (1992). Autonomic nervous system differences among emotions. *Psychological Science, 3*, 23–27.

Levenson, R. W. (1994). The search for autonomic specificity. In P. Ekman & R. J. Davidson (Eds.), *The nature of emotion* (pp. 252–257). New York, NY: Oxford University Press.

Lindquist, K. A., Wager, T. D., Kober, H., Bliss-Moreau, E., & Barrett, L. F. (2012). The brain basis of emotion: A meta-analytic review. *Behavioral and Brain Sciences, 35*, 121–143.

MacLean, P. D. (1986). Ictal symptoms relating to the nature of affects and their cerebral substrate. In R. Plutchik & H. Kellerman (Eds.), *Emotion: Theory, research, and experience: Vol. 3. Biological foundations of emotion* (pp. 61–90). Orlando, FL: Academic Press.

Magnusson, A., & Partonen, T. (2005). The diagnosis, symptomatology, and epidemiology of seasonal affective disorder. *CNS Spectrums, 10*, 625–634.

Mandler, G. (1984). *Mind and body: Psychology of emotion and stress*. New York, NY: W. W. Norton.

Mandler, G. (1990). William James and the construction of emotion. *Psychological Science, 3*, 179–180.

Mauss, I. B., Levenson, R. W., McCarter, L., Wilhelm, F. H., & Gross, J. J. (2005). The tie that binds? Coherence among emotion experience, behavior, and physiology. *Emotion, 5*, 175–190.

Mauss, I. B., & Robinson, M. D. (2009). Measures of emotion: A review. *Cognition and Emotion, 23*, 209–237.

Morris, W. N. (1992). A functional analysis of the role of mood in affective systems. In M. S. Clark (Ed.), *Review of personality and social psychology: Vol. 13. Emotion* (pp. 256–293). Newbury Park, CA: Sage.

Murray, G., Allen, N. B., & Trinder, J. (2001). A longitudinal investigation of seasonal variation in mood. *Chronobiology International, 18,* 875–891.

Nesse, R. M., & Ellsworth, P. C. (2009). Evolution, emotions, and emotional disorders. *American Psychologist, 64,* 129–139.

Nieuwenhuyse, B., Offenberg, L., & Frijda, N. H. (1987). Subjective emotion and reported body experience. *Motivation and Emotion, 11,* 169–182.

Oatley, K., & Johnson-Laird, P. N. (1990). Semantic primitives for emotions: A reply to Ortony and Clore. *Cognition and Emotion, 4,* 129–143.

Ortony, A., & Turner, T. J. (1990). What's basic about basic emotions? *Psychological Review, 97,* 315–331.

Plutchik, R. (1980). *Emotion: A psychoevolutionary synthesis.* New York, NY: Harper & Row.

Plutchik, R. (1984). Emotions: A general psychoevolutionary theory. In K. R. Scherer & P. Ekman (Eds.), *Approaches to emotion* (pp. 197–219). Hillsdale, NJ: Lawrence Erlbaum.

Raz, G., Touroutoglou, A., Wilson-Mendenhall, C., Gilam, G., Lin, T., Gonen, T., . . . Maron-Katz, A. (2016). Functional connectivity dynamics during film viewing reveal common networks for different emotional experiences. *Cognitive, Affective, and Behavioral Neuroscience, 16,* 709–723.

Reisenzein, R. (1983). The Schachter theory of emotion: Two decades later. *Psychological Bulletin, 94,* 239–264.

Rosenberg, E. L., & Ekman, P. (1994). Coherence between expressive and experiential systems in emotion. *Cognition and Emotion, 8,* 201–229.

Ruch, W. (1995). Will the real relationship between facial expression and affective experience please stand up: The case of exhilaration. *Cognition and Emotion, 9,* 33–58.

Russell, J. A. (1991). Culture and the categorization of emotions. *Psychological Bulletin, 110,* 426–450.

Russell, J. A. (2009). Emotion, core affect, and psychological construction. *Cognition and Emotion, 23,* 1159–1283.

Saarimäki, H., Gotsopoulos, A., Jääskeläinen, I. P., Lampinen, J., Vuilleumier, P., Hari, R., . . . Nummenmaa, L. (2016). Discrete neural signatures of basic emotions. *Cerebral Cortex, 26,* 2563–2573.

Schachter, S., & Singer, J. E. (1962). Cognitive, social, and physiological determinants of emotional state. *Psychological Review, 69,* 379–399.

Shaver, P., Schwartz, J., Kirson, D., & O'Connor, C. (1987). Emotion knowledge: Further exploration of a prototype approach. *Journal of Personality and Social Psychology, 52,* 1061–1086.

Shuchter, S. R., & Zisook, S. (1993). The course of normal grief. In M. Stroebe, W. Stroebe, & R. Hansson (Eds.), *Handbook of bereavement: Theory, research, and intervention* (pp. 23–43). Cambridge: Cambridge University Press.

Smith, T. W. (1979). Happiness: Time trends, seasonal variations, intersurvey differences, and other mysteries. *Social Psychology Quarterly, 42,* 18–30.

Stephens, C. L., Christie., I. C., & Friedman, B. H. (2010). Autonomic specificity of basic emotions: Evidence from pattern classification and cluster analysis. *Biological Psychology, 84,* 463–473.

Talbot, L. S., McGlinchey, E. L., Kaplan, K. A., Dahl, R. E., & Harvey, A. G. (2010). Sleep deprivation in adolescents and adults: Changes in affect, *Emotion, 10,* 831–841.

Tracy, J. L., & Robins, R. W. (2004). Show your pride: Evidence for a discrete emotion expression. *Psychological Science, 15,* 194–197.

Tracy, J. L., & Robins, R. W. (2007). Emerging insights into the nature and function of pride. *Current Directions in Psychological Science, 16,* 147–150.

Traffanstedt, M. K., Mehta, S., & LoBello, S. G. (2016). Major depression with seasonal variation: Is it a valid construct? *Clinical Psychological Science, 4,* 825–834.

Udry, J. R. (1980). Changes in the frequency of marital intercourse from panel data. *Archives of Sexual Behavior, 9,* 319–325.

van Thriel, C., & Ruch, W. (1994). The role of surprise in humor appreciation. Unpublished manuscript, University of Düsseldorf, Düsseldorf, Germany.

Verduyn, P., Delvaux, E., Van Coillie, H., Tuerlinckx, F., & Van Mechelen, I. (2009a). Predicting the duration of emotional experience: Two experience sampling studies. *Emotion, 9,* 83–91.

Verduyn, P., Van Mechelen, I., & Tuerlinckx, F. (2011). The relation between event processing and the duration of emotional experience, *Emotion, 11*, 20–28.

Verduyn, P., Van Mechelen, I., Tuerlinckx, F., Meers, K., & Van Coillie, H. (2009b). Intensity profiles of emotional experience over time. *Cognition and Emotion, 23*, 1427–1443.

Wager, T. D., Kang, J., Johnson, T. D., Nichols, T. E., Satpute, A. B., & Barrett, L. F. (2015). A Bayesian model of category-specific emotional brain responses. *PLOS Computational Biology, 11*, e1004066.

Watson, D. (2000). *Mood and temperament*. New York, NY: Guilford.

Watson, D., & Clark, L. A. (1994a). Emotions, moods, traits, and temperaments: Conceptual distinctions and empirical findings. In P. Ekman & R. J. Davidson (Eds.), *The nature of emotion* (pp. 89–93). New York, NY: Oxford University Press.

Watson, D., & Clark, L. A. (1994b). *The PANAS-X: Manual for the Positive and Negative Affect Schedule—Expanded Form*. Retrieved August 28, 2003, from www.psychology.uiowa.edu/faculty/clark/PANAS-X.pdf.

Watson, D., Wiese, D., Vaidya, J., & Tellegen, A. (1999). The two general activation systems of affect: Structural findings, evolutionary considerations, and psychobiological evidence. *Journal of Personality and Social Psychology, 76*, 820–838.

Westrin, Å., & Lam, R. W. (2007). Seasonal affective disorder: A clinical update. *Annals of Clinical Psychiatry, 19*, 239–246.

White, G. L., Fishbein, S., & Rutsein, J. (1981). Passionate love and the misattribution of arousal. *Journal of Personality and Social Psychology, 41*, 56–62.

Williams, D. (1956). The structure of emotions reflected in epileptic experiences. *Brain, 79*, 29–67.

Zillmann, D. (1978). Attribution and misattribution of excitatory reactions. In J. H. Harvey, W. Ickes, & R. F. Kidd (Eds.), *New directions in attribution research* (pp. 335–368). Hillsdale, NJ: Lawrence Erlbaum.

Zillmann, D. (1984). *Connections between sex and aggression*. Hillsdale, NJ: Lawrence Erlbaum.

CHAPTER 14

Emotions as Motives

The face is the image of the soul.

Cicero, 80 BC

More grievous than tears is the sight of them.

Antonio Porchia, "Voces," 1943

How do emotions unfold and for what function? This question along with the following guides the reading of this chapter:

1. Does the situation determine what emotion is experienced?
2. Does appraisal of the situation also contribute to what emotion is experienced?
3. What is the nature of the link between an emotional feeling and a facial expression?
4. What function do facial expressions serve?
5. How do emotions motivate cognitive activity and behavior?
6. What motivational features does happiness provide?

APPRAISAL OF THE EMOTION EVENT

As the chapter title indicates, emotions can serve as motives that push an individual into action. As noted in Chapter 2, the French philosopher Descartes (1649/1968) believed that the effect of an emotion was first to instill the goal of the emotion into a person's consciousness. The second effect was to prepare the mind and body to achieve that goal. Descartes's theory implies that fear wills a person to flee toward safety and anger wills a person to fight in order to redress an insult. The observation by Descartes serves to tie emotions to motivation—that is, emotions are an internal source of motivation that push humans into action toward specific aims.

In trying to describe emotional feelings, a person can describe the situation that induced it. For example, happiness is what you feel when hearing good news, while disappointment is what you feel when someone lets you down. Is it possible that all emotions in the same category are evoked by similar circumstances, while emotions in different categories are evoked by different circumstances? So how do the characteristics of a situation lead to the unfolding of a particular emotion? Does the appraisal of a situation also affect the unfolding of an emotion?

Characteristics of the Emotion-Inducing Event

Emotions unfold from stimulus changes that impact an individual. They serve as adaptations to those changes. What is the nature of those stimulus changes?

Situational definitions of emotion. The **situational definition** approach examines what features of stimulus changes are responsible for emotions. It assumes that emotions are caused by people's interactions with changing events but ignores how people might appraise those events. Table 14.1 shows that the situational definition of emotion relies on two factors: the valence of the stimulus and people's relationship to it. Valence means that stimuli are experienced as negative or unpleasant and as positive or pleasant. Relationships refer to psychological interactions with the event, such as moving closer to, moving further away from, or being blocked from the stimulus. The interaction between valence of and relationship with the stimulus determines the emotion. To illustrate, sadness results when a dear friend (high positive valence) moves away. The move marks an increase in psychological distance from a person (see Table 14.1). Fear results when a spider (negative valence) approaches the arm of a spider phobic. And frustration or anger results when an individual blocks your goal, such as when your roommate's phone conversation hinders your concentration.

Several components are involved in the situational definition approach to understanding emotions. First, as described in Chapter 13, emotions have evolutionary significance and thus the stimulus changes are assumed to signal important concerns in the lives of people (Brosch et al., 2010; Nesse & Ellsworth, 2009). Emotion-inducing events are often threats to an individual's welfare. For example, being "stood up" for an appointment suggests a threat to the need to belong. Second, each cell in Table 14.1 can accommodate a variety of events based on the appropriate combination of valence and relationship. The fear category contains events such as robbers pointing guns at their victims but also poisonous snakes in the vicinity—that is, negative

TABLE 14.1 Situational Definition of Basic Emotion Categories

	Changes in Psychological Distance from Stimulus		
Valence of stimulus	Decreases	Increases	Blocked
Negative stimulus	relief	fear	gratitude
Positive stimulus	sad	happy	anger

stimuli in close proximity to the person. The anger category contains events such as being cut off in traffic but also from being continuously insulted, needled, and harangued. In these examples, an individual is blocked from positive stimuli, such as unimpeded driving or maintaining an intact self-esteem. According to Brosch and coresearchers (2010), such examples are rapidly classified into the appropriate emotion categories. As a consequence, all events placed in the same category activate similar responses. For example, anger evokes retaliation in order to remove any goal-blocking obstacles. The third characteristic is that the emotion category provides additional information so that the appropriate adaptive reaction results (Brosch et al., 2010). In other words, the emotion provides the basis for adapting to the situation in terms of physiological arousal and readiness for action in line with the aim of the emotion. Thus, such adaptation involves being set to flee for the fear category, being set to fight for the anger category, and tears plus disengagement for the sad category. Notice, however, that situational definition approach (see Table 14.1) is too simple to account for all emotion categories presented in the previous chapter (see Table 13.1). Love, disgust, and the self-conscious emotions are not accounted for.

Emotion-eliciting situations. Do people's actual emotional experiences fit into any of the cells in Table 14.1? In order to answer this question, Shaver and associates (1987) attempted to identify various elicitors of different emotions. Respondents in the study were asked to think of incidents during which they experienced emotions such as fear, sadness, anger, joy, or love. They were then to describe in detail the events that led them to experience the emotion. Their reports resembled situational outcomes in Table 14.1. For example, experiencing a positive stimulus or event evokes joy, such as achieving a task, receiving acceptance and love, or attaining what was wanted. Losing a positive incentive or experiencing a negative outcome—such as experiencing rejection, loss of love, or a negative surprise—evokes sadness. A threat to a person's well-being results in fear, especially when the threat is severe and unexpected. For example, participants reported being afraid in the dark or walking alone. Anger occurred in reaction to blocked goals, losses, and injustices. The positive emotion of love, however, was inspired from the ability of other individuals to induce good feelings in the participant. Script writers and directors have great insight into what induces emotions in people. They use this knowledge to create movie scenes to produce various emotions (Schaefer et al., 2010).

Event–Appraisal–Emotion Sequence

As joke tellers know, a listener's reaction can range from amused laughter to disgusted groans. An explanation of these varied reactions is that individuals appraise jokes differently. In a review of theories concerned with the appraisal of emotion-inducing events, Roseman and Smith (2001) derived some common assumptions. First, different appraisals of the same event produce different emotions. For example, the breakup of their romantic relationship induces sadness in one partner and relief in the other. Second, the same appraisal of different events produces the same emotion. For example, a student who earned a C on an exam is as satisfied as one who earned an A, provided that both grades were proportional to the amount of exam preparation. Third, the outcome of the appraisal process elicits the involuntary unfolding of an emotion. For instance, at times a person cannot help but feel disappointed or elated. Finally, appraisal can occur above and also below an individual's cognitive awareness—for instance, gut-level reactions that occur without knowledge of their cause.

Figure 14.1 gives an overview of the event–appraisal–emotion sequence. The process begins with the occurrence of an emotion-inducing event or stimulus and ends with the unfolding of the components of emotion. During the pre-aware phase, a rough nonconscious appraisal occurs of the negative and positive aspects of the stimulus. During this phase, the process is biased to detect negative features prior to any positive ones. Are there any features that are dangerous rather than safe, damaging rather than beneficial, unpleasant rather than pleasant, or to be avoided rather than approached? A few milliseconds later, the situation is appraised cognitively and more extensively, with awareness occurring along emotion-relevant dimensions. This phase includes information obtained during the pre-aware appraisal process. Ellsworth and Scherer (2003) raise the possibility that early in the appraisal process an individual becomes emotional although this may be more akin to undifferentiated arousal. This early arousal in turn influences the nature of further appraisal until eventually a fully formed emotion unfolds. Early arousal causes individuals to focus on the emotion-inducing event, thus ensuring optimal appraisal and subsequent efficient coping (Mather & Sutherland, 2011). Later, especially during the awareness phase, Smith and Lazarus (1990) maintain that a person appraises a situation in a manner consistent with her attitudes, personality, needs, and goals. This process is quite flexible, so there may be no close correspondence between the actual stimulus and the appraised stimulus. Two people who are in the same actual situation may appraise it quite differently. For example, what if the stimulus is receiving a C in a course? To one student this may be a cause of happiness, if failure had been expected. To another student, however, a C may be a cause of disappointment, if a higher grade had been expected.

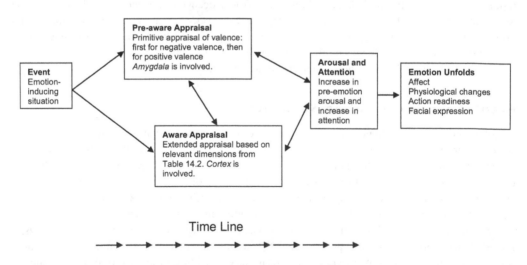

Time Line

FIGURE 14.1 Event Appraisal, Awareness, Arousal, and Emotion Unfolds. Appraisal of the emotion stimulus can begin prior to cognitive awareness. With involvement of the amygdala, negative features receive more attention during this initial appraisal process. More extensive appraisal entails cognitive awareness and involves the cortex. Appraisal increases arousal and attention until eventually an emotion unfolds. Appraisal is an ongoing process.

The Appraisal Process

Nonhuman animals and people once lived in an environment faced with continual challenges detrimental to their well-being and very survival. According to evolutionary psychology, the natural and sexual selection of emotions resulted in the increased ability and motivation to solve these problems. The benefits were improved chances of survival. An obvious example is the emotion of fear, which evolved to motivate avoidance and escape from danger. The evolutionary benefit of emotion begins with the appraisal of those environmental challenges. On what bases are situational changes appraised? And is it beneficial for appraisals to be fast and to focus on what is dangerous?

Appraisal dimensions. The situational definition emphasizes the power of the stimulus event to evoke an emotion. Appraisal, in contrast, emphasizes how the stimulus event as evaluated or as appraised evokes the emotion. Following pre-aware appraisal, people realize they are appraising a situation even though an emotion might follow automatically. Is a situation or event appraised using a universal set of dimensions? Do these dimensions separate emotions from one another? One set of dimensions in Table 14.2 is useful for differentiating among emotions. Scherer (1997) had respondents from 37 different countries answer questions similar to the ones listed in Table 14.2. The results indicate that there seems to be high agreement around the world on what appraisal dimensions are responsible for evoking emotions. For example, joy was induced by goal-compatible events that could be easily coped with. Sadness, however, was the result of events produced by others that hindered one's goals and that were difficult to cope with. Most indicative of fear was its unpleasantness rating, its external causation, and difficulty in being coped with. Anger-evoking situations were appraised as being unfair and resulting from hindered goals. The most striking appraisal dimension for disgust was its unpleasantness, with external causation also being important. Smith and Kirby (2009) provide the importance or value of a stimulus change as an additional appraisal dimension (Table 14.2). This dimension refers to the magnitude of stimulus change, which determines the strength of the emotion (Verduyn et al., 2009).

Stimulus changes that induce emotion are seldom clear cut in daily life and thus are subject to a variety of different appraisals. The type of appraisal, in turn, influences the emotion that actually unfolds. Psychologists have investigated the effects of appraisal themes on emotions both in the laboratory and from daily life. Both types of investigation have produced complementary findings

TABLE 14.2 Appraisal Dimensions for Emotion-Inducing Situations

Dimension	Definition
Novelty/Expectedness	To what extent did the person expect the situation?
Unpleasantness/Pleasantness	To what extent was the situation considered unpleasant or pleasant?
Goal hindrance/Helpfulness	To what extent did the situation hinder or help a person achieve her goals?
Unfairness/Fairness	To what extent was the event unjustified or undeserved versus justified?
Internal/External Causation	Who or what was responsible for the situation: yourself or other?
Coping Ability	How powerful or capable does a person feel in coping with the situation?
Immorality/Morality	To what extent did the person responsible for the situation act appropriately?
Self-Consistency	To what extent did the situation affect the person's self-confidence or self-esteem?
Importance or Value	What is the degree of importance or the value of the event to the individual?

Source: Based on Scherer (1997) but importance/value based on Smith & Kirby (2009).

about the link between appraisals and emotions. First, an emotion may depend on either the situation or on the appraisal, since different situations lead to different appraisals (Nezlek et al., 2008). However, the effects of appraisal are apparent when the same objective situation is identical for all participants (Siemer et al., 2007). Second, negative emotions such as guilt, shame, and sadness result from a person's decreased control of the situation whereas pleasure results from increased control. Third, emotions also differ on whether individuals hold themselves or someone else responsible. Self-responsibility leads to guilt, sadness, and shame, while other-responsibility leads to anger and amusement. Finally, several appraisal dimensions may be involved in the unfolding of an emotion. For example, joy stems from being in control, not holding others responsible, and experiencing success. Sadness stems from experiencing a loss and not feeling in control.

Pre-awareness of emotion event processing. One winter day walking behind two students on a snowy path, I observed that when one fell down her friend burst out laughing. The laughter occurred so quickly that any cognitive appraisal of the event must have been very rapid. "You looked so funny," she said to her fallen friend. In another instance, a male student and a female student were reading a bulletin board in the hall. He was standing behind her left shoulder and out of her line of vision. When turning to leave, she was immediately startled on detecting his presence. Her reaction happened so quickly that any appraisal of him must have been instantaneous. She said, "Oh, you scared me."

These examples illustrate that the appraisal process can occur very rapidly even before individuals are cognitively aware of focusing their attention on the situation (Roseman & Smith, 2001; Smith & Lazarus, 1990). Nonconscious appraisal below the level of awareness can be demonstrated with a procedure known as *subliminal priming* (sub = below, limen = threshold) (Tamietto & de Gelder, 2010). For example, an emotion word or picture is presented on a screen so fast that an individual did not detect it. Or an odor stimulus is presented, but so faintly that a person reports being unable to smell it. Although cognitively unaware, appraising subliminal stimuli occurs in an area of the brain labeled the **amygdala** (Liddell et al., 2005; Tamietto & de Gelder, 2010). This refers to a brain area that receives visual, auditory, taste, and smell information and uses that to make a quick and rough evaluation of the stimulus for a person's well-being. Evaluation can occur even when stimuli occur below the level of the individual's cognitive awareness (Costafreda et al., 2007).

For instance, the amygdala can detect some facial expressions of emotion prior to conscious awareness. Liddell and coresearchers (2005) presented photos depicting neutral or fear expressions below their participants' conscious awareness. Using fMRI, they were able to measure increased activity in the amygdala in response to the fear faces compared to neutral faces. The researchers hypothesized that the amygdala would be partly responsible for alerting the cortex, which is then in charge of instigating behavior to cope with the fear stimulus. The amygdala is also sensitive to happy faces. Juruena and coresearchers (2010) presented photos depicting happy, sad, and neutral expressions below the level of their participants' conscious awareness. Also using fMRI, they were able to measure increased activity in the amygdala in response to happy faces but not to sad faces when compared to neutral faces. The researchers reasoned that the salience of a sad face may not differ enough from a neutral face compared to the contrast between a happy and a neutral face.

Furthermore, stimuli presented below conscious awareness can also create positive or negative affect, which in turn influences conscious preferences (Winkielman & Berridge, 2004). For example, wearing cologne or perfume can both attract and repel others: attract if the odor is mild, repel if too strong. However, what if it were possible to pique someone's romantic interest in you by wearing a scent that is below that person's level of awareness? In this potential case, an individual experiences positive affect below his conscious awareness, but which can influence his conscious feelings of you. Li and coresearchers (2007) investigated this possibility using odors and likeability for facial expressions. The researchers presented their participants with pleasant (lemon), neutral, or unpleasant (sweat) odors. The intensity of each odor was below the participant's level of conscious awareness such that they claimed not to have smelled anything. Following this procedure, participants rated neutral facial expressions for likeability: *extremely unlikable* to *extremely likable*. The results of the ratings indeed indicated that faces were rated more likable following the pleasant odor and less likable following the unpleasant odor compared to ratings following the neutral odor. In this experiment, odor-induced affect acted nonconsciously— that is, below the individuals' level of awareness, but which influenced the likeability of neutral facial expressions.

Subliminally primed affect can also motivate behavior that fulfills the aim of the emotion. Thus, an individual may not be aware why she feels anxious, happy, or angry yet those emotional feelings will motivate avoidance, approach, or confrontational behavior, respectively. For instance, Wyer and Calvini (2011) subliminally primed their participants to feel threatened, tense, and sensitive to a menacing stimulus of a hostile person represented by a man in a hoodie. The experiment was conducted in Plymouth, England, where according to the Oxford English Dictionary a hoodie is "a young person who wears a hoodie and is typically regarded as socially disruptive . . . a hooligan, a thug" (p. 1231). A control group was subliminally presented the same young man but without his hoodie, a neutral prime. A follow-up evaluation indicated that the participants were unaware of the priming stimuli. Nevertheless, the subliminal presentation of the hoodie made the participants more anxious and threatened. They focused more strongly on threatening words on the computer screen, such as agony, coffin, or disease than did the control participants. It was important to verify this existence of sensitivity to threat because it explained the participants' subsequent avoidance behavior.

In the next phase of the experiment, participants were informed they had to work with another person who was temporarily out of the room. However, this individual's jacket and backpack were on a chair positioned at the far end of a table. The participants, however, were told they could begin work and to position their own chair for where they would like to sit. The experimenter measured the distance between the position of the participant's chair and the chair of the absent stranger. According to Wyer and Calvini (2011), this distance represents the participants' avoidance of the stranger. Did the prior subliminal priming with a threat stimulus and threat sensitivity influence the distance the participant chose to sit from the unknown individual? Yes, as shown in Figure 14.2. The participants experienced the subliminally primed anxiety and increased sensitivity to threat. This feeling, in turn, made them wary of strangers. Thus, they chose to sit farther away compared to the sitting distance of control participants, who had been primed with a neutral stimulus.

Priority of negative stimulus appraisal. Emotion-inducing events contrast with the background on which they occur. For example, shouts of anger, a friend's smile, or strange noises in the dark all stand out. However, are emotion stimuli equally noticeable or are potentially harmful stimuli noticed sooner than positive stimuli, as indicated in Figure 14.1? Based on evolutionary

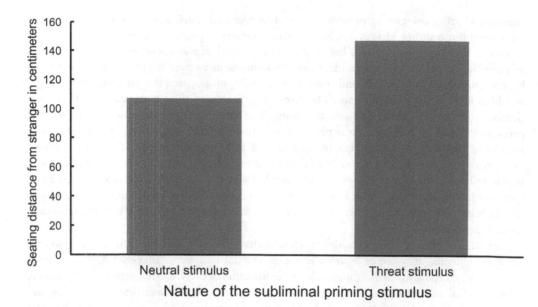

FIGURE 14.2 Subliminally Activated Threat Influences Avoidance Behavior. A subliminally presented threat stimulus (picture of a man in a hoodie) resulted in sitting further away from a stranger compared to the effect of a subliminally presented neutral stimulus (picture of same man without hoodie).

Source: Adapted from "Don't Sit So Close to Me: Unconsciously Elicited Affect Automatically Provokes Social Avoidance" by N. A. Wyer and G. Calvini, 2011, *Emotion, 11*, p. 1232.

psychology, a person benefits from quick appraisal of negative stimuli (danger), since fast escape leads to safety. Slow appraisal and slow escape, however, could result in injury or death. Speed of appraisal or approach to positive stimuli is not as crucial. Is there any evidence that appraisal of negative stimuli occurs prior to the appraisal of positive stimuli? Yes, dangerous stimuli grab attention sooner than safe stimuli. For instance, Fox and coresearchers (2007) measured whether a person could detect a snake or gun faster than a flower or mushroom. In the experiment, on some trials the picture of a single snake or gun was shown among four pictures of either flowers or mushrooms. On other trials, a single picture of a mushroom or flower was shown among four pictures of either snakes or guns. Which single picture will be detected sooner: snake or gun versus flower or mushroom? The results showed that snakes and guns were detected faster than flowers or mushrooms.

Do snakes have particular features that signal danger? For example, when walking in the woods are you more likely to detect stimuli shaped like an S versus a W? The S-shape resembles a snake while the W-shape resembles sticks. LoBue (2014) discovered that indeed people are able to identify and respond more quickly to wavy line stimuli compared to jagged line stimuli. Thus, individuals are biased to detect curvilinear shapes, which are representative of snakes. Furthermore, when anxious and fearful, people identify wavy lines even faster (LoBue, 2014).

These evaluation tendencies occur automatically and are also associated with behavioral tendencies. Negatively evaluated stimuli are associated with avoidance tendencies (to flee, withdraw), while positively evaluated stimuli are associated with approach tendencies (to contact, approach). One way to determine if stimuli and response tendencies of the same valence are automatically associated together is to see what happens when they are made incompatible—that is, avoidance responses are required to positive stimuli and approach responses are required to negative stimuli. Marsh and coresearchers (2005) reasoned that faces that indicate anger are perceived as aversive, since they signal danger and potential harm. Faces that indicate fear, on the other hand, are perceived to signal surrender and affiliation instead. Participants had to push or pull a computer joystick in response to whether an anger face or fear face appeared on the screen. In one condition, the requirement was to push a computer joystick away (avoidance) in response to anger faces and pull the joystick toward (approach) for fear faces. In the other condition, the requirement was the opposite: pull toward (approach) in response to anger faces and push away (avoidance) for fear faces. The results in Figure 14.3 show that avoidance responses were faster to the anger face than to the fear face. Approach responses, on the other hand, were faster to the fear face than to the anger face. The results of this experiment with faces show that action readiness is automatically attached to stimulus valence and occurs very early in the unfolding of emotions. In addition, the fastest action corresponds to the valence of the stimulus. Avoidance is faster to negative stimuli and approach is faster to positive stimuli.

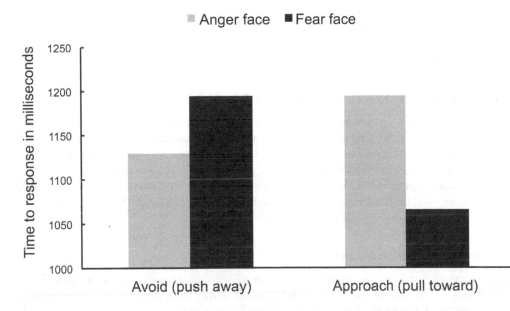

FIGURE 14.3 Speed of Reaction to Anger and Fear Faces. Avoidance responses (push away) were faster to anger faces than to fear faces while approach responses (pull toward) were faster to fear faces than to anger faces. Lower bars mean faster reaction times.

Source: Adapted from "The Effects of Fear and Anger Facial Expressions on Approach- and Avoidance-Related Behaviors" by A. A. Marsh et al., 2005, *Emotion, 5,* Table 1, p. 121.

Section Recap

According to the *situational definition* of emotion, it is the nature of an evolutionarily significant stimulus change that determines what emotion unfolds. All emotions in the same category stem from a similar set of stimulus changes. For example, approach of a positive stimulus defines happiness, its retreat defines disappointment, and being blocked promotes anger. The approach of a negative stimulus defines fear, its retreat defines relief, and being blocked produces gratitude. In addition, joy stems from gains, sadness from losses, fear from threat, anger from frustration or threat, and love from close association with other people. Emotion evolved to cope with consistent environmental problems that occurred in our evolutionary past, such as those described by the situational definition approach.

Emotion-inducing situations are complex and it is the outcome of the appraisal process that produces the emotions and not as a direct reaction to the unappraised situation. The event–appraisal–emotion sequence refers to the unfolding of an emotion that began with the evaluation of stimulus change and ended with the emotional reaction. Initial appraisal scans for negative features that may denote harm before proceeding with a more extensive analysis. Appraisal of emotion-inducing events occurs along several dimensions, such as expectedness, pleasantness, causation, coping ability, fairness, and importance. Evaluation of the emotion stimulus can occur very rapidly, without awareness, and impact physiological responses and behavior. The *amygdala* makes it possible to conduct a quick and crude analysis of the situation and do so below cognitive awareness. In the appraisal process, negative stimuli are detected sooner than positive stimuli. Negative and positive subliminal stimuli that are presented below awareness can evoke unpleasant and pleasant affect respectively and influence preferences. Furthermore, avoidance responses are more strongly associated with negative stimuli, while approach responses are associated with positive stimuli.

EMOTIONS MOTIVATE FACIAL EXPRESSIONS

Based on evolutionary psychology, the *response coherence postulate* is a working assumption regarding the function of emotions. Presumably, there is a master program that coordinates the different channels along which emotions operate much like an orchestra conductor synchronizes the individual musicians. This coordination is necessary in order to effectively deal with the environmental demands that people encounter (Tooby & Cosmides, 2005). Facial expression is one such channel. How well do facial expressions synchronize with other channels? What is the function of a facial expression for the self and for others?

Expression–Feeling Link

Facial expressions and emotional feelings (affect) are joined in an **expression–feeling link** (Izard, 1994). This means that different facial expressions are linked with different emotional feelings (see photos in Table 13.1). Thus, a smile is linked with happiness and tears are linked with sadness. Furthermore, as the intensity of the emotional feeling increases, the linked facial expressions become more vivid. What is the nature of this link?

One hypothesis is that the affective experience and expression simply correlate with each other. One does not cause the other, but both are in response to an emotion stimulus (Buck,

1984, 1985). For example, viewing sad movie scenes can evoke tears, moist eyes, and the urge to cry along with feelings of depression, sadness, and decreased happiness (Marston et al., 1984; Martin & Labott, 1991). Viewing a playful puppy, however, evokes a smile and feelings of happiness (Ekman et al., 1980a). Viewing cartoons evokes smiles, laughs, and feelings of amusement (Deckers, 1994). Comedy scenes evoke facial expressions showing pleasantness along with pleasant feelings. Unpleasant scenes such as traffic accidents and ritual suicides, however, evoke facial expressions indicating that the feelings are unpleasant (Zuckerman et al., 1981). Disgusting odors are considered very unpleasant and evoke facial expressions signifying disgust, while good-smelling odors are considered pleasant and evoke pleasant facial expressions (Kraut, 1982). A conclusion from these examples is that both affective experiences and facial reactions jointly occur in reaction to the emotion-inducing event.

Another view is that the affective experience produces the facial expression. Feeling happy results in a smile, while feeling sad results in tears. In fact, neural activity in the brain responsible for the subjective feeling is also responsible for movement of the facial muscles. According to the **efference hypothesis**, the activated brain circuit sends information to the facial muscles, which generate the expression that is synonymous with the emotional feeling (Camras et al., 1993; Izard, 1993). For example, an activated fear circuit stimulates facial muscles that produce the expression of fear, while a disgust circuit stimulates looks of disgust. The efference hypothesis supposes that emotion circuits exist in the brain. However, this assumption has been challenged (Barrett, 2017). If there are no circuits, then facial expressions are best considered as direct reactions to an external emotion stimulus.

Innateness of Facial Expression of Emotion

Facial expression is the public channel of emotion. Face-to-face conversation is difficult without attending to the nonverbal cues the face provides. But what is the function of these cues? Is it to inform others of what we feel or is it to signal to others what we want? Furthermore, from Figure 3.2, just as the area of a rectangle equals length × width, facial expressions result from heredity × experience. In other words, learning to express ourselves interacts with our existing innate disposition to do so. How can we show that facial expressions have both innate and learning components?

Facial expression in early life. Facial expressions occur long before learning could have had much influence. Recall from Chapter 3 that newborn infants made facial reactions to various taste stimuli. In reaction to sweet, sour, and bitter tastes, infants made sweet, sour, and bitter faces. A person might argue that taste sensations are not emotions. However, the infants were making facial expressions consistent with adult taste experiences (Mennella & Beauchamp, 1998; Steiner, 1977).

In addition to reacting to taste, infants show facial expressions of emotion within the first few months of life. Izard and associates (1995) recorded the expressions made by 2.5 to nine-month-old infants during pleasant or mildly stressful interactions with their mothers. During these interactions a mother showed interest and joy while playing with her infant, or she showed a sad, angry, or still expression. Infants at 2.5 months were already sensitive to their mothers. They exhibited facial expressions of interest, joy, sadness, and anger. Furthermore, the infants' expressions also depended on their mothers' emotional expressions. For instance, at six months of age infants expressed sadness, anger, and decreased joy to their mothers' sadness and expressed more anger and interest in reaction to their mothers' anger. However, infants generally showed a much greater frequency of positive expressions in reaction to their mothers' positive expressions.

Facial expression in deaf and blind children. The rudiments of facial expressions of emotion are present in children who are blind and deaf. Eibl-Eibesfeldt (1973) observed six such children smiling, laughing, crying in distress and anger, frowning, pouting, and showing surprise. Furthermore, the situations producing these expressions were the same for deaf and blind children as for normally developed children. Of particular interest was Sabine, who was born with no eyesight and was totally deaf. Yet she exhibited expressions in much the same manner as a hearing and seeing child. For example, Sabine smiled "when she sat by herself in the sun patting her face with the palms of her hands" (p. 175). She also smiled when she was patted, tickled, or engaged in social play. Sabine exhibited angry crying when someone persistently presented her with an object that she did not like or social contact that she did not want. She would also pout afterward. Sabine exhibited surprise when she sniffed a pungent-smelling object, much like a hearing and seeing person would. Eibl-Eibesfeldt (1973) felt that these facial expressions were innate and concluded that learning refines facial expressions. "The deaf-and-blind often lack the minute gradation of an expression. An expression suddenly appears, and equally suddenly wanes without warning leaving a completely blank face" (p. 192).

The YouTube channel for the California Academy of Sciences contains a link to a YouTube video titled "Facial expressions of emotion for seeing and blind individuals" here: www.youtube.com/user/calacademy and here: www.youtube.com/watch?v=5G6ZR5lJgTI.

Learning and fine-tuning of expressions. Eibl-Eibesfeldt's (1973) conclusion that the blind lack "minute gradation of an expression" implies a role for learning. Does experience interact with innate factors to form facial expressions in sighted individuals? For instance, Ekman and associates (1980b) instructed five-, nine-, and 13-year-old children to display facial expressions of anger, disgust, fear, happiness, and sadness. The ability of the children to make these facial movements increased with age. Blind children, however, did not become better at posing as they got older; they became less adept. Fulcher (1942) photographed sighted children and blind children while they posed with a happy, sad, angry, or afraid expression. Fulcher rated how close the child's pose matched the expression judged to be appropriate for that particular emotion. His ratings showed that facial poses of sighted children were judged to be more adequate than the poses of blind children. The poses of blind children became less precise as they got older, while those of the sighted children became more refined.

More recent research shows that learning allows for fine-tuning of expressions. Rinn (1991; cited in Galati et al., 1997) concluded that blind individuals do not develop suitable control over their facial muscles because they lack practice and do not benefit from feedback. Galati and associates (1997) had individuals blind from birth and normally sighted individuals portray neutral, surprise, anger, joy, disgust, sadness, and fear expressions. A different group of sighted individuals was then asked to identify what emotional expression was being conveyed. It was easiest for judges to identify the expression of joy. They had more difficulty, however, identifying the expressions of surprise, anger, disgust, and a neutral expression of blind individuals compared to those of sighted individuals. In a later study, with children younger than four years, different facial intensities between positive and negative emotions were also clearer in normally sighted children than in blind children (Galati et al., 2001).

Universality of facial expression of emotion. Emotion researchers have assumed that basic emotions are common in all humans and that each has a corresponding unique facial expression. Furthermore, since these facial expressions are innate, they should be recognizable in different cultures. Izard (1971) and Ekman (1973; Ekman & Friesen, 1971) conducted a series of **emotion recognition** studies in which they asked people in different countries to identify the emotion portrayed by various facial expressions. Slides of facial expressions are shown on a screen, and you are to identify the emotion it portrays from a list containing these options: happiness, disgust, surprise, anger, sadness, and fear. If facial expressions are universal, then participants the world over should agree on what emotions are represented. Ekman's (1973) study employed participants from five different countries representing a variety of cultures and languages: Argentina, Brazil, Chile, Japan, and the United States. They were shown several photographs representing a specific emotion. Members of the different countries showed high agreement in identifying what emotions each facial expression represented. Izard (1971) showed pictures of facial expressions representing eight basic emotions to people from the United States, Europe, Greece, Japan, and Africa. He also found high agreement among the different cultures in identifying these expressions. Furthermore, Ekman and Friesen (1971) also found that a culture whose members had never seen movies or television could still correctly identify the facial expressions of emotion in Westerners.

High agreement, however, in identifying emotional expressions is not the same as perfect agreement. In a closer analyses of eight such experiments, Russell (1994) noticed that emotion identification was not perfect (see Figure 14.4). First, participants from Western countries were better at identifying facial expressions than were individuals from non-Western countries. Second, happiness was the easiest expression to recognize in both sets of countries. However, recognition was lower for negative emotions. Sadness, fear, disgust, and anger were identified correctly an average of 81 percent of the time by individuals from Western countries but only about 65 percent of the time by individuals from non-Western countries. This analysis in Figure 14.4 questions whether each basic emotion has a specific corresponding facial expression.

Specificity of facial expression of emotion. If expressions are not recognized equally by all cultures, does that mean that facial expressions of emotion are not universal but instead are specific to a culture? Does culture modify the innate configuration of an emotion expression? Modified configurations illustrate differences in the **dialect of facial expressions**. In the case of language, for instance, dialects refer to differences in word pronunciation, meaning, and grammar that occur in various regions of a country or with groups of people. Differences in the dialect of expressions make identifying facial displays of emotion more difficult among cultures. In a relevant investigation, Elfenbein and coresearchers (2007) took photos of facial expressions of participants from two different cultures: Gabon, on the western coast of Africa, and Quebec. The researchers hypothesized that cultural differences in the expression of emotion should make cross-culture identification more difficult than same-culture identification. Dialect differences were evident in two ways. First, facial muscle movement was different between the two cultures, especially for emotions that send signals to other people, such as anger, happiness, sadness, and shame. Second, a same-culture advantage was evident in correctly identifying facial expressions of those same emotions. Participants identified facial expressions of their own culture more accurately than that of the other culture.

Cultural differences also show up for facial movements that are identified as emotional. A facial movement is expressive of an emotion provided that a person recognizes it as such.

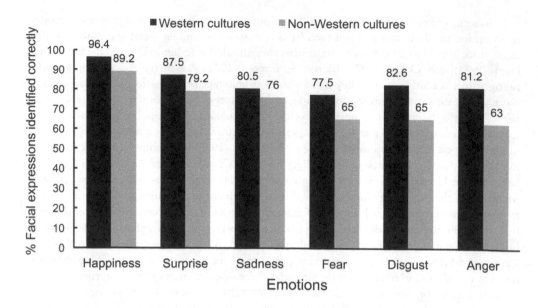

FIGURE 14.4 Identifying Facial Expressions of Emotion across Cultures. In eight different investigations, individuals from Western and non-Western cultures indicated the basic emotion shown on a face. The graph shows the median percentage of correct identifications. Happy expressions were classified correctly the most while fear, disgust, and anger were classified correctly the least, especially for non-Western cultures such as China, Japan, Malaysia, and Ethiopia.

Source: Adapted from "Is There Universal Recognition of Emotion from Facial Expressions? A Review of the Cross-Cultural Studies" by J. A. Russell, 1994, *Psychological Bulletin, 115,* Table 2, p. 108.

For example, imagine a face that makes random movements. Some movements will be unfamiliar and meaningless, while others will indicate emotions. Will people of different cultures identify identical or different movements as indicating emotions? Jack and coresearchers (2012) displayed random facial movements on a computer screen to individuals from the West and from East Asia (Chinese). Participants indicated when they perceived an emotion on the display. Cultural differences emerged regarding what facial movement indicated an emotion. East Asians focused on the eyes sooner for identifying anger, disgust, fear, and happiness. Western participants, on the other hand, relied more on other aspects of the face for identifying those emotions. Furthermore, Westerners showed clear distinctions in identifying basic emotions, while East Asians did this to a lesser extent. They embraced more overlap among emotion categories, especially for anger, disgust, fear, and surprise. The researchers concluded that innate facial expressions of emotion have been modified to meet the social requirements of a specific culture.

Function of Facial Expression

Can you put your emotional feelings into words, or do you leave that up to songwriters, poets, and novelists? Perhaps our faces do a better job. People often judge us by the facial communication of our feelings and not by what we say, as if the face, rather than words, is a more accurate conveyor of emotion. As described earlier, the efference hypothesis maintains that an emotion circuit in the brain sends information to the facial muscles to create an expression (Camras et al., 1993). What is the function of these expressions? To answer this question, two hypotheses have emerged.

Two hypotheses on the function of facial expression. "Pass the salt!" Does this mean I have a craving for salt or that I simply want you to hand me the shaker, since I cannot reach it? Similarly, do tears indicate sadness, or are they a plea for help? Does a smile mean happiness, or is it a reward one friend bestows on another?

According to the **readout hypothesis**, a facial expression conveys an individual's emotional feeling to another individual (Buck, 1984, 1991, 1994; Ekman, 1984). A facial expression is like a dial that registers the emotional feelings, much like the car's gas gauge is a readout of the amount of gasoline in the tank or the thermometer indicates the room temperature. This relationship is the *expression–feeling link*. According to Buck (1984), "It is useful for social animals to be able to communicate their internal states of anger, fear, interest, sexual excitement, and so forth, to their fellows without actually having to engage in overt behaviors associated with those states" (p. 36). Thus, tears communicate sadness and a smile communicates happiness. In contrast, according to the **behavioral ecology hypothesis**, facial expressions "are issued to serve one's social motives" in a particular situation and need not be linked to emotional feelings (Chovil & Fridlund, 1991; Fridlund, 1991, 1992, 1994). Fridlund (1991) points out that "if we exhibit social inclinations and we are emotional, our faces signal the former and not the latter" (p. 69). Table 14.3 compares the meaning of facial expressions according to the readout hypothesis and the behavioral ecology hypothesis.

People are able to infer social motives from the facial expressions that other individuals exhibit. Yik and Russell (1999) presented photos of facial expressions that displayed surprise, happiness, disgust, sadness, anger, fear, and contempt. The participants (who were Canadian, Hong Kong Chinese, and Japanese) were required to match the faces with a list of social messages—for example, what face matches the statement "Back off or I'll attack" or matches "Don't hurt me! I give up"? The matching results showed that all groups were able to identify a face with its corresponding social message and also with the emotion a face displayed.

Motivational power of facial expressions. Are you affected by another person's smile or tears? The smiles and tears of adults also motivate other adults with the smile being the most obvious. First, people definitely prefer to see genuine smiles in other individuals compared to polite smiles.

TABLE 14.3 Interpretations of Facial Expressions According to the Readout Hypothesis and the Behavioral Ecology Hypothesis

Facial Expression	Readout Hypothesis: Face Communicates	Behavioral Ecology Hypothesis: Face Communicates
Smile	Happiness	Friendship, friendliness, no threat
Cry	Sadness, grief	Need for help, readiness to receive help/comfort
Anger	Annoyance, anger, fury	Verbal attack, physical attack
Fear	Worry, fear, terror	Readiness to submit, desire to be rescued
Disgust	Offended, disgusted, sickened	Reaction to bad-smelling or bad-tasting object
Blush	Ashamed, embarrassed	Make amends, reduce salience of others

Genuine smiles also serve as better social reinforcers than polite (fake) smiles do (Shore & Heerey, 2011). Second, smiles are more likely to elicit helping behavior compared to neutral expressions. In one naturalistic experiment, researchers in Amsterdam asked passers-by to "please participate in an investigation?" (Vrugt & Vet, 2009, p. 1253). This request concluded by the experimenter exhibiting either a clear smile or a neutral expression. Passers-by were more likely to agree to help when the experimenter had smiled. Furthermore, the passers-by reported a higher positive mood when the experimenter smiled at them compared to the neutral expression. Third, people are more likely to approach smiling individuals than those showing neutral expressions. Willis and coresearchers (2011) showed their participants individuals who exhibited either happy (smile) or neutral facial expressions. Next, participants were asked to imagine approaching such an individual in a crowd with the intent of asking directions. Participants reported being more likely to approach an individual with a smiling face compared to a neutral face.

The sight of tears is another powerful motivator of behavior. Hendriks and Vingerhoets (2006) showed their participants photos of people posing with the following expressions: crying, anger, fear, and a neutral expression. Participants rated these faces for whether they would react with emotional support, such as calming, comforting, helping, sympathizing, or crying along with that person. Emotional support reactions were highest toward individuals who posed with crying expressions than with fear expressions and lowest for those with neutral poses. In a follow-up experiment, Hendriks and coresearchers (2008) presented participants with different social vignettes. In one version, individuals cried while in others they did not. For example, you are at a funeral or party or have met someone who won the lottery. In some vignettes one of the characters cries, while in the other version the same character does not. Participants rated their degree of emotional support for the individual on such dimensions as calming, comforting, or helping him or her. Participants clearly indicated greater emotional support when the character in the vignette was crying compared to not crying.

Whereas smiles and tears tend to elicit approach behavior, anger expressions motivate avoidance behavior. Willis and coresearchers (2011) asked participants to imagine approaching a person exhibiting an angry, happy, or neutral expression. Participants reported being unlikely to approach an individual exhibiting an angry compared to a happy or neutral expression. Hendriks and Vingerhoets (2006) showed their participants people exhibiting crying, anger, fear, or neutral faces. Participants also rated how they would react to people exhibiting such expressions, such as avoiding, ignoring, or getting angry with that person. These reactions were strongest toward a person exhibiting an angry expression and lowest to a crying expression. However, people will approach an angry face if that expression signals a social challenge that must be overcome in order to reach one's goal (Wilkowski & Meier, 2010).

Social facial vasodilation. Blood rushing to a person's face during shame and embarrassment is a curious reaction because it is not universally visible in all individuals. Visibility depends on skin color, which in some cases masks blushing. To investigate this possibility, Simon and Shields (1996) asked university students of various racial/ethnic groups the following questions: when you blush, does your face (1) get hot plus change color, (2) change color only, or (3) get hot only? The answers depended on the skin color of the students. The majority of light-skinned students reported that their face got hot and changed color, while the majority of dark-skinned students reported that their face got hot but did not noticeably change color. Nevertheless, blushing implies getting "red in the face." Since this is not readily observable in all people, Leary and coresearchers (1992) have suggested the term **social facial vasodilation**, which means that during certain social situations the small blood vessels of the face and neck expand to permit increased blood flow into those areas. But, if blushing is not observable in all individuals, then what is its function for communication?

Generally, undesired social attention is the major circumstance that elicits social facial vasodilation, such as being evaluated, scrutinized, stared at, criticized, or praised excessively. Blushing also results if the person violated social norms and is considered incompetent, rude, or immoral or if the person has not lived up to a public self-image as a result of criticism or from being overly praised. There may be two reasons, in accordance with the behavioral ecology hypothesis, why people blush: appeasement and escape from unwanted attention (Leary et al., 1992). The appeasement function is to show that the person cares about social norms and wants to repair any social damage that was caused. It is an attempt to admit error, apologize, or placate the offended individuals in order to deter retaliation, aggression, or banishment. For example, your cell phone sounded during your professor's lecture. The skin of your face became red or darkened in order to appease the professor and surrounding students—that is, you are truly sorry for disturbing the class. The escape function also notes that blushing is often accompanied by the lowering of one's head and averting one's gaze. These actions are designed to escape or deflect the scrutiny of others and thereby make those individuals less salient or noticeable. In this case, when the cell phone rings, individuals also avert their gaze from others in order to make the scrutiny of others less salient or noticeable.

Display rules for facial expressions. Is that smile real or fake? Are those tears real or fake? These questions imply that real expressions are spontaneous (occur involuntarily), while fake expressions are voluntary (occur at will). Several differences exist between these two types of expression. First, a spontaneous facial expression is elicited by an external stimulus, while a voluntary expression is emitted and does not require a stimulus. Second, a spontaneous expression occurs immediately after the eliciting stimulus, while a voluntary expression can also occur immediately or after a delay. Third, the intensity of the spontaneous expression is directly related to the intensity of the eliciting stimulus, while a voluntary expression can occur independently of stimulus intensity. Fourth, the spontaneous/voluntary distinction is reflected in the facial muscles that are responsible for a smile. A spontaneous smile of enjoyment involves the outer portion of the muscle circling the eye, whereas a voluntary or deceitful smile does not (Ekman et al., 1990). Finally, another useful distinction concerns their brain origins. Spontaneous expressions originate from an evolutionary older part of the brain known as the extrapyramidal system. Voluntary expressions, on the other hand, originate in what is known as the cortical motor strip (Rinn, 1984). Both sources send information to the facial nerves, which connect onto facial muscles for the formation of an expression.

The question of whether an expression is real or fake implies that a person can shape an expression to serve his or her purpose. The expressions are not spontaneous but instead are voluntary and governed by social situations. **Display rules** refer to social conventions that govern the expressions individuals must exhibit in public. They need not be linked to emotional feelings (Ekman & Friesen, 1975; Matsumoto et al., 2005). According to Matsumoto and coresearchers (2005), "display rules are cognitive representations of social conventions about emotional displays" (p. 29). For example, do you know what expression to display when receiving a gift, when being reprimanded, and when angry with your boss or romantic partner?

TABLE 14.4 Displays from the *Display Rule Assessment Inventory*

Amplify	Intensify or exaggerate the expression of your feelings
Not inhibit	Express your feelings naturally
Deamplify	Reduce the intensity of the expression of your feelings
Qualify	Express your feelings but add an accompanying expression (e.g., smile)
Neutralize	Show a neutral face not indicative of any emotional feeling
Mask	Show a different expression than what you are feeling; cover up with a smile

Source: Adapted from "Development and Validation of a Measure of Display Rule Knowledge: The Display Rule Assessment Inventory" by D. Matsumoto et al., 2005, *Emotion, 5,* p. 40.

The *Display Rule Assessment Inventory* measures the extent that people feel they should alter their facial expressions in the presence of family members, close friends, colleagues, and strangers in various situations (Matsumoto et al., 2005). The *Inventory* describes six different facial management techniques, which are shown in Table 14.4. With the not-inhibit procedure, individuals display facial expressions that match their emotional feelings. If you see an anger expression on her face, then she is angry with you. If you see a smile on his face, then he is happy to see you. The other procedures, however, are used by the individuals to alter their facial expressions independent of their emotional feelings. For example, a father might feel it is necessary to amplify his smile of appreciation when he receives a valentine card from his young son. However, a person might feel she should inhibit her expression of anger at a dining companion. Perhaps one feels he should use a mask technique in order to hide the disappointment when a friend lets him down. Finally, the boss reprimands a worker for making an error but feels it necessary to add a qualifying smile in order to indicate absence of anger.

The web page of David Matsumoto (Research Tools) provides a link to the *Display Rule Assessment Inventory* (DRAI) here: www.davidmatsumoto.com and here: www.davidmatsumoto. com/content/AbridgedDRAI.pdf.

Section Recap

According to the *expression–feeling link*, a spontaneous facial expression is linked to the emotional feeling. The *efference hypothesis* holds that a specific emotion circuit in the brain connects to the facial muscles to generate the unique expression linked with the emotion. Spontaneous facial expressions are innate but then modified by experience. Expressions occur very early in life, are present in blind and deaf children, and are fine-tuned by experience. In *emotion recognition* studies, participants identify the emotion shown on a facial expression. Smiles of happiness are identified the most accurately the world over while negative emotions are recognized accurately in about 81 percent of the cases by Westerners and 65 percent by non-Westerners. Facial expressions show the effects of *dialect of facial expressions*, which means that each culture molds the innate expressions to their liking. Dialect results in an in-group advantage, which means we can more accurately recognize the facial expression of someone from our culture compared to a different culture.

The function of facial expression is to communicate a person's emotional feeling according to the *readout hypothesis*. A smile communicates happiness, and tears communicate sadness. Facial expressions can also signal a person's intent or social motive, according to the *behavioral ecology hypothesis*. A person smiles, for example, as a signal to maintain contact with another person whereas tears are requests for help. People are more likely to approach individuals who smile or cry but tend to avoid anger expressions. *Social facial vasodilation* refers to blood rushing to a person's face, which is commonly known as blushing. A person blushes as appeasement for having violated a social norm and to repair any social damage. Two types of facial muscle movements produce emotional expressions. Voluntary control of facial movement is made at will and independent of or without any emotion stimulus. Spontaneous movements, on the other hand, are considered involuntary, are evoked by the emotion stimulus, and accompany emotional feelings. Voluntary movements are often governed by social customs or *display rules*, which dictate what expression an individual should exhibit in public. For example, an individual smiles when receiving a gift.

THE MOTIVATING FUNCTION OF EMOTIONS

Emotions motivate behavior toward some designated end, which is the goal or aim of the emotion. But, how are behaviors and thoughts channeled to achieve that goal?

Emotions as Motives for Behavior

If a stimulus is dangerous or disgusting, then wouldn't it be appropriate for the person to run away from danger or spit out the disagreeable substance? And if a situation is beneficial, then shouldn't it be preserved? In each of these examples, emotion serves as a **motive for action** to induce the individual to deal specifically with the emotional event (Frijda, 1994). The person is in a state of *action readiness*, which is the impulse or urge to behave in a particular manner (Frijda, 1986, 2007). Some action tendencies of emotion are innate, as if they are already wired into the nervous system. Other action tendencies result from learning and occur only after some deliberation (Clark & Watson, 1994; Scherer, 1994).

Different emotions have different goals. Some possible goals of basic emotions and the actions they motivate are summarized in Table 14.5 (Ellsworth & Smith, 1988; Frijda, 1994; Izard, 1993). Joy acts like a reward for achievement and accompanies consummatory behavior. For sadness, the event is appraised as an irrevocable or uncontrollable loss. The goal of sadness is to signal others for help when we cannot help ourselves. In fear, we appraise a stimulus as dangerous and harmful. The goal of fear is to motivate avoidance and escape behavior in order to reach safety. For anger, we appraise a situation or other person as blocking our goal or as detrimental to our well-being. The goal of anger is to motivate a person to remove the obstacle or person who is potentially harmful to us. The goal of disgust is to avoid becoming ill or contaminated. This is achieved by an active rejection of the repelling substance. Self-conscious emotions of shame, guilt, embarrassment, and pride serve as social motives for a person's interactions with others (Leary, 2007; Tangney et al., 2007). Shame is the result of a self-evaluation that focused on the self as a bad or unworthy person. Guilt is the negative evaluation of some misdeed. The goal of shame is to maintain the respect of others along with one's self-esteem. Shame motivates denying or escaping shame-inducing situations and avoiding and withdrawing from other individuals (Barrett & Campos, 1987). Guilt, however, motivates attempts to make amends, apologies, and in general undo the effects of one's misdeeds (Ellsworth & Smith, 1988; Tangney et al., 2007). Embarrassment results when a person violates a social norm and others derive a negative conclusion of that person (Leary, 2007). The goal of embarrassment is to promote

TABLE 14.5 Goals of Emotions and the Actions They Motivate

Emotion	Goal	Action Tendency
Joy/Happiness	To reward goal achievement To motivate consummatory behavior (eating, sex)[a] To maintain social interaction[b]	Any instrumental behavior achieving goals, leading to consummatory behavior, or maintaining interactions
Sadness	To seek help to make harm or loss easier to bear[c] To bring people together To scrutinize the cause of the sadness[b] To promote disengagement from the lost object/person[a]	Sad facial expression signals others to help;[c] behavioral and thinking activities slow down[b]
Fear	To motivate escape from danger[a,b] To focus attention on stimulus for danger[b,c]	Avoid, escape, freeze, tonic immobility depending on the stimulus and situation
Anger	To remove obstacle blocking goal[c] To discourage another's anger or aggression[a,b]	Actual removal of goal-blocking obstacle;[c] angry state discourages other's aggression[b]
Disgust	To maintain clean environment for survival[b] To keep person from harmful substances[b]	Nausea, vomiting, escaping, avoiding the disgusting object
Shame	To maintain respect of others, restore self-esteem[f]	Escape, avoid situation and people[d]
Guilt	To undo effect of one's misdeeds[c,f]	Make amends, apologize[c,f]
Embarrassment	To restore harmonious social relationships[e]	Withdraw, apologize, explain[e]
Pride	To reinforce successful achievement of socially valued behaviors[g]	Act altruistically, treat others well[g]

Notes:

a Frijda, 1994.
b Izard, 1993.
c Ellsworth and Smith, 1988.
d Barrett and Campos, 1987.
e Keltner and Anderson, 2000.
f Tangney et al., 2007.
g Tracy and Robins, 2007.

appeasement through withdrawal, apologies, or explanations as the means of restoring harmonious social relations (Keltner & Anderson, 2000). In contrast, pride is a positive emotion that reinforces successful achievement and behaviors that are socially valued. Thus, pride motivates a person to act altruistically and to treat others well (Tracy & Robins, 2007).

Emotions as Motives for Cognitive Activity

Does how we feel influence how we think, evaluate, and decide on an action? When happy, are we optimistic in what is achievable, but when unhappy does pessimism reign? In addition to motivating behavior, emotions motivate thinking. Emotional feelings influence decision-making in various ways (Lerner et al., 2015). The feelings can arise in the current situation or carry over from other events. For example, taking a test evokes anxiety currently and thus influences your exam performance. But your exam performance may also suffer from a feeling of sadness that carried over from a different situation, such as having been jilted. Affect sways the valence and scope of an individual's thinking and accordingly biases appraisal, judgment, and decision-making. In addition, a person's affect can alter the scope and depth of that thinking.

Emotions influence decisions. An emotion stimulus can alter a person's affect, which in turn influences cognitive appraisal. But, rather than a specific emotion, it may be that the valence of the emotion influences appraisal and judgment. For instance, we think optimistically when happy but pessimistically when anxious or sad. Anxiety and sadness are both negative emotions and thus influence our thinking the same way. However, according to Lerner and Keltner's (2000) **appraisal tendency hypothesis**, each emotion has a unique influence on people's judgments. For example, Lerner and Keltner (2001) induced feelings of anger or fear in their participants by having them describe events that made them most angry or most fearful. Next, participants rated hypothetical situations for the extent they would feel in control and for the extent such situations were predictable. Even though both anger and fear are negative emotions, they affected the ratings differently. Angered participants rated themselves as having more personal control and felt the situations were more predictable than fearful participants did.

The unique feel of an emotion can also affect a person's judgments about unrelated events. In a field experiment, Lerner and coresearchers (2003) had 973 respondents reply to e-mail messages that were designed to induce either fear or anger. Following the inducement, participants were asked to evaluate the likelihood of future risks, such as another terrorist attack on the United States or on themselves. Risk estimates depended on the emotion that had been induced. Angered respondents rated the likelihood of these risks to be lower than frightened respondents did. The respondents were also asked to rate their level of support for the following two government policies: (1) "Deport foreigners in the U.S. who lack valid visas" or (2) "Strengthen ties with countries in the Muslim world." The ratings showed that, when angered, respondents were more likely to retaliate—that is, more in favor of deporting foreigners who lacked visas. However, when afraid, respondents were more likely to be conciliatory—that is, more in favor of trying to establish better relations with Muslim countries. In addition, feelings of anger that resulted from the actual September 11 terrorist attacks also resulted in greater endorsement of the policy to deport foreigners and less endorsement of strengthening ties with the Muslim world.

Do our emotional feelings also influence the common dilemma of choosing between a small immediate reward versus a large delayed reward? As described in Chapter 10, decisions may involve a choice between a small reward available now versus a larger reward available later. For example, choose between $25 available now versus $50 available in three months. Would your decision be based on your emotions? Lerner and coresearchers (2013) speculate that, in the case of sadness, people are impatient. Sad individuals decide on a small reward immediately in order to feel better right away. A feeling of disgust, on the other hand, produces an avoidance orientation that involves ejecting an aversive substance. In this orientation, people may be more willing to wait for the larger reward. To test these ideas, Lerner and coresearchers (2013, exp. 2) used video clips to induce sadness, disgust, or a neutral feeling. Afterwards, participants wrote essays to further intensify these feelings. Next, participants made a series of choices between Amazon gift cards worth different amounts. The choices ranged from a $50 gift card available immediately versus a card worth $55 to $105 available three months later. Before making their choices, participants were also asked to list what thoughts were going through their minds. Did these thoughts favor receiving the money now, later, both, or neither?

Thus, the procedure required participants to choose between a $50 gift card available immediately versus a larger gift card available after three months. For example, decide between each of the following choices:

Choice 1: $50 card now versus $55 card in three months.
Choice 2: $50 card now versus $60 card in three months.
Choice 3: $50 card now versus $65 card in three months.
(and so on to the last choice, i.e., choice 11)
Choice 11: $50 card now versus $105 card in three months.

When will individuals who feel sad, disgusted, or neutral switch from the $50 card to the larger gift card available in three months? If sad participants are indeed impatient, then they should persist longer at choosing the $50 card, since it is available immediately—that is, no waiting. More money will need to be added to the delayed card for sad participants to switch, since they will now have to wait. Disgusted and neutral participants, on the other hand, who are patient and willing to wait, should switch sooner to a larger delayed gift card. Less money needs to be added to the delayed card, since they are willing to wait anyway. The results confirmed these hypotheses. As shown in Figure 14.5, sad participants required more money to become patient. In other words, not until $31 had been added were they willing to wait the three months for the more valuable delayed card—that is, not until it exceeded $81 did they choose it. Disgusted and neutral participants, however, showed their patience by choosing the delayed gift card when only $23 had been added to it—that is, when it exceeded $73 they chose it. Thus, more money is required to motivate sad participants to wait compared to what is required for disgusted and neutral participants. Impatience was also reflected in the thoughts of the sad participants. They listed more impatient thoughts and listed them sooner compared to the thought listings of the disgusted and neutral participants. The latter two did not differ in their thoughts. Sadness, rather than disgust or neutral, fostered thoughts about receiving a reward sooner, even if smaller. These thoughts provided the reasons for deciding to choose the more immediate gift card.

Effects of affect intensity. The intensity of affect also influences the scope of an individual's thinking. As noted a century and a quarter ago by Paulhan (1887/1930), emotions flood consciousness. As a consequence, our attention is drawn to both the valence and intensity of affect. Presumably as intensity increases, the focus of attention increases and thereby restricts the scope of thought. For example, if the noise in the kitchen frightens an individual, then not much thought will be spent on planning dinner but instead will be focused on the noise. On the other hand, if you realize the noise is your roommate, then the relief allows you to think about many other things, including dinner plans. Is there any empirical support for these conjectures—that is, does the valence and intensity of affect influence the scope of thinking?

Reasoning from Paulhan's conjecture, one idea is that as affect intensity increases the scope of cognitive processing decreases (Gable & Harmon-Jones, 2010a). One method that determines the scope of cognitive processing is to determine on what stimulus properties a person focuses. For example, what is the first thing that you see in the two stimuli in Table 14.6: large T and F or small Fs and Ts? If you claim to see either the larger letter T or F, then you have engaged

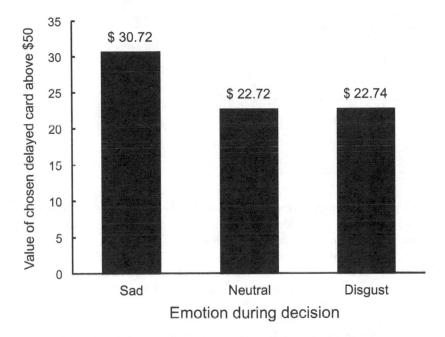

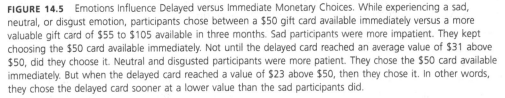

FIGURE 14.5 Emotions Influence Delayed versus Immediate Monetary Choices. While experiencing a sad, neutral, or disgust emotion, participants chose between a $50 gift card available immediately versus a more valuable gift card of $55 to $105 available in three months. Sad participants were more impatient. They kept choosing the $50 card available immediately. Not until the delayed card reached an average value of $31 above $50, did they choose it. Neutral and disgusted participants were more patient. They chose the $50 card available immediately. But when the delayed card reached a value of $23 above $50, then they chose it. In other words, they chose the delayed card sooner at a lower value than the sad participants did.

Source: Adapted from "The Financial Costs of Sadness" by J. S. Lerner et al., 2013, *Psychological Science, 24,* p. 75.

in broad or *global processing*. However, if you focused on the smaller Fs and Ts that compose the large letters, then you have engaged in narrow *local processing*. In actual experiments, participants are instructed to make a decision as fast as possible about the location of the large T or F or about the location of the smaller Fs or Ts. Faster decision-reaction times to the large stimuli indicate a broad or global focus of attention, while a faster decision-reaction time to the small letters indicates narrow or local focus of attention (Gable & Harmon-Jones, 2010a).

As affect intensity increases, there is a tendency to change from global to local processing regardless of the valence of the affect. Gable and Harmon-Jones (2008, exp. 4) manipulated the intensity of positive affect by having participants view either neutral pictures, pictures of dessert, or pictures of dessert with the expectation of eating it at the conclusion of the experiment. These mood induction procedures were followed by the letter-position decision task. Participants in the neutral condition had faster decision times to the large letters than to the small ones, which indicated they had a broad focus of attention. The reverse was true for participants who expected to eat the dessert. Their decision time to the large letters was much slower than that

TABLE 14.6 On What Do You Focus First?

TTTTT	FFFFFFF
T	F
TTTT	F
T	F
T	F

On what do you focus first?
Large F and T or small Ts and Fs?

Global attention for large letters
Focal attention for small letters

of the neutral condition participants, which indicates that their global attention span had reduced. Thus, when positive affect is of low intensity, more attention can be devoted to exploring the environment. However, when positive affect is of high intensity, less attention is paid to the environment and more is devoted to affect itself and the aim of that affect.

The influence of affect intensity has been replicated with negative emotions. In one experiment, Gable and Harmon-Jones (2010b) presented sad pictures to their participants in order to induce sadness. In a second experiment, they presented disgusting pictures in order to induce disgust. The researchers reasoned that sadness is a negative emotion of low intensity, while disgust is a negative emotion of high intensity. Each experiment contained a control group, which saw neutral pictures. Mood induction was followed by the letter-position decision task. The results indicated that the sad participants made faster decisions regarding the large T and F and slower decision times regarding the small Fs and Ts. This result meant that sadness as a weak emotion promoted a global attention span. The results for disgust, on the other hand, showed the opposite effect. Decision times were relatively faster for the small Fs and Ts than for the large T and F, which indicates a reduction in global processing—that is, a more narrow or local focus of attention. Thus, a weak emotion such as sadness broadens an individual's cognitive focus, while a strong emotion such as disgust decreases that focus.

Motivational Nature of Positive Emotions

Emotions divide into two categories: negative and positive. Negative emotions serve as current motives for immediate action. They support impulsive behaviors that bring about immediate rather than delayed outcomes. For example, anger is felt in the present and motivates immediate action to redress a wrong. Likewise, fear motivates escape behavior toward safety, right now, not later. Positive emotions, such as happiness, act more like positive incentives. Their motivating effect comes from anticipating their occurrence in the future. So, what effects do positive emotions such as happiness have on thought and behavior?

Happiness. What is happiness? **Subjective well-being** or happiness is a private experience that an individual strives to bring into consciousness while its opposite or unhappiness an individual strives to drive out of consciousness. To be happy means that a person is highly satisfied with life and experiences positive affect (glad, cheerful) more frequently than negative affect (anxious, gloomy). In addition, an individual feels purposeful and autonomous and has positive social relationships. Happiness is operationally defined or measured with different questionnaires, such as the *Subjective Happiness Scale*, the *Oxford Happiness Questionnaire*, or a single-item scale (Lyubomirsky & Lepper, 1999; Hills & Argyle, 2002; Abdel-Khalek, 2006; respectively). Table 14.7 provides some items that are representative of each scale but written in a question format. Scales that measure happiness are important because they can be used to show what factors determine a person's level of happiness and how happiness relates to various behaviors.

Happiness serves as a positive incentive for behaviors that will produce this feeling. Psychologists have uncovered a number of effective behaviors that can make this happen—that is, promote happiness (Sin & Lyubomirsky, 2009). Such positive behaviors include acting kindly, counting one's blessings, mindfulness meditation, visualizing an ideal future self, writing letters of gratitude, and thinking about things for which a person is grateful. Lyubomirsky and Layous (2013) hypothesize that these behaviors increase well-being directly but also through their effects on positive emotions, positive thoughts, and positive behaviors. In addition, these behaviors can provide for psychological need satisfaction, such as the need for autonomy and relatedness. However, these activities are only considered positive if they increase the pleasantness of thoughts, emotions, and behaviors (Lyubomirsky & Layous, 2013).

Set point level of happiness. Every individual is assumed to have a baseline level of emotional valence, which resembles a set point. It is the level of unhappiness or happiness to which people consistently return—that is, their **set point level of happiness**, much like the thermostat setting in a house. Some experiences reduce happiness and others increase happiness. However, eventually people return to their set point level.

Psychologists have discovered three factors that determine people's habitual level of unhappiness or happiness (Lyubomirsky et al., 2005b). First, the happiness set point is genetically determined. For example, Lykken and Tellegen (1996) report that identical twins are more alike than fraternal twins in well-being or happiness even when identical twins have been raised by different families. Furthermore, these consistencies remain in effect even when measured 10 years apart. Weiss and coresearchers (2008) also found that identical twins were more alike than fraternal twins in subjective well-being. A second factor is that happiness has been linked to some of the big five

TABLE 14.7 Questions about Subjective Happiness Derived from Happiness Scales

Respondents are required to rate themselves on each question to the extent it is true of them or the extent they agree with the statement. For example, individuals may rate themselves on each question using the following scale: not at all to very much so

Are you very happy?

Do you often experience joy and elation?

Do you feel happy in general?[a]

Is your life satisfactory?

Do you consider yourself happy when compared to others of your sex and age?

Notes:

A higher score on these psychological scales indicates a higher level of happiness

a from Abdel-Khalek (2006)

personality traits. The traits of neuroticism, extraversion, and agreeableness are definitely associated with happiness (see Figure 9.6). The happiest students were those ranked low in neuroticism, high in extraversion, and high in agreeableness (Diener & Seligman, 2002). Weiss and coresearchers (2008) confirmed these findings, especially for extraversion and neuroticism. Well-being correlated positively with extraversion and negatively with neuroticism.

A third factor is that positive and negative events only affect happiness temporarily. According to the idea of a **hedonic treadmill**, people return to their set point level of happiness because they habituate to changes in their life circumstances (Brickman & Campbell, 1971). Lyubomirsky and coresearchers (2005a) liken the hedonic treadmill to walking up a down-escalator. Walking up resembles trying to improve life's circumstances in order to increase happiness while the descent of the escalator shows that people return to their set point level. However, there are some refinements to the set point level of happiness. First, as Diener and coresearchers (2006) point out, a person's habitual level of happiness is not zero as a neutral point would suggest but is actually a bit higher. Most people are at least a little bit happy. For example, using the *Subjective Happiness Scale* psychologists found that students from eight different campuses scored, on average, above the midpoint of that scale. Second, a return to set point happiness may not always occur. Diener and coresearchers (2006) observe that some negative life events have lasting impacts so that people do not return to their set point. For example, using data from longitudinal surveys, Lucas (2007) found that people do not return to their initial level of life satisfaction after they experience divorce, widowhood, unemployment, or disability even up to seven years after the event.

Subjective well-being can motivate behavior. Psychologists assume that happiness motivates success or leads to successful outcomes. However, does happiness cause success or does success cause happiness? Does hard work produce an A grade, which then causes happiness? Or does happiness motivate hard work, which results in the A grade? One way out of this quandary is to examine longitudinal studies in which happiness existed well before the occurrence of any behavior that could influence it (Lyubomirsky et al., 2005a). To illustrate by analogy, foot size determines the size of shoe a person buys, not the reverse. A person's foot size existed well before she or he bought a pair of shoes.

There are numerous findings based on longitudinal investigations to support the idea that happiness produces beneficial outcomes (Lyubomirsky et al., 2005a). For example, happiness leads to better job performance, such as work quality and productivity. Prior happiness predicts higher incomes, more successful marriages, greater longevity, and both better physical and mental health. For instance, longitudinal data show that prior happiness contributes to marital satisfaction. On a scale from 1 to 10, how satisfied are you with your life? Does this measure of subjective well-being relate to the likelihood of a successful marriage? To answer this question, Lucas (2005, 2007) examined data from a long-term longitudinal study conducted in Germany. He observed a couple of interesting trends. First, people's set point level of happiness prior to marriage predicts marital success. Happier people are more likely to remain married than unhappier people are. Second, happier people experienced a small rise in happiness from marriage, while unhappier people did not.

A second type of evidence for the effects of happiness on motivation comes from experiments. Different degrees of happiness are created in different groups in order to see the effects on subsequent behavior. In general, based on experimental research, increases in happiness cause increases in achievement behavior (Lyubomirsky et al., 2005a). In one illustrative experiment, by Erez and Isen (2002), a small increase in happiness was created in the experimental group by giving its members a bag of candy prior to the start of the experiment. The control group was not given any candy at that time but received candy after the experiment concluded. The candy procedure resulted in greater positive affect in the experimental group than in the control group as measured by the PANAS. An anagram-solving task was used to measure three effects of happiness: number of anagrams solved, persistence at solving, and future motivational interest in the task. The measure of motivation involved asking participants the extent to which they would look forward to taking the same anagram-solving test in the future. Participants were provided with 25 minutes to solve 10 anagrams, although only six of them had a solution. The results showed that the positive affect from the candy had a facilitative effect. The experimental group solved more anagrams and persisted longer than the control group did. In addition, the experimental group reported a higher level of future motivation for solving anagrams.

A downside to happiness. Happiness may also have a dark side (Gruber et al., 2011). First, happiness may provide benefits up to a certain point, with further increases being detrimental. Extreme happiness may lead to unintended consequences, such as reduced creativity, reckless behavior, and reduced well-being. Second, happiness may occur at inappropriate times. Thus, happiness, compared to fear, may cause a person to be slower in detecting danger. If a person expresses happiness when sadness is more appropriate, then this expression may indicate to friends that the situation is fine when it is not. Third, the pursuit of happiness could be done inappropriately and lead to disappointment if it is not achieved. Furthermore, higher expected amounts of happiness will lead to greater disappointment if a person fails to achieve it. Also, spending money to acquire material goods, for example, will provide less happiness than using that money for activities with friends (Van Boven, 2005). Finally, not all types of happiness have equal utility. Some types of happiness may cause social disruption, such as having too much pride might irritate other people. There are cultural differences in what types of happiness are valued, such as contentment versus pride or happiness obtained from individual versus group endeavors.

In addition, happiness may not lead to greater success in all endeavors, especially in instances where happiness improves one activity but is a detriment to another. An example is the divergence between studying and socializing. Nickerson and coresearchers (2011) examined how well the positive affect of entering students predicted their cumulative GPA at graduation. The researchers used ratings of cheerfulness as the substitute for happiness. Upon entering various universities, over 17,000 students were asked to rate themselves for cheerfulness when compared with the average student of their own age "on a 5-point scale: 1 = *lowest* 10%, 2 = *below average*, 3 = *average*, 4 = *above average*, and 5 = *highest* 10%" (p. 723). These ratings were correlated with their cumulative GPA years later at graduation. Surprisingly, the correlation between cheerfulness ratings and cumulative GPA was negative but extremely low (r = −0.07). One reason that Nickerson and coresearchers proposed revolves around sociability. Students derive their happiness from other people and thus devote more time socializing than studying, wiping out any gain that happiness may have provided. Okun and coresearchers (2009) found support for this hypothesis. Using the *Subjective Happiness Scale*, they found that when happiness was channeled into peer relationships, there was a negative relationship with cumulative GPA. They conjectured that happier students spend more time in social interaction in order to build social relationships, which are successful in many areas of life. However, increased social time means less time for academic pursuits, which is detrimental to the students' GPA.

Section Recap

Emotions serve as *motives for action* that have either evolved or were learned in order to achieve the goal of the emotion. Each emotion has a different goal or aim, which is to alter a person's relationship with the emotion-inducing situation. For instance, fear motivates running away in order to reach safety while anger motivates asserting oneself in order to unblock a goal. Self-conscious emotions motivate behavior to restore the goal of group harmony. Emotional feelings inform the individual how a situation has been appraised. For example, fear means danger and sadness means a loss. An emotion also serves to guide thinking by influencing an individual's cognitive processes in appraising a situation and in making decisions. According to the *appraisal tendency hypothesis*, a specific emotion influences cognitive judgments in a manner congruent with the emotion's affective feeling. Both positive and negative affect intensity influences the depth and breadth of thinking. As affect intensity increases, the focus of thought changes from broad to narrow as if more attention is being devoted to the emotional feeling. For instance, angered participants downplay risks and are more willing to retaliate than frightened participants are willing to do. For money decisions, sad participants, compared to neutral or disgusted participants, are impatient—that is, they prefer immediate small rewards over large delayed rewards. Immediate rewards help alleviate sadness sooner, while neutral and disgusted participants are more patient and willing to wait for larger rewards.

In contrast to unpleasant emotions, pleasant emotions act like positive incentives, since a person behaves to attain pleasant affect. *Subjective well-being* or happiness means that a person experiences positive affect more than negative affect and is satisfied with life. A *person's set point level of happiness* refers to her habitual level of happiness or unhappiness. The set point depends on a person's genetic makeup, level of extraversion, neuroticism, and agreeableness. Happiness has a stable set point according to the *hedonic treadmill*. Decreases or increases in happiness are temporary, since people habituate to changes in their circumstances. Greater happiness seems to produce positive developments in life in those cases where happiness has existed beforehand; for example, happier people prior to marriage are less likely to divorce. However, major negative life changes such as divorce and unemployment can lower one's level of happiness for many years. Experimentally created positive affect increases motivated behavior, such as more success and persistence in an anagram-solving task. However, happiness can also have a down side if it occurs inappropriately, crowds out other emotions, and prevents long-term achievement. Pursuit of happiness in one endeavor (socializing) may lead to decreases in happiness from another endeavor (studying).

GLOSSARY

Term	Definition
Amygdala	Location (or nuclei) in the brain that conducts a quick and crude analysis of an emotional situation for a person's well-being
Appraisal Tendency Hypothesis	A specific emotion influences people's cognitive judgment of a stimulus; emotion influences the evaluation of events
Behavioral Ecology Hypothesis	Facial expressions occur to serve a person's social motives, e.g., a smile serves as a reward and tears are a request for help

continued . . .

GLOSSARY Continued

Term	Definition
Dialect of Facial Expressions	Like dialects in language, culture modifies the innate configuration of an expression; facial expressions of emotion differ somewhat among cultures
Display Rules	Social conventions that govern the emotional expressions that individuals must exhibit in public and need not be linked to emotional feelings
Efference Hypothesis	An activated brain circuit sends information to the facial muscles, which generates the expression that is synonymous with the emotional feeling
Emotion Recognition	When people are able to identify the emotions that are portrayed by various facial expressions
Expression–Feeling Link	The association between different emotional feelings (affect) and their corresponding facial expressions, e.g., smile linked with happiness
Hedonic Treadmill	Changes in happiness are temporary because people return to their set point level of happiness as a result of habituating to changes in life's experiences
Motive for Action	The function of an emotion is to induce an individual to deal specifically with the emotional event, which is to achieve the aim of the emotion
Readout Hypothesis	The idea that a facial expression conveys (reads out) an individual's private emotional feeling to another individual
Set Point Level of Happiness	Baseline level of emotional valence and serves as the level of happiness or unhappiness to which a person consistently returns
Situational Definition	Emotions are defined by changes in the environment to which people react, e.g., losses evoke negative emotions and gains evoke positive emotions
Social Facial Vasodilation	Blood rushing to a person's face, which is commonly known as blushing when a person feels ashamed or embarrassed
Subjective Well-Being	A feeling that individuals strive to bring into consciousness, being happy or satisfied with life, and experiencing positive affect more than negative affect
Subliminal Priming	Presentation of a stimulus below a person's level of awareness (sub = below, limen = threshold) in order to evoke components of an emotion

REFERENCES

Abdel-Khalek, A. M. (2006). Measuring happiness with a single-item scale. *Social Behavior and Personality: An International Journal, 34*, 139–150.

Barrett, K. C., & Campos, J. J. (1987). Perspectives on emotional development II: A functionalist approach to emotions. In J. D. Osofsky (Ed.), *Handbook of infant development* (pp. 555–578). New York, NY: Wiley.

Barrett, L. F. (2017). *How emotions are made: The secret life of the brain*. Boston, MA: Houghton Mifflin.

Brickman, P., & Campbell, D. T. (1971). Hedonic relativism and planning the good society. In M. H. Appley (Ed.), *Adaptation level theory* (pp. 287–302). New York, NY: Academic Press.

Brosch, T., Pourtois, G., & Sander, D. (2010). The perception and categorisation of emotional stimuli: A review. *Cognition and Emotion, 24*, 377–400.

Buck, R. (1984). *The communication of emotion*. New York, NY: Guilford.

Buck, R. (1985). Prime theory: An integrated view of motivation and emotion. *Psychological Review, 92*, 389–413.

Buck, R. (1991). Social factors in facial display and communication: A reply to Chovil and others. *Journal of Nonverbal Behavior, 15*, 155–161.

Buck, R. (1994). Social and emotional functions in facial expression and communication: The readout hypothesis. *Biological Psychology, 38*, 95–115.

Camras, L. A., Holland, E. A., & Patterson, M. J. (1993). Facial expression. In M. Lewis & J. M. Haviland (Eds.), *Handbook of emotions* (pp. 199–208). New York, NY: Guilford.

Chovil, N., & Fridlund, A. J. (1991). Why emotionality cannot equal sociality: Reply to Buck. *Journal of Nonverbal Behavior, 15*, 163–167.

Clark, L. A., & Watson, D. (1994). Distinguishing functional from dysfunctional affective responses. In P. Ekman & R. J. Davidson (Eds.), *The nature of emotion* (pp. 131–136). New York, NY: Oxford University Press.

Costafreda, S. G., Brammer, M. J., David, A. S., & Fu, H. Y. (2007). Predictors of amygdale activation during the processing of emotional stimuli: A meta-analysis of 385 PET and fMRI studies. *Brain Research Reviews, 58*, 57–70.

Deckers, L. (1994, June). *The relationship between facial reactions of humor and funniness ratings within and across subjects*. A poster presented at the International Humor Studies Conference, Ithaca, NY.

Descartes, R. (1649/1968). The passions of the soul. In E. S. Haldane & G. R. T. Ross (Eds.), *The philosophical works of Descartes*. Cambridge: Cambridge University Press.

Diener, E., Lucas, R. E., & Scollon, C. N. (2006). Beyond the hedonic treadmill: Revising the adaptation theory of well-being. *American Psychologist, 61*, 305–314.

Diener, E., & Seligman, M. E. P. (2002). Very happy people. *Psychological Science, 13*, 81–84.

Eibl-Eibesfeldt, I. (1973). The expressive behaviour of the deaf-and-blind-born. In M. von Cranach & I. Vine (Eds.), *Social communication and movement* (pp. 163–194). New York, NY: Academic Press.

Ekman, P. (1973). Cross-cultural studies of facial expression. In P. Ekman (Ed.), *Darwin and facial expression* (pp. 169–222). New York, NY: Academic Press.

Ekman, P. (1984). Expression and the nature of emotion. In K. R. Scherer & P. Ekman (Eds.), *Approaches to emotion* (pp. 319–344). Hillsdale, NJ: Lawrence Erlbaum.

Ekman, P., Davidson, R. J., & Friesen, W. V. (1990). The Duchenne smile: Emotional expression and brain physiology II. *Journal of Personality and Social Psychology, 58*, 342–353.

Ekman, P., & Friesen, W. V. (1971). Constants across cultures in the face and emotion. *Journal of Personality and Social Psychology, 17*, 124–129.

Ekman, P., & Friesen, W. V. (1975). *Unmasking the face*. Englewood Cliffs, NJ: Prentice-Hall.

Ekman, P., Friesen, W. V., & Ancoli, S. (1980a). Facial signs of emotional experience. *Journal of Personality and Social Psychology, 39*, 1125–1134.

Ekman, P., Roper, G., & Hager, J. C. (1980b). Deliberate facial movement. *Child Development, 51*, 886–891.

Elfenbein, H. A., Beaupré, M., Lévesque, M., & Hess, U. (2007). Toward a dialect theory: Cultural differences in the expression and recognition of posed facial expressions. *Emotion, 7*, 131–146.

Ellsworth, P. C., & Scherer, K. R. (2003). Appraisal processes in emotion. In R. J. Davidson, K. R. Scherer, & J. H. Goldsmith (Eds.), *Handbook of affective sciences* (pp. 572–595). Oxford: Oxford University Press.

Ellsworth, P. C., & Smith, C. A. (1988). From appraisal to emotion: Differences among unpleasant feelings. *Motivation and Emotion, 12*, 271–302.

Erez, A., & Isen, A. M. (2002). The influence of positive affect on the components of expectancy motivation. *Journal of Applied Psychology, 87*, 1055–1067.

Fox, E., Griggs, L., & Mouchlianitis, E. (2007). The detection of fear-relevant stimuli: Are guns noticed as quickly as snakes? *Emotion, 7*, 691–696.

Fridlund, A. J. (1991). Evolution and facial action in reflex, social motive, and paralanguage. *Biological Psychology, 32*, 3–100.

Fridlund, A. J. (1992). The behavioral ecology and sociality of human faces. In M. S. Clark (Ed.), *Review of personality and social psychology: Vol. 13. Emotion* (pp. 90–121). Newbury Park, CA: Sage.

Fridlund, A. J. (1994). *Human facial expression: An evolutionary view*. San Diego, CA: Academic Press.

Frijda, N. H. (1986). *The emotions*. Cambridge: Cambridge University Press.

Frijda, N. H. (1994). Emotions are functional, most of the time. In P. Ekman & R. J. Davidson (Eds.), *The nature of emotion* (pp. 112–122). New York, NY: Oxford University Press.

Frijda, N. H. (2007). *The laws of emotion*. Mahwah, NJ: Lawrence Erlbaum.

Fulcher, J. S. (1942). "Voluntary" facial expression in blind and seeing children. *Archives of Psychology, 272*, 2–49.

Gable, P., & Harmon-Jones, E. (2008). Approach-motivated positive affect reduces breadth of attention. *Psychological Science, 19*, 476–482.

Gable, P., & Harmon-Jones, E. (2010a). The motivational dimensional model of affect: Implications for breadth of attention, memory, and cognitive categorisation. *Cognition and Emotion, 24*, 322–337.

Gable, P., & Harmon-Jones, E. (2010b). The blues broaden, but the nasty narrows: Attentional consequences of negative affects low and high in motivational intensity. *Psychological Science, 21*, 211–215.

Galati, D., Miceli, R., & Sini, B. (2001). Judging and coding facial expression of emotions in congenitally blind children. *International Journal of Behavioral Development, 25*, 268–278.

Galati, D., Scherer, K. R., & Ricci-Bitti, P. E. (1997). Voluntary facial expression of emotion: Comparing congenitally blind with normally sighted encoders. *Journal of Personality and Social Psychology, 73*, 1363–1379.

Gruber, J., Mauss, I. B., & Tamir, M. (2011). A dark side of happiness? How, when, and why happiness is not always good. *Perspectives on Psychological Science, 6*, 222–233.

Hendriks, M. C. P., Croon, M. C., & Vingerhoets, A. J. J. M. (2008). Social reactions to adult crying: The help-soliciting function of tears. *Journal of Social Psychology, 148*, 22–41.

Hendriks, M. C. P., & Vingerhoets, A. J. J. M. (2006). Social messages of crying faces: Their influence on anticipated person perception, emotions and behavioural responses. *Cognition and Emotion, 20*, 878–886.

Hills, P., & Argyle, M. (2002). The Oxford Happiness Questionnaire: A compact scale for the measurement of psychological well-being. *Personality and Individual Differences, 33*, 1073–1082.

Izard, C. E. (1971). *The face of emotion*. New York, NY: Appleton-Century-Crofts.

Izard, C. E. (1993). Four systems for emotion activation: Cognitive and noncognitive processes. *Psychological Review, 100*, 68–90.

Izard, C. E. (1994). Innate and universal facial expressions: Evidence from developmental and cross-cultural research. *Psychological Bulletin, 115*, 288–299.

Izard, C. E., Fantauzzo, C. A., Castle, J. M., Haynes, O. M., Rayias, M. F., & Putnam, P. H. (1995). The ontogeny and significance of infants' facial expressions in the first 9 months of life. *Developmental Psychology, 31*, 997–1013.

Jack, R. E., Garrod, O. G., Yu, H., Caldara, R., & Schyns, P. G. (2012). Facial expressions of emotion are not culturally universal. *Proceedings of the National Academy of Sciences, 109*, 7241–7244.

Juruena, M. F., Giampietro, V. P., Smith, S. D., Surguladze, S. A., Dalton, J. A., Benson, P. J., . . . Fu, C. H. Y. (2010). Amygdala activation to masked happy facial expressions. *Journal of the International Neuropsychological Society, 16*, 1–5.

Keltner, D., & Anderson, C. (2000). Saving face for Darwin: The functions and uses of embarrassment. *Current Directions in Psychological Science, 9*, 187–192.

Kraut, R. E. (1982). Social presence, facial feedback, and emotion. *Journal of Personality and Social Psychology, 42*, 853–863.

Leary, M. R. (2007). Motivational and emotional aspects of the self. *Annual Review of Psychology, 58*, 317–344.

Leary, M. R., Britt, T. W., Cutlip II, W. D., & Templeton, J. L. (1992). Social blushing. *Psychological Bulletin, 112*, 446–460.

Lerner, J. S., Gonzalez, R. M., Small, D. A., & Fischhoff, B. (2003). Effects of fear and anger on perceived risks of terrorism: A national field experiment. *Psychological Science, 14*, 144–150.

Lerner, J. S., & Keltner, D. (2000). Beyond valence: Toward a model of emotion-specific influences on judgment and choice. *Cognition and Emotion, 14*, 473–493.

Lerner, J. S., & Keltner, D. (2001). Fear, anger, and risk. *Journal of Personality and Social Psychology, 81*, 146–159.

Lerner, J. S., Li, Y., Valdesolo, P., & Kassam, K. S. (2015). Emotion and decision making. *Psychology, 66*, 799–823.

Lerner, J. S., Li, Y., & Weber, E. U. (2013). The financial costs of sadness. *Psychological Science, 24*, 72–79.

Li, W., Moallem, I., Paller, K. A., & Gottfried, J. A. (2007). Subliminal smells can guide social preferences. *Psychological Science, 18*, 1044–1049.

Liddell, B. J., Brown, K. J., Kemp, A. H., Barton, M. J., Das, P., Peduto, A., . . . Williams, L. M. (2005). A direct brainstem-amygdala-cortical "alarm" system for subliminal signals of fear. *NeuroImage, 24*, 235–243.

LoBue, V. (2014). Deconstructing the snake: The relative roles of perception, cognition, and emotion on threat detection. *Emotion, 14*, 701–711.

Lucas, R. E. (2005). Time does not heal all wounds. *Psychological Science, 16*, 945–950.

Lucas, R. E. (2007). Adaptation and the set-point model of subjective well-being. *Current Directions in Psychological Science, 16*, 75–79.

Lykken, D., & Tellegen, A. (1996). Happiness is a stochastic phenomenon. *Psychological Science, 7*, 186–189.

Lyubomirsky, S., King, L., & Diener, E. (2005a). The benefits of frequent positive affect: Does happiness lead to success. *Psychological Bulletin, 131*, 803–855.

Lyubomirsky, S., & Layous, K. (2013). How do simple positive activities increase well-being? *Current Directions in Psychological Science, 22*(1), 57–62.

Lyubomirsky, S., & Lepper, H. S. (1999). A measure of subjective happiness: Preliminary reliability and construct validation. *Social Indicators Research, 46*, 137–155.

Lyubomirsky, S., Sheldon, K. M., & Schkade, D. (2005b). Pursuing happiness: The architecture of sustainable change. *Review of General Psychology, 9*, 111–131.

Marsh, A. A., Ambady, N., & Kleck, R. E. (2005). The effects of fear and anger facial expressions on approach- and avoidance-related behaviors. *Emotion, 5*, 119–124.

Marston, A., Hart, J., Hileman, C., & Faunce, W. (1984). Toward the laboratory study of sadness and crying. *American Journal of Psychology, 97*, 127–131.

Martin, R. B., & Labott, S. M. (1991). Mood following emotional crying: Effects of the situation. *Journal of Research in Personality, 25*, 218–244.

Mather, M., & Sutherland, M. R. (2011). Arousal-biased competition in perception and memory. *Perspectives on Psychological Science, 6*, 114–133.

Matsumoto, D., Yoo, S. H., Hirayama, S., & Petrova, G. (2005). Development and validation of a measure of display rule knowledge: The Display Rule Assessment Inventory. *Emotion, 5*, 23–40.

Mennella, J. A., & Beauchamp, G. K. (1998). Early flavor experiences: Research update. *Nutrition Reviews, 56*, 205–211.

Nesse, R. M., & Ellsworth, P. C. (2009). Evolution, emotions, and emotional disorders. *American Psychologist, 64*, 129–139.

Nezlek, J. B., Vansteelandt, K., Van Mechelen, I., & Kuppens, P. (2008). Appraisal-emotion relationship in daily life. *Emotion, 8*, 145–150.

Nickerson, C., Diener, E., & Schwarz, N. (2011). Positive affect and college success. *Journal of Happiness Studies, 12*, 717–746.

Okun, M. A., Levy, R., Karoly, P., & Ruehlman, L. (2009). Dispositional happiness and college student GPA: Unpacking a null relation. *Journal of Research in Personality, 43*, 711–715.

Paulhan, F. (1887/1930). *The laws of feeling* (C. K. Ogden, trans.). London: Kegan Paul, Trench, Trubner.

Rinn, W. E. (1984). The neuropsychology of facial expression: A review of the neurological and psychological mechanisms for producing facial expressions. *Psychological Bulletin, 95*, 52–77.

Rinn, W. E. (1991). Neuropsychology of facial expression. In R. Feldman & B. Rime (Eds.), *Fundamentals of nonverbal behavior* (pp. 3–70). Cambridge: Cambridge University Press.

Roseman, I. J., & Smith, C. A. (2001). Appraisal theory: Overview, assumptions, varieties, controversies. In K. R. Scherer, A. Schorr, & T. Johnstone (Eds.), *Appraisal processes in emotion: Theory, methods, research* (pp. 3–19). New York, NY: Oxford University Press.

Russell, J. A. (1994). Is there universal recognition of emotion from facial expressions? A review of the cross-cultural studies. *Psychological Bulletin, 115*, 102–141.

Schaefer, A., Nils, F., Sanchez, X., & Philippot, P. (2010). Assessing the effectiveness of a large database of emotion-eliciting films: A new tool for emotion researchers. *Cognition and Emotion, 24*, 1153–1172.

Scherer, K. R. (1994). Emotion serves to decouple stimulus and response. In P. Ekman & R. J. Davidson (Eds.), *The nature of emotion: Fundamental questions* (pp. 127–130). New York, NY: Oxford University Press.

Scherer, K. R. (1997). Profiles of emotion-antecedent appraisal: Testing theoretical predictions across cultures. *Cognition and Emotion, 11*, 113–150.

Shaver, P., Schwartz, J., Kirson, D., & O'Connor, C. (1987). Emotion knowledge: Further exploration of a prototype approach. *Journal of Personality and Social Psychology, 52*, 1061–1086.

Shore, D. M., & Heerey, E. A. (2011). The value of genuine and polite smiles. *Emotion, 11*, 169–174.

Siemer, M., Mauss, I., & Gross, J. J. (2007). Same situation—different emotions: How appraisals shape our emotions. *Emotion, 7*, 592–600.

Simon, A., & Shields, S. A. (1996). Does complexion color affect the experience of blushing? *Journal of Social Behavior and Personality, 11*, 177–188.

Sin, N. L., & Lyubomirsky, S. (2009). Enhancing well-being and alleviating depressive symptoms with positive psychology interventions: A practice-friendly meta-analysis. *Journal of Clinical Psychology, 65*, 467–487.

Smith, C. A., & Kirby, L. D. (2009). Putting appraisal in context: Toward a relational model of appraisal and emotion. *Cognition and Emotion, 23*, 1352–1372.

Smith, C. A., & Lazarus, R. S. (1990). Emotion and adaptation. In L. Pervin (Ed.), *Handbook of personality theory and research* (pp. 609–637). New York, NY: Guilford.

Steiner, J. E. (1977). Facial expressions of the neonate infant indicating the hedonics of food-related chemical stimuli. In J. M. Weiffenbach (Ed.), *Taste and development* (pp. 173–189). Bethesda, MD: U.S. Department of Health, Education, and Welfare.

Tamietto, M., & de Gelder, B. (2010). Neural bases of the non-conscious perception of emotional signals. *Nature Reviews Neuroscience, 11*, 697–709.

Tangney, J. P., Stuewig, J., & Mashek, D. J. (2007). Moral emotions and moral behavior. *Annual Review of Psychology, 58*, 345–372.

Tooby, J., & Cosmides, L. (2005). Conceptual foundations of evolutionary psychology. In D. Buss (Ed.), *The handbook of evolutionary psychology* (pp. 5–67). Hoboken, NJ: John Wiley & Sons.

Tracy, J. L., & Robins, R. W. (2007). Emerging insights into the nature and function of pride. *Current Directions in Psychological Science, 16*, 147–150.

Van Boven, L. (2005). Experientialism, materialism, and the pursuit of happiness. *Review of General Psychology, 9*, 132–142.

Verduyn, P., Van Mechelen, I., Tuerlinckx, F., Meers, K., & Van Coillie, H. (2009). Intensity profiles of emotional experience over time. *Cognition and Emotion, 23*, 1427–1443.

Vrugt, A., & Vet, C. (2009). Effects of a smile on mood and helping behavior. *Social Behavior and Personality, 37*, 1251–1258.

Weiss, A., Bates, T. C., & Luciano, M. (2008). Happiness is a personal(ity) thing: The genetics of personality and well-being in a representative sample. *Psychological Science, 19*, 205–210.

Wilkowski, B. M., & Meier, B. P. (2010). Bring it on: Angry facial expressions potentiate approach-motivated motor behavior. *Journal of Personality and Social Psychology, 98*, 201–210.

Willis, M. L., Palermo, R., & Burke, D. (2011). Judging approachability on the face of it: The influence of face and body expressions on the perception of approachability. *Emotion, 11*, 514–523.

Winkielman, P., & Berridge, K. C. (2004). Unconscious emotion. *Current Directions in Psychological Science, 13*, 120–123.

Wyer, N. A., & Calvini, G. (2011). Don't sit so close to me: Unconsciously elicited affect automatically provokes social avoidance. *Emotion, 11*, 1230–1234.

Yik, M. S. M., & Russell, J. A. (1999). Interpretation of faces: A cross-cultural study of a prediction from Fridlund's theory. *Cognition and Emotion, 13*, 93–104.

Zuckerman, M., Klorman, R., Larrance, D. T., & Spiegel, N. H. (1981). Facial, autonomic, and subjective components of emotion: The facial feedback hypothesis versus the externalizer-internalizer distinction. *Journal of Personality and Social Psychology, 41*, 929–944.

Index